Handbook on Trade and the Environment

Edited by

Kevin P. Gallagher

Boston University, USA

Edward Elgar
Cheltenham, UK • Northampton, MA, USA

Published by
Edward Elgar Publishing Limited
The Lypiatts
15 Lansdown Road
Cheltenham
Glos GL50 2JA
UK

Edward Elgar Publishing, Inc.
William Pratt House
9 Dewey Court
Northampton
Massachusetts 01060
USA

A catalogue record for this book
is available from the British Library

Library of Congress Cataloguing in Publication Data

Handbook on trade and the environment/edited by Kevin P. Gallagher.
    p.   cm. (Elgar original reference)
   Includes bibliographical references and index.
    1. Commerce—Environmental aspects. 2. International trade—
Environmental aspects. 3. Commercial policy—Environmental aspects.
4. Environmental policy—Economic aspects. 5. Environmental policy—
Political aspects. I. Gallagher, Kevin, 1968–   .
HF1008.H375   2008
333.7—dc22
                                                                2008040341

PEFC/16-33-111
CATG-PEFC-052
www.pefc.org

ISBN 978 1 84720 454 7 (cased)

Printed and bound in Great Britain by MPG Books Ltd, Bodmin, Cornwall

Contents

PART III   TRADE AND ENVIRONMENTAL POLICY

Figures and tables

Contributors

Frank Ackerman is an economist who has written extensively about the economics of environmental policy in areas including international trade, climate change and chemicals policy. His most recent books, published in 2008, are *Poisoned for Pennies: The Economics of Toxics and Precaution* (Island Press) and *Can We Afford the Future? Economics for a Warming World* (Zed Press). He has written numerous academic and popular articles, and has directed policy reports for clients ranging from Greenpeace to the European Parliament. At Tufts University's Global Development and Environment Institute (GDAE) since 1995, he now works jointly with the Stockholm Environment Institute–US Center, also located at Tufts. He received a PhD from Harvard University, and has taught economics at Tufts and at the University of Massachusetts.

Philipp Aerni graduated in Geography and Economics at the University of Zurich in 1996 and received his PhD from the Institute of Agricultural Economics at the Swiss Federal Institute of Technology (ETH) in Zurich in 1999. From January 2000 to April 2002, he continued his research as a postdoctoral research fellow in the Science, Technology and Innovation Program at the Center for International Development at Harvard University, Cambridge, MA, USA. Apart from his research at the World Trade Institute, he is currently heading two National Science Foundation Projects (NFP 59). Philipp Aerni is also co-founder and member of the management steering team of the Geneva-based NGO 'Africa Technology Development Forum' (ATDF). The main objective of ATDF is to promote science, technology and entrepreneurship in Africa.

James Van Alstine is a Fellow in Environmental Policy Studies and a PhD candidate in the Department of Geography and Environment at the London School of Economics and Political Science. His research focuses on the social and environmental risks of industrial development, the governance of resource extraction in developing countries, and the dynamics of institutional and organizational change. His dissertation explores the contestation of corporate environmentalism in the South African petrochemical industry.

David Angel holds the Laskoff Professorship in Economics, Technology and the Environment at Clark University where he is also Professor of Geography, Provost and Vice President for Academic Affairs. His current work focuses on global economic change and the environment, with a particular focus on rapidly industrializing economies in Asia. Recent books include: *Asia's Clean Revolution: Industry, Growth and the Environment* (with Michael T. Rock, 2000, Greenleaf Publishers), *Effective Environmental Regulation: Learning from Poland's Experience* (with Halina Brown and Patrick Derr, 2000, Praeger Press) and *Industrial Development in the Developing World* (with Michael T. Rock, 2005, Oxford University Press).

Nicholas A. Ashford is Professor of Technology and Policy at the Massachusetts Institute of Technology, where he teaches courses in 'Sustainability, Trade and Environment'. He is the co-author of a new textbook on *Environmental Law, Policy, and Economics: Reclaiming the Environmental Agenda* (MIT Press, 2008) and a forthcoming textbook/reader on

Technology, Globalization, and Sustainability. He has published several hundred articles in peer-reviewed journals and law reviews. Dr Ashford was a public member and chairman of the National Advisory Committee on Occupational Safety & Health, served on the EPA Science Advisory Board, and was chairman of the Committee on Technology Innovation & Economics of the EPA National Advisory Council for Environmental Policy and Technology. Dr Ashford is a Fellow of the American Association for the Advancement of Science and former chair of its Section on Societal Impacts of Science and Engineering. He served as an advisor to the United Nations Environment Programme and is also legislation, regulation and policy editor of the *Journal of Cleaner Production* and serves on the editorial board of the *Journal of Environmental Technology and Management*. He currently serves as co-chair of the US–Greece Council for the Initiative on Technology Cooperation with the Balkans.

Edward B. Barbier is the John S. Bugas Professor of Economics, Department of Economics and Finance, University of Wyoming. He has over 25 years' experience as an environmental and resource economist, working on natural resource and development issues as well as the interface between economics and ecology, and has published widely in these fields.

J. Samuel Barkin is Associate Professor of Political Science at the University of Florida. His research interests are international organization and international environmental politics. Within the latter category, he has published work on issues such as the relationship between international trade and the environment, and international fisheries politics, in journals such as *Global Environmental Politics*, *Environment and Politics* and *Global Governance*.

Thomas Bernauer is Professor of Political Science (International Relations) in ETH Zurich's Department of Social Sciences and Humanities (D-GESS). He heads a group of around ten persons that forms part of the Center for Comparative and International Studies (CIS) and the Institute for Environmental Decisions (IED). Bernauer teaches primarily in D-GESS and the Department of Environmental Sciences (D-UWIS). Currently he also serves as director of the CIS and is a member of the Swiss National Science Foundation's Research Council. In his research and teaching, Thomas Bernauer focuses on international economic and environmental issues. His book publications include *Genes, Trade and Regulation* (Princeton University Press, 2003), *Staaten im Weltmarkt* (*States in World Markets*; Leske+Budrich, 2000), *The Politics of Positive Incentives in Arms Control* (University of South Carolina Press, 1999), *Handel und Umwelt* (*Trade and the Environment*; Westdeutscher Verlag, 1999) and *The Chemistry of Regime Formation* (Dartmouth Publishers, 1993). He has published in journals such as *British Journal of Political Science*, *European Journal of International Relations*, *Water Resources Research*, *International Organization*, *Journal of Public Policy*, *Zeitschrift für Internationale Beziehungen*, *PVS*, *European Journal of Political Research*, *Business and Politics*, *World Development*, *Journal of Environment and Development*, *Aquatic Sciences*, *Environmental Politics*, *International Journal of BioTechnology*, *Swiss Political Science Review*, *Bulletin of Peace Proposals* and *Security Dialogue*.

James K. Boyce teaches economics at the University of Massachusetts, Amherst, where he directs the program on development, peacebuilding and the environment at the Political Economy Research Institute. His books include *The Political Economy of the Environment* (Edward Elgar, 2002), *Natural Assets: Democratizing Environmental Ownership* (Island Press, 2003) and *Reclaiming Nature: Environmental Justice and Ecological Restoration* (Anthem Press, 2007). He is a member of the steering committees of the *Forum on Social Wealth* and *E3: Economics for Equity and the Environment*. He received his BA from Yale University and his PhD from Oxford University.

Steve Charnovitz is Associate Professor of Law at George Washington University Law School. He writes frequently in the field of international law. He is the author of *Trade Law and Global Governance* (2002).

Sachin Chaturvedi is a Fellow at the Research and Information System for the Developing Countries. His areas of specialization include trade and economic issues related to technology and innovation systems, and possible linkages with frontier technologies. He has also served as a consultant to the UN Food and Agriculture Organization, the World Bank, UNESCAP, UNESCO, OECD, the Commonwealth Secretariat, IUCN, the Ministry of Environment and Forests and Department of Biotechnology and the Government of India, among other organizations. He was Visiting Fellow at the University of Amsterdam (1996), the Institute of Advanced Studies, Shimla (2003) and the German Development Institute (2007). His experience and assignments include working at the University of Amsterdam for a project supported by the Dutch Ministry of External Affairs on International Development Cooperation and Biotechnology for Developing Countries, and he has been a member of IGSAC Committee of Experts to evolve a framework of cooperation for conservation of biodiversity in the SAARC (South Asian Association for Regional Cooperation) region. He is on the editorial board of *Biotechnology Development Monitor, The Netherlands,* and *Asian Biotechnology Development Review*, New Delhi. He is author of two books and has published several research articles in various prestigious journals.

Carol Chouchani Cherfane is the Acting Team Leader of the Technology and Enterprise Development Team in the Sustainable Development and Productivity Division of the United Nations Economic and Social Commission of Western Asia (ESCWA) in Beirut, Lebanon. She also provides training and technical assistance in support of the Program on Trade and Environment Capacity Building in the Arab Region on behalf of ESCWA in cooperation with the League of Arab States and United Nations Environment Program. The subject of her doctoral research at the Fletcher School of Law and Diplomacy is trade and environment decision-making in the Arab region. The views expressed in this book are those of the author and do not necessarily reflect the views of the United Nations.

Jennifer Clapp is Professor of Environmental Studies and a CIGI Research Chair in International Governance at the University of Waterloo. Her most recent book is *Paths to a Green World: The Political Economy of the Global Environment* (with Peter Dauvergne, MIT Press). She is the author of a number of research articles on the global political economy of agriculture, food and the environment.

Brian R. Copeland is Professor and Head of the Department of Economics at the University of British Columbia. His research has focused on developing analytical techniques to study the interaction between international trade and the environment. He has published in the leading economics journals, including the *American Economic Review*, *Quarterly Journal of Economics*, *Journal of International Economics* and the *Journal of Economic Literature*. He and his colleague Scott Taylor are the authors of the book, *Trade and the Environment: Theory and Evidence* (Princeton University Press, 2004). He was previously co-editor of the *Journal of Environmental Economics and Management* and is currently an associate editor of the *Journal of International Economics*. Professor Copeland is the recipient of several awards, including the Purvis Prize and a UBC-Killam research prize.

James J. Corbett conducts technology-policy research related to transportation, including groundbreaking research on air emissions from maritime transport, energy and environmental impacts of freight transportation, and assessment of technological and policy control strategies for goods movement. Dr Corbett is Associate Professor in the Marine Policy Program of the College of Marine and Earth Studies, and Associate Professor of Civil and Environmental Engineering in the College of Engineering at the University of Delaware. Dr Corbett's experience includes work as a licensed officer in the US Merchant Marine, a Naval Reserve Engineering Duty Officer, and consulting for industry and government in industrial operations, energy and environmental performance. He has more than 30 peer-reviewed publications related to shipping and multimodal transportation; he co-authored the 2000 *IMO Study on Greenhouse Gases from Ships*, and wrote the 'Marine Transportation and Energy Use' chapter in the 2004 *Encyclopedia of Energy*.

Christopher Costello is Associate Professor of Environmental and Resource Economics at the Donald Bren School of Environmental Science & Management, UC Santa Barbara. His research is primarily in the area of environmental regulation and natural resource management under uncertainty, with a particular emphasis on information, its value, and its effect on management decisions. He is also interested in the process and design of adaptive management programs in which learning (to resolve uncertainty or asymmetric information) is actively pursued. Topical interests include biological diversity, introduced species, regulation of polluting industries and marine policy. Costello frequently collaborates with research outside of economics such as statistics, ecology, biogeography and mathematics.

Elizabeth R. DeSombre is Frost Professor of Environmental Studies and Professor of Political Science at Wellesley College. Her research is on global environmental politics, particularly relating to issues of the global commons. Her recent books include *Flagging Standards: Globalization and Environmental, Safety, and Labor Standards at Sea* (MIT Press, 2006) and *Global Environmental Institutions* (Routledge, 2006). Her first book, *Domestic Sources of International Environmental Policy: Industry, Environmentalists, and U.S. Power* (MIT Press, 2000) won the 2001 Chadwick F. Alger Prize for the best book published in 2000 in the area of international organization, and the 2001 Lynton Caldwell Award for the best book published on environmental policy. A second edition of her textbook, *The Global Environment and World Politics* (London: Continuum, 2002) was published in 2007.

Kelly Sims Gallagher, Adjunct Lecturer in Public Policy, is director of the Energy Technology Innovation Policy (ETIP) research group at the Harvard Kennedy School's Belfer Center for Science and International Affairs. Her work is focused on studying, informing and shaping US and Chinese energy and climate-change policy. USA–China energy cooperation and energy-technology innovation, including technology transfer, are important themes in her work. She has specialized particularly on energy policy related to transportation and coal in both countries. She is currently serving on the Task Force on Innovation for the China Council for International Cooperation on Environment and Development, and as Counselor-at-Large for the Asia Society–Council on Foreign Relations–Brookings Institution Initiative for USA–China Cooperation on Energy and Climate. She previously worked for Fluor Daniel Environmental Services, the Office of Vice President Al Gore, and Ozone Action. She speaks Spanish and basic Mandarin Chinese, and is the author of *China Shifts Gears: Automakers, Oil, Pollution, and Development* (MIT Press, 2006).

Kevin P. Gallagher is an assistant professor of international relations at Boston University. He is the author of *The Enclave Economy: Foreign Investment and Sustainable Development in Mexico's Silicon Valley* (with Lyuba Zarsky) (MIT Press, 2007), and *Free Trade and the Environment: Mexico, NAFTA, and Beyond* (Stanford Law and Politics, 2004). He has been the editor or co-editor of a number of books, including *Putting Development First: The importance of Policy Space in the WTO and IFIs* (Zed Books, 2005), *International Trade and Sustainable Development* (Earthscan, 2002), and others. He is a research fellow at the Frederick S. Pardee Center for the Study of the Longer-Range Future, where he directs the Global Economic Governance Initiative. Professor Gallagher is also a research associate at the Global Development and Environment Institute of the Fletcher School of Law and Diplomacy at Tufts University, the Political Economy Research Institute at the University of Massachusetts, Amherst, an adjunct fellow at the Research and Information System for Developing Countries in Delhi, India, and a member of the US–Mexico Futures Forum.

A.Y. Hoekstra is Professor in Multidisciplinary Water Management at the University of Twente, The Netherlands. His research focuses on integrated water resources planning, river basin management and global water issues. His books include *Perspectives on Water* (International Books, 1998) and *Globalization of Water* (with A.K. Chapagain) (Blackwell, 2008).

Jennifer A. Keahey is a PhD student in sociology and Research Assistant for the Center for Fair & Alternative Trade Studies at Colorado State University. Her primary research interests focus on the gender and empowerment dimensions of fair trade in Africa. She has worked in Ghana with a small-scale farmer organization seeking to strengthen indigenous low-external-input technologies and rural women's groups engaged in income generation projects. Her past research focuses also on the organic movement in Latvia.

Chad Lawley is a PhD candidate in the Department of Agricultural and Resource Economics at the University of Maryland.

Carol McAusland is Assistant Professor at the University of Maryland, Department of Agricultural and Resource Economics. Her research focuses on the interaction between globalization, politics, and the provision of environmental and other public goods.

Alejandro Nadal is a full professor at the Center for Economic Studies at El Colegio de México. He has carried out research on macroeconomics, general equilibrium theory, technical change and sustainable resource management. Recent publications include (with Frank Ackerman) *The Flawed Foundations of General Equilibrium: Critical Essays in Economic Theory* (Routledge, 2005), 'Stability and capital flows in the open economy model' (in *Experiencias de crisis y estrategia de desarrollo: autonomía económica y globalización*, El Colegio de México, 2006) and 'Coasean fictions: law and economics revisited' (*Seattle Journal of Social Justice*, forthcoming). He is chair of the Theme on the Environment, Macroeconomics, Trade and Investment (TEMTI) of the World Conservation Union (IUCN). He writes a weekly column on economics and sustainability in *La Jornada*, one of Mexico's leading national newspapers.

W.A.W. Neilson is Professor Emeritus of Law, University of Victoria, Canada. His recent work and publications have been in comparative legal regimes, regional trade agreements, parliamentary law-making and the intersection between intellectual property and competition law fields, particularly in transitional economies in Asia.

Eric Neumayer is Professor of Environment and Development in the Department of Geography and Environment at the London School of Economics and Political Science (LSE). He has broad research interests all relating to evidence-based public policy making. He has published widely in a range of journals across different social science disciplines. His recent books include *Handbook of Sustainable Development* (Edward Elgar, 2007, co-edited with Dr Giles Atkinson and Dr Simon Dietz), *Weak versus Strong Sustainability: Exploring the Limits of Two Opposing Paradigms* (Edward Elgar, revised edition, 2003), *The Pattern of Aid Giving: The Impact of Good Governance on Development Assistance* (Routledge, 2003) and *Greening Trade and Investment: Environmental Protection without Protectionism* (Earthscan, 2001).

Peter Newell is Professor of Development Studies at the University of East Anglia and James Martin Fellow at the Oxford University Centre for the Environment. He has researched and published widely on the relationship between the global political economy and environmental governance. In recent years he has been involved in research on civil society and trade politics in Latin America in general, and environmental politics in Argentina in particular.

David Naguib Pellow is Professor of Ethnic Studies at the University of California, San Diego, where he teaches courses on social movements, environmental justice, globalization, immigration, and race and ethnicity. He has published a number of works on environmental justice issues in communities of color in the USA and globally. His books include: *The Treadmill of Production: Injustice and Unsustainability in the Global Economy* (with Kenneth Gould and Allan Schnaiberg, Paradigm Press, 2008); *Resisting Global Toxics: Transnational Movements for Environmental Justice* (MIT Press, 2007); *The Silicon Valley of Dreams: Environmental Injustice, Immigrant Workers, and the High-tech Global Economy* (with Lisa Sun-Hee Park, New York University Press, 2002); *Garbage Wars: The Struggle for Environmental Justice in Chicago* (MIT Press, 2002); *Urban Recycling and the Search for Sustainable Community Development* (with Adam Weinberg and Allan Schnaiberg, Princeton University Press, 2000); *Power, Justice, and the Environment: A Critical Appraisal of the Environmental Justice Movement* (editor, with Robert J. Brulle, MIT Press, 2005); and *Challenging the Chip: Labor Rights and Environmental Justice in the Global Electronics Industry* (co-editor, with Ted Smith, David Sonnenfeld and Leslie

Byster, Temple University Press, 2006). Pellow is the director of the California Cultures in Comparative Perspective – an international research initiative based at University of California, San Diego. He has served on the boards of directors of several community-based, national and international organizations that are dedicated to improving the living and working environments for people of color, immigrants and working-class communities.

Laura T. Raynolds is co-director of the Center for Fair & Alternative Trade Studies and Professor of Sociology, Colorado State University. She has done extensive research on fair/alternative trade, global agro-food networks and gendered labor forces. Recent publications in these areas include: *Fair Trade: The Challenges of Transforming Globalization* (with D. Murray and J. Wilkinson, Routledge, 2007), as well as over two dozen book chapters and articles in journals such as *World Development*, *Sociologia Ruralis*, *Gender & Society*, and *Agriculture and Human Values*.

Michael T. Rock is the Harvey Wexler Professor of Economics at Bryn Mawr College, USA. His published research focuses on the environment and development, and the role of industrial policy in the second-tier newly industrializing economies of Southeast Asia. His most recent books included *Industrial Transformation in the Developing World* (with David Angel, Oxford University Press, 2005) and *Pollution Control in East Asia* (Institute for International Economics, 2002). Rock is currently working on a book on democracy and development in Southeast Asia.

Henrik Selin is Assistant Professor in the Department of International Relations at Boston University. Educated at universities in Sweden and England, he was a Wallenberg Research Fellow in Environment and Sustainability at the Massachusetts Institute of Technology, USA before taking up his current faculty position. His research and teaching focuses on international and European politics, policy-making and implementation on environment and sustainability issues. He has published numerous book chapters and journal articles on these issues in, among others, *Journal of European Public Policy*, *Review of European Community & International Environmental Law*, *Global Environmental Politics*, *International Environmental Agreements: Politics, Economics and Law*, *Global Governance* and *Ambio*. His current research focuses on the history of sustainable development, and European, North American and global policy developments on hazardous substances, hazardous wastes and climate change.

Robert K. Stumberg is Professor of Law at Georgetown University and director of Georgetown's Harrison Institute for Public Law. His experience in law and public policy includes serving as counsel to the Forum on Democracy & Trade, policy director for the Center for Policy Alternatives, and legislative counsel to local governments in the Washington, DC area. He has published analysis of trade policy and climate change, utility regulation, investor rights, prescription drug programs, and the authority of subnational governments to promote human rights.

Chris Tollefson is Professor of Law and Executive Director of the Environmental Law Centre at the Faculty of Law, University of Victoria, Canada. His current research interests include access to justice and environmental governance, regional trade agreements, and indigenous rights and resource management. His most recent publication is *Setting* *the Standard: Certification, Governance and the Forest Stewardship Council* (2008, UBC Press).

Stacy D. VanDeveer is Associate Professor of Political Science at the University of New Hampshire. His research interests include international environmental policy-making and its domestic impacts, the connections between environmental and security issues, and the role of expertise in policy-making. His current research projects include assessment of climate change politics and policy-making across North America, transatlantic environmental and trade relations, and the structure and effects of fair trade campaigns. He has received fellowships from the Belfer Center for Science and International Affairs at Harvard University's John F. Kennedy School of Government and the Watson Institute for International Studies at Brown University. His work been funded by the US National Science Foundation, the European Union and the Swedish Foundation for Strategic Environmental Research (MISTRA), among others. In addition to authoring and co-authoring numerous articles, book chapters, working papers and reports, he co-edited *EU Enlargement and the Environment: Institutional Change and Environmental Policy in Central and Eastern Europe* (Routledge, 2005) and *Saving the Seas: Values, Science and International Governance* (Maryland Sea Grant Press, College Park, MD, 1997).

James J. Winebrake, PhD, is a teacher and researcher working to solve problems in the energy and environmental fields. His research applies analytical tools to study such topics as alternative transportation technologies, greenhouse gas reduction policies, health impacts of transportation pollution, and transportation systems dynamics. His most recent work involves the application of life-cycle analysis tools, technology optimization modeling and uncertainty analysis to better understand how to mitigate the environmental impacts of personal and freight transportation. Dr Winebrake is currently chair of the Department of Science, Technology & Society/Public Policy at Rochester Institute of Technology (RIT). He also serves as co-director of the RIT Laboratory for Environmental Computing and Decision Making, and is a partner in the consulting firm Energy and Environmental Research Associates, LLC in Pittsford, NY. Before his position at RIT, Dr Winebrake taught for seven years at James Madison University and worked for the US Department of Energy, Office of Energy Efficiency and Renewable Energy. He lives with his wife, Susan, and four children in upstate New York.

Timothy A. Wise is deputy director and researcher at the Global Development and Environment Institute at Tufts University. He is the former executive director of Grassroots International, a Boston-based international aid organization, and co-author of *Confronting Globalization: Economic Integration and Popular Resistance in Mexico* (Kumarian Press, 2004). His current research focuses on globalization's impact on small farmers and the environment.

Lyuba Zarsky is Associate Professor in the International Environmental Policy Program of the Monterey Institute of International Studies in Monterey, California. Her research focuses on policy-relevant studies of globalization, sustainable development and market governance. In the 1990s, she co-founded and co-directed the Nautilus Institute for Security and Sustainability, based in Berkeley. She has also worked for the government of Australia in designing a national sustainable development strategy, and has consulted with a wide range of international organizations, including the OECD, the Asian Development Bank and the UN Development Program. Her recent books include *Enclave Economy, Foreign Investment and Sustainable Development in Mexico's Silicon Valley* (with Kevin Gallagher, MIT Press, 2007), *International Investment for Sustainable Development: Balancing Rights and Rewards* (Earthscan, 2005) and *Human Rights and the Environment: Conflicts and Norms in a Globalizing World* (Earthscan, 2003). She is a Senior Research Fellow with the Global Development and Environment Institute at Tufts University in Boston, and an International Research Fellow at the International Institute for Environment and Development in London.

Abbreviations

ABS	access and benefit-sharing
AFRM	alternative fuels and raw materials
APEC	Asia–Pacific Economic Cooperation
APHIS	Animal and Public Health Information System
ASEAN	Association of Southeast Asian Nations
ATDF	Africa Technology Development Forum
AUSTFA	Australia–US Free Trade Agreement
BAN	Basel Action Network
BAU	business as usual
BEA	British Environment Agency
BECC	Border Environmental Cooperation Commission (USA–Mexico)
BITs	bilateral investment treaties
BSE	bovine spongiform encephalopathy
CAGR	compound annual growth rate
CAMRE	Council of Arab Ministers Responsible for the Environment
CBD	Convention on Biological Diversity
CCAMLR	Convention for the Conservation of Antarctic Marine Living Resources
CERES	Coalition for Environmentally Responsible Economies
CFCs	chlorofluorocarbons
CIS	Center for Comparative and International Studies
CITES	Convention on International Trade in Endangered Species of Wild Fauna and Flora
CoP	Conference of Parties
CSR	corporate social responsibility
CTBC	Computer TakeBack Campaign
CTE	Committee on Trade and the Environment (WTO)
DDA	Doha Development Agenda
EEZ	Exclusive Economic Zone (EU)
EFSA	European Food Safety Authority
EHS	environmental health and safety
EIA	Energy Information Administration (USA)
EKC	environmental Kuznets curve
ENGO	environmental non-government organization
EPA	Environmental Protection Agency (USA)
EPPs	environmentally preferable products
ESCWA	UN Economic and Social Commission for Western Asia
ESG	environmental, social and governance
ESP	electro-static precipitator
ETH	Swiss Federal Institute of Technology (Zurich)
ETIP	Energy Technology Innovation Policy (US research group)

FAO	Food and Agriculture Organization
FDA	Food and Drug Administration (USA)
FDI	foreign direct investment
FLO-I	Fairtrade Labelling Organizations International
FOC	flag of convenience
FTA	free trade agreement
FTAA	Free Trade Area of the Americas
GAFTA	Greater Arab Free Trade Area
GATS	General Agreement on Trade in Services
GATT	General Agreement on Tariffs and Trade
GC	Global Compact (UN)
GDAE	Global Development and Environment Institute (USA)
GDP	gross domestic product
GMO	genetically modified organism
GRI	Global Reporting Initiative
GRRN	GrassRoots Recycling Network
HACCP	Hazard Analysis and Critical Control Point
HFO	heavy fuel oil
HS	Harmonized System (EU)
IAS	invasive alien species
ICA	international commodity agreement
ICC	International Chamber of Commerce
ICRT	International Campaign for Responsible Technology
ICSID	International Centre for the Settlement of Investment Disputes
IEA	International Energy Agency
IED	Institute for Environmental Decisions
IGC	Inter-Governmental Committee
IIA	international investor agreement
IISD	International Institute for Sustainable Development
IKS	indigenous knowledge system
ILO	International Labor Organization
IMO	International Maritime Organization
IMS	international minimum standard
IO	international organization
IPPC	International Plant Protection Convention
IPR	intellectual property rights
ITF	International Transport Workers' Federation
ITPGRFA	International Treaty on Plant Genetic Resources for Food and Agriculture
IUCN	World conservation Union (formerly International Union for Conservation of Nature and Natural Resources)
JCEDAR	Joint Commission for Environment and Development in the Arab Region
JPAC	Joint Public Advisory Committee (NAFTA)
LAS	League of Arab States
LDC	less developed country

LMICs	low- and middle-income countries
LNG	liquefied natural gas
LSE	London School of Economics and Political Science
MA	market access
M&A	mergers and acquisitions
MEA	multilateral environmental agreement
MDO	marine distillate oil
MFN	most favored nation
MGO	marine gas oil
MIR	marginal invasion risk
MISTRA	Swedish Foundation for Strategic Environmental Research
MMPA	Marine Mammal Protection Act (USA)
MNC	multinational corporation
MOU	Memorandum of Understanding
MW	megawatt
NAAEC	North American Agreement on Environmental Cooperation
NACEC	North American Commission for Environmental Cooperation
NAFTA	North American Free Trade Agreement
NGO	non-governmental organization
NIS	non-indigenous species
NT	national treatment
NTB	non-tariff barrier
OECD	Organisation for European Co-operation and Development
PCB	polychlorinated biphenyl
PCT	Patent Cooperation Treaty
PFC	perfluorocarbon
PIC	prior informed consent
PLT	Patent Law Treaty
PP	precautionary principle
PPMs	processes and production methods
PPP	purchasing power parity
PRI	Principles for Responsible Investment
PSC	port state control
R&D	research and development
RCRA	Resource Conservation and Recovery Act (USA)
REACH	Registration, Evaluation, and Authorization of Chemicals
RIT	Rochester Institute of Technology (USA)
RMALC	Mexican Action Network on Free Trade
RoHS	Restriction on Hazardous Substances (EU)
SAARC	South Asian Association for Regional Cooperation
S&DT	special and differential treatment
SARS	severe acute respiratory syndrome
SCC	Stockholm Chamber of Commerce
SCM	Subsidies and Countervailing Measures (Agreement)
SPLT	Substantive Patent Law Treaty
SPS	Sanitary and Phytosanitary Measures

SVTC	Silicon Valley Toxics Coalition
TBT	Technical Barriers to Trade
TNC	transnational corporation
TREM	trade-related environmental measure
TRIPs	Trade-Related Aspects of Intellectual Property (Rights)
TRQ	tariff rate quota
UNCED	UN Conference on Trade and Development
UNCITRAL	UN Commission on International Trade Law
UNCLOS	UN Convention on the Law of the Sea
UNCTAD	UN Conference on Trade and Development
UNDP	UN Development Program
UNEP/ROWA	UN Environment Program/Regional Office for West Asia
UNESCAP	UN Economic and Social Commission for Asia and the Pacific
UNESCO	UN Educational, Scientific and Cultural Organization
URAA	Uruguay Round's Agreement on Agriculture
USDA	US Department of Agriculture
USPTO	US Patent and Trademark Office
WEEE	Waste from Electrical and Electronic Equipment (EU Directive)
WHO	World Health Organization
WIPO	World Intellectual Property Organization
WSSD	World Summit on Sustainable Development
WTO	World Trade Organization

Introduction: international trade and the environment
Kevin P. Gallagher

Over the course of almost 20 years a burgeoning field of interdisciplinary research and policy work has emerged surrounding the issues of international trade and the environment. The purpose of this book is to provide a comprehensive but not exhaustive study of the thinking and policy around these issues. The contributors comprise close to 30 of the world's academic experts in the field, each of whom addresses the topics in his or her sub-field. The volume will serve as a guide for both undergraduate and graduate students, as well as for scholars wishing to start research in this field and to policy-makers wanting a quick and comprehensive reference to research on trade and environment.

The world economy is witnessing a new wave of economic globalization, defined qualitatively as the integration of the world's economies through an increasing array of multilateral, regional, and bilateral trade and investment agreements, as well as numerous examples of governments that are unilaterally reducing the role of the state in economic affairs. This in part has led to large increases in the volumes of international trade and investment in the world economy. According to the World Bank, trade (exports plus imports) as a percentage of world gross domestic product (GDP) was 24 percent in 1960, 38 percent in 1985 and 52 percent in 2005. In other words, over half of all economic activity in the world economy, which is close to US$50 trillion in size, is traded.

The environment has also experienced profound change during this period. According to the recent Millennium Ecosystem Report conducted by 1300 experts from 95 countries, '60 percent of the ecosystem services that support life on Earth – such as fresh water, capture fisheries, air and water regulation, and the regulation of regional climate, natural hazards and pests – are being degraded or used unsustainably' (UNDP, 2005). Such degradation is proving to be costly in economic terms. The World Bank and other international agencies estimate that the economic costs of environmental degradation range from 6 to 10 percent of GDP on an annual basis.

How closely are these trends related? In other words, to what extent is the integration of the world's economies and the subsequent rise in world trade and investment affecting the environment and its politics and policies? Early political debates in the late 1980s and 1990s were rife with contention over this issue. In what are now seen as rather simplistic depictions of a very complex set of interactions, many argued that increased trade would automatically improve the environment, while others said that trade automatically makes the environment worse off. In the politics that ensued, for example in the negotiations surrounding the North American Free Trade Agreement (NAFTA), environment became the 'make-or-break issue' that led to the passage of the agreement.

The literature on trade and environment, mirrored in part by policy discussions on the subject, can be divided into three sub-categories:

1. *Trade and environmental quality*: this body of work examines the extent to which trade and investment flows, and the policies that lead to increases in such flows, affect

1

environmental quality both positively and negatively. This literature consists of work largely (but not exclusively) conducted by economists and natural scientists.

2. *Trade and environmental politics*: here scholars examine the political economy of environmental aspects of trade policy and conversely the trade aspects of environmental policy. This work is largely conducted by political scientists.

3. *Trade and environmental policy*: this sub-field examines the extent to which new trade rules affect the ability of nations and the global governance institutions outside the trade regime to deploy effective environmental policy. There is also a literature on the extent to which new environmental policies will affect the ability of firms to compete internationally. This literature is often conducted by legal scholars, economists and political scientists.

After almost 20 years of research that includes countless volumes, special journal issues, articles, testimony and so forth, a number of the more contentious issues that arose at the beginning of debates over trade and environment have reached close to consensus. However, some are as controversial as ever. This brief introduction provides a context for these three sub-fields and casts the chapters included in the book in this light.

Trade and environmental quality
Political and policy debates over trade and environment stem from conceptions regarding the impact that trade will have on environmental quality. Since the early 1990s some have contended that trade liberalization would lead to economic growth and that once nations reached a certain level of income they would begin to reduce their negative impacts on the environment. Others countered that trade liberalization would lead to a mass migration of pollution-intensive firms to nations with weaker environmental laws. This would lead to increases in pollution in the developing world and put downward pressure on environmental regulations in nations with stringent norms. Such debates jump-started what has become a substantial literature on these questions. Ironically, there is now an emerging consensus in academic thinking regarding these questions, yet the policy community is often still mired in older debates.

The theory of international trade
In theory international trade and the environment can be mutually compatible, and perhaps even reinforcing. According to independent theories of international trade on the one hand, and environmental economics on the other, trade liberalization can bring economic benefits that can be distributed so as to reduce poverty and protect the environment.

The economist David Ricardo showed that because countries face different costs to produce the same product, if each country produces and then exports the goods for which it has comparatively lower costs, then all parties benefit. The effects of comparative advantage (as Ricardo's notion became called) on factors of production were developed in the 'Heckscher–Ohlin' model. This model assumes that in all countries there is perfect competition, technology is constant and readily available, there is the same mix of goods and services, and that factors of production (such as capital and labor) can move freely between industries.

Within this rubric, the Stolper–Samuelson theorem adds that international trade can increase the price of products (and therefore the welfare) in which a country has a comparative advantage. Foreign direct investment (FDI) can contribute to development by increasing employment and by human capital and technological 'spillovers' where foreign presence 'crowds in' new technology and investment. In theory, the gains from trade accruing to 'winning' sectors freed to exploit their comparative advantages have the (Pareto) possibility to compensate the 'losers' of trade liberalization. Moreover, if the net gains from trade are positive, there are more funds available to stimulate growth and reduce poverty. In a perfect world, then, free trade and increasing exports could indeed be unequivocally beneficial to all parties.

These theories have been extended to conceptualize the trade and environment relationship. The impacts on the environment can be seen as direct and indirect effects. Direct effects are the least studied but can be the most grave. Chapters in this volume by Christopher Costello, Chad Lawley and Carol McAusland, and by James J. Corbett and James J.Winebrake, examine the impacts of international trade on the introduction of alien invasive species and on global shipping emissions respectively. In a January 2000 article in the journal *BioScience*, noted scientist David Pimentel and his colleagues estimated that the annual economic costs of alien invasive species in the USA could amount to $137 billion. According to Pimentel et al., roughly 90 percent of these invasives enter the USA through trade. Therefore the trade-related economic costs are approximately $123 billion (Pimentel et al., 2000).

A recent study found that total emissions from ships are largely increasing due to the increase in foreign commerce (or international trade). The economic costs of SO_2 pollution range from $697 million to $3.9 billion during the period examined, or $77 million to $435 million on an annual basis. The bulk of the cost is from foreign commerce, where the annual costs average to $42 million to $241 million. For NO_x emissions the costs are $3.7 billion over the entire period, or $412 million per year. Because foreign trade is driving the growth in US shipping, we also estimate the effect of the Uruguay Round on emissions. Separating out the effects of global trade agreements reveals that the trade-agreement-led emissions amounted to $96 million to $542 million for SO_2 between 1993 and 2001, or $10 million to $60 million per year. For NO_x they were $745 million for the whole period, or $82 million per year (Gallagher, 2005a). The article by DeSombre in this volume (Chapter 16) gives an in-depth analysis of the politics of global shipping and the environment.

A useful framework for thinking about the indirect effects of trade on the environment has been proposed by Gene Grossman and Alan Krueger (1993). They identify three mechanisms by which trade and investment liberalization affect the environment: scale, composition and technique effects. Scale effects occur when liberalization causes an expansion of economic activity. If the nature of that activity is unchanged but the scale is growing, then pollution and resource depletion will increase along with output. Composition effects occur when increased trade leads nations to specialize in the sectors where they enjoy a comparative advantage.

When comparative advantage is derived from differences in environmental stringency, the composition effect of trade will exacerbate existing environmental problems in the countries with relatively lax regulations. Race-to-the-bottom discussions are perfectly plausible in economic theory. The Hecksher–Ohlin (H–O) theory in trade economics postulates that nations will gain a comparative advantage in those industries where they are factor abundant. Applying the H–O theory to pollution, then, it could be argued that a

Table I.1   Stolper–Samuelson and sustainable development: winners and losers in trade liberalization

	Economic	Environmental
Winners	*Export sectors*	*Export sectors* Pollution haloes Composition effects
Losers	*Import sectors*	*Export sector* Scale and composition effects Worker health and safety *Import sector* Liabilities Genetic diversity

country with less stringent environmental standards would be factor abundant in the ability to pollute. Therefore trade liberalization between a developed and a developing nation where the developed nation has more stringent regulations may lead to an expansion in pollution-intensive economic activity in the developing country with fewer regulations. As Brian Copeland discusses in this volume (Chapter 4), the developing country with the less stringent regulations becomes a 'pollution haven' for pollution-intensive economic activity.

Technique effects, or changes in resource extraction and production technologies, can potentially lead to a decline in pollution per unit of output for two reasons. First, the liberalization of trade and investment may encourage multinational corporations to transfer cleaner technologies to developing countries. Second, if economic liberalization increases income levels, the newly affluent citizens may demand a cleaner environment.

The economic and environmental dimensions of trade and sustainable development are outlined in Table I.1. From an economic perspective, when liberalization occurs and nations trade where they have a comparative advantage, the 'winners' are those sectors that can now export more of their goods or services. Theoretically this will not only cause expansion of exports but also of employment and wages in such sectors. The 'losers' in trade liberalization are those sectors that will find it harder to face an inflow of newly competitive imports. In those sectors one would expect a contraction, layoffs and wages decreases. If the gains to the export sector outweigh the losses to the import sector, the net gains are positive. This leaves the 'possibility' that the winners can compensate the losers, or that the gains from trade can be used to stimulate pro-poor growth.

Column 3 in Table I.1 outlines potential environmental winners and losers. There may be environmental benefits from being an economic winner. First, this can occur if trade liberalization causes a compositional shift toward less environmentally degrading forms of economic activity. Second, there is also the possibility of environmental improvements in relatively environmentally destructive sectors if those sectors attract large amounts of investment from firms that transfer state-of-the-art environmental technologies to the exporting sector.

Trade liberalization can also have negative effects. It can cause a composition effect where the economy moves toward more pollution-intensive industry. Edward Barbier

(Chapter 5) shows that trade can shift the composition of exports from a country back toward resource-intensive industries and accentuate 'Dutch disease'. In this case a resource export boom will increase the value of a domestic currency, crowd out other export sectors and deepen the composition of exports toward an environmentally unsound extractive industry while at the same time pushing the poor into more marginal existences that can also harm the environment. Hoekstra (Chapter 8) shows that trade can shift the composition of water-intensive imports and exports for countries as well. Scale effects can also adversely impact the environment, and the health and safety of the workers in economically expanding plants that may have to handle increasing amounts of pollution-intensive inputs (see Pellow, Chapter 18).

It is often overlooked that there can also be adverse environmental effects of being a trade policy 'loser'. Some analysts argue that the shrinking of a sector that is environmentally degrading is beneficial for an economy because by definition less economic activity will equal less pollution. On the other hand, a shrinking sector can bring with it environmental liabilities that may cost taxpayers increased amounts. Moreover, from a political-economy perspective, shrinking sectors may put pressure on governments to turn a blind eye to environmental performance in order to maintain an economic presence (in other words causing a worsening technique effect).

Losing economic comparative advantages can also hurt the environment when losing sectors are those related to positive externalities. In two separate chapters James Boyce and Tim Wise (Chapters 7 and 9) discuss how this occurred in Mexico, where smallholder maize growers are finding it hard to compete with a flood of US corn imports after the North American Free Trade Agreement (NAFTA) was signed. Mexico is the center of origin for maize and the cradle of maize crop genetic diversity. Thus pressure to leave the land or convert it to other crops is threatening such diversity and global food security. Smallholders cultivating maize are generating positive externalities of protecting a global public good and maintaining diversity. Yet such prices are not reflected in their goods. Boyce provides similar examples for jute production in Bangladesh.

In theory, then, trade liberalization can benefit the environment but only if winners compensate the social and environmental losers with the gains from trade in the form of institution-building for sustainable development. This is very difficult in developing countries for political, cultural and economic reasons. On the political level, trade liberalization costs a great deal of political capital to begin with. It is then very difficult to get the winners of a trade policy to agree to give away a portion of their gains. What's more, many in developing countries may not accept compensation for losing. Indigenous groups see themselves as having ancient rights to land and resources, and may not be willing to be 'bought off' (Kanbur, 2001). Even if they could be bought off, at what price would this come? The fields of ecological and environmental economics have made great strides in recognizing that the environment has values that need to be incorporated into the price scheme to allocate resources in a more socially optimal manner. However, the methodologies for identifying the exact prices for those values are very much in their infancy, controversial, and often inappropriate – especially in developing-country contexts (Ackerman and Heinzerling, 2004).

The evidence on the environmental effects of trade is mixed as well. Economic integration is contributing to worldwide environmental degradation, but not so much because the developing world is serving as a 'pollution haven' for developed-world pollution. In

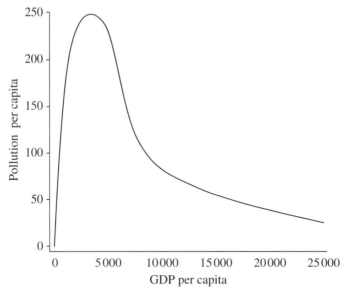

Figure I.1   The environmental Kuznets curve

1992, the World Bank's *World Development Report* made the case that while trade-led growth may cause sharp increases in environmental degradation during the early stages of economic development, such degradation would begin to taper off as nations reached 'turning points' ranging between $3000 and $5000 GDP per capita (World Bank, 1992). The Bank was generalizing from a landmark 1991 paper by economists Gene Grossman and Alan Krueger. This article examined the relationship between ambient concentrations of criterial air pollutants and GDP per capita. When they plotted their regression results they found that lower-income nations had higher rates of pollution per capita whereas the reverse occurred for higher-income nations (Grossman and Krueger, 1993).

This relationship became known as the EKC(the environmental Kuznets curve), borrowing its name from the landmark article by Simon Kuznets that found a similar relationship between income inequality and GDP per capita in a cross-section of countries in the 1950s (Kuznets, 1957). For the developed countries, the three factors described earlier (scale, composition and technique effects) are seen to be interacting: as income has grown, the composition of industry has shifted toward relatively less pollution-intensive economic activity while at the same time improvements in technology and environmental regulation have occurred. Although overall levels of growth (scale) have vastly increased, they have been offset by composition and technique effects.

To this day, generalizations of these findings have been used to make the claim that nations should grow now through trade liberalization and worry about the environment later (Bhagwhati and Daly, 1993). EKC studies have become a cottage industry, with close to 100 articles published since the original 1991 piece (see Stern, 2004). As Van Alstine and Neumayer show in their chapter in this volume (Chapter 3), what is ironic is that at as the policy community has rushed to generalize the EKC in the political realm, the consensus in the peer-reviewed academic literature on the EKC has become much more cautious. Most importantly, the literature shows that the empirical evidence for the EKC is relatively weak and limited. The chapter by Michael Rock and David Angel in this volume (Chapter 10) shows that as East Asian 'miracle' nations grew, they indeed polluted the environment significantly. The authors show that over time these nations began to improve environmental governance and performance, but this did not happen automatically. Indeed, it was conscious orchestration by the state, which integrated environmental policy into industrial and innovation policies, that led to success.

Yet opponents of free trade often claim that trade liberalization will result in a mass migration of pollution-intensive industry from developed countries with stringent environmental regulations to developing countries with lax environmental standards. Not only will such migration cause increases in pollution in developing countries; they argue that pressure will then be exerted on developed-country standards in the name of competition – effectively creating a 'race to the bottom' in standards.

As in the EKC literature, Brian Copeland in this volume (Chapter 4) shows that it is also ironic that the majority of the peer-reviewed literature has found very limited evidence for pollution havens but that some in the policy community continue to cite it as a dire consequence of trade liberalization. Very recently, however, a handful of studies have indeed found evidence of pollution havens in the world economy. A study by Cole (2004) examines North–South trade flows for ten air and water pollutants. Cole finds evidence of pollution haven effect, but claims that such effects are quite small relative to other explanatory variables. Another study, by Kahn and Yoshino (2004), looks at bilateral trade data over the years 1980 to 1997 for 128 nations in 34 manufacturing industries, and examines how low-, middle- and high-income nations differ regarding their income elasticity in exporting pollution-intensive products. They find that among nations outside of regional trade blocs there is general support for the pollution haven hypothesis. As national incomes rise, exports of pollution-intensive products decrease relative to exports of 'cleaner' goods. Nations participating in regional trading arrangements have slightly weaker pollution haven effects than those observed outside of regional trading blocs.

The reason why so many of these studies fail to find evidence for pollution havens (or find small effects) in developing countries is that the economic costs of environmental degradation are relatively much smaller than many other factors of production – especially those that determine comparative advantage. In general, the developing world is factor abundant in unskilled labor that takes the form of manufacturing assembly plants. On average, such manufacturing activity is relatively less pollution intensive than more capital-laden manufacturing activities such as cement, pulp and paper, and base metals production. A full review of this literature is beyond the scope of this chapter (see Jaffe et al., 1995; Neumayer, 2001 for comprehensive reviews of this literature).

Another misconception held by some in policy circles is that since there is weak evidence of a pollution haven, there is no rationale for linking trade and environmental policy. However, such claims overlook that the pollution haven hypothesis is a theory of firm location, and does not provide a framework for analyzing the environmental impacts of firms when they do move to another country, albeit for other reasons. The chapters in this volume by Zarsky and Sims Gallagher (Chapters 6 and 11) shed light on this. Zarsky provides an overview of the interaction between foreign investment and environment, showing that firms have the potential to be 'pollution haloes' whereby they bring better environmental practices to developing nations and can help them 'leapfrog' to higher standards. Indeed, Zarsky also demonstrates cases where this has occurred. Sims Gallagher, however, shows that in the auto sector US firms brought dated cars without catalytic converters to China.

Trade and environmental politics

The contentious issues discussed in the previous section certainly spill over into the political realm.

The analysis that is thus far the most comprehensive in scope has been conducted by David Vogel. Vogel (1997) primarily draws from theories of political power (realist) and domestic politics to argue that trade liberalization and environmental protection are not incompatible. In an investigation of the EU, the WTO and the NAFTA he notes that, by and large, trade liberalization has strengthened rather than weakened the ability of nations to protect the environment. Importantly, however, he acknowledges that this did not happen automatically. Indeed, he concludes that the impact of trade liberalization on regulatory standards is a function of the preferences of powerful states (which are in part informed by domestic politics) and the level of economic integration (in other words the stronger the trade institution) between the negotiating partners. According to Vogel, 'California effects' occur when powerful (often correlating with wealthy) nations prod their trading partners to strengthen their policies in the integration process. 'Delaware effects' arise when the opposite occurs.

In this light, Vogel concludes that a 'trade' occurs: market access is granted by powerful states in exchange for raising consumer and environmental standards. It was the EU's strong commitment to integration that empowered Germany (in turn empowered by its environmental community) to influence the environmental policies of other European states, whereas, in the case of the GATT, a much weaker institution, the ability of strong and wealthy countries to influence its partners was more diffuse. To Vogel, NAFTA falls in the middle. While it allows the USA to influence Mexican environmental policy more than was possible under the WTO, it does not go as far as the EU. Evoking the work of Albert Hirschman, a former student of Vogel has added that the key condition that powerful countries use to lure weaker ones into protecting their environment is access to the powerful countries' markets (Steinberg, 1997).

The role of domestic politics is key to the formation of the powerful state's environmental preferences. Interestingly, Vogel explains how 'baptist and bootlegger' coalitions are formed to push hegemons toward advocating environmental policy in trade agreements. During prohibition in the USA, two constituencies had an interest in keeping the southern states 'dry.' First were baptists, who had a moral case to outlaw alcohol. Second were bootleggers, who stood to gain from keeping alcohol sales illegal. In a trade and environment setting, Vogel explains:

> For producers who wish to maintain or increase trade barriers, the convergence of trade and regulatory policies provides them with two significant political benefits. First, it furnishes them with an argument for trade restrictions that has relatively wide political appeal: consumer or environmental regulation. They can argue against the removal of trade barriers on similar grounds. Second, it provides them with an important new source of political support, as consumer and environmental organizations enjoy considerable influence in a number of capitalist nations. (Vogel, 1997, p. 21)

Baptist and bootlegger coalitions can arise in various forms. DeSombre has shown how such coalitions form to increase the stringency of environmental regulations in other countries. In this case, industry is interested in such action because it fears that, since it is subject to such regulation, it will not be able to compete with firms that are not (DeSombre, 2001). So in this case industry supports trade liberalization. For NAFTA, baptist and bootlegger coalitions were also formed in opposition to trade liberalization – but the coalitions were formed for similar reasons to DeSombre's. Under NAFTA, certain industries allied with anti-NAFTA NGOS for fear of having to compete with foreign firms that did not have to adhere to such regulation (Vogel, 1997). This coalition was even broader under NAFTA: baptists and bootleggers were joined by conservative political constituencies led by leaders such as Patrick Buchanan and Ross Perot, who questioned NAFTA's ability to uphold the sovereignty of US regulation. Both DeSombre and Vogel describe coalitions that form for fear of being unable to compete because firms overseas *do not* have to comply with stringent environmental standards.

Interestingly, the USA is not always the home of stronger standards and therefore coalitions to increase standards abroad – as Henrik Selin and Stacy VanDeveer discuss in this volume (Chapter 15), as do Thomas Bernauer and Philipp Aerni (Chapter 14). Indeed, the most recent baptist and bootlegger coalition in the USA has arisen because of stringent standards for genetically modified organisms (GMOs) in Europe. Europe is a large market for US farm products, but increasingly requires that all crops sold in Europe not include GMOs. While many industries still fight such efforts, some are joining with environmental groups in the USA to push for GMO standards in that country, thus securing access to European markets for US farmers. In an attempt to draw out general lessons, then, Vogel concludes that trade liberalization is more apt to cause a California effect when the most powerful among a group of negotiating nations has influential domestic constituencies that support more stringent environmental standards. To summarize, the stronger the commitment of nations to coordinate policy, the more powerful is the California effect (Vogel, 1997; 1999).

Vogel's work is an in-depth and pioneering analysis of the politics of trade and environment. However, while he eloquently shows how power, markets, institutions and interest groups all play a role in the formation of trade and environment regimes, he falls short of weighing the relative importance of each of these variables. Such an effort has been undertaken in two studies of NAFTA. In a volume that describes the passage of NAFTA, Frederick Mayer (1998) devotes considerable attention to explaining the determinants of the trade and environment regime that arose as a result of NAFTA. To Mayer, this regime was a necessary condition for the passage of NAFTA as a whole. Where Vogel could be said to have drawn from primarily realist and institutional approaches to trade and environment, Mayer's explanation simultaneously blends realist, liberal and constructivist theories to explain the creation of a trade and environment regime. Drawing from game theory and process-tracing through a gamut of confidential documents and interviews, Mayer outlines three major episodes that together led to the creation of such a regime under NAFTA: the need to secure fast-track negotiating authority in the USA; the negotiations themselves; and the ratification process. With political power as a constant force in all three stages, Mayer argues that it was institutional factors that determined the first stage of NAFTA, interests the second, and constructivisim the third.

For Mayer, each stage of NAFTA was determined by interactions among institutions, interests and social construction. From an institutional perspective, US fast-track and ratification policies loomed over the entire period. Interest groups saw that they would be key brokers in seeing that these institutional hurdles were cleared and began linking their demands to the negotiations. During the elections of 1992, Bill Clinton needed to support NAFTA but also had to distinguish himself from his opponent, then President George Bush. Seeing the support of interests such as environment and labor as seminal to his election campaign, he decided to support NAFTA *and* labor and environmental-side agreements (Mayer, 1998). By doing so he automatically opened the door to even more interest-group involvement.

In an in-depth analysis of environmental NGO involvement during NAFTA, John Audley (1997) showed how NGOS performed different roles during each stage of the process. Some used grassroots tactics to threaten the ability of the agreements to succeed, while others used that leverage to be included in the negotiating process and directly influence the outcome. Referring to these classic 'good cop, bad cop' tactics as pre-emptive leverage and accommodating politics, Audley shows how procedural rules (institutions) enabled NGOS to pre-empt negotiations. However, both pre-emptive leverage and accommodating politics were essential to gain concessions from negotiators. He also reveals that such tactics may have backfired in the end. Indeed, he argues that the coalition of accommodating environmental groups used their access to trade policy-makers and their general support for the principles of free trade to neutralize any opposition to NAFTA's passage by the more adversarial pre-emptive groups (Audley, 1997).

The campaign to finally ratify and pass NAFTA, however, lends itself, in Mayer's view, to constructivist analysis. In the effort to win voters during the ratification process, clashing interests waged symbolic campaigns to make their points. The final debates over NAFTA were not about its actual effect, but about what it symbolized. Those against NAFTA associated it with images of corporate greed and as triggering a 'giant sucking sound' of jobs and environmental regulations going south of the border. Conversely, those in favor of NAFTA attempted to create images of unanimous support by lining up all living ex-presidents with the chairs of many influential CEOs, and so forth (Mayer, 1998). Peter Newell in this volume (Chapter 13) demonstrates how similar forces have come into play in clashes over trade and environment in social movements across Latin America.

In short, the particular institutional framework (US elections and the fast-track process) in the USA that gives interest groups a number of opportunities to engage in trade policy, coupled with the ability of such interests (and the interests of the government) to wage symbolic campaigns both supporting and against NAFTA, led to a final outcome that included environmental provisions in the NAFTA text and in the form of formal and informal side agreements. For the other two parties involved, Mexico and Canada, who didn't have these constraints, NAFTA's environmental package was more of a formality.

Trade and environmental policy

The evidence just summarized underscores the need to couple any economic integration with social and environmental policy at the local, national and/or international level. The fact that there is only mixed evidence that trade liberalization is associated with growth shows that trade must be coupled with institution-building. The fact that there is limited evidence for the EKC shows that economic integration cannot be relied on for automatic environmental improvements. Indeed, the evidence shows that the lack of effective institutions in the presence of economic integration has exacerbated longstanding problems in the developing world.

However, a silver lining lies in the fact that there is little evidence of pollution havens. This suggests that strengthening environmental institutions and standards in developing and developed countries alike will not deter foreign and domestic investments. Because the abatement costs of pollution are so small relative to other key costs, firms will not move to or from developing countries as regulations rise (at least to US levels). Nicholas Ashford in this volume (Chapter 24) draws the key links between environmental regulation, innovation and global trade. Michael Porter's hypothesis (Porter, 2002) that regulation-inspired innovation to reduce environmental degradation can lead to reduced costs and therefore increased competitiveness, also deserves to be spelled out. Environmental regulation can lure firms to seek ways of increasing resource productivity and therefore reduce the costs of inputs. Such 'innovation offsets' can exceed the costs of environmental compliance. Therefore the firm that leads in introducing cleaner technologies into the production process may enjoy a 'first-mover advantage' over those industries in the world economy that continue to use more traditional, dirtier production methods (for a critical rebuttal see Palmer et al., 1995).

Rhys Jenkins (1998) has offered a synthesis of the Porter hypothesis, arguing that regulation is more likely to lead to 'innovation offsets' under three conditions. Note that each condition requires that a firm have substantial market power in an industry in which there is substantial innovative activity. First, because cost reductions are more likely to occur where new clean technologies are developed rather than in industries that adopt end-of-pipe solutions, the level of R&D is likely to be a factor in determining the impact on competitiveness. Second, innovation offsets are more likely in industries or firms that have the ability to absorb environmental costs, which is most often determined by profit margins and firm size. Finally, they are more likely in firms that have the ability to pass on increased costs to consumers in the form of higher prices.

Creative policy does not have to be designed by government. Conroy (2002) analyzes how advocacy organizations have used certification processes to reward firms that produce and trade goods that use high social and environmental standards in their production processes. Through such efforts, the Forest Stewardship Council has certified 60 million acres of forest between 1995 and 2001, accounting for more than 5 percent of the world's working forests. Working on the demand side of the equation, advocacy groups set up market campaigns to pressure firms to buy these products. Indeed, some retail giants are now actually seeking to participate in these processes. When governments or citizens' groups recognize more sustainable practices in the developing world, there are avenues to gain market access for production processes that would be deemed inefficient by an unfettered marketplace. Laura T. Raynolds and Jennifer A. Keahey in this volume (Chapter 17) present a case study on fair trade certification in Africa.

Although developing countries agreed to enter a new round of trade negotiations only on the condition that development would be the centerpiece, there are growing concerns that this promise will go unfulfilled. Key among those concerns is the notion that a new trade agreement will not give the developing world the 'policy space' to use the very instruments and tools that many industrialized nations took advantage of to reach their current levels of environmental protection and development. The jury is still out on this, but new agreements must give countries the space to establish the necessary institutions to steer growth toward development. If that doesn't occur, the world trading system will continue to confuse the means of increasing trade and investment with their ends of sustainable development.

Besides preserving the space for national efforts, as J. Samuel Barkin demonstrates in this volume (Chapter 26), three models of institutions have emerged that deal with trade and sustainable development linkages at the regional and global levels. On the one hand the EU has a very deep set of linkages between integration and sustainable development, whereas the WTO has quite limited linkages. Trade arrangements negotiated by the USA are situated somewhere in the middle.

The EU has made reducing economic, social and environmental disparities a cornerstone of its regional integration strategies. According to Anderson and Cavanagh (2004), the EU made $324 billion in development grants to this end between 1961 and 2001. Annual aid for a new member of the EU can be as high as 4 percent of GDP. As a result, the relatively less well-off European countries have improved their social and environmental situations as well as having benefited economically from integration. Coupled with development funds, the EU has established regional social and environmental ministries that set independent standards and allow for civil society participation and monitoring as well.

In its regional arrangements, the USA allows for a much more limited level of linkages between trade and sustainable development. The majority of regional trade arrangements (such as the US agreements with Chile, Jordan, Morocco, Singapore, Central America and others) have text concerning environmental matters but leave out social concerns completely, set up no institutions, and have very limited avenues for civil society participation. Indeed, according to Anderson and Cavanagh (2004), EU development funds total approximately ten times the amount of US economic assistance grants to all of Latin America. In the largest US regional arrangement, the NAFTA, a parallel agreement set up an environmental institution called the Commission for Environmental Cooperation. With an annual budget of $9 million, the institution can do little more than provide technical assistance to the parties involved, but it does allow interesting levels of civil society participation. NAFTA does not include any mechanism to address regional inequality. Thus the experience of Ireland, Spain and Greece with EU development funds has resulted in increasing standards of living as well as social and environmental improvements. Mexico, on the other hand, has become worse off since NAFTA: incomes have grown a mere 1 percent annually and poverty and inequality have worsened. What's more, the economic costs of environmental degradation have reached 10 percent of GDP annually (Gallagher, 2004).

On the world stage, the WTO has limited formal linkage between sustainable development and trade, although that may be changing. At the social end, the WTO (and the GATT before it) has allowed for 'special and differentiated treatment' for developing countries, allowing them to deploy many of the development policies that were used in the developed world in the past but are now not allowed. However, successive rounds of WTO negotiations are shrinking the policy space for such policies. Agreements on intellectual property rights, investment rules and services have all made it much more difficult for developing nations to deploy the development policies used by middle- and high-income nations in the twentieth century (Gallagher, 2005b).

Steve Charnovitz's overview of the trade and environment issue in Chapter 19 is impeccable. On the environmental front, there has been a longstanding controversy regarding the extent to which WTO laws restrict the ability of nations and the world community to establish effective environmental policy. At the national level, numerous cases have gone before the WTO claiming that national environmental policies have served as unfair trade barriers to member nations. Two famous cases involving tuna and shrimp respectively occurred when developing-country governments challenged US laws that restricted imports of these fish when they were caught using techniques that also killed dolphins or sea turtles. Developing countries saw such laws as unfair trade barriers. The WTO has ruled that it does not object to environmental policy *per se*, but to environmental policies that are trade restrictive. The USA has since amended these laws (Neumayer, 2001).

The divide between developed and developing countries on trade issues is just as contentious. The widely publicized tuna–dolphin dispute is a case in point. The US Marine Mammal Protection Act (MMPA) enables the USA to impose sanctions on nations whose fishing practices harm dolphins and other protected marine life. Indeed, this is one of the effective forms of domestic internationalization discussed in the work of DeSombre. However, in the late 1980s, under MMPA the USA imposed an embargo on Mexico and Venezuela because their fishing practices were ensnaring dolphins in the process of catching tuna. Mexico filed a complaint under the GATT, arguing that GATT rules forbid nations from restricting the import of a product on the basis of how it is produced. Later that year a GATT panel ruled that the tuna embargo violated the US GATT obligations. Environmentalists went berzerk, and argued that as environmental policy was moving increasingly toward focusing on the environmental impacts of products through their life cycle – including production, distribution, use and disposal – the world trading regime was moving in the opposite direction (French, 1998).

While thus far the clash of environment and trade regimes has occurred over national environmental laws, many are concerned that the key compliance mechanisms in many multilateral environmental agreements (MEAs) will be deemed illegal under the WTO. At least seven MEAs have actual trade provisions in their text: the Convention on International Trade in Endangered Species of Wild Fauna and Flora (CITES); the Montreal Protocol on Substances that Deplete the Stratospheric Ozone Layer; the Basel Convention on the Control of Transboundary Movements of Hazardous Wastes and their Disposal; the Convention on Biological Diversity and the Cartagena Protocol on Biosafety; the Framework Convention on Climate Change and its subsequent Kyoto Protocol; in addition to the Rotterdam Convention on the Prior Informed Consent (PIC) Procedure for Certain Hazardous Chemicals and Pesticides in International Trade (UNEP/IISD, 2000). The trade provisions of these MEAs, such as the threat of sanctions under the Montreal Protocol and CITES, have in some cases been key to their success (Barrett, 1994). Although a provision of a specific MEA has not yet been called into question by the WTO, some scholars argue that the possibility of such questioning is 'chilling' the regimes of MEAs so that they cannot carry out their mandates effectively. Indeed, certain export bans in the Basel Convention have been seen as an unsound precedent by the trade community, and it is possible that this is affecting the development of newer MEAs (Krueger, 1999).

As Charnovitz points out in this volume (Chapter 19), from a legal perspective, these conflicts can be boiled down to two issues that can violate a core norm in the trade regime, that of 'non-discrimination' – treating producers in a domestic economy in the same manner as producers that one relies on for imported goods. The two issues are those over the tools to enforce environmental policies, and environmental policies aimed at the production methods of environmentally degrading products. Many of the policies that have been the subject of WTO conflict concern attempts to enhance national (or international) environmental protection through government intervention of various forms. Interventions that use subsidies, quantitative restrictions and of course sanctions are often questioned as not being the 'least trade restrictive' measures to achieve environmental goals. Another set of conflicts relates to the production processes of various goods and services. Environmental policy is often concerned with processes in the 'life cycle' of a product that could harm or benefit the environment. What causes problems in trade law is when government measures are seen as 'discriminatory', that is, pertaining to one set of producers (for example those wishing to sell in a domestic market) but not others (such as domestic producers) (Sampson, 2000). The Technical Barriers to Trade (TBT) agreement under the WTO prohibits the discrimination of products on the basis of their production methods. Again, non-discrimination is the principal norm of the trade regime.

The beef hormone and tuna–dolphin cases were only the beginning of trade and environmental disputes in the world trading system. Since tuna–dolphin there have been numerous other conflicts. Among these have been cases to do with environmental aspects of food safety, fuel economy standards in cars, devices to protect endangered turtles and sanctions to protect endangered rhinoceros and tiger stocks in the wild (Schlingemann, 1998; WTO, 2001). And fears about MEAs continue to loom as well. This all came to a head in 1999 at the Seattle Ministerial of the WTO, intended to launch a new round of trade negotiations. While the USA and Europe bickered over agricultural subsidies and food safety regulations, the developing countries criticized both the EU and the USA for wanting to impose environmental regulations that developing countries saw as 'veiled protectionism'. Outside of the negotiations hundreds of thousands from across the planet echoed these and many other concerns.

Although there has never been a WTO case to this effect, at the multilateral level there is growing concern that MEAs will be overridden by WTO laws. Many MEAs use trade restrictions as an enforcement mechanism, and the fear is that such mechanisms would be deemed WTO illegal and thus reduce the effectiveness of MEAs and 'chill' the negotiations of future MEAs (Neumayer, 2001). In response to this, the Doha Round of WTO negotiations (2001– present) is charged with examining the relationship between MEAs and the WTO.

Some scholars and policy-makers argue that more needs to be done, that indeed a 'World Environmental Organization' should be established in order to serve as a counterweight to the WTO (Esty, 1997; Speth, 2004). Indeed, such an institution has also been proposed by none other than former WTO head Renalto Ruggerio: 'I would suggest that we need a similar multi-lateral rules-based system for the environment – a World Environment Organization to also be the institutional or legal counterpart to the WTO' (Ruggiero, 1999). Discussion of a World Environmental Organization has become quite controversial, with many in the environmental community arguing against it on numerous grounds. Some say that the existing global environmental regime (surrounding such bodies as the UN Environment Program) has not been able to fulfill its mandate and the focus should be on reforming the existing architecture, not creating new institutions that could become plagued with the same problems (Najam, 2003).

This brief and far from exhaustive introduction to the field opens the door to over 25 chapters that may comprise the most comprehensive treatment of the trade and environment literature in academia.

References

Ackerman, Frank and Lisa Heinzerling (2004), *Priceless: On Knowing the Price of Everything and the Value of Nothing*, New York: New Press.

Anderson, Sarah and John Cavanagh (2004), *Lessons of European Integration for the Americas*, Washington, DC: Institute for Policy Studies.

Audley, John (1997), *Green Politics and Global Trade: NAFTA and the Future of Environmental Politics*, Washington, DC: Georgetown University Press.

Barrett, Scott (1994), 'Self-enforcing international environmental agreements', *Oxford Economic Papers*, **46**(0), 878–94.

Bhagwati, Jagdish N. and Herman E. Daly (1993), 'Debate: does free trade harm the environment?', *Scientific American*, November, 41–57.

Cole, Matthew A. (2004), 'Trade, the pollution haven hypothesis and the EKC', *Ecological Economics*, **48**, 71–9.

Conroy, Michael (2002), *Can Advocacy-Led Certification Systems Transform Global Corporate Practices? Evidence, and some theory*, PERI Working Paper No. 21.

DeSombre, Elizabeth (2001), *Domestic Sources of International Environmental Policy*, Cambridge, MA: MIT Press.

Esty, Daniel (1997), *Greening the GATT*, Washington, DC: Institute for International Economics.

French, Hilary (1998), *Vanishing Borders: Protecting the Planet in the Age of Globalization*, New York: Norton.

Gallagher, Kevin P. (2004), *Free Trade and the Environment: Mexico, NAFTA, and Beyond*, Palo Alto, CA: Stanford University Press.

Gallagher, Kevin (2005a), 'International trade and air pollution: estimating the economic costs of air emissions from waterborne commerce vessels in the United States', *Journal of Environmental Management*, **77**(2), 99–103.

Gallagher, Kevin P. (ed.), (2005b), *Putting Development First: The Importance of Policy space in the WTO and IFIs*, London: Zed Books.

Grossman, Gene and Alan Krueger (1993), 'Environmental impacts of a North American Free Trade Agreement', in Peter Garber (ed.), *The US–Mexico Free Trade Agreement*, Cambridge, MA: MIT Press, pp. 13–56.

Jaffe, Adam, Steven Peterson, Paul Portney and Robert Stavins (1995), 'Environmental regulation and the competitiveness of U.S. manufacturing: what does the evidence tell us?', *Journal of Economic Literature*, **33**, 132–63.

Jenkins, Rhys (1998), 'Environmental regulation and international competitiveness: a review of the literature', INTECH Working Paper No. 9801, Maastricht, United Nations University.

Kahn, Mathew E. and Yutaka Yoshino (2004), 'Testing for pollution havens inside and outside of regional trading blocs', *Advances in Economic Analysis & Policy*, **4**(2), Article 4.

Kanbur, Ravi (2001), 'Economic policy, distribution, and poverty: the nature of disagreements'. http://people.cornell.edu/pages/sk145/papers/Disagreements.pdf.

Krueger, Jonathan (1999), *International Trade and the Basel Convention*, London: Earthscan.

Kuznets, Simon (1957), 'Economic growth and income inequality', *American Economic Review*, **45**(1), 1–28.

Mayer, Frederick (1998). *Interpreting NAFTA: The Science and Art of Political Analysis*, New York: Columbia University Press.

Najam, Adil (2003), 'The case against a new international environmental organization', *Global Governance*, July, 367–84.

Neumeyer, Eric (2001), *Greening Trade and Investment*, London: Earthscan.

Palmer, Karen, Wallace E. Oates and Paul R. Portney (1995), 'Tightening environmental standards: the benefit–cost or the no-cost paradigm', *Journal of Economic Perspectives*, **9**(4), Fall, 119–32.

Pimentel, D., L. Lach, R. Zuniga and D. Morrison (2000), 'Environmental and economic costs associated with non-indigenous species in the United States', *Bioscience*, **5**(1), 53–65.

Ruggerio, Renalto (1999), Address to the World Trade Organization, March.

Sampson, Gary (2000), *Trade, Environment, and the WTO: The Post-Seattle Agenda*, Washington, DC: Overseas Development Council.

Schlingemann, Fritz (1998), 'Trade vs. environment: the evidence', *Trade and Environment: Conflict or compatibility?* London: Earthscan.
Steinberg, Richard (1997), 'Trade–environment negotiations in the EU, NAFTA, and WTD: regional trajectories of rule development', *American Journal of International Law*, 231–67.
Speth, Gustave (2004), *Red Sky at Morning: America and the Crisis of the Global Environment*, New Haven, CT: Yale University Press.
Stern, David (2004), 'The rise and fall of the environmental Kuznets curve,' *World Development*, **32**(8), 1419–39.
UNDP (2005), *Millennium Ecosystem Assessment*, New York: United Nations.
UNEP/IISD (2000), *Trade and the Environment: A Handbook*, Winnipeg, Canada: International Institute of Sustainable Development.
Vogel, David (1997), *Trading Up: Consumer and Environmental Regulation in a Global Economy*, Cambridge, MA: Harvard University Press.
Vogel, David (1999), 'The Politics of Trade and Environment in the United States', BRIE Working Paper No. 94.
World Bank (1992), *World Development Report*, Washington, DC.
World Trade Organization (2001), *Doha Ministerial Declaration*, www.wto.org.

PART I

TRADE AND ENVIRONMENTAL QUALITY

1   Pre-empting NIS introductions: targeting policy

Christopher Costello, Chad Lawley and
Carol McAusland

Introduction

Invasives are non-indigenous species (NIS) that out-compete native species for resources and become pests in a host region. Because they are excellent competitors, invasives impose costs on their hosts by displacing native species (facilitating species loss) and heightening control costs. Costs from NIS can be considerable:[1] the USA spends roughly $1.5 billion to $2.3 billion annually on herbicides to combat non-native crop weeds (OTA, 1993) and suffers $1 billion a year in fouling from zebra mussels alone (Pimentel et al., 2005). Worldwide, competition from exotic species is the second leading cause of species loss; invasives are implicated in the decline of 400 of the 958 species listed as endangered in the USA (Wilcove et al., 1998). Pimentel et al. (2005) estimate that the annual cost of dealing with harmful NIS is almost $120 billion.

Trade in goods and services plays a central role in many NIS Introductions. The purpose of this chapter is to present a framework for tailoring trade (and other pre-emptive policies) to NIS characteristics. We find that most NIS problems can be classified, for policy response purposes, into a handful of categories, each with a specified policy response. For example, sometimes the traded product is the source of the introduction, as with imports of horticultural stock.[2] In other cases NIS introductions are purely accidental, as when individuals hitchhike on imported goods, tourists, or packing materials. Asian Tiger mosquitoes probably entered the USA in the wells of used tires (Hawley et al., 1987), SARS (Severe acute respiratory syndrome) entered Canada via a returning tourist (Varia et al., 2003), and Asian longhorned beetle entered the USA on wood packing crates (Normile, 2004). Finally, NIS can also stow away in vessels transporting traded goods, such as in airplane holds, or in ship ballast water, as was likely the case with zebra mussels; since 1959, 24 animal NIS introduced via shipping became established in the North American Great Lakes (Holeck et al., 2004). Our analysis extends to both intentional and unintentional introductions.

Policies aimed at stemming damages from NIS take two broad forms: pre-emptive policies – those designed to prevent NIS introductions in the first place – and reactive, such as efforts to control or eradicate NIS once they are established in the host region. We focus primarily on the former. True, as we argue below, the benefits from pre-emptive measures will depend on the types of control measures taken to combat NIS making it through a country's borders. However, in many cases it is easy to incorporate damages resulting from NIS introduction as a function of the process. As such, we can treat the damages resulting from introductions as an exogenously determined function, one that will be determined by the optimal control/eradication policy.[3]

In this chapter we develop a taxonomy of NIS characteristics that focuses on the following four characteristics:

- *Observability*: how easy is it to detect the presence of an NIS?
- *Separability*: how easily can importers/exporters disentangle unwanted NIS from wanted goods and services?
- *Traceability*: if an invasion occurs, how finely can the source of the release be pin-pointed?
- *Predictability*: what do policy-makers know about the growth function, physical and economic impacts associated with individual NIS?

We use this taxonomy to build a framework for tailoring pre-emptive NIS policy. Our goal is to assist policy-makers in identifying which instruments are best able to target NIS damage, given the economic and ecological characteristics of the problem at hand. Along the way, we identify areas where NIS introductions and generic trade and environment problems overlap, and so policy-makers interested in NIS can look to general research on trade and environment problems for solutions. We also identify research gaps, paying particular attention to research prompted by NIS problems that can inform policy on a wider range of problems.

Trade and invasives – the causal link
Traded goods and services, as well as the vessels that deliver these traded commodities, are a principal conduit for NIS introductions. We begin our review with the following question: is the assumption that trade flows drive NIS introductions borne out by the data? This question has received relatively little empirical study.

Dalmazzone (2000) conducts a cross-country regression using as a dependent variable the ratio of established exotics to indigenous species. She finds '[n]either trade as a share of GDP nor tourism . . . [provides] statistically significant explanations of vulnerability to plant invasions' (p. 23). She does find, however, that merchandise imports and import duties are positively and negatively, respectively, correlated with the exotics ratio, although only the import duties measure is statistically significant.

Levine and D'Antonio (2003) examine the relationship between international trade and NIS establishment in the USA. They construct species-import curves using historical trade and NIS establishment data on cumulative totals beginning in 1920. Trade forecasts are used to predict the number of new NIS expected to become established in the US between 2000 and 2020: conservative estimates predict 115 new insect species and five new plant pathogens.

The Levine and D'Antonio (2003) analysis does not differentiate NIS and trade data on the basis of biogeographic origin. Costello et al. (2007) estimate the NIS invasion risk posed by different regions of the world to the San Francisco Bay. They find that invasion risk is differentiated by region of origin and that the number of introductions from a region is a concave function of imports. A related literature in marine ecology establishes a firm causal link between certain NIS pathways, ballast water carried by ships in particular, and NIS introductions; see Ruiz et al. (1997) and Holeck et al. (2004).

In sum, the few extant empirical studies suggest that NIS introductions are positively correlated with trade. For the rest of this review, we take this as a maintained assumption.

Targeting
Trade facilitates NIS introductions. Logic would suggest that any instrument reducing import volumes would thereby reduce introductions and NIS-related damage in turn. The

crudest such instrument is a general tariff on trade. However, the seemingly simple relationship between trade restrictions and damage outlined above may fail for at least two reasons. First, as pointed out theoretically by Rosenzweig (1995) for species accumulation in general, and empirically by Levine and D'Antonio (2003), Solow and Costello (2004) and Costello et al. (2007), there exists an attenuation of the introduction rate from a given host to a given destination. This arises from the erosion of the 'introducible' species pool in the host region. So, *ceteris paribus*, a constant tariff may have a declining effect on introductions over time. Second, general equilibrium interactions may even reverse a tariff's effect. Costello and McAusland (2003) adopt a general equilibrium framework with competitive industries; they point out that import tariffs on agricultural goods will lead to agricultural expansion in the protected country, expanding the platform for NIS invasions and associated damage. Thus, even though tariffs may reduce the overall rate of NIS introductions, they may lead to higher NIS damage overall.[4] Finally, Acquaye et al. (2005) point out that direct measures of costs from restricting imports for NIS prevention purposes may be overstated if analysts neglect to consider concurrent distortions such as commodity programs (i.e. subsidies). They find subsidy interactions from restrictions aimed at citrus canker reduce estimates of US consumer, producer and taxpayer losses by $10 million.

Pre-emptive policies
The principle of targeting advocates policy instruments aimed at acts most closely linked to the externality of interest. There is a wide array of policy instruments available for pre-empting NIS introductions, ranging from price-based instruments to process standards to liability rules and quarantine. Below we give examples of applications of the different policy instruments.

Price-based instruments

Inspection-recovery fees   The quarantine service in New Zealand is required to recover costs where possible (Mumford, 2002). In the USA, APHIS (Animal and Public Health Information System) inspects incoming propagative and non-propagative cargo as well as air passengers, collecting user fees to partially recover the cost of inspections (GAO, 2006).

Taxes   In 2007, Hawaii's legislature passed Senate Bill 1066 imposing a $1 fee on each shipping container entering Hawaii (State of Hawaii, S.B. No. 1066); the governor's subsequent veto was overridden by 2/3 votes in both the House and Senate. Although revenues go into a Pest Inspection, Quarantine, and Eradication Fund to offset inspection costs, the tax is levied on all incoming shipments, regardless of whether they are ultimately searched.

Tariffs   Although not set with NIS risk in mind, tariff escalation has the effect of encouraging imports of raw products, which are more likely to have higher NIS risk (Tu et al., forthcoming).

Quantitative import restrictions/import bans
The US import ban on Mexican avocados was partially lifted in 1993 when avocados were allowed entry into Alaska. In 2005, avocados grown in Michoacán, Mexico were

permitted entry into all states except California, Florida and Hawaii. As of 2007, avocados can be imported into all 50 states (ERS, 2006). Import bans are imposed on exporting countries following the discovery of bovine spongiform encephalopathy (BSE) or foot and mouth disease (Josling et al., 2004). Exports of US fruits and vegetables (including apples, cherries, citrus, pomegranates, potatoes, raspberries and stone fruit) to a variety of countries are banned due to phytosanitary concerns (FAS, 2005).

Product standards
The International Plant Protection Convention (IPPC) approved an International Standard of Phytosanitary Measure for wood packing material (IPPC, 2006). Pallets must now be heat-treated, treated with methyl bromide, or replaced by plastic pallets if they are used for goods traded internationally (Mumford, 2002).

Process standards
In the USA, chemical treatments may include applications of fumigants such as methyl bromide, while non-chemical treatments can include cold treatment, heat treatment and irradiation (USDA, 2002). In 2002, APHIS issued a final rule allowing irradiation as a phytosanitary treatment of fruits and vegetables imported into the USA (Federal Register, 2002). In April 2007, the USA began to allow imports of irradiated mangoes imported from India; before this, Indian mangos were banned entry into the USA (http://www.aphis.usda.gov/newsroom/hot_issues/indian_mango/indian_mango.shtml).

The International Convention for the Control and Management of Ships Ballast, Water & Sediments and the US National Aquatic Invasive Species Act regulate the discharge of ballast water from transoceanic vessels. The USA requires that ships discharge ballast water in the ocean before entering the Great Lakes (Costello et al., 2007). Between 2001 and 2005, the USDA had a 'winter shipping only' restriction on imports of Mexican avocados (Josling et al., 2004). Currently, all pet birds imported into the USA (from non-US and non-Canadian origin) require a 30-day quarantine in a USDA animal import quarantine facility at the owner's expense (http://www.aphis.usda.gov/NCIE/pet-bird-non-us.html).

Criminal and civil liability
Releasing NIS, either intentionally or through carelessness, may be punishable by law. The UK's Wildlife and Countryside Act of 1981 renders the 'intentional or negligent introduction of an alien animal or subsequent release "of an already introduced animal"' a criminal offense (Shine et al., 2000, p. 81). 'In Poland, any person may bring a civil action for damages against a person responsible for an introduction . . . .' (ibid., p. 82).

A taxonomy of NIS characteristics
When and where particular instruments are appropriate depends on the characteristics of the NIS problem at hand. To this end we provide a taxonomy of NIS characteristics. In this section we also provide an overview of the research useful in matching policy design with NIS characteristics. In addition to the literature specific to NIS policy, we include the literature on trade policy in the presence of externalities, and regulation in the presence of uncertainty and asymmetric information. As outlined above, there are four characteristics that loosely define individual NIS problems: observability, separability, traceability and predictability.

Observability

In some cases the presence of NIS in a traded good may be obvious, as when the traded good is an NIS itself, as with some nursery stock. At the other extreme, detecting NIS presence may be costly, as when commodities harbor NIS that are not easily identified visually such as tephritid fruit flies (Follett and Neven, 2006).

McAusland and Costello (2004) examine the tradeoff between tariffs and the intensity of costly inspections to deter entry of a single NIS with known damages. They find that, while it is always desirable to impose a positive tariff (even in the absence of terms-of-trade considerations, scale economies, or political-economy concerns), there are circumstances under which inspections are not advisable. Specifically, if inspection costs are high, or the proportion of infested products is either high or zero, it might be preferable to either ban the product outright or to accept it uninspected but with a high associated import tax.

Harboring is not exclusive to NIS. An extensive literature analyzes policy for preventing contaminated commodities from entering the food supply. Much of this literature focuses on minimizing accidental contamination. Policy debates have focused on the relative efficiency of performance versus process standards (Antle, 1996; MacDonald and Crutchfield, 1996) and the impact of these standards on trade in food products (Caswell and Hooker, 1996; Josling et al., 2004). Since foodborne microbial contamination has low incidence and is costly to detect, process standards such as mandatory adoption of Hazard Analysis and Critical Control Point (HACCP) may be more efficient than product standards such as end product testing (MacDonald and Crutchfield, 1996; Unevehr and Jensen, 1996).

There are also parallel literatures on identifying strategies for preventing intentional harboring, ranging from bioterrorism to smuggling. To date few cases of malicious NIS introductions have been documented. The trade of smallpox-infected blankets to Native Americans in the 1700s is a notorious exception. Nevertheless, some of this research has obvious overlaps with the search for NIS. Persico (2002) argues that statistical discrimination can raise the effectiveness of search for contraband materials; this parallels the recommendation that inspections vary by trade partner according to infection rates.

The literature on commodity taxes and smuggling may also be relevant for NIS policy. It is well established that raising commodity taxes induces smuggling of goods that would otherwise be traded legally (but face high taxes). However, this smuggling does not necessarily undermine the preventive power of these instruments; in fact Merriman (2002) argues that the health benefits of commodity taxes are identical with and without smuggling. As Merriman (2002) points out concerning cigarette taxes, smuggling is a costly alternative to legal trade. Thus, relative to a counterfactual with neither taxes nor smuggling, commodity taxes will still dampen cigarette consumption even when smuggling occurs. Applying Merriman's argument to NIS, we would expect that tight border inspections will drive some trade in potentially NIS-harboring products underground, and that the overall cost of imports will rise (relative to no taxes or inspections). This results in less trade, and thus a smaller platform for NIS introductions. The analogy is imperfect, though. While the marginal damage from cigarettes depends only on characteristics determined at the point of manufacture, with NIS it also depends on the mode of transport. Smuggled goods may spend less or more time in transit. They are also less likely to undergo post-production treatment (such as heat treatment or spraying) and visibly infested units will not be detained by port inspectors. As a result, we would expect smuggled imports to exhibit a higher risk of harboring NIS than legally imported goods. In short, it is conceivable that commodity taxes and strict port inspections may actually raise NIS damage in the presence of smuggling. This has some of the same flavor as Fischer's (2004) argument that sanctioning some trade in endangered species parts may reduce stigma from illicit trade, with feedback effects on poaching rates overall.

Poor observability creates an obvious obstacle to liability rules. As Shine et al. (2000) note, for large captive animals it may be possible to establish compulsory registration and marking systems, so that the owner of a released NIS can be easily identified. But for most NIS this is not possible. As summarized by Europe's Standing Committee for the Convention on the Conservation of European Wildlife and Natural Habitats,

> [w]here invasive alien species (IAS) cause damage, conventional approaches to liability are usually difficult to apply. This is partly because of difficulties in proving causation and/or fault (time lag, scientific uncertainty, number of users involved) and partly because many existing IAS were introduced to the environment in the past by businesses operating under legal standards and permits. (2003, p. 20)

Separability
Even if detection is easy, if a product and its contaminants are easily separated it might make more sense merely to undertake processes that achieve separation, even for products that may be clean from the start. In some cases this can be achieved by imposing product standards, as mentioned above.

Wilson and Anton (2006) examine the substitutability of mitigation strategies, such as treatments that reduce the NIS infection rate, and border measures, such as tariffs and import bans. Calibrating an example of preventing foot and mouth disease from entering the USA, they find that mitigation strategies (culling and vaccination) generate net welfare gains and that it is optimal to apply mitigation strategies first, complemented by a tariff if necessary.

Alternately, process standards may be in order, such as requiring products to be irradiated as with US imports of mangoes from India. Similarly, many countries (in compliance with WHO and International Civic Aviation Organization guidelines) engage in 'disinsection' – the spraying of airline passengers with insecticides to reduce the risk of importing harmful NIS (Gratz et al., 2000).

As is well known from the literature on environmental regulation, performance and technology standards are blunter tools than emission taxes or tradable permits. The problem with applying direct contamination taxes for NIS is the observability trait described above. Some researchers have proposed a variation on the tradable permit theme. For example, Horan and Lupi (2005) propose tradable risk permits; risk levels would be judged based on biosecurity measures undertaken.

Fullerton and West (2002) point out that in cases where the undesirable attribute is unobservable, employing a series of subsidies to inputs complementary to abatement, taxes on inputs that are substitutes to abatement, as well as a tax/subsidy to the product overall, can act as an equivalent to a tax on emission intensity. In the case of traded products likely to harbor NIS, the appropriate panoply of substitute instruments may include an import tariff that is partially rebated depending on the individual exporter's efforts to 'pre-clean' products as evidenced by undertaking certified management practices.

Traceability

An alternative to punitive taxes and seizures is to impose liability rules on importers and consumers of imported goods. When an outbreak or release can be traced back to the party responsible for the original release, this policy channel has potential. This may be a likely candidate in the case of nursery stock, where the NIS risk is clear and present to all parties, and genetic forensics can in theory identify the source of an invasion with precision. However, as is well known from the literature on liability as a tool for regulating pollution from nonpoint sources, when the source of an accident is difficult to identify, liability rules become a blunt tool for preventing release. With respect to NIS, in many cases we do not observe an infestation until long after its introduction, rendering the causal link difficult to establish (see Costello and Solow, 2003).

Thomas and Randall (2000) examine liability and assurance bonds to reduce intentional introductions of (what turn out to be) harmful species. They propose a mixed policy under both imperfect *ex ante* knowledge about damage and imperfect *ex post* revocability. In the general context of uncertain environmental damages, Shogren et al. (1993) examine bonds as a mechanism for compliance. They provide a useful taxonomy of cases in which bonds cannot be effectively implemented (e.g. due to liquidity or legal constraints).

Predictability

Probably the key dimension along which NIS differ from other trade and environment problems is predictability. Unlike most other defects in traded goods – e.g. lead in paint – NIS reproduce. Thus an importer's ultimate damages from NIS introductions may be only weakly related to the size of its initial exposure. To the extent that native, but harmful, bacteria can reproduce and contaminate a considerable fraction of a nation's food supply depending on its distribution system, NIS reproduction has many parallels with food safety research.

Growth   A small literature on regulation under uncertainty regarding growth dynamics focuses on NIS (e.g. see Olson and Roy, 2002). The substantially larger non-NIS literature on resource extraction under uncertainty focuses primarily on beneficial resources, where the 'take' is economically valuable and the goal is to maintain the reproducing population (see, e.g., Reed, 1979). In the NIS context, however, the emphasis is reversed: the goal is usually to eradicate, if possible, the invasive population and the 'take' usually has no economic value. While the insights from this literature are instructive for designing post-introduction policy, it sheds little light on pre-emptive policy design.

Before import, the growth function for an NIS (and the associated damage) is unknown. While recent modeling efforts enhance predictive power, our ability to forecast damage, before first introduction, is weak (Simberloff, 2006). Further, because host and native regions differ climactically and geographically, exhibit different populations of competing and complementary species, and experience different levels of disturbance, observing growth dynamics in the NIS' native region gives an imperfect indicator of dynamics in the host region. Accordingly, there may be some scope for learning about NIS susceptibility. Intentional releases of NIS for biological control programs are used to assess the performance of both the introduced NIS and the native ecosystem (NRC, 2002; Grevstad, 1999). Many Agricultural Extension programs currently engage in cooperative agreements with farmers to test new crops, including NIS. Although we can find no evidence that these tests are designed in part so as to quantify the risk that these crop species will become invasive, this would seem justified.

Simberloff (2006) argues that, due to our incomplete understanding of which species pose the largest risk, countries should take a precautionary approach with regard to permissible imports of NIS. However, research on learning under uncertainty suggests that, when damages and control costs are uncertain and can only be learned through experience, erring on the side of caution may be advisable (Kolstad, 1996). In terms of policy prescriptions, this suggests that countries may want to employ grey lists instead of white or black lists: rather than either banning (black list) or granting unimpeded entry (white list) to unknown species, countries may want to grant restricted entry to unknown species so that more can be learned about them (as was practiced by the aforementioned US policy on avocado imports from Mexico).

Learning can also take place by observing the outcomes of a given introduction in other countries. Calzolari and Immordino (2005) examine this possibility with respect to new products with uncertain human health effects (such as genetically modified crops) which can be learned over time – through experience. They conclude that each country wants the other to allow the new product and provide the safety information. This incentive to free-ride results in an inefficiently low level of learning globally.

Damage   Without doubt, reactive policy, particularly eradication and control, is essential to managing NIS damages. In some instances reactive and pre-emptive policy can be analyzed separately. For example, when budgets are unconstrained, research on the optimal pre-emption program can treat the damages from allowing entry of X individuals as an exogenous function $D(X)$, where $D(X)$ measures the expected loss arising when the optimal post-introduction control policy is applied. X may represent a vector of traits: e.g. if individuals vary genetically, then X will measure the invading population's genetic composition. Alternately, if the structure of the host economy varies with the type of instrument used, then X will include information on domestic and international prices. The function $D(X)$ then embeds an optimal post-introduction response. While not the purpose of this review, it is noteworthy that the post-introduction response literature includes analysis of both deterministic and stochastic growth (see Olson and Roy, 2002). Finally, if there is uncertainty regarding the number of individuals introduced, X may be a random variable. Olson and Roy (2005) show that the (relative) benefits of control and prevention depend only on the expected introduction rate if marginal damages are constant; however, when damages are variable, additional information is needed.

However, when agency budgets for preventing and controlling NIS are jointly constrained, $D(X)$ cannot be treated as exogenous: the revenue-generating/depleting properties of pre-emptive policies such as tariffs and inspections will impact damages from actual introductions.

Finnoff et al. (2006) look at the preferences of managers for prevention relative to control of invasive species; they observe that managers tend to prefer control because its productivity is less variable. Leung et al. (2005) evaluate prevention versus control with an application to zebra mussel invasions into lakes with power plants. Finnoff et al. (2005a, 2005b) examine a framework wherein a government agency chooses optimal prevention and control of a zebra mussel invasion in a Midwest lake, taking into account feedback effects due to the response of private firms and the risk of invasion. Horan et al. (2002) evaluate optimal prevention measures when damages are uncertain (marginal damage after the first invasion is assumed zero). They show it is optimal to allocate more resources to confront high-damage events with non-negligible probability of occurring, but possibly no resources to low-probability events, even those carrying very high damages conditional on occurrence.

Uncertainty and the scope for protectionist policy

For better or for worse, uncertainty over NIS damages provides governments with the scope to manipulate trade-related NIS policy for protectionist purposes. It is well recognized that governments in large countries have an incentive to erect import tariffs for the purposes of lowering the international price of imported goods. Governments in small countries may also want to manipulate policy so as to shift rents to politically powerful import-competing interests. Margolis et al. (2005) adapt the Grossman–Helpman model of lobbying to show that a politically captured regulator will set tariffs to reflect both marginal damages from admitted pests and internal rent shifting. They argue that it is difficult to distinguish between disguised protectionism and legitimate damage internalization unless damages are commonly known.

When tariffs are constrained, governments have an incentive to distort other policy instruments for protectionist purposes. In the case of NIS, phytosanitary regulations may serve this goal.[5] Margolis and Shogren (2007) show that equilibrium inspections may lead to higher levels of effective protection when tariffs are constrained as opposed to unconstrained. Lichtenberg and Lynch (2006) examine pest-free certification schemes involving costly monitoring and eradication protocols. As with eco-labels in general, they find exports may optimally choose to eradicate but eschew certification. Importing countries also have an incentive to set inefficiently strict certification requirements for protectionist purposes.

Importing governments may also be tempted to cite uncertainty to justify discriminatory trade policy. As Paarlberg and Lee (1998), McAusland and Costello (2004) and Wilson and Anton (2006) all conclude, pre-emptive policy should vary with infection risk and damage from introduced NIS. These invariably vary by trade partner, not only because precautionary measures may vary by exporter, but also because the risk that a hitchhiking NIS will ultimately become a damaging invader also varies by the importer–exporter pair according to climo-geographic similarities. For example, China is considered a likely source for introductions of NIS into the USA due in part to a comparable range of physical environments within the two countries (NRC, 2002). Costello et al. (2007) estimate marginal invasion risk (MIR) from imports into San Francisco Harbor; they show that MIRs vary considerably across trade partners and over time, in general attenuating with imports. They show that, in general, general barriers to trade designed to reduce expected NIS introductions do not pass a rough cost–benefit test. Moreover, the levels of crude import restrictions achieving the same ecological goal vary considerably across trade partners: in order to reduce the number of NIS introductions from the West Pacific region (which includes China and Japan) expected by 2020, trade with the West Pacific would have to be reduced by 2 percent; achieving an equivalent one-NIS reduction from the region with the next largest MIR (the Atlantic–Mediterranean region) would require a 90 percent reduction in imports. Given the considerable variance in MIRs across regions, and the potentially subjective nature of assessments of future risk, the scope for protection-motivated discrimination may be great.

Research gaps
The biggest gap in our understanding of the relationship between trade and invasive species is clearly empirical. Few studies have tested the strength of the relationship between trade volumes, patterns and biological invasions. Moreover, despite the preponderance of anecdotal evidence suggesting that marginal invasion risk (MIR) varies across export partners, mode of transport and commodity type, virtually no empirical studies to date have allowed MIR to vary by type. Costello et al. (2007) is one exception, finding that MIR varies widely across trading regions, however, these authors restrict their attention to a single importing region, a single transport mode (ocean vessel), and a generic measure of imports (tonnage).

Another topic needing further research concerns stepping-stone invasions: a species native to region A that invades region B becomes a risk to B's trade partner C even if countries A and C refrain from trading with one another. Drake and Lodge (2004) use shipping data to estimate a uniform rate of port-to-port infections. Among other things, they conclude that some of the ports that are *observed* to be most highly infected, San Francisco Bay and the North American Great Lakes in particular, may in fact be relatively unimportant sources of secondary infections; they explain this discrepancy by pointing to the variations in search intensity (for NIS) across ports. Even if an NIS is unable to establish itself in a stepping-stone location, it may nevertheless be able to contaminate outgoing traffic, as documented by Apte et al. (2000) for Mytilus galloprovincialis in Pearl Harbor. The role of secondary infections and the role of policy, in particular preferential trade zones and hub–spoke shipping arrangements, need further empirical and theoretical exploration.

Incorporating an importer's ecological history into policy is another area requiring further study. Most extant trade and invasives research maintains the assumption that damages from a particular exotic species are a function only of the size of the introduced population. However, ecological research suggests that damages depend critically on interactions with other species present, both native and invasive. Species interactions have been studied in the context of reactive policy (e.g. Simberloff et al., 1997) but not for pre-emptive policy. Given that trade policies can themselves induce substitutions across commodities, trade partners and transport modeds, the general equilibrium consequences of type-specific policies need to be better understood.

As we stressed earlier in this review, we believe that a critical aspect of trade and invasives interactions lies with uncertainty. Researchers often presume an exogenous degree of uncertainty, e.g. per individual damages are a random variable with known distribution. However, in practice the degree of uncertainty borne by policy-makers is a choice. Policy-makers can assign resources to learning more about an invasives problem via observation, adaptive management and restricted trials. In short, governments can invest funds to reduce uncertainty. Investment is costly because it reallocates resources away from prevention efforts such as inspections and enforcing quarantine. The optimal tradeoff between investment and search/enforcement will ultimately depend on the relative costs of type I and II errors. Liberal entry policy will allow too much contaminated trade, prompting ecological damage. Restrictive treatment of imports will unnecessarily raise prices in the importing country, generating consumption and production distortions.

As the relative size of type I and II errors will itself depend on trade flows and restrictions, trade policy and risk assessment must be considered in tandem.

Finally, we raise again the problem of imperfect enforcement. The trade and invasives literature uniformly assumes that all imports are legal. This is questionable. In 1999, officials seized 41 000 pounds of illegally imported plant and animal materials from retailers, wholesalers and such in the Los Angeles area (Kreith and Golino, 2003). As noted above, it seems theoretically possible that strict pre-emptive policies may actually raise NIS damages; policy-makers would benefit from advice along this dimension.

Notes

1. Many NIS are beneficial: corn, wheat and rice are all crop plants that were introduced into the USA. This review is concerned with non-beneficial NIS.
2. Some species are intentionally released directly into the wild: European starlings were introduced as part of a private campaign to establish in North America the different birds listed in Shakespeare's writings (Cabe, 1998). Asian kudzu was planted by the US Soil Erosion Service and Civilian Conservation Corp; it was many decades before its approval for erosion control was revoked as a result of the plant's invasiveness (Forseth and Innis, 2004).
3. For more general reviews of control and prevention strategies, see Olson (2006) for terrestrial invasives and Lovell et al. (2006) for aquatics.
4. Tu and Beghin (2006) extend the analysis to allow for intra-industry trade. They find that imports of differentiated products needn't crowd out production, while intra-industry liberalization tends to increase invasive species damage.
5. A number of empirical studies have examined the effect of phytosanitary barriers to trade in agriculture. James and Anderson (1998) find that Australia's ban on banana imports is not justified if the welfare of Australian consumers is considered. Calvin and Krissoff (1998) find that Japan's phytosanitary restrictions on imports of US apples (US apples are assumed to be perfect substitutes for Japanese apples) protect Japanese producers at the expense of social welfare. Yue et al. (2006) assume that Japanese and US apples are imperfect substitutes and find that Japanese phytosanitary restrictions had little impact on US apple exports to Japan.

References

Acquaye, Albert K.A., Julian M. Alston, Hyunok Lee and Daniel Sumner (2005), 'Economic consequences of invasive species policies in the presence of commodity programs: theory and application to citrus canker', *Review of Agricultural Economics*, 27(3), 498–504.

Antle, John M. (1996), 'Efficient food safety regulation in the food manufacturing sector', *American Journal of Agricultural Economics*, 78(5), 1242–7.

Apte, Smita, Brenden S. Holland, L. Scott Godwin and Jonathan P.A. Gardner (2000), 'Jumping ship: a stepping stone event mediating transfer of a non-indigenous species via a potentially unsuitable environment', *Biological Invasions*, 2(1), 75–9.

Cabe, Paul R. (1998), 'The effects of founding bottlenecks on genetic variation in the European starling (Sturnus vulgaris) in North America', *Heredity*, 80, 519–25.

Calvin, Linda and Barry Krissoff (1998), 'Technical barriers to trade: a case study of phytosanitary barriers and U.S.–Japanese apple trade', *Journal of Agricultural and Resource Economics*, 23(2), 351–66.

Calzolari, Giacomo and Giovanni Immordino (2005), 'Hormone beef, chlorinated chicken and international trade', *European Economic Review*, 49, 145–72.

Caswell, Julie A. and Neal H. Hooker (1996), 'HACCP as an international trade standard', *American Journal of Agricultural Economics*, 78(3), 775–9.

Costello, Christopher and Carol McAusland (2003), 'Protectionism, trade, and measures of damage from exotic species introductions', *American Journal of Agricultural Economics*, 85(4), 964–75.

Costello, Christopher J. and Andrew R. Solow (2003), 'On the pattern of discovery of introduced species', *Proceedings of the National Academy of Sciences*, 100(3), 321–23.

Costello, Christopher, John M. Drake and David M. Lodge (2007), 'Evaluating an invasive species policy: ballast water exchange in the Great Lakes', *Ecological Applications*, 17(3), 655–62.

Costello, Christopher, Michael Springborn, Carol McAusland and Andrew Solow (2007), 'Unintended biological invasions: does risk vary by trading partner?', *Journal of Environmental Economics and Management*, 54(3), 262–76.

Dalmazzone, S. (2000), 'Economic factors affecting vulnerability to biological invasions', in C. Perrings, M. Williamson and S. Dalmazzone (eds), *The Economics of Biological Invasions*, Cheltenham, UK and Northampton, MA, USA: Edward Elgar, pp. 17–30.

Drake, J.M. and D.M. Lodge (2004), 'Hotspots for biological invasions determined from global pathways for non-indigenous species in ballast water', *Proceedings of the Royal Society of London*, Series B **271**(1539), 575–80.

Economic Research Service (2006), 'Linking risk and economic assessments in the analysis of plant pest regulations: the case of US imports of Mexican avocados', CCR-25. ERS/USDA, http://www.ers.usda.gov/publications/ccr 25/ccr 25.pdf.

Federal Register (2002), *Rules and Regulations*, **67**(205), 23 October. http://www.senasa.gob.pe/eng/importer_exporter/orientation/international_phyto_zoo_regulations/Irradiation_Final_Rule_102302.pdf.

Finnoff, David, Jason F. Shogren, Brian Leung and David Lodge (2005a), 'The importance of bioeconomic feedback in invasive species management', *Ecological Economics*, **52**(3), 367–81.

Finnoff, David, Jason F. Shogren, Brian Leung and David Lodge (2005b), 'Risk and nonindigenous species management', *Review of Agricultural Economics*, **27**(3), 475–82.

Finnoff, David, Jason F. Shogren, Brian Leung and David Lodge (2006), 'Take a risk: preferring prevention over control of biological invaders', *Ecological Economics*, **62**, 216–22.

Fischer, Carolyn (2004), 'The complex interactions of markets for endangered species products', *Journal of Environmental Economics and Management*, **48**(2), 926–53.

Follett, Peter A. and Lisa G. Neven (2006), 'Current trends in quarantine entomology', *Annual Review of Entomology*, **51**, 359–85.

Foreign Agricultural Service (2005), *FAS Guide to World Horticultural Trade: US Specialty Crops Trade Issues Edition*, Circular Series FHORT 1-05 FAS/USDA, http://www.fas.usda.gov/htp/Hort_Circular/2005/05-05/Trade%20Issues%20Circular%202005%20_Publication%20Version%20_.pdf.

Forseth, Irwin N. Jr and Anne F. Innis (2004), 'Kudzu (Pueraria montana): history, physiology, and ecology combine to make a major ecosystem threat', *Critical Reviews in Plant Sciences*, **23**(5), 401–13.

Fullerton, Don and Sarah E. West (2002), 'Can taxes on cars and on gasoline mimic an unavailable tax on emissions?', *Journal of Environmental Economics and Management*, **43**, 135–57.

Government Accountability Office (2006), *Management and Coordination Problems Increase Vulnerability of U.S. Agriculture to Foreign Pests and Diseases*, GAO-06-644, Washington, DC.

Gratz, Norman G., Robert Steffen and William Cocksedge (2000), 'Why aircraft disinsection?' *Bulletin of the World Health Organization*, **78**(8), 995–1004.

Grevstad, F.S. (1999), 'Experimental invasions using biological control introductions: the influence of release size on the chance of population establishment', *Biological Invasions*, **1**(4), 313–23.

Hawley, W.A., P. Reiter, R.W. Copeland, C.B. Pumpuni and G.B. Craig, Jr (1987), '*Aedes albopictus* in North America: probable introduction in used tires from northern Asia', *Science*, **236**, 1114–6.

Holeck, Kristen T., Edward L. Mills, Hugh J. MacIsaac, Margaret R. Dochoda, Robert I. Colautti and Anthony Ricciardi (2004), 'Bridging troubled waters: biological invasions, transoceanic shipping, and the Laurentian Great Lakes', *BioScience*, **54**(10), 919–29.

Horan, Richard D. and Frank Lupi (2005), 'Tradeable risk permits to prevent future introductions of invasive alien species into the Great Lakes', *Ecological Economics*, **52**, 289–304.

Horan, Richard D., Charles Perrings, Frank Lupi and Erwin H. Bulte (2002), 'Biological pollution prevention strategies under ignorance: the case of invasive species', *American Journal of Agricultural Economics*, **84**(5), 1303–10.

International Plant Protection Convention (2006), *Guidelines for Regulating Wood Packaging Material in International Trade*, http://www.apawood.org/perf_panels/133703_ISPM15_2002_with_Ann.pdf.

James, Sallie and Kym Anderson (1998), 'On the need for more economic assessment of quarantine policies', *The Australian Journal of Agricultural and Resource Economics*, **42**(4), 425–44.

Josling, Tim, Donna Roberts and David Order (2004), *Food Regulation and Trade: Towards a Safe and Open Global System*, Washington, DC: Institute for International Economics, March.

Kolstad, Charles D. (1996), 'Learning and stock effects in environmental regulation: the case of greenhouse gas emissions', *Journal of Environmental Economics and Management*, **31**(1), 1–18.

Kreith, Marcia and Deborah Golino (2003), 'Regulatory framework and institutional players', in D.A. Sumner (ed.), *Exotic Pests and Diseases: Biology and Economics for Biosecurity*, Ames, IA: Iowa State Press, pp. 19–38.

Leung, Brian, David Finnoff, Jason F. Shogren and David Lodge (2005), 'Managing invasive species: Rules of thumb for rapid assessment', *Ecological Economics*, **55**(1), 24–36.

Levine, Jonathan M. and Carla M. D'Antonio (2003), 'Forecasting biological invasions with increasing international trade', *Conservation Biology*, **17**(1), 322–6.

Lichtenberg, Erik and Lori Lynch (2006), 'Exotic pests and trade: when is pest-free certification worthwhile?', *Agricultural and Resource Economics Review*, **35**(1), 52–62.

Lovell, S.J., S.F. Stone and L. Fernandez (2006), 'The economic impacts of aquatic invasive species: a review of the literature', *Agricultural and Resource Economics Review*, **35**(1), 195–208.

MacDonald, James M. and Stephen Crutchfield (1996), 'Modeling the costs of food safety regulation', *American Journal of Agricultural Economics*, **78**(5), 1285–90.

Margolis, Michael, Jason F. Shogren and Carolyn Fischer (2005), 'How trade politics affect invasive species control', *Ecological Economics*, **52**, 305–13.

Margolis, Michael and Jason F. Shogren (2007), 'The political economy of disguised protectionism and contaminated imports', Working paper.

McAusland, Carol and Christopher Costello (2004), 'Avoiding invasives: trade-related policies for controlling unintentional exotic species introductions', *Journal of Environmental Economics and Management*, **48**, 954–77.

Merriman, David (2002), 'Cigarette smuggling does not reduce the public health benefits of cigarette taxes', *Applied Economics Letters*, **9**, 493–6.

Mumford, J.D. (2002), 'Economic issues related to quarantine in international trade', *European Review of Agricultural Economics*, **29**(3), 329–48.

National Research Council (2002), *Predicting Invasions of Nonindigenous Plants and Plant Pests*, Washington, DC: National Academy Press.

Normile, Dennis (2004), 'Expanding trade with China creates ecological backlash', *Science*, **306**(5698), 968–9.

Office of Technology Assessment (1993), *U.S. Congress Harmful Non-Indigenous Species in the United States*, OTA-F-565, Washington, DC: US Government Printing Office. http://www.wws.princeton.edu/ota/disk1/1993/9325_n.html.

Olson, Lars J. (2006), 'The economics of terrestrial invasive species: a review of the literature', *Agricultural and Resource Economics Review*, **35**(1), 178–94.

Olson, Lars J. and Santanu Roy (2002), 'The economics of controlling a stochastic biological invasion', *American Journal of Agricultural Economics*, **84**(5), 1311–16.

Paarlberg, Philip L. and John G. Lee (1998), 'Import restrictions in the presence of a health risk: an illustration using FMD', *American Journal of Agricultural Economics*, **80**(1), 175–83.

Persico, Nicola (2002), 'Racial profiling, fairness, and effectiveness of policing', *American Economic Review*, **92**(5), 1472–97.

Pimentel, David, Rodolfo Zuniga and Doug Morrison (2005), 'Update on the environmental and economic costs associated with alien-invasive species in the United States', *Ecological Economics*, **52**, 273–88.

Reed, William J. (1979), 'Optimal escapement levels in stochastic and deterministic harvesting models', *Journal of Environmental Economics and Management*, **6**(4), 350–63.

Rosenzweig, M.L. (1995), *Species Diversity in Space and Time*, Cambridge, UK: Cambridge University Press.

Ruiz, Gregory M., James T. Carlton, Edwin D. Grosholz and Anton H. Hines (1997), 'Global invasion of marine and estuarine habitats by non-indigenous species: mechanisms, extent, and consequence', *American Zoologist*, **37**(6), 621–32.

Shine, Clare, Nattley Williams and Lothar Gündling (2000), *A Guide to Designing Legal and Institutional Frameworks on Alien Invasive Species*, Gland, Switzerland and Cambridge, UK: IUCN.

Shogren, Jason F., Joseph A. Herringes and Ramu Govindasamy (1993), 'Limits to environmental bonds', *Ecological Economics*, **8**(2), 109–33.

Simberloff, Daniel (2006), 'Risk assessments, blacklists, and white lists for introduced species: are predictions good enough to be useful?', *Agricultural and Resource Economics Review*, **35**(1), 1–10.

Simberloff, D., D. Schmitz and T. Brown (1997), *Strangers in Paradise*, Washington, DC: Island Press.

Solow, Andrew R. and Christopher J. Costello (2004), 'Estimating the rate of species introductions from the discovery record', *Ecology*, **85**(7), 1822–5.

Standing Committee for the Convention on the Conservation of European Wildlife and Natural Habitats (2003), *European Strategy on Invasive Alien Species*, Council of Europe.

Thomas, M.H. and A. Randall (2000), 'Intentional introductions of nonindigenous species: a principal–agent model and protocol for revocable decisions', *Ecological Economics*, **34**(3), 333–45.

Tu, Anh T. and John C. Beghin (2006), 'Intra-industry trade, multilateral trade integration, and invasive species risk', Center for Agricultural and Rural Development, Iowa State University, Working Paper 06-WP 439.

Tu, Anh, John C. Beghin and Estelle Gozlan (forthcoming), 'Tariff escalation and invasive species risk', *Ecological Economics*.

United States Department of Agriculture (2002), *Treatment Manual*, http://www.aphis.usda.gov/import_export/plants/manuals/ports/downloads/treatment.pdf.

Unnevehr, Laurian J. and Helen H. Jensen (1999), 'The economic implications of using HACCP as a food safety regulatory standard', *Food Policy*, **24**(6), 625–35.

Varia, Monali, Samantha Wilson, Shelly Sarwal, Allison McGeer, Effie Gournis, Eleni Galanis and Bonnie Henry (2003), 'Investigation of a nosocomial outbreak of severe acute respiratory syndrome (SARS) in Toronto, Canada', *Canadian Medical Association Journal*, **169**(4), 285–92.

Wilcove, David S., David Rothstein, Jason Dubow, Ali Phillips and Elizabeth Losos (1998), 'Quantifying threats to imperiled species in the United States', *Bioscience*, **48**(8), 607–15.

Wilson, Norbert L.W. and Jesus Anton (2006), 'Combining risk assessment and economics in managing a sanitary–phytosanitary risk', *American Journal of Agricultural Economics*, **88**(1), 194–202.

Yue, Chengyan, John C. Beghin and Helen H. Jensen (2006), 'Tariff equivalent of technical barriers to trade with imperfect substitution and trade costs', *American Journal of Agricultural Economics*, **88**(4), 947–60.

2 International trade and global shipping
James J. Corbett and James J. Winebrake

The freight transportation system is the network of specialized vessels, the ports they visit, and transportation infrastructure from factories to terminals to distribution centers to markets (MARAD, 1999). Within such a definition, it is nearly impossible to consider ocean shipping separately from the goods movement context. On a worldwide basis, nearly 50 000 oceangoing vessels move cargo more than 33 billion tonne-km annually. In the European Union, marine transportation moves more than 70 percent (by volume) of all cargo traded with the rest of the world; in the USA, more than 95 percent of imports and exports are carried by ships (MARAD, 2000). This work is accomplished by ships using 2 to 4 percent of the world's fossil fuels (Corbett, 2004).

These inbound and outbound freight flows through national ports are connected to truck and train movement of goods through a transportation network. In fact, ocean shipping can be considered to be a 'trip-generator' for intermodal cargoes in global trade, blending with domestic freight movements on nations' roads and rails. This intermodal context is important when considering impacts of ocean shipping, particularly where modal tradeoffs in energy intensity and emissions differ. This chapter discusses the role of ocean shipping within the context of international goods transportation, with specific attention paid to the energy and environmental impacts of such shipping.

Multimodal freight context
International maritime shipping is a critical element in the global freight transportation system that includes ocean and coastal routes, inland waterways, railways and roads, and air freight. The freight transportation network connects locations by multiple modal routes, functioning as modal substitutes (see Figure 2.1a) A primary example is containerized shortsea shipping, where the shipper or logistics provider has some degree of choice about how to move freight between locations. However, international maritime transportation is more commonly a complement to other modes of transportation (see Figure 2.1b). This is particularly true for intercontinental containerized cargoes[1] and for liquid and dry bulk cargoes, such as oil and grain. International shipping connects roads, railways, and inland waterways through ocean and coastal routes.

Mode choice (especially for containerized cargo movement) involves balancing tradeoffs to facilitate trade among global corporations and nations. In the current global economy, competing factors have been time, cost and reliability of delivery. Low-cost modes may be less preferred than faster modes if the cargo is very time sensitive; however, slower, lower-cost modes often carry much more cargo and, with proper planning, these modes can reliably deliver larger quantities to meet just-in-time inventory needs.

Mode share in freight transportation can be measured in several ways, but a common metric is work done in cargo tonne-km (tkm). The EU and the USA have similar mode shares for trucking, about 45 percent of total freight transport work (EPA, 2005a; Mantzos and Capros, 2006). However, it is important to note that European waterborne

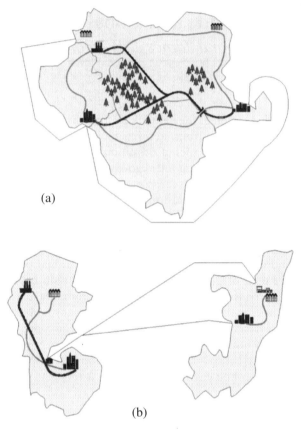

(a)

(b)

Source: Skjølsvik et al. (2000).

Figure 2.1   Ocean shipping (a) as a substitute and (b) as a complement to other freight modes

freight (inland river and shortsea combined) is second in mode share, moving about 40–44 percent of the cargo tkm in recent years (Mantzos and Capros, 2006; ECDGET and Eurostat, 2006); in the USA, rail freight tkm is nearly equal to road freight. Moreover, these mode-share summaries ignore the 46 000 giga-tkm (one Gtkm $= 10^9$ tkm) of seaborne trade moving cargoes among all trading nations from distances outside the domains from which national statistics are reported. For context, seaborne trade is some 30 times greater than the seaborne mode share in the EU, and 12 times greater than all freight tkm in the EU. Figure 2.2 summarizes these mode-share comparisons.

Categorizing environmental impacts of ocean shipping
Environmental impacts from ocean shipping can be summarized in different contexts. For this overview, the impacts are categorized as either episodic or routine. These designations help to explain why some aspects of ocean shipping, such as stack emissions, are so challenging to address. Example environmental impacts under this taxonomy are listed in Table 2.1. Some

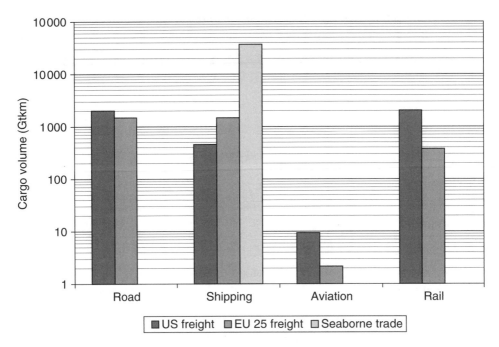

Figure 2.2 Comparison of freight-mode shares (tonne-km) for the USA and Europe

pollution related to ocean shipping is not directly from the ships, but from efforts to serve the ocean shipping sector through port infrastructure maintenance and fleet modernization.

Episodic pollution discharges are among those best understood by the commercial industry and policy-makers, as evidenced by the international conventions and national regulations addressing them. The dominant mitigation approach is to prohibit pollution episodes from occurring (as in ocean dumping), to design systems that are safer (as in double hulls to prevent oil spills or traffic separation schemes to avoid collisions), to confine activities that produce untreated discharges to safer times or locations (e.g. environmental windows for dredging), to require onboard treatment before discharge (e.g. oily water separators), and/or to provide segregated holding and transfer to reception facilities at port (as in sewage handling).

Routine pollution releases are different than episodic discharges because they represent activities necessary for the safe operation of the vessel, whether at sea or in port. Regulation of routine releases has lagged policy action to address episodic discharges, partly because these impacts were not so well understood in the past, and partly because operational behavior must change and/or new technology is required.

Freight energy and emissions
Energy use by mode is generally proportional to the work done (cargo tkm) by each freight mode, with intermodal adjustments for differences in energy intensities. Energy

Table 2.1   Overview of types of ocean shipping pollution

Episodic environmental events	Routine environmental events
Vessel-based	
Oil spills	Engine air emissions
Ocean dumping	Volatile cargoes emissions (petroleum)
Sewage discharges	Invasive species introductions
Oily wastewater	(ballast water/hull fouling)
Vessel collisions	Hull coating toxics releases
Ship-strikes with marine life	Underwater noise
Port-based	
Dredging	Stormwater runoff
Port expansion	Vessel wake erosion
Ship construction, breaking	Cargo-handling air emissions

intensities are a function of cargo payload-to-capacity ratios, and fuel economy differences among the engines used by the modes (Mantzos and Capros, 2006; ECDGET and Eurostat, 2006; Davis, 2003).

Shipping and rail are not only among the least costly modes of transportation, they are also the most energy efficient (with some exceptions generally proportional with high vessel speed and low service capacity). Because fuel costs can represent between 20 and 60 percent of shipping costs, operators have strong economic motivation to operate ships efficiently and to employ propulsion technologies that reduce fuel consumption per cargo tkm.

However, a consequence of marine engine technologies is increased air pollution. Among freight modes, waterborne transportation has been shown to cause significant air pollution locally in port communities, add to long-range pollution transport in coastal regions of heavy trade, and contribute to climate change on a global scale (Skjølsvik et al., 2000; Corbett and Koehler, 2004; 2003; Capaldo et al., 1999; Corbett and Fischbeck, 1997; Corbett et al., 1999; Endresen et al., 2003; Kasibhatla et al., 2000; Lawrence and Crutzen, 1999). Oceangoing shipping is also the least regulated freight mode, at least for air pollution.

Together with ocean shipping, emissions associated with other freight modes are significant (Skjølsvik et al., 2000; OECD, and Hecht, 1997; IEA, 1998). According to the US EPA, heavy-duty truck, rail and water transport together account for more than 25 percent of US CO_2 emissions, about 50 percent of NO_x emissions, and nearly 40 percent of PM (particulate matter) emissions from all mobile sources (EPA, 2005a; 2005b). In Europe, these modes generate more than 30 percent of the transportation sector's CO_2 emissions (Bates et al., 2001).

Fleet energy and emissions[2]
Most energy in marine transportation is used by cargo or passenger transport vessels – ships that move cargo or passengers from one place to another in trade. A profile of the internationally registered fleet of ships greater than 100 gross tons is shown in Table 2.2 (LMIS, 2002). Transport vessels account for almost 60 percent of the ships and nearly 80 percent of the enery demand of the internationally registered fleet (not including

Table 2.2　*Profile of world commercial fleet, number of main engines, and main engine power*

Ship type	Number of ships	% of fleet	Number of main engines	% of main engines	Installed power (MW)	% of total power	% of energy demand[1]
Cargo fleet							
Container vessels	2 662	2	2 755	2	43 764	10	13
General cargo vessels	23 739	22	31 331	21	72 314	16	22
Tankers	9 098	8	10 258	7	48 386	11	15
Bulk/combined carriers	8 353	8	8 781	6	51 251	11	16
Non-cargo fleet							
Passenger	8 370	8	15 646	10	19 523	4	6
Fishing vessels	23 371	22	24 009	16	18 474	4	6
Tugboats	9 348	9	16 000	11	16 116	4	5
Other (research, supply)	3 719	3	7 500	5	10 265	2	3
Registered fleet Total	88 660	82	116 280	77	280 093	62	86
Military vessels2	19 646	18	34 633	23	172 478	38	14
World fleet total	108 306	100	150 913	100	452 571	100	100

Notes:
1. Percentage of energy demand is not directly proportional to installed power because military vessels typically use much less than their installed power except during battle. Average military deployment rate is 50% under way time per year (US Navy, 1996); studies indicate that when under way, naval vessels operate below 50% power for 90% of the time (NAVSEA, 1994). Energy demand was adjusted to reflect these facts.
2. The data upon which military vessel power was based specified the number of engines aboard naval ships.

Sources:　Adapted from Corbett (2004); Corbett and Koehler (2003).

military ships). Other vessels are primarily engaged in extraction of resources (e.g. fishing, oil or other minerals), or primarily engaged as support vessels (vessel-assist tugs, supply vessels). Because non-transport ships operate within specific regions, often at low power, to extract the ocean resources, these ships require much less energy than ships engaged in commercial trade.

To reduce operating expenses, marine engines have been designed to burn the least costly of petroleum products in high-temperature, high-pressure engines. Residual fuels, also known as heavy fuel oil (HFO), are a blend of various oils obtained from the highly viscous residue of distillation or cracking after the lighter (and more valuable) hydrocarbon fractions have been removed. Of the two-stroke, low-speed engines, 95 percent use HFO and 5% are powered by marine distillate oil (MDO). Fuel consumed by 70% of the four-stroke, medium-speed engines is HFO, with the remainder burning either MDO or marine gas oil (MGO). Four-stroke, high-speed engines all operate on MDO or MGO. The remaining engine types are small, high-speed diesel engines all operating on MDO or MGO, steam turbines powered by boilers fueled by HFO, or gas turbines powered by MGO. Residual fuels are preferred if ship engines can accommodate their poorer quality, unless there are other reasons (such as environmental compliance) to use more expensive fuels.

Table 2.3   International marine fuel sales by nation, 1990–99

% of total sales	Nations selling residual bunkers (% in parentheses)	Nations selling other bunkers (% in parentheses)
>15	USA (18)	USA (22)
6–15	Singapore (9), Russia (9), Netherlands (8), United Arab Emirates (8)	Saudi Arabia (12)
2–5	Japan, Saudi Arabia, Belgium, South Korea, Spain, South Africa, Greece	Hong Kong, Singapore, Netherlands, South Korea, UK, Spain, Russia
~1	France, Taiwan, China, Italy, Egypt, Netherlands Antilles, Hong Kong, UK, Germany	Thailand, Greece, India, Belgium, Italy, Brazil, Indonesia, Denmark, Egypt, Venezuela, Germany
<1	47 other countries	92 other countries

Sources: Adapted from Corbett (2004); Corbett et al. (1999).

Nations with strong interests in the cargoes or services provided by ships sell the most fuel. OECD nations account for roughly half of these fuel sales and provide one illustration of historical consumption trends in the overall fleet (IEA, 1977–97; EIA, 2001).

Table 2.3 presents a summary of the top nations selling international marine fuels during the 1990s, according to the World Energy Database (EIA, 2001). The USA provides most of the world's marine fuels by far, and together the top 20 nations selling international marine fuels (shown in Table 2.3) account for more than 80% of total marine fuel sales.

The term 'international marine fuel' introduces a classification problem for environmental assessments. The basic issue is whether international sales statistics describe total energy consumption by shipping or whether they describe only those sales classified as international sales for EIA purposes. International marine fuels statistics were used to differentiate those fuels within a nation's domestic stock from those not eligible for emergency allocation calculations within the oil emergency sharing system (Scott, 1994; IEA, 1987; Houghton et al., 1997). Depending on whether sales data or activity data are used to estimate fuel consumption in shipping, estimates may vary (Corbett and Koehler, 2004; 2003; Corbett and Fischbeck, 1997; Corbett et al., 1999; Houghton et al., 1997; Browning et al., 2005; Thomas et al., 2002; UNFCCC and Subsidiary Body for Scientific and Technological Advice, 2004). Recent estimates based on ship activity and installed engine power also conclude that the world fleet of ships (including cargo, non-cargo and military vessels) consumes some 280 million tonnes of fuel per year, with more than 200 million tonnes required for cargo ships alone. Some debate continues, but the major elements of activity-based inventories are widely accepted (Endresen et al., 2003, 2005, 2004). Considering the range of current estimates using activity-based input parameters, ocean-going ships consume 2–4 percent of world fossil fuels.

Figure 2.3 summarizes emissions estimates from various sources, including NO_x (as elemental nitrogen), SO_x (as elemental sulfur), and particulate matter (PM_{10}), hydrocarbons and methane (from both engines and cargoes), black carbon and organic carbon (constituents of PM with climate implications), and refrigerants. The figure shows estimated ranges of fuel use and carbon dioxide alongside the other emissions using a log scale.

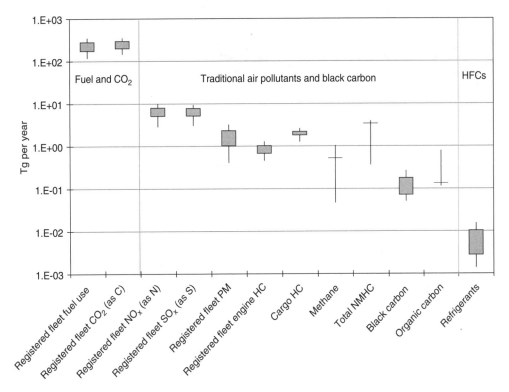

Notes: Box-plots represent the 5th and 95th percentile results from uncertainty analysis; whiskers extend to lower and upper bounds; emissions do not represent comparative climate impacts.

Figure 2.3   *Summary of estimated ranges in global emissions from maritime shipping*

Representing spatial (and temporal) activity of commercial shipping is fundamentally similar to modeling any mobile source: the location and intensity of the fleet activity must be depicted. Two global ship-reporting datasets, ICOADS and the Automated Mutual-assistance Vessel Rescue system (AMVER), have previously been used as proxies of ship traffic to geographically resolve the global emissions inventories (Corbett and Fischbeck, 1997; Corbett et al., 1999; Endresen et al., 2003; Wang, 2006; Wang and Corbett, 2005). Recently, a global shipping network has been developed (see Figure 2.4); this network has been used to combine the best of the bottom-up and top-down approaches (Wang, 2006; Wang and Corbett, 2005; Corbett et al., 2006a; 2006b; Wang et al., 2006; Corbett et al., 2007).

Freight energy and emissions trends[3]
The multimodal and multicargo freight context must be considered when forecasting oceangoing environmental trends. This is because all freight modes respond to common drivers of change (e.g. economic growth, population demographics, energy prices), and cross-mode influences need to be included (e.g. metropolitan road congestion around one port diverting some cargoes to other ports). This applies whether one is considering air

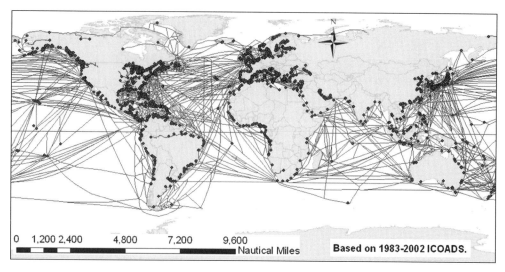

0   1,200 2,400   4,800   7,200   9,600
                                                  Nautical Miles   **Based on 1983-2002 ICOADS.**

Source: Wang et al. (2007).

Figure 2.4   Global shipping network of routes and ports

quality, climate change, or other environmental impacts. Three critical questions for forecasting freight activity and environmental impacts include:

1. *Baseline conditions*: what are freight energy and activity patterns?
2. *Rates of change*: what are the forecast trends for these energy and activity patterns?
3. *Patterns of change*: where will future freight activity be located?

While interrelated, these questions are to some extent independent, given uncertainty. Convergence is emerging on baseline estimates – at least in terms of major insights – through academic dialogue about uncertainty ranges in oceangoing energy and emissions.

Freight transportation, particularly international cargoes, are an important and increasing contributor to global and national economic growth, as well as regional economic growth in and around major cargo ports. For example, international trade is increasing as a proportion of US gross domestic product (GDP) – i.e. freight transportation is growing faster than US GDP (BEA, 2006; US Department of Transportation et al., 2006). Economic activity related to imports and exports contributes about 22% of US GDP in recent years, whereas goods movement contributed only about 10% of GDP in the 1970s. Moreover, the dominance of containerized cargoes in seaborne trade suggests that truck and containerized shipments may double by 2025 or sooner (Giuliano and Godwin, 2006). This freight-sector growth rate in terms of dollar value is reflected in the observed ~6.3 to 7.2 percent annual growth rates of 'high-value' containerized trade volumes, particularly from Asia (Vickerman, 2006). The US Bureau of Transportation Statistics (BTS) recently released a report that describes North American freight activity and trends (US Department of Transportation et al., 2006). This document reports growth rates for North America above 7.4% for international trade and above 7.2% across all measures of value.

Growth factors embedded in mobile source energy and emissions models appear to capture this economic-driven growth in freight transportation (EIA, 2003; EPA et al., 2004; EPA, 1998; 2003). Importantly, some trend reports claim that freight energy growth will slow over the next two decades (Mantzos and Capros, 2006), although these analyses seem inconsistent with global trade economic projections for imported goods. A basic insight when adopting growth patterns based on the economic drivers of freight is that growth rates in GDP and trade volumes are coupled. In other words, if growth in GDP and trade volumes is compounded as forecast by economic and transportation demand studies, then growth in energy requirements cannot be linear without decoupling (changes in energy intensity). Even with efficiency improvements, compounding increases in trade volumes are likely to outstrip energy conservation efforts unless a technological or operational breakthrough in goods movement emerges.

Previous studies have described global growth rates for maritime shipping, based on fleet size, trade growth and/or cargo tkm, mostly calibrated to linear or conservative extrapolations of historic data. The *IMO Study on Greenhouse Gas Emissions from Ships* and other studies (Skjølsvik et al., 2000; EC and ENTEC UK, 2002) used fleet growth rates based on two market forecast principles, validated by historical seaborne trade patterns: (1) world economic growth will continue; and (2) demand for shipping services will follow the general economic growth. The IMO study correctly stated that growth in demand for shipping services was driven by both increased cargo (tonnage) and increased cargo movements (ton-miles), and considered that these combined factors made extrapolation from historic data difficult. None the less, their forecast for future seaborne trade (combined cargoes in terms of tonnage) was between 1.5% and 3% annually. The IMO study applied these rates of growth in trade to represent growth in energy requirements.

Eyring et al. (2005b) estimated 'future world seaborne trade in terms of volume in million tons for a specific ship traffic scenario in a future year' using a linear fit to past data. Except for the Eyring et al. work, these linear extrapolations appear to present growth rates slower than the economy. Linear extrapolations are likely biased on the low side, because shipping growth rates have actually grown faster than the economy. Studies for Southern California (San Pedro Bay) ports confirm that growth in cargo volumes equivalent to 6–7% compounding annual growth rates is expected for some major ports (NNI Task Force, 2005; Mercator Transportation Group et al., 2005; Meyer Mohaddes Associates, 2004; Parsons Transportation Group, 2004). However, increased cargo throughput may not produce a corresponding increase in port calls, as some studies suggest (Mercator Transportation Group et al., 2005). Historic data on port calls to San Pedro Bay have shown that the number of ship calls remained between 5000 and 7000 calls per year since the 1950s (Port of Los Angeles et al., 1994). Furthermore, proportional relationships between environmental impacts and goods movement trends are reflected in recent port and regional studies of economic activity and goods transportation, particularly those focused on Southern California ports (NNI Task Force, 2005; California Air Resources Board, 2006; Southern California Association of Governments, 2006; Port of Los Angeles, 2006).

Forecasting of environmental impact from shipping is constrained by the quality of shipping and trade forecasts (Stopford, 1997). At the global scale, we evaluate available trends in energy use and/or emissions from published literature with the seaborne cargo

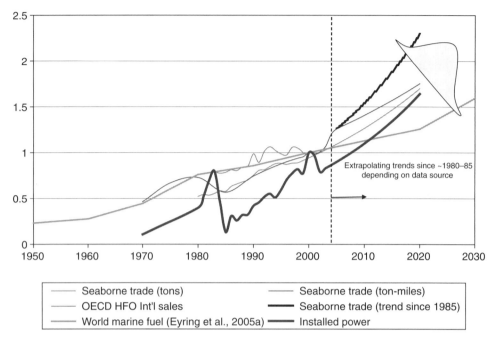

Figure 2.5   Global indices for seaborne trade, ship energy/fuel demand, and installed power

and trade data discussed earlier. We compare world fleet trends in installed power (derived from average power by year of build) with energy trends (work by Eyring et al. and fuel sales), with trade-based historical data (tons and ton-miles). Activity-based energy results for similar base years (2001 or 2002) are within close agreement (Corbett and Koehler, 2004; 2003; Eyring et al., 2005a). This allows us to index trends to nearly the same value and year, to index trade-based trends similarly, and to compare these with trends in installed power (Figure 2.5).

Three insights emerge from this global comparison. Extrapolating past data (with adjustments) produces a range of trends that is bounded and reveals convergence around a set of similar trends; in other words, while the range of growth may vary within bounds of a factor of two, one cannot get 'any forecast one wants' out of the data. If we consider that global trade and technology drivers mutually influence future trends, then we may interpret convergence within the bounds as describing a likely forecast of global shipping activity.

World shipping activity and energy use are on track to double from 2002 by about 2030 (~2015 if one considers seaborne trade since 1985, ~2050 if one considers Eyring et al.'s BAU (business as usual) trend). Growth rates are not likely to be reduced without significant changes in freight transportation behavior and/or changes in shipboard technology.

Confirming earlier discussion, trends in installed power are clearly coupled with trends in trade and energy. This reinforces the analysis of installed power as a proxy for forecasting growth, not only for use in baseline inventory estimates.

Change in energy and emissions could be a modified growth curve from the growth in cargo activity, depending on change in energy intensity and/or emissions through investments in economies of scale, fuel conservation measures, or emissions control measures. If so, one indication would be different rates of change for installed power on ships providing goods movement compared to changes in cargo volume. In other words, if a fleet of ships can carry more cargo without a proportional increase in installed power, then it must be adopting improved technologies (e.g. hull forms, engine combustion systems, plant efficiency designs) or innovating its cargo operations (e.g. payload utilization).

In fact, the opposite trend is observed over the past 20 to 30 years, where fleet installed power has grown at rates faster than global trade growth. Observed trends in average installed power reveal a compound annual growth rate (CAGR) for installed power since 1985 is ~10.7% per year, more than twice the rate of world seaborne trade growth, driven by increases in containership power, which grew at more than 16% CAGR over these two decades. Rephrasing, ocean shipping may have become more energy intensive, not more energy conserving. This seemingly counter-intuitive observation is typical of other transportation modes, particularly on-road freight and passenger vehicles, and readily explainable in terms of trade globalization and containerization of international trade. Globalization produced longer shipping routes, and containerization served just-in-time (or at least on-time) liner schedules; both of these drivers motivated economic justification for larger and faster ships which require greater power to perform their service. Introduction of the fastest, largest ships first occurred on the most valuable trade routes (e.g. serving North America and Europe) where economics most justified the higher-performing freight services. Increasingly over the past two decades, ships serving all routes became faster and larger through intentional expansion and aging fleet transition from prime routes to secondary markets.

Even assuming that efficiency improvements from economies of scale reduce energy intensity and emissions rather than being directed to larger and faster ships (e.g. container ships), compounding increases in trade volumes outstrip energy conservation efforts unless technological or operational breakthroughs in goods movement emerge.

However, technological change might offset this trend, if fleets can achieve greater efficiencies while increasing installed power (Wartsila NSD, 1998; Harrington, 1992; Heywood, 1998). In other words, if fuel economy (energy input) is not directly proportional over time to energy output (proportional to rated power), then improved propulsion technologies can explain the decoupling of increased power and fuel use. Adjusting power-based trends for a number of factors, including fleet modernization and shipping cycles, we estimate a world growth trend ranging between 3.8% and 4.5% CAGR. Coincidentally, averaging bounding extrapolations yields between 3.8% and 4.5% CAGR growth in installed power, nearly the same 4.1% CAGR as observed for past world seaborne trade. In other words, this explains and confirms the use of seaborne trade growth to project ship fuel use and emissions, as other studies have done. Consistent with the market-forecast principles reflected in the IMO study, and given the strong relationship observed between cargo moved (work done) and maritime emissions (fuel energy used), we adopt for our forecasts the world average growth rate of 4.1%.

Mitigation alternatives for shipping
Reduction of traditional air pollutants has received greater attention. Air emissions technologies are generally adapted or marinized from similar engines in other industries (Wartsila NSD, 1998; Alexandersson et al., 1993; Corbett and Fischbeck, 2001;

Winebrake et al., 2005; Farrell et al., 2002; Quandt, 1996, MAN B&W Diesel, 1997; Cooper, 2001; Wartsila NSD, 1994). Emissions controls have been categorized as either pre-combustion, in-engine, or post-combustion controls (Corbett and Fischbeck, 2002). Technologies that reduce NO_x emissions can be divided into three groups: those that require engine modifications (in-engine controls), those that are implemented in the fuel or air system (pre-engine technologies), and those that are on the exhaust system (post-engine technologies). An important consideration identified in reducing air quality pollutants through technologies and alternative fuels is that nearly all increase the energy requirements on a system basis by 1–5%, thereby increasing CO_2 emissions attributed to shipping proportionally.

Fewer studies have considered directly how to mitigate CO_2 emissions; the IMO study of greenhouse gases from ships presented a suite of alternatives for both new and existing vessels (Skjølsvik et al., 2000). The IMO study estimated that new vessel CO_2 emissions could be reduced by 5–20% through technological measures, with hull and propeller modifications and engine optimization for efficiency (rather than power) offering the greatest potential. Other new-engine technologies offered only modes CO_2 reductions (0.5–5%), although a hypothetical combination of technological measures to could achieve a maximum range of 5–30% reduction. The IMO study estimated that reducing CO_2 from existing vessels (e.g. through retrofit technologies) would be more challenging, with reductions from individual measures ranging from 1 to 7%. Some reasonable combinations put CO_2 reductions in a range of 5–12%, with a hypothetical combination of all technological measures at 5–20%.

Alternative marine fuels (other than for performance improvement or cost reduction) were first studied following the 1970s reaction to the energy crisis (National Research Council, 1980). The possibility of alternative fuels in ocean shipping is receiving renewed attention, based primarily on environmental concerns about climate change and air quality (Intertanko, 2006; Wang and Corbett, 2007). Alternative fuels choices should not be made only on the basis of operating ship fuel consumption, but should also add impacts of extracting, refining and delivering new fuels to replace marine heavy fuel oil (residual fuel). Assessing complete emissions from marine transportation (and to compare these emissions with landside alternatives), a total fuel life-cycle emissions analysis is needed (Winebrake et al., 2007a; 2007b; Winebrake et al., 2006). These analyses consider emissions and energy use along the entire fuel pathway – from extraction to use. In any case, the freight sector overall, and perhaps oceangoing shipping in particular, may offer some advantages in a shift to alternate transportation fuels (Farrell et al., 2003).

More directly, environmental mitigation through behavior change is also an option (Kågeson and Nature Associates, 1999; Theis et al., 2004). Operational measures, primarily fleet and logistics planning, offer greater potential CO_2 reductions. For example, air emissions reductions can be achieved through speed reductions, as studied by IMO and as implemented through voluntary agreements with industry (Skjølsvik et al., 2000; Corbett, 2004; Los Angeles Board of Harbor Commissioners et al., 2001). For a given vessel, 10% reduction in speed (e.g. from 22 to 20 knots) can reduce energy requirements for that voyage by more than 20%. Importantly, operational measures can also reduce air quality pollutants such as NO_x and SO_x (both of which have climate-scale influences through ozone and aerosols).The IMO study estimated CO_2 reductions from operational changes to range from 1 to 40%.

Especially where these operational changes may affect global trade, these issues are not single-mode concerns for oceangoing ships. International trade needs to be considered as an intermodal/multimodal network responding to common drivers differently than other mobile sources (autos) and coupled with larger sustainability issues such as land use, resource extraction, labor and population. Within this context, both technological and operational measures can achieve more sustainable goods movement involving marine transportation.

Summary

Considering mitigation options involves valuing and comparing their characteristics in terms of decision criteria that may vary among stakeholders facing competing objectives. For example, when emissions reduction is clearly merited for reasons other than cost (e.g. health-based impacts), the valuation of alternatives may require a cost-effectiveness evaluation to select the most preferred options; however, considering whether action is merited on an economic basis may require a more difficult full accounting of direct and indirect costs and benefits. With regard to cost-effectiveness, studies show that shipping is among the least regulated and most cost-effective transportation sectors with regard to NOx and SO$_x$ control (Skjølsvik et al., 2000; Corbett and Fischbeck, 2002, 2001; Corbett, 1999; Friedrich et al., 2007). Ongoing and recent studies are quantifying impacts of current and forecast fleet activity in terms of air quality, environmental impacts (e.g. acidification), human health and climate change, many being led or funded in Europe.

Notes

1. Air freight is also a mode connecting intercontinental logistics. Air freight tends to move the highest-value, most time-sensitive freight; while a significant mode in trade value, aircraft move much less global freight by volume, and at significant energy per unit shipped.
2. This discussion is adapted or excerpted from the author's work published in the *Encyclopedia of Energy* and other work (Giuliano and Godwin, 2006; Vickerman, 2006; EIA, 2003).
3. This section is adapted or excerpted from other work (Giuliano and Godwin, 2006; Vickerman, 2006; EIA, 2003; Mercator Transport Group et al., 2005).

References

Alexandersson, A. et al. (1993), *Exhaust Gas Emissions from Sea Transportation*, Gothenburg, Sweden: Swedish Transportation Research Board.

Bates, J. et al. (2001), *Economic Evaluation of Emissions Reductions in the Transport Sector of the EU: Bottom-up analysis, UPDATED, Final Report*, Abingdon, UK: AEA Technology Environment.

Browning, I.C. Louis and E.P.S.L. Kathleen Bailey (eds) (2005), *Best Practices in Preparing Port Emission Inventories: Draft for review*, prepared for Office of Policy, Economics and Innovation, US Environmental Protection Agency, Fairfax, VA: ICF Consulting, p. 39.

Bureau of Economic Analysis (2006), 'Table 1.1.6: real Gross Domestic Product, chained dollars', in *National Income and Product Accounts Tables*, Washington, DC: US Department of Commerce, available at: http://www.bea.gov/bea/dn/nipaweb/index.asp.

California Air Resources Board (2006), *Goods Movement and Ports*, Sacramento, CA: California Air Resources Board.

Capaldo, K.P. et al. (1999), 'Effects of ship emissions on sulphur cycling and radiative climate forcing over the ocean', Nature, **400**, 743–6.

Corbett, J.J. (2004a), 'Marine transportation and energy use', in C.J. Cleveland (ed.), *Encyclopedia of Energy*, San Diego, CA: Elsevier Science, pp. 745–8.

Corbett, J.J. (2004b), *Verification of Ship Emission Estimates with Monitoring Measurements to Improve Inventory and Modeling*, Newark, DE: University of Delaware 47.

Corbett, J.J. (1999), 'An assessment of air pollution and environmental impacts from international maritime transportation including engineering controls and policy alternatives', *Engineering and Public Policy*, Pittsburgh, PA: Carnegie Mellon University.

Corbett, J.J. and P.S. Fischbeck (1997), 'Emissions from ships', Science, **278**(5339), 823–4.
Corbett, J.J. and P.S. Fischbeck (2001a), *Commercial Marine Emissions and Life-Cycle Analysis of Retrofit Controls in a Changing Science and Policy Environment*, Marine Environmental Engineering Technology Symposium (MEETS) 2001, Arlington, VA: ASNE/SNAME.
Corbett, J.J. and P.S. Fischbeck (2001b), 'International technology-policy: challenges in regulating ship emissions', in P.S. Fischbeck and S. Farrow (eds), *Improving Regulation: Cases in Environment, Health and Safety*, Washington, DC: RFF Press, pp. 282–309.
Corbett, J.J. and P.S. Fischbeck (2002), 'Commercial marine emissions and life-cycle analysis of retrofit controls in a changing science and policy environment', *Naval Engineers Journal*, **114**(1), 93–106.
Corbett, J.J. and H.W. Koehler (2003), 'Updated emissions from ocean shipping', *Journal of Geophysical Research – Atmospheres*, **108**(D20), 4650–66.
Corbett, J.J. and H.W. Koehler (2004), 'Considering alternative input parameters in an activity-based ship fuel consumption and emissions model', *Journal of Geophysical Research – Atmospheres*, **109**(D23303), 8.
Corbett, J.J., P.S. Fischbeck and S.N. Pandis (1999), 'Global nitrogen and sulfur emissions inventories for ocean-going ships', *Journal of Geophysical Research*, **104**(D3), 3457–70.
Corbett, J.J., C. Wang and J. Firestone (2006a), *Estimation, Validation, and Forecasts of Regional Commercial Marine Vessel Inventories, Tasks 3 and 4: Forecast inventories for 2010 and 2020*, Draft Report, Sacramento, CA: State of California Air Resources Board.
Corbett, J.J., C. Wang and J. Firestone (2006b), *Estimation, Validation, and Forecasts of Regional Commercial Marine Vessel Inventories, Tasks 1 and 2: Baseline Inventory and Ports Comparison, Final Report*, Sacramento, CA, and Montreal, Quebec: State of California Air Resources Board and the Commission for Environmental Cooperation of North America.
Corbett, J.J., C. Wang and J. Firestone (2007), *Estimation, Validation, and Forecasts of Regional Commercial Marine Vessel Inventories, Final Report*, Sacramento, CA: State of California Air Resources Board, the California Environmental Protection Agency and the Commission for Environmental Cooperation of North America.
Cooper, D.A. (2001), 'Exhaust emissions from high speed passenger ferries', *Atmospheric Environment*, **35**(24), 4189–200.
Davis, S. (2003), *Transportation Energy Data Book: Edition 23*, Oak Ridge, TN: Oak Ridge National Laboratory.
Endresen, Ø. et al. (2003), 'Emission from international sea transportation and environmental impact', *Journal of Geophysical Research*, **108**(D17), 45–60.
Endresen, Ø. et al. (2004), 'Substantiation of a lower estimate for the bunker inventory: comment on "Updated emissions from ocean shipping" by James J. Corbett and Horst W. Koehler', *Journal of Geophysical Research – Atmospheres*, **109**(D23302).
Endresen, Ø. et al. (2005), 'Improved modelling of ship SO_2 emissions – a fuel-based approach', *Atmospheric Environment*, **39**(20), 3621–8.
Energy Information Administration (EIA) (2001), *World Energy Database and International Energy Annual 2001*, Washington, DC: Department of Energy.
Energy Information Administration (EIA) (2003), *Annual Energy Outlook 2003, With Projections to 2025*, Washington, DC: Department of Energy.
Environmental Protection Agency (EPA) (1998), *Locomotive Emissions Standards Regulatory Support Document*, Washington, DC: US Environmental Protection Agency.
Environmental Protection Agency (EPA) (2003), *Final Regulatory Support Document: Control of Emissions from New Marine Compression-Ignition Engines at or Above 30 Liters per Cylinder*, Washington, DC: US Environmental Protection Agency.
Environmental Protection Agency (2005a), *Inventory of U.S. Greenhouse Gas Emissions and Sinks: 1990–2003*, Washington, DC: US Environmental Protection Agency.
Environmental Protection Agency (EPA) (2005b), *National Air Pollutant Emission Trends, 1970–2002*, Washington, DC: US Environmental Protection Agency.
Environmental Protection Agency (EPA) et al. (2004), *MOVES2004 Highway Vehicle Population and Activity Data, Draft*, Washington, DC: US Environmental Protection Agency.
European Commission Directorate-General for Energy and Transport and Eurostat (2006), *European Energy and Transport in Figures 2006*, Brussels, Belgium: European Commission.
European Commission (EC) and ENTEC UK Ltd (2002), *Quantification of Emissions from Ships Associated with Ship Movements between Ports in the European Community*, Brussels: European Commission, DG ENV.C1.
Eyring, V. et al. (2005a), 'Emissions from international shipping: 1. The last 50 years', *Journal of Geophysical Research – Atmospheres*, **110**(D17), D17305.
Eyring, V. et al. (2005b), 'Emissions from international shipping: 2. Impact of future technologies on scenarios until 2050', *Journal of Geophysical Research – Atmospheres*, **110**(D17), D17306.

Farrell, A., J.J. Corbett and J.J. Winebrake (2002), 'Controlling air pollution from passenger ferries: cost effectiveness of seven technological options', *Journal of the Air & Waste Management Association*, **52** (December), 1399–410.

Farrell, A.E., D.W. Keith and J.J. Corbett (2003), 'A strategy for introducing hydrogen into transportation', *Energy Policy*, **31**(13), 1357–67.

Friedrich, A. et al. (2007), *Air Pollution and Greenhouse Gas Emissions from Oceangoing Ships: Impacts, Mitigation Options and Opportunities for Managing Growth*, Washington, DC: International Council on Clean Transportation (ICCT).

Giuliano, G. and S. Godwin (2006), *Critical Issues in Transportation*, TRB Executive Committee, Washington, DC: Transportation Research Board.

Harrington, R.L. (ed.) (1992), *Marine Engineering*, Jersey City, NJ: Society of Naval Architects and Marine Engineers.

Heywood, J.B. (1988), *Internal Combustion Engine Fundamentals*, New York: McGraw-Hill.

Houghton, J. et al. (eds) (1997), *Revised 1996 IPCC Guidelines for National Greenhouse Gas Inventories*, IPCC/OECD/IEA, Bracknell, UK: IPCC WGI Technical Support Unit.

International Energy Agency (IEA) (1977–97), *Quarterly Oil Statistics*, various issues, Paris: OECD.

International Energy Agency (IEA) (1987), *Energy Statistics 1970–1985 and Main Series from 1960*, Vol. I, Paris: OECD.

International Energy Agency (IEA) (1998), *Energy Efficiency Initiative, Volume 1: Energy Policy Analysis*, Paris: International Energy Agency.

Intertanko (2006), 'Revisions of MARPOL Annex VI, the NO_x Technical Code and relevant guidelines in Intersessional Meeting of the BLG-WGAP, BLG Working Group on Air Pollution', IMO submittal, Intersessional Meeting of the BLG Working Group on Air Pollution, 1st session, Agenda item 2, London.

Kågeson, P. and Nature Associates (1999), *Economic Instruments for Reducing Emissions from Sea Transport*, Göteborg, Sweden and Brussels, Belgium: Swedish NGO Secretariat on Acid Rain, The European Federation for Transport and Environment (T&E) and the European Environmental Bureau (EEB).

Kasibhatla, P. et al. (2000), 'Do emissions from ships have a significant impact on concentrations of nitrogen oxides in the marine boundary layer?', *Geophysical Research Letters*, **27**(15), 2229–33.

Lawrence, M. and P. Crutzen (1999), 'Influence of NO_x emissions from ships on tropospheric photochemistry and climate', *Nature*, **402**(6758), 167–70.

Lloyds Maritime Information System (LMIS) (2002), *The Lloyds Maritime Database*, London: Lloyd's Register, Fairplay Ltd.

Los Angeles Board of Harbor Commissioners et al. (2001), *Memorandum of Understanding for the Use of Emission Reductions from Voluntary Commercial Cargo Ship Speed Reductions to Meet the Goals of the 1994 State Implementation Plan and the 1997 South Coast Air Quality Management Plan for Marine Vessel Emissions Control Strategies*, Los Angeles, CA: Los Angeles Board of Harbor Commissioners, US Environmental Protection Agency, State of California Air Resources Board, South Coast Air Quality Management District, City of Long Beach, City of Los Angeles, Steamship Association of Southern California, the Pacific Merchant Shipping Association, and the Marine Exchange of LA/LB Harbor.

MAN B&W Diesel (1997), *Emission Control: Two-Stroke Low-Speed Diesel Engines*, MAN B&W Diesel.

Mantzos, L. and P. Capros (2006), *European Energy and Transport, Trends to 2030 – Update 2005*, Brussels, Belgium: European Commission.

MARAD (1999), *Maritime Transportation System Brochure*, Maritime Administration, US Department of Transportation.

MARAD (2000), website pages, Maritime Administration, US Department of Transportation.

Mercator Transport Group, Herbert Engineering Corporation, and MDS Transmodal Ltd (2005), *Forecast of Container Vessel Specifications and Port Calls Within San Pedro Bay: Final Cunningham Report*, Bellevue, WA: Mercator Transport Group, Herbert Engineering Corporation, and MDS Transmodal Ltd.

Meyer Mohaddes Associates Inc. (2004), *Port of Los Angeles Baseline Transport Study*, Los Angeles, CA: Port of Los Angeles.

National Research Council (US), Committee on Alternative Fuels for Maritime Use (1980), *Alternative Fuels for Maritime Use*, prepared by the Committee on Alternative Fuels for Maritime Use of the Maritime Transportation Research Board, Commission on Sociotechnical Systems, National Research Council, Washington, DC: National Academy of Sciences.

NAVSEA (1994), *U.S. Navy Marine Diesel Engine and Gas Turbine Exhaust Emissions*, Washington, DC: Naval Sea Systems Command, 03X31.

NNI Task Force (2005), *Report to Mayor Hahn and Councilwoman Hahn by the No Net Increase Task Force*, Los Angeles, CA: Port of Los Angeles.

Organisation for Economic Co-operation and Development (OECD) and J. Hecht (1997), *The Environmental Effects of Freight*, Paris: OECD.

Parsons Transportation Group (2004), *San Pedro Bay Ports Rail Market Study, TM-1b, Draft Report*, Los Angeles, CA: Port of Los Angeles.

Port of Los Angeles (2006), *Goods Movement Projects*, Los Angeles, CA: Port of Los Angeles.

Port of Los Angeles et al. (1994), *Control of Ship Emission in the South Coast Air Basin: Assessment of the Proposed Federal Implementation Plan Ship Fee Emission Fee Program*, Los Angeles, CA: Port of Los Angeles and Port of Long Beach.

Quandt, E. (1996), *European Technology for Reducing Exhaust Pollution from Naval Ship Engines*, Bethesda, MD: Carderock Division, Naval Surface Warfare Center.

Scott, R. (1994), *IEA: The First Twenty Years – Volume I: Origins and Structure*, Paris: OECD.

Skjølsvik, K.O. et al. (2000), *Study of Greenhouse Gas Emissions from Ships (MEPC 45/8 Report to International Maritime Organization on the Outcome of the IMO Study on Greenhouse Gas Emissions from Ships)*, Pittsburg, PA: MARINTEK Sintef Group, Center for Economic Analysis, Carnegie Mellon University and Trondheim, Norway: Det Norske Veritas.

Southern California Association of Governments (2006), *Goods Movement*, Los Angeles, CA: Southern California Association of Governments.

Stopford, M. (1997), *Maritime Economics*, 2nd edn, London: Routledge, Taylor and Francis Group.

Theis, M. et al. (2004), 'The role of technology in achieving environmental policy goals in the MTS', *Transportation Research Record*, **1871**, 42–9.

Thomas, R. et al. (2002), 'Shipping activities, Chapter B842', in K. Lavender et al. (eds), *EMEP/CORINAIR Emission Inventory Guidebook – October 2002 Update*, Copenhagen, Denmark: European Environment Agency.

UNFCCC and Subsidiary Body for Scientific and Technological Advice (2004), *Methodological Issues Relating to Emissions from International Aviation and Maritime Transport: Note by the Secretariat*, Bonn: United Nations Framework Convention on Climate Change, Subsidiary Body for Scientific and Technological Advice.

US Department of Transportation, Research and Innovative Technology Administration, and Bureau of Transportation Statistics (2006), *North American Freight Transportation*, Washington, DC: Bureau of Transportation Statistics.

US Navy (1996), *Navy News Service Message*, Naval Media Center Publishing.

Vickerman, M.J. (2006), 'North American marine trade and transportation trends', in *Transystems: Industry Presentations*, Kansas City, MO: Transystems, available at http://www.transystems.com/industry_presentations.asp?industry_id=8.

Wang, C. (2006), 'A study of geographical characterization of ship traffic and emissions and a cost-effectiveness analysis of reducing sulfur emissions from foreign waterborne commerce for the U.S. West Coast', Marine Policy Program, College of Marine Studies, University of Delaware, Newark.

Wang, C. and J.J. Corbett (2005), 'Geographical characterization of ship traffic and emissions', *Transportation Research Record*, **1909**, 90–99.

Wang, C. and J.J. Corbett (2007), 'A preliminary estimation of costs and benefits for reducing sulfur emissions from cargo ships in the U.S. west coastal waters', paper 07-3402 presented at the Transportation Research Board 86th Annual Meeting, Washington, DC: Transportation Research Board.

Wang, C., J.J. Corbett and J. Firestone (2006), 'Modeling energy use and emissions from North American shipping: an application of ship traffic, energy and environment model', *Environmental Science & Technology* (revision in review).

Wang, C., J.J. Corbett and J. Callahan (2007), 'Geospatial modeling of ship traffic and air emissions', paper presented at the 2007 ESRI International User Conference, San Diego, CA.

Wartsila NSD (1994), *Wartsila Diesel Group Customer Journal: Marine News*, Annapolis, MD: Wartsila NSD Corporation.

Wartsila NSD (1998), *Wartsila 32: Technology Review*, Annapolis, MD: Wartsila NSD Corporation.

Winebrake, J.J. et al. (2005), 'Optimal fleetwide emissions reductions for passenger ferries: an application of a mixed-integer nonlinear programming model for the New York–New Jersey Harbor', *Journal of Air and Waste Management*, **55**(4), 458–66.

Winebrake, J.J., J.J. Corbett and P.E. Meyer (2006), 'Total fuel-cycle emissions for marine vessels: a well-to-hull analysis with case study', paper presented at the 13th CIRP International Conference on Life Cycle Engineering, Leuven, Belgium.

Winebrake, J.J., J.J. Corbett and P.E. Meyer (2007a), 'A total fuel life-cycle analysis of energy and emissions from marine vessels', Paper No. 07-0817 presented at the Transportation Research Board 86th Annual Meeting, Washington, DC.

Winebrake, J.J., J.J. Corbett and P.E. Meyer (2007b), 'Energy use and emissions from marine vessels: a total fuel cycle approach', *Journal of Air and Waste Management*, **57** (January), 102–10.

3 The environmental Kuznets curve
James Van Alstine and Eric Neumayer

Introduction

The presumption is often made that economic growth and trade liberalization are good for the environment. The risk is that policy reforms designed to promote growth and liberalization may be encouraged with little consideration of the environmental consequences (Arrow et al., 1995). At the early stages of the environmental movement some scientists began to question how natural resource availability could be compatible with sustained economic growth (Meadows et al., 1972). Neoclassical economists, on the other hand, fiercely defended that limits to growth due to resource constraints were not a problem (e.g. Beckerman, 1974). Thus the debate between the so-called environmental pessimists and optimists began as centered on non-renewable resource availability. Although the debate has continued throughout the years (e.g. Beckerman, 1992; Lomborg, 2001; Meadows et al.,1992; 2004), the pessimists were perhaps naïve in extrapolating past trends without considering how technical progress and a change in relative prices can work to overcome apparent scarcity of limits (Neumayer, 2003b, p. 46).

In the 1980s, issues such as ozone layer depletion, global warming and biodiversity loss began to refocus the debate around the impacts of economic growth on environmental degradation. Interest was shifting away from natural resource availability towards the environment as a medium for assimilating wastes (i.e. from 'source' to 'sink') (Neumayer, 2003b, p. 47). Also, following the Brundtland Report (WCED, 1987), the discourse of sustainable development largely embraced the economic growth logic as a way out of poverty, social deprivation and also environmental degradation, particularly for the developing world. Thus the relationship between economic growth and the environment came under increased scrutiny.

In the 1990s, the empirical literature on the link between economic growth and environmental pollution proliferated (see Cole and Neumayer, 2005; Stern, 2003; 2004 for overviews). Much of this literature sought to test the environmental Kuznets curve (EKC) hypothesis, which posits that in the early stages of economic development environmental degradation will increase until a certain level of income is reached (known as the turning point) and then environmental improvement will occur. This relationship between per capita income and pollution is often shown as an inverted U-shaped curve. This curve is named after Kuznets (1955), who hypothesized that economic inequality increases over time and then after a threshold becomes more equal as per capita income increases further. In the early 1990s the EKC was introduced and popularized with the publication of Grossman and Krueger's (1991) work on the potential environmental impacts of NAFTA, and the 1992 World Bank Report (Shafik and Bandyopadhyay, 1992; World Bank, 1992).

This chapter will critically review the theoretical and empirical literature on the EKC. We find that recent improvements in empirical methods address a number of past criticisms, which adds robustness to the EKC results for certain environmental pollutants.

However, economic growth and liberalization should not be thought of as a panacea for environmental problems, particularly in the developing world. Recent work has demonstrated the unpleasant implications for many less developed countries (LDCs) that are entering the stage of economic development where emission levels are set to rise rapidly (Cole and Neumayer, 2005).

The theoretical case
Why might economic growth benefit the environment? There are a number of theoretical explanations that suggest the sink side of the environment will be less impacted as incomes rise. First, environmental quality is often cited as a normal good, if not even a luxury good. In other words, the income elasticity of demand for environmental quality is greater than zero, possibly even greater than one. In other words, as income grows, environmental concern rises as well, perhaps even more than proportionally so (Beckerman, 1992; World Bank, 1992). In addition, rich countries may be better able to meet the higher demands for environmental protection through their higher institutional environmental capacity (Neumayer, 2003b, p. 77). However, it is contested whether rich people care more about the environment than the poor (e.g. Martinez-Alier, 1995), and the available evidence is far from conclusive (see Kriström and Riera, 1996). Second, it is likely that economic growth increases the possibility that more modern and less pollution-intensive man-made capital and technology are introduced (Grossman and Krueger, 1995). Yet, while pollution per unit of output might go down, absolute pollution levels might very well go up as economic growth increases. Therefore the effect of technological change on pollution is in principle ambiguous (Lopez, 1992).

Third, as economic development progresses and income grows, the share of industry will go down as the share of services goes up; thus sectoral changes may favor less-polluting sectors (e.g. Jänicke et al., 1997). Yet if starting from low income levels, structural changes in the economy will most likely have a detrimental effect on the environment. Pollution will increase as the share of agriculture goes down and that of industry goes up. Also there may be limitations in the scope of these changing patterns of output, given that people's revealed preferences indicate that pollution-intensive material goods are still highly valued (Neumayer, 2003b, p. 81). It is also suspected that high-income countries have become cleaner because they have exported their pollution-intensive industry to LDCs; this is known as the 'pollution haven hypothesis'. By importing goods that are resource or pollution intensive, developed countries' environmental track records appear cleaner than they actually are. Despite some recent evidence for such claims, the empirical record for this argument remains somewhat inconclusive (see our discussion further below).

Fourth, rising income brings population growth rates down, therefore population pressure on the environment decreases. Although not all agree that population growth is detrimental to the environment (Simon, 1996), the evidence is clear: larger populations generate more emissions (Cole and Neumayer, 2003). However, with considerable variance in the data, it is clear that population growth is determined by factors other than a country's income level as well (Neumayer, 2003b, p. 82). Thus economic growth is neither a necessary nor a sufficient condition for reducing population growth. For example, it is argued that investing in education for women and providing retirement insurance schemes are the best ways to reduce population growth (ibid.).

Underpinning the above arguments is the assumption that economic growth is not log-

Environmental degradation

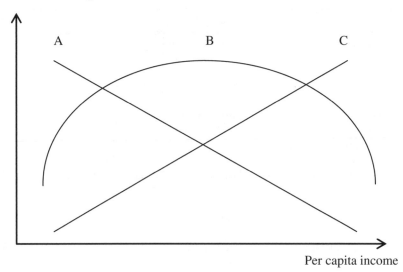

Figure 3.1   Environmental degradation and per capita income

ically equivalent to rising output in material terms but to rising output in value terms (Pezzey, 1992, p. 324). Thus economic value needs to be decoupled from resource depletion and environmental destruction. However, from the theoretical discussion above no conclusive answer is found that explains how this decoupling will occur.

Examining the empirical evidence
As we have discussed, the theoretical explanations are mixed: economic growth may or may not benefit the environment. Therefore we shall now examine the empirical literature on the link between economic growth and the environment.

Unfortunately, results from empirical studies have also been mixed, for both different environmental indicators and also, perhaps more worryingly, for different studies looking at the same environmental indicator. But the results overall point to three qualitative ideal-type cases to be distinguished (see Figure 3.1).

Formally, in the majority of studies, the basic EKC equation that is estimated is of the following form:

$$E_{it} = (\alpha + \beta_i F_i) + \delta Y_{it} + \phi (Y_{it})^2 + k_t + \varepsilon_{it} \tag{3.1}$$

where E denotes the environmental indicator, either in per capita form or in the form of concentrations, Y denotes per capita income, F denotes country-specific effects, k refers to year-specific dummies or a linear time trend and i and t refer to country and year, respectively. In equation (3.1), if δ is negative and statistically significant but ϕ is statistically insignificant, then we get pattern A. These are indicators that show an unambiguous improvement with rising per capita income, such as access to clean water and adequate sanitation. If δ is positive and statistically significant but ϕ is statistically

Table 3.1   Estimated turning points for various pollutants and studies

Pollutant	Study	Turning point ($)
Arsenic (concentration)	Grossman and Krueger (1995)	4 900
Biological oxygen demand	Grossman and Krueger (1995)	7 623
Chemical oxygen demand	Grossman and Krueger (1995)	7 853
CO (emissions)	Selden and Song (1994)	6 241
	Cole et al. (1997)	9 900
Dissolved oxygen	Grossman and Krueger (1995)	2 703
Fecal coliform	Grossman and Krueger (1995)	7 955
Lead (concentration)	Grossman and Krueger (1995)	1 887
Mercury (concentration)	Grossman and Krueger (1995)	5 047
Nickel (concentration)	Grossman and Krueger (1995)	4 113
Nitrates (concentration)	Grossman and Krueger (1995)	10 524
	Cole et al. (1997)	25 000
NO_x (emissions)	Selden and Song (1994)	12 041
	Cole (2003)	14 810
SPM (ambient concentration)	Shafik (1994)	3 280
	Grossman and Krueger (1995)	6 151
SPM (emissions)	Selden and Song (1994)	9 811
	Cole et al. (1997)	7 300
SO_2 (ambient concentration)	Shafik (1994)	3 670
	Grossman and Krueger (1995)	4 053
SO_2 (emissions)	Selden and Song (1994)	8 916
	Cole (2003)	8 691
	Stern and Common (2001) (non-OECD only)	18 039
Total coliform	Grossman and Krueger (1995)	3 043

Source: Cole and Neumayer (2005), p. 310.

insignificant, then we get pattern C. These are indicators that show an unambiguous deterioration as incomes increase. These include per capita CO2 emissions. It is possible that these indicators will follow the EKC pattern but at much higher per capita income turning points that no countries have yet reached (Neumayer, 2003b, p. 84). The pattern most often encountered is B, which follows if δ is positive and statistically significant and φ is negative and statistically significant. In this case, the estimated EKC has a maximum turning point per capita income level, calculated as $Y^* = (-\delta/2\phi)$. Table 3.1, taken from Cole and Neumayer (2005), provides the estimated turning points from a large number of EKC studies. Examples include suspended particulate matter, sulfur dioxide, carbon monoxide and nitrogen oxide emissions, fecal and total coliforms and the quality of ambient air (Neumayer, 2003b, pp. 83–4).

A number of caveats should be kept in mind when looking at the results of empirical studies. For some aspects of the environment, no turning point is in sight. Examples include CO_2 emissions, already mentioned, direct material flows (Seppala et al., 2001, but see Canas et al., 2003 for contrary evidence) and biodiversity loss (Asafu-Adjaye, 2003).

Econometric evidence captures historical/contemporary evidence. But it is not deterministic, i.e. future forecasts are highly problematic. We come back to this point later on, when we discuss the implications of the EKC literature for LDCs. Even if an EKC relationship is found, there is the possibility of a second turning point. To check for this possibility, studies would need to add a cubic per capita GDP term to equation (3.1). Studies that have found second turning points include De Bruyn and Opschoor (1997) and Binder and Neumayer (2005).

Country-specific fixed and year-specific time effects are often required, but sometimes not included. Country fixed effects are required if per capita GDP or some other explanatory variables are correlated with country-specific time-invariant factors, such as geographical factors (climate, land size and resource endowments – see Neumayer, 2002a; 2004), or institutional quality. Year-specific time effects are required if there are global changes in environmental indicators, perhaps due to global advances in technology, that have a roughly equal impact on countries at any given point of time. Where country-specific fixed effects are included, the results are conditional on these effects and are contingent to the sample at hand. Strictly speaking, no out-of-sample predictions are possible for such estimation results.

If the environmental indicator and GDP per capita are both trending over time (in technical terms: are non-stationary), then spurious regression results are possible. Year-specific time dummies mitigate, but do not solve, the problem. Estimating the model in first differences might work as a solution. Co-integration is superior, but only if both variables are truly co-integrated. Very few studies have taken this potential problem seriously (Galeotti et al., 2006; Perman and Stern, 2003; Stern, 2000; Stern and Common, 2001; Wagner and Müller-Fürstenberger, 2005).

Where EKC exists, this could be partly due to a trade effect, i.e. rich countries may have become clean partly by importing products that are polluting in production from lower-income countries. See our discussion below.

Even where EKCs exist, with median GDP per capita far below mean GDP per capita the environmental implications can be unpleasant for many low-income countries for many years to come (Cole and Neumayer, 2005).

Why is there a distinction between these three different groups of environmental indicators? One possible explanation is that those that are very important to human health, such as local public goods, are not easily externalized and tend to improve at low levels of income, whereas those that are global public goods, and are quite easy to externalize to others, such as CO_2 emissions, worsen with economic growth (Shafik, 1994, p. 768). However, one of the key questions that academics have addressed since the EKC hypothesis came under scrutiny is whether or not the EKC relationship is quasi-automatic or policy induced (Grossman and Krueger, 1995), to which we now turn.

EKC and policy

The reduced-form econometric models that have commonly been used in EKC studies do not test the pro-growth hypotheses as discussed above (Grossman and Krueger, 1995, p. 372). However, other studies have analyzed the factors that influence environmental change on a more disaggregate level (Neumayer, 2003b, p. 84). Selden et al. (1999) analyzed scale, composition and technique effects at the sector level to decompose changes in various US emissions.[1] Scale is indicated by the growth of emissions when the ratio of emissions to GDP remains constant. Composition effects are changes in emissions due to differential growth rates among sectors within an economy, and technique effects are all other changes in emissions per unit of output at the sectoral level, including energy efficiency, energy mix, and other technique effects.

Selden et al. find that increased economic growth will trigger a compositional shift of economic activity away from heavy manufacturing to services, and that economic growth may also generate environmental benefits through the development and adoption of new technology, i.e. cleaner production and improved energy efficiency. Therefore the policy prescription for alleviating at least some environmental problems may be more economic growth, but their finding that emissions abatement technology played a significant role in bringing about improvement in environmental quality points towards a policy-induced response. They also find that global energy prices may signal emissions downturns because price incentives most likely provide incentives for increased energy efficiency. Therefore the question remains if emissions will rise again as international energy prices fall from their peaks or if policy is not introduced.

The empirical literature has also examined a range of other factors that may influence environmental quality, such as democracy, literacy, income inequality and civil society strength. Using the panel data with which Grossman and Krueger (Grossman and Krueger, 1993; 1995) established the EKC, Torras and Boyce (1998) define higher political and civil liberties and increased literacy rate as constituting a more equitable power distribution. They find that a more equitable power distribution tends to result in better environmental quality and that literacy and rights appear to be strong predictors of pollution levels in low-income countries. Therefore the policy implications may be not to put a brake on economic growth in LDCs, but to focus on interventions that may lead to a more equitable power distribution, such as increased literacy and rights.

Barrett and Graddy (2000), using the same data, find that for air and water pollution, an increase in civil and political freedoms significantly improves environmental quality. They find, especially with SO_2, that a low-freedom country with an income level near the peak of the EKC can reduce its pollution at least as much by increasing freedoms as it can by increasing income per capita. However, freedoms show up as significant for measures directly related to human health but not for others; therefore perhaps something other than an induced policy response lies behind the EKC relationships for water quality measures (e.g. nitrates).

In contrast to these studies, Neumayer (2002b) argues that there is at best weak evidence for a link between democracy and environmental outcomes. He shows that there is much stronger evidence for a link between democracy and international environmental commitment. For example, democracies are more likely to ratify multilateral environmental agreements than non-democracies. Even if democracy were to have a positive effect on environmental outcomes, we need to understand what it is about democracies that impacts on environmental commitments – is it rule of law, specific types of institutions, etc? Binder and Neumayer (2005), using the same data as Torras and Boyce (1998), find that environmental non-government organization (ENGO) strength is associated with lower air pollution levels even after controlling for variation in income, democracy, business lobby strength, literacy and income inequality. Thus they highlight that ENGOs are important drivers of policy-induced responses. Furthermore, Neumayer (2003a) finds that countries with left-wing governments improve environmental quality more than those with right-wing governments, whereas the effect of a corporatist governance of the economy is largely ambiguous. Cole (2007) reports that more corrupt countries have a worse environmental record than countries with less corruption. Thus there are a myriad of factors that may influence increased demand for environmental regulation as incomes rise.

EKC and trade

The EKC provides a framework with which to test the role of trade in the economic growth and environment relationship as well. Similar to the debate on economic growth, the debate on trade is typically divided between the so-called optimists and pessimists who believe that trade as a driver of economic growth is either good or bad for the environment (see, e.g., Bhagwati, 1993; Daly, 1993). Studies have found that the EKC inverted-U relationship may be a result of the changing scale, composition and technique patterns that appear to accompany liberalized trade and economic growth (Grossman and Krueger 1993; 1995; Heil and Selden, 2001; Suri and Chapman, 1998). However, these structural changes from heavy industry towards services in the now rich countries may be a result of the South's specialization in the extraction of natural resources and the production of labor- and pollution-intensive goods (Stern, 1998). The fact that developed countries may now be importing their pollution-intensive output from the developing world may therefore explain the reductions in local air pollution experienced in most developed countries in recent years (Cole and Neumayer, 2005).

The pollution haven hypothesis, as previously mentioned, is one attempt to explain these changes in trade patterns. It claims that less stringent regulation in developing countries will provide them with a comparative advantage in the production of pollution-intensive goods over developed countries (Cole, 2004). Therefore the North will specialize in clean production but the South in pollution-intensive production. However, the data are mixed. Some studies find no evidence to suggest that the stringency of a country's environmental regulation significantly impacts on competitiveness of pollution-intensive firms (Jaffe et al.,1995; Jänicke et al., 1997), whereas others have found some evidence of pollution haven pressures (Antweiler et al., 2001; Cole and Elliott, 2003; 2005). Cole (2004) examined North–South trade flows for pollution-intensive products, and found evidence of pollution haven effects, but did not find they were widespread. In fact, he found that they may be small compared to other EKC explanatory variables such as increased demand for environmental regulations, increased investment in abatement technologies, trade openness, structural change away from manufacturing, and increased imports of pollution-intensive outputs.

The effect of trade on the environment is not restricted to potential pollution haven effects, however. Indeed, there is some evidence that trade openness may have beneficial effects on the environment as well. Neumayer (2002c) reports evidence suggesting that countries more open to foreign trade have a higher likelihood of ratifying multilateral environmental agreements. Perkins and Neumayer (2008) examine the claim that outward orientation helps countries to reduce their pollution intensity, that is the amount of pollution generated per unit of GDP. They find that countries that import a larger share of their machinery and manufactured goods from countries with lower pollution intensity manage to lower their CO_2 and SO_2 pollution intensity faster than others.

EKC and LDCs

One of the key issues that the EKC has raised is whether the same pattern of growth versus environmental impact can be replicated by the now poor countries in the future. Is the policy ramification for poor countries that they should grow themselves out of environmental problems rather than implementing stricter regulation now? Recent research has engaged with these important questions.

Cole and Neumayer (2005) examine the implications of the EKC for pollution trends in LDCs. They first review the robustness of the EKC critique, suggesting that the EKC may be more robust than some studies have claimed. Then they explore whether LDCs are likely to follow the compositional changes that developed countries have followed. They demonstrate evidence that the emissions reductions in now rich countries are in part due to export of pollution-intensive domestic production to LDCs, thus suggesting that current poor countries will not be able to replicate this experience. They then examine how long it will take different regions in the developing world to reach EKC turning points according to three economic growth projections and the most widely cited EKC studies. They come to the unsettling conclusions that environmental quality is predicted to get worse for many years to come, even under high economic growth scenarios. Cole and Neumayer (2005) contribute to the literature by explicitly considering whether LDCs can expect to follow an EKC or when they can expect to experience an improvement in environmental quality. Also, while some studies have predicted future global emission trajectories of certain air pollutants, no analysis had been undertaken at the regional level.

In Dasgupta et al.'s (2002) critical review of the EKC they discuss four different viewpoints regarding the EKC relationship. First is the view that pollution rises to a horizontal line of maximum emissions as globalization forces a 'race to the bottom' in environmental standards. Second, in a similar pessimistic outlook, some believe that environmental impacts will continue to increase as 'new toxics', such as CO_2 emissions and carcinogens, replace traditional pollutants that may have exhibited an inverted U-shaped curve. Third is the conventional EKC, and fourth is the 'revised EKC' where pollution begins falling at lower income levels. Dasgupta et al. remain optimistic (with caveats) that the EKC is lowering and flattening in LDCs through increased formal and informal regulation.

However, we cannot take for granted that LDCs will experience an increased demand for environmental regulations. We need to consider what mechanisms are needed to translate society's preferences into policy-making. For example, if the technique effect is emphasized through policy, then LDCs may be able to tunnel through the EKC, as the technology is already there. However, many criticisms of the EKC suggest that estimated turning points may not be indicative of expected turning points for developing countries, given that most such turning points have been estimated using only OECD data.

Furthermore, there are other reasons why moving up the first part of the EKC curve could lead to very unpleasant implications for LDCs. What if environmental thresholds or irreversible environmental degradation occurs? Neumayer (2003b, p. 88) cautions that there are no guarantees that the external and internal conditions of low-income countries are now the same as those of high-income countries at the time of their development.

Conclusions

This chapter has critically reviewed the theoretical and empirical literature on the EKC. Explanations for the inverted U-shaped relationship between income and environmental degradation are complex and perhaps context specific, but recent improvements in empirical methods address a number of past criticisms, which adds robustness to the EKC results for certain environmental pollutants.

However, recent studies have raised important questions with serious ramifications for LDCs. Should today's developing countries follow the 'grow now, clean up later' logic that has characterized the development paths of today's rich countries? Given predictions that some LDCs will not reach EKC turning points for decades to come, it is even more imperative that economic growth and liberalization should not be thought of as a solution for environmental problems. Therefore it might not be optimal, particularly for LDCs, to follow an EKC pathway for a variety of reasons, including: the likelihood of high environmental damage costs; the high cost of raising environmental quality after the damage has occurred; and the potential of reaching environmental thresholds and causing irreversible environmental damage. A precautionary approach suggests that in order to decouple economic value from environmental degradation, policy responses are needed from the earliest stages of economic development. Thus alternative socioeconomic factors that would induce increased demand for environmental regulations should be given incentives, along with measures to spur economic growth.

Note

1. The emissions include particulates, SO_x, NO_x, non-methane volatile organic compounds, carbon monoxide and lead over the time period from 1970 to 1990.

References

Antweiler, W., B.R. Copeland and M.S. Taylor (2001), 'Is free trade good for the environment?', *American Economic Review*, **91**(4), 877–908.

Arrow, K. et al. (1995), 'Economic growth, carrying capacity, and the environment', *Science*, **268**, 520–21.

Asafu-Adjaye, J. (2003), 'Biodiversity loss and economic growth: a cross-country analysis', *Contemporary Economic Policy*, **21**(2), 173–85.

Barrett, S. and K. Graddy (2000), 'Freedom, growth and the environment', *Environment and Development Economics*, **5**, 433–56.

Beckerman, W. (1974), *In Defence of Economic Growth*, London: Jonathan Cape.

Beckerman, W. (1992), 'Economic growth and the environment: whose growth? Whose environment?', *World Development*, **20**(4), 481–96.

Bhagwati, J. (1993), 'The case for free trade', *Scientific American*, 18–23.

Binder, S. and E. Neumayer (2005), 'Environmental pressure group strength and air pollution: an empirical analysis', *Ecological Economics*, **55**, 527–38.

Canas, A., P. Ferrao and P. Conceicao (2003), 'A new environmental Kuznets curve? Relationship between direct material input and income per capita: evidence from industrialised countries', *Ecological Economics*, **46**, 217–29.

Cole, M.A. (2003), 'Development, trade and the environment: how robust is the environmental Kuznets curve?', *Environment and Development Economics*, **8**(4), 555–80.

Cole, M.A. (2004), 'Trade, the pollution haven hypothesis and the environmental Kuznets curve: examining the linkages', *Ecological Economics*, **48**, 71–81.

Cole, M.A. (2007), 'Corruption, income and the environment: an empirical analysis', *Ecological Economics*, **62**, 637–47.

Cole, M.A. and R.J.R. Elliott (2003), 'Determining the trade–environment composition effect: the role of capital, labor and environmental regulations', *Journal of Environmental Economics and Management*, **46**(3), 363–83.

Cole, M.A. and R.J.R. Elliott (2005), 'FDI and the capital intensity of "dirty" sectors: a missing piece of the pollution haven puzzle', *Review of Development Economics*, **9**(4), 530–48.

Cole, M.A. and E. Neumayer (2003), 'Examining the impact of demographic factors on air pollution', *Population and Environment*, **26**(1), 5–21.

Cole, M.A. and E. Neumayer (2005), 'Environmental policy and the environmental Kuznets curve: can developing countries escape the detrimental consequences of economic growth?', in P. Dauvergne (ed.),

International Handbook of Environmental Politics, Cheltenham, UK and Northampton, MA, USA: Edward Elgar, pp. 298–318.

Cole, M.A., A.J. Rayner and J.M. Bates (1997), 'The environmental Kuznets curve: an empirical analysis', *Environment and Development Economics*, **2**, 401–16.

Daly, H. (1993), 'The perils of free trade', *Scientific American*, 24–9.

Dasgupta, S., B. Laplante, H. Wang and D. Wheeler (2002), 'Confronting the environmental Kuznets curve', *Journal of Economic Perspectives*, **16**(1), 147–68.

De Bruyn, S.M. and J.B. Opschoor (1997), 'Developments in the throughput–income relationship: theoretical and empirical observations', *Ecological Economics*, **20**(3), 255–68.

Galeotti, M., M. Manera and A. Lanza (2006), 'On the robustness of robustness checks of the environmental Kuznets curve', Working Paper 22, Milan, Italy: Fondazione Eni Enrico Mattei.

Grossman, G.M. and A.B. Krueger (1991), 'Environmental impacts of the North American Free Trade Agreement', Working paper 3914, NBER.

Grossman, G.M. and A.B. Krueger (1993), 'Pollution and growth: what do we know?', in I. Goldin and L. Winters (eds), *The Economics of Sustainable Development*, Cambridge, MA: MIT Press, pp. 19–45.

Grossman, G.M. and A.B. Krueger (1995), 'Economic growth and the environment', *Quarterly Journal of Economics*, **110**(2), 353–77.

Heil, M. and T.M. Selden (2001), 'International trade intensity and carbon emissions: a cross-country econometric analysis', *Journal of Environment & Development*, **10**, 35–49.

Jaffe, A.B., S.R. Peterson, P. R. Portney and R.N. Stavins (1995), 'Environmental regulation and the competitiveness of U.S. manufacturing: what does the evidence tell us?', *Journal of Economic Literature*, **33**(1), 132–63.

Jänicke, M., M. Binder and H. Mönch (1997), ' "Dirty industries": patterns of change in industrial countries', *Environmental and Resource Economics*, **9**, 467–91.

Kriström, B. and P. Riera (1996), 'Is the income elasticity of environmental improvements less than one?', *Environmental and Resource Economics*, **7**(1), 45–55.

Kuznets, S. (1955), 'Economic growth and income inequality', *American Economic Review*, **49**, 1–28.

Lomborg, B. (2001), *The Skeptical Environmentalist: Measuring the real state of the world*, Cambridge, UK: Cambridge University Press.

Lopez, R. (ed.) (1992), *The Environment as a Factor of Production: The economic growth and trade policy linkages*, Washington DC: World Bank.

Martinez-Alier, J. (1995), 'The environment as a luxury good or "too poor to be green"?', *Ecological Economics*, **13**(1), 1–10.

Meadows, D., D. Meadows and J. Randers (1992), *Beyond the Limits: Global Collapse or a Sustainable Future*, London: Earthscan.

Meadows, D., D. Meadows and J. Randers (2004), *The Limits to Growth: The 30-Year Update*, White River Junction, VT: Chelsea Green Publishing Company.

Meadows, D., D. Meadows, J. Randers and W.W. Behrens III (1972), *The Limits to Growth*, New York: Universe Books.

Neumayer, E. (2001), 'Pollution havens: an analysis of policy options for dealing with an elusive phenomenon', *Journal of Environment & Development*, **10**(2), 147–77.

Neumayer, E. (2002a), 'Can natural factors explain any cross-country differences in carbon dioxide emissions?', *Energy Policy*, **30**(1), 7–12.

Neumayer, E. (2002b), 'Do democracies exhibit stronger international environmental commitment? A cross-country analysis', *Journal of Peace Research*, **39**(2), 139–64.

Neumayer, E. (2002c), 'Does trade openness promote multilateral environmental cooperation?', *World Economy*, **25**(6), 815–32.

Neumayer, E. (2003a), 'Are left-wing party strength and corporatism good for the environment? A panel analysis of 21 OECD countries, 1980–1998', *Ecological Economics*, **45**(2), 203–20.

Neumayer, E. (2003b), *Weak versus Strong Sustainability*, Cheltenham, UK and Northampton, MA, USA: Edward Elgar.

Neumayer, E. (2004), 'National carbon dioxide emissions: geography matters', *Area*, **36**(1), 33–40.

Perkins, R. and E. Neumayer (forthcoming 2008), 'Fostering environment-efficiency through transnational linkages? Trajectories of CO_2 and SO_2, 1980–2000', *Environment and Planning A*.

Perman, R. and D.I. Stern (2003), 'Evidence from panel unit root and cointegration tests that the environmental Kuznets curve does not exist', *Australian Journal of Agricultural and Resource Economics*, **47**, 325–47.

Pezzey, J. (1992), 'Sustainability: an interdisciplinary guide', *Environmental Values*, **1**(4), 321–62.

Selden, T.M. and D. Song (1994), 'Environmental quality and development: is there a Kuznets curve for air pollution emissions?', *Journal of Environmental Economics and Management*, **27**, 147–62.

Selden, T.M., A.S. Forrest and J.E. Lockhart (1999), 'Analyzing the reductions in U.S. air pollution emissions: 1970 to 1990', *Land Economics*, **25**(1), 1–21.

Seppala, T., T. Haukioja and J. Kaivo-oja (2001), 'The EKC hypothesis does not hold for direct material flows', *Population and Environment*, **23**(2), 217–38.

Shafik, N. (1994), 'Economic development and environmental quality: an econometric analysis', *Oxford Economic Papers*, **46**(5), 757–73.

Shafik, N. and S. Bandyopadhyay (1992), 'Economic growth and environmental quality: time series and cross-country evidence', Background Paper for the World Development Report 1992, Washington, DC: The World Bank.

Simon, J.L. (1996), *The Ultimate Resource*, Princeton, NJ: Princeton University Press.

Stern, D.I. (1998), 'Progress on the environmental Kuznets curve?', *Environment and Development Economics*, **3**(2), 173–96.

Stern, D.I. (2000), 'Applying recent developments in time series econometrics to the spatial domain', *Professional Geographer*, **52**, 37–49.

Stern, D.I. (2003), 'The environmental Kuznets curve', *Online Encyclopedia of Ecological Economics*.

Stern, D.I. (2004), 'The rise and fall of the environmental Kuznets curve', *World Development*, **32**(8), 1419–39.

Stern, D.I. and M.S. Common (2001), 'Is there an environmental Kuznets curve for sulfur?', *Journal of Environmental Economics and Management*, **41**, 162–78.

Suri, V. and D. Chapman (1998), 'Economic growth, trade and energy: implications for the environmental Kuznets curve', *Ecological Economics*, **25**, 195–208.

Torras, M. and J.K. Boyce (1998), 'Income, inequality, and pollution: a reassessment of the environmental Kuznets curve', *Ecological Economics*, **25**, 147–60.

UNDP (1999), *Human Development Report Statistics CD-ROM*, New York: UNDP.

Wagner, M. and G. Müller-Fürstenberger (2005), *The Carbon Kuznets Curve: A Cloudy Picture Emitted by Bad Econometrics?*, Bern, Switzerland: University of Bern, Department of Economics.

WCED (1987), *Our Common Future*, Oxford, UK: Oxford University Press.

World Bank (1992), *World Development Report*, New York: Oxford University Press/World Bank.

4 The pollution haven hypothesis
Brian R. Copeland

At the heart of the debate over how globalization affects the environment is the question of whether trade and investment liberalization will cause pollution-intensive industry to concentrate in countries with relatively weak environmental policy. This is known as the pollution haven hypothesis.

If the pollution haven hypothesis were correct, the level and incidence of global pollution would be affected. The average pollution intensity of production would increase as polluting industry moved to those parts of the world with the weakest environmental standards. Moreover, an exodus of polluting industry from countries with stringent environmental policy could create a political backlash because of concerns about losses of jobs and investment. This could lead to a 'race to the bottom' as governments weaken environmental policy in response to such pressures. Because the stringency of environmental regulation is highly correlated with national income, polluting industry would tend to concentrate in relatively poor countries. This could exacerbate the effects of pollution on health and mortality because poor countries are less able to afford the infrastructure and medical treatments to protect their populations from the effects of pollution. Increased environmental degradation could also lead to long-run income losses for those at the lower end of the income distribution in poor countries because of their dependence on natural capital.

To assess the pollution haven hypothesis, it is useful to break it into two parts. First, we need to know whether more stringent environmental policy adversely affects international competitiveness in polluting industry. We shall refer to this as the competitiveness hypothesis. Second, the pollution haven hypothesis asks whether the effect of environmental policy on competitiveness is strong enough to determine the pattern of trade. The competitiveness and pollution haven hypotheses are closely related, but different conceptual experiments lie behind each. The competitiveness hypothesis takes the trade regime as given and ask what happens if we tighten environmental policy in one country. The pollution haven hypothesis takes environmental policy differences across countries as given and asks what happens if we reduce trade barriers.

Most of the literature on the pollution haven hypothesis has focused on production-generated pollution from manufacturing. However, much pollution is also generated from consumption. Pollution regulations that target consumption-generated pollution have very different effects on competitiveness than pollution regulations targeting production-generated pollution. Hence it is important to distinguish between these two broad classes of pollution. A focus on manufacturing pollution has also led much of the literature to neglect the role of environmental capital. Environmental capital is a critical input in renewable resources, such as fisheries, forestry and agriculture. If environmental degradation depletes environmental capital, then the productive capacity of the economy will be reduced, and this can have an important effect on competitiveness. In what follows, I first focus on cases where natural capital is not significantly affected by environmental damage; later in the chapter, I discuss cases where environmental capital is significantly affected.

Competitiveness hypothesis under production-generated pollution: theory

The theory behind the competitiveness hypothesis is straightforward. Consider an industry where pollution is generated during production, and suppose that more stringent environmental policy increases production costs. Higher production costs shift domestic supply curves inward and reduce net exports or increase net imports. Hence the domestic industry becomes less internationally or regionally competitive.

This theory predicts that more stringent environmental policy will, all else equal, shift some pollution-intensive production away from the jurisdiction that tightens environmental policy. But it does not predict that the production will move to a region with weaker environmental policy. Production will move to a region with lower costs, but there are many factors in addition to environmental policy that affect costs. It is, for example, consistent with the competitiveness hypothesis for production to shift to a region with more stringent environmental policy, but with lower labor costs.

The main alternative to the competitiveness hypothesis is the Porter hypothesis. Porter and van der Linde (1995) argue that more stringent environmental policy can increase international competitiveness and shift supply curves outward. Many economists are skeptical because if firms are profit maximizing, they should already be using least-cost production methods, and so it is difficult to see how imposing additional constraints on firms via regulation can lower their costs. However, some authors have developed models consistent with the Porter hypothesis. In Greaker (2006), tighter environmental policy increases the demand for abatement technology, and this can spur innovation in the environmental services sector. If the cost-reducing effect of such induced innovation is greater than the cost-increasing effect of tighter regulation, then the polluting industry could become more competitive.

Competitiveness hypothesis: evidence

The competitiveness hypothesis predicts that, all else equal, jurisdictions with more stringent environmental policy should attract less pollution-intensive industry and have higher net imports (or lower net exports) of pollution-intensive goods. To test this hypothesis, researchers need data on trade or investment flows, the stringency of environmental policy, and other factors that affect trade and investment. These data are needed for a large number of different jurisdictions, and it is desirable to have panel data with time series and cross-sectional variation. Unfortunately, such data sets are rare.

The major challenge for researchers in this field has been to come up with a cross-jurisdictional series of data on the stringency of environmental policy. Such data are not available for most countries, and as a result, much of the available research has used data from the USA. Pollution taxes would be ideal, but they are rarely used by governments. China has adopted a system of pollution charges and some authors, such as Dean et al. (2005), have used variation in these charges across provinces in China to test the competitiveness hypothesis. Levinson (1999) used taxes on hazardous waste across US states. Most countries have fuel taxes, but these are imposed for many reasons and so they are not a good proxy for a pollution tax. A number of studies have used county-level non-attainment of the air quality standards in the US Clean Air Act as a proxy for stringent environmental policy. The idea here is that US states are required to have a plan to bring all counties into compliance with the federally mandated air quality standards. Hence those counties that have not met the standards should on average have experienced an increase in the stringency of environmental regulations after the Act came into effect.

Many studies use abatement costs (usually from the USA) as a proxy for the stringency of environmental policy. This is problematic for several reasons. First, the data are obtained from firm-level surveys. It is difficult for firms to isolate abatement costs from other production costs, especially when the design of the production facility has been influenced by the environmental policy regime. Moreover, firms have incentives to be strategic in reporting abatement costs if they think the information might influence future environmental regulation. Even if abatement costs are accurately reported, they are endogenous and, as Keller and Levinson (2002) have emphasized, this can create biases. To see this, suppose there is heterogeneity across firms within an industry in the costs of responding to pollution regulations. If the competitiveness hypothesis is correct, then stringent environmental policy will drive away the firms with the highest abatement costs. When firms are surveyed and asked about their abatement costs, only the low-abatement-cost firms will remain. So in cases where the competitiveness hypothesis holds, measured abatement costs may be low even in regions with stringent environmental policy.

To test the competitiveness hypothesis, researchers estimate the effects of the stringency of environmental policy on the pattern of trade, direct foreign investment, or plant location decisions. Early studies in this area used cross-sectional data, and almost universally found no support for the competitiveness hypothesis (see Jaffe et al., 1995 and Levinson, 1996 for surveys). The environmental policy variable was either insignificant or had a sign opposite to what was predicted (that is, it was sometimes found that more stringent environmental policy was positively correlated with inward investment or export success in pollution-intensive industries).

For example, Tobey (1990) used a sample of data on net exports of pollution-intensive goods from 23 countries. He used a country-level measure of the stringency of environmental policy and estimated its effect on trade flows. Data on factor endowments controlled for other factors that affect trade flows. The environmental policy variable was not statistically significant. Kalt (1988), Grossman and Krueger (1993) and others used US data and asked whether industry-level variation in the stringency of environmental policy (measured using industry-level abatement costs) affected US industry-level net trade. Data on other industry characteristics (such as tariffs, skilled labor intensity, etc.) controlled for other factors that affect trade flows. These studies found either that abatement costs are not statistically significant or (as in the case of Kalt, 1988) that higher pollution abatement costs were associated with increased net exports. Levinson (1996) and others used similar techniques to estimate the effect of environmental policy on plant location and again found little or no support for the competitiveness hypothesis.

Although some interpreted these results as support for the Porter hypothesis, recent research has shown that omitted-variable bias and endogeneity problems are the most likely factors responsible for the failure to find support for the competitiveness hypothesis in early studies.

Omitted-variable bias arises when factors correlated with the stringency of environmental policy, and which also affect trade and investment flows, are not controlled for. As an example, consider countries that are rich because they are capital abundant and have highly developed infrastructures that support industrial manufacturing. And suppose manufacturing is pollution intensive. Then we would expect such countries to have relatively stringent environmental policy because of their high income. But we would also expect such countries to be net exporters of manufacturing goods if the effects of their infrastructure and capital abundance are stronger than the effects of environmental policy in determining production location. Consequently it would not be surprising to find a positive correlation between the stringency of pollution policy and net exports of pollution-intensive goods. However, it would be an error to conclude from this that tightening up environmental policy would increase exports of manufacturing. In fact the reverse is true in our example.

To deal with this problem, one could control for capital abundance and infrastructure. But there are many other factors that affect trade and investment flows, and the researcher cannot control for all of them. This is the problem of unobserved heterogeneity, which can lead to omitted variable bias. Recent work has used panel data to deal with such problems. A good example is Keller and Levinson (2002), who looked at the effects of the stringency of environmental policy on foreign investment inflows into US states. They had a panel of data with both time series and cross-sectional variation. First they pooled all of their data and replicated earlier work that found no effect of environmental regulation on investment flows. But when they used state-level fixed effects to control for unobserved heterogeneity, they found support for the competitiveness hypothesis: all else equal, more stringent environmental policy reduced net foreign investment into a state.

Endogeneity bias has also affected results. As an example, suppose that governments are less likely to tighten up environmental policy in industries that are subject to strong pressure from imports. Then we would expect to see a negative correlation between the stringency of environmental policy and net imports. This is opposite to what the competitive hypothesis would predict, even though it is competitive pressure that is causing governments to act in this way and induce the negative correlation. These types of problems have been dealt with by explicitly confronting the endogeneity problem using techniques such as instrumental variables. Levinson and Taylor (forthcoming) and Ederington and Minier (2003) studied the effect of US environmental policy on US net imports. Both studies found evidence of endogeneity bias and both found strong support for the competitiveness hypothesis once they corrected for endogeneity using instrumental variables.

There is now a growing body of evidence coming from studies using panel data that are consistent with the competitiveness hypothesis. Levinson (1999) found that (all else equal) states with high taxes on the processing and disposal of hazardous waste were less likely to attract shipments of such waste. Some of the most convincing evidence comes from a series of studies that have found that the Clean Air Act in the USA has had a significant effect on the location of new plants (at the country level) in pollution-intensive industries. Becker and Henderson (2000) found that new plant births in pollution-intensive industries were 26–45 percent lower in counties that were not in compliance with air quality standards required by the Clean Air Act (plants in such counties are subject to more stringent environmental policy).

Evidence on outward direct investment from the USA is more mixed. Hanna (2006) found evidence that the Clean Air Act induced multinational firms to shift some production out of counties with more stringent environmental policy. Eskeland and Harrison

(2003) found little or no evidence that US abatement costs affect the flow of investment to a sample of four developing countries; however, the small sample of host countries in this study leaves little scope for controlling for unobserved heterogeneity.

While a number of recent studies found evidence supporting the competitiveness hypothesis, most rely on US data. More work using data from other jurisdictions, especially developing countries, is needed.

To conclude the discussion of the competitiveness hypothesis, it is worth reviewing what this evidence does not imply. First, evidence that more stringent environmental policy affects trade and investment flows is not enough to conclude that the pollution haven hypothesis is correct. To assess this hypothesis, we need to assess whether the effects of environmental policy are strong or weak when compared to other factors. Second, evidence that more stringent environmental policy reduces competitiveness in polluting industry does not imply that such policy reduces welfare. Rather, it is better seen as evidence that environmental policy works. Weak environmental policy is an implicit subsidy to pollution-intensive industries. It results in excessive production of pollution-intensive goods. When environmental policy is tightened, the subsidy is reduced, and pollution-intensive output contracts as the pattern of production adjusts to reflect true social costs of all inputs, including access to the environment.

Pollution haven hypothesis: theory
The pollution haven hypothesis predicts that trade or investment liberalization will cause production of pollution-intensive goods to shift to countries with relatively weak environmental policy. This production shift may occur as a result of either trade or direct foreign investment. In both cases, the reallocation of production may be augmented by capital flows. In the trade version, the hypothesis is simply that countries with relatively weak environmental policy have a comparative advantage in pollution-intensive production. In the investment version, it is a hypothesis about what determines the direction of foreign investment flows.

Pethig (1976) developed the first pollution haven model. He starts with the simple Ricardian model of trade and considers two countries that are completely identical except that one country (North) has a higher pollution tax than the other (South). Since differences in pollution taxes are the only motive for trade, the model predicts that South has a comparative advantage in the pollution-intensive good, and North has a comparative advantage in the clean good.

In Pethig's model, pollution taxes are exogenous; hence the model does not make any predictions about what type of countries become pollution havens. Moreover, because pollution havens are exogenous, governments are not given the opportunity to respond to inflows or outflows of pollution-intensive production. Copeland and Taylor (1994) developed the first pollution haven model with endogenous environmental policy. They consider two countries that are identical except that North is a scaled-up version of South; hence North is richer than South. The key assumptions that lead to a pollution haven prediction in their model are (1) the demand for environmental quality increases with income (this assumption is backed up by a large body of evidence – see Copeland and Gulati, 2006 for a review); and (2) governments are responsive to the preferences of their citizens when implementing pollution policy. Because North's income is higher than South's, North's government imposes more stringent environmental policy than South's. Because there is no other source of comparative advantage in their model, this leads to the prediction that South has a comparative advantage in the pollution-intensive good. Trade liberalization shifts pollution-intensive production to South, and so the relatively poor country becomes a pollution haven when trade is liberalized.

The Copeland/Taylor model also highlights the importance of distinguishing between positive and normative predictions concerning the pollution haven hypothesis. In their model, pollution policy in each country is assumed to be fully optimal. The model predicts that trade will shift pollution-intensive production to the low-income country. However, it also predicts that trade will be welfare increasing in each country. South could choose to tighten up its environmental policy to the same level as North's and prevent itself from attracting polluting industry; however, it prefers not to do so because South is more willing than North to trade off a deterioration in its environmental quality in return for increased income. Hence the fact that trade causes pollution-intensive production to move in or out of a country is not sufficient information to conclude that trade is 'bad'. On the other hand, if environmental policy is not optimal because governments are corrupt, responsive to special interest groups, or ineffectual, then a country that becomes a pollution haven as a result of pollution policy that is too weak may lose from trade because the increased environmental damage can more than offset other gains from trade (see Copeland and Taylor, 2003).

If capital is internationally mobile, the tendency for countries with weak environmental policy to become pollution havens can be reinforced. Rauscher (1997) develops a simple model in which capital is mobile and North has more stringent pollution policy than South. South's weak environmental policy increases its rate of return on capital; hence it attracts capital from North and becomes a pollution haven.

The models described above all generate predictions consistent with the pollution haven hypothesis by setting up a scenario in which a difference in pollution policy is the only motive for trade and investment. In reality, there are many motives for trade. To develop a model of the pollution haven hypothesis suitable for empirical testing, Antweiler et al. (2001) and Copeland and Taylor (2003) consider a model in which North is both richer and more capital abundant than South. Pollution-intensive production is assumed to be capital intensive and so capital in this model should be thought of as a proxy for factors that make a country attractive as a location for pollution-intensive production. North's richness results in stringent pollution policy, which tends to give South a comparative advantage in the polluting good. But North's capital abundance makes it an attractive place for pollution-intensive manufacturing, and this tends to give North a comparative advantage in the polluting good. If the effects of capital abundance are more important than the effects of pollution policy in determining the direction of trade, then North will have a comparative advantage in the polluting good, and trade liberalization will shift pollution-intensive production from South to North. That is, even if the competitiveness hypothesis is correct, trade liberalization may nevertheless shift pollution-intensive production to countries with relatively stringent environmental policy if such countries have other attributes which make them cost-effective producers in those sectors. Testing the pollution haven hypothesis amounts to determining which of these factors are more important in affecting the pattern of trade.

Pollution haven hypothesis: evidence
There has been surprisingly little work that directly tests the pollution haven hypothesis. A number of studies have looked for circumstantial evidence. Low and Yeats (1992), Mani and Wheeler (1997) and others have found that the share of pollution-intensive goods in exports from developing countries has risen since the 1960s, while the share of such goods in exports from OECD countries has fallen over time. This is consistent with the pollution haven hypothesis since trade was liberalized during this period. But it is also consistent with other hypotheses, such as economic growth and capital accumulation in developing countries.

Ederington et al. (2004) calculated estimates of the pollution generated during the production of US imports and exports during the period 1992–94 and found that the pollution content of US imports from developing countries declined relative to the pollution content of its exports during this period. This is opposite to what the pollution haven hypothesis would predict. To test the pollution haven hypothesis directly, they estimate the effects of trade liberalization on import flows. They hypothesize that if the pollution haven hypothesis is correct, then the response of US imports to tariff reductions should be larger in industries with high abatement costs (which proxies for stringent environmental policy). Instead, they find the opposite – imports in high-abatement-cost industries are less responsive to trade liberalization than imports in other sectors.

Antweiler et al. (2001) estimate the response of sulfur dioxide (SO_2) pollution to increased openness to trade, controlling for scale, proxies for policy, and other factors in a sample of both rich and poor countries. This is intended to isolate the pure effect of increased openness to trade on the composition of production within a country. The pollution haven hypothesis predicts that trade should cause the composition of production to become cleaner in rich countries and dirtier in poor countries. Antweiler et al. find the opposite. All else equal, increased openness has tended to increase SO_2 pollution in rich countries and reduce it in poor countries. Since SO_2-intensive industries are also capital intensive, Antweiler et al.'s results are consistent with the view that the capital abundance of rich countries has given them a comparative advantage in SO_2-intensive production, despite their more stringent environmental policy. In terms of the theory sketched out above, other motives for trade are more important than pollution regulation in determining the pattern of trade.

Overall, while there is growing evidence supporting the competitiveness hypothesis, there is very little evidence to support the pollution haven hypothesis.

Consumption-generated pollution
Most of the literature on both the competitive and pollution haven hypotheses has focused on pollution generated by manufacturing production. Much pollution is, however, generated during consumption. Examples include automobile emissions, consumption waste and emissions from home heating. McAusland (2007) has emphasized that the effects of pollution regulation on competitiveness are very different for consumption-generated pollution. Regulations affecting pollution generated during consumption often take the form of product standards – for example, automobiles have to satisfy emission standards and consumer goods may be subject to regulations on packaging. These regulations apply to all goods sold within a country, regardless of whether the goods are produced domestically or imported. Since all producers are subject to the

same regulations, domestic producers need not be put at a competitive disadvantage relative to foreign producers when domestic regulations are tightened up.

It is possible that tighter domestic pollution regulations aimed at consumption pollution could give domestic producers a competitive advantage. The logic is the same as that outlined in Salop and Scheffman's (1983) paper on 'Raising rivals' costs'. If the new regulations are easier for domestic producers than foreign producers to comply with, then domestic costs will go up less than foreign costs and domestic market share will increase. The controversy over European restrictions on genetically modified food is a good example. A ban would raise costs in both the USA and Europe, but because the use of such food is much more pervasive in the USA than in Europe, then costs of complying with a ban are higher for US producers than for European producers.

As yet there has been no empirical work that I am aware of that explicitly distinguishes between consumption- and production-generated pollution when testing the competitiveness or pollution haven hypotheses. However, theory suggests that it is important to do so, and that the effects of environmental policy on international competitiveness will be very different for the two types of pollution.

Natural capital

Environmental regulation affects competitiveness by affecting production costs. But environmental degradation can also affect competitiveness by depleting natural capital. In industries reliant on natural capital, it is important to consider both effects.

It is useful to focus on two channels via which environmental capital can be degraded. First, pollution from one industry can harm environmental capital used by a different industry. For example, water pollution from manufacturing can kill fish, excessive forest harvesting can cause soil erosion and flooding that reduces productivity in agriculture and fishing, and industrial pollution can reduce the appeal of a region for tourists. I shall refer to these types of examples as cross-sectoral pollution. The second possibility is that activities in an industry can deplete environmental capital used by that same industry. Renewable resources are a good example of this: excessive fishing can deplete the fish stock, which reduces productivity for the fishing industry. While the case of renewable resources goes beyond the strict interpretation of the pollution haven hypothesis (since the environmental problem is not caused by pollution), the logic and concerns are very similar.

Cross-sectoral pollution

Copeland and Taylor (1999) study the implications of cross-sectoral pollution for the pattern of trade. Their analysis implies that cross-sectoral pollution reinforces the effects of weak environmental policy on trade patterns. The following example illustrates the point. Suppose that pollution damages environmental capital needed for the tourism sector. A weakening of environmental policy increases the competitiveness of the industrial sector relative to the tourist sector in two ways: production costs in industry fall because environmental regulations are weak; and increased industrial pollution kills off more environmental capital in the tourist sector, causing the tourist sector to contract and free up more resources for use by the industrial sector. Hence, in theory, the presence of cross-sectoral pollution that depletes environmental capital should reinforce the competitiveness effect of environmental policy. This is an issue that has not yet been explored empirically.

Renewable resources

To illustrate how environmental capital can be critical for determining trade patterns in renewable resource industries, consider the example of fisheries. As is well known, open access fisheries are vulnerable to depletion because of stock externalities. The fish stock needs to be maintained at a healthy size so that it produces more fish for harvest in the future. But in an open access fishery, a fisher who chooses to invest in the fish stock by reducing his or her harvest rate will not reap the full benefits of that investment because the fish will be available for others to catch. Hence theory predicts underinvestment in conservation of the stock.

Now consider the analogue of the pollution haven hypothesis. Suppose there are two countries, North and South. Assume that North has stringent conservation policy, and that South's fishery is open access. As in the pollution haven models discussed above, we assume the countries are otherwise identical to highlight the role of conservation policy in affecting trade patterns. Would we expect trade liberalization to shift fishing effort from North to South and exacerbate the depletion of South's renewable resources?

Chichilnisky (1994) and Brander and Taylor (1997) studied this scenario. The result depends on the strength of the demand for fish. If the demand for fish is low, so that the fish stock in South is just mildly depleted prior to trade, then the logic of the pollution haven hypothesis applies. North's stringent conservation policy increases harvest costs, and so South has a comparative advantage in fishing. Trade liberalization causes South's fishing industry to expand and puts increased pressure on its resource. Trade therefore increases environmental degradation in South. Suppose, however, that the demand for fish is high. In this case, South's fishery will have faced huge fishing pressure prior to trade and its stock will be severely depleted. Because of its depleted environmental capital (fish stock), its fishing costs will be relatively high and fish harvest rates will be low. North, on the other hand, with its stringent conservation policy, will have been able to maintain a healthy fish stock despite the high demand for fish. Hence when trade opens, North's relatively abundant environmental capital (fish stock) will give it a comparative advantage in fishing. Hence in this case a pollution haven type of result does not obtain – it is the high-regulation country that ends up exporting fish.

Conclusion

Fears that trade liberalization will cause an exodus of polluting industry to poor countries with weak environmental policy appear to be unfounded. Although there is evidence that stringent environmental policy does reduce competitiveness in industries intensive in production-generated pollution, there is no evidence that it is the most important factor affecting trade and investment flows.

That being said, there are still a number of channels via which pollution-intensive production could shift from rich to poor countries. If pollution policy were to tighten up at a faster rate in rich countries than in poor countries, then the competitiveness hypothesis implies that we would expect to see a gradual relocation of polluting production to poorer countries. Industries that are both polluting and intensive in the use of unskilled labor will expand in developing countries as trade liberalization occurs: weak environmental policy reinforces an already existing comparative advantage in such cases. And capital accumulation in developing countries will stimulate the growth of capital-intensive polluting industries.

Most of the world's industrial pollution has been generated by relatively rich countries. As other parts of the world grow, their capacity to generate industrial pollution will also grow for reasons that have little to do with the pollution haven hypothesis.

References

Antweiler, W., B.R. Copeland and M.S. Taylor (2001), 'Is free trade good for the environment?', *American Economic Review*, **91**(4), 877–90.

Becker, R. and V. Henderson (2000), 'Effects of air quality regulations on polluting industries', *Journal of Political Economy*, **108**(2), 379–421.

Brander, J.A. and M.S. Taylor (1997), 'International trade between consumer and conservationist countries', *Resource and Energy Economics*, **19**, 267–98.

Chichilnisky, G. (1994), 'North–south trade and the global environment', *American Economic Review*, **84**(4), 851–74.

Copeland, B.R. and S. Gulati (2006), 'Trade and the environment in developing economies', in R. Lopez and M.A. Toman (eds), *Economic Development and Environmental Sustainability: New Policy Options*, Oxford: Oxford University Press, pp. 178–216.

Copeland, B.R. and M.S. Taylor (1994), 'North-south trade and the environment', *Quarterly Journal of Economics*, **109**, 755–87.

Copeland, B.R. and M.S. Taylor (1999), 'Trade, spatial separation, and the environment', *Journal of International Economics*, **47**, 137–68.

Copeland, B.R. and M.S. Taylor (2003), *Trade and the Environment: Theory and Evidence*, Princeton, NJ: Princeton University Press.

Copeland, B.R. and M.S. Taylor (2004), 'Trade, growth and the environment', *Journal of Economic Literature*, **42**(1), 7–71.

Dean, J.M., M.E. Lovely and H. Hwang (2005), 'Are foreign investors attracted to weak environmental regulations? Evaluating the evidence from China', mimeo.

Ederington, W.J and J. Minier (2003), 'Is environmental policy a secondary trade barrier? An empirical analysis', *Canadian Journal of Economics*, **36**, 137–54.

Ederington, W.J. A. Levinson and J. Minier (2004), 'Trade liberalization and pollution havens', *Advances in Economic Analysis and Policy*, **4**(2), Article 6. Berkeley, CA: Berkeley Electronic Press.

Eskeland, G.S. and A.E. Harrison (2003), 'Moving to greener pastures? Multinationals and the pollution haven hypothesis', *Journal of Development Economics*, **70**, 1–23.

Greaker, M. (2006), 'Spillovers in the development of new pollution abatement technology: a new look at the Porter-hypothesis', *Journal of Environmental Economics and Management*, **52**, 411–20.

Grossman, Gene M. and Alan B. Krueger (1993), 'Environmental impacts of a North American Free Trade Agreement', in Peter M. Garber (ed.), *The Mexico–U.S. Free Trade Agreement*, Cambridge, MA and London: MIT Press, pp. 13–56.

Hanna, R. (2006), 'U.S. environmental regulation and FDI: evidence from a panel of U.S. based multinational firms', NYU Development Research Institute Working Paper, 23, March.

Jaffe, A., S. Peterson, P. Portney and R. Stavins (1995), 'Environmental regulation and the competitiveness of U.S. manufacturing: what does the evidence tell us?' *The Journal of Economic Literature*, **33**, 132–63.

Kalt, J.P. (1988), 'The impact of domestic environmental regulatory policies on U.S. international competitiveness', in A.M. Spence and Heather A. Hazard (eds), *International Competitiveness*, Cambridge, MA: Harper & Row/Ballinger, pp. 221–62.

Keller, W. and A. Levinson (2002), 'Pollution abatement costs and foreign direct investment inflows to US states', *Review of Economics and Statistics*, **84**, 691–703.

Levinson, A. (1996), 'Environmental regulations and industry location: international and domestic evidence', in Jagdish N. Bhagwati and Robert E. Hudec (eds), *Fair Trade and Harmonization: Prerequisites for Free Trade*, Cambridge, MA: MIT Press, pp. 429–57.

Levinson, A. (1999), 'State taxes and interstate hazardous waste shipments', *American Economic Review*, **89**, 666–77.

Levinson A. and M.S. Taylor (forthcoming), 'Trade and the environment: unmasking the pollution haven effect', *International Economic Review*.

Low, P. and A. Yeats (1992), 'Do "dirty" industries migrate?', in P. Low (ed.), 'International trade and the environment', World Bank Discussion Paper No. 159, 89–104.

Mani, M. and D. Wheeler (1997), 'In search of pollution havens: dirty industry migration in the world economy', World Bank Working Paper No. 16.

McAusland, Carol (2007), 'Trade, politics, and the environment: tailpipe vs. smokestack', mimeo, University of Maryland.

Pethig, R. (1976), 'Pollution, welfare, and environmental policy in the theory of comparative advantage', *Journal of Environmental Economics and Management*, **2**, 160–69.

Porter, Michael E. and Claas van der Linde (1995), 'Toward a new conception of the environment–competitiveness relationship', *Journal of Economic Perspectives*, **9**(4), 97–118.

Rauscher, M. (1997), *International Trade, Factor Movements, and the Environment*, Oxford: Clarendon Press.

Salop, S.C. and D.T. Scheffman (1983), 'Raising rivals' costs', *American Economic Review*, **73**, 267–71.

Tobey, James A. (1990), 'The effects of domestic environmental policies on patterns of world trade: an empirical test', *Kyklos*, **43** (2), 191–209.

5 Trade, natural resources and developing countries
Edward B. Barbier

In the current era of globalization two concerns have been expressed about the environmental effects of expanding world trade. The first, which is a more frequently heard criticism, is that trade is 'bad' for the environment. Economic arguments underlying this view usually cite alarm over economic scale relative to ecological limits and the implied effects of globalization on incentives for domestic environmental regulation (see Daly and Goodland, 1994; Rees, 2006). The counter-argument in economics has been that 'in general, trade is not the root cause of environmental problems, which are due to market and intervention failures' (OECD, 1994, p. 8; see also Copeland and Taylor, 2003). Many of the other chapters in this handbook address this trade versus environment debate; therefore it will not be the focus of the following chapter. Instead, I shall focus here on a second concern, which suggests that trade could be 'bad' for development: many developing countries are currently failing to manage their natural resources efficiently and sustainably for successful development, and 'opening to trade' could be perpetuating the mismanagement problem. This view stems from recent empirical findings that many resource-dependent developing countries – those countries with a high percentage of resource-based commodities to total exports or to GDP – tend to have lower levels of real GDP per capita, lower growth rates, higher poverty levels and a higher proportion of their populations living in poverty (Barbier, 2005; Bulte et al., 2005; Ding and Field, 2005; Mehlum et al., 2006; Neumeyer, 2004; Rodríguez and Sachs, 1999; Sachs and Warner, 1997; 2001). As summarized by Jurajada and Mitchell (2003, p. 130).

> the main upshot of this literature is two-fold: first, natural resources, if not well-managed in well-built markets, will impede growth through rent-seeking; and second, an abundance of natural resources leads to serious policy failures: for example, if the windfall from a natural-resource boom is poorly invested, it can have long-run detrimental effects.

The following chapter explores more closely this perceived relationship between trade, natural resource mismanagement and long-run development. First, we clarify that this concern is a new one; although it appears to be related to a somewhat older criticism of trade, i.e. the postwar 'unequal develoment' thesis that primary product exports fail to provide the 'engine of growth' for developing economies, we argue that this is a misleading analogy. Second, we show that, while the concern about resource dependence and the poor economic growth performance in modern devleoping economies may be justified, it addresses only two of the four 'stylized facts' concerning natural resource use in these economies. To understand more fully the relationship between trade, natural resources and long-run development, it is necessary to assess the implications of all four stylized facts.

Resource dependence and unequal development
The recent concern over the relationship between resource dependence and the poor economic growth performance of many developing economies has revived the older 'unequal

development' criticism that dependence on primary product exports is in itself detrimental to long-term development. The failure of primary product exports to provide the 'engine of growth' for developing economies in the post-World War II era led some authors to conclude that there is a structural imbalance in the global pattern of trade and international division of labor that keeps the 'undeveloped periphery' trapped in a perpetual state of underdevelopment and specialized in the production and export of primary products. Proponents of the unequal development doctrine in the past have included Marxist and dependencia writers (e.g. Amin, 1974; Emmanuel, 1972; Frank, 1978; Wallerstein, 1974), and also less radical authors (Dixon and Thirwall, 1975; Myrdal, 1957; Prebisch, 1950; 1959; Seers, 1962; Singer, 1950).

One of the testable hypotheses to emerge from this literature as to why unequal development should occur between the industrial core and the primary-producing periphery in the world economy is the Prebisch–Singer thesis. Examining long-run international data, Prebisch (1950; 1959) and Singer (1950) noted that the terms of trade of developing countries' primary product exports relative to imports of manufacturing goods were falling. The long-run tendency for international prices of primary products to fall in relation to manufactures may not in itself be a problem; for example, if they are the result of increased technical progress they allow a country to export more and improve its world market position. However, Prebisch and Singer argued that falling terms of trade do affect a developing country's growth prospects given that the income elasticity of demand for manufactured goods is much higher than the income elasticity for primary commodities. The combination of relatively low income elasticities and falling terms of trade for developing countries' exports means that their capacity to pay for imported capital goods is lowered, thus affecting development and growth prospects.

Empirical evidence on whether the long-run relative terms of trade of primary products are falling remains fairly mixed, with recent studies suggesting a modest fall in the region 0 to 0.8 percent annually, with larger 'shocks' occurring as the result of major world events, such as the Great Depression and the 1980s oil crisis (Bleany and Greenaway, 1993; Kellard and Wohar, 2006; Zarias, 2005; Ziesemer, 1995). More importantly, the basic premise of the Prebisch–Singer thesis, the tendency of long-run (non-oil) primary product prices to fall relative to manufacturing prices, is now generally accepted and is no longer 'such a heretical proposition as in 1950' (Raffer and Singer, 2001, p. 23). What has changed is that the thesis is no longer used, as Prebisch (1950; 1959) argued, to justify import substitution policies in developing countries as a means to reduce dependence on primary product exports and jump-start industrialization. Most protectionist import substitution efforts in the postwar era have produced disappointing, if not disastrous, results for developing countries, largely 'because protectionism has led to imports of capital goods higher than the imports substituted by domestic production' (Ziesemer, 1995, p. 18). Instead, as suggested by Raffer and Singer (2001, p. 25), the policy recommendations emerging from the Prebisch–Singer thesis seem to accord with more 'mainstream' economic advice to developing countries:

> It appears that poorer countries with static comparative advantages in (non-oil) primary commodities, or in low-tech manufactures, would be well advised to try to create different and more dynamic comparative advantages in higher-tech manufactures or services. Otherwise, they may well be caught in the trap of deteriorating terms of trade and may be at the wrong end of the distribution of gains from trade and investment. Hence our conclusion emphasizes the

importance of education, and development of skills and of technological capacity. In the light of recent mainstream thinking on growth and trade, there is nothing startling about this conclusion.

However, if there is now universal agreement on the policy prescription, why has it been so difficult to achieve? Or, as Hayami (2001, p. 114) has stated, ever since the development theories of Hla Myint (1958) and W. Arthur Lewis (1954), it has been well known that

> whether economic growth based on exploitation of natural resource slack could lead to sustained growth and increased welfare of indigenous people depended critically on mobilization of resource rent for investment in human capital and on improvements in both physical and institutional infrastructure for efficient functioning of the market mechanism.

Resource dependence and the resource curse

One proposed explanation of the poor performance of resource-dependent economies is the resource curse hypothesis. This phenomenon is often linked to the 'Dutch disease' effect arising from sudden trade liberalization or a resource price boom.[1] There are two components to the 'resource curse'. First, economies with large natural resource sectors relative to manufacturing and services will grow more slowly, even if no resource boom occurs. Because manufacturing and advanced services lead to a more complex division of labor and innovation, these sectors are more dynamic and will produce more economy-wide growth. For example, Matsuyama (1992) has shown that trade liberalization in a land-intensive economy could actually slow economic growth by inducing the economy to shift resources away from manufacturing (which produces learning-induced growth) towards agriculture (which does not). Second, a resource price boom or windfall may lead to increased growth initially, but this will be only a temporary gain.[2] As a result of the boom, the natural resource sector will expand and draw economic resources away from the more dynamic sectors, such as manufacturing. The result is that in the long run the economy will become more specialized in natural resource production and export, and thus growth may even slow down.

Sachs and Warner (1999) find over the period 1960–94 in Latin America that only in Ecuador did a resource boom have a positive and lasting effect on GDP per capita. In Chile and Colombia there appears to have been a resource boom effect but with little impact on economic development, and in Bolivia, Mexico, Peru and Venezuela the resource boom actually produced a negative impact on GDP per capita. On balance, resource booms appear to frustrate economic growth in Latin America, most likely through a 'Dutch disease' resource boom effect. Sachs and colleagues have also conducted other cross-country analyses that seem to verify that countries with a high ratio of natural resource exports to GDP have tended to grow less rapidly than countries that are relatively resource poor (Rodríguez and Sachs, 1999; Sachs and Warner, 1997; 2001).[3] Other studies have also shown that resource dependence is negatively correlated with growth across countries (Bulte et al., 2005; Ding and Field, 2005; Mehlum et al., 2006; Neumeyer, 2004).

Special features of certain developing countries may make them particularly vulnerable to this type of commodity boom impact. For example, by examining eight country case studies – Cameroon, Ecuador, Gabon, Indonesia, Mexico, Nigeria, Papua New

Guinea and Venezuela – Wunder (2003) maintains that the resource curse is particularly relevant for oil-producing tropical countries. In these countries, the 'Dutch disease' effect of the discovery of new reserves or oil price increases caused the oil and non-traded sectors of the economy to expand at the expense of non-oil trade sectors. In tropical developing countries, such as the eight countries examined by Wunder, the key non-oil trade sectors are typically agriculture, fisheries, forestry and non-oil mining, which are likely to stagnate as a result of the rising terms of trade from the oil boom.[4] Hausmann and Rigobon (2002) show that if a country has a sufficiently large non-resource tradable sector, relative prices can be stable, even when a commodity boom in the resource sector generates significant volatility in the demand for non-tradables. However, when the non-resource tradable sector disappears, prices in the economy become much more volatile, mainly because Dutch-disease-induced shocks to the demand for non-tradables will not be accommodated by movements in the allocation of labor but instead by expenditure-switching. The inefficiency of financial markets in the country further reinforces this impact, especially as the presence of bankruptcy costs makes interest rates dependent on relative price volatility. These two effects interact, causing the economy to specialize inefficiently away from non-resource tradables: the less it produces of them, the greater the volatility of relative prices, and the higher the interest rate the sector faces, causing it to shrink even further until it disappears. An increase in resource income will therefore lead to specialization in the resource sector, higher interest rates and a lower level of capital and output in the non-tradable sector, ultimately causing a large and permanent decline in welfare.

Auty (2001) also emphasizes that different types of natural resource endowments may have different impacts on the economic performance of a country. In particular, he distinguishes between the potential effects of point resources (e.g. mineral and energy resources) and diffuse resources (e.g. cropland). Some studies have sought to distinguish natural resource endowments in this way, and have concluded that countries endowed with abundant point resources tend to grow more slowly or be more susceptible to the 'Dutch disease' impacts of a resource commodity boom (Bulte et al., 2005; Leite and Weidmann, 1999; Stijns, 2006; Wunder, 2003). Others question whether the resource curse hypothesis is valid, even for countries endowed mainly with energy and mineral resources (Davis, 1995; Manzano and Rigobon, 2001). For instance, Manzano and Rigobon (2001) re-examine the period of analysis of Sachs and colleagues in the 1970s and 1980s and conclude that the poor performance of countries highly dependent on primary product exports is less likely the result of the 'resource curse' than of 'debt overhang'.

Despite some compelling evidence in favor of a 'resource curse' arising from a commodity price boom, many recent studies suggest that the 'Dutch disease' and other economic impacts of the resource curse cannot be explained adequately without also examining political-economy factors, in particular the existence of policy and institutional failures that lead to myopic decision-making, fail to control rent-seeking behavior by resource users and weaken the political and legal institutions necessary to foster long-run growth (Ascher, 1999; Auty, 1994; 1997; Baland and Francois, 2000; Broad, 1995; Bulte et al., 2005; Gylfason, 2001; Karl, 1997; Lane and Tornell, 1996; Leite and Weidmann, 1999; Ross, 1999; Stevens, 2003; Tornell and Lane, 1998; 1999; Mehlum et al., 2006; Torvik, 2002).[5] The encouragement of rent-seeking behavior has received the most attention of late (Ascher, 1999; Gylfason, 2001; Mehlum et al., 2006; Tornell and Lane,

1998; 1999; Torvik, 2002). In short, natural resource abundance, windfall commodity price booms and the discovery of valuable new reserves can all encourage private agents to compete vigorously for the increased resource rents, and in states with weak political and legal institutions, governments are overwhelmed by the special interest pressures of rent-seekers, thus leading to distorted economic and resource management policies that favor the rent-seekers and generate problems of corruption, institutional breakdown and of course dissipation of resource rents. Certain types of natural resource endowments may generate these opportunities for rent-seeking behavior and corruption. For instance, several studies suggest that this is the case for 'point resources', which include energy and mineral resources as well as timber forests (Auty, 2001; Bulte et al., 2005; Karl, 1997; Leite and Weidmann, 1999; Ross, 1999).

If 'bad' policies and institutions lie at the heart of translating resource abundance and windfall gains into negative economy-wide effects, then 'good' policies and institutions may explain why some developing economies with resource wealth may have avoided the 'resource curse'. However, judging by available empirical evidence, very few resource-dependent developing economies have achieved such success. For example, Gylfason (2001, p. 566) examined the long-run growth performance of 85 economies and concluded:

> Of this entire group there are only four resource-rich countries which managed to achieve (a) long-term investment exceeding 25% of GDP on average in 1965–1998, equal to that of various successful industrial states lacking raw materials, and (b) per capita economic growth exceeding 4% per year on average during the same period . . . These countries are Botswana, Indonesia, Malaysia and Thailand. The three Asian countries achieved this success by diversifying their economies and by industrializing; Botswana without doing so.[6]

The 'stylized facts' of resource use in developing countries
While the concern about resource dependence and the poor economic growth performance in modern developing economies may be justified, to understand more fully the relationship between trade, natural resources and long-run development it is necessary to understand further some of the key structural features, or 'stylized facts', of natural resource use in these economies. As outlined by Barbier (2005), four such 'stylized' facts can be identified:

1. The majority of low- and middle-income countries (LMICs) are highly dependent on primary product exports.
2. Resource dependence – usually measured as primary product exports as a share of total exports – in LMICs is associated with poor economic performance.
3. Development in LMICs is associated with increased land conversion.
4. A significant share of the population in LMICs is concentrated in 'fragile' lands.

The problem with all the 'resource curse' explanations of the possible negative impacts of resource dependence on trade and long-run devleopment is that such explanations address the first two stylized facts, but not the third and fourth. The latter are worth examining further.

As stylized fact 3 indicates, in all LMICs, expansion of this agricultural land base is occurring rapidly through conversion of forests, wetlands and other natural habitat (Chomitz et al., 2007; FAO, 1995; 2001; Fischer and Heilig, 1997). This trend for greater land use appears to be occurring in all low- and middle-income countries, regardless of their resource dependence or economic performance. This is a persistent, long-term trend that is unlikely to abate in coming decades. Over 1970–90 increased harvested area accounted for 31% of the additional crop production in these countries, and over 1990–2010 this contribution is expected to rise to 34% (FAO, 1995). Throughout the developing world, cultivated land area is expected to increase by over 47% by 2050, with about 66% of the new land coming from deforestation and wetland conversion (Fischer and Heilig, 1997).

Stylized fact 4 is the outcome of two important trends in rural population growth in developing countries. First, in the coming decades rural population growth will be much higher for those low- and middle-income economies that are more resource dependent; and second, a large share of the rural populations in these economies is concentrated in poor, or 'fragile', lands (World Bank, 2003). The World Bank defines 'fragile lands' as 'areas that present significant constraints for intensive agriculture and where the people's links to the land are critical for the sustainability of communities, pastures, forests, and other natural resources' (ibid., p. 59). Currently one quarter of the people in developing countries – almost 1.3 billion – survive on fragile lands, which include 518 million living in arid regions with no access to irrigation systems, 430 million on soils unsuitable for agriculture, 216 million on land with steep slopes and more than 130 million in fragile forest systems. Barbier (2005) has shown that resource-dependent LMICs contain large concentrations of their populations in fragile lands. Moreover, greater resource dependence is associated with a large percentage of population on fragile land. For example, as the concentration of populations on fragile lands in low- and middle-income economies increases from 20–30% to 30–50% to 50–70% to over 70%, the average share of primary products in exports rises from 62.9% to 72.8% to 87.6% to 98.3% respectively.

Each of the four stylized facts on its own has important development implications. However, taken together, these facts also suggest some key underlying relationships between exploiting new land and resource frontiers and unsustainable economic development in LMICs.

For example, the first three stylized facts suggest that developing countries today are embarking on a pattern of resource-dependent development that culminates in frontier resource exploitation, particularly in the form of agricultural land expansion and commercial raw material exploitation, but the end results do not yield much in the way of sustained economic progress. Stylized fact 4 indicates an additional 'symptom' of malaise associated with frontier-based development today: in many developing economies a significant proportion of extremely poor households are concentrated on fragile lands, and both rural population growth and the share of population on fragile lands seem to increase with the degree of resource dependence of a developing economy. That is, frontier land expansion appears to be serving mainly as an outlet for the rural poor in many developing countries.

There is now some empirical evidence to support these structural linkages in developing countries. For example, Barbier (2003; 2005; 2007) demonstrates that for the majority of today's developing countries long-run agricultural land conversion appears to be associated with lower GDP per capita levels. The analysis was extended to prove oil and natural gas reserves, experienced expansion of those reserves, and the expansion in these resources is also associated with lower GDP per capita levels. Similarly, Stijns (2006) finds that arable land per capita is significantly associated with total years of education, the net secondary enrollment rate, and the share of aggregate expenditure devoted to public education when examining all economies – developed and underdeveloped. However, when he restricts his analysis to just developing countries he finds a result similar to that of Birdsall et al. (2001): the relationship between arable land per capita and human capital indicators is negative.

In fact, a closer look at the four 'stylized facts' suggests that most low- and middle-income economies fall into a persistent pattern of resource use that is very relevant to the problem of resource degradation, poverty and chronic underdevelopment. Table 5.1 reveals this pattern by grouping low- and middle-income economies by three types of indicators: the first indicator is the degree of resource dependence of an economy, as measured by the share of primary commodities in total exports. For instance, an economy with a primary product export share of 50% or more would be considered highly resource dependent. As stylized facts 1 and 2 imply, if a developing country is highly resource dependent, then its 'take-off' into sustained and structurally balanced economic growth and development is still some time away, and thus the dependence of the overall economy on natural resources will persist over the medium and long term. The second and third indicators depicted in Table 5.1 illustrate the extent to which both a high degree of rural poverty and a high concentration of the rural poor in marginal land areas occur in low- and middle-income economies. The former indicator is the share of the rural population living under conditions of absolute poverty, whereas the latter is the share of the total population concentrated on fragile lands, as defined by the World Bank (2003, p. 59) and discussed above in connection with stylized fact 4. Combining these two indicators gives us an approximate benchmark, or '20–20 rule', for the degree of rural poverty–resource degradation linkage within a developing economy: a country with 20% or more of its population concentrated on fragile land and 20% or more of its rural population living in poverty shows evidence that poverty, frontier land expansion and resource degradation are persistent problems in rural areas.

Table 5.1 combines the above two sets of indicators for 72 low- and middle-income economies. The countries are grouped in terms of their degree of resource dependence, as measured by the share of primary products in total exports, and the extent to which their populations are concentrated on fragile land. The figure in parentheses by each country also indicates the percentage of the rural population below the national poverty line. According to the table, 56 out of the 72 economies have a primary product export share of 50% or more, and therefore display evidence of high resource dependence. All 72 economies have 20% or more of their population on fragile land, and all but seven also have 20% or more of the rural population living in absolute poverty. Thus by the '20–20 rule', virtually all the economies listed in Table 5.1 show signs of a high incidence of rural poverty–resource degradation linkage within the economy. What is more striking is that, with the exception of the Yemen Arab Republic and Indonesia, all 56 highly resource-dependent countries also satisfy the '20–20 rule'.[7] That is, three-quarters of the countries listed in Table 5.1 show considerable evidence of a high degree of resource dependence as well as a high incidence rural poverty–resource degradation linkage. Of the 16 countries that are not highly resource dependent, i.e. they have a primary product export share of less than 50%, many of the countries nevertheless display evidence that poverty, frontier

Table 5.1   Low- and middle-income countries and patterns of resource use

	Share of population on fragile land, ≥ 50%	Share of population on fragile land, 30–50%	Share of population on fragile land, 20–30%
Primary product export share ≥ 90%	Burkina Faso (61.2) Chad (67.0) Congo Dem. Rep. (NA) Laos (53.0) Mali (72.8) Niger (66.0) Papua New Guinea (NA) Somalia (NA) Sudan (NA) Yemen A.R. (19.2)	Algeria (30.3) Angola (NA) Benin (33.0) Botswana (NA) Cameroon (32.4) Comoros (NA) Eq. Guinea (NA) Ethiopia (31.3) Gambia (64.0) Guyana (NA) Iran (NA) Mauritania (57.0) Nigeria (36.4) Rwanda (51.2) Uganda (55.0)	Ecuador (47.0) Congo, Rep. (NA) Liberia (NA) Zambia (88.0)
Primary product export share 50–90%	Egypt (23.3) Zimbabwe (31.0)	Central Af. Rep. (66.6) Chad (67.0) Guatemala (71.9) Guinea (40.0) Kenya (46.4) Morocco (27.2) Senegal (40.4) Sierra Leone (76.0) Syria (NA) Tanzania (51.1)	Bolivia (79.1) Burundi (36.2) Côte d'Ivoire (32.3) El Salvador (55.7) Ghana (34.3) Guinea-Bissau (48.7) Honduras (51.0) Indonesia (15.7) Madagascar (77.0) Mozambique (37.9) Myanmar (NA) Panama (64.9) Peru (64.7) Togo (32.3) Trinidad & Tobago (20.0)
Primary product export share <50%		Costa Rica (25.5) Haiti (66.0) Lesotho (53.9) Nepal (44.0) Pakistan (36.9) South Africa (11.5) Tunisia (21.6)	China (4.6) Dominican Rep. (29.8) India (36.7) Jamaica (33.9) Jordan (15.0) Malaysia (15.5) Mexico (10.1) Sri Lanka (20.0) Vietnam (57.2)

Notes:
Primary commodity export share is the average export share 1990/99 for low- and middle-income countries.
Share of population on fragile land is from World Bank (2003), Table 4.3.
Figures in parentheses are the percentage of the rural population below the national poverty line, from World Bank (2002), *World Development Indicators*.

land expansion and resource degradation may be chronic in rural areas. For example, Haiti, Lesotho, Nepal and Pakistan have 30–50 % of their populations on fragile land and display an incidence of rural poverty of 30–70%. The Dominican Republic, India, Jamaica and Vietnam have 20–30 % of their populations living in fragile areas and around 30–60 % of their rural populations in poverty. Only China and Mexico, and to a lesser extent Jordan and Malaysia, do not conform very strongly to the '20–20 rule' for population concentrated on fragile land and the degree of rural poverty.

Final remarks
The relationship between trade, natural resources and economic development is a complicated one. The persistence of underdevelopment in many low- and middle-income economies, combined with the fact that many of them remain fundamentally dependent on primary product exports, has led to various explanations over the years attempting to link these phenomena, from the 'unequal development' thesis of the 1960s and 1970s to the more recent 'resource curse' hypothesis. This chapter suggests that, although such arguments are often compelling and may have some empirical validity, they cannot explain fully how most low- and middle-income economies fall into a persistent pattern of resource use that is very relevant to the problem of resource degradation, poverty and chronic underdevelopment. Resource dependence may in fact be a symptom of 'chronic underdevelopment' rather than the cause of it. As summarized by Barbier (2005), to break out of this pattern may be possible, but to do so requires a new development strategy in resource-dependent low- and middle-income economies aimed at setting four long-term goals:

1. Reinvesting resource rents in more productive and dynamic sectors of the economy, which in turn are linked to the resource-exploiting sectors of the domestic economy.
2. Developing political and legal institutions to discourage rent-seeking behavior by wealthy investors in the natural resource sectors of the economy.
3. Instigating widespread reform of government policies that favor wealthier investors in markets for valuable natural resources, including arable land.
4. Targeting additional policies and investments to improve the economic opportunities and livelihoods of the rural poor, rather than relying on frontier land expansion and urban migration as the principal outlet for alleviating rural poverty.

Notes
1. Auty (1993) is often credited with naming this phenomenon a 'resource curse'. However, Auty (1994) gives credit to Mahon (1992) for also suggesting a 'variant' of the resource curse theme as an explanation of why resource-rich Latin American countries have often failed to adopt sensible industrial policies. The resource curse is often linked to the 'Dutch disease' effect. In the wake of the oil-price shocks of the 1970s and 1980, 'Dutch disease' models focused on the problems caused for a primary product-exporting economy by 'resource booms' that led to overvalued commodities (e.g., see Corden, 1984; van Wijnbergen, 1984). Either the discovery of large reserves of a valuable natural resource or a boom in commodity prices will cause an expansion in primary product exports and lead to overvaluation of the exchange rate. This will reduce manufacturing and service exports that are more conducive to growth, and may also reduce total exports eventually.
2. Some economists have placed greater emphasis on the revenue volatility of primary product exports, rather than the windfall price effects of a commodity boom, as a significant factor in the resource curse (Auty 1997; Gylfason et al., 1999). Thus Gylfason et al. (1999, p. 204) state: 'the volatility of the primary sector generates real-exchange-rate uncertainty and may thus reduce investment and learning in the secondary sector and hence also growth'.

3. In these studies Sachs and colleagues refer to their measure of 'resource dependence, primary products exports as a percentage of GDP', as a measure of a country's 'resource abundance'. Strictly speaking, such a variable cannot be a true indicator of 'resource abundance' *per se*, as it is not a measure of the total resource endowment or stocks of a country. In fact, there is an ongoing debate in the 'resource curse' literature over what indicator should be used as a measure of 'resource abundance', with most authors agreeing that some measure of total resource stock availability, such as total land area per capita, cropland per capita and mineral resources per capita, would be the preferred indicators (Auty, 2001; Stijns, 2006). Ding and Field (2005) find that resource dependence may have a negative effect on growth but abundant natural resource endowments may not.
4. Wunder (2003) also notes that, because these economic activities in the non-oil trade sector are also mainly responsible for much of the forest conversion occurring in oil-producing tropical countries, one unintended but potential side effect of the 'Dutch disease' impact of an oil boom is a decline in tropical deforestation.
5. Drawing from the political science literature, Ross (1999, p. 308) categorizes 'political explanations for the resource curse' in terms of cognitive, societal and statist theories: 'Cognitive, societal, and statist approaches to the resource curse each take resource windfalls (rents) as their independent variable and economic stagnation as their dependent variable. Cognitive theories suggest that windfalls produce myopic disorders among policymakers; societal theories argue that windfalls empower social groups that favor growth-impeding fiscal or trade policies; and statist approaches suggest that windfalls can weaken state institutions that are necessary to foster long-term economic development.'
6. However, Gylfason (2001, p. 566 n. 12) suggests that Indonesia should be considered at best only a qualified success, given the widespread corruption in the country and because Indonesia has recovered much less well from the 1997–98 Asian crisis compared to Malaysia and Thailand.
7. In fact, with over 50% of its population in fragile areas and with a rural poverty incidence of 19.2%, Yemen shows distinct signs of a rural poverty–resource degradation linkage. Indonesia is also not far off from satisfying the '20–20 rule', given that the country has over 20% of its population on fragile land and 15.7% of its rural population in absolute poverty.

References

Amin, Samir (1974), *Accumulation on a World Scale: A Critique of the Theory of Underdevelopment*, New York: Monthly Review Press.
Ascher, W. (1999), *Why Governments Waste Natural Resources: Policy Failures in Developing Countries*, Baltimore, MD: Johns Hopkins University Press.
Auty, Richard M. (1993), *Sustaining Development in Mineral Economies: The Resource Curse Thesis*, London: Routledge.
Auty, Richard M. (1994), 'Industrial policy reform in six large newly industrializing countries: the resource curse thesis', *World Development*, **22**(1), 11–26.
Auty, Richard M. (1997), 'Natural resource endowment, the state and development strategy', *Journal of International Development*, **9**(4), 651–63.
Auty, Richard M. (2001), 'The political economy of resource-driven growth', *European Economic Review*, **45**(4–6), 839–46.
Baland, Jean-Marie and Patrick Francois (2000), 'Rent-seeking and resource booms', *Journal of Development Economics*, **61**, 527–42.
Barbier, Edward B. (2003), 'The role of natural resources in economic development', *Australian Economic Papers*, **42**(2), 259–72.
Barbier, Edward B. (2005), *Natural Resources and Economic Development*, Cambridge, UK: Cambridge University Press.
Barbier, Edward B. (2007), 'Frontiers and sustainable development', *Environmental and Resource Economics*, **37**, 271–95.
Birdsall, N., T. Pinckney and R. Sabot (2001), 'Natural resources, human capital, and growth', in R.M. Auty (ed.), *Resource Abundance and Economic Growth*, Oxford: Oxford University Press, pp. 57–75.
Bleany, Michael and David Greenaway (1993), 'Long-run trends in the relative price of primary commodities and in the terms of trade of developing countries', *Oxford Economic Papers*, **45**(3), 349–63.
Broad, Robin (1995), 'The political economy of natural resources: case studies of the Indonesian and Philippine forest sectors', *The Journal of Developing Areas*, **29**, 317–40.
Bulte, E.H., R. Damania and R.T. Deacon (2005), 'Resource intensity, institutions and development', *World Development*, **33**, 1029–44.
Chomitz, Kenneth M. et al., (2007), *At Loggerheads? Agricultural Expansion, Poverty Reduction, and Environment in the Tropical Forests*, Washington, DC: The World Bank.
Copeland, Brian and M. Scott Taylor (2003), *Trade and the Environment: Theory and Evidence*, Princeton, NJ: Princeton University Press.

Corden, W. Max (1984), 'Booming sector and Dutch disease economics: survey and consolidation', *Oxford Economic Papers*, **36**, 359–80.

Daly, Herman and Robert Goodland (1994), 'An ecological-economic assessment of deregulation of international commerce under GATT', *Ecological Economics*, **9**(1), 73–92.

Davis, Graham A. (1995), 'Learning to love the Dutch disease: evidence from the mineral economies', *World Development*, **23**(1), 765–79.

Ding, N. and B.C. Field (2005), 'Natural resource abundance and economic growth', *Land Economics*, **81**, 496–502.

Dixon, R. and A.P. Thirwall (1975), 'A model of regional growth rate differences on Kaldorian lines', *Oxford Economic Papers*, **27**, 201–14.

FAO (1995), *World Agriculture: Towards 2010 – an FAO study*, Rome and New York: FAO and John Wiley & Sons.

FAO (2001), *Forest Resources Assessment 2000: Main Report*, Forestry Paper 140. Rome: FAO.

Fischer, Günther and Gerhard K. Heilig (1997), 'Population momentum and the demand on land and water resources', *Philosophical Transactions of the Royal Society Series B*, **352**(1356), 869–89.

Frank, André Gunder (1978), *Dependent Accumulation and Development*, London: Macmillan.

Gylfason, Thorvaldur (2001), 'Nature, power, and growth', *Scottish Journal of Political Economy*, **48**(5), 558–88.

Gylfason, Thorvadulr, T.T. Herbertsson and G. Zoega (1999), 'A mixed blessing: natural resources and economic growth', *Macroeconomic Dynamics*, **3**, 204–25.

Hausmann, Ricardo and Roberto Rigobon (2002), 'An alternative interpretation of the "resource curse": theory and policy implications', Working Paper No. 9424, Cambridge, MA: NBER.

Hayami, Yujiro (2001), *Development Economics: From the Poverty to the Wealth of Nations*, 2nd edn, Oxford: Oxford University Press.

Jurajada, Štěpán and Janet Mitchell (2003), 'Markets and growth', in Gary McMahon and Lyn Squire (eds), *Explaining Growth: A Global Research Project*, New York: Palgrave Macmillan, pp. 117–58.

Karl, Terry L. (1997), *The Paradox of Plenty: Oil Booms and Petro-States*, Berkeley, CA: University of California Press.

Kellard, Neil and Mark E. Wohar (2006), 'On the prevalence of trends in primary commodity prices', *Journal of Development Economics*, **79**, 146–67.

Lane, Philip R. and Aaron Tornell (1996), 'Power, growth and the voracity effect', *Journal of Economic Growth*, **1**, 213–41.

Leite, Carlos and Jens Weidmann (1999), 'Does Mother Nature corrupt? Natural resources, corruption and economic growth', Working Papers WP/99/85, Washington DC: IMF.

Lewis, W. Arthur (1954), 'Economic development with unlimited supplies of labor', *Manchester School of Economic and Social Studies*, **22**, 139–91.

Mahon, J.E. (1992), 'Was Latin America too rich to prosper? Structural and political obstacles to export-led industrial growth', *Journal of Development Studies*, **28**, 241–63.

Manzano, Osmel and Roberto Rigobon (2001), 'Resource curse or debt overhang?', Working Paper No. 8390, Cambridge, MA: NBER.

Matsuyama, Kimoru (1992), 'Agricultural productivity, comparative advantage, and economic growth', *Journal of Economic Theory*, **58**, 317–34.

Mehlum, H., K. Moene and R. Torvik (2006), 'Institutions and the resource curse', *Economic Journal*, **116**, 1–20.

Myint, Hla (1958), 'The classical theory of international trade and the underdeveloped countries', *Economic Journal*, **68**, 315–37.

Myrdal, Gunnar (1957), *Economic Theory and Under-developed Regions*, London: Duckworth.

Neumayer, E. (2004), 'Does the "resource curse" hold for growth in genuine income as well?', *World Development*, **32**, 1627–40.

OECD (1994), *The Environmental Effects of Trade*, Paris, France: OECD.

Prebisch, Raúl (1950), 'The economic development of Latin America and its principal problems', *Economic Bulletin for Latin America*, **7**(1), 1–22.

Prebisch, Raúl (1959), 'Commercial policy in the underdeveloped countries', *American Economic Review*, **59**(2), 251–73.

Raffer, K. and H.W. Singer (2001), *The Economic North–South Divide: Six Decades of Unequal Development*, Cheltenham, UK and Northampton, MA, USA: Edward Elgar.

Rees, William E. (2006), 'Globalization, trade and migration: undermining sustainability', *Ecological Economics*, **59**(2), 220–25.

Rodríguez, Francisco and Jeffery D. Sachs (1999), 'Why do resource-abundant economics grow more slowly?', *Journal of Economic Growth*, **4**(3), 277–303.

Ross, Michael L. (1999), 'The political economy of the resource curse', *World Politics*, **51**, 297–322.

Sachs, Jeffrey D. and Andrew M. Warner (1997), 'Fundamental sources of long-run growth', *American Economic Review*, **87**(2), 184–8.

Sachs, Jeffrey D. and Andrew M. Warner (1999), 'The big push, natural resource booms and growth', *Journal of Development Economics*, **59**, 43–76.

Sachs, Jeffrey D. and Andrew M. Warner (2001), 'The curse of natural resources', *European Economic Review*, **45**, 827–38.

Seers, Dudley (1962), 'A model of comparative rates of growth in the world economy', *Economic Journal*, **72**, 285.

Singer, Hans W. (1950), 'The distribution of gains between investing and borrowing countries', *American Economic Review*, **40**, 478.

Stevens, P.A. (2003), 'Firms' expectations and employment behavior: evidence from a panel of UK manufacturing firms', *Economics Letters*, **81**(3), 305–8.

Stijns, Jean-Philippe (2006), 'Natural resource abundance and human capital accumulation', *World Development*, **34**(6), 1060–83.

Tornell, Aaron and Philip R. Lane (1998), 'Are windfalls a curse? A non-representative agent model of the current account', *Journal of International Economics*, **44**, 83–112.

Tornell, Aaron and Philip R. Lane (1999), 'The voracity effect', *American Economic Review*, **89**, 22–46.

Torvik, Ragnar (2002), 'Natural resources, rent seeking and welfare', *Journal of Development Economics*, **67**, 455–70.

Van Wijnbergen, S. (1984), 'The "Dutch disease": a disease after all?', *Economic Journal*, **94**, 41–55.

Wallerstein, Immanuel (1974), *The Modern World-System*, New York: Academic Press.

World Bank (2003), *World Development Report 2003*, Washington, DC: World Bank.

Wunder, Sven (2003), *Oil Wealth and the Fate of the Forest: A Comparative Study of Eight Tropical Countries*, London: Routledge.

Zarias, George P. (2005), 'Testing for trends in the terms of trade between primary commodities and manufacturing goods', *Journal of Development Economics*, **78**, 49–59.

Ziesemer, T. (1995), 'Growth with imported capital goods, limited export demand and foreign debt', *Journal of Macroeconomics*, **7**(1), 31–53.

6 Foreign direct investment and sustainable industrial development

Lyuba Zarsky

Introduction

In August 2005, some 300 leaders of the world's biggest corporations gathered in Sydney for a conference convened by the world's richest man: billionaire, publisher and one-time US presidential candidate Steven Forbes. While hundreds of noisy anti-globalization protestors climbed fences outside the Sydney Opera House, a visibly irate Forbes told an evening television reporter that global capitalism was not the problem but the solution to global poverty. Echoing neoliberal orthodoxy, Forbes proclaimed that, for developing countries, foreign investment by multinational corporations is '*the* ladder to development' (emphasis in original). Is he right?

This chapter probes the interface between foreign direct investment (FDI) and development – or more precisely, sustainable industrial development. The crisis of global ecosystems, most pointedly threats of global warming, suggests that ecologically unconditioned development paths are not economically viable (Millennium Ecosystem Assessment, 2005). On the other hand, the profound crisis of global poverty makes urgent the quest for sustainable livelihoods. Despite recent attention to the environment, development theory and policy focus mainly on the role of FDI in increasing economic growth. On the other hand, environmentalists tend to assume that FDI delivers economic benefits and focus on environmental externalities.

The concept of sustainable industrial development used in this chapter is innovative in two ways.[1] First, it defines a development path based on the integration of economic and environmental objectives, with the latter defined as a reduction in the ecological 'footprint' of industrial growth. Second, it defines the key economic objective not as growth *per se* but as sustainable increases in the local capacities of workers and firms to 'upgrade' industry, that is to produce and innovate in ways that can generate sustainable livelihoods. An increase in local productive capacities means that host countries can better capture opportunities presented by globalization, while being more resilient to its vagaries – including pullout by MNCs. It also means that host countries have better technologies and skills by which to improve the environmental performance of industry.

The chapter has two interrelated arguments. First, the primary channel by which FDI can potentially promote sustainable industrial development is by generating spillovers – 'leakages' of knowledge, technology and expertise to local workers and firms that generate social and environmental benefits. In later sections, the chapter explores spillovers that generate two types of social benefits: industry upgrading and improved environmental performance. For both types, the chapter presents an analytical framework to identify channels for FDI spillovers and then evaluates evidence that spillovers have actually been captured. Based on the evidence, the chapter concludes with the second and central argument, i.e. that the capture of benefits from FDI for sustainable industrial development is not automatic but requires strategic and proactive government policy.

Spillovers for industry upgrading
Foreign direct investment (FDI) by multinational corporations (MNCs) is the core industrialization strategy for many developing countries. Accordingly, investment and industry policies aim to maximize the quantity of FDI by attracting MNCs, assuming that spillovers for industry upgrading will follow. Industry upgrading is important not only to generate sustainable livelihoods but also to promote environmentally cleaner economic growth. The optimistic view about FDI is encapsulated in a recent report from the OECD:

> The overall benefits of FDI for developing country economies are well documented. Given appropriate host country policies and a basic level of development, a preponderance of studies shows that FDI triggers technology spillovers, assists human capital formation, contributes to international trade integration, helps create a more competitive business environment and enhances enterprise development. All of these contribute to higher economic growth, which is the most potent tool for alleviating poverty in developing countries . . . (OECD, 2002, p. 5)

Analytical framework
The most powerful way that FDI can promote industry upgrading is through 'knowledge spillovers'. MNCs are considered to possess a 'bundle of assets' – technology, technical and management expertise, links to global markets – that makes FDI more productive and environmentally sustainable than domestic investment. Because many of these special assets are a source of rents – for example, through technology patents – MNCs work to keep them tightly in-house. None the less, some knowledge 'spills over' outside the firm.

Depending on the stage of industrial development, spillovers may enable local firms to: (1) achieve scale economies that allow them to expand their domestic regional or national markets; (2) increase labor productivity and product quality that enable them to be integrated into global value chains as suppliers to MNCs; or (3) enhance capacities for product and process design that promote the evolution of local firms into globally competitive producers and exporters in their own right.

Host-country spillovers from FDI can be captured by:

1. MNC subsidiaries
2. Other firms in the same industry as the MNC (horizontal spillovers)
3. Downstream suppliers to the MNC (vertical spillovers)
4. Firms in upstream and other industries.

Except for MNC subsidiaries, whose access to knowledge is directly determined by their corporate parents, spillovers may occur in five ways:

- *Human capital*: MNCs hire and train both skilled and unskilled workers who can apply their knowledge either in starting their own firms or in working for domestic firms in the same industry.
- *Demonstration effects*: domestic firms may adopt and produce technologies introduced by MNCs through imitation or reverse engineering. They may also adopt higher, productivity-enhancing standards of MNCs in relation to inputs, quality control, environmental management and labor. Governments may codify these standards in new regulation, spawning further gains in efficiency.

- *Competition effects*: except in sectors where there are no indigenous firms or where they are offered a monopoly status, MNCs will compete with local firms for domestic and export markets. The presence of MNCs may exert pressure on domestic firms to adopt new technology or to utilize existing technology more efficiently.
- *Backward linkages*: domestic suppliers of intermediate inputs to MNCs may capture spillovers through technical training to meet specifications, as well as requirements and training to meet global standards. If MNCs purchase a substantial volume of inputs locally, and/or if they help their local suppliers find additional export markets, they may also allow local suppliers to capture economies of scale, thus increasing productivity and potentially 'crowding in' domestic investment.
- *Forward linkages*: MNC-produced goods and services may enter into and increase the productivity of production processes of firms in upstream and other industries. The hope is that developing countries will attract 'quality' FDI which – through positive spillovers – generates a 'virtuous circle' of higher productivity, skills and industry upgrading. However, it is possible that FDI will instead lock developing countries into non-globally competitive growth paths, or have negative externalities leading to de-skilling and de-industrialization. Theodore Moran (2006, p. 142) argues:

> FDI in manufacturing and assembly comes in two distinct forms – full-scale plants with cutting-edge technology and management practices, often export-oriented and integrated into the supply chain of the parent; and subscale plants protected from international competition with older technology and management practices and little prospect of becoming competitive in world markets.

Empirical evidence

Over the past 30 years, a large literature has emerged seeking to determine empirically whether and in what circumstances FDI generates spillovers for industry upgrading in developing countries.

Statistical studies searching for horizontal spillovers – that is, increases in the productivity of domestic competitors to MNCs – have had disappointing results. In a review of 28 studies, a World Bank paper found, once statistical biases were corrected, no instances of positive horizontal spillovers in developing countries (Gorg and Greenaway, 2003). Moreover, six studies found evidence of negative spillovers – domestic firms contracted or went out of business. In the classic study, Aitken and Harrison (1999) analyzed a panel of over 4000 manufacturing firms in Venezuela between 1976 and 1989. They found that the total factor productivity of local firms in the same industry dropped in the presence of MNCs.[2]

Case studies present a more optimistic, though still mixed, assessment. Amsden and Chu (2003) found that partnerships with MNCs in the 1960s and 1970s helped build globally competitive electronics firms in Taiwan. China successfully leveraged joint venture requirements with MNCs in the 1980s and 1990s to build a globally competitive computer industry (Dussell, 2005). On the other hand, Malaysia, despite large MNC investment in its electronics sector, 'failed to develop a sufficiently diversified and deep industrial structure, to induce a critical mass of corporate investment in specialized skills and innovative capabilities' (Ernst, 2003, p. 17). In Trinidad and Tobago, substantial inflows of FDI in the 1990s failed to stimulate domestic development in the natural gas industry (Barclay, 2003).

Given that MNCs seek to prevent knowledge leakages to competitors but want and need to transfer it to local suppliers, spillovers are more likely to be vertical than horizontal (Saagi, 2002). A study of FDI in Lithuania, for example, found evidence of positive spillovers to local suppliers in the manufacturing sector (Smarzynska, 2003).

Case studies, too, provide support for spillovers from MNCs to local supplier firms. Moran (1998) found that FDI by the 'big three' US car companies in the 1980s worked to upgrade technology and global competitiveness of Mexican auto supply firms. Singapore heavily depended on MNC investment to develop a dense network of local supply firms in its electronics sector in the 1970s and 1980s (Moran, 1998; Wong, 2003). India's domestic auto components firms developed substantial new capacities to supply global MNC auto companies who invested in India following liberalization (Tewari, 2005). Other case studies, however, found that MNCs generate few backward linkages to local firms. In northern Mexico, one study found that despite 25 years of FDI, Mexican material inputs accounted for less than 2 percent of value added in *maquiladora* plants. Based on surveys with plant managers and corporate purchasing agents, the study found that MNC purchasing strategies favored imports over domestic firms (Brannon et al., 1994).

More recently, Gallagher and Zarsky (2007) found that FDI had negative spillovers for Mexican firms in the IT industry in Guadalajara, driving some 45 out of 50 local firms out of business by sourcing from foreign contract manufacturers and creating an import-dependent 'enclave economy' based on assembly and sub-assembly. They argue that Mexican policy at the national and regional levels failed to anticipate and to counteract the MNC bias towards foreign suppliers by nurturing the capacities of local firms built up under policies of import substitution. Government support for research and development, for example, was only 0.36 percent of GDP in 2000, compared to 2.60 percent in South Korea. Generally, Latin American governments have adopted a passive policy approach to FDI – and FDI has had a poor performance in generating spillovers or promoting business linkages and employment. Ernst (2005, p. 1) found that:

> economic opening in Argentina, Brazil and Mexico did not lead to export dynamism and had a disappointing impact on employment . . . only Mexico experienced an export surge in manufacturing production and employment during the second half of the 1990s, mainly due to the booming maquiladora sector. However, the maquiladora industry did not develop significant links with the rest of the economy. There was no upgrading of production even for the more sophisticated exports, since the import content of exports also rose significantly. Moreover, the maquiladora industry has declined significantly since 2000 thus reducing drastically formal job creation in Mexico.

In Asia, where many governments have adopted pro-active policies to capture FDI spillovers, performance has been better. While policies differ by country, all aim generally to overcome market failures, such as the lack of access to credit by local firms, and provide public goods to raise general productive capacity, such as support for education and R&D. Singapore, for example, aggressively supported R&D, education, infrastructure investment, and science and technology policies. China effectively used joint venture agreements with MNCs and access to domestic markets to promote industry upgrading in the IT sector (Dedrick and Kramer, 2002). India used tariffs and supplier training programs to build a globally competitive local supply base for global auto companies (Tewari, 2005).

Environmental spillovers

A central promise of FDI is that it will promote not just economic growth but the growth of more environmentally sustainable industries in developing countries. 'FDI has the potential to bring social and environmental benefits to host economies', advises the OECD, 'through the dissemination of good practices and technologies within MNEs (multinational enterprises) and through their subsequent spillovers to domestic enterprises.' While it cautions that there is a risk that foreign-owned enterprises may jeopardize sustainable industrial development by exporting old technologies and 'not-so-good' practices banned in home countries, the OECD optimistically concludes that 'there is little empirical evidence to support the risk scenario' (OECD, 2002, p. 5).

FDI potentially delivers three types of environmental spillovers for sustainable industrial development:

- *Clean technology transfer*: transfer to MNC affiliates of production technologies which are less polluting and more input efficient than those used by domestic firms.
- *Technology leapfrogging*: transfers of state-of-the-art production and pollution-control technologies by MNCs which allow developing countries to leap to the global technology frontier.
- *Pollution halo*: diffusion among domestic firms, including suppliers, of 'best practice' in environmental management.

The existence of environmental spillovers in developing countries rests on four assumptions. First, because they are subjected to global competition, MNCs are more technologically dynamic than domestic firms. Technological change tends to promote efficiency in the use of production inputs, which reduces both pollution and resource intensity.

Second, MNCs transfer their cleanest, state-of-the-art production technologies to developing countries. They do so because developing-country production sites are integrated into MNC global production and marketing strategies. Competing for global markets requires companies to maximize efficiency in all production sites.

Third, originating primarily in OECD countries, MNCs are subject to higher environmental standards in their home countries than are domestic firms in developing countries. Reflected in both government regulation and consumer preferences, higher environmental standards force MNCs to direct R&D funds towards cleaner and safer process technologies and products. They also nudge MNCs 'beyond compliance' with mandatory environmental regulation and towards adopting best practice in environmental management as a way of demonstrating corporate social responsibility. Increasingly, best practice includes corporate oversight not only of foreign-based subsidiaries but also of supply chains.

Fourth, to minimize transaction and reputation costs and liability risks, MNCs operate with global, company-wide environmental standards. These centralized standards are based either on those of the MNC home country or on higher internal or international standards.[3] It is 'standard operating procedure' for MNCs to diffuse these standards to foreign affiliates and monitor performance.

Where these assumptions hold, it is reasonable to expect that FDI will generate sustainable development spillovers. However, they may not hold for all or even most MNCs.

In terms of technological dynamism, industries and industry subsectors are subjected to differing degrees of global competition and other drivers of technological change. The mining industry, for example, is far less dynamic in terms of innovation in process technology and final products than the informatics industry. Even within a relatively dynamic industry, companies are not homogeneous: there are leaders and laggards in terms of both technological and managerial innovation, including in environmental management (Mazurek, 1999; Leighton et al., 2002). Whether FDI generates sustainable development spillovers is thus likely to be contingent on the technological trajectory within a particular industry, as well as the innovation culture of particular companies. Second, like cutting-edge technology more generally, MNCs have incentives to protect intellectual property in environmentally cleaner technology and/or better management practices. Even in technologically dynamic industries and companies, MNCs may find it cost-effective to slough off older, lower-margin, dirtier technologies to developing countries rather than transfer state-of-the-art production technologies.

The assumption that environmental regulation of industry generally is more stringent in OECD than in developing countries is probably warranted. However, although they tend to converge, government regulation and social expectations are not uniform in OECD countries. The European Union, in particular, has in recent years adopted more stringent standards for industry, including regulation of industrial chemicals, than North America. European MNCs have also voluntarily adopted 'best practice' at a higher rate than those in North America, Australasia, or Japan.[4] In addition, MNCs increasingly are emerging from non-OECD countries, including China, Singapore and Malaysia (UNCTAD, 2002). Environmental practices and the influence of civil society are not only generally lower but more diverse than in highly developed countries. In short, the environmental management practices that MNCs bring to developing countries are conditioned by their source country and are thus highly diverse.

Finally, the assumption that MNCs uniformly adopt and implement global standards as a strategy for cross-border environmental management is overly optimistic. In many developing countries, environmental regulation is non-existent, weak or not enforced. In this context, foreign firms have a choice of four strategies: (1) follow (or set) local practice; (2) comply with host-country regulation; (3) follow home-country standards; (4) operate with higher standards set by the company or by an international agency (Hansen, 1999). Which strategy they choose depends on their determination of costs and risks. Tradeoffs between costs and risks are complex and conditioned by a host of factors, including global market dynamics within a particular sector and the size and global strategy of particular MNCs. On the one hand, the adoption of global standards reduces transaction and information costs entailed in producing to a myriad of different national environmental and occupational health standards. Some MNCs operate in dozens of countries. High company-wide standards may also reduce production costs by increasing eco-efficiency, that is, reducing inputs per unit output and reducing pollution. Moreover, high company-wide standards reduce the risk of liability and adverse publicity resulting from high-profile environmental disasters and/or targeted activist campaigns.

On the other hand, two factors militate against MNC adoption of high company-wide standards, whether based on home-country, internally set, or international standards. First, MNC liability for environmental harm in developing countries is generally limited to compliance with domestic law. In international law, the concept of 'environmental rights' with the right of redress is generally limited to governments and to cross-border environmental harms. New forms of liability, including financial institutions that make loans to MNCs and home-country governments, are still at an early stage.[5]

Second, reputation costs are negligible for MNCs without high-visibility consumer products and brands. Even for those MNCs vulnerable to loss of consumer confidence, the probability of suffering reputation costs due to poor environmental practice may be low because of poor monitoring, reporting and information mechanisms. Put simply, they have a low risk of getting caught or being held to account if they engage in 'bad practice', not least because of the limited resources of advocacy groups, who are the information bridge to consumers.

Examining the evidence
The analytical arguments presented above both support and challenge the idea that FDI generates spillovers for sustainable industrial development in developing countries. In this section, we examine the empirical evidence.

Are foreign firms cleaner than domestic firms? A detailed case study of FDI in Chile's mining sector in the 1970s and 1980s found that the two foreign-owned companies performed (far) better than domestic companies. Following their corporate parents, Exxon Minerals Chile and Fluor Corporation, the two companies put in place an environmental policy framework requiring 'responsible practices' at a time when there was as yet no coherent government regulation of the mining industry (Lagos and Velasco, 1999). Ten years later, domestic mining companies followed suit.

Using survey methodology, a study of MNCs in India's manufacturing sector likewise found that foreign firms, that is, MNC affiliates, were cleaner than domestic firms (Ruud, 2002). MNCs transferred state-of-the-art production (though not necessarily pollution control) technologies to their affiliates. In addition, MNC affiliates were strongly influenced by corporate parents to improve environmental management.

Other case studies, however, suggest that MNCs follow poor local practice or, in cases where domestic companies do not exist, engage in 'bad practice'. In explorations for oil and natural gas off Sakhalin Island, for example, Exxon openly flaunted new Russian laws requiring environmental review and zero water discharge. Only the pressure of environmental jurists and activists, as well as the European Bank for Reconstruction and Development, forced Exxon to comply with the law (Rosenthal, 2002). Case studies of FDI in the petroleum industry, including in Nigeria, Ecuador, Azerbaijan and Kazakhstan, likewise find that MNCs operate in developing countries with 'double standards' – environmental and human rights practices that would be fined or prosecuted in their home countries (Leighton et al., 2002).

Statistical studies are likewise mixed. Using energy use per unit of output as a proxy for energy emissions, one World Bank study found that foreign ownership was associated with cleaner and lower levels of energy use in Mexico, Venezuela, and Côte d'Ivoire (Eskeland and Harrison, 1997). In China, foreign investment in electricity generation was linked to improvements in energy efficiency and emission reduction (Blackman and Wu, 1998). Besides transferring advanced generating technologies and better management, FDI stimulated competition among Chinese companies in the electricity generation sector.

Another group of World Bank researchers, however, found that foreign firms and plants performed no better than domestic companies. Based on firm-level data in Mexico (manufacturing) and Asia (pulp and paper), the New Ideas in Pollution Regulation group found firm environmental performance to depend on: (1) the scale of the plant (bigger is better); and (2) the strength of local regulation, both government and 'informal' (Hettige et al., 1996; Dasgupta et al., 1997). In addition, a study of the manufacturing sector in Korea found that domestic firms performed better than foreign-owned firms, a result the authors attributed to the sensitivity of Korean *chaebol* to public criticism (Aden et al., 1999).

Does FDI promote technology leapfrogging?   Technology gaps between developed and developing countries can be very large. In this context, MNCs can transfer technology that is cleaner than that currently in use in developing countries, yet which is not state of the art. Moreover, production processes, especially in manufacturing, are complex and multi-stage. MNCs may transfer a mixture of older and state-of-the-art technologies.

The concept of technology leapfrogging is that, through transfer by MNCs of the most efficient, least polluting technologies, developing countries can move to the global production frontier. The economic benefits include developing globally competitive industries, potentially even out-competing producers with older technologies. The reduction in the pollution intensity of developing country production (and consumption) brings environmental benefits both locally and, in the case of global pollutants such as carbon emissions, globally.

Three studies of the Mexican steel industry found that foreign firms were cleaner than domestic firms and that FDI generates environmentally beneficial technology leapfrogging. Mercado (2000) found that foreign firms in the Mexican steel sector, or firms that serve foreign markets, were more apt than domestic firms to comply with environmental regulations. Gentry and Fernandez (1998) found that the Mexican government played a key role, brokering an early agreement with Dutch steel firms whereby the government took on some of the environmental liabilities associated with steel production. Later, the foreign firms began investing in environmental improvements.

Most tellingly, Gallagher (2004) found that steel production in Mexico is 'cleaner' per unit of output, in terms of criteria air pollutants, than in the US.[6] The primary reason is that FDI, as well as domestic investment in new plants, deployed newer and more environmentally benign mini-mill technology rather than more traditional and dirtier blast furnaces.

But a recent study of FDI by US auto companies in China had less optimistic findings (Sims Gallagher, 2006). Based on extensive interviews with plant managers at Ford, GM and Jeep affiliates, the study found that US firms transferred outdated automotive pollution control technologies. While 'somewhat cleaner' automotive technologies were transferred, potential environmental benefits will be outweighed by the increase in the number of vehicles. Most importantly, FDI did little to improve Chinese technological capabilities because 'US companies have transferred products, but not much knowledge, to China' (ibid., p. 9). As a result, China (and the world) will reap neither the environmental nor the economic benefit of producing at the global technology frontier. In earlier work, Sims Gallagher (2006) posited that there are 'limits to leapfrogging' through technology transfer from foreign firms via FDI. In the case of substantially cleaner automotive technologies in China, these limits included, first and foremost, the lack of strategic and consistent Chinese government policies that aimed to achieve environmental and energy-technology leapfrogging.[7] In addition, China had weak technological capabilities, and MNCs were unwilling to transfer cleaner or more efficient technologies beyond those required by standards. She concludes that, for China to leapfrog to the technological frontier of clean automobiles, '[A] coherent, concerted, consistent, and long-term effort of government, industry, and civil society cooperation' would be required (ibid., p. 10).

Pollution halo: do MNCs diffuse good environmental management to domestic firms?
Beyond transferring clean technology and good environmental management to their affiliates, MNCs can create a 'pollution halo' by diffusing good environmental management to domestic firms. One of the primary channels is through the supply chain; that is, MNC requirements that suppliers meet their internally set environmental standards. Environmental management training opportunities for suppliers accelerate diffusion. Another channel is the demonstration effect. Domestic firms may voluntarily copy foreign firms, while host-country governments may adopt MNC standards as local regulation. A third channel is upstream markets, that is, firms and consumers who purchase more eco-efficient MNC products, thus raising the overall level of environmental performance in the country. A fourth channel is industry collaboration to promote better environmental management in developing countries through self-regulation. Examples include the Responsible Care Program of the chemical industry and the Electronics Industry Code of Conduct.

What is the evidence that 'pollution halos' exist? Evidence in support of the pollution halo hypothesis is provided by Eskeland and Harrison (1997). Using energy use per unit of output as a proxy for energy emissions, they found that foreign ownership was associated with cleaner and lower levels of energy use in the three countries of their sample (Mexico, Venezuela and Côte d'Ivoire). A study by Blackman and Wu (1998) also found significant support for the conclusion that foreign investment in electricity generation in China increased energy efficiency and reduced emissions. The primary reason is that FDI targeted advanced generating technologies. Better management and the introduction of competition are also part of the halo effect.

A number of other studies, however, have found no significant effect of foreign ownership or financing. In a study of Mexican foreign and domestic manufacturing firms, Dasgupta et al. (1997) found that 'OECD influence' did not affect the degree of firm 'environmental effort'. The degree of effort was measured by two variables: the adoption of ISO 14000 type procedures and the use of plant personnel for environmental inspection and control. Using survey methodology, the researchers found that new technology was not significantly cleaner and there was no evidence that plants with new equipment had better environmental performance.

What did matter to environmental performance in Mexico was the size of the plant and multi-plant status (larger size and multi-plant firms were positively correlated with more effort), recent experience of regulatory pressure (inspections), and public scrutiny. For company compliance with its own internal environmental guidelines, the most important variable is strong regulation. The foreign connection in general was not significant. 'We do not find', they conclude, 'a significant role for any OECD linkage: multinational ownership, trade, management training, or management experience' (ibid., p. 18).

Three other studies in Asia, summarized in Hettige et al. (1996), also found foreign ownership, financing, or links to OECD markets to be insignificant in firm-level environmental performance. Huq and Wheeler (1993) examined fertilizer and pulping plants in Bangladesh; Hartman et al. (1995) examined determinants of pollution abatement among 26 pulp and paper plants in Bangladesh, India, Indonesia and Thailand; and Pargal and Wheeler (1996) conducted an econometric analysis of determinants of performance among plants across a number of sectors in Indonesia.

Like the Mexican study, these studies in Asia found that the scale of the plant or firm was positively associated with environmental performance – i.e. the bigger the better. They also found that 'rapidly spreading multinational facilities are relatively clean' because they employ newer technology (Hettige et al., 1996, p. 1901). The most important factor, however, was not ownership (i.e. domestic versus foreign), but the newness of the facilities: new plants, whether domestic or foreign owned, are likely to be cleaner because of newer technology. In a surprising twist, a recent study of manufacturing plants in Korea by Aden et al. (1999) found that domestic firms apparently perform better than foreign firms. The variable examined was plant-level spending on pollution abatement. The authors speculate that the reason that domestic firms spend more might stem from the attempt by the unpopular Korean *chaebol* to shield themselves from public criticism.

All these studies suggest that, despite the lack of effective regulation, environmental performance of many firms is improving. Rather than pollution-intensive production across the board, Hettige et al. (1996) conclude that, 'Despite weak or non-existent formal regulation and enforcement, there are many clean plants in the developing countries of South and Southeast Asia' (p. 1891). What accounts for this? While scale and technology effects are important, what emerges from these studies (as well as from the Mexican study) as the most significant determinant of firm performance is community pressure.

The actual mechanisms by which communities pressure firms to clean up are not clearly spelled out in these studies (with the exception of Korea, where communities have signed formal agreements with companies). Instead, what the studies show is a high correlation between the income and/or education level of a particular community and the overall level of environmental performance by firms located in that community. This result is strong in Indonesia and Thailand, in China (Afseh et al., 1996), and in South Asia. Apparently, richer and more educated communities are able to bargain effectively with firms. Poorer and less educated communities are not.

In addition to community pressure, the Mexican and Korean studies suggest that strong regulation matters. Firms adjust their effort and their performance based on expectations of enforcement, especially site inspection visits and sanctions. In Korea, regulators apply an increasingly intrusive monitoring program and escalating sanctions depending on past performance.

A study of MNCs in the chemical industry in Latin America found that US companies played a leading role in diffusing the Responsible Care Program to domestic companies in Mexico and Brazil (Garcia-Johnson, 2000). Developed in the early 1980s in Canada by the chemical industry in response to the Bhopal disaster, the program aims to raise industry self-regulation beyond mandatory government standards in the areas of environmental impact, employee health and safety, facility security and product stewardship.[8] By 2005, chemical industry associations in 45 countries had signed up to the Responsible Care Program, including 17 in developing countries.[9]

A volume of case studies in Latin America found evidence that better environmental management practices were diffused through FDI, including through supply chains (Gentry, 1998). One example was the cooperation of the US company Chiquita Brands International, the largest banana grower in the world, in the Better Banana Project. Started by the Rainforest Alliance, the project uses NGO monitors to certify that growers meet strict environmental and social standards in the areas of toxic chemical use, pollution, water and soil conservation, and worker health and safety (Rainforest Alliance, 2000; BSR, 2003).

In India's manufacturing sector, however, Ruud (2002) found no evidence that MNCs diffused better environmental management practices to local partners, suppliers or consumers. While MNC affiliates were cleaner then domestic firms, they apparently operate as 'islands of environmental excellence in a sea of dirt'. He concludes that local norms and institutions are central in determining MNC practice and that 'FDI inflows do not automatically create a general improvement in environmental performance' (ibid., p. 116).

One impediment to the capture of environmental spillovers is the tendency of FDI in developing countries to agglomerate in urban enclaves and rely intensively on imported components rather than local suppliers. If procurement linkages are thin, there is little opportunity for MNCs to diffuse good environmental practices through supply chains. Gallagher and Zarsky (2007), for example, found that FDI in the information technology industry in Guadalajara, Mexico generated few environmental spillovers to local firms, primarily because MNC contract manufacturers imported over 95 percent of components.

Conclusion: enhancing the benefits of FDI

Theoretical frameworks suggest that FDI can potentially generate benefits for host communities in the form of knowledge and technology spillovers that promote industry upgrading and enhance environmental performance. Empirical evidence, however, reveals a gap between theory and reality and suggests that the capture of spillovers is not guaranteed: some countries have successfully captured them, while others have not. The capture of FDI spillovers requires pro-active government policy, including, *inter alia*, regulation of and partnerships with MNCs, worker and supplier training, provision of credit to SMEs, support for R&D, investment in primary and tertiary education, and science and technology policies.

Interestingly, many policies that support SME growth can, with only a little effort, support more environmentally sustainable growth. For example, making credit available to enable SMEs to develop supply capacities could be extended to purchase pollution control and energy efficiency technologies. Likewise, support for supplier training could be designed to encompass both quality control and environmental management.

Most importantly, the capture of spillovers requires that desired goals from FDI be articulated and integrated into overarching development strategies. To be successful, such strategies must marry location-specific social and economic assets with effective pro-active policies to develop local firms, both as suppliers and competitors to MNCs. Despite Mr Forbes's confident expectation, FDI can only be a ladder to development if there is a blueprint that channels it.

Notes

1. In other work, I have also explored a 'social' dimension of sustainable industrial development, defined as an increase in equity-enhancing employment (Gallagher and Zarsky, 2007).
2. They also show that, had the authors used cross-sectional data, they would have come to the opposite conclusion.
3. Some companies adopt the highest applicable standard, whether it is national or sub-national, as the global company standard. Intel, for example, which is subject to state-level water quality regulation in each of its semiconductor production sites within the USA, applies the highest standard at home to its global operations. See Leighton et al. (2002), pp. 126–30.
4. For example, 39 European companies were among the top 50 companies rated as having the best sustainability reports in 2002. Only five US companies were in the top 50 (SustainAbility, 2005).
5. A landmark legal settlement in the USA in April 2005 expanded liability in home countries for MNC actions in host countries. In two suits brought in California and federal courts, the California-based oil and gas company Unocal agreed to compensate Burmese villagers for complicity in human rights abuses suffered at the hands of the Burmese military, who provided security for the building of the company's natural gas pipeline in southern Burma. See Dimmock (2005).
6. Criteria air pollutants are non-toxic air pollutants such as nitrogen oxide (NO_x), sulfur oxide (SO_x), sulfur dioxide (SO_2), nitrogen dioxide (NO_2), volatile organic compounds (VOC), all particulates and carbon monoxide.
7. Sims Gallagher (2006) suggests that these policies include the reduction of sulfur levels in fuels, fuel-efficiency standards, tighter air-pollution-control standards, fuel pricing that reflects the true costs of fuel consumption, perhaps through a carbon tax, and economic incentives and disincentives.
8. For more information see http://www.responsiblecare-us.com. See also information from the International Council of Chemical Associations, http://www.icca-chem.org/.
9. See http://www.ccpa.ca/ResponsibleCare/GlobalPartners.aspx.

References

Aden, J., A. Kyu-Hong and Michael Rock (1999), 'What is driving pollution abatement expenditure behavior of manufacturing plants in Korea?', *World Development*, **27**(7), 1203–14.
Afseh, S., B. Laplante and David Wheeler (1996), 'Controlling industrial pollution: a new paradigm', Policy Research Working Paper No.1672, Washington, DC: World Bank.
Aitken, B. and A. Harrison (1999), 'Do domestic firms benefit from foreign direct investment?', *American Economic Review*, **89**(3), 605–18.
Amsden, Alice and Wan-Chen Chu (2003), *Beyond Late Development: Taiwan's Upgrading Policies*, Cambridge, MA: MIT Press.
Barclay, Lou Anne (2003), 'FDI-facilitated development: the case of the natural gas industry of Trinidad and Tobago', United Nations University, Institute for New Technologies, Discussion Paper No. 2003–7, September.
Blackman, A. and X. Wu (1998), *Foreign Direct Investment in China's Power Sector: Trends, Benefits, and Barriers*, Washington, DC: Resources for the Future.
Brannon, Jeffrey T., Dilmus D. James and William G. Lucker (1994), 'Generating and sustaining backward linkages between *maquiladoras* and local suppliers in northern Mexico', *World Development*, **22**(12), 1933–45.
BSR (2003), *Monitoring Global Supply Chain Practices*, Business for Social Responsibility Issue Brief, http://www.bsr.org.
Dasgupta, S., B. Laplante and N. Pramingi (1997), 'Pollution and capital markets in developing countries', The World Bank Development Reasearch Group, October.
Dasgupta, Susmita, Hemamala Hettige and David Wheeler (2000), 'What improves environmental performance? Evidence from Mexican industry', *Journal of Environmental Economics and Management*, **38**, 39–66.
Dedrick, J. and K.L. Kramer (2002), 'Enter the dragon: China's computer industry', *Perspectives*, February, 28–36.
Dimmock, Matthew (2005), 'Burma: victory for human rights', *Green Left Outline Weekly*, Issue #629, 8 June.
Dussell, Enrique (2005), *Economic Opportunities and Challenges Posed by China for Mexico and Central America*, German Development Institute.
Eskeland, G.S. and A.E. Harrison (1997), 'Moving to greener pastures? Multinationals and the pollution haven hypothesis', Washington, DC: World Bank.
Ernst, Christopher (2005), 'Trade liberalization, export orientation and employment in Argentina, Brazil and Mexico', Employment Strategy Papers, Employment Strategy Department, No. 14.
Ernst, Dieter (2003), 'How sustainable are benefits from global production networks? Malaysia's upgrading prospects in the electronics industry', East–West Centre Working Papers, **57** (June), http://www.eastwestcenter.org/stored/pdfs/econwpo57.pdf.

Gallagher, Kevin P. (2004*)*, *Free Trade and the Environment: Mexico, NAFTA, and Beyond*, Palo Alto, CA: Stanford University Press.

Gallagher, Kevin P. and Lyuba Zarsky (2007), *Enclave Economy, Foreign Investment and Sustainable Development in Mexico's Silicon Valley*, Cambridge, MA: MIT Press.

Garcia-Johnson, Ronie (2000), *Exporting Environmentalism: U.S. Multinational chemical corporations in Brazil and Mexico*, Cambridge, MA: MIT Press.

Gentry, Bradford (ed.) (1998), *Private Capital Flows and the Environment*: *Lessons from Latin America*, Cheltenham, UK and Northampton, MA, USA: Edward Elgar.

Gentry, Bradford and L.O. Fernandez (1998), 'Mexican steel', in Bradford Gentry (ed.,) *Private Capital Flows and the Environment: Lessons from Latin America*, Cheltenham, UK and Northampton, MA, USA: Edward Elgar, pp. 37–41.

Gorg, Holger and David Greenaway (2003), 'Much ado about nothing? Do domestic firms really benefit from foreign direct investment?', IZA Discussion Paper 944, November.

Hansen, M.W. (1999), 'Cross border environmental management in transnational corporations: an analytical framework', Occasional paper no. 5, UNCTAD/CBS Project, June.

Hartman, R.S., M. Huq, and David Wheeler (1995), 'Why paper mills clean up: determinants of pollution abatement in four Asian countries', *New Ideas in Pollution Regulation*, No. 1710 Washington, DC: World Bank.

Hettige, Hemalala, M. Huq, S. Pargal and D. Wheeler (1996), 'Determinants of pollution abatement in developing countries: evidence from south and southeast Asia', *World Development*, **24**(12), 1891–904.

Huq, M. and David Wheeler (1993), 'Pollution reduction without formal regulation: evidence from Bangladesh', Working Paper No. 1993–39, Washington, DC: World Bank, Environment Department.

Lagos, Gustavo and Patricio Velasco (1999), 'Environmental policies and practices in Chilean mining', in Alyson Warhurst (ed.), *Mining and the Environment: Case Studies from the Americas*, Ottawa, Canada: International Development Research Centre, pp. 101–36..

Leighton, Michelle, Lyuba Zarsky and Naomi Roht-Arriaza (2002), *Beyond Good Deeds: Case Studies and a new policy agenda for corporate accountability*, San Francisco, CA: Natural Heritage Institute.

Mazurek, Jan (1999), *Making Microchips: Policy, Globalization and Economic Restructuring in the Semiconductor Industry*, Cambridge, MA: MIT Press.

Mercado, A. (2000), 'Environmental assessment of the Mexican steel industry', in R. Jenkins (ed.), *Industry and the Environment in Latin America*, London: Routledge, pp. 218–44.

Millennium Ecosystem Assessment (2005), *Ecosystems and Human Well-Being*, Washington, DC: Island Press.

Moran, Theodore H. (1998), *Foreign Direct Investment and Development: The New Agenda for Developing Countries and Economies in Transition*, Washington, DC: Institute for International Economics.

Moran, Theodore H. (2006), *Harnessing Foreign Direct Investment for Development: Policies for Developed and Developing Countries*, Washington, DC: Center for Global Development.

Moran, Theodore H., Edward M. Graham and Magnus Blomstrom (2005), *Does Foreign Direct Investment Promote Development?*, Washington DC: Institute for International Economics and Center for Global Development.

OECD (2002), *Foreign Direct Investment for Development: Maximising Benefits, Minimising Costs, Overview*, Paris: OECD.

Pargal S. and Wheeler David (1996), 'Informal regulation of industrial pollution in developing countries: evidence from Indonesia', *Journal of Political Economy*, **104**(6), 1314–27.

Rainforest Alliance (2000), 'News from the front: Banana eco-labeling program is world's largest', *The Canopy*, January/February.

Rosenthal, Erika (2002), 'Conflicts over transnational oil and gas development off Sakhalin Island in the Russian Far East: a David and Goliath tale', in Lyuba Zarsky (ed.), *Human Rights and the Environment: Conflicts and Norms in a Globalizing World*, London: Earthscan, pp. 96–122.

Ruud, Audun (2002), 'Environmental management of transnational corporations in India: are TNCs creating islands of environmental excellence in a sea of dirt?', *Business Strategy and the Environment*, **11**(2), 103–18.

Saagi, K. (2002), 'Trade, foreign direct investment, and international technology transfer: a survey', Background paper for the World Bank's Microfoundations of International Technology Diffusion project, Southern Methodist University Department of Economics.

Sims Gallagher, Kelly (2006), *China Shifts Gears: Automobiles, Oil, Pollution, Development*, Cambridge, MA: MIT Press.

Smarzynska, Beta K. (2003), 'Does foreign direct investment increase the productivity of domestic firms? In search of spillovers through backward linkages', William Davidson Working Paper 548, University of Michigan Business School, March.

SustainAbility (2005), 'Trust us: the Global Reporters 2002 Survey of Corporate Sustainability Reporting', available at: http:// www.sustainability.com.

Tewari, Meenu (2005), 'Foreign direct investment and the transformation of Tamil Nadu's automotive supply base', in Yves-André Faure, Loraine Kennedy and Pascal Labazée (eds), *Local Production Systems and Global Markets in Emerging Economies: Brazil, India, Mexico*, Paris: IRD/Karthala.

UNCTAD (2002), *World Investment Report, Transnational Corporations and Export Competitiveness*, Geneva: United Nations Publications.

Wong, Poh Kam (2003), 'From using to creating technology: the evolution of Singapore's national innovation system and the changing role of public policy', in Sanjaya Lall and Shujiro Urata (eds), *Competitiveness, FDI and Technological Activity in East Asia*, Cheltenham, UK and Northampton, MA, USA: Edward Elgar, pp. 191–238.

7 Globalization and the environment: convergence or divergence?

James K. Boyce[*]

Introduction

In the early 1990s, the environmental movement in the USA underwent an acrimonious split over whether to support the proposed North American Free Trade Agreement (NAFTA). Some groups backed the treaty, agreeing that 'the best way to ensure that Mexico's environment is cleaned up is to help Mexico become a prosperous country, and that means NAFTA'.[1] Others opposed it, arguing that 'the competition to attract investment will result in a lowest common denominator for environmental statutes' and that 'the country with the least restrictive statutes will become the floor, and others will harmonize downward to that floor'.[2]

Despite their differences, both sides made a common assumption: Mexico's environmental practices were inferior to those of the USA and Canada. The only point of contention was whether free trade would pull the USA and Canada down to Mexico's level, or lift Mexico to the plane of its northern neighbors. Partly as a result, both sides were oblivious to what may turn out to be NAFTA's most serious environmental impact: the erosion of Mexico's rich biological diversity in maize ('corn' in US parlance), as Mexican *campesino* farmers abandon traditional agriculture in the face of competition from cheap corn imported from the USA.[3]

In this chapter, I question the assumption that the global North is relatively 'green' and the global South relatively 'brown'. I also argue that neither theoretical reasoning nor empirical evidence supports the axiomatic claims that 'globalization' will promote a convergence toward better environmental practices, or toward worse environmental practices, or instead a growing divergence in environmental practices across countries.

Environmental convergence: four scenarios

In debates on North–South trade, it is often assumed that production processes in the global South tend to be more environmentally degrading than those in the global North, by virtue of weaker demand for environmental quality (ascribed to low incomes), the weaker ability of governments to promulgate and enforce environmental regulations, or both. Hence trade occurs on a tilted playing field, where southern producers have a competitive advantage over their Northern counterparts thanks to their greater scope for externalization of costs.

Economic theory is often invoked to maintain that a level playing field – one with no international differences in environmental standards – is not necessarily optimal: the marginal costs and benefits of environmental quality are likely to vary across locations.[4] Two points should be noted in this connection. First, this does not imply that existing variations in standards across countries are optimal, nor that moves toward greater harmonization would not be welfare improving in conventional terms. Second, international differences in

97

Direction of change	'Harmonization upward'	'Race to the bottom'
Environmental quality gradient		
North > South	Ecological modernization	Environmental protectionism
South > North	Greening the North	Environmental imperialism

Figure 7.1   Environmental convergence: four scenarios

the 'optimal' level of environmental quality are partly – perhaps mainly – attributable to differences in ability to pay: in this sense it is 'efficient' for poorer people to breathe dirtier air. This distribution-blind notion of optimality is unexceptional in neoclassical economics, but its wider normative appeal as a basis for policy is questionable. Elsewhere I have suggested that a rights-based allocation of access to a clean and safe environment – a principle enshrined in dozens of national constitutions around the world – is an attractive alternative to the wealth-based allocation principle founded on willingness to pay.[5]

Here, however, our concern is not normative prescription but rather positive description. As in the NAFTA debate, the question is whether economic integration will lead to 'harmonization upward' in which the South becomes more like the North, or a 'race to the bottom' in which the opposite occurs. These opposing outcomes are labeled 'ecological modernization' and 'environmental protectionism,' respectively, in Figure 7.1, based on prominent schools of thought that have emphasized these possibilities.

In principle we can distinguish two further paths of convergence, in which the North–South environmental gradient is reversed: that is, southern production is cleaner and more sustainable than that of competing sectors in the North. That this is not a purely hypothetical possibility will be illustrated below. In Figure 7.1, these paths are labeled the 'Greening the North' (when the North moves up the gradient, becoming more like the South) and 'Environmental imperialism' (when the South moves down the gradient to become more like the North).

Of course, these stylized scenarios simplify complex processes. One scenario need not fit all environmental problems; it is quite possible, for example, that in some respects the environmental gradient runs from North to South while in others it runs in the opposite direction. Harmonization may occur not at either end of the spectrum, but rather somewhere in the middle. And in some cases globalization may promote divergence rather than convergence. To begin mapping out the possibilities, this section considers the four convergence scenarios in turn.

Ecological modernization

The term 'ecological modernization' was coined in the 1980s by European sociologists to describe recent changes in production and consumption in industrialized countries. In many cases these have reduced use of natural resources and emissions of pollutants per unit of output, and in some cases these reductions have been substantial enough to generate net environmental improvements alongside economic growth (see, e.g., Weale, 1992, Spaargaren and Mol, 1992).

Ecological modernization theorists interpret these transformations as a response not only to market signals, but more importantly to the growth of environmental concerns among the public and policy-makers.[6] Although originally put forward as an analysis of trends in industrialized countries, the theory has been extended globally by some of its proponents. In so doing, most have accepted the conventional premise that the environmental-quality gradient runs from North to South. Thus Mol (2001, p. 157) writes of 'the need to harmonize environmental capacities and regimes up to at least the level that has been achieved in the [Europe–North America–Japan] triad countries'. Mechanisms identified as vehicles for such harmonization upward include income growth, foreign direct investment, international agreements, and 'governance from below'.

A positive effect from income growth is premised on the view that globalization leads to rising per capita incomes, and that the latter in turn lead to greater effective demand for environmental quality (often referred to as a better ability to 'afford' a cleaner environment). During the NAFTA debate, for example, Mexican president Carlos Salinas proclaimed, 'Only through widespread prosperity can we have the resources to channel toward the protection of land, air and water' (quoted by Hogenboom, 1998, p. 180). Both links – from globalization to rising incomes, and from rising incomes to a better environment – are open to question. With respect to the latter link, it is important to recognize that many aspects of environmental quality are public goods. To be politically effective, demand for environmental quality therefore must be articulated through institutions that overcome both the free-rider problem and political opposition from the beneficiaries of cost externalization. I return to this issue in the next section.

Foreign direct investment is sometimes portrayed as a vehicle for environmental improvement on the grounds that foreign firms have superior technological know-how, derived from production in countries with stricter regulations, and that they find it efficient to use standardized processes to produce standardized products. In addition, foreign firms may be more sensitive to reputational concerns than local firms, and more subject to media scrutiny and pressure from public opinion. In keeping with this prediction, some empirical studies have found evidence of 'pollution halos' – above-average environmental performance – associated with foreign investment. In a review of this literature, Zarsky (1999, p. 14) concludes that the evidence is mixed, and that 'the most significant determinant of firm performance is community pressure' rather than the origin of investment *per se*.[7]

International agreements can also promote upward harmonization in environmental practices. Examples of such agreements include the treaties on oceanic pollution, transport of hazardous waste, and ozone-depleting chemicals. Neumayer (2002) finds that the degree of democracy – as measured by indices of political rights and 'voice and accountability' – is a strong predictor of whether countries will enter into environmental agreements, again pointing to the importance of political variables in determining outcomes.

'Governance from below' refers to *de facto* rules that are imposed not by governments, but by 'civil society' and public opinion. A series of studies at the World Bank, for example, has found that 'informal regulation' by local communities can limit industrial pollution even in the absence of formal regulation (see Pargal and Wheeler, 1996; Pargal et al., 1997). These studies generally find average income and education of communities to be strongly correlated with successful informal regulation. Transnational environmental alliances also can increase the bargaining power of local communities (see, e.g., Keenan et al., 2007). In addition to directly influencing the decisions of private firms and government officials, informal actors have developed third-party certification and 'eco-labeling' initiatives that respond to and influence consumer demands.[8]

Environmental protectionism
Instead of harmonization upward, many environmentalists maintain that globalization promotes a 'race to the bottom', in which competition for private investment undermines environmental regulation. In its weaker variant, this argument holds that global competition impedes new regulation so that South countries remain 'stuck at the bottom' (Porter, 1999) and Northern countries are 'stuck in the mud' (Zarsky, 1997). In its stronger variant, globalization spurs the competitive lowering of standards in the North, ultimately leading to convergence on the lowest common denominator. Hence the claim in the NAFTA debate that the trade agreement would 'sabotage' US environmental laws.[9]

The usual policy recommendation flowing from this analysis is that Northern countries should use compensating tariffs or other trade restrictions to prevent 'ecological dumping' – the sale of products at prices below their marginal social cost of production by virtue of externalization of environmental costs.[10] Hence this school of thought is here termed 'environmental protectionism'.

The logic rests on the uneven globalization of markets and governance:

> International trade increases competition, and competition reduces costs. But competition can reduce costs in two ways: by increasing efficiency or by lowering standards. A firm can save money by lowering its standards for pollution control, worker safety, wages, health care and so on – all choices that externalize some of its costs . . . Nations maintain large legal, administrative and auditing structures that bar reductions in the social and environmental standards of domestic industries. There are no analogous international bodies of law and administration; there are only national laws, which differ widely. Consequently, free international trade encourages industries to shift their production activities to the countries that have the lowest standards of cost internalization – hardly a move toward global efficiency. (Daly, 1993, p. 52)

Empirical studies generally have concluded that environmental regulation does not, in fact, have much effect on firms' competitiveness (for a review, see Jaffe et al., 1995). At the same time, however, studies of 'revealed comparative advantage' in pollution-intensive industries (such as pulp and paper, mining, chemicals, and petroleum products) have found that countries in the global South and Eastern Europe account for a rising share of world exports.[11] This relocation of 'dirty industries' – a policy infamously recommended by the World Bank's chief economist in the early 1990s (*The Economist*, 1992) – occurs mainly via net additions to the capital stock, given sunk costs in existing Northern facilities.

Even if there were robust evidence that dirty industries are migrating from North to South, this would not automatically put downward pressure on environmental standards in the North, as envisaged in the strong variant of the race-to-the-bottom logic. It is conceivable that instead northern countries would allow, or even encourage, the displacement of environmental costs to the South, with international trade allowing them to import raw materials, intermediate inputs, and final products at prices held down by cost externalization.[12] In other words, the North could maintain higher environmental standards domestically, while reaping 'ecological subsidies' from the South, a possibility to which I return below.

Greening the North

I now turn to scenarios where the environmental-quality gradient runs from South to North – that is, where southern production is cleaner and more sustainable than competing production in the North. At first blush this may seem implausible, given the deeply ingrained assumption that environmental quality is a luxury that only the affluent can afford, or at least a normal good for which demand rises with income. Indeed, it is often assumed that the 'bottom billion' – the world's poorest people – 'cause a disproportionate share of environmental degradation' (Myers, 1993, p. 23).

This demand-driven model neglects the supply side of environmental quality. We know that the global North's share of world income – and hence of world production and consumption – far exceeds that of the global South. In the year 2000, those countries with the richest 20 percent of the world's population, in terms of per capita incomes, accounted for 67 times as much income as the countries with the poorest 20 percent. The ratio narrows when computed on the basis of purchasing-power parity (PPP), but even then the average income of the richest quintile exceeded that of the poorest quintile by a ratio of 16 to 1 (Sutcliffe, 2003, p. 10).

Environmental degradation per unit of income may vary across countries or income classes. If degradation were sufficiently concave in income, the poorest quintile in theory could generate more environmental degradation than the richest quintile. But merely to *equal* the degradation generated by the top quintile, the environmental degradation per unit of PPP-adjusted income in the bottom quintile would have to be 16 times greater. Such a disparity seems improbable. In some respects, at least, environmental degradation per unit of income may even be greater for the rich. Contrast, for example, the pollution generated by automobiles compared to bicycles, the amount of non-renewable resources used to produce a bushel of grain in the USA compared to India, or the pollution generated in the production and disposal of synthetic as opposed to natural fibers.

If there is indeed a gradient along which certain aspects of environmental quality are better in the South than in the North, then an optimistic view of globalization is that it will promote the 'greening of the North' (Sachs et al., 1998). This is akin to the ecological modernization school of thought in that it emphasizes possibilities for harmonization upward, but with the difference that it reverses the relative positions of North and South.

Broadly speaking, there are two routes by which greening of the North could come about. The first is via reductions in northern consumption levels, a change that could be brought about by either falling incomes or a shift in preferences away from goods in favor of leisure, as advocated by the 'voluntary simplicity' movement in the USA. There is little historical precedent, however, for expecting either to happen on a meaningful scale in the foreseeable future.

The second is via transformations of production and consumption that reduce environmental degradation per unit of income. This is the sort of change envisioned by the ecological modernization school, but in this scenario it is the North that 'catches up' with the South in terms of environmental practices.

Several recent trends in agriculture in the industrialized countries illustrate this possibility. In the USA, for example, organically grown products are now the fastest-growing segment of the food market, with sales rising at more than 20 percent annually in the past decade (Dimitri and Greene, 2002). Urban agriculture and community-supported agriculture have also grown substantially, and even when these are not 'organic' (in the sense of zero use of agrochemicals), they minimize negative externalities in transportation, as well as generating positive externalities in the form of community amenities (Pinderhughes, 2003). On a related front, the 'slow food' movement that originated in Italy in the late 1980s is promoting the conservation and revival of traditional agricultural practices (Petrini, 2003).[13] Such 'greening of the North' is by no means a uniform process, however: it has come about partly as a reaction against other features of globalization, such as the use of genetically modified organisms in agriculture and the spread of multinational fast-food restaurant chains.

Environmental imperialism
In the final convergence scenario, globalization undermines relatively clean, sustainable production in the global South. I term this 'environmental imperialism' to evoke the parallel with economic and political subordination of South to North. Here I illustrate this possibility by means of two examples: the displacement of jute by polypropylene, and the displacement of Mexican maize by US maize.

Jute versus polypropylene   Since World War II, international markets for renewable natural raw materials such as cotton, jute, sisal and rubber have faced increasingly tough competition from synthetic substitutes.[14] The former are produced mainly in the global South, the latter mainly in the global North. While the production of natural raw materials can have substantial negative environmental impacts (as in the case of pesticide-intensive cotton cultivation), in general synthetics entail greater environmental costs. The competition between jute and polypropylene is a case in point.

Jute, traditionally used to produce hessian (burlap) cloth and carpet backing, is the second most important natural fiber in world trade after cotton. In the late 1960s, stimulated by US military orders for sandbags for the Vietnam War, polypropylene began to compete with jute. Between 1970 and 1992, jute imports to North America and Western Europe plummeted from 1.0 million to 52 000 metric tons, and jute's real price fell by 70 percent (Boyce, 1995). This collapse hit particularly hard the incomes of small farmers and agricultural laborers in Bangladesh, the world's premier jute-exporting country.

The environmental impacts of jute production are modest. Bangladeshi farmers use only modest amounts of chemical fertilizers and little pesticide on the crop. The country's flooded jute fields support diverse fish populations, an important positive externality for rural people. Like all plants, jute sequesters atmospheric carbon, a further positive externality. At the end of the product life cycle, jute biodegrades in the soil.

Polypropylene, jute's main competitor, is manufactured by multinational petrochemical firms. The USA is the world's leading producer. Polypropylene production generates emissions of numerous air pollutants, including particulates, sulfur oxides, nitrogen oxides, carbon monoxide, volatile organic compounds, and other toxins, in addition to carbon dioxide. Since it is not biodegradable, polypropylene generates further environmental costs in the form of landfill disposal, incineration, or litter at the end of the product life cycle.

The price advantage that has helped polypropylene to displace jute arises in no small measure from the failure of market prices to internalize environmental costs.[15] The result of the global competition between the two has been the displacement of a relatively 'green' southern product by a relatively 'brown' northern product. Even within Bangladesh, plastic shopping bags have begun to replace jute ones.

Maize: Mexico versus the USA   Maize is the leading crop in both Mexico and the USA. Competition between producers in the two countries has intensified in recent years, as the Mexican government has cut support to small farmers and lowered maize tariffs.

Mexico is the historic center of origin of maize, and the modern center of the genetic diversity in the crop. In the hilly lands of southern and central Mexico, campesino farmers grow thousands of different varieties of maize in small plots that botanists call 'evolutionary gardens' (Wilkes, 1992). On these farms, the maize plant continues to evolve with the assistance of the human hand – in the process Darwin called 'artificial selection' – in response to climate change and newly emerging strains of pests and plant diseases. The campesinos thus provide a valuable positive externality to humankind – the *in situ* conservation and evolution of genetic diversity in one of our main food crops.

In the USA, fewer than a dozen varieties account for half of total acreage under maize. Only a few hundred varieties, many of them closely related, are commercially available. The crop therefore suffers from genetic vulnerability – the eggs-in-one-basket syndrome – a problem dramatically revealed in 1970 when a new strain of leaf blight destroyed one-fifth of the nation's corn harvest. In the effort to remain a step ahead of evolving pests and pathogens, US plant breeders run a 'varietal relay race', constantly developing new varieties that incorporate resistance to new threats. The average commercial lifespan of a US corn variety is only seven years. The raw material for this race is the genetic diversity found in the evolutionary gardens of traditional agriculture.

By the measuring stick of market prices, US farmers are more 'efficient' than their Mexican counterparts. Before NAFTA, US maize sold at roughly $110/tonne at the border, whereas Mexican growers received $240/tonne. Several factors contribute to the price advantage of US corn: (i) natural conditions such as better soils, more regular rainfall, and a killing frost that limits pest populations; (ii) farm subsidies that reduce US market prices; (iii) the externalization of environmental costs, such as groundwater contamination by pesticides; and (iv) the failure of market prices to internalize the value of sustaining genetic diversity provided by Mexican farmers.[16]

Since NAFTA took effect, Mexican imports of US corn have risen from less than 1 million tonnes/year to more than 5 million tonnes/year. Meanwhile the price of maize in Mexico has fallen by more than 70 percent.[17] If these trends persist, they are likely to accelerate genetic erosion – the loss of intra-specific diversity – in the crop.[18]

Some comfort can be taken from the fact that samples of many Mexican maize varieties are stored in 'seed banks' at agricultural research institutes in Mexico and elsewhere. But seed banks are insecure, subject to the perennial hazards of underfunding, accidents and war. Most of the maize stored in the world's single largest collection, at the Vavilov Institute in St Petersburg, today is believed to be non-viable due to inadequate maintenance. Moreover, having seeds 'in the bank' is not the same as knowing about varietal properties such as pest resistance and climate sensitivity, information that is most readily obtained in the field. And even at best, seed banks can conserve only the existing stock of genetic diversity; they cannot replicate the ongoing process of evolution that takes place in the farmers' fields.[19]

As in the case of jute and polypropylene, the competition between Mexican and US maize pits relatively 'green' production in the South against relatively 'brown' production in the North. If we view globalization through a long-term lens, looking back to the era of colonialism and the Industrial Revolution, this may have been the more common type of race to the environmental bottom.

Environmental polarization
Rather than convergence, globalization instead could promote polarization: widening disparities in environmental quality across countries. The most likely polarization scenario, discussed in this section, would combine environmental improvements in the global North together with increasing environmental degradation in the global South. Regardless of whether a 'green' North and 'brown' South is a good description of the current situation, it could be a prediction of where the world is headed.

The impacts of pollution and natural resource depletion are often concentrated in specific localities. This fact opens possibilities for 'environmental cost shifting' so as to separate those who benefit from an economic activity from those who bear its external costs (Opschoor, 1992, p. 36). Globalization increases possibilities for environmental cost shifting by widening the spatial distance across which economic interactions take place. It also can widen what can be termed the 'social distance' between the beneficiaries of cost externalization and those who bear these costs, making the latter less able to influence the actions of the former. The likelihood of polarization hinges on whether globalization also promotes countervailing forces, such as the development of global civil-society networks, which offset these effects by reducing social distance.

To frame the discussion, I begin this section with a brief overview of the political economy of environmental degradation. In contrast to the neoclassical treatment of environmental problems as simply a result of missing markets and impersonal governance failures, political economy suggests that the identities of those who gain and lose by virtue of cost externalization help to determine the extent of corrective action undertaken by institutions of governance. I then review evidence on the impact of power disparities within countries on the magnitude of environmental degradation. I then turn to the impacts of globalization on prospects for environmental cost shifting.

Political economy of environmental degradation

Environmentally degrading economic activities generally involve winners who benefit from these activities as well as losers who bear their costs. Without winners, the activities would not occur. Without losers, their environmental impacts would not matter from the standpoint of human well-being.

In analyzing the dynamics of environmental degradation, we can therefore ask why it is that the winners are able to impose environmental costs on the losers. When market failures take the form of environmental externalities, why do the institutions of governance fail to remedy them? There are three possible reasons:

1. The losers may belong to future generations who are not here to defend themselves. In such cases, the only remedy for governance failure is a social commitment to an ethic of intergenerational responsibility.
2. The losers may lack adequate information as to the extent or sources of environmental burdens. It is often difficult, for example, to link health problems to pollution, and to track pollution to its source. In such cases, environmental education and right-to-know legislation are crucial elements of a solution.
3. The losers may lack sufficient power to alter the behavior of the winners. In such cases, a change in the balance of power between winners and losers is a necessary condition for greater environmental protection.

Here I focus on the third explanation – power disparities – since this is most directly affected by globalization.

In the past two decades, a growing body of literature has documented the uneven distribution of environmental burdens within countries, and their correlation with disparities in political power. In the USA, studies of 'environmental justice' have shown that communities with lower incomes and higher percentages of racial and ethnic minorities tend to face disproportionate environmental hazards.[20] For example, even when controlling for income, Ash and Fetter (2004) find that African Americans tend to reside not only in metropolitan areas with above-average levels of point-source air pollution, but also in localities that have higher-than-average pollution levels for the metropolitan area.

In their analysis of informal regulation in Indonesia, Pargal and Wheeler (1996) similarly find that communities with lower-than-average incomes and educational attainments tend to have higher levels of industrial water pollution, even after controlling for other variables such as the volume of output and the age of nearby factories. They attribute this to differences in the 'implicit price' of pollution, which they define as 'the expected penalty or compensation exacted by the affected community'. Following this logic, Hettige et al. (2000, p. 452) write that 'cost-minimizing firms with flexible abatement choices will control pollution to the point where their marginal abatement costs equal the "price" exacted for pollution by the affected parties'. The latter may include local communities, government officials, non-governmental organizations, stockholders and consumers – all parties who are 'in a position to impose some cost on a firm or plant if its emissions exceed the norms adopted by that group'. The resulting 'price' of pollution varies across localities.

Pollutees (those who bear costs from environmental degradation) can influence the decisions of polluters in two broad ways. The first is when their well-being enters directly into the polluters' utility function. This can be termed internalization through sympathy.

Following Sen (1975, p. 23), we can represent the degree of sympathy by means of a para-meter, h, that indicates the weight placed on the well-being of others relative to one's own well-being. When $h_i = 0$, the polluter is indifferent to the well-being of the ith individual. When $h_i = 1$, the polluter values impacts on the ith individual the same as impacts on oneself. If $h_i = 1$ for all i individuals impacted by pollution, there is full internalization.

The second way pollutees can influence the decisions of polluters is through the polit-ical process. This can be termed internalization through governance, with governance understood to encompass both formal and informal rules that constrain behavior. Like sympathy, the ability of pollutees to use governance to alter the behavior of polluters is a matter of degree. Let the parameter π_i represent the power of the ith individual to affect social decisions regarding pollution. Where $\pi_i = 0$ for all pollutees, the 'price' of pollution (set implicitly by informal regulation or formal standards, or explicitly by pollution taxes or tradable permits) is likewise zero.

More generally, we can describe environmental governance outcomes as following a power-weighted social decision rule (Boyce, 2002, chs 4,6):

$$\max \sum_i \pi_i b_i$$

where b_i = the net benefit that individual i derives from an environmentally degrading activity (net cost if $b_i < 0$).[21] Where the power of those who benefit – as producers via higher incomes, or as consumers via lower prices – exceeds the power of those who bear net costs, the social decision rule leads to weaker environmental governance than when the reverse is true. In general, the social decision rule yields outcomes that are 'efficient' in the conventional cost–benefit sense only in the special case where π_i is the same for everyone.

The social distance between the winners and the losers affects both types of internal-ization. As Princen (1997, p. 235) observes, the obscuring of environmental costs and their displacement onto others 'impede ecological and social feedback and create cogni-tive, institutional, and ethical lags between initial benefits and eventual full costs'. When those who benefit from polluting activities do not have any social ties to those who bear the costs – when they do not know them, or see them, or perhaps even know that they exist – there is little scope for internalization through sympathy. When the winners are very powerful relative to the losers, the scope for internalization through governance is corre-spondingly limited.

Power disparities and the environment
The power-weighted social decision rule generates two testable hypotheses. The first is that the distribution of environmental burdens is correlated with power-related variables such as income, education, race and ethnicity. Communities whose residents are poorer, less educated, or belong to historically marginalized racial and ethnic groups will tend to bear greater burdens than communities whose residents are affluent, well educated, or belong to historically dominant racial and ethnic groups.

As noted above, a substantial empirical literature has emerged on this topic. In general, its findings are broadly consistent with this hypothesis. There is room for debate, as always, regarding causal explanations for observed correlations. Some researchers have suggested, for example, that the inverse relation between average incomes and toxic hazards often found by studies in the USA. may arise not from disproportionate siting of hazardous facilities near low-income neighborhoods, but rather from market dynamics in which low-income people are drawn to these locations by lower property values.[22] This logic would have to be stretched, however, to explain correlations between hazards and race that persist even after controlling for income.[23]

The second hypothesis is that societies with wider power disparities tend to have more environmental degradation. That is, power disparities affect the magnitude of pollution and resource depletion, as well as their distributional incidence. This hypothesis is based on the assumption that there is a positive correlation between net benefits (b_i) and power (π_i), an assumption that seems reasonable in that both are likely to be correlated with wealth.[24]

Empirical studies of this second hypothesis remain scarce, but support for it can be drawn from several recent cross-country studies that have investigated the impact of political variables on environmental performance. These studies were sparked by research suggesting that environmental degradation – or at least some types of it – is concave in income, and that high-income countries have passed a turning point beyond which further income gains are associated with environmental improvements. In an early example, the World Bank (1992, p. 41) reported an inverted U-shaped relationship of this type between atmospheric sulfur dioxide and per capita income.

This relationship has been dubbed the 'environmental Kuznets curve' (EKC), due to its likeness to the original Kuznets curve depicting a relationship between income inequality and per capita income (see Figure 7.2). As in the case of its namesake, the EKC has sometimes been taken to imply that problems that accompany economic growth will be resolved, more or less automatically, by growth itself. Thus Beckerman (1992) writes, 'in the end the best – and probably the only – way to attain a decent environment in most countries is to become rich'.

Notwithstanding the allusion to Kuznets's earlier work on income inequality, few studies of the EKC have examined the relationship between environmental quality and inequalities of income, wealth, or power. Yet combining the two inverted-U curves (and assuming that the income levels at which they reach their turning points are roughly comparable), we can infer a positive correlation between environmental degradation and income inequality, as depicted in Figure 7.2. Such a correlation does not prove causation, of course, but it is intriguing. And because the curves themselves (when found to exist at all) are statistical relationships, rather than iron laws, there are many outliers – for example, countries with relatively low income inequality and low per capita income – making it possible to attempt to distinguish econometrically between the environmental impacts of income and inequality.

To investigate the impacts of power disparities on environmental quality, Torras and Boyce (1998) analyzed cross-country variations in air pollution (ambient concentrations of sulfur dioxide, smoke and heavy particles), water pollution (concentrations of dissolved oxygen and fecal coliform), and the percentages of the population with access to safe water and sanitation facilities. In addition to per capita income and the Gini ratio of income distribution, their analysis included two other explanatory variables – adult literacy and an index of political rights and civil liberties – regarded as relevant to the distribution of power. In low-income countries, the estimated coefficients on the rights and literacy variables had the expected signs in all cases: higher literacy and greater rights were associated with better environmental quality. These coefficients were statistically significant in the majority of cases. Controlling for these other variables, the estimated

(a) The 'Kuznets curve'

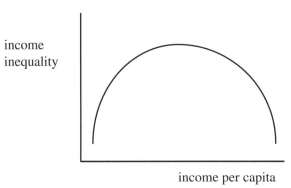

(b) The 'environmental Kuznets curve'

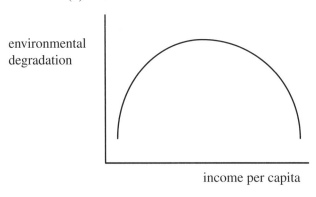

(c) Environment–inequality relation

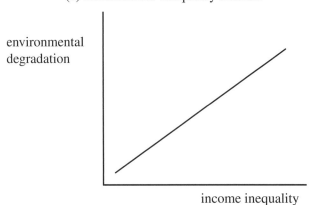

Figure 7.2   Environmental degradation, income inequality and per capita income

effects of income inequality were inconsistent, and the authors suggest that either rights and literacy capture more important aspects of power disparities or the quality of the income distribution data is poor (or both).[25] They obtain weaker results for the high-income countries, suggesting that rights and literacy are most important when average incomes are low.

Other cross-country studies have also suggested that political rights can be an important determinant of environmental outcomes. Scruggs (1998) found greater rights to have a statistically significant favorable effect on sulfur dioxide concentrations, favorable but weaker effects on particulates and fecal coliform pollution, and an adverse effect on dissolved oxygen. Barrett and Graddy (2000) found air pollution by sulfur dioxide, smoke and particulates to be 'monotonically decreasing in the extent of democratic freedoms'; for water pollutants, they found statistically significant favorable effects in the cases of fecal coliform, arsenic and lead. Harbaugh et al. (2000) also found a strong statistical relationship between an index representing democratic participation in government and atmospheric concentrations of sulfur dioxide, smoke and particulates.

Further empirical support for the hypothesis that power disparities have an adverse impact on environmental quality comes from a cross-sectional study of the 50 US states by Boyce et al. (1999). The authors derived a power-distribution index from state-level data on voter participation, tax fairness, access to health care and educational attainment. In a recursive econometric model, they found that states with more equitable distributions of power had stronger environmental policies, and that these in turn were associated with better environmental quality.

Globalization and environmental cost shifting
As globalization extends the arena for environmental cost shifting, the profound inequalities in the worldwide distribution of power and wealth become more relevant to the political economy of environmental degradation. As Sutcliffe (2003) observes, income inequality at the global level exceeds that at the national level even in the most unequal of countries, such as Brazil and South Africa (with the possible exception of Namibia). This is hardly surprising, since a global measure of inequality puts the richest strata of the population in the global North in the same universe as the poorest strata of the global South. The 'power equivalents' of this income distribution – a phrase coined by Kuznets (1963, p. 49) – may likewise be more unequal globally than at the national level. If so, the foregoing analysis suggests that globalization may lead both to environmental polarization between North and South and to an increase in the total magnitude of environmental degradation worldwide.

Having widened environmentally relevant disparities by putting the global rich and the global poor into the same basket, globalization eventually may reduce these disparities by promoting faster growth in the incomes of the poor than of the rich. But the evidence for such a trend is mixed at best.[26] More promising, perhaps, is the possibility of social developments – the other side of Polanyi's 'double movement' – that increase the political effectiveness of demand for environmental protection in low-income countries. Here too, however, the record to date is not terribly encouraging. While Weidner and Jänicke (2002, p. 440) find some evidence of a global convergence between North and South in environmental policies, at the same time they conclude that capacities for policy implementation have become more unequal, resulting in 'convergence of policies but divergence of outcomes'.

But countervailing forces are set in motion by globalization, too. Advances in telecommunications can shrink social distances, increasing the scope for internalization through sympathy by giving faces and voices to the people who bear environmental costs, and at the same time giving the latter greater access to information and the power that comes with it. Alliances across national boundaries, among local communities, non-governmental organizations (NGOs), workers, shareholders and consumers, can alter balances of power. And as discussed in the next section, the phenomenon of global environmental change – where there is little or no scope for cost shifting – may not only give impetus to global environmental governance, but also create new opportunities for globally egalitarian politics.

To illustrate these opposing forces, consider the rapid growth of industrial shrimp farming in the coastal areas of tropical countries. This has been accompanied by the widespread and often violent appropriation of land and aquatic resources from local residents, and by adverse environmental impacts on local communities, spurring polarization (Stonich and Vandergeest, 2001). At the same time, however, the spread of shrimp farms has sparked international alliances of environmental and peasant-based NGOs that defend and reassert community rights to natural assets (Stonich and Bailey, 2000). Similarly, export markets for beef, timber and minerals have been a major stimulus to Amazonian deforestation. Again, international alliances have emerged to support local people who traditionally have relied on the forest for their livelihoods. These were instrumental in the creation of extractive reserves in Brazil, where local communities have secured their right to harvest latex and other forest products while preventing forest clearing (Hall, 1997). As these examples suggest, globalization not only poses risks of environmental polarization and increased environmental degradation, but also creates opportunities for countervailing forces.

Concluding remarks
This chapter has viewed globalization as a process of economic integration that embraces governance as well as markets. In principle, the globalization of governance can counter adverse environmental impacts arising from the globalization of market failure that accompanies the integration of world markets. But there is nothing automatic about this outcome – it rests on human agency, and on balances of power between those who stand to gain and lose from environmental governance.

In assessing the effects of globalization, my main focus has been its impacts on environmental quality in the global North and global South. Closely related to this, however, is a concern with impacts on human well-being. Environmentalists tend to conflate the two, seeing current and future human well-being as dependent on environmental quality. Economists tend to emphasize the tradeoffs that can and do arise between environmental quality and the satisfaction of other human needs and wants. Such tradeoffs pose the positive question of how they are made in practice, as well as the normative question of how they ought to be made. I have suggested above that both questions are intimately bound up with the issue of interpersonal tradeoffs in the well-being of different people.

With respect to the positive question of how societies choose to make tradeoffs, I have suggested that these are guided by a power-weighted social decision rule, in which benefits and costs are weighed by the power of those to whom they accrue. This leads to the hypotheses that power disparities affect the distributional incidence of environmental degradation and its overall magnitude.[27] As noted, there is a growing body of empirical literature that has reported findings consistent with these hypotheses.

With respect to the normative question of how societies ought to make tradeoffs, I have noted the important difference between the wealth-based approach used in conventional cost–benefit analysis, in which values are conditioned by ability and willingness to pay, and a rights-based approach in which all individuals have equal entitlements to a clean and safe environment. As I have discussed at greater length elsewhere, these two approaches can have quite different prescriptive implications.[28] Under the wealth-based approach, for example, if globalization were to promote environmental polarization, in which improvements in the North were coupled with increasing environmental degradation in the South, this might be argued to be welfare maximizing; indeed, in the extreme case, pollution imposed on people who have no ability to pay to avoid it is regarded as costless. Under a rights-based approach, environmental costs and benefits are not weighed by the purchasing power of those to whom they accrue. The normative stance that ultimately is adopted by formal and informal institutions for environmental governance will have profound implications for how globalization affects both the distribution of power and access to environmental quality.

This chapter has questioned several tenets of conventional thinking about the environmental impacts of globalization. I have argued that the assumption that production practices in the global North are environmentally superior to those in the global South – shared by many champions and critics of globalization alike – can be quite misleading, and can lead to the neglect of important environmental issues. I have maintained that globalization can promote environmental convergence via 'harmonization upward', as argued by its proponents, and via a 'race to the bottom', as argued by its opponents, but that neither outcome is assured on *a priori* grounds. I have also noted that instead of convergence, globalization could foster environmental polarization – 'greening' the North and 'browning' the South. Whether this occurs will depend on the extent to which those who face environmental burdens are able to take advantage of new opportunities to bridge social distances and narrow power disparities, so as to promote internalization through sympathy and governance.

The environmental impacts of globalization not only remain to be seen; they remain to be determined. The outcome will not be dictated by an inexorable logic. Rather it will depend on how the new opportunities created by the globalization of markets and governance alter balances of power, both within countries and among them. As its critics fear, globalization could accelerate worldwide environmental degradation and deepen environmental inequalities. Yet globalization also gives impetus to countervailing forces that could bring about a greener and less divided world. The history of the future is still to be written.

Notes

* An earlier version of this chapter was published as 'Green and brown? Globalization and the environment', in the *Oxford Review of Economic Policy*, **20**(1), 2004.
1. Senator John Chafee, quoted in Behr (1993).
2. 'Sabotage of America's Health, Food & Safety, and Environmental Laws', advertisement in *The Washington Post*, 14 December 1992, by the Sierra Club, Greenpeace USA, Friends of the Earth, and others; quoted in Commission for Environmental Cooperation (1996, p. 29).
3. For discussion, see below.
4. See, for example, Barrett (2000), who also points out that there may be differences between harmonization of emission standards and harmonization of environmental quality standards.

5. See Boyce (2000), reprinted in Boyce (2002, ch. 2).
6. Thus Mol (2001, p. 211) writes that economic mechanisms 'will always fall short in fully articulating environmental interests and pushing environmental reforms, if they are not constantly paralleled and propelled by environmental institutions and environmental movements'.
7. Both community pressure and firm responsiveness may differ when foreign firms outsource to unbranded suppliers. In a study of northern Mexico, Gallagher (2004) found that outsourcing by US firms had adverse environmental impacts.
8. For examples, see Conroy (2007).
9. There is an obvious analogy with labor standards; see Singh and Zammit (2004). Indeed environmental protectionism is sometimes depicted by its critics as a smokescreen for other protectionist interests (see, e.g., Bhagwati, 1993).
10. 'Ecological dumping' need not be intentional. Rauscher (1994, p. 825) proposes a more restrictive definition: 'a scenario in which environmental standards are tighter in the non-tradables than in the tradables sector.' While this comes closer to the notion of dumping as a deliberate instrument of trade policy, it is possible that inter-sectoral disparities in environmental standards are not wholly intentional. In any event, proponents of environmental protectionism are more concerned with the effects of ecological dumping than its causes.
11. Low and Yeats (1992) found a rising share of pollution-intensive exports from developing countries (particularly in Southeast Asia) in the period 1965-88, albeit from a fairly small base. Extending this analysis to the period 1992–2000, Bouvier (2003) finds that this trend has continued, with some Eastern European countries also emerging as major exporters.
12. If this is accompanied by declining terms of trade for environment-intensive products, the result could be both 'environmental improvement and economic growth in the North and environmental deterioration and economic stagnation in the South' (Muradian and Martinez-Alier, 2001, p. 286).
13. See also http://www.slowfood.com/.
14. Maizels (1992, p. 189; 1995, p. 108) reports that substitution by synthetics reduced the developed market-economy countries' consumption of natural raw materials by 2.9 percent per year from 1963–65 to 1971–73, 0.9% per year from 1971–73 to 1978–80, and 1.2 percent per year from 1978–80 to 1984–86.
15. For details, see Boyce (1995).
16. For further discussion, see Boyce (1996).
17. For accounts of the social impacts in rural Mexico, see Weiner (2002) and Becker (2003).
18. So far, however, relatively few *campesinos* appear to have abandoned maize cultivation, in part because of the lack of other economic opportunities; see Ackerman et al. (2003).
19. For further discussion of the value of *in situ* (in-the-field) crop genetic diversity, see Brush (2000) and Thrupp (1998).
20. For literature surveys, see Bullard (1994), Szasz and Meuser (1997), Bowen (2001) and Pastor (2003).
21. 'Power' here plays a role analogous to that of 'influence' in Becker's (1983) model of fiscal policy.
22. See, e.g., Been (1994). In a longitudinal study in southern California, one of the few to examine empirically the siting versus 'move-in' question, Pastor et al. (2001) found strong evidence of disproportionate siting.
23. See, for example, Bouwes *et al.* (2003) and Ash and Fetter (2002).
24. Where b_i and π_i are negatively correlated, the result will be 'too little' environmental degradation, by the usual efficiency standard, rather than too much. For discussion, see Boyce (2002, pp. 37–38, 51).
25. For further discussion of the impacts of income inequality on environmental quality, see Boyce (2007).
26. For a review of the evidence, see Sutcliffe (2003).
27. As noted above, the power of those who bear environmental costs relative to those who benefit from cost externalization can also be described in terms of their ability to put an implicit or explicit 'price' on environmental degradation.
28. See Boyce (2002, chs 2 and 4).

References

Ackerman, Frank et al. (2003), 'Free trade, corn, and the environment: environmental impacts of US–Mexico corn trade under NAFTA', Global Development and Environment Institute Working Paper 03-06, Medford, MA: Tufts University, http://ase.tufts.edu/gdae/Pubs/wp/03-06-NAFTACorn.PDF.
Ash, Michael and T. Robert Fetter (2004), 'Who lives on the wrong side of the environmental tracks? Evidence from the EPA's risk-screening environmental indicators model', *Social Science Quarterly*, **85**(2), 441–62.
Barrett, Scott (2000), 'Trade and environment: local versus multilateral reforms', *Environment and Development*

Economics, **5**, 349–59.

Barrett, Scott and Kathryn Graddy (2000), 'Freedom, growth, and the environment', *Environment and Development Economics*, **5**, 433–56.

Becker, Elizabeth (2003), 'U.S. corn subsidies said to damage Mexico', *New York Times*, 27 August.

Becker, Gary (1983), 'A theory of competition among pressure groups for political influence', *Quarterly Journal of Economics*, **48**, 371–400.

Beckerman, Wilfred (1992), 'Economic growth and the environment: whose growth? Whose environment?', *World Development*, **20**, 481–96.

Been, Vicki (1994), 'Locally undesirable land uses in minority neighborhoods: disproportionate siting or market dynamics', *Yale Law Journal*, **103**, 1383–22.

Bhagwati, Jagdish (1993), 'The case for free trade', *Scientific American*, November, 41–9.

Bouvier, Rachel (2003), 'Three essays on income, inequality, and environmental degradation', PhD dissertation, University of Massachusetts at Amherst.

Bouwes, Nicolaas W., Steven M. Hassur and Marc D. Shapiro (2003), 'Information for empowerment: the EPA's risk-screening environmental indicators project', in James K. Boyce and Barry G. Shelley (eds), *Natural Assets: Democratizing Environmental Ownership*, Washington, DC: Island Press, pp. 117–34.

Bowen, William M. (2001), *Environmental Justice through Research-Based Decision-making*, New York: Garland Publishing.

Boyce, James K. (1995), 'Jute, polypropylene, and the environment: a study in international trade and market failure', *Bangladesh Development Studies*, **23**(1–2), 49–66.

Boyce, James K. (1996), 'Ecological distribution, agricultural trade liberalization, and *In Situ* genetic diversity', *Journal of Income Distribution*, **6**(2), 263–84.

Boyce, James K. (2000), 'Let them eat risk: wealth, rights, and disaster vulnerability', *Disasters*, **24**(3), 254–61.

Boyce, James K. (2002), The *Political Economy of the Environment*, Cheltenham, UK and Northampton, MA, USA: Edward Elgar.

Boyce, James K. (2007), 'Inequality and environmental protection', in Jean-Marie Baland, Pranab Bardhan and Samuel Bowles (eds), *Inequality, Collective Action, and Environmental Sustainability*, Princeton, NJ: Princeton University Press, pp. 314–48.

Boyce, James K., Andrew R. Klemer, Paul H. Templet and Cleve E. Willis (1999), 'Power distribution, the environment, and public health: A state-level analysis', *Ecological Economics*, **29**, 127–40.

Brush, Stephen B. (2000), 'The issues of *in situ* conservation of crop genetic resources', in Stephen B. Brush (ed.), *Genes in the Field: On-Farm Conservation of Crop Diversity*, Boca Raton FL: Lewis Publishers, pp. 3–26.

Bullard, Robert D. (ed.) (1994), *Unequal Protection: Environmental Justice and Communities of Color*, San Francisco, CA: Sierra Club Books.

Commission for Environmental Cooperation (1996), *Potential NAFTA Effects: Claims and Arguments, 1991–94*, Environment and Trade Series, 2, Montreal: CEC. http://www.cec.org/files/pdf/ECONOMY/claimse_EN.pdf.

Conroy, Michael (2007), *Branded! How the 'Certification Revolution' is Transforming Global Corporations*, Vancouver, Canada: New Society Publishers.

Daly, Herman (1993), 'The perils of free trade', *Scientific American*, November, 50–57.

Dimitri, Carolyn and Catherine Greene (2002), *Recent Growth Patterns in the U.S. Organic Foods Market*, Agriculture Information Bulletin Number 777, Washington, DC: US Department of Agriculture, Economic Research Service, Market and Trade Economics Division and Resource Economics Division.

The Economist (1992), 'Let them eat pollution', *The Economist*, **8** (February), 66.

Gallagher, Kevin P. (2004), *Free Trade and the Environment: Mexico, NAFTA, and Beyond*, Stanford, CA: Stanford University Press.

Hall, Anthony (1997), *Sustaining Amazonia: Grassroots Action for Productive Conservation*, Manchester, UK: Manchester University Press.

Harbaugh, William, Arik Levinson and David Wilson (2000), '*Reexamining the empirical evidence for an environmental Kuznets curve*', Working Paper 7711, Cambridge, MA: National Bureau of Economic Research.

Hettige, H., M. Mani and D. Wheeler (2000), 'Industrial pollution in economic development: the environmental Kuznets curve revisited', *Journal of Development Economics*, **62**, 445–76.

Hogenboom, Barbara (1998), *Mexico and the NAFTA Environment Debate: The Transnational Politics of Economic Integration*, Utrecht, The Netherlands: International Books.

Jaffe, Adam. B. et al (1995), 'Environmental regulation and the competitiveness of U.S. manufacturing: what does the evidence tell us?', *Journal of Environmental Literature*, **33**(1), 132–63.

Keenan, Karyn, Jose de Echave and Ken Traynor (2007), 'Mining rights and community rights: poverty amidst wealth', in James K. Boyce, Sunita Narian and Elizabeth A. Stanton (eds), *Reclaiming Nature: Environmental*

Justice and Ecological Restoration, London and Chicago, IL: Anthem Press, pp. 181–202.

Kuznets, Simon (1963), 'Quantitative aspects of the economic growth of nations', *Economic Development and Cultural Change*, **11** (2/II), 1–80.

Low, Patrick and Alexander Yeats (1992), 'Do "dirty" industries migrate?', in P. Low (ed.), *International Trade and the Environment*, Washington, DC: World Bank Discussion Paper 159.

Maizels, A. (1992), *Commodities in Crisis: The Commodity Crisis of the 1980s and the Political Economy of International Commodity Prices*, Oxford: Clarendon Press.

Maizels, A. (1995), 'The functioning of international markets for primary commodities: key policy issues for developing countries', in UNCTAD, *International Monetary and Financial Issues for the 1990s: Research Papers for the Group of Twenty-Four*, Volume V, New York and Geneva: UN, pp. 81–114.

Mol, Arthur P.J. (2001), *Globalization and Environmental Reform: The Ecological Modernization of the Global Economy*, Cambridge, MA: MIT Press.

Muradian, Roldan and Joan Martinez-Alier (2001), 'Trade and the environment: from a "southern" perspective', *Ecological Economics*, **36**, 281–97.

Myers, Norman (1993), *Ultimate Security: The Environmental Basis of Political Stability*, New York: Norton.

Neumayer, Eric (2002), 'Do democracies exhibit stronger international environmental commitment? A cross-country analysis', *Journal of Peace Research*, **39**(2), 139–64.

Opschoor, Johannes B. (1992), 'Sustainable development, the economic process and economic analysis', in J.B. Opschoor (ed.), *Environment, Economy and Sustainable Development*, Amsterdam: Wolters-Noordhoff, pp. 25–52.

Pargal, Sheoli and David Wheeler (1996), 'Informal regulations in developing countries: evidence from Indonesia', *Journal of Political Economy*, **104**(6), 1314–27.

Pargal, Sheoli et al. (1997), 'Formal and informal regulation of industrial pollution: comparative evidence from Indonesia and the United States', *World Bank Economic Review*, **11**(3), 433–50.

Pastor, Manuel (2003), 'Building social capital to protect natural capital: the quest for environmental justice', in James K. Boyce and Barry G. Shelley (eds), *Natural Assets: Democratizing Environmental Ownership*, Washington, DC: Island Press, pp. 77–97.

Pastor, Manuel, Jim Sadd and John Hipp (2001), 'Which came first? Toxic facilities, minority move-in, and environmental justice', *Journal of Urban Affairs*, **23**, 1–21.

Petrini, Carlo (ed.) (2003), *Slow Food*, New York: Columbia University Press.

Pinderhughes, Raquel (2003), 'Poverty and the environment: the urban agriculture connection', in James K. Boyce and Barry G. Shelley (eds), *Natural Assets: Democratizing Environmental Ownership*, Washington, DC: Island Press, pp. 299–312.

Porter, Gareth (1999), 'Trade competition and pollution standards: "race to the bottom" or "stuck at the bottom"?', *Journal of Environment and Development*, **8**(2), 133–51.

Princen, Thomas (1997), 'The shading and distancing of commerce: when internalization is not enough', *Ecological Economics*, **20**, 235–53.

Rauscher, Michael (1994), 'On ecological dumping', *Oxford Economic Papers*, **46**, 822–40.

Sachs, Wolfgang et al. (1998), *Greening the North: Post-Industrial Blueprint for Ecology and Equity*, London: Zed.

Scruggs, Lyle A. (1998), 'Political and economic inequality and the environment', *Ecological Economics*, **26**, 259–75.

Sen, Amartya (1975), *Employment, Technology, and Development*, Oxford: Oxford University Press.

Singh, Ajit and Ann Zammit (2004), 'Labour standards and the "race to the bottom": rethinking globalization and workers' rights from developmental and solidaristic principles', *Oxford Review of Economic Policy*, **20**, 85–104.

Spaargaren, Gert and Arthur P.J. Mol (1992), 'Sociology, environment, and modernity: ecological modernisation as a theory of social change', *Society and Natural Resources*, **5**, 323–44.

Stonich, Susan and Conner Bailey (2000), 'Resisting the blue revolution: Contending Coalitions surrounding industrial shrimp farming', *Human Organization*, **59**(1), 23–36.

Stonich, Susan and Peter Vandergeest (2001), 'Violence, environment, and industrial shrimp farming', in Michael Watts and Nancy Peluso (eds), *Violent Environments*, Ithaca, NY: Cornell University Press, pp. 261–86.

Sutcliffe, Bob (2003), 'A more or less unequal world? World income distribution in the 20th century', Working Paper No. 54, Amherst, MA: Political Economy Research Institute, available at: http://www.umass.edu/peri/pdfs/WP54.pdf.

Szasz, Andrew and Michael Meuser (1997), 'Environmental inequalities: literature review and proposals for new directions in research and theory', *Current Sociology*, **45**(3), 99–120.

Thrupp, Lori Ann (1998), *Cultivating Diversity: Agrobiodiversity and Food Security*, Washington, DC: World Resources Institute.

Torras, Mariano and James K. Boyce (1998), 'Income, inequality, and pollution: a reassessment of the environmental Kuznets curve', *Ecological Economics*, **25**, 147–60.

Weale, A. (1992), *The New Politics of Pollution*, Manchester, UK: Manchester University Press.

Weidner, Helmut and Martin Jänicke (2002), 'Environmental capacity building in a converging world', in H. Weidner and M. Jänicke (eds), *Capacity Building in National Environmental Policy: A Comparative Study of 17 Countries*, Berlin: Springer, pp. 409–43.

Weiner, Tim (2002), 'In corn's cradle, U.S. imports bury family farms', *New York Times*, 26 February, p. A4.

Wilkes, H. Garrison (1992), *Strategies for Sustaining Crop Germplasm Preservation, Enhancement, and Use*, Washington, DC: Consultative Group for International Agricultural Research.

World Bank (1992), *World Development Report 1992: Development and the Environment*, Oxford: Oxford University Press.

Zarsky, Lyuba (1997), 'Stuck in the mud? Nation-states, globalization and the environment', Paper prepared for the Globalization and Environment Study, The Hague: OECD Economics Division, May. Available at: http://www.nautilus.org/papers/enviro/zarsky_mud.html.

Zarsky, Lyuba (1999), 'Havens, halos and spaghetti: untangling the evidence about foreign direct investment and the environment', Paper presented at the Conference on Foreign Direct Investment and the Environment, The Hague: OECD Environment Directorate, January. Available at: http://www.nautilus.org/papers/enviro/zarsky_oecdfdi.html.

8   The relation between international trade and water resources management

A.Y. Hoekstra

Unlike oil, water is generally not regarded as a global resource. Whereas in most countries the energy sector has an obvious international component, this is different for the water sector. The international component of water is recognized only in the case of transboundary rivers. The relation between international trade and water management is generally not something that water sector officials think about. The reason is that water is not traded internationally, due to its bulky properties. Besides, there is no private ownership of water, so that it can also not be traded as in a market (Savenije, 2002). Water sector specialists often forget, however, that water is traded in virtual form, i.e. in the form of agricultural and industrial commodities. Although invisible, import of 'virtual water' can be an effective means for water-scarce countries to preserve their domestic water resources (Allan, 2001a).

Water sector specialists do not usually explicitly study the relation between water use and import or export. At the same time, trade specialists and economists engaged in or studying international trade generally do not bother much about the implications of international trade for the water sector. The reason here is that the water inputs generally hardly contribute to the overall price of traded commodities. This seems to justify the conclusion that water cannot be a significant factor influencing trade patterns. The fact that water inputs are generally heavily subsidized by national governments is hereby ignored. Trade specialists also tend to forget that external effects of water use can be very significant, but are never included in the price of water, and that no country charges a scarcity rent for water inputs even though water is sometimes very scarce. When one merely looks at the prices of traded commodities one will indeed get the impression that water scarcity cannot be a driving force of or limiting factor to international trade.

One of the principles widely accepted in water resources management is the subsidiarity principle, according to which water issues should be settled at the lowest community level possible (GWP, 2000). In cases where upstream water users affect downstream users, it has been recognized that it is necessary to take the perspective of a river basin as a whole, considering water as a river-basin resource. Regarding water as a global resource is very uncommon. To illustrate this, read what the Global Water Partnership writes about how to come towards good water resources management (GWP, 2000, pp. 28 and 33):

> In order to achieve efficient, equitable and sustainable water management . . ., a major institutional change will be needed. Both top-down and bottom-up participation of all stakeholders will have to be promoted – from the level of the nation down to the level of a village or a municipality or from the level of a catchment or watershed up to the level of a river basin. The principle of subsidiarity, which drives down action to the lowest appropriate level, will need to be observed.

There is no word about the fact that there might be a global dimension to water management.

Considering water management from a local, national or river-basin perspective is, however, not always sufficient. Many water problems bear an international trade component (Hoekstra and Chapagain, 2008). Subsidized water in Uzbekistan is overused to produce cotton for export; Thailand experiences water problems due to irrigation of rice for export; Kenya depletes its water resources around Lake Naivasha to produce flowers for export to the Netherlands; Chinese rivers get heavily polluted through waste flows from factories that produce cheap commodities for the European market. Not only water problems, but also water solutions have an international trade component. Jordan and various other countries in the Middle East meet their demand for food and save their scarcely available water resources through food imports from overseas. Mediterranean countries will expectedly experience increased water scarcity due to climate change, forcing them into the direction of increased import of water-intensive products. Apparently there are more connections between seemingly local or national water issues and international trade than recognized at first sight.

This chapter reviews current knowledge with respect to three questions:

1.   What is the effect of international trade on domestic water resources?
2.   What is the effect of water availability on international trade?
3.   Can international trade increase global water-use efficiency?

The chapter concludes with a discussion of risks and opportunities associated with the intensification of international trade in water-intensive commodities.

The effect of international trade on domestic water resources
An obvious effect of international trade on water-intensive commodities is that it generates water savings in the countries that import those commodities. This effect has been discussed since the mid-1990s (Allan, 2001b; Hoekstra, 2003). The national water saving associated with import can be estimated by multiplying the imported product volume by the volume of water that would have been required to produce the product domestically. The other side of international trade in water-intensive commodities is that it takes water in the exporting countries that can no longer be used for other (domestic) purposes. Besides, the social and environmental costs that are often associated with water use remain in the exporting countries; they are not included in the price paid for the products by the consumers in the importing countries.

Import of water-intensive commodities reduces national water demand
In many countries international trade in agricultural products effectively reduces domestic water demand. These countries import commodities that are relatively water intensive while they export commodities that are less water intensive. In the period 1997–2001, Japan, the largest (net) importer of water-intensive goods in the world, annually saved 94 billion m^3 from its domestic water resources. This volume of water would have been required, in addition to its current water use, if Japan had produced all imported products domestically. In a similar way, Mexico annually saved 65 billion m^3, Italy 59 billion m^3, China 56 billion m^3 and Algeria 45 billion m^3 (Chapagain et al., 2006).

One of the water-scarce countries that most heavily depends on imports of water-intensive commodities is Jordan. It imports 5 to 7 billion m^3 of water in virtual form per year, which is in sharp contrast with the 1 billion m³ of water withdrawn annually from domestic water sources (Haddadin, 2003; Hoekstra and Chapagain, 2007, 2008). People in Jordan thus survive owing to the fact that their 'water footprint' has largely been externalized to other parts of the world, for example the USA. Intelligent trade largely covers up Jordan's water shortage: export of goods and services that require little water and import of products that need a lot of water. The good side of Jordan's trade balance is that it preserves the scarce domestic water resources; the downside is that the people are heavily water dependent.

For countries that depend on the import of water-intensive products, it is important to know whether the water thus saved has higher marginal benefits than the additional cost involved in importing these products. Let us consider the example of Egypt, a country with a very low rainfall – the mean rainfall is only 18 mm/yr – and with most of its agriculture being irrigated. The import of wheat in Egypt implies a saving of their domestic water resources of 3.6 billion m³/yr, which is about 7 percent of the total volume of water Egypt is entitled to according to the 1959 agreement on the use of the Nile. The national saving is made with the investment of foreign exchange of US$593 million/yr (ITC, 2004), so that the cost of the virtual water is US$0.16/m³ at most. In fact, the cost will be much lower, because the costs of the imported wheat cover not only the cost of water, but also the costs of other input factors such as land, fertilizer and labor. In Egypt, fertile land is also a major scarce resource. The import of wheat not only releases the pressure on the disputed Nile water, but also reduces pressure to increase the area of land under agriculture. Greenaway et al. (1994) and Wichelns (2001) have shown that in the international context Egypt has a comparative disadvantage in the production of wheat, so that the import of wheat into Egypt implies not only a physical water saving, but also an economic saving.

Export of water-intensive commodities raises national water demand
Water is not merely a local resource to meet local demands for water-based products. In the period 1997–2001, 16 percent of world water use was not for producing products for domestic consumption but for making products for export (Hoekstra and Chapagain, 2007; 2008). The nations with the largest net annual water use for producing export products were the USA (92 billion m³), Australia (57 billion m³), Argentina (47 billion m³), Canada (43 billion m³), Brazil (36 billion m³) and Thailand (26 billion m³). The main products behind the national water use for export from the USA were oil-bearing crops and cereal crops. These products are grown partly rain-fed and partly irrigated. In Australia and Canada, the water use for export was mainly related to the production of cereals and livestock products. In Argentina and Brazil, water use for export was primarily for producing oil-bearing crops. The national water use for export in Thailand was mainly the result of export of rice. Much of the rice cultivation in Thailand is done during the rainy season, but irrigation is widespread, to achieve two harvests per year. In the period 1997–2001, Thailand used 27.8 billion m³/yr of water (sum of rainwater and irrigation water) to produce rice for export, mostly grown in the central and northern regions (Maclean et al., 2002). The monetary equivalent of the rice export was US$1556 million/yr (ITC, 2004). Hence Thailand generated a foreign exchange of US$0.06/m³.

Recall that currently 16 percent of the water use in the world is not for producing products for domestic consumption but for making products for export and let us simply assume that, on average, agricultural production for export does not cause significantly more or fewer water-related problems (such as water depletion or pollution) than production for domestic consumption. That means that roughly one-sixth of the water problems in the world can be traced back to production for export. Consumers do not see the effects of their consumption behavior due to the teleconnection between areas of consumption and areas of production. The benefits are on the consumption side, but since water is generally grossly underpriced, the costs remain on the production side. From a water resources point of view it would be wise for the exporting countries in the world to review their water use for export and see to what extent this is good policy given the fact that the foreign income associated with the exports generally does not cover most of the costs associated with the use of water. The construction of dams and irrigation schemes and even operation and maintenance costs are often covered by the national or state government. Negative effects downstream and the social and environmental costs involved are not included in the price of the export products either.

The effect of international trade on local water pollution
International trade brings another phenomenon: natural cycles of nutrients such as nitrogen and phosphorus are disturbed through depletion of the soil in some places, excessive use of fertilizers in others, long-distance transfers of food and animal feed, and concentrated disposal of nutrient-rich wastes in densely populated areas of the world (Grote et al., 2005). This has already led and will further lead to depletion of the soil in some areas (Sanchez, 2002; Stocking, 2003) and eutrophication of water elsewhere (McIsaac et al., 2001; Tilman et al., 2001). The surplus of nutrients in the Netherlands, for instance, is partially related to deforestation, erosion and soil degradation in those areas of the world that export food and feed to the Netherlands, for example in Brazil, which exports large amounts of soybeans for Dutch pigs and chickens. This implies that the nutrient surplus in the Netherlands is not an issue that can simply be understood as a Dutch issue. Dutch water pollution is part of the global economy.

The disturbance of nutrient cycles is not the only mechanism through which international trade influences the quality of water resources worldwide. Meybeck (2004) shows how other substances are also dispersed into the global environment and change the quality of the world's rivers. Nriagu and Pacyna (1988) set out the specific impacts of the use of trace metals in the global economy on the world's water resources. The regular publication of new reports on global pollution shows that this phenomenon in itself is no longer news; what is now gradually being uncovered and is therefore relatively new is the fact that pollution is not simply 'global' because pollution is so 'widespread', but that it is interlinked with how the global economy works and is therefore a true global problem. Water pollution is intertwined with the global economic system to such an extent that it cannot be dealt with independently from that global economy. Indeed, pollution can be tackled by end-of-pipe measures at or near the location of the pollution, but a more cause-oriented approach would be to restructure the (rules for the) global economy, with the aim to close the element cycles.

The effect of water availability on international trade
There is an immense volume of literature on international trade, but few scholars address the question of to what extent international trade is influenced by regional differences in water availability. Rather, international trade is explained in terms of differences in labor

productivities, availability of land, domestic subsidies to agriculture, import taxes, production surpluses and associated export subsidies, etc. It will be hard to find evidence that regional water abundance benefits the export of water-intensive commodities and that regional water scarcity promotes the import of water-intensive commodities.

According to international trade theory that goes back to Ricardo ([1817] 2006), nations can gain from trade if they specialize in the production of goods and services in which they have a comparative advantage, while importing goods and services in which they have a comparative disadvantage. The meaning of the principle for the field of water resources has been elaborated by Wichelns (2004). The economic efficiency of trade in a water-intensive commodity between two countries should be evaluated based on a comparison of the opportunity costs of producing the commodity in each of the trading nations. Export of a water-intensive commodity is attractive if the opportunity cost of producing the commodity is comparatively low. This is the case when there is a relatively high production potential for the water-intensive commodity due to, for example, relative abundance of water and/or a relatively high water productivity (yield per unit of water input) in the country. Import of a water-intensive commodity (instead of producing it domestically) is attractive if the opportunity cost of producing the commodity is comparatively high, for example because water is relatively scarce and/or water productivity in the country is low.

The most convincing research providing evidence that water availability influences international trade has been carried out by Yang et al. (2003; 2007). As they have quantitatively shown, cereal imports have played a crucial role in compensating water deficits in various water-scarce countries. They demonstrate that below a certain threshold in water availability, an inverse relationship can be identified between a country's cereal import and its per capita renewable water resources. In the early 1980s the threshold was at about 2000 m^3 per capita per year. At the end of the 1990s it had declined to about 1500 m^3 per capita per year. Countries with less water than the threshold cannot do without the import of staple foods. The threshold has declined over the past couple of decades due to the improvement in water productivities and the expansion of irrigated areas.

There is clear evidence that the trade balance of countries with very low water availability (per capita) is partly determined by the fact that those countries have a comparative disadvantage in producing water-intensive products. One does not need to be an economist to see that; the available water resources simply fall short in some countries to produce the food to survive. Most international trade in the world, however, has little to do with the intentional trade in water-intensive commodities to countries with low water availability from countries with higher water availability. The driving force behind international trade in water-intensive products may be water scarcity in the importing countries, but more often other factors play a decisive role (Yang et al., 2003; De Fraiture et al., 2004).

International trade in agricultural commodities depends on many more factors than differences in water scarcity in the trading nations, including differences in availability of land, labor, knowledge and capital, and differences in economic productivities in various sectors. The existence of domestic subsidies, export subsidies, or import taxes in the trading nations will also influence the trade pattern. As a consequence, international virtual-water transfers usually cannot – or can only partly – be explained on the basis of differences in water availability and productivity.

In some cases, the relation between water availability and the actual trade pattern is even counter-intuitive. North China, for instance, has a very low availability of water per capita, unlike South China, but nevertheless, there is a very significant trade in food from North to South China (Ma et al., 2006). Of course, this does intensify the water problems in the North. A similar case can be found in India, where water has become relatively scarce in the northern states of Punjab, Uttar Pradesh and Haryana. Nevertheless, these states export significant volumes of food to the eastern states of Bihar, Jharkhand and Orissa, which have much larger water endowments than the northern states (Verma et al., 2008). No simple explanation will suffice to explain the counter-intuitive situations with respect to internal trade within China and India, because various factors will play a role, including historical, political and economic ones. One factor that may play a role as well is that in water-scarce regions the incentives to increase water productivity are highest. As a result, it becomes attractive to produce in those regions, which however enhances the scarcity of the water. This may be a factor in northern India, where water productivities are indeed much higher than in the eastern states, providing them with a comparative advantage although the water availability in absolute terms is much lower.

Global water-use efficiency
In the water sector, the term water-use efficiency is most often used to refer to the inverse of local water productivity. The latter is expressed as the amount of product made per unit of water (in the agricultural sector known as 'crop per drop'). Water-use efficiency is expressed as the volume of water required to make one unit of product. A water user can increase local water-use efficiency by producing the same with less water input. Water users can be encouraged to do so by charging them a water price that is based on full marginal cost, by stimulating them to adopt water-saving technology, or by creating awareness that saving water is good for the environment.

The local view on water-use efficiency is only one way of looking at the subject; there are two other levels at which one can consider the efficiency of water use (Hoekstra and Hung, 2005). At the catchment or river-basin level, water-use efficiency refers to the efficiency of water allocation to alternative uses. Water-use efficiency at this level can be enhanced by reallocating water to purposes with higher marginal benefits (Rogers et al., 1998). At the global level, water-use efficiency can be increased if nations use their comparative advantage or disadvantage in producing water-intensive goods to either encourage or discourage the use of domestic water resources for producing export commodities.

Much research effort has been dedicated to studying water-use efficiency at the local and river-basin levels. The research on global water-use efficiency is of more recent date. Only four studies have been carried out so far, all of them focusing on the quantification of physical water savings as a result of global trade, not on the associated economic savings. All four studies indicate that the current pattern of international trade results in a substantial global water saving (Oki and Kanae, 2004; De Fraiture et al., 2004; Chapagain et al., 2006; Yang et al., 2006).

Volume of water saved as a result of international trade
The most comprehensive study on global water saving in relation to international trade was the one carried out by Chapagain et al. (2006). According to their study, the global water use for producing agricultural products for export amounted to 1250 billion m³/yr (in the

period 1997–2001). If the importing countries were to have produced the imported products domestically they would have required a total of 1600 billion m³/yr. This means that the global water saving by trade in agricultural products was 350 billion m³/yr. So the average water saving accompanying international trade in agricultural products has been (350/1600=) 22 percent. The global volume of water used for agricultural production is 6400 billion m³/yr. Without trade, supposing that all countries had to produce the products domestically, agricultural water use in the world would amount to 6750 instead of 6400 billion m³/yr. International trade thus reduces global water use in agriculture by 5 percent.

The above figures do not differentiate between the use of green water (rainwater) and the use of blue water (ground and surface water). The global water saving associated with a certain trade flow can refer to either a global blue or a global green water saving (or a combination of both). Even if there is a net global water loss from a trade relation, there might be a saving of blue water at the cost of a greater loss of green water or vice versa. From an economic point of view there is a substantial difference between blue and green water saving, because the opportunity costs of blue water are generally much higher than the opportunity costs of green water. As a result, trade with an associated blue water saving but a greater green water loss could still be efficient from an economic point of view.

The downside of virtual-water import as a solution to water scarcity
Saving domestic water resources in countries with relative water scarcity through virtual-water import (import of water-intensive products) looks very attractive. There are, however, a number of drawbacks that have to be taken into account. First, saving domestic water through import should explicitly be seen in the context of the need to generate sufficient foreign exchange to import food that otherwise would be produced domestically. Some water-scarce countries in the world are oil rich, so they can easily afford to import water-intensive commodities. However, many water-scarce countries lack the ability to export energy, services or water-extensive industrial commodities in order to afford the import of water-intensive agricultural commodities. Second, import of food carries the risk of moving away from food self-sufficiency. This plays an important role in the political considerations in countries such as China, India and Egypt. Third, import of food will be bad for the domestic agricultural sector and lead to increased urbanization, because import reduces employment in the agricultural sector. It will also result in an economic decline and worsening of land management in rural areas. Fourth, in many water-scarce developing countries, where an important part of the agriculture consists of subsistence farming, promoting food imports may threaten the livelihoods of those subsistence farmers and reduce access to food for the poor. Finally, increases in virtual-water transfers to optimize the use of global water resources can relieve the pressure on water-scarce countries but may create additional pressure on the countries that produce the water-intensive commodities for export. The potential water saving from global trade is sustainable only if the prices of the export commodities truly reflect the opportunity costs and negative environmental impacts in the exporting countries. Otherwise the importing countries are simply gaining from the fact that they would have had to bear the cost of water depletion if they had produced domestically whereas the costs remain external if they import the water-intensive commodities instead.

Discussion

International transfers of water in virtual form are substantial and likely to increase with continued global trade liberalization (Ramirez-Vallejo and Rogers, 2004). Intensified trade in water-intensive countries offers both opportunities and risks. The most obvious opportunity of reduced trade barriers is that virtual water can be regarded as a possibly cheap alternative source of water in areas where freshwater is relatively scarce. Virtual-water import can be used by national governments as a tool to relieve the pressure on their domestic water resources. This import of virtual water (as opposed to real water, which is generally too expensive) will relieve the pressure on the nation's own water resources. For water-abundant countries an argument can be made for export of virtual water. Trade can physically save water if products are traded from countries with high to countries with low water productivity. For example, Mexico imports wheat, maize and sorghum from the USA, which requires 7.1 billion m^3 of water per year in the USA. If Mexico were to produce the imported crops domestically, it would require 15.6 billion m^3 of water per year. Thus, from a global perspective, the trade in cereals from the USA to Mexico saves 8.5 billion m^3/yr. Although there are also examples where water-intensive commodities flow in the opposite direction, from countries with low to countries with high water productivity, the available studies indicate that the resultant of all international trade flows works in a positive direction. We showed that international trade in agricultural commodities reduces global water use in agriculture by 5 percent. Liberalization of trade seems to offer new opportunities to contribute to a further increase of efficiency in the use of the world's water resources.

A serious drawback of trade is that the indirect effects of consumption are externalized to other countries. While water in agriculture is still priced far below its real cost in most countries, an increasing volume of water is used for processing export products. The costs associated with water use in the exporting country are not included in the price of the products consumed in the importing country. Consumers are generally not aware of – and do not pay for – the water problems in the overseas countries where their goods are being produced. According to economic theory, a precondition for trade to be efficient and fair is that consumers bear the full cost of production and impacts. Another downside of intensive international virtual-water transfers is that many countries increasingly depend on the import of water-intensive commodities from other countries. Jordan annually imports a virtual-water volume that is five times its own annual renewable water resources. Other countries in the Middle East, but also various European countries, have a similar high water import dependence. The increasing lack of self-sufficiency has made various individual countries, but also larger regions, very vulnerable. If for whatever reason food supplies cease – be it due to war or a natural disaster in an important export region – the importing regions will suffer severely. A key question is to what extent nations are willing to take this risk. The risk can be avoided only by promoting national self-sufficiency in water and food supply (as Egypt and China do). The risk can be reduced by importing food from a wide range of trade partners. The current worldwide trend, however, facilitated by the World Trade Organization, is toward reducing trade barriers and encouraging free international trade, and reducing interference by national governments.

The current global trade pattern significantly influences water use in most countries of the world, either by reducing domestic water use or by enhancing it. Future national and regional water policy studies should therefore include an assessment of the effects of trade on water policy. For water-scarce countries, it would also be wise to do the reverse: study the possible implications of national water scarcity on trade. In short, strategic analysis for water policy-making should include an analysis of expected or desirable trends in international or inter-regional virtual-water flows.

References

Allan, J.A. (2001a), 'Virtual water – economically invisible and politically silent – a way to solve strategic water problems', *International Water and Irrigation*, November, 39–41.

Allan, J.A. (2001b), *The Middle East Water Question: Hydropolitics and the Global Economy*, London: I.B. Tauris.

Chapagain, A.K., A.Y. Hoekstra and H.H.G. Savenije (2006), 'Water saving through international trade of agricultural products', *Hydrology and Earth System Sciences*, **10**(3), 455–68.

De Fraiture, C., X. Cai, U. Amarasinghe, M. Rosegrant and D. Molden (2004), 'Does international cereal trade save water? The impact of virtual water trade on global water use', Comprehensive Assessment Research Report 4, Colombo: IWMI.

Greenaway, F., R. Hassan and G.V. Reed (1994), 'An empirical analysis of comparative advantage in Egyptian agriculture', *Applied Economics*, **26**(6), 649–57.

Grote, U., E. Craswell and P. Vlek (2005), 'Nutrient flows in international trade: ecology and policy issues', *Environmental Science and Policy*, **8**, 439–51.

GWP (2000), 'Integrated water resources management', TAC Background Paper No 4, Stockholm: Global Water Partnership.

Haddadin, M.J. (2003), 'Exogenous water: a conduit to globalization of water resources', in A.Y. Hoekstra, *Virtual Water Trade: Proceedings of the International Expert Meeting on Virtual Water Trade*, Value of Water Research Report Series No. 12, Delft: UNESCO–IHE, pp. 159–69.

Hoekstra, A.Y. (ed.) (2003), *Virtual Water Trade: Proceedings of the International Expert Meeting on Virtual Water Trade*, Value of Water Research Report Series No. 12, Delft, The Netherlands: UNESCO–IHE.

Hoekstra, A.Y. and A.K. Chapagain (2007), 'Water footprints of nations: water use by people as a function of their consumption pattern', *Water Resources Management*, **21**(1); 35–48.

Hoekstra, A.Y. and A.K. Chapagain (2008), *Globalization of Water: Sharing the Planet's Freshwater Resources*, Oxford: Blackwell Publishing.

Hoekstra, A.Y. and P.Q. Hung (2005), 'Globalisation of water resources: International virtual water flows in relation to crop trade', *Global Environmental Change*, **15**(1), 45–56.

ITC (2004), PC-TAS version 1997–2001, Harmonized System CD-ROM, Geneva: International Trade Centre.

Ma, J., A.Y. Hoekstra, H. Wang, A.K. Chapagain and D. Wang (2006), 'Virtual versus real water transfers within China', *Philosophical Transactions of the Royal Society of London B*, **361**(1469), 835–42.

Maclean, J.L., D.C. Dawe, B. Hardy and G.P. Hettel (2002), *Rice Almanac: Source Book for the Most Important Economic Activity on Earth*, Los Baños, Philippines: International Rice Research Institute.

McIsaac, G.F., M.B. David, G.Z. Gertner and D.A. Goolsby (2001), 'Eutrophication: nitrate flux in the Mississippi river', *Nature*, **414**(6860), 166–7.

Meybeck, M. (2004), 'The global change of continental aquatic systems: dominant impacts of human activities', *Water Science and Technology*, **49**(7), 73–83.

Nriagu, J.O. and J.M. Pacyna (1988), 'Quantitative assessment of worldwide contamination of air, water and soils by trace metals', *Nature*, **333**, 134–9.

Oki, T. and S. Kanae (2004), 'Virtual water trade and world water resources', *Water Science and Technology*, **49**(7), 203–9.

Ramirez-Vallejo, J. and P. Rogers (2004), 'Virtual water flows and trade liberalization', *Water Science and Technology*, **49**(7), 25–32.

Ricardo, D. ([1817] 2006), *On the Principles of Political Economy and Taxation*, New York: Cosimo.

Rogers, P., R. Bhatia and A. Huber (1998), 'Water as a social and economic good: how to put the principle into practice', TAC Background Papers No. 2, Stockholm: Global Water Partnership.

Sanchez, P.A. (2002), 'Soil fertility and hunger in Africa', *Science*, 295(5562), 2019–20.

Savenije, H.H.G. (2002), 'Why water is not an ordinary economic good, or why the girl is special', *Physics and Chemistry of the Earth*, **27**, 741–4.

Stocking, M.A. (2003), 'Tropical soils and food security: the next 50 years', *Science*, **302**(5649), 1356–9.

Tilman, D., J. Fargione, B. Wolff, C. D'Antonio, A. Dobson, R. Howarth, D. Schindler, W.H. Schlesinger, D. Simberloff and D. Swackhamer (2001), 'Forecasting agriculturally driven global environmental change', *Science*, **292**(5515), 281–4.

Verma, S., D.A. Kampman, P. Van der Zaag and A.Y. Hoekstra (2008), 'Going against the flow: a critical analysis of virtual water trade in the context of India's National River Linking Programme', *Physics and Chemistry of the Earth*, submitted.

Wichelns, D. (2001), 'The role of "virtual water" in efforts to achieve food security and other national goals, with an example from Egypt', *Agricultural Water Management*, **49**(2), 131–51.

Wichelns, D. (2004), 'The policy relevance of virtual water can be enhanced by considering comparative advantages', *Agricultural Water Management*, **66**(1), 49–63.

Yang, H., P. Reichert, K.C. Abbaspour and A.J.B. Zehnder (2003), 'A water resources threshold and its implications for food security', *Environmental Science and Technology*, **37**, 3048–54.

Yang, H., L. Wang, K.C. Abbaspour and A.J.B. Zehnder (2006), 'Virtual water trade: an assessment of water use efficiency in the international food trade', *Hydrology and Earth System Sciences*, **10**, 443–54.

Yang, H., L. Wang and A. Zehnder (2007), 'Water scarcity and food trade in the Southern and Eastern Mediterranean countries', *Food Policy*, **32**, 585–605.

9   The environmental costs of Mexico–USA maize trade under NAFTA
Timothy A. Wise

The North American Free Trade Agreement (NAFTA) had a profound impact on maize trade between the USA and Mexico. Negotiated quota and tariff reductions and the Mexican government's decision not to charge some tariffs to which it was entitled contributed to a tripling of US exports to Mexico. US corn now supplies about one-fifth of Mexican demand, primarily for feed grain, corn sweetener and processed foods. Although US exports to Mexico account for only about 2 percent of total US production, corn is such a large crop in the USA that the marginal impacts of trade cannot be ignored.

The changes in USA–Mexico corn trade had significant environmental impacts on both sides of the border. Corn production in the USA has heavy negative impacts, while the production of maize in Mexico predominantly involves positive environmental externalities associated with the stewardship of genetic diversity in the world's center of origin for maize. Neither the environmental costs of pollution-intensive US production nor the benefits of Mexico's biodiverse maize production are reflected in international prices. These externalities allow US corn to be priced below its true costs of production, while traditional Mexican maize prices do not reflect their full value.

The linking of these two dynamics through deregulated trade results in overall environmental impacts that are worse than the simple sum of their parts, as underpriced US corn threatens to displace undervalued Mexican maize, a process referred to as the globalization of market failure (Boyce, 1999).

An analytical framework
The concept most widely associated with the effects of trade on the environment is the pollution haven. According to this theory, rising trade and declining restrictions on the movement of capital and goods between an industrialized and a developing country will lead pollution-intensive companies to relocate production to areas in which regulations and/or enforcement of environmental laws are more lax. Following this theory, it was feared that NAFTA would produce an exodus of pollution-intensive industries from the USA to Mexico to take advantage of Mexico's weaker environmental enforcement. This fear has largely not proven to be a widespread phenomenon, although there are certainly instances of dirtier industries relocating production to avoid stricter US environmental regulations. (See Copeland and Taylor, 2003 for a good review of this literature.)

The assumption embedded in the pollution haven concept is that the flow of environmental degradation will be from North to South, from the more developed toward the less developed country. This is based on the assumption that cleaner technology and rising expectations for a clean environment will make practices in the North more sustainable than those in the South. This is a false assumption for at least some agricultural trade. Agricultural practices in US corn production are far less sustainable than the traditional Mexican practices of maize cultivation using – and continuing to steward – diverse seed varieties of benefit to humankind as a whole. The shift in corn production from Mexico to the USA, a trend reinforced by NAFTA, has the net effect of increasing environmental degradation. Contrary to the common applications of the pollution haven hypothesis, trade has not brought cleaner production through the introduction of developed-country technology. Rather, it has brought more environmentally damaging practices.

Economist James Boyce has offered a particularly useful concept to the discussion of the environmental impacts of trade: the globalization of market failure. He bases his analysis on field studies of traditional jute production in Bangladesh, which is being displaced by imported synthetic fibers, and traditional corn production in Mexico, which is threatened by hybrid corn imports from the USA following trade liberalization. He argues that economic integration links imperfect markets in environmentally destructive ways. In both cases, the market prices for modern, Northern products fail to incorporate significant negative environmental externalities. The international economic playing field is tilted even further against traditional producers, who go uncompensated for the positive environmental externalities associated with traditional production. As trade – and trade agreements – bring together these two forms of production, distorted in opposite ways by environmental externalities, the result is unfair competition with net environmental costs. Boyce demonstrates, for example, that nearly the entire price advantage enjoyed by synthetics over jute – about 35 percent – would be eliminated if environmental externalities were factored into prices (Boyce, 1999).

As we shall see in the case of changing maize trade between Mexico and the USA, the flow of pollution-intensive economic activity is from South to North. And economic liberalization, of which NAFTA is a key component, has fueled the globalization of market failure, increasing environmental damage in the USA while threatening an irreplaceable environmental (and economic) global good in the South – Mexico's rich reservoir of maize diversity.

Changing maize trade under NAFTA

Maize and beans were included in NAFTA very late in the negotiations due to resistance within Mexico to liberalizing the country's two most important staple crops and food sources. Over farmer objections, Mexico agreed to liberalize maize and beans, along with other crops, using a tariff-rate quota (TRQ) system to phase in imports and phase out tariffs. Maize and beans got the maximum 15-year TRQ. For maize, the initial import quota was set at 2.5 million tons, with 215 percent tariffs on imports above quota. The quota was set to increase by 3 percent each year, reaching 3.6 million tons by 2008, while the tariffs on over-quota imports were negotiated to decrease gradually over the same period, reaching zero by 2008 (Nadal, 2000).

The stated goal of the 15-year TRQ was to allow a slow transition to full competition, recognizing the wide productivity differences between US and Mexican maize producers. Those differences are dramatic. The USA farms nearly four times the area and achieves yields over three times those in Mexico. This gives the USA 11 times the production, which at the time NAFTA was passed sold for roughly half the price of Mexican maize. US farm subsidies also give US producers an advantage, with direct subsidies per hectare about three times the levels in Mexico (Wise, 2004).

Claiming production shortfalls and inflationary pressures, the Mexican government declined to enforce any of the TRQs it had negotiated for agricultural products, including maize. For maize, the negotiated 15-year transition to free trade was eliminated (Nadal, 2000). From NAFTA's inception in 1994 the TRQ was not enforced. Beginning in 1996, US exports to Mexico increased dramatically, from a pre-NAFTA average (1990–93) of 1.6 million tons to 6.3 million tons. With annual fluctuations, US exports have averaged around 5 million tons since 1996, a 323 percent increase from the pre-NAFTA period (FATUS, 2003).

In Mexico, the flood of imports produced a significant drop in producer prices. Real prices fell by 25 percent in the years following NAFTA. By 2002 they were 47 percent below their pre-NAFTA levels (SIACON, 2003).

US environmental impacts

The changes since the adoption of NAFTA have resulted in an increase in exports to Mexico from 0.8 percent to 2.1 percent of total US corn production. Thus the growth in trade amounts to an additional 1.3 percent of the US corn crop, and can be credited with 1.3 percent of the impacts of corn production, both positive and negative, in the USA. US corn production remained fairly stable during this period, so rising exports to Mexico did not result in an increase in corn production. Rather, rising Mexican demand prevented a possible decline due to reduced demand in other export markets.

It is important to use a broad approach in assessing NAFTA's impact. NAFTA cannot be usefully separated from the set of trade liberalizing policies of which it is a part. NAFTA's North American Commission for Environmental Cooperation, in its analytical framework, calls for a broad interpretation of NAFTA's economic and environmental impacts, noting that even where the agreement did not have a direct effect it may have stabilized and reinforced trends already under way (NACEC 1999). Some analysts attribute a smaller portion of rising US exports to NAFTA, arguing that some of these increases would have occurred even without the tariff reductions under NAFTA (see, e.g., Porter, 2002; Zahniser and Link, 2002). While I recognize the usefulness in some instances of isolating those impacts that are directly attributable to NAFTA's provisions, here a broader interpretation is used.

Environmental impacts of increased US corn production for the Mexican market fall into four basic categories:

1. Intensive agrochemical use, with its resulting environmental impacts
2. The increasing use of genetically modified seed varieties, despite continued uncertainty about their risks to human health or the environment
3. Unsustainable water use in areas where irrigation is needed
4. Reduced biodiversity due to corn cultivation on grasslands and wetlands.

Looking first at chemical use, corn is one of the country's largest and most chemical-intensive crops. Corn is planted on some 28 million hectares, 20 percent of all US harvested land, and 3.7 percent of the entire land area of the contiguous 48 states (Anderson et al., 2000). Chemical fertilizers are used on the vast majority of US corn crops. The runoff is a major source of water pollution, affecting drinking water throughout the corn belt in the center of the country. Runoff also pollutes rivers and streams. The great quantities of nitrogen carried by the Mississippi river have been implicated in the large 'dead zone' in the Gulf of Mexico where ocean life has been killed off (Keeney and Muller, 2000;

Runge, 2002; Goolsby et al., 1999). Corn production is a major contributor to this effect both through direct nitrogen runoff from fertilizer application on farms and through the use of corn as a feed for livestock whose manure contributes to water pollution.

US corn is also intensive in its use of herbicides and insecticides. Atrazine, the most common herbicide used in corn production, among other crops – and the most common pesticide detected in groundwater nationwide – is an endocrine disrupter and possible human carcinogen (it causes cancer in rats). Exposure to atrazine creates risks for farm workers, consumers of corn products, and users of groundwater downstream from farm areas (EPA, 2001a; Repetto and Baliga, 1996; Ribaudo and Bouzaher, 1994; Briggs and Council, 1992). Metolachlor and S-Metolachlor, both leading herbicides, are possible human carcinogens (EPA, 2000; Briggs and Council, 1992). Chlorpyrifos, the most common insecticide used on cornfields, is a neurotoxin that poses risks for children who are exposed to it at high levels; it is also used on other foods, and for residential cockroach and termite control (EPA, 2001b; Briggs and Council, 1992).

Due to important technological improvements, the intensity of herbicide use has declined in recent years, although atrazine and other chemical herbicides still pollute drinking water supplies (Benbrook, 2001a).

Pesticide intensity has remained roughly constant, which is disappointing given the growing use of genetically modified corn. By 2004, just eight years since the introduction of genetically modified corn varieties in the USA, nearly half of all corn land was planted in GM crops. More than 30 percent of US corn was planted in varieties engineered with the Bt (*Bacillus thuringiensis*) endotoxin to fight some common pests, most notably the European corn borer. Roughly 15 percent of US corn was genetically engineered for herbicide tolerance (USDA–NASS, 2004). While there are widespread concerns about the risks of such crops to human health and to the environment, their widespread adoption has not yet produced the environmental benefit they promised: reduced pesticide applications (Clark, 1999; Heimlich et al., 2000; Benbrook, 2001b).

In addition, rising exports of unlabeled corn to Mexico, which contain high levels of GM varieties, have caused significant concern in Mexico since the discovery of traditional maize varieties contaminated with transgenic corn. This will be discussed later, in the examination of the environmental impacts of changing USA–Mexico corn trade on Mexico.

In terms of unsustainable water use, although only about 15 percent of US corn is irrigated, the vast majority of irrigated corn land is found in four states: Nebraska, Texas, Colorado and Oklahoma. These states rely for their irrigation on water from the vast Ogallala aquifer, an underground reservoir the size of Lake Huron. The Ogallala is being depleted at unsustainable rates, calling into question the wisdom of expanding corn production in areas lacking adequate rainfall (NRC, 1996; Opie, 2000).

Two additional environmental impacts from US corn production are worth examining briefly: soil erosion and biodiversity impacts. Conversion to cropland has carried with it rising problems with soil erosion. Some historical studies suggest that conservation tillage practices have significantly reduced erosion rates since the 1930s. This would suggest that expanding corn production may have little impact on soil erosion rates.

Biodiversity impacts are still of concern with expanded corn production. In sharp contrast to the situation in Mexico, biodiversity in the corn crop itself is long gone in the USA. Commercially distributed hybrid varieties have been the norm in US production for decades. In addition to the dangers of Bt contamination and rising pesticide resistance among insects, there is one other way in which US corn production can impact biodiversity within the USA. The long-term expansion of cultivated area in the USA has reduced the area of grasslands and wetlands, while the growth in average farm size has eliminated many field edges that have been important habitats for birds and other species (Runge, 2002). While proponents of biotechnology argue that increased yields from transgenic crops will reduce the need for cultivated land, this is an oversimplification: higher yields will not automatically lead to the return of existing cropland to wild habitat (Batie and Ervin, 2001).

While corn production has not expanded during this period, access to the Mexican market has allowed the USA to keep corn land in production when it would otherwise have been turned over to other crops. Increased exports to Mexico due to trade liberalization – the threefold increase recorded since NAFTA – represent 1.3 percent of total US production and should therefore be considered responsible for 1.3 percent of the environmental impacts of corn production. Given the scale of US production, these are considerable, representing, for example, 100 000 additional tons of nitrogen, phosphorous and potassium-based loadings to US water each year. These externalized environmental costs are not reflected in US corn prices.

Mexico environmental impacts

In Mexico corn production accounts for over two-thirds of the gross value of agricultural production. Corn covers half of the total area under cultivation for all crops (Sistema Dinámico de Información y Análisis Agroalimentanó, DIAGRO). Roughly 3 million people are employed in the cultivation of corn, more than 40 percent of the labor force involved in agriculture or about 8 percent of Mexico's total labor force (Nadal, 2000). This supports some 18 million people.

Mexico has the world's second highest annual per capita corn consumption (127 kg) after Malawi (Morris, 1998). The pattern of consumption in Mexico is distinct from that in the USA and other industrial countries since 68 percent of all corn is directly used as food. In the world as a whole, just 21 percent of total corn production is consumed as food. In industrial countries, including the USA, corn is more often used as livestock feed or as an industrial input – a trend that is recently beginning to appear in Mexico.

In Mexico maize is the basic staple food for human consumption. One study found that on average about 59 percent of human energy intake and 39 percent of protein intake was provided by maize grain in the form of 'tortilla' (cooked corn dough) (Bourges and Lehrer, 2004, in Turrent-Fernandez et al.,1997). Five thousand years of maize domestication has generated more than 40 races of maize specialized for direct human consumption. By contrast, in the last hundred years, the industrialized countries have specialized in developing hybrid varieties of maize for animal consumption and industrial use (CIMMYT, 2001).

Mexico is the ancestral home of maize, and possesses a unique and irreplaceable genetic diversity of varieties. Most of the country's maize production comes from traditional landraces cultivated by peasant farmers from seeds that they preserve from their own crops and from the exchange of seeds with neighbors in their communities (Wilkes, et al., 1981; Serratos-Hernandez et al., 2001). Such *in situ* conservation of maize genetic resources is considered essential to the long-term security of this important food crop, which has particular economic value because it serves as the basis for crop breeding (Brush, 2000).

While the principal environmental impacts of shifting corn trade relate to biodiversity, Mexico has a significant number of modern growers, geographically concentrated in the northern state of Sinaloa. In a detailed case study for the North American Commission for Environmental Cooperation, de Ita Rubio (2003) assessed the environmental impacts of expanding industrial maize production in Sinaloa. Due to price incentives and other market distortions that temporarily favored maize and bean production, modern producers dramatically increased production in the mid-1990s. With the removal of price supports, irrigated land planted in maize dropped 40 percent nationally between 1989 and 2001 (de Ita Rubio, 2003). There was a decline in acreage in Sinaloa as well, but a tripling of yields allowed production in Sinaloa to rise to ten times its pre-NAFTA level (SIACON, 2003).

Not surprisingly, the impacts mirror those in the USA: high chemical use, with its accompanying environmental impacts; and unsustainable water use for heavily irrigated farms. GM maize cultivation is still banned in Mexico, so potential damage from Bt maize is not present in Sinaloa at the time of writing.

While Sinaloa's share of national production increased dramatically during the 1990s, production in more traditional sectors of Mexico's maize economy has stagnated or declined. Trade threatens Mexican maize diversity in two ways. First, and most important, the flood of imports from the USA has brought producer prices down nearly 50 percent, increasing economic pressure on marginal maize farmers. If they leave the land or leave maize farming, the traditional knowledge and practices that sustain this resource will go with them.

In Mexico, the map of rural poverty closely mirrors the map of genetic diversity, with the poorest and most diverse farms concentrated in the southern and eastern parts of the country. This is not surprising. Traditional agricultural practices tend to prevail in more marginal environments, where native landraces have been selected over the generations to provide unique advantages not available in high-yield hybrid seeds. The map of cultural diversity would also show similar shadings, as indigenous farmers concentrated in the southeastern section of the country tend to use the widest diversity of seeds while also suffering the highest levels of poverty and marginalization.

While many – including some in the Mexican government – predicted that NAFTA would lead to an exodus from maize, this has largely not occurred. Data suggest that production has remained relatively constant, and even increased in some of the states dominated by traditional production (Ackerman et al., 2003).

Nadal (2000) notes that prices for other traditional crops suffered declines similar to or greater than that of maize, making a shift to other crops less viable. Pointing to evidence of expanding cultivation and declining yields in some traditional areas, he attributes the apparent persistence of traditional production to survival strategies of peasant farmers, who bring more marginal lands under cultivation in order to grow for subsistence. Yúnez-Naude and Barceinas Paredes (2003) suggest that a significant proportion of corn farmers grow for subsistence and are likely to remain isolated from market forces, reducing the impact of falling prices and the threat to maize genetic diversity. However, Taylor and Dyer (2003) found that there has indeed been a significant increase in rural migration to the USA since the mid-1980s, and that trend has been particularly rapid since NAFTA took effect, showing an increase of 175 percent from 1994 to 2002.

It is difficult to believe that such large-scale migratory trends will not eventually translate into losses in maize production, local knowledge and maize diversity. The threats to agro-biodiversity are long term in nature. To the extent that they reside in the migration patterns of traditional farmers, we know that families do not generally abandon the land en masse but rather export labor, generally younger family members, over time, sustaining the homestead with remittances from migrant family members. Given the legal rights in Mexico associated with maintaining an active farm, there is an incentive to keep the land planted by keeping some family members at home. Thus, figures on production or planted area or even migration can mask trends that are leading to the gradual loss of traditional knowledge in the process of seed selection, which is the basis for the ongoing evolution and stewardship of maize genetic diversity.

One recent analysis using disaggregated national data, correlated with data on maize diversity, suggested there is cause for concern. Those farmers employing the greatest diversity of native seeds were found to suffer the highest levels of poverty, and this has remained true from 1990 to 2000. These farmers, who represented two-thirds of Mexico's maize producers in 1990, expanded the area planted in maize since 1990, by 26 percent and 33 percent. Output has increased as well, although susceptibility to crop failure remains highest for this group, suggesting that they are bringing more marginal land under cultivation in order to cope with rising economic pressures. Also consistent with previous analysis is the finding that international migration remains most intense not for the poorest, most diverse producers but for those showing relatively low diversity and slightly lower poverty rates. But internal migration is common for poorer producers, who may well be migrating to Mexico's modern horticulture fields initially, then moving on to the USA when they earn enough to afford the trip (Nadal and Wise, 2004).

These initial findings should serve as a warning to those who would conclude that agro-biodiversity in maize is secure. The long-term expulsion of family members from the households of those farming the most diverse varieties of maize is likely to interrupt the transmission of local knowledge, undermining the seed selection upon which agro-biodiversity depends. By all accounts, stagnation or decline in Mexican agriculture and in other sectors of the Mexican economy has limited the options available to farmers suffering the effects of low maize prices. This may have slowed the feared exodus from traditional maize, but it may not have prevented it.

Paradoxically, things could get worse for agro-biodiversity if things get better for the Mexican economy. Better opportunities elsewhere – in agriculture, in the Mexican service sector, or in the USA – could offer traditional maize farmers viable alternatives to producing for subsistence or selling maize in the market at the prevailing low prices.

The second threat to maize diversity is the contamination of traditional fields by GM corn from the USA. Mexico has banned the cultivation of GM maize since 1998. Yet studies have verified the presence of Bt and herbicide-tolerant transgenic traits in traditional landraces in several states, leading to widespread fears that such gene flow from GM varieties to landraces may be more rapid and widespread than previously thought. It is widely assumed the contamination came from US grain, which enters Mexico unsegregated and unlabeled, and until recently was distributed in rural areas as food by a government anti-poverty program. Unwitting farmers are presumed to have experimented with the grain as seed, and the pollen contaminated traditional varieties.

An exhaustive study by the Commission for Environmental Cooperation, the agency set up by NAFTA's side agreement, concluded that the threat to maize diversity from GM contamination is neither imminent nor negligible. Experts highlighted the uncertainty of the science of gene flow and the wide variety of potential risks to Mexico's ecosystems, agricultural practices, communities and cultures. The scientific consensus was that a precautionary approach was warranted. While current levels of contamination may not pose a significant threat to Mexico's agro-biodiversity, it is difficult to know for certain since the only field testing has been done in the USA, so not under conditions found in Mexico, and only in the short term. The authors recommended that all corn imported from the USA be ground beforehand, to prevent the possibility of planting, at least until the USA segregates its GM corn and provides adequate labeling (NACEC, 2004). The US and Mexican governments have ignored the recommendations.

Conclusion

The case of Mexican maize clearly calls into question the wisdom of across-the-board agricultural trade liberalization. Looking at Latin America and other parts of the developing world, there are clearly other crops and countries that share Mexico's status as a center of important genetic diversity for traded food crops. Potatoes in the Andean highlands would be a clear example. Positive environmental externalities are present in many traditional forms of agricultural production, from low chemical use to soil-stabilizing farming techniques. Where traditional production continues to be a significant part of developing-country agriculture, it is important to assess the environmental benefits of such activities before throwing such producers into unmediated competition with their more industrialized, pollution-intensive counterparts.

If agro-biodiversity is a common global good that is worth preserving, and if the market is unlikely to internalize these benefits any time soon, then non-market mechanisms will be needed to shelter such sectors in the economic integration process. Government intervention will be critical to overcoming the globalization of market failures. In the end, tariffs may prove the best way to protect environmentally valuable farm sectors, while government policies will also need to develop the productivity of traditional farming sectors.

On the positive side, trade creates growing demand for some agricultural products, such as feed grain, corn sweetener and corn flour in the case of Mexico. This demand has been largely filled by imports from the USA. But a different set of trade arrangements and government policies could allow rising demand to serve as the economic stimulus to improve the livelihoods and long-term economic prospects of traditional farmers. This would represent a dramatic and welcome shift in Mexican agricultural policies.

References

Ackerman, F., T.A. Wise et al. (2003), 'Free trade, corn, and the environment: environmental impacts of US–Mexico corn trade under NAFTA', in North American Commission for Environmental Cooperation (ed.), *Trade and Environment in North America: Key Findings for Agriculture and Energy*, Montreal: North American Commission for Environmental Cooperation.

Anderson, W., R. Magleby et al. (2000), *Agricultural Resources and Environmental Indicators, 2000*, Washington, DC: US Dept. of Agriculture, Economic Research Service, Resource Economics Division.

Batie, S.S. and D.E. Ervin (2001), 'Transgenic crops and the environment: missing markets and public roles', *Environment and Development Economics*, **6**(4), 435–57.

Benbrook, C.M. (2001a), *Factors Shaping Trends in Herbicide Use*, Sandpoint, ID: Northwest Science and Environmental Policy Center.

Benbrook, C.M. (2001b), 'Do GM crops mean less pesticide use?', *Pesticide Outlook*, 204–8.

Bourges, H. and S. Lehrer (2004), 'Assessment of human health effects. Article 13 report: maize and biodiversity: the effects of transgenic maize in Mexico', Montreal: NACEC.

Boyce, J.K. (1999), *The Globalization of Market Failure? International Trade and Sustainable Agriculture*, Amherst, MA: Political Economy Research Institute (PERI).

Briggs, S.A. and R.C. Council (1992), *Basic Guide to Pesticides: Their Characteristics and Hazards*, Washington, DC: Taylor & Francis.

Brush, S.B. (2000), *Genes in the Field: On-Farm Conservation of Crop Genetic Diversity*, New York: Lewis Publishers.

CIMMYT (2001), *Draft Consensus Document on the Biology of Zea mays subsp. mays (maize)*, OECD Program of Work on Harmonization of Regulatory Oversight in Biotechnology.

Clark, E.A. (1999), 'Ten reasons why farmers should think twice before growing GE crops', Retrieved April 2003, accessed at: http://www.plant.uoguelph.ca/research/homepages/eclark/10reasons.htm.

Copeland, B.R. and M.S. Taylor (2003), *Trade and the Environment: Theory and Evidence*, Princeton, NJ: Princeton University Press.

de Ita Rubio, A. (2003), *Los Impactos Socioeconomicos y Ambientales de la Liberalizacion Comercial de los Granos Basicos en el Contexto del TLCAN: El Caso de Sinaloa*, Mexico City: North American Commission for Environmental Cooperation.

EPA (2000), 'Acetochlor home page', 2 October, US Environmental Protection Agency, retrieved 12 December 2001, accessed at: http://www.epa.gov/oppefed1/aceto/index.htm.

EPA (2001a), 'Revised preliminary human health risk assessment: atrazine', Washington DC: US Environmental Protection Agency, Reregistration Branch 3, Health Effects Division, Office of Pesticide Programs, 117.

EPA (2001b), 'Organophosphate pesticides: documents for Chlorpyrifos-Methyl', US Environmental Protection Agency, retrieved 14 December 2001, accessed at: http://www.epa.gov/pesticides/op/chlorpyrifos-methyl.htm.

FATUS (2003), Foreign Agricultural Trade of the United States – Database Search, retrieved 16 March 2004, accessed at http://www.ers.usda.gov/db/fatus/.

Goolsby, D.A., W.A. Battaglin, G.B. Lawrence, R.S. Artz, B.T. Aulenbach, R.P. Hooper, D.R. Keeney and G.J. Stensland (1999), 'Flux and source of nutrients in the Mississippi-Atchafalaya River Basin: Topic 3 report', NOAA report, accessed at: http://www.nos.noaa.gov/pdflibrary/hypox_t3final.pdf.

Heimlich, R.E., J. Fernandez-Cornejo et al. (2000), 'Genetically engineered crops: has adoption reduced pesticide use'?, *Agricultural Outlook*, August, AGO-273, 13–17.

Keeney, D. and M. Muller (2000), 'Nitrogen and the Upper Mississippi River', Minneapolis: Institute for Agriculture and Trade Policy, 15.

Morris, M.L. (1998), *Overview of the World Maize Economy: Maize Seed Industries in Developing Countries*, Boulder, Co: Lynne Rienner Publishers, Inc. and CIMMYT, Int.

NACEC (1999), 'Assessing environmental effects of the North American Free Trade Agreement (NAFTA): an analytic framework (Phase II)', in *Assessing Environmental Effects of the North American Free Trade Agreement*, Montreal: Commission for Environmental Cooperation, pp. 1–64.

NACEC (2004), *Symposium: Maize and Biodiversity: The Effects of Transgenic Maize in Mexico*, Maize and Biodiversity Symposium, Oaxaca, Mexico: North American Commission for Environmental Cooperation.

Nadal, A. (2000), *The Environmental & Social Impacts of Economic Liberalization on Corn Production in Mexico*, Gland, Switzerland and Oxford: WWF International and Oxfam GB, pp. 1–13.

Nadal, A. and T.A. Wise (2004), 'The environmental costs of agricultural trade liberalization: Mexico–U.S. maize trade under NAFTA', Working Group Discussion Paper DP04, Medford, MA: Working Group on Development and Environment in the Americas.

NRC (1996), *A New Era for Irrigation*, Washington DC: National Academy Press.

Opie, J. (2000), *Ogallala: Water for a Dry Land*, Lincoln, NE: University of Nebraska Press.

Porter, G. (2002), 'Subsidies and the environment: an overview of the state of knowledge', Workshop on Environmentally Harmful Subsidies, Paris: OECD.

Repetto, R. and S.S. Baliga (1996), *Pesticides and the Immune System: The Public Health Risks*, Washington, DC: World Resources Institute.

Ribaudo, M.O. and A. Bouzaher (1994), 'Atrazine: environmental characteristics and economics of management', Washington, DC: US Department of Agriculture, Economic Research Service, 22.

Runge, C.F. (2002), *US Agricultural Policy in 2002: A Four Dimensional Disaster*, Winnipeg: George Morris Centre.

Serratos-Hernandez, J.A., F. Islas Gutierrez et al. (2001), *Producción de maíz, razas locales y distribución del teozintle en México: Elementos para un análisis GIS de flujo genético y valoración de Riesgos para la liberación de maíz transgénico*, Campo Experimental Valle de Mexico, Instituto Nacional de Investigaciones Forestales Agícolas y Pecuarias (INIFAP), Centro de Biotecnología Aplicada Centro Internacional de Mejoramiento de Maíz y Trigo (CIMMYT).

SIACON (2003), SIACON database, retrieved 15 March 2004.

Taylor, E. and G. Dyer (2003), 'NAFTA, trade, and migration', unpublished manuscript, Washington, DC.

Turrent-Fernandez, A.N., J.L. Gomez-Montiel et al. (1997), *Plan de investigación del sistema maíz-tortilla en los Estados Unidos Mexicanos*, Internal Document, INIFAP–SAGAR.

USDA–NASS (2004), USDA–NASS Agricultural Statistics 2004, retrieved 13 December 2005, accessed at: http://www.usda.gov/nass/pubs/agr 00/acro00.htm.

Wilkes, G.,C. W. Yeatman et al. (eds) (1981), *Plant Genetic Resources: A Conservation Imperative*, American Association for the Advancement of Science selected symposium, Boulder, CO: Westview Press.

Wise, T. A. (2004), *The Paradox of Agricultural Subsidies: Measurement Issues, Agricultural Dumping, and Policy reform*, Medford, MA: Global Development and Environment Institute.

Yúnez-Naude, A. and F. Barceinas Paredes (2003), *The Agricultural Sector of Mexico After Ten Years of NAFTA*, Washington, DC: Carnegie Endowment for International Peace.

Zahniser, S. and J. Link (2002), *Effects of North American Free Trade Agreement on Agriculture and the Rural Economy*, Washington DC: US Department of Agriculture.

10 The impact of open trade and investment regimes on environmental outcomes in East Asia's capitalist developmental states
Michael T. Rock and David Angel

Introduction

The burgeoning literature on trade and the environment suggests that the impact of openness to trade and investment on the environment depends on whether positive technique effects are large enough to overcome the negative scale and composition effects of openness. Copeland and Taylor (2003) suggest that they are, at least for SO_2, while Managi (2007) argues that these results do not hold for developing economies.

Our contribution to this literature takes a decidedly different tack by demonstrating that in the rapidly developing East Asian newly industrializing economies these technique effects depend on a development strategy and a set of institutions and incentives that encourage local firms to invest in the hard slog of building their technological capabilities, including their environmental capabilities. Our argument proceeds in three steps. The first section describes the evolution of the two major institutional innovations in this group of economies – the capitalist developmental state, which emphasizes technological learning through the export of manufactures, and policy integration, or the integration of environmental policies and institutions with the institutions of industrial policy. Our aim is to demonstrate how capitalist developmental states in this region harnessed technological learning around the export of manufactures and the practice of policy integration to reduce environmental intensities expressed as environmental impact per unit of output. The second section demonstrates, through industry and firm-level examples, how this particular configuration rewarded firms investing in technological learning to reap the positive technique effects associated with globalization. The final section concludes our argument.

The capitalist developmental state and policy integration

Since the 1960s, the economies in rapidly developing East Asia have been going through a historically unprecedented process of high-speed industrial technological catch-up with the West. This process, which began in Japan (1981), spread first to Korea (Amsden,1989), Taiwan Province of China (Wade, 1990), Hong Kong, China (Haggard, 1990) and Singapore (Huff, 1999) and subsequently to Indonesia (Hill, 1996; Rock, 2003; 1999), Malaysia (Jomo, 1986) and Thailand (Pasuk and Baker, 1995; Rock, 1994). While there are significant differences among this group of rapidly developing economies, including differences in their ability to upgrade their technological capabilities, their development strategies have been led by what Johnson (1982) refers to as capitalist developmental states.

East Asia's capitalist developmental states possess a number of important institutional innovations that distinguish them from the rest of the developing world. To begin with, governing elites committed to development provided long-term political stability lengthening the time horizons of business. Those elites also built more or less capable public sector bureaucracies that enjoyed embedded autonomy with the private sector (Evans, 1995). Embeddedness meant that technocrats in government understood the real problems faced by business. Autonomy meant that technocrats were able to escape capture by their private sector clients.

Long-term commitments to development, substantial bureaucratic capabilities and embedded autonomy were used to create a set of institutions and incentives that enticed firms to build their technological capabilities so that they could successfully penetrate world export markets for manufactures. Those institutions and incentives included maintaining political and macroeconomic stability; investing in reliable infrastructural services – transport, telecommunication and power – at competitive prices; and eschewing protection of labor and the creation of social welfare states in favor of investing in education that provided firms with the skilled and unskilled labor they needed at competitive wages (World Bank, 1993). Because the institutions used to promote technological learning and the incentives offered firms and industries were firm and industry specific, promotional privileges were selective.

Institutional structures

Since governments recognized that technological catch-up had to be carried out by firms, they worked hard to develop contextually appropriate firm and industry structures. In Japan, Korea, Indonesia and Thailand, governments organized business into large-scale conglomerated firms – Japanese *zaibatsu* (Johnson, 1982), Korean *chaebols* (Amsden, 1989), Sino-Indonesian conglomerates run by *cukong* entrepreneurs (Hill, 1996), and Sino-Thai conglomerates (Rock, 1994). In Taiwan, the government used the power of the state to keep firms small and medium sized (Wade, 1990). In Singapore (Huff, 1999) and Malaysia (Rasiah, 1995), governments followed a catch-up strategy based on attracting foreign direct investment and linking local small and medium-sized firms as suppliers to OECD multinationals. Governments also took historically unique and direct roles in promoting technological catch-up. Three distinct strategies are evident.[1]

Taiwan built the public sector institutions of a national technology system and tightly linked them to the country's small and medium-sized enterprises (SMEs) and the international economy (Wade, 1990). A public sector investment promotion agency identified industries and technologies thought to be most applicable to each stage of industrial development. A public sector science and technology institute acquired these technologies, reverse-engineered them, and diffused them to the country's numerous SMEs. Another public sector agency linked the country's larger firms to clusters of smaller firms that became suppliers to the larger firms. In numerous instances, state-owned enterprises in upstream industries were used to acquire technological capabilities in scale-intensive industries which in turn supplied downstream users with high-quality and competitively priced intermediate inputs (Wade, 1990).

The Republic of Korea and, to a lesser extent, Indonesia and Thailand focused new government institutions and new incentives on building large indigenous national firms with substantial technological capabilities that could compete with developed-country multinational corporations. This strategy housed technological capabilities in firms and de-emphasized the role of the public sector in technical change. Korea did this by allocating performance-based promotional privileges, particularly subsidized credit from state-owned banks, to a small number of what turned out to be very large conglomerates (Amsden, 1989; Jones and Sakong, 1980; Rhee et al., 1984; Westphal, 1981). Those firms relied on the government's Foreign Capital Inducement Act to severely restrict foreign investment and rigorously review foreign firms' requests for licensing and technical assistance agreements so as to ensure that such agreements hastened the building of local technological capabilities (Mardon, 1990). Governments in Indonesia and Thailand adopted similar strategies but were less capable than Korea (Rock, 2000; 1995; 1994; MacIntyre, 2000; 1994). Despite this fact, governments in both targeted promotional privileges to a relatively few but very large national firms engaged in joint ventures with large developed-country multinational corporations (Rock, 1999; 1994). As in Korea, those firms dominated the industrial economy and initially served the local rather than export markets. Over time, promotional privileges shifted to encourage the export of manufactures.

Singapore and Malaysia focused on creating an institutional framework and developing the physical infrastructure and human capital to attract multinationals from developed countries (Huff, 1999; Times Academic Press, 1993; Rasiah, 1995). In both, investment promotion agencies scoured the globe for firms and industries to attract, and export processing zones (EPZs) were built to meet foreign investors' needs for reliable, high-quality and reasonably priced infrastructure services. Both also invested in skilled labor, controled wage rates, and severely restricted workers' rights to unionize and strike (Huff, 1999; and Jomo and Todd, 1994). Initially, this approach did not assume the necessity of creating an indigenously owned industrial base or an indigenous class of entrepreneurs, but eventually the model was extended to include the participation of indigenous SMEs in the global value chains coordinated by OECD multinationals (Battat et al., 1996; Rasiah, 2001). This was accomplished through local industry upgrading programmes or vendor development programmes that linked investment promotion agencies, multinationals and local supplying SMEs in long-term relationships.

Policy integration
Initially, governments in all these economies followed 'grow first, clean up later' environmental strategies. But once the costs of environmental degradation became visible, governments built effective command-and-control environmental agencies. Those agencies set ambient and emissions standards, monitored performance relative to standards, and enforced standards by imposing duties on polluters (Rock, 2002). In the most successful cases, ambient air and water quality approached that in economies in the OECD (Angel and Rock, 2003).

But a number of governments went further by integrating their command-and-control environmental agencies into the institutions of industrial policy. While this linkage, labeled policy integration by Rock and Angel (2006), took different forms in different political economies, it drove further improvements in ambient environmental quality, contributed to reductions in environmental intensities in specific industries, and encouraged shifts from pollution abatement to pollution prevention and clean production.

The specifics of policy integration varied significantly across economies. In Singapore, policy integration was achieved by linking the promotional decisions of the Economic Development Board (EDB), an investment promotion agency, to the infrastructure decisions of its premier infrastructure agency, the Jurong Town Corporation, and by requiring firms receiving support from these agencies to meet the environmental requirements of its environmental agency, the Ministry of the Environment (ENV) (Rock, 2002). In Taiwan, the government bypassed its premier industrial policy agency, the Industrial Development Board (IDB), by creating a strong environmental agency that had the legal authority, technical capabilities and the administrative discretion to impose sanctions on firms that failed to meet emissions standards (Rock, 2002). By this action, the government signalled to the IDB that it was serious about environmental clean-up. This led the IDB to devise its own industrial environmental improvement programme – one that benchmarked the environmental performance of Taiwanese firms in particular industries against international best practices. In this way, the government followed a pathway to industrial environmental improvement that integrated environmental considerations into its national innovation system. In Malaysia, a somewhat weaker environmental agency reduced wastewater emissions in the crude palm oil (CPO) industry by establishing and relying on close relations to CPO firms, a powerful palm oil industry association, and the Palm Oil Research Institute of Malaysia (PORIM) (Rock, 2002).

Capturing international technique effects
There is a growing body of research which suggests that process technologies in OECD industries have lower energy, materials and pollution intensities than their counterparts in the developing world. Both Reppellin-Hill (1999), who focused on the steel industry, and Wheeler and Martin (1992), who analyzed the pulp and paper industry, concluded that technique effects are quite substantial and that access to them by local producers is conditioned on openness of developing economies to trade and investment. However, questions remain as to whether these results follow automatically from openness to OECD capital and technology or whether they depend upon the incentives that exist for adopting such capital and technologies (Rock, 2002; Brandon and Ramankutty, 1993). If they do not flow automatically from openness, improved environmental performance within particular industries may well depend upon the coexistence of two conditions: access to technologies that are less energy, materials and pollution intensive, and incentives to select these technologies and adapt them to local conditions.

Technique effects in cement and pulp and paper
What do we know about the coexistence of these two conditions in the East Asian newly industrializing economies? While there is not much evidence on this question, two recent studies (Angel and Rock, 2005; Rock, 2006) in notably dirty and energy-intensive industries – cement and pulp and paper – in four East and Southeast Asian economies – China, Indonesia, Malaysia and Thailand – provide evidence that supports the need for these conditions. The findings of these studies suggest quite large technique effects in both industries where access to and incentives for the adoption of environmentally friendly technologies were present. With respect to cement production, the energy-intensity benefits of openness to trade, foreign investment and foreign technology range from a low of 15% (a saving of 131 kilocalories per kilogram of clinker) to a high of 93% (658 kilocalories per kilogram of clinker). The impact of openness to trade, foreign investment and foreign technology, and regulatory pressure on pollution intensity is even more dramatic – it declines by more than 90% when plants import OECD cement kilns with OECD pollution control equipment and are either part of a joint venture with an OECD multinational or export. Similar findings emerge in pulp and paper plants, where liberalization of

policies toward this industry and openness to trade and investment lowered energy intensity by more than 50% and pollution intensity by about 20% (Rock, 2006, pp. 15–16). While these results are encouraging and consistent with a range of other studies (Repellin-Hill, 1999; Wheeler and Martin, 1992), they ultimately tell us too little about how such technique effects actually occur in globalizing industries or those that upgrade their technologies through international relationships. To remedy this problem, we examine technological learning in two firms in these economies.

Technique effects in firms
The first study (Rock and Angel, 2006) focuses on long-term technological learning in a large leading Thai cement conglomerate – Siam City Cement – and the impact of environmental learning before and after the firm became a joint venture partner with an OECD multinational corporation. The second focuses on the emerging environmental relationship between an OECD electronics multinational, Motorola, its wholly owned subsidiary in Penang, Malaysia, and that subsidiary's suppliers following adoption of two new EU environmental directives affecting electronics firms (Rock et al., 2006). We chose these two examples because they represent different aspects of the technological upgrading process attending globalization – one focuses on the linkages between an OECD multinational and a local lead firm (cement), while the other focuses on linkages between an OECD multinational and its local small and medium-sized suppliers (electronics). Both demonstrate how technological learning, policy integration and interaction with OECD multinationals can contribute to substantial environmental technique effects. Both also demonstrate the growing importance of OECD multinational firm-based global environmental standards.

Siam City Cement Company (SCCC) began operations in 1972 when it established a turnkey contractual relationship with a European engineering firm to build its first cement kiln. This kiln was the first modern dry kiln with a pre-heater in Thailand. The company's second kiln, a modern dry kiln with a pre-heater, was built in 1981, also as a turnkey operation. Numerous production-related problems with both kilns convinced management that they had to invest in building their technological capabilities. Their first major capabilities investment occurred in the late 1970s when rising energy prices led them to modify the firing systems in the kilns so they could use coal lignite rather than bunker fuel. This effort cut fuel use.

In 1983, adaptive technological learning continued when the company achieved international best practice fuel efficiency by adding a pre-calciner to its first kiln line. During the 1980s, the company added four more kilns. For the third kiln, engineers worked with a European engineering firm on the design, construction, and identification and oversight of suppliers for various parts. Through this process, company engineers learned to conduct investment feasibility studies, organize activities associated with establishing a new cement plant, and manage the information, skills and technology associated with overseeing the project's subcontractors. In 1989, 1992 and 1996, the company added its fourth, fifth and sixth kilns. Each time its engineers took on more of the design, construction and subcontracting responsibilities. By 1996 the company was able to successfully manage all project phases independently.

SCCC's investment, production and linkage capabilities extended to pollution management. From the very beginning, engineers at SCCC worked with their European suppliers on the operation of air pollution control equipment. They subsequently learned how to install and operate both electro-static precipators (ESP) and bag filters (BF). By 2002, SCCC had 87 BFs and 9 ESPs installed in factory 1, 168 BFs and 13 ESPs installed in factory 2, and 223 BFs and 13 ESPs installed in factory 3 (SCCC, 2002). Because SCCC has been so successful in acquiring environmental capabilities, dust and SO_2 emissions from its kiln stacks are quite low (varying from 23 to 85 mg/m^3 of dust between 1999 and 2001, and 1.71 ppm to 3.41 ppm SO_2).

Following the East Asian financial crisis, Holcim Ltd, a Swiss cement multinational, acquired a 30% share in SCCC. This linkage enabled engineers at SCCC to further advance their production and environmental process capabilities. Engineers at SCCC learned through Holcim's internal plant benchmarking process that a number of their production lines were the most productive, efficient,[2] and least polluting plants in the Holcim group. Moreover, SCCC's environmental performance exceeds Holcim's guidelines for emissions of dust, NO_x and SO_2. SCCC engineers also learned how to design, manage and implement an aggressive alternative fuels and raw materials (AFRM) program introduced by Holcim – one that significantly reduced CO_2 emissions (SCCC, 2002, pp. 20–21).

SCCC's long-term investments in technological capabilities building appear to have paid off. Beyond very significant energy cost savings, the pollution intensity of cement production at SCCC converged to international best practice. This would have been impossible without SCCC's internal investments in technological learning and its international ties to the Holcim group.

Similar environmental improvements are visible at Motorola and Motorola's wholly owned subsidiary in Penang, Malaysia. There the company worked closely with its local suppliers to insure that its electronics products would be compliant with the Restriction of certain Hazardous Substances (RoHS) and Waste from Electrical and Electronic Equipment (WEEE) directives of the EU. But Motorola's attention to firm-based environmental standards cannot be separated from a broader set of institutional developments within the corporation that began with the creation of the Motorola Training and Education Center in the 1970s (MTEC) (Meyer, 1996a, 1996b). While MTEC focused on continuous quality improvements in production (Meyer, 1996b), it was subsequently expanded to cover all aspects of Motorola's business (Barney, 2002), including environmental health and safety (EHS).

Integration of environmental health and safety concerns into quality management practices began in 1993 when Motorola conducted a series of environmental audits of its facilities worldwide.[3] In the midst of these site-specific audits, the company moved to a common EHS management system requiring all subsidiaries to meet a set of corporate environmental expectations (Motorola, 2002). Subsequently, the Motorola–Penang facility replaced its health and safety team with an EHS committee while Motorola introduced a set of global firm-based environmental standards that covered performance, procedures and suppliers.

With respect to performance, Motorola developed specific global firm-wide quantitative environmental goals for reducing volatile organic compounds, hazardous air emissions, perfluorocarbon (PFC) use, hazardous waste, and water and energy consumption (Motorola, 2002). These operational goals are buttressed by longer-range improvement goals including zero waste, benign emissions and closed-loop recycling of all natural resources (ibid.). Motorola also developed product performance goals for environmentally preferred products (EPPs) (ibid.).

With respect to procedures, Motorola maintains a suite of specific internal protocols and reporting requirements that must be followed by all plants worldwide. Each site is required to report on a standard set of environmental metrics consistent with corporate environmental goals (Motorola, 2002). In addition, the firm uses a variety of proprietary global and subsidiary-specific software tools to drive it toward continuous environmental improvement. A Motorola Toxicity Index (MTI) is used to identify each of the chemicals used in a product and to weigh each chemical by its toxicity. This, in turn, enables the company to develop a simple aggregate measure of the toxicity of each product. The Green Design Advisor (GDA) is used in the project design stage to improve the recyclability of new products while designing out toxicity (Feldman et al., 1999). Motorola also maintains a specifications list, the W 18 list, of banned substances and those that can only be used if they fall below certain concentration levels.

With respect to suppliers, Motorola has numerous requirements to ensure compliance with environmental expectations. All first-tier-qualified suppliers must be ISO 14001 certified. Suppliers are not permitted to use ozone-depleting substances. Suppliers must also complete detailed materials disclosure sheets for all the parts they supply. These sheets identify the use of particular materials in components supplied to the MNC (e.g. lead and all heavy metals) and detail the amount of those materials in each product supplied. These supply chain requirements are 'enforced' by the use of a Parts Information Management System (PIMS), an electronic tool that identifies each part in each product by a part number, supplier and set of technical specifications. Motorola is in the process of implementing a new database system called Compliance Connect (Kierl, 2004). Compliance Connect will enable Motorola to electronically identify each part in each Motorola product by a part number, preferred global supplier, technical specifications, and by toxic substance and toxicity level.

How have Motorola's global firm-based standards affected its wholly owned subsidiary in Penang and this subsidiary's suppliers in Penang and Malaysia? There are several answers to this question. Because Motorola benchmarks individual plants against firm-wide performance standards, the Penang facility is benchmarked on such performance measures as water and electricity use, hazardous waste generation and waste recycling. This has encouraged substantial improvements in environmental performance at the plant – between 2000 and 2003 hazardous materials per unit built has fallen by 75%, the scrap recycling rate has increased by 100% and water use has declined from 35 liters per person-hour to 15 liters per person-hour.

Pursuit of corporate environmental objectives forced Motorola–Penang to work more closely with its local suppliers. This began when plant engineers realized that they could not meet Motorola's deadline for phasing out chlorofluorocarbons (CFCs) without getting their suppliers to eliminate the use of CFCs in the parts they supplied. More recently, regulatory developments elsewhere[4] suggested to Motorola–Penang that continued access to those markets might depend on their ability to meet new stringent hazardous substances requirements.

Faced with this problem, Motorola-Penang turned to Motorola's Corporate EHS Department, the Real Environmental Assessment Lab (REAL) in Wiesbaden, Germany, and the Environmental Materials Assessment Lab in China for help. Much of the initial back and forth focused on how to interpret and define the EU's directive banning or limiting the use of certain hazardous substances in each 'homogeneous element'[5] in each product. Once Motorola decided that the term 'homogeneous element' would be applied to each distinct element in each distinct part in each Motorola product, Motorola-Penang brought its EHS personnel, its design engineers, manufacturing engineers and supply chain managers together to sort through how the subsidiary would organize itself and how it would interact with its suppliers to meet these requirements. This *ad hoc* group broke each product down into its constituent 'homogeneous elements' and analyzed each element to determine whether it met the RoHS Directive. Because some of these homogeneous elements were provided to Motorola-Penang by local and/or global suppliers, Motorola-Penang began asking its suppliers to provide additional detailed documentation on the use of hazardous materials in the production of the parts they supplied. This documentation was double checked at Motorola-Penang and at one of Motorola's labs.

But work with suppliers extends beyond requests for information and testing of supplied parts. Increasingly, Motorola-Penang has been working with suppliers on problems related to increasing the compliance rate of its products with RoHS and WEEE. In one instance, Motorola-Penang worked with several chemical suppliers, other Motorola subsidiaries and Motorola corporate to develop a new no-clean flux tin/lead solder paste. A similar process was used in developing halogen-free printed wiring boards (PWBs) and flex.[6] In another instance, Motorola–Penang worked closely with its Indian suppliers of leather cases for hand phones produced by Motorola–Penang to reduce the level of chromium in these cases. This required working with chemical and leather suppliers to find an alternative process for 'softening' the leather cases. As a result, the leather suppliers have been able to reduce the concentration of chromium by 99.99%.

Taken together, Motorola's longstanding program of continuous improvement along the supply chain, coupled with its extension of this program to an evolving set of firm-based environmental standards, helped the company integrate traditional price, quality and on-time delivery expectations with environmental standards for its suppliers. When this was combined with growing global pressures to reduce the toxicity and increase the recyclability of its products, Motorola went a step further by using corporate environmental standards and its own protocols to meet these new external standards and to force and entice its wholly owned subsidiaries and first-tier suppliers to specify the toxicity of the parts they manufacture.

Conclusions

Our research suggests that globalization has had some significant environmental effects in several industries in East Asia where industrial development strategies have been based on two institutional innovations, the capitalist developmental state and policy integration. Together these appear to be driving firms in this region to upgrade their technological and environmental capabilities. This has been largely an imitative process by which local firms have imported, adopted and adapted newer OECD-derived process technologies, including pollution control technologies and clean production processes, in particular industries. But none of this was automatic and it took time, energy and some failure before governments figured out how to create the institutional environment that would get firms to invest heavily in such technological learning. Because investment in technological learning is costly, difficult and uncertain, governments recognized that they had to provide the enabling conditions, the incentives and the institutions so that firms would undertake it. While the evidence suggests that governments in these economies were more rather than less successful in these efforts, the early environmental consequences of this development strategy were quite negative.

As local industries and economies grew and became more integrated in the world economy, it became increasingly evident that governments had to complement their industrial polices and institutions with better pollution management. Consequently, governments invested in the creation of cost-effective command-and-control regulatory agencies and integrated these agencies into the institutions of industrial development. It appears that a development strategy that emphasizes technological learning,and forces multinationals to transfer their technologies, while practicing policy integration, made it easier for local firms to tap into environmental technique effects associated with openness to trade and investment. This finding suggests that tapping into these effects may well require more than opening an economy. As our case studies in cement and electronics demonstrate, when these factors are combined with environmental pressures in OECD markets, they just may be sufficient to get multinationals to adopt stringent firm-based environmental standards which they can then impose on their developing-country joint venture partners and suppliers. When they do this, the positive technique effects associated with an industrial technological catch-up development strategy are reinforced.

Notes

1. These broad approaches identify the dominant approach to technological development in particular economies. In practice, governments in most East Asian countries adopted elements of more than one approach. For example, while Taiwan focused most of its technological development strategy on small and medium-sized firms, it also promoted larger firms in upstream industries.
2. The average cost of producing a ton of cement in the Holcim group in 2001 and 2002 was nearly twice the cost of producing a ton of cement at SCCC.
3. Unless otherwise noted, what follows is based on a series of in-depth interviews conducted in October 2003 and January 2004 at Motorola-Malaysia.
4. There is discussion in Japan, California (Proposition 65) and China about adopting EU-like RoHS and WEEE directives.
5. Although the term 'homogeneous element' does not appear in the EU's RoHS Directive, it does appear in an EU Commission stakeholder document, which can be found at http://www.intertek-cb.com/newsitetest/news.rohsresources.shmtl.
6. Flex refers to flexible wiring boards, which are used in numerous electronics products such as cellphones.

References

Amsden, A. (1989), *Asia's Next Giant*, New York: Oxford University Press.
Angel, D.P. and M.T. Rock (2001), 'Policy integration: environment and development in Asia', paper prepared for the *Asian Environmental Outlook Series*, Manila: Asian Development Bank.
Angel, D. P. and M.T. Rock (2003), 'Engaging economic development agencies in environmental protection: the case for embedded autonomy', *Local Environment*, 8(1), 45–59.
Angel, D.P. and M.T. Rock (2005), 'Global standards and the environmental performance of industry', *Environment and Planning*, 37, 1903–18.
Barney, M. (2002), 'Motorola's second generation', *Six Sigma Forum Magazine*,1(3), 1–5.
Battat, J., I. Frank and X. Shen (1996), 'Suppliers to MNCs: linkage programs to strengthen local companies in developing countries', Foreign Investment Advisory Service Occasional Paper, 6, Washington, DC: World Bank.
Brandon, C. and R. Ramankutty (1993), *Toward an Environmental Strategy for Asia*, Washington, DC: World Bank.
Copeland, B.R. and M. Scott Taylor (2003), *Trade and Environment: Theory and Evidence*, Princeton,NJ: Princeton University Press.

Evans, P.B. (1995), *Embedded Autonomy: States and Industrial Transformation*, Princeton,NJ: Princeton University Press.

Feldmann, K., O. Meedt, S. Trautner, H. Scheller and W. Hoffman (1999), 'The "Green Design Advisor": a tool for design for the environment', *Journal of Electronics Manufacturing*, **9**(1), 17–28.

Haggard, S. (1990), *Pathways from the Periphery*, Ithaca, NY: Cornell University Press.

Hill, H. (1996), *The Indonesian Economy Since 1966*, Cambridge, UK: Cambridge University Press

Huff, W.G. (1999), 'Singapore's economic development: four lessons and some doubts', *Oxford Development Studies*, **21**(1), 33–5.

Johnson, C. (1982), *MITI and the Japanese Miracle*, Palo Alto, CA: Stanford University Press.

Jomo, K.S. (1986), *A Question of Class: Capital, the State and Uneven Development in Malaya*, Singapore: Oxford University Press.

Jomo, K.S. and P. Todd (1994), *Trade Unions and the State in Peninsular Malaysia*, Kuala Lumpur: Oxford University Press.

Jones, L. and I. Sakong (1980), *Government, Business and Entrepreneurship: The Korean Case*, Cambridge, MA: Harvard University Press.

Kierl, B. (2004), *iDEN Compliance Connect Hands On Training*, Plantation, FL and Schaumburg, IL: Motorola, Inc.

MacIntyre, A. (1994), 'Power, prosperity, and patrimonialism: business and government in Indonesia', in A. MacIntyre (ed.), *Business and Government in Industrializing Asia*, Ithaca, NY: Cornell University Press,pp. 244–67.

MacIntyre, A. (2000), 'Funny money: fiscal policy, rent-seeking and economic performance in Indonesia', in M.H. Khan and K.S. Jomo (eds), *Rents, Rent-Seeking and Economic Development: Theory and Evidence from Asia*, Cambridge, UK: Cambridge University Press,pp. 248–73.

Managi, S. (2007), *International Trade, Economic Growth and the Environment in High and Low Income Economies*, Yokohama, Japan: International Graduate School of the Social Sciences, Yokohama National University.

Mardon, R. (1990), 'The state and the effective control of foreign capital', *World Politics*, **43** (October), 111–38.

Meyer, K.A. (1996a), *Motorola (A)*, Harvard Business School Case, Boston, MA: Harvard Business School Publishing.

Meyer, K.A. (1996b), *Motorola (B)*, Harvard Business School Case, Boston, MA: Harvard Business School Publishing.

Motorola, Inc. (2002), *Motorola: 2002 Global Corporate Citizenship Report*, Schaumburg, IL: Motorola, Inc.

Pasuk, P. and C. Baker (1995), *Thailand: Economy and Politics*, New York: Oxford University Press.

Rasiah, R. (1995), *Foreign Capital and Industrialization in Malaysia*, Basingstoke, UK: Macmillan.

Repellin-Hill, V. (1999), 'Trade and the environment: an empirical analysis of the technology effect in the steel industry', *Journal of Environmental Economics and Management*, **38**, 283–30.

Rhee, Y. H., B. Ross-Larson and L. Westphal (1984), *Korea's Competitive Edge: Managing Entry into World Markets*, Baltimore, MD: Johns Hopkins University Press.

Rock, M.T. (1994), 'Transitional democracies and the shift to export-led industrialization: lessons from Thailand', *Studies in Comparative International Development*, **29**(1), 18–37.

Rock, M.T. (1995), 'Thai industrial policy: how irrelevant was it to export success?' *Journal of International Development*, **7**(5), 745–57.

Rock, M.T. (1999), 'Reassessing the effectiveness of industrial policy in Indonesia: can the neo-liberals be wrong?', *World Development*, **27**(4), 691–704.

Rock, M.T. (2000), 'Thailand's old bureaucratic polity and its new semi-democracy', in M.H. Khan and K.S. Jomo (eds), *Rents, Rent-Seeking and Economic Development: Theory and Evidence from Asia*, Cambridge, UK: Cambridge University Press, pp. 182–206.

Rock, M.T. (2002), *Pollution Control in East Asia: Lessons from the Newly Industrializing Economies*, Washington, DC: Resources for the Future, and Singapore: Institute for Southeast Asian Studies.

Rock, M.T. (2003), 'The Politics of Development Policy-Making in New Order Indonesia', paper presented at the Seminar on Economic Policy Reform in Asia, Department of Political Science and the William Davidson Institute, University of Michigan, Ann Arbor, 12 September, 2002.

Rock, M.T. (2006), 'The impact of liberalization, privatization and globalization on environmental intensities in the pulp and paper industry in China', paper presented at the Industrial Transformation in Asia Conference, Beijing, China, 12–13 January.

Rock, M.T. and D.P. Angel (2006), *Industrial Transformation in the Developing World*, Oxford: Oxford University Press.

Rock, M. T., D. P. Angel, and P. L. Lim (2006), 'Impact of multinational corporations' firm-based environmental standards on subsidiaries and their suppliers: evidence from Motorola-Malaysia', *The Journal of Industrial Ecology*, **10**(1–2), 257–78.

SCCC (2002), *Environmental Initiatives*, Bangkok, Thailand: Siam City Cement Public Company Limited.

Times Academic Press (1993), *Challenge and Response: Thirty Years of the Economic Development Board*, Singapore: Times Academic Press.

Wade, R.H. (1990), *Governing the Market*, Princeton, NJ: Princeton University Press.

Westphal, L. (1981), '*Korea's industrial competence: where it came from*', Staff Working Paper No. 469, Washington, DC: World Bank.

Wheeler D. and P. Martin (1992), 'Prices, policies and the international diffusion of clean technology: the case of wood pulp production', in P. Low (ed.), *International Trade and the Environment*, Washington, DC: World Bank, pp. 197–224.

World Bank (1993), *The East Asian Miracle*, New York: Oxford University Press.

11 Foreign direct investment and clean technology leapfrogging in China
Kelly Sims Gallagher

It has often been assumed that foreign direct investment (FDI) in developing countries brings with it more advanced technologies from the home country. Embedded in this assumption is the notion that foreign investors also bring cleaner technologies with them, thereby allowing the developing countries to 'leapfrog' to the most advanced environmental technologies available. Contrary to this notion is the pollution haven hypothesis, wherein large multinational companies move to developing countries because of their weaker environmental standards.

Some scholars and policy-makers have taken the wrong lesson from the empirical evidence regarding the pollution-haven hypothesis. As the chapter by Copeland in this volume (Chapter 4) demonstrates, most multinational companies do not move to developing countries because of their weaker environmental standards. Some policy-makers have interpreted these findings to mean that one not need formulate policies to address the environmental impact of foreign investment. From a scholarly perspective, though, the pollution-haven hypothesis is strictly a 'firm location' theory, and makes no pretense about explaining the behavior of foreign firms once they have already invested in or moved to a developing country.

This chapter looks mainly at the environmental behavior of multinational corporations investing in China, specifically taking the case of the US automotive firms as they formed joint ventures with Chinese counterparts. The US Big Three automakers clearly did not move to China in order to exploit its weaker environmental laws but instead they invested in order to serve China's exploding domestic automobile market. They saw China as the next big emerging market for the industry. This chapter, however, which draws on a larger book on the subject, demonstrates that the US firms did not automatically transfer state-of-the-art environmental technologies to China when they started their operations there due to a stark lack of incentives to do so (Gallagher, 2006a). There is evidence of this lack of technological leapfrogging from FDI in other industries elsewhere in China, and this is reviewed as well. The main lesson for research and policy, then, is that FDI will not automatically transfer cleaner technologies to developing countries – and therefore that environmental leapfrogging is not automatic through FDI. A coherent incentive structure largely composed of policies and institutions must be in place in order to elicit cleaner technology transfer.

This chapter first reviews the existing theories of the impact of FDI on environmental quality. It then examines the current situation in China in terms of trends in environmental quality, and the situation with FDI in China. The case of FDI in the auto industry in China is discussed in some detail before turning to the lessons for research and policy.

FDI and the environment
That FDI will bring cleaner technologies to developing countries, enabling technological leapfrogging, is a persistent and attractive notion. Numerous cases from around the world, however, show that FDI does not automatically bring cleaner technologies with it (Gentry, 1999; Araya, 2002). There are three principal theories to explain this phenomenon of foreign investors transferring outdated or more pollution-intensive technologies to the recipient country: the pollution haven hypothesis; the race-to-the-bottom hypothesis; and the stuck-in-the-mud hypothesis. But it is perhaps better to try to understand not whether FDI is good or bad for the environment, but rather under what conditions it can be beneficial (Araya, 2002). As Gentry (1999) notes, FDI is neither 'boon nor bane' for the environment; it is both.

The pollution haven hypothesis posits that multinational corporations will relocate to developing countries due to their weaker environmental standards (and therefore lower compliance costs). As mentioned above, this hypothesis is one regarding firm location, not firm performance, once the firm has already invested. The empirical evidence for the pollution haven hypothesis is thin (Chudnovsky and Lopez, 2002; Gallagher, K.P., 2004). The main reason why so little evidence for the pollution haven hypothesis has accumulated seems to be that environmental compliance costs are relatively insignificant as compared with the other potential benefits of moving to developing countries, such as substantially lower labor costs.

The race-to-the-bottom and stuck-in-the-mud hypotheses are connected. The race-to-the-bottom hypothesis is that countries wishing to attract more FDI will weaken their environmental standards in order to do so. This weakening could be done through relaxing existing standards (though this is rare), or through offering reduced non-compliance fees or exemptions for certain projects. A variation on this theory is the 'stuck-in-the-mud' or 'regulatory chill' theory, where recipient countries – mainly developing countries – will not raise environmental standards for fear of losing FDI to other countries (Zarsky, 1999). Here the evidence is more mixed.

Extending the 'regulatory chill' theory, a 'competitive-disadvantage–vicious-circle' hypothesis has been posited (Gallagher, 2006a), where recipient countries do not raise environmental standards for fear that domestic industries cannot compete with the foreign-invested firms because the unaffiliated domestic firms lack the technology to comply. The developing country delays raising environmental standards for fear of putting the domestic firms out of business, but meanwhile the foreign firms further innovate to meet ever-more stringent standards abroad. Thus the environmental–technological gap continues to widen between domestic firms and their foreign counterparts, putting further pressure on the recipient government to delay imposition of stricter pollution policies.

Grossman and Krueger (1991) decomposed the effect of trade liberalization in a manner that is useful for considering the environmental impact of FDI as well: scale, composition and technique effects. Scale effects refers to when the environmental impact is large because the scale of economic activity is large. Composition effects refers to structural changes in the economy resulting in increased or reduced pollution, such as if heavy, pollution-intensive industry grows as a result of FDI. Technique effects refers to the impact of technological changes such as introduction of pollution control technologies.

FDI in China

China's economy is the fourth largest in the world, with a GDP of $2.7 trillion in 2006, but the second largest in the world on a purchasing-power-parity basis. It continues to grow rapidly, with an average annual growth rate of 10 percent since 1978 (Xinhua, 2007). The success of China's economic development strategy has lifted 400 million people out of absolute poverty, although an estimated 200 million remain in poverty (World Bank, 2007).

Until 2007, China's economic growth strategy was investment and export led. The Chinese government poured its own resources into its own firms while simultaneously requiring them to improve product quality, to export more and more to integrate China into the global economy, and to improve competitiveness. The government also actively pursued FDI. Between 1990 and 2000, China received $30 billion per year in inward FDI on average, but this amount has grown substantially since then, with China receiving $69 billion in 2006, accounting for 18 percent of total FDI into developing economies (UNCTAD, 2007).

The environmental situation in China

The environmental situation in China is becoming increasingly grave as its unfettered economic growth continues. By nearly every indicator of environmental quality, the situation is getting worse. Sulfur dioxide emissions rose 42 percent between 2000 and 2005. Soot emissions rose 11 percent during the same time period. Water pollution is also a serious problem. Between 2001 and 2005, on average 54 percent of the water from the seven main rivers was deemed unsafe for human consumption (World Bank, 2007). One-third of China's cities do not have wastewater treatment plants (CCICED, 2008). Acid rain costs 9 billion yuan annually in crop damage. A recent report estimated that, in total, water and air pollution costs in 2003 were 362 billion yuan, equivalent to 3 percent of China's GDP that year (World Bank, 2007). Other estimates of the economic cost of China's pollution have been much higher. The situation has become so dire that local protests have become strikingly frequent. In 2006, Minister Zhou Shengxian of China's State Environmental Protection Administration (SEPA) announced that there were 51 000 environmental protests in 2005, nearly 1000 per week (Economy, 2007). In many of these cases, dumping of hazardous wastes and toxic substances into local water supplies is a primary cause of protest. In terms of climate change, Chinese carbon dioxide emissions are rising rapidly. In 2007, China surpassed the USA in terms of total aggregate greenhouse gas emissions, although its per capita emissions are approximately one-fifth those of the USA, now the second-largest emitter of greenhouse gas emissions (IEA, 2007).

Many of China's environmental problems are driven by its heavy reliance on coal. China consumes twice as much coal as does the USA, and coal accounts for 70 percent of commercial energy supply. In 2006, power plants and industry reportedly consumed 2.8 billion metric tons (tonnes) of coal, which was 70 percent higher than in 2001. The growth in China's power sector has been incredibly fast, unrivaled anywhere else. In 1995, power plant capacity was 217 GW. Five years later, in 2000, it surpassed 319 GW. Between 2005 and 2006, electricity generation capacity grew by 20 percent from 517 GW to 622 GW, nearly all of which was coal-fired power (Zhao and Gallagher, 2007).

The Chinese government is actively tackling most of these environmental challenges and is making some progress. Desulfurization equipment has been installed on 200 GW of coal-fired power plants, which is approximately 40 percent of thermal power plant capacity in China (Zeng, 2007). The government has issued strong targets for energy efficiency and renewable energy, although its progress toward meeting these goals has been uneven. China has issued six main environmental laws and nine natural resources laws, though, again, enforcement of these laws is inconsistent. The State Council has released 28 environmental administrative regulations, and SEPA has published 27 environmental standards. Reportedly, more than 900 local environmental rules have been promulgated as well (Liu, 2007). The Chinese government issued its first fuel efficiency standards for automobiles in 2005, and they were strengthened in 2008. China now leads the world in total installed renewable energy capacity at 42 GW, largely due to its widespread deployment of solar thermal technology. In 2005, China passed a renewable energy law that requires grid operators to purchase electricity from renewable generators and it set a target of 10 percent of electric power generation coming from renewable energy sources by 2010, not including large hydropower (Gallagher, 2007).

In China's big cities, most of the urban air pollution comes from motor vehicles. The car population in China has grown dramatically, going from less than 100 000 total in 1990 to approximately 25 million in 2007. All the new cars on the road are causing oil imports to rise, and China is now the second-largest consumer of oil in the world and the third-largest oil importer. By 2000, total Chinese automobile oil consumption equaled total oil imports at 1.2 million barrels per day (Xu, 2002). Although the growth in new cars has been astounding, the total number is still small compared with the situation in the USA, which has a car and sport utility vehicle (SUV) population of 230 million. With 20 percent of the world's population, the Chinese own only 1.5% of the cars in the world (Davis and Diegel, 2007).

The Chinese government has imposed four kinds of environmental regulations on passenger vehicles in China: tailpipe pollution control standards, fuel quality standards, fuel-efficiency standards, and a system of administrative fees based on engine size. The first pollution control standards took effect in the year 2000, and at that time China adopted the European system for pollution control, imposing the Euro 1 standard. This standard was very weak in comparison with other industrialized countries at the time. In 2004, China tightened the pollution control standards to the Euro 2 level, and then moved to Euro 3 levels in 2007. Fuel quality standards have lagged behind, and this has proved to be a major obstacle for reducing tailpipe emissions in China because, with high-sulfur fuels, it is impossible to achieve low emissions since the fuels erode the pollution-reducing catalytic converters. The first fuel quality standards were also imposed in 2000, and tightened in 2005. But policy towards improving fuel quality has stagnated due to the Chinese government's unwillingness to require its refiners to install expensive desulfurization equipment. As in the USA, some of the big cities have moved beyond the national standards and imposed more stringent standards themselves, Beijing and Shanghai among them. These cities are requiring low-sulfur fuel, which in turn forces the refiners to import more expensive sweet crude.

As the price of oil increased and China became a net oil importer, the Chinese government got serious about reducing demand for oil, which has many co-benefits in terms of reduced air pollution and greenhouse gas emissions. China issued its first fuel-efficiency standards for vehicles in 2005, and they were tightened at the beginning of 2008 in the second phase. In addition, the government created a system to impose higher taxes on vehicles with larger engines in an effort to encourage consumers to buy smaller, efficient cars. This system took effect in 2006.

FDI and the environment in China
Because there has been so much foreign investment in China, there are now more cases where one can examine the extent to which FDI has been correlated with environmental technology leapfrogging as compared with cases available regarding other countries. The evidence is mixed.

In some cases, FDI has contributed to better environmental performance. Eriksen and Hansen (1999) describe the joint venture between Novo Nordisk and Suzhou Hangda Group, which introduced a production process that eliminated the discharge of untreated water in accordance with Novo Nordisk's own corporate environmental policies. Christmann and Taylor (2001) argue that global ties increase 'self-regulation' pressures on firms in 'low-regulation' countries in a sample of 188 firms operating in China, and in particular, they showed that firms that were providing products to multinational corporations in China or to foreign customers were more likely to adopt the ISO 14000 system than other firms. In the case of wind energy development in China, China's large government wind tenders have local content requirements that increased from 50 percent in 2003 to 70 percent at the time of writing, in essence requiring foreign firms to look for ways to shift their manufacturing base to China (Lewis and Wiser, 2007). In general, the case studies of positive environmental spillovers in China seem to show that when there are environmental corporate norms on the part of the foreign investor or when a product is being exported to a country with higher environmental standards, then the Chinese-foreign joint venture firm will acquire and use cleaner technologies.

On the other hand, there are numerous cases where no environmental benefit is associated with FDI, putting aside the large potential 'scale' effect that one would expect to result from the FDI spurring greater economic output, which in turn will increase pollution, all things being equal. Xian et al. (1999) provide several examples of poor environmental performance by foreign investors in China, particularly on the part of other Asian investors in the toy, leather, footwear and plastics industries. Ohshita and Ortolano (2002) show that in the case of the clean coal technology transfer program of the Green Aid Program of Japan's Ministry of International Trade and Industry, there was a total failure of deployment of cleaner coal technologies due to the lack of effective mechanisms to enforce the environmental policies that would have made the use of clean coal technologies mandatory. Since the policies were not enforced, there was no need to pay additional money to transfer more expensive technology to China. In his examination of the chemical industry in China, Stalley (2005) also found that the simple lack of enforcement of existing environmental laws in China created a disincentive for cleaner technologies to be transferred and utilized.

Technology transfer in the Chinese auto industry
The US auto industry was among the very first industries of any kind to invest in China. The first investment was that of American Motors Corporation (AMC), maker of the Jeep brand all-terrain vehicle at the time, when AMC formed a joint venture with Beijing Auto Works (BAW) in 1983. Shortly thereafter, German firm Volkswagen was the second foreign firm to invest in the automobile industry, forming its own joint venture with the

Shanghai Automobile Industry Corporation (SAIC). These two pioneering foreign investments blazed the trail for all others that followed. Much later, General Motors eventually formed a joint venture with VW's same partner in Shanghai, and finally Ford Motor Company made its own foreign investment after China entered the World Trade Organization around the turn of the century. Now, all major foreign automobile firms are heavily invested in China. In this section, the environmental impact of the FDI for each of the three Sino-US joint ventures described during the period of 1984–2002 above will be evaluated drawing on a larger book on this subject (Gallagher, 2006a).

Beijing Jeep Corporation (BJC) was the first Sino-foreign automobile joint venture in China. Originally a joint venture of AMC and BAW, first Renault and then Chrysler took over the US side of the joint venture. The Chinese partner remained the same, although BAW's parent, Beijing Automobile Industry Corporation (BAIC), eventually dissolved and absorbed BAW when it consolidated. The motivations for the joint venture greatly diverged between the two partners. AMC saw China as the next huge passenger car market, forgetting that most of China's one billion consumers at the time were far too poor to buy a car. BAW, and the Chinese government more broadly, was anxious to acquire a modern, soft-top all-terrain vehicle for military purposes. The older model currently available in China, the BJ212, had been transferred to China by the Soviet Union before the Sino-Soviet split. BAW was the primary producer of these vehicles that served the Chinese military. The Chinese government was also experimenting, through BAW, the idea of developing a world-class automobile industry, even though there was much debate then within the Chinese leadership about whether or not it would be possible for China to catch up to the rest of the world given how far behind they were after the Cultural Revolution.

After much debate, AMC accepted a minority stake in the joint venture for a term of 20 years, and agreed to transfer AMC's Jeep Cherokee XJ model. This technological choice was a compromise solution because AMC refused to redesign any vehicles for the Chinese market, so the Chinese desire for a soft-top model, for example, was denied. The old model, the BJ212, was to be continued temporarily. There were no provisions for environmental or energy-efficient technology transfer. Thus, for nearly 20 years, all of the Beijing Jeep models were sold without any pollution control technology such as catalytic converters whatsoever. In addition, because the old BJ212 was so much cheaper, it continued to be sold for the next two decades and, actually, to be the top-selling model. Once China imposed its first vehicle emissions control standard in 2000, Beijing Jeep introduced Euro 1-level technology. Because Beijing had a more stringent standard, the Euro 2 standard, Beijing Jeep had to bring its vehicles into compliance as well and by 2003, all of the Beijing Jeep vehicles purportedly met the Euro 2 standard.

Shanghai GM was formed in 1997 as a partnership between the Shanghai Automotive Industry Corporation (SAIC) and General Motors (GM). GM aggressively pursued this joint venture because SAIC was considered to be one of the most successful and profitable Chinese automotive firms. Like all other foreign investors, GM was anxious to get into the Chinese market because it saw it as a big growth opportunity. In 1994, the Chinese government had finally issued its first Auto Industry Policy, which strongly emphasized enhancing the indigenous technological capabilities of the Chinese industry through technology transfer, so GM knew it would have to respond to this policy. GM transferred to China by far the most advanced technology to date of any foreign investor. As mentioned above, SAIC had a prior joint venture with Volkswagen, Shanghai VW, which was technologically stagnant. Shanghai VW had been producing the same old version of the Santana for many years with no updates at all. For the Shanghai GM joint venture, SAIC wanted to use the Buick brand due to its greater name recognition in China, and so the first model that was introduced was a Buick Regal (New Century) sedan, aimed at serving the government/official consumer market. The Chinese also insisted that GM establish a technical center, and so the Pan-Asia Technical Automotive Center (PATAC) was established as a separate joint venture to provide engineering services. The second model to be launched was aimed at private consumers in the burgeoning Chinese middle class, and it was a version of the Brazilian Chevrolet Corsa (which in turn was based on the original German Opel Corsa), named in China the Buick Sail. This small compact sedan had dual air bags and antilock brakes as standard features, a first for a compact car in China. Although the Buick Sail was far from being a new technology, many modifications had to be made before it could be introduced to China, including modifying the suspension, calibrating the engine, altering exterior styling and so forth. Shanghai GM started production of the Sail with 70 percent local content, the highest ever for a joint venture in China at the time.

Production of Shanghai GM vehicles began in December 1998. At the same time, China's first tailpipe pollution control emission standards for passenger vehicles were announced. The first emission control standards took effect in 2000, and at that time, China required all new vehicles to meet the Euro 1 emission control standard, which was the standard required by Europe for European vehicles in 1992. Some of the big cities went a step further and required Euro 2 standards, so Shanghai GM complied with the more stringent Euro 2 standard, which was the level required by Europe in 1994. But, as of 2000, Europe had already moved on to Euro 3 levels and the USA had imposed its Tier 1 standard, which was even more strict than European levels in some respects. Thus it cannot be said that GM transferred environmental technologies to China comparable to the ones they sold in the USA. GM argued that one reason why they did not was that fuel quality was so much worse in China. Poor fuel quality harms advanced vehicular pollution control technology and makes it increasingly ineffective.

The final case of Chang'An Ford is the most recent. Chang'An Ford was established in 2001, a joint venture between Chang'An Automobile (Group) Corp., based in Chongqing, and Ford Motor Company of Dearborn, MI. Ford was risk averse due to major concerns about intellectual property, and Ford was not willing to negotiate seriously with Chang'An until after the Permanent Normal Trade Relations (PNTR) negotiations between the USA and China were concluded as part of China's accession to the World Trade Organization. Among the many concessions that the USA sought, relaxation of restrictions on foreign investors in the automotive sector was a major point of contention. The USA succeeded in dismantling many of the restrictions, including a key provision that disallowed any requirements for technology transfer. After PNTR was finally signed into law, Ford concluded its negotiations with Chang'An in April 2001. The joint venture was split equally into a 50–50 ownership structure. For the first car model, Ford was willing to transfer only the Ford Fiesta to its counterparts in China, and this model was actually a 'Fiesta-based' Ford Ikon, which was already in production in India. The Ikon–Fiesta model to be produced in China was essentially the same as the one already being produced in India, other than being adapted for left-hand driving and automatic transmission. Chang'An was disappointed with this choice because it wanted to compete directly with the Buick Sail, and Chang'An feared that the technology was too outmoded. But Ford would not relent and together they built a new factory to produce the Fiesta in Chongqing. When it went into production, 62 percent of the Fiesta parts were domestically sourced. The Fiesta was not a success. So Ford reversed course, agreeing to introduce a version of the more modern Ford Focus in a new factory that was later built in Nanjing.

Similar to the Shanghai GM case, all of the Chang'An Ford vehicles met the Euro 2 standard, which was required by the Chinese government as of 2000. The Chang'An Ford vehicles did not go beyond the Euro 2 standard, so the pollution control technology in the Chang'An Ford vehicles was not as good as it is in Ford's US vehicles.

Lessons for research and policy

Based on the prior evidence and the cases presented above, there are several lessons that can be learned about the environmental impact of FDI in China. First, policy matters. In the absence of any environmental policy, no pollution control technologies were transferred to China. As soon as the Chinese government imposed its first pollution control standard, all of the foreign-invested joint ventures immediately complied and the foreign companies transferred the technologies sufficient to meet the local standards. Interestingly, none of the companies went 'beyond compliance', even though the Chinese pollution-control standards were considerably weaker than US or European standards. So long as the technology was good enough to meet the standard, that level of technology was all that was be transferred – a phenomenon that can be called the 'good enough phenomenon' (Gallagher, 2006b). Thus a second lesson to be learned is that environmental technology transfer correlates to the incentives in place. The stronger the incentive in place, the better the technological response. Third, no environmental technological leapfrogging took place in the sense that the Chinese skipped over previous generations of environmental technology. Instead, by virtue of the Chinese government decision to start at the relatively weak Euro 1 standard and then gradually make the standard more stringent (as had been done in Europe during the 1990s), the firms responded by meeting only the standard imposed by the Chinese government, and never surpassing it.

Another important lesson is that technological leapfrogging is not automatic. Incentives that push and pull the technologies into the market must exist. These cases demonstrate that environmental policy can create a highly effective incentive structure to require that technologies are transferred from foreign firms to their joint venture partners, thereby pulling them into China from abroad. In the automotive cases discussed above, although they did not choose to do so, it is also conceivable that the Chinese firms could have bargained for pollution-control technologies themselves during their joint venture negotiations. There is no evidence that the Chinese firms asked for environmental technologies; nor is there evidence that the foreign firms offered more environmental technologies.

References

Araya, Monica (2002), 'Environmental benefits of foreign direct investment: a literature review,' OECD Working Paper ENV/EPOC/GSP(2001)10/FINAL.
CCICED (2008), 'Report of Task Force on Innovation in Environmental Technologies', China Council for International Cooperation on Environment and Development, November.

Christmann, Petra and Glen Taylor (2001), 'Globalization and the environment: determinants of firm self-regulation in China', *Journal of International Business Studies*, **32**(3), 439–58.

Chudnovsky, Daniel and A. Lopez (2002), 'Globalization, foreign direct investment, and sustainable human development,' in K.P. Gallagher and J. Werksman (eds), *The Earthscan Reader on International Trade and Sustainable Development*, London: Earthscan, pp. 45–76.

Davis, Stacy and Susan Diegal (2007), *Transportation Energy Data Book*, Oak Ridge National Lab, Edition 26.

Economy, Elizabeth C. (2007), 'The great leap backwards? The costs of China's environmental crisis', *Foreign Affairs*, **86**(5), 38–59.

Eriksen, J. and M. Hansen (1999), 'Environmental aspects of Danish foreign direct investment in developing countries', Report, Copenhagen Business School, available from http://www.earthscape.org.

Gallagher, Kelly Sims (2006a), *China Shifts Gears: Automakers, Oil, Pollution, and Development*, Cambridge, MA: The MIT Press.

Gallagher, Kelly Sims (2006b), 'Limits to leapfrogging? Evidence from China's automobile industry,' *Energy Policy*, **34**, 383–94.

Gallagher, Kelly Sims (2007), 'China's place in the sun,' *Current History*, November/December, 389–94.

Gallagher, Kevin P. (2004), *Free Trade and the Environment: Mexico, NAFTA, and Beyond*, Stanford, CA: Stanford University Press.

Gentry, Bradford (1999), 'Foreign direct investment and the environment: boon or bane?', in OECD (ed.), *Foreign Direct Investment and the Environment*, Paris: Organisation for Economic Co-operation and Development.

Grossman, G.M. and A. Krueger (1991), *Environmental Impacts of a North American Free Trade Agreement*, Cambridge, MA: National Bureau of Economic Research.

IEA (2007), *World Energy Outlook*, Paris: International Energy Agency.

Lewis, Joanna I. and Ryan H. Wiser (2007), 'Fostering a renewable energy technology industry: an international comparison of wind industry policy support mechanisms', *Energy Policy*, **35**, 1844–57.

Liu, Xielin (2007), 'Building an environmentally-friendly society through innovation: challenges and choices', Background Paper, China Council for International Cooperation on Environment and Development.

Ohshita, Stephanie B. and Leonard Ortolano (2002), 'The promise and pitfalls of Japanese cleaner coal technology transfer to China', *International Journal of Technology Transfer and Commercialisation*, **1**(1–2), 56–81.

Stalley, Phillip (2005), 'Foreign investment and the implementation of domestic environmental regulation in China', *The International Journal of Environmental, Cultural, Economic and Social Sustainability*, **1**(4), 119–26.

UNCTAD (2007), World Investment Report Country Fact Sheet, Geneva.

World Bank (2007), *Cost of Pollution in China: Economic Estimates of Physical Damages*, The World Bank and China State Environmental Protection Administration, Washington, DC, The World Bank.

Xian, Guoming, Zhang, Cheng, Zhang Yangui, Ge Shunqi and James Zhan (1999), 'The interface between FDI and the environment: the case of China', Occasional Paper No. 3, Copenhagen Business School, available from http://www.unctad-10.org/pdfs/preux_fdipaper 3.en.pdf.

Xinhua (2007), 'China's GDP grows annual average of 9.67% from 1978 to 2006', Xinhua News Agency, Xinhua.net, 05/07/07, downloaded 12/07/07 from http://news.xinhuanet.com/english/2007-05/07/content_6064981.htm.

Xu, B. (2002), 'Arrangement on auto fuel economy standards and fuel efficiency promotion policies of China', Workshop on Cleaner Vehicles in the US and China sponsored by Harvard University, China Ministry of Science and Technology and China Automotive Technology and Research Center, Beijing.

Zarsky, Lyuba (1999), 'International investment rules and the environment: stuck in the mud?', *Foreign Policy in Focus*, **4**(22), 1–3.

Zeng, Peiyuan (2007), Speech delivered by Vice Premier of China, Beijing, China.

Zhao, Lifeng and Kelly Sims Gallagher (2007), 'Research, development, demonstration, and early deployment policies for advanced coal technology in China', *Energy Policy*, **35**, 6467–77.

PART II

TRADE AND
ENVIRONMENTAL POLITICS

12 Global mechanisms for greening TNCs: inching towards corporate accountability?
Jennifer Clapp

Introduction

There has been heightened concern in recent years with respect to the environmental impact of transnational corporations (TNCs) and foreign direct investment (FDI) (Dauvergne, 2001; Leighton et al., 2002; Gallagher and Zarsky, 2007). The past few decades have seen the emergence of a number of international mechanisms designed to enhance or improve the performance of TNCs with respect to the environment. Some of these mechanisms are undertaken by individual firms; some have been derived from within a particular industry; some have been developed in conjunction with other actors (state and non-state); and some are overseen by intergovernmental organizations. A key debate has been whether mechanisms to green TNCs should be industry driven and voluntary, or mandatory, as part of government regulation. All of the international mechanisms thus far put into place are voluntary. But many claim that such measures lack teeth, and there have been mounting calls for a more state-based regulatory approach at the global level to ensure corporate accountability.

This chapter provides a brief survey of the main international instruments for corporate greening that aim to improve the environmental performance of TNCs and FDI. The chapter first provides an outline and discussion of the various mechanisms and debates that have arisen with respect to these instruments. It then goes on to discuss the idea of a corporate accountability treaty, which some non-state actors have suggested as a means by which to provide more teeth to corporate greening initiatives. I argue that although there is at present too wide a range of existing corporate greening mechanisms – which makes the corporate greening landscape rather convoluted and diffused – there is a lack of political support at the present time for an overarching legally binding international treaty on corporate accountability. Efforts to link and strengthen existing mechanisms to give them more coherence and teeth may well be the best available strategy at this time at the global level for greening TNCs and FDI.

Global mechanisms for corporate greening

TNCs tend to invest in sectors that have potentially high environmental impact. They are key players in the manufacturing sector, which includes electronics, chemicals and heavy industry, as well as in the primary sector, which includes resource extraction – from forests to oil to minerals. Each of these industries is seen to have potentially high environmental impact, and recent research has documented environmental damage resulting from TNC behavior in these sectors, especially in the developing world.[1] In the past few years, growth in FDI has been especially strong in the primary sector (UNCTAD, 2006, p. 7), in particular in mining and oil, industries that are particularly prone to negative environmental consequences. It has also been noted that TNCs play a significant role in contributing to climate change (Morgera, 2004, p. 215).

It is not just the fact that TNCs tend to invest in high environmental impact sectors that has led to calls for corporate greening. The focus on the environmental impact of TNCs also has much to do with the remarkable growth of these entities and their increasing weight in the global economy in recent years, as the sheer volume of their activity alone has environmental consequences that must be considered, regardless of the sector in which they operate. As of 2005 there were some 77 000 TNCs (some 20 000 of which are headquartered in developing countries) and over 770 000 foreign affiliate firms in operation globally. These firms account for around one-tenth of global GDP and make up around one-third of world exports (UNCTAD, 2006, p. 10; 2001, p. 9; 2002, pp. xv and 272). The value of FDI has also grown remarkably in recent decades. In 1970 the level of FDI inflows stood at US$9.2 billion, and by 2005 it was US$916 billion (UNCTAD, 2006).

In this context of growing numbers of TNCs and growing value of FDI, combined with heightened concern with respect to the environmental impact of this investment, a number of international instruments have emerged over the past few decades to encourage corporate good environmental practice (KMPG and UNEP, 2006). These initiatives are primarily voluntary in nature, and aim to provide both guidance and standardization to corporate greening efforts at the international level. Some of these initiatives have emerged from within industry itself. But others have been put in place by other actors, although all initiatives work in close cooperation and coordination with industry itself. Because of the high degree of industry participation in such initiatives, many have seen these developments as a kind of 'privatization' of global environmental governance (Clapp, 1998), though with a complex relationship to government authority (Falkner, 2003).

The idea of greening TNCs and FDI is not entirely new. The UN Centre for Transnational Corporations sought to impose a global code of conduct for TNCs back in the 1970s, with the idea of holding TNCs accountable for the negative impacts of their global activities (FOE, 1998; Clapp, 2005). The initiative, however, was stopped short in the run-up to the Rio Earth Summit in 1992, where industry was incorporated into the global dialogue on 'sustainable development'. At Rio and in its aftermath, voluntary industry measures were promoted as being the appropriate governance mechanism by which to clean up the environmental impact of the activities of global firms. The result was the emergence of an array of voluntary initiatives at the international level to address different aspects of corporate greening, rather than pursuing a single regulatory approach at the global level.

The number of such initiatives is large, and appears to be still growing, with new initiatives being adopted almost yearly since 2000. Although each of these international mechanisms addresses a different need and niche with respect to corporate greening, the landscape has become somewhat crowded and confusing. The principal mechanisms and types of mechanisms are outlined below.

Global Reporting Initiative
In an effort to provide information on the environmental and social dimensions of their business operations, many TNCs began voluntarily in the 1990s to issue regular sustainability and corporate social responsibility (CSR) reports (Lamberton, 2005). Because these reports were mainly the product of self-analysis, with no oversight of the extent to

which firms disclosed information on the environmental impact of their operations and products, many early reports were seen to be mainly public relations exercises, rather than proper disclosure documents. To address this weakness in such reporting, the Global Reporting Initiative (GRI) emerged in 1997, the product of a collaboration between the Coalition for Environmentally Responsible Economies (CERES) and the United Nations Environment Program. The GRI sets guidelines as a means to establish a standardized framework for corporate sustainability reports and to ensure that such reports adequately and accurately reflect firm performance on a variety of fronts, including environmental.

The GRI's first set of guidelines was released in 2000 with some 50 firms following the reporting guidelines. The guidelines were revised in 2002, and again in 2006. Today there are over 1000 firms that adhere to some degree to the GRI guidelines. Initially based in CERES, a coalition of investors and environment and public interest groups in North America, the GRI became a permanent organization in 2002. It is also a collaborating center with the UNEP and in addition cooperates with the UN Global Compact, discussed below (GRI website: www.globalreporting.org). With GRI now a stand-alone organization, and with its guidelines becoming somewhat of an oversight and quality control mechanism for corporate sustainability reports, the reporting requirements for firms that sign on to this standard of reporting have increased over the years. The GRI guidelines, however, have several categories of adherence, which firms self-declare or have verified externally by a third party.

While encouraging corporations to disclose information about the environmental and social impacts of their operations can go some way to encouraging firms to improve their performance on these fronts, sustainability reporting has been critiqued as a weak mechanism for corporate greening. It relies heavily on self-reporting with no real external oversight of compliance (Utting, 2005). Because there are several categories of adherence to the GRI guidelines, it is easy for firms to sign on to the least demanding of these – preparing their reports with reference to the GRI guidelines without having them externally verified – and still advertise that they are GRI compliant.

UN Global Compact
The Global Compact (GC) is a pact between the UN and global business players that calls on corporations to adhere to a set of ten social, environmental and human rights goals. The GC, launched by then UN Secretary General Kofi Annan in July 2000, requests firms to incorporate these goals into their mission statements as well as into their operations (Therien and Pouliot, 2006). With respect to the environment, corporations are specifically asked to support the precautionary approach (Principle 7), to undertake initiatives to promote environmental responsibility (Principle 8), and to develop and diffuse environmentally friendly technologies (Principle 9). By 2007, some 3100 firms had signed on to the GC as participants. However, there are no strict reporting or membership requirements other than making a public pledge and providing an annual communication of progress to the UN (for which firms can now submit their sustainability reports provided they follow GRI guidelines). Because there is no oversight or monitoring, it is very easy for firms to join the GC.

NGOs have critiqued the GC as 'bluewash' (Bruno and Karliner, 2002). They claim that TNCs are using the GC as a way to associate themselves in the UN, which helps to improve their public image, without having to do much in terms of changing their actual practices. These critiques with respect to the lack of monitoring and oversight of the corporations that have signed on to the GC prompted the introduction of new integrity measures in 2004. Corporations that fail to provide their communication of progress for two years in a row are de-listed from the GC. As of mid-2007, some 791 firms had been listed as inactive. While the integrity measures may go some way toward reducing the incentive for firms to sign on without making an effort to adhere to the rules, the GC is still entirely voluntary and still lacks any stringent sanctions against firms that fail to adhere to the principles.

OECD Guidelines on Multinational Enterprise
The OECD Guidelines on Multinational Enterprises is a set of voluntary guidelines within OECD countries, which account for some 90 percent of FDI (Macklem, 2005, p. 283). First adopted in 1976, these guidelines cover a wide range of issues such as information disclosure, taxation, labor relations and the environment. A chapter on environmental protection was added in 1991, and updated in 2000 (Bunn, 2004, p. 1277). These updates included a recommendation for extraterritorial application of the guidelines for MNEs operating in non-OECD countries. The guidelines promote environmental management standards already in existence, such as the ISO 14000. At the same time, however, they encourage governments to employ performance standards rather than simply management standards. But the OECD Guidelines do not set performance standards; they also recommend extensive consultation with communities affected by TNCs, as well as improved access to information on the environmental activities of TNCs (OECD, 2000).

Although the guidelines promote improved environmental performance rather than simply improved management, which some see as a positive step, some environmental groups have expressed disappointment with the guidelines because they lack any sort of monitoring or enforcement mechanism (FOE Netherlands, 2002). Further, the guidelines do not place any legal obligations on TNCs with respect to their performance. They are merely guidelines for OECD member countries to encourage their TNCs to follow voluntarily. For this reason, environmental NGOs have been somewhat skeptical of the ability of the guidelines in their current form to engender true change in TNC environmental practices.

Environmental management standards
Environmental management standards are standards for management within firms, rather than product or performance standards. The ISO 14000 standards, perhaps the best known of the international environment management standards, were established by the International Organization for Standardization (ISO) and are applied by firms around the world (see Prakash and Potoski, 2006). These standards were established in the early 1990s following industry promises to self-regulate at the Rio Earth Summit. The ISO 14000 series of standards provides guidance on a number of fronts, and the ISO 14001 standard, on environmental management systems, is the only one to which firms can certify their facilities. This standard calls on firms to be aware of environmental regulations and to follow those regulations in the countries in which they operate as well as to continually improve their internal performance. As of 2005 some 111 000 firms operating in 138 countries had certified to the standard (ISO, 2006).

Whether the ISO 14000 standards have made improvements in firms' environmental performance has been a subject of much debate in recent years. Early on, the standards were critiqued on the grounds that they were management standards rather than product or performance standards (Krut and Gleckman, 1998). Further, some have pointed out that while the ISO is an international organization, it is dominated by industry actors that would have the incentive to set standards that were easy to meet. While these standards have become a *de facto* prerequisite for doing international business, questions have also been raised regarding their effectiveness in terms of improving environmental perfor-mance of firms, particularly those operating in developing countries (Clapp, 1998). Recent research, however, indicates that in the USA adherence to ISO 14001 resulted overall in lower toxic emissions and higher rates of regulatory compliance, particularly for firms with environmental performance in the middle range (Prakash and Potoski, 2006).

Industry-specific codes of conduct and certification schemes
A range of industry-wide codes of conduct and product certification schemes has emerged over the past decade with the aim of enhancing firms' social and environmental performance (Cashore, 2002). Most of these schemes are specific to a particular industry or product, typically one with a high environmental impact. Some of these schemes are controlled entirely within the industry to which it is geared, or have involvement of non-governmental organizations or other non-state actors as independent input and over-sight providers. As a result, private standards such as these have a wide diversity in terms of the role of independent actors as standard-setters, and in monitoring and enforcement mechanisms.

Industry-wide standards for production and management include, for example, pro-grams such as Responsible Care, a set of principles for environmental, health and safety practices that are voluntary (although some national chemical associations require members to sign on to the principles). These standards are set by the International Council for Chemical Associations, an industry group (see Prakash, 2000). In the mining sector, the International Council on Mining and Metals (ICMM) established Principles of Sustainable Development in 2003 (http://www.icmm.com/icmm_principles.php). All members of the ICMM are asked to commit to these principles, although there is no inde-pendent monitoring and enforcement of this commitment. In 2005, however, the ICMM asked members to act in accordance with GRI reporting standards (highest level), and the GRI and ICMM have collaborated to develop a mining sector supplement for sustain-ability reporting. An industry-wide set of principles also exists in the forestry sector, as promoted by the Forest Stewardship Council. The FSC has membership that includes not just industry players, but also NGOs and other stakeholders, which some say give its prin-ciples more teeth and a more objective ability to monitor and enforce the standards (Cashore, 2002; Pattberg, 2005).

In addition to standards and principles that guide the general practices within a specific industry, there is also a growing number of certifiable standards and requirements specific to particular products within an industry. Certifications are usually established for prod-ucts that are seen to be environmentally friendly, such as fair trade and organic foods (Raynolds, 2000), sustainable forest products (Cashore, 2002), and increasingly retail food items, particularly fresh produce that is grown using 'good agricultural practices'

(Hatanaka et al., 2005; Tallontire, 2007). Because of the diversity with respect to independent actors' roles in standards-setting for industries as a whole and for specific products, as well as in monitoring and enforcement, some of these standards are seen to be stronger than others. Standards that are certifiable and independently verified by third parties are seen to be more stringent and likely to be more effective than those that are not.

International investment standards

Standards for international investment by financial institutions have also emerged. The Equator Principles, launched in 2003, provide a set of social and environmental benchmarks for private financial institutions to assess project finance in developing countries. Formulated by private sector banks in consultation with non-governmental organizations and the World Bank's private lending arm, the International Finance Corporation, the principles are voluntary for those banks that adopt them. The idea is to ensure that private financial institutions do not fund projects in developing countries that may be unsustainable, either socially or environmentally. In 2006, the principles were revised and strengthened. Although they are strictly voluntary for financial institutions, the principles have been widely adopted, with some 50 private banks now adhering to them (http://www.equator-principles.com/).

Principles for Responsible Investment (PRI) is a set of voluntary principles, adopted in April 2006 on the initiative of the United Nations Environment Program finance initiative and the UN Global Compact, that institutional investors signed on to. These principles influence corporations indirectly as investors who sign on to them ask their clients to report and provide information with respect to environmental, social and governance (ESG) issues. The PRI call for investors to incorporate ESG issues into their investment analysis and decision-making, to incorporate these issues into ownership policies and practices, to seek appropriate disclosure on ESG issues by entities in which they invest, to promote the principles more broadly in the investment industry, to work together to enhance the effectiveness of the principles, and to report on their activities with respect to implementing the principles (PRI, 2007). As of July 2007, some 200 institutional investors, representing over $10 trillion in assets, had signed on to these principles, and more than half of the signatories had asked the companies they invested in to provide standardized reporting with respect to ESG issues (PRI 2007).

These investment initiatives are a relatively new form of standards for greening TNCs via the pressure from investors – both shareholders and financial institutions. Some critics have noted, however, that these new standards, although a positive step, are still quite limited in scope. The Equator Principles, for example, apply only to project finance, a relatively small percentage of the activities of private banks. The principles are further seen to be lacking in transparency (Missbach, 2004).

Toward corporate accountability?

All of the above instruments are voluntary in nature and had strong industry representation and consultation in their development. Because of their voluntary and non-legally binding nature, these measures have been characterized as 'soft law'. The close involvement of industry players in the rules that govern them has led critics to argue that although in theory these various instruments could help to mitigate the environmental impact of TNCs and FDI, none has sufficiently strict external enforcement mechanisms to ensure that this actually happens. Morever, when comparing the number of global firms that have taken on such voluntary initiatives to the total number of TNCs in existence, it becomes clear that only a very small percentage of these firms are engaging actively in these corporate greening efforts.

Further critiques have also emerged. Although current voluntary measures are wide ranging and diverse, they still only cover certain environmental and social issues, while completely ignoring others. For example, while there may be explicit requirements in the Global Reporting Initiative to report on activities to mitigate climate change or conserve energy, little is included on similar activities to mitigate the spread of genetically modified organisms to jurisdictions where they are not legal. And while there may be an industry-wide code with respect to chemical safety or sustainable mining, there is not a similar industry code or set of principles for other sectors, such as agricultural biotechnology, which also has important environmental implications (see Clapp, forthcoming). The weaknesses of these various instruments has led critics to conclude that there is a need for stronger legal mechanisms at the international level to ensure that transnational investment and corporate activity is not harmful to the environment (Clapp and Utting, forthcoming).

Over the past decade, a corporate accountability movement has gathered momentum in an attempt to push for stronger regulatory mechanisms to rein in and keep watch over corporate activities that have potentially negative social and environmental consequences (Bendell, 2004; Broad and Cavanagh, 1999). Key to this idea of corporate accountability is to push for stronger regulatory measures than are available under the corporate responsibility agenda, including financial and legal accountability on the part of firms (Bunn, 2004). This movement has advocated the imposition of legal liability on firms, that is, damages to those affected in cases of malpractice. Also important to this idea is a reassertion of the key role played by government as 'final authority' (WRI, 2003, pp. 135, 108). Some in the movement have also called for 'foreign direct liability', which would enable lawsuits to be undertaken in the home country of a TNC for environmental and social impacts of their activities in other countries (Ward, 2001).

In the run-up to the World Summit on Sustainable Development in 2002, several proposals were put on the table advocating for a legally binding international corporate accountability treaty (Bendell, 2004; Morgera, 2004). A fairly detailed proposal for such a treaty was put forward by Friends of the Earth International. This proposal stressed the need to ensure that corporations are legally accountable not only to their shareholders, as is currently the case, but also to the broader public. The proposal envisioned much more detailed reporting on social and environmental practices of corporations, as well as a requirement to consult with affected communities before undertaking new investments and activities. It further promoted the extension of corporations' liability to their directors when there is a breach of national environmental or social laws, and to directors and corporations for breaches of international laws or agreements. The proposal also called for rights of redress for citizens, community rights to control and access resources, and minimum environmental, social, labor and human rights standards. Sanctions would be imposed on firms that breached the requirements under the treaty (FOEI, 2001).

At the same time, Greenpeace International advocated a set of principles, called the 'Bhopal Principles on Corporate Accountability'. Although this proposal was for the global adoption of a set of voluntary principles to hold corporations accountable, the clear intention was to then ratchet up the principles to the status of a legally binding treaty. The Bhopal Principles included measures to ensure that corporations follow key principles of the Rio Declaration, including those on liability for damages, avoidance of double standards in the global operations of TNCs, and application of the precautionary principle and the polluter pays principle (Greenpeace International, 2002).

The idea of a corporate accountability treaty did not receive a warm welcome from industry groups at the World Summit on Sustainable Development (see Clapp, 2005). Although early drafts of the Plan of Implementation included a commitment to 'launch negotiations for a multilateral agreement on corporate accountability' (cited in Graymore and Bunn, 2002, p. 1), this commitment was watered down in the final version. NGOs promoting the idea of a treaty blame the removal of this commitment on the intense lobbying by industry at the summit (CEO, 2001). The Plan does encourage active promotion of both corporate responsibility and accountability, however, and mentions the importance of intergovernmental agreements and measures, along with other mechanisms. Some see this as leaving the door open for future discussions on a corporate accountability treaty (Morgera, 2004, p. 219). Although discussions on a legally binding corporate accountability treaty have not been launched as yet, it is important to assess the pros and cons of such an approach.

There are some clear advantages to a legally binding international corporate accountability treaty over the myriad of disparate voluntary efforts for corporate greening currently available, each of which would contribute to the enhancement of the actual environmental performance of global firms. Having a single, legally binding instrument would remedy the limited reach of domestic regulations in the international sphere. With current legal systems based on domestic regulations, it is often difficult, if not impossible, for communities in developing countries to launch a formal complaint and seek redress for environmental damages caused by foreign corporations (Macklem, 2005). A single treaty would also help to eliminate overlap and duplication of efforts. A common set of foundational principles would be established by a global instrument, providing a regulatory 'floor' (Waddock, 2004), avoiding the problem we have at present where some initiatives have more stringent regulations than others. Consolidation of efforts into one treaty with common principles would also ensure that corporations could not pick and choose which standards to follow, as they currently do. Monitoring and enforcement would also be stronger than the current situation. Because the treaty would be signed by states, which would oblige them to implement and enforce the treaty, there would be stronger state incentive to ensure compliance. At present, because the current voluntary measures are not state mandated, states have employed a very hands-off attitude toward them. Civil society does play a role in some monitoring and enforcement in some of the current mechanisms, but this role could be strengthened and reinforced with an internationally legally binding treaty. Further, the threat of legal liability for infractions, which many see as central to such a treaty, would be a strong motivator of industry to green practices.

Although there are some clear advantages to pursuing a single legally binding treaty at the global level to ensure corporate accountability, there are also reasons why pursuit of such a strategy may be extremely difficult in practice at the present time. First, as was made clear at the World Summit on Sustainable Development in 2002, industry is not in favor of the idea, which it sees as a 'one size fits all' approach. Industry has argued that the current myriad of voluntary and sector-specific approaches is more appropriate and viable because they provide flexibility to industry to adopt measures that best suit their needs (Moody Stuart, 2002). Although such a treaty would be negotiated and implemented among governments, corporate actors do exert power and influence over such exercises, in a variety of ways (Fuchs, 2005). For this reason, as long as industry is opposed to the idea of such a treaty, the likelihood that negotiations will be launched to put it into place is slim.

In addition to strong industry opposition to the idea, there is also currently a lack of political will among states to pursue this option. Emerging economies that are increasingly host to TNCs, such as China, as well as a number of OECD countries that are the source of much of the world's FDI, would probably be strong opponents of a global treaty on TNC activity that is so general in scope and that may undermine or contradict the bilateral investment treaties currently being negotiated between states. Even if talks were launched, enormous effort might go into negotiating such a treaty, but it could be reduced to the least common denominator and would lose its effectiveness if weakened. How to prove environmental damage and assign liability, assign a value to damages and enforce payments, would all be highly contentious issues. Further, pursuing a corporate accountability treaty could also have legal ramifications that proponents might not want to encourage, such as enhancing the legal personality of TNCs in the global arena (Macklem, 2005, p. 289).

Conclusion

The current wide-ranging suite of voluntary mechanisms that promote corporate greening at the global level is far from perfect. There are at present many different, disparate and overlapping voluntary mechanisms for corporate greening. This leads to a crowded corporate greening landscape, confusion about the differences between the various measures, and a lack of a clear overarching articulation of what is necessary for greening global investment. Moreover, while the present instruments outlined in the first part of this chapter may address certain sorts of environment problems, they ignore others and lack real enforcement mechanisms and performance criteria. And with such a diverse set of arrangements on the menu, corporations have been able to pick and choose what they do in terms of CSR environmental measures. Strong critiques have been made of the available instruments, and it is now largely understood that most of these mechanisms are weak overall in terms of eliciting major change in corporate practice. These problems have translated into patchy and uneven progress in terms of actual corporate greening.

At the same time, the political climate at the moment does not seem right for the pursuit of a corporate accountability treaty. Although a single legally binding instrument for corporate accountability could embody key sustainability principles across a number of industries, be applied globally, and have a built-in strength to spur corporate change by holding corporations legally liable, there are a number of obstacles to seeing such a treaty adopted in the near future.

While this might appear to present a dilemma for those wishing to promote corporate accountability on the environmental front, recent developments within the existing mechanisms suggest that there may be some scope for consolidation and ratcheting up to give them more coherence and more teeth. The Global Compact appears to be playing a key role in seeking out collaboration with many of these various mechanisms, such as the PRI and the GRI. The ISO is also currently developing a new series of standards on social responsibility, to be launched in 2008, and is collaborating closely with the GC and the GRI to ensure compatibility. At the same time, there is also evidence of some measures to ratchet up the monitoring and enforcement aspects of these existing mechanisms. Responsible Care, for example, moved from being primarily self-monitored by industry to incorporating third-party verification. The GC's efforts to introduce integrity measures, as well as the institutionalization of the GRI, can be interpreted as steps toward strengthening the ability of these mechanisms to engender change in corporate practice.

While these developments may signal a consolidation and ratcheting up of the existing global mechanisms for corporate greening, the process thus far has been slow, and for many still falls short of achieving corporate accountability. Although there are different views on this question, it is possible to pursue both strategies simultaneously. Indeed, the goal of achieving corporate accountability may well be brought closer by continuing to push for corporate accountability measures such as a legally binding treaty at the same time as strengthening and ratcheting up existing mechanisms. In other words, it may well be that without the pressure for more corporate accountability, efforts to improve voluntary measures would be weak or non-existent. Further, it may be that the two ideas eventually merge. This may not be what either side of the debate is ideally hoping for, but it could be a step further toward achieving corporate accountability.

Note

1. See, e.g, Gedicks (2001) on oil and mining; Dauvergne (2001) on logging; and Leighton et al. (2002) on chemicals and electronics.

References

Bendell, Jem (2004), *Barricades and Boardrooms: A Contemporary History of the Corporate Accountability Movement*, Programme on Technology, Business and Society, Programme Paper No. 13, Geneva: UNRISD.

Broad, Robin and John Cavanagh(1999), 'The corporate accountability movement: lessons and opportunities', *The Fletcher Forum of World Affairs*, **23**(2), 151–69.

Bruno, Kenny (with Joshua Karliner) (2002), *Greenwash + 10: The UN's Global Compact, Corporate Accountability and the Johannesburg Earth Summit*, Corporate Watch, available online at www.corpwatch.org/un.

Bunn, Isabella (2004), 'Global advocacy for corporate accountability: transatlantic perspectives from the NGO community', *American University International Law Review*, **19**(6), 1265–306.

Cashore, Benjamin (2002), 'Legitimacy and the privatization of environmental governance: how non-state market-driven (NSMD) governance systems gain rule-making authority', *Governance*, **15**(4), 503–29.

Clapp, Jennifer (1998), 'The privatization of global environmental governance: ISO 14000 and the developing world', *Global Governance*, **4**(3), 295–316.

Clapp, Jennifer (2005), 'Global environmental governance for corporate responsibility and accountability',. *Global Environmental Politics*, **5**(3) 23–34.

Clapp, Jennifer (forthcoming), 'Corporate accountability in the agro-food sector: the case of illegal GMO releases', in P. Utting and J. Clapp (eds), *Corporate Accountability and Sustainable Development*, Delhi: Oxford University Press.

Clapp, Jennifer and Peter Utting (forthcoming), 'Corporate responsibility, accountability and law: an introduction' in P. Utting and J. Clapp (eds), *Corporate Accountability and Sustainable Development*, Delhi: Oxford University. Press.

Corporate Europe Observer (CEO) (2001), 'Industry's Rio+10 strategy: banking on feelgood PR', *The CEO Quarterly Newsletter*, **10**, December.

Dauvergne, Peter (2001), *Loggers and Degradation in the Asia-Pacific: Corporations and Environmental Management*, New York: Cambridge University Press.

Falkner, Robert (2003), 'Private environmental governance and international relations: exploring the links', *Global Environmental Politics*, **3**(2), 72–87.

Friends of the Earth (FOE) England, Wales and Northern Ireland (1998), 'A history of attempts to regulate the activities of transnational corporations: what lessons can be learned?', available at http://www.corporate-accountability.org/docs/FoE-US-paper-history_TNC-Regulation.doc.

Friends of the Earth (FOE) Netherlands (2002), *Using the OECD Guidelines for Multinational Enterprises: A Critical Starterkit for NGOs*, Amsterdam: FOE Netherlands.

Friends of the Earth International (FOEI) (2001), *Towards Binding Corporate Accountability*, available at http://www.foei.org/publications/corporates/accountability.html.

Fuchs, Doris (2005), *Understanding Business Power in Global Governance*, Baden-Baden, Germany: Nomos.

Gallagher, Kevin and Lyuba Zarsky (2007), *The Enclave Economy: Foreign Investment and Sustainable Development in Mexico's Silicon Valley*, Cambridge, MA: MIT Press.

Gedicks, Al (2001), *Resource Rebels: Native Challenges to Mining and Oil Corporations*, Cambridge, MA: South End Press.

Graymore, Daniel and Isabella Bunn (2002), 'A world summit for business development?', Christian Aid, available at www.christian-aid.org.uk/indepth/0208wssd/report.htm2002.

Greenpeace International (2002), *Corporate Crimes: The Need for an International Instrument on Corporate Accountability and Liability*, Amsterdam: Greenpeace.

Hatanaka, Maki, Carmen Bain and Lawrence Busch (2005), 'Third party certification in the global agrifood system', *Food Policy*, **30**, 354–69.

International Organization for Standardization (2006), *ISO Survey of Certifications 2005*, summarized online at http://www.iso.ch/iso/en/iso9000-14000/pdf/survey2005.pdf.

KPMG Global Sustainability Services and United Nations Environment Program (UNEP) (2006), *Carrots and Sticks for Starters: Current Trends and Approaches in Voluntary and Mandatory Standards for Sustainability Reporting*, Paris: UNEP.

Krut, Riva and Harris Gleckman (1998), *ISO 14001: A Missed Opportunity for Global Sustainable Industrial Development*, London: Earthscan.

Lamberton, Geoff (2005), 'Sustaining accounting – a brief history and conceptual framework', *Accounting Forum*, **29**(1), 7–26.

Leighton, Michelle, Naomi Rhot-Arriaza and Lyuba Zarsky (2002), *Beyond Good Deeds: Case Studies and a New Policy Agenda for Corporate Accountability*, Berkeley, CA: Nautilus Institute for Security and Sustainable Development.

Macklem, Patrick (2005). 'Corporate acountability under international law: the misguided quest for universal jurisdiction', *International Law Forum*, **7**, 281–9.

Missbach, Andreas (2004), 'The Equator Principles: drawing the line for socially responsible banks? An interim review from an NGO perspective', *Development*, **47**(3), 78–84.

Moody Stuart, Mark (2002), 'Globalization in the 21st century: an economic basis for development', *Corporate Environmental Strategy*, **9**(2), 115–21.

Morgera, Elisa (2004), 'From Stockholm to Johannesburg: from corporate responsibility to corporate accountability for the global protection of the environment?', *RECIEL*, **13**(2), 214–22.

OECD (Organisation for Economic Co-operation and Development) (2000), *The OECD Guidelines for Multinational Enterprises*, available at http://www.oecd.org/dataoecd/56/36/1922428.pdf.

Pattberg, Philipp (2005), 'The institutionalization of private governance: how business and nonprofit organizations agree on transnational rules', *Governance*, **18**(4), 589–610.

Prakash, Aseem (2000), 'Responsible Care: an assessment'. *Business & Society*, **39**(2), 183–209.

Prakash, Aseem and Matthew Potoski (2006), *The Voluntary Environmentalists: Green Clubs, ISO 14001, and voluntary environmental regulations*, Cambridge: Cambridge University Press.

Principles for Responsible Investment (2007), *PRI Report on Progress 2007*, Geneva: UNEP, available online at http://www.unpri.org/report07/PRIReportOnProgress2007.pdf.

Raynolds, Laura (2000), 'Re-embedding global agriculture: the international organic and fair trade movements', *Agriculture and Human Values*, **17**(1), 297–309.

Tallontire, Anne (2007), 'CSR and regulation: towards a framework for understanding private standards initiatives in the agri-food chain', *Third World Quarterly*, **28**(4), 775–91.

Therien, Jean-Philippe and Vincent Pouliot (2006), 'The Global Compact: shifting the politics of international development?', *Global Governance*, **12**, 55–75.

UNCTAD (2001), *World Investment Report 2001: Promoting Linkages*, New York and Geneva: UN.

UNCTAD (2002), *World Investment Report 2002: Transnational Corporations and Export Competitiveness*, New York and Geneva: UN.

UNCTAD (2006), *World Investment Report 2006 – FDI from Developing and Transition Economies: Implications for Development*, New York and Geneva: UN.

Utting, Peter (2005), *Rethinking Business Regulation: From Self-Regulation to Social Control*, UNRISD Paper No. 15.

Waddock, Sandra (2004), 'Creating corporate accountability: foundational principles to make corporate citizenship real', *Journal of Business Ethics*, **50**, 313–27.

Ward, Halina (2001), *Governing Multinationals: The Role of Foreign Direct Liability*, Briefing Paper No. 18, The Royal Institute of International Affairs, February.

World Resources Institute (2003), *World Resources: 2002–2004*, Washington, DC: WRI.

13 Civil society participation in trade policy-making in Latin America: the case of the environmental movement
Peter Newell

Introduction

The challenge of civil society participation in trade policy has risen to prominence for a series of complex, but interrelated, reasons. First, involving civil society actors in economic policy can be seen as a legitimating exercise in the face of powerful critiques about the secrecy in which key decisions regarding trade and investment get taken. Crucial to public trust is evidence that governments' policies reflect a careful consideration of issues including non-economic social and environmental concerns, and are not merely designed to serve special interests. Institutionalized public participation is seen as an important vehicle by which states can defend their claims to represent a broad notion of the public interest.

Instrumentally, an informed public and open debate can help to raise key issues and participation can allow for more complete information and priority-setting and therefore better-quality decision-making. Civil society organizations can inject new ideas and specialized expertise, and lend technical support to delegations lacking capacity. Perhaps most crucially, the involvement of civil society can help to

> build public support for the trade agreement that emerges. By engaging their parliaments and the public in the formulation of national trade policy objectives, trade negotiators can develop trade initiatives with a clear sense of the standards and benchmarks which legislators and the public expect them to meet, (Fisher, p. 2002 191)

This also makes it more likely that civil society groups will provide much-needed support to get accords through national parliaments, as well as help to monitor the implementation of agreements. Conversely, their exclusion undermines support for trade agreements. The Hemispheric Social Alliance (HSA) has claimed as one of its mobilizing rationales in this regard 'the desire to stop being merely spectators in a game that affects all our lives but is played only by people with the power and money, to determine our own destiny' (Púlsar, 2001, my translation).

Added to these generic challenges, there are specific challenges for Latin America. In large parts of the region, democratic processes remain, in historical terms, relatively new. In particular, there is a long history of confrontation between civil society and the state in Latin America. At an institutional and regional level, the challenge of participation in trade policy is also a relatively new one, despite the existence of mechanisms for consultation with business and labour within the Andean Pact, for example (Botto and Tussie, 2003, p. 31). There is a strong sense, however, in which NAFTA definitively broke with previous models of thinking about participation in trade policy in the region. The FTAA (Free Trade Area of The Americas) opens up the possibility of extending this change across the whole hemisphere. Ministerial statements from the summits have called for mechanisms for incorporating non-governmental views other than business through consultation and dialogue, but there is a gap between the rhetoric and the reality, with many Latin American governments actively resisting attempts to open up trade decision-making to greater input from civil society.

There is a series of historical and political reasons for this suspicion regarding the participation of civil society actors in trade policy in Latin America. Besides the Mexican government's bitter experience of the NAFTA negotiations, which I discuss below, there is also a prevailing fear about loss of competence or sovereignty for decision-making in this area. This relates to a concern that the numerical and financial superiority of organized civil society in North America would serve to compound existing underrepresentation of less developed countries within the region in trade negotiations. With the exception of Mercosur (the Common Market of the South), many of the initiatives for the inclusion of civil society actors in trade-negotiating processes within the Americas have come from North American governments, a path set most clearly by the Clinton Administration in the context of the NAFTA negotiations.

The politics of mobilization

This section explores the forms of mobilization within the environmental movement, around each of the three key trade agreements. The aim is to generate insights into how groups claim rights to participation, and to make use of those spaces that exist within trade policy arenas described in the next section or protest either the lack of such spaces or the limits imposed by the ways in which they are currently constituted.

The NAFTA and its handling of environmental issues generated significant, though uneven, degrees of mobilization by environmental groups in each of the three countries party to the agreement. The emergence of transnational relations between environmental NGOs (ENGOs) in Mexico, the USA and Canada was, in many ways, unprecedented. Initially, this was centred around collaboration between border organizations in the USA and Mexico, but developed well beyond this. There were nevertheless important differences in structure, constituency and strategies that organizations adopted that were, to some extent, determined by nationality (Hogenboom, 1998, p. 141).

In some cases such differences were a driver of the transnational alliances that were formed. In Mexico, for example, the lack of openings at state level was an important reason for Mexican ENGOs' alignment with foreign groups which had more political clout. Mexican groups also relied on counterparts elsewhere for access to information about the negotiations, which their own government was failing to provide. This was particularly true of more critical groups with less access to government. RMALC (Mexican Action Network on Free Trade), for example, worked with the Canadian group 'Common Frontiers' and the Alliance for Responsible Trade and the Citizens' Trade Campaign in the USA. Such transnational ties served to amplify the influence of weaker groups in Mexico that, through connections with allies in North America, got to participate in key policy arenas where decisions on NAFTA were being taken. This participation took the form of hearings in the US Congress which, through exposure in the USA, helped to secure access to Mexican officials, evidence of what Keck and Sikkink (1998) call the 'boomerang effect'. For US groups, ties to Mexican groups helped to improve their credibility in presenting positions that went beyond their own narrow interests as well as permitting them to act as vehicles for transmitting information from the 'front line' about environmental problems confronting Mexico.

The process of alliance-building has not been without its difficulties. The different organizational structures of groups often prove to be a point of contention. In the context of NAFTA, the fact that, compared with large membership-based organizations from the USA and Canada, many Mexican groups had fewer official members created tensions about how wide a group of citizens was being adequately represented. This has been an issue in the FTAA negotiations too, with trade unions in particular questioning who NGOs represent, occasionally referring to them in dismissive terms as 'non-governmental individuals'. NGOs, in turn, have been critical of the overly hierarchical and bureaucratic nature of some trade unions (Korzeniewicz and Smith, 2003, p. 69).

In the NAFTA context, both the scale of funding disparities between groups from Mexico and North America and, particularly, the extent of corporate funds received by the latter, also created suspicions among some Mexican ENGOs about how far those groups' agendas were influenced by their funding sources – companies that stood to benefit from NAFTA (Hogenboom, 1998, pp. 153–4). Despite these issues, united positions were possible, such as the Common Declaration on NAFTA in 1991 issued by a group of more than 20 Mexican, US and Canadian ENGOs calling, among other things, for the inclusion of environmental issues in NAFTA, a review of the environmental effects of NAFTA and the participation of environmental experts in the negotiations.

The point of departure for many of these coalitions was not to claim that NAFTA was responsible for the social and environmental problems they were experiencing, but that it was accelerating them. A tactic on the part of NAFTA proponents was to characterize those against the plan as protectionist, encouraging some groups to demonstrate that they are not against trade and investment, but rather in favour of different frameworks of rules. Some went about articulating that alternative in the form of the 'Just and Sustainable Trade and Development Initiative for North America'. Following inputs from other groups within the region, the agreement was broadened to become 'Alternatives for the Americas: Building a Peoples' Hemispheric Agreement'.

The timing of NAFTA also made a difference to the issues around which groups mobilized. Signed in 1992 and coming into effect in January 1994, the agreement emerged at a time of high levels of environmental concern on the back of UNCED in 1992. With global attention focused on the way in which NAFTA mediated the relationship between trade and environment, greater pressure was felt by those negotiating its terms to strengthen environmental provisions. By contrast, ongoing negotiations within Mercosur and FTAA have been, to some extent, overshadowed by economic crises within the region (Argentina in 2000/2001 and previously Brazil's massive currency devaluation in January 1999) such that the very project of regional integration has been in doubt at key moments (Carranza, 2003).

Timing also made a difference in terms of the types of alliance that were possible. Coming as it did in the early 1990s, NAFTA managed to bring into loose alliance coalitions of labor and environmental interests to combat threats to hard-fought regulation. As Obach notes (2004, p. 63); 'Although unions and environmentalists had distinct concerns in regard to NAFTA, the common threat the agreement presented created the impetus for labor–environmental cooperation.' At times working independently, at other times together, national coalitions were formed that included many of the major labor and environmental actors such as the Citizens' Trade Campaign and the Alliance for Responsible Trade.

Although trade negotiations become focal points from cross-sectoral and transnational mobilizing, it should be made clear that many groups also chose not to engage with trade policy processes. This was either because they are not seen to be relevant to a group's core activities, because financial and/or technical barriers meant that mobilizing around these issues was not a realistic possibility, or as a conscious strategy of rejection of the aims and conduct of the process: in other words a positive choice to remain on the outside. There also often appears to be a divide between capital-city-based groups that are more geared to addressing national and international policy agendas, and environmental and *campesino* groups based in rural areas that attach a lower priority to these agendas. As Hogenboom notes in the context of Mexico, 'Their distance from the political centre of Mexico city, a lack of finance and experience, and poor access to information about NAFTA discouraged their participation in the NAFTA debate' (1998, p. 146).

Differences in perspective regarding the relationship between trade and environment played out between groups in the context of NAFTA within each of the countries party to the agreement. Similar divisions have also emerged in the context of the FTAA discussions, with some groups adopting a critical position within the HSA and other groups investing in efforts to identify and advance 'win–win' linkages between environmental protection measures and trade liberalization.

One element of this strategy of engagement has been to build bridges with industry. Audley (1997, p. 83) notes in the case of the National Wildlife Federation, for example, a policy 'of constructive engagement with industry elites convinced them that a dialogue between business and responsible environmental organisations could result in effective changes in investment patterns and improve the chances for environmental quality through trade'. Sometimes the strategy is aimed at shaping the negotiating stance of government. In Mexico in relation to NAFTA, 30 ENGOs organized themselves in the Union of Environmental Groups, which sought to foster positive relations with the Mexican government in order to have a say in Mexico's official position on environmental safeguards in NAFTA. Despite their insider status, aided by the fact that one of the Unión de Grupos Ambientalistas (UGAM's) advisers was a prominent environmental lawyer, they faced many of the same barriers to effective participation as outsiders in terms of poor access to official information and the lack of state capacity to handle inputs from civil society. Their input, along with that of organizations such as the Group of Hundred, was restricted to some 'side-room' discussions during negotiations on the supplemental environmental agreement.

The extent to which groups mobilize around trade agreements seems to reflect not only the formal political and institutional opportunity structures, but also their sense of where their campaigning energies are most likely to yield change. The lack of spaces for engagement with Mercosur and the deliberate undermining of its environmental provisions has led some groups to abandon it and focus their attentions on FTAA, which is in any case potentially much more far-reaching in economic and environmental impact. This 'strategic turn' perhaps also reflects a broader power play in which the USA is seeking to outmanoeuvre Mercosur by speeding up negotiations towards FTAA (Teubal and Rodriguez, 2002).

Opposition to FTAA within civil society has been widespread, reflecting both what is at stake in political and economic terms and the number of countries and associated civil societies involved. A large number of anti-FTAA movements have developed positions that place themselves outside the process (Newell, 2007). The forms of protest in many ways mirror, and build on, experiences of campaigning around trade issues in the WTO and investment issues associated with the aborted MAI (Multilateral Agreement on Investment). 'Virtual' alliances held together through exchange of information and formulation of positions through exchange over the internet, combined with joint demonstrations around key summits such as Quito and Quebec, are indicative of this form of mobilizing. Such protests have been aimed at challenging the secrecy of the process, as well as the sustainability of the development model being promoted.

Within these coalitions, environmental groups critical of the process and sceptical about the compatibility of trade liberalization with sustainable development have articulated concerns which resonate with a much broader critique of neoliberal development models. There are concerns about the potential for mobile capital to exploit lower environmental standards, as it is claimed has occurred in the *maquiladoras*, or to encourage 'regulatory chill' among states competing for their investment. The environmental impact of increased volumes of trade has also been a focus for groups such as Acción Ecológica that argue, 'FTAA implies a direct increase in the consumption and therefore production of fossil fuels, this implies an increase in CO_2 emissions which the US does not want to control' (Acción Ecológica, 2004, my translation).

Institutionalized participation and political opportunity structures
The purpose of this section is to look at those mechanisms of participation that exist within the formal arenas created by NAFTA, Mercosur and FTAA respectively, with a view to understanding for whom such processes are working and which groups and interests are effectively screened out of current regional trade debates by the ways these institutional channels have been constructed.

NAFTA
The impact of campaigns on institutional structures is often not easy to discern in the short term, but may yield longer-term benefits for groups in the future. Hence with NAFTA, although environmental concerns over trade policy did not substantively alter the norms and principles of trade policy, some (minor) changes to institutional procedures were achieved that may create windows of opportunity for future activism around NAFTA. Audley notes (1997, p. 118), 'While NAFTA did not alter the practice of using trade experts as panelists, panel members may now call upon experts from the environmental community to provide them with information relevant to the case.' The Border Environmental Cooperation Commission (BECC) was also created in response to concerns expressed by NGOs about the effect of trade expansion on the Mexico–USA border. Previously operating as a bi-national institution, the BECC now constitutes a ten-person board of directors which includes representatives of the 'general public'. Many environmentalists are, nevertheless, 'fuming that the BECC operates behind closed doors' (Timmons Roberts and Demetria Thanos, 2003, p. 57). Alongside this, there is an 18-member advisory board, made up of residents of the border region, which is meant to ensure that interests of state and local communities affected by BECC decisions are

represented. Members of the public are required to submit a request to speak at a public meeting 15 days in advance, and the board retains full discretion regarding who can speak at meetings.

The environmental side agreement of NAFTA also creates a Joint Public Advisory Committee (JPAC) to the NACEC (North American Commission for Environmental Cooperation) designed to provide input from NGOs and the private sector to the NACEC's governing council (Fisher, 2002). The JPAC normally consists of 15 members, with each nation appointing an equal number of representatives, although it currently stands at 14 with one fewer representative from Canada than the other NAFTA members. The committee seeks public input and recommendations to help determine the advice it provides to the Environmental Council. According to Fisher (2002, p. 189), 'By consistently working to seek public input and incorporate the insights and expertise of civil society into its activities and projects, the NACEC's initiatives have been greatly enhanced.' Articles 14 and 15 of the side agreement provide that any citizen or NGO from the parties may send to the secretariat a submission asserting that a party is failing effectively to enforce its environmental law in order to promote exports or investment. In response, the NACEC's secretariat may be obliged to provide a factual record, though without legal value or the ability to trigger trade sanctions.

Despite these institutional innovations and the degree of interest the agreement generated, and continues to generate, NAFTA has been criticized for its top-down approach and lack of consultation with civil society in the negotiation process. A key lesson from this experience has been that merely having the mechanisms in place does not mean that they are used effectively. To date (from 1995 to 2007), the NACEC had received just 61 citizen submissions, 12 of which were under review and 49 had been closed, many because they did not meet the established criteria.

Resources, perceptions of return on effort and shifts in strategic priorities mean that the extent to which groups make use of or engage these mechanisms will change over time. For example, since the heyday of NAFTA, leading environmental groups such as the Sierra Club have shifted their focus away from daily participation in the activities of trade bodies and sought to focus their attention instead on raising the level of interest in trade policy among their members. Lack of resources, even among the accommodating groups, inhibits further participation. Costly engagement is more difficult to justify in a context of pervading frustration with lack of leverage in the process. The concern about lack of progress is compounded by the proliferation in the number of forums where dialogue takes place, each requiring time, personnel and money, and the strong sense that the window of political opportunity to advance trade policy reform has closed.

Mercosur

In comparison with NAFTA, Mercosur's mechanisms of participation are underdeveloped. While ambitious in its economic and commercial dimensions, Mercosur is weak in the construction of political dimensions that facilitate participation and representation of citizens that make up its member states. This is despite the fact that the Agreement of Florianopolis, the Environmental Framework Agreement in Mercosur, spells out in two places the importance members attach to civil society participation 'in the treatment of environmental questions' and more generally 'in the protection of the environment and the use of sustainable natural resources' (Decision No. 2/01-Annex; preamble and chapter

1(e)). There is a Foro Consultivo Económico y Social, created by the Protocol of Ouro Preto in 1994, which has spaces designed for businesses and unions, but offers few opportunities for environmental or other activists (Botto and Tussie, 2003, p. 32). Indeed, business groups actively sought to exclude other social groups from this consultative forum. In the case of both the Foro and the Comisión, described below, Hochstetler concludes (2003b, p. 212 [my translation]) they 'only have consultative functions that make them cul de sacs for political participation'.

It is important to emphasize that control of decision-making has rested with national governments within Mercosur. The majority of decisions regarding Mercosur are taken by national presidents and their economic and diplomatic advisers with little input from citizens. The process has been led by national ministers and ministries of foreign affairs and economy through bodies such as the Mercosur Consejo del Mercado Común. Primary responsibility for implementation is given to the Grupo del Mercado Común, made up of representatives from the national economic and foreign ministries and central banks. Unlike NAFTA, the dispute resolution mechanisms within Mercosur, which in theory could provide an opening for citizen engagement, are underdeveloped and, specifically, there are no environmental dispute resolution mechanisms. As Hochstetler (2003a, p. 13) puts it 'in practice, most conflicts are resolved through direct negotiations among the region's national presidents, a forum not especially open to broad social participation'. Even the joint parliament (Comisión Parlamentaria Conjunta) is made up simply of selected members of the national congresses of the member countries and, while in theory this provides more opportunities for engagement by civil society actors, it is structurally very weak and therefore plays a limited role in key decision-making.

NGOs often have fewer established ties and points of access to those ministries leading the Mercosur negotiations. This reflects a broader trend within trade policy-making where ministries with the weakest ties to environmental groups have the strongest influence over the direction of policy. As Alanis-Ortega and González-Lutzenkirchen (2002, p. 44) note,

> Within Mexico, the Economic Ministry exerts extensive influence on environmental policy decision-making, regulations and practices that could influence economic or trade activity. At the international level, Mexico's Economic Ministry actively negotiates for Mexico in multilateral environmental forums where trade questions arise.

In this sense, officials from these ministries get to exercise a veto over environmental policy measures with which they disagree.

Those regional environmental institutions of Mercosur that do exist are essentially a gathering of the (currently) four national environmental agencies. The working subcommittees of Mercosur have no permanent agenda or roles, except in the most general sense to enable the realization of the goals of the Treaty of Asunción, leaving them little capacity to act as autonomous policy entrepreneurs. Weak institutions in this regard equate with fewer channels of access or mechanisms of influence, however indirect, regarding key power brokers within the foreign and trade ministries. It is clear, then, that the majority of opportunities that environmental activists could make use of within the Mercosur decision-making structure are confined to environmental areas that are considered secondary problems by the key Mercosur bodies. Hochstetler (2003,p. 15) notes, 'Given the limited agenda and powers of the Environmental Sub-committee, it is not surprising that SGT6 has not become a major focus for environmentalists in the region, even though it has tried to include non-governmental actors.'

There are many restrictions on meaningful NGO participation in Mercosur proceedings. There are difficulties in accessing information about decisions in the process of being made, or even those that have already been made within Mercosur (CEDA, 2002). Documents are not routinely distributed in advance, so, as Hochstetler (2003a,p. 15) suggests, 'meetings can consist of observers sitting at the margins of a room while SGT6 members sit at a central table and make cryptic comments about negotiating documents, without divulging their actual content'. Another mechanism that permits decision-makers within Mercosur to deny NGO access to their meetings is to call 'extraordinary' rather than 'ordinary' meetings, which means that NGOs cannot even attend the first day of the meeting. There is also evidence that levels of participation have actually decreased over time, perhaps reflecting the dynamic, already noted, whereby some NGOs choose to disengage from a process that offers few returns, especially after the diluting of the protocol on environmental issues and the continued narrow pro-trade bias of SGT6.

FTAA

In contrast to Mercosur, the involvement of diverse social actors has been on the agenda of FTAA from the very beginning. From Quebec onwards, the summits of the Americas have pronounced on the importance of civil society participation in FTAA deliberations. The Ministerial reunion in San José in 1998 produced a declaration to this effect. At the Santiago summit, governments confirmed that they encouraged 'all sectors of civil society to participate and to contribute in a constructive manner their points of view through mechanisms of consultation and dialogue created in the process of the FTAA negotiations' (Ricco, 2004, p. 7, my translation). Efforts to promote transparency, access to information through the internet (such as text being negotiated between states), public reports and participation in seminars are held up as evidence of efforts to reach out to civil society, even if concerns remain about the technical nature of information provided which is difficult for citizens to make sense of (Ricco, 2004).

It is the establishment of a Committee of Government Representatives on the Participation of Civil Society that forms the centrepiece of FTAA's architecture of participation, however. The FTAA draft declares the objectives of the committee to be information exchange, establishing procedures for accepting submissions, issuing status reports on the negotiations and managing civil society inputs. It is dismissed by critics, meanwhile, as a meaningless side-show. This is due to its absence of authority, work plan and lack of a real mandate, operating more as a 'drop box' for comments from civil society than a serious forum for debate. According to FTAA's own website, 'Vice-Ministers and Ministers are to decide the treatment and response to be given to these contributions' (ALCA, 2004). Groups can submit recommendations to the committee, 'but the committee is not obligated to actually consider the views expressed' (Blum, 2000,p. 6). This lack of follow-up on the impact of proposals submitted has led to sharp criticism of its effectiveness as a mechanism of participation. Global Exchange (n.d.) argue, for example:

> Despite repeated calls for the open and democratic development of trade policy, the FTAA negotiations have been conducted without citizen input. A process has been set up to solicit citizens' views, but there is no real mechanism to incorporate the public's concerns into the actual negotiations. The public has been given nothing more than a suggestion box. At the same time,

however, hundreds of corporate representatives are advising the US negotiators and have advance access to the negotiating texts. While citizens are left in the dark, corporations are helping to write the rules for the FTAA.

The underlying political purpose of the committee is made clear in the FTAA draft:

> The aim of the Committee of Government Representatives (CRG) on the Participation of Civil Society is to build broad public understanding of and support for hemispheric trade liberalization by serving as a channel of communication between civil society at the regional level and the FTAA negotiations. (Cited in Blum, 2000, p. 6)

It is also open only to those groups that express their views in a 'constructive manner', a device clearly intended to screen out critics. The chief negotiator of NAFTA for Mexico under the administration of Ernesto Zedillo, Herminio Blanco Mendoza stressed the limited role of the committee in the following terms: 'This is no study group, no negotiating group, it's a committee that receives proposals and presents them to ministers' (cited in Blum, 2000, p. 7). The short summaries produced by the committee of inputs from civil society for the Trade Negotiations Committee led environmentalists to react by saying: 'We just don't think it's a good use of our time . . . We don't want our view mediated by a bunch of bureaucrats' (ibid.). For all its limitations, the committee remains the only remaining official avenue for consideration of the environmental implications of the FTAA, given that the negotiating groups have failed to identify specific opportunities for raising environmental concerns directly. Even the existing body has faced opposition from a number of Latin American countries.

Since its creation, the CRG has met numerous times and extends open invitations to civil society groups to present contributions regarding the FTAA process, the first of which was issued on 1 November 1998 and the most recent on 21 November 2003. The first two calls received 70 contributions, the third received 56 and the fourth 43, many of which came from US-based industry associations. Declining interest perhaps reflects both greater enthusiasm in response to the first call, the first such innovation of its sort, and subsequent frustration with the 'drop-box' model of participation (CIECA, 2003, p. 337). No formal process links the civil society dialogue and any of the FTAA's nine negotiating groups. Deere and Esty (2002, p. 7) suggest that 'In fact, no procedures even exist to guide the consideration of submissions from civil society, let alone analysis of them.' They claim that there has been no substantive analysis of the submissions received from various groups and organizations since the committee was established, only the brief summaries mentioned above. On this basis, they argue,

> Although the Civil Society Committee nominally reports directly to the FTAA trade ministers [through the Trade Negotiations Committee], it does so in terms that are far too general to be of any real use. Such lip service to critical issues and to the process of public participation promises to become a serious obstacle when it comes to ratify the FTAA'.

Alongside this, there have been government-led initiatives carried forward by individual administrations within the FTAA process to improve the participation of civil society in decision-making on environmental issues. Examples include the initiative between the Bolivia government and the World Resources Institute, or the roles created by the governments of the USA and Canada for processes led by groups such as Fundación Futuro

Latinoamericano, the North–South Center of the University of Miami and latterly Corporación PARTICIPA and Fundación Esquel at key summits (Botto, 2003). Civil society groups have also created their own parallel conferences to register their views and make their voices heard, including on environmental issues. The Cumbres de los Pueblos (Peoples' Summits) that have been held alongside summits of the Americas as well as more recent summits of the South American Community of Nations bring together activists from across the region to generate alternative proposals for integration that advance social and environmental agendas.

While the focus of this section has been on the institutional opportunity structures available to civil society within regional trade accords, we should not overlook the importance of sub-regional agreements such as CAFTA (Central America Free Trade Agreement) or bilateral accords. Bilateral trade accords provide a potentially important policy space for civil society participation. The Chile–Canada Agreement on Environmental Cooperation, negotiated in parallel with their bilateral free trade agreement, is held up as a positive model for handling environmental protection measures, but also contains a provision that allows citizens and NGOs of the two parties to make submissions alleging a party's failure to effectively enforce its environmental laws. Such submissions may not include complaints affecting a private individual or a specific productive activity, although they may be filed against the parties if they fail to enforce their own environmental legislation (Matus and Rossi, 2002, p. 266). In practice, critics allege that many of the provisions regarding public participation in the agreement have too many weaknesses to be effectively utilized (CEDA, 2002), but procedures concerning transparency, access to justice and procedural guarantees give others grounds for hope (Cordonier-Segger, 2005a, p. 204).

It is equally true that bilateral trade accords between unequal partners can be used to undermine environmental protection measures. The bilateral investment agreement between the USA and Bolivia, said to have been 'negotiated on behalf of US mining companies to protect their investments in the mineral rich Andean country' (Cordonier-Segger, 2005b, p. 156) offers few openings for public input regarding the social and environmental impacts of mining, for example, and there are no provisions for the pulic release of documents nor stakeholder participation in investor-state tribunals. Likewise the bilateral trade agreement negotiated between Peru and the USA opens the way to the entry of GMOs into a susbsistence-based economy, which is a centre of origin for potatoes, by requiring Peru to synchronize its sanitary and phytosanitary measures with those of the USA, potentially undermining policy autonomy conferred upon Peru by its membership of the Cartagena Protocol on Biosafety. There are also fears that measures to strengthen intellectual property protection in line with US demands will threaten the genetic resources and traditional knowledge base of indigenous communities in the country (TWN, 2006).

Conclusions

It is clear that top-down mechanisms of participation in trade policy often serve to reinforce inequities within civil society. In the run-up to ministerial meetings of FTAA, for example, space was made available for academics, think-tanks and consultants, and not other elements within civil society. Attempts to construct virtual mechanisms of engagement where groups can deposit suggestions are essentially only taken up by these same actors: academics, business foundations and a sprinkling of NGOs, principally from

North and Central America. As noted above, many are sceptical of the value of engaging with initiatives such as this when there is no way of monitoring the impact of the proposals. There is also a degree of political screening at work in so far as these groups play a key role in consensus-building because these actors, while perhaps disagreeing on the roadmaps to get there, support the basic principles of market liberalization.

There is a delicate balance to strike between attempting to construct ambitious mechanisms of consultation on a hemispheric, or even regional, basis and focusing attention on improving national mechanisms of consultation that, in the final instance, is where responsibility resides for considering the public interest in the formulation of trade policy. As we have seen, groups with poor access to national decision-making structures often value openings at regional level to make their voices heard. Ensuring that they are in a position to exploit those openings means overcoming barriers they face in terms of funding to attend meetings and the personnel implications of stretching often small staffs even further by engaging in regional processes. Those who benefit most from participatory mechanisms in regional trade accords appear to be those who also have open to them channels of influence at national level; hence the concern about getting 'two bites of the apple': privileged access in both national and regional policy-making arenas. While this scenario prevails, we can expect the debate about trade and environment in the Americas to be framed by those who view the relationship as mutually supportive and not the rising tide of opposition to neoliberal environmentalism in Latin America which raises questions about whose resources are being traded and on whose behalf.

References

Acción Ecológica (2004), http://www.accionecologica.org/alca.htm, accessed 5 October.
Alanis-Ortega, Gustavo and Ana Karina González-Lutzenkirchen (2002), 'No room for the environment: the NAFTA negotiations and the Mexican perspective on trade and environment', in Carolyn L. Deere and Daniel Esty (eds), *Greening the Americas: NAFTA's Lessons for Hemispheric Trade*, Cambridge,MA: MIT Press, pp. 41–61.
Albán, María Amparo (2003), 'Sociedad civil: Tras un derecho a participar en la ALCA', *La Ley: Suplemento de Derecho Ambiental*, 14 July, Buenos Aires, p. 7.
ALCA (2004), http://www.alca-ftaa.org/English Version/view.htm.
Audley, John (1997), *Green Politics and Global Trade: NAFTA and the Future of Environmental Politics*, Washington, DC: Georgetown University Press.
Blum, Jonathan (2000), 'The FTAA and the fast track to forgetting the environment: a comparison of the NAFTA and Mercosur environmental models as examples for the hemisphere', *Texas International Law Journal*, **35**(3), pp. 435–58, available online at http://gateway.proquest.com/openurl, pp. 1–33.
Botto, Mercedes (2003), 'Mitos y realidades de la participación no gubernamental', in Diana Tussie and Mercedes Botto (eds), *El ALCA y las cumbres de las Americas: una nueva relacion publico–privada?*, Buenos Aires: Biblos, pp. 237–61.
Botto, Mercedes and Diana Tussie (2003), 'Introducción. La internacionalización de la agenda de participación: El debate regional', in Diana Tussie y Merceded Botto (eds), *El ALCA y las cumbres de las Americas: Una nueva relacion publico–privada?*, Buenos Aires: Biblos, pp. 27–47.
Carranza, M. (2003), 'Can Mercosur survive? Domestic and international constraints on Mercosur', *Latin American Politics and Society*, **45**(2), 67–103.
CEDA (Centro Ecuatorio de Derecho Ambiental) (2002), 'Hacia la participación de la sociedad civil en las Americas', *Memorias de los talleres sobre comerico y ambiente en la reunión ministerial del ALCA*, Quito, 29 and 30 October, pp. 62–75.
CIECA (Centro de Investigación Económica para el Caribe) (2003), 'ALCA y la participación de la sociedad civil', in Herman Blanco,Mónica Araya and Carlos Murillo (eds), *ALCA y medio ambiente: ideas desde Latinoamérica*, Santiago, Chile: C1PMA-GETS-C1NPE, pp. 333–53.
Cordonier-Segger, M.C. (2005a), 'Enhancing social and environmental cooperation in the Americas', in M.C. Cordonier-Segger and M.L. Reynal (eds), *Beyond the Barricades: The Americas' Trade and Sustainable Development Agenda*, Aldershot: Ashgate, pp. 181–225.

Cordonier-Segger, M.C. (2005b), 'From protest to proposal: options for an Americas investment regime?', in M.C. Cordonier-Segger and M.L. Reynal (eds), *Beyond the Barricades: The Americas Trade and Sustainable Development Agenda*, Aldershot: Ashgate, pp. 145–65.

Deere, Carolyn L. and Daniel Esty (eds) (2002), *Greening the Americas: NAFTA's Lessons for Hemispheric Trade*, Cambridge, MA: MIT Press.

Fisher, Richard (2002), 'Trade and environment in the FTAA: learning from the NAFTA', in Carolyn L. Deere and Daniel Esty (eds), *Greening the Americas: NAFTA's Lessons for Hemispheric Trade*, Cambridge, MA: MIT Press, pp. 183–201.

Global Exchange (n.d.),'*Top ten reasons to oppose the Free Trade of the Americas*', http://www.globalexchange.org/campaigns/ftaa/topten.html, accessed 2 August 2004.

Hochstetler, K. (2003a), 'Fading green? Environmental politics in the Mercosur Free Trade Agreement', *Latin American Politics and Society*, **45**(4), 1–33.

Hochstetler, K. (2003b), 'Mercosur, ciudadania y ambientalismo', in Elisabeth Jelin (ed.), *Mas alla de la nation: Las escalas multiples de los movimientos sociales*, Buenos Aires: Libros de Zorzal, pp. 203–45.

Hogenboom, Barbara (1998), *Mexico and the NAFTA Environment Debate*, Utrecht: International Books.

Keck, Margaret E. and Kathryn Sikkink (1998), *Activists Beyond Borders: Advocacy Networks in International Politics*, Ithaca, NY and London: Cornell University Press.

Korzeniewicz, Roberto Patricio and William Smith (2003), 'Redes transnacionales de la sociedad civil: entre la protesta y la colaboración', in D. Tussie and M. Botto (eds), *El ALCA y las cumbres de las Americas: Una nueva relacion publico-privada?* Buenos Aires: Biblos, pp. 47–77.

Matus, Mario and Edda Rossi (2002), 'Trade and environment in the FTAA: a Chilean perspective', in Carolyn L. Deere and Daniel Esty (eds), *Greening the Americas: NAFTA's Lessons for Hemispheric Trade*, Cambridge, MA: MIT Press, pp. 259–73.

Newell, P. (2007), 'Trade and environmental justice in Latin America', *New Political Economy*, **12**(2), 237–59.

Obach, Brian (2004), *Labor and the Environmental Movement: The Quest for Common Ground*, Cambridge, MA: MIT Press.

Púlsar (Agencia Informativa) (2001), 'México: movimientos sociales ante ALCA', 4 May, http://www.correodelsur.ch/articulos/mex_ante-alca.html, accessed 2 August 2004.

Ricco, Víctor, H. (2004), 'El ambiente y la participación pública en el proceso del ALCA', *La ley: suplemento de derecho ambiental*, 25 June, Buenos Aires, pp. 6–7.

Teubal, Miguel and Javier Rodríguez (2002), *Agro y alimentos en la globalizacion: una perspectiva crítica*, Buenos Aires: La Colmena.

Third World Network (2006), 'US FTA likely to open Peru to GMOs?' 2 October, Kuala Lumpur, Malaysia: TWN Biosafety Information Service.

Timmons Roberts, J. and Nikki Demetria Thanos (2003), *Trouble in Paradise: Globalization and Environmental Crisis in Latin America*, London: Routledge.

14 Trade conflict over genetically modified organisms
Thomas Bernauer and Philipp Aerni

In 2003 the USA, seconded by Argentina and Canada, initiated litigation in the World Trade Organization (WTO) against the European Union's regulatory policy for genetically modified organisms (GMOs). The three plaintiffs claimed that the EU's GMO policy was creating illegal trade restrictions. Specifically, they argued (1) that the EU had implemented a *de facto* moratorium on approval of new biotech crop varieties; that (2) the EU had failed to approve some particular GM crops for which US firms were seeking approval; and (3) that several EU countries were unilaterally banning the import and marketing of GM crops that had been approved at the EU level. The WTO Dispute Settlement Panel's verdict (a 2000-page document!), issued in September 2006, supports the plaintiffs' position to a large extent and asks the EU to bring its GMO approval process in line with WTO rules. As of December 2007, it appeared very unlikely that the EU would be willing or able to comply with the WTO verdict. The EU's GMO legislation had been overhauled even before the WTO panel issued its verdict. But the EU decision-making process for GMO approvals has remained complex and subject to political considerations rather than scientific risk assessment alone: it involves the European Food Safety Authority (EFSA), which has an advisory role, as well as the EU Commission and Council of Ministers, which hold the decision-making authority.

Why does the WTO trade dispute on GMOs, one of more than 300 WTO disputes since 1995, deserve a full chapter in this book? We submit that this dispute is interesting because it pits countries with a predominantly GMO-adverse public (Europe) against countries whose GMO policy is driven by large, export-oriented farmers and the biotech industry (primarily the USA, to some extent also Argentina and Canada). These circumstances raise difficult questions with respect to legitimate justifications for trade-restricting environment, health and safety policies. Most European governments and the EU take the position that the precautionary principle (a 'better safe than sorry' approach to regulation in the presence of uncertainty about risks posed by GMOs) and the prevailing GMO skepticism among consumers and voters are sufficient justification for a restrictive policy. The USA, in contrast, claims that WTO rules, particularly those of the Agreement on Sanitary and Phytosanitary Measures (SPS Agreement), mandate a strong 'sound science' discipline. From the latter perspective, trade-restricting GMO policies are permitted only to the extent that they are supported by scientific evidence on risks.

The analytical (positive) and normative issues raised by the transatlantic GMO dispute extend far beyond the dispute itself. Analytically, the GMO dispute raises the question of why regulatory policies in the USA and the EU have, over the past 10–15 years, moved in different directions. It will be noted that GMOs is not the only area where this has been the case. Several other environment, health and safety policy issues have followed a similar pattern, e.g. electronic waste regulation, toxic waste trade policy and climate change policy. From a normative viewpoint, the GMO dispute raises the question of whether science and global institutions with judicial authority (such as the WTO) relying on scientific evidence can be effective arbiters in cases where democratic justifications (what consumers and voters want) do not line up with scientific justifications (risks identified by science). It also raises questions about the consequences that the GMO trade dispute between the two biggest economic powers in the global system has for other countries, and poor countries in particular.

The following section describes the polarization of regulatory policies for GMOs. In Section 2 we examine why GMO regulations in the EU and the USA have moved in different directions. Section 3 looks at the WTO dispute on GMOs. In Section 4 we explore the effects on developing countries. In Section 5 we conclude by discussing normative issues and policy options for moving beyond deadlock.

1. Genetically modified (GM) crops and regulatory polarization

The first 'green revolution' started in the 1930s. It brought rapid yield increases throughout the 1970s in corn and other temperate-climate crops through increasingly effective fertilizers, pesticides, crop species, machinery and farm management. The average farmer in modern agriculture is thus able to feed up to 30 non-farmers. The second green revolution took place in the 1960s and 1970s: it carried the same technologies to the developing world and crops grown in the tropics (particularly rice). Genetic engineering in agriculture may lead to a third green revolution, although it is still at an early stage. It emerged in the 1970s and was commercialized in the 1990s. The proponents of this technology claim that it will result in another massive increase in agronomic productivity and also provide qualitative improvements in the food supply (e.g. healthier food).

One of the big differences between the first two green revolutions and the (potentially) third one is that the latter has not been greeted with unqualified enthusiasm. In fact, we have witnessed a process of global regulatory polarization as EU countries have imposed severe regulatory constraints on GMOs, whereas the USA has opened its market to most agri-biotech applications. Other countries have either aligned with one or the other of the world's two largest economies, or they have been struggling to find some middle ground.

This process of polarization is quite surprising. In the mid-1980s, the GMO policies of West European countries, the USA and other nations were similar. But at the end of the 1980s, they began to drift apart. From 1990 on, the EU and its member states turned to ever more stringent approval and labeling standards for GMOs, with strong emphasis on the precautionary principle. The result is that very few agricultural biotech applications have been approved for commercialization in the EU. Commercial planting of GM crops in EU countries accounts only for a tiny fraction of total crop cultivation. And the number of GM crop field trials is much smaller than in the USA. The number of labeled GM food products on the EU market has approached zero as food processors and retailers have chosen to avoid rather than label GM foods. The EU's market for GM food products has shrunk to GM food ingredients and animal feed not subject to mandatory labeling.

Policy-makers in the USA have opted for an entirely different approach. They have embraced agricultural biotechnology. They view genetic engineering as a new and innovative food and feed production technology that does not *per se* make produced food or feed less safe than their conventional counterparts. The US Food and Drug Administration (FDA), the Department of Agriculture (USDA), and the Environmental Protection Agency (EPA) have installed relatively simple notification procedures, have left pre-market risk assessments to industry, and have approved most industry requests for field-testing and commercialization of GM products very quickly. Producers and/or retailers may voluntarily label GM foods but are not required by law to do so. While the EU has imposed the (involuntary) burden of labeling on producers and/or vendors of GM products, the USA imposes the (voluntary) burden of labeling on producers of non-GM products: there is a US market for labeled non-GM products, but not for labeled GM products. More than 60 GM crop varieties are approved and grown in the USA. Many more GM varieties have been authorized for field-testing. GM crop acreage increased dramatically between 1996 and 2007. And GM ingredients can be found in thousands of processed food products.

These transatlantic differences are associated, at the global level, with an increasing gap between GMO-promoting and GMO-restricting countries, in terms of both approval and labeling regulation and at the market level. The pro-biotech camp clusters around the USA and includes in particular Argentina and Canada. The other camp clusters around the EU and also includes several non-EU states in Europe, such as Norway, Switzerland, and various Central and Eastern European countries. An unusual case in this respect is Switzerland, whose citizens approved by large majority an initiative that imposes a five-year moratorium (2006–10) on the commercial cultivation of GM crops. We shall return to this case because it pits fundamental principles of democracy against economic freedom and scientific risk assessment.

Many other countries (e.g. Australia, Brazil, China, India, Japan, Mexico, Russia and South Africa) have moved towards stricter approval procedures. Many countries (e.g. Australia, China, Japan, South Korea and Russia) have also adopted mandatory labeling requirements for GM food. These regulations differ very much with respect to their stringency. On average they position these countries somewhere in between the EU and the USA.

Most developing countries have experienced great difficulties in trying to make sense of scientific and political controversies about risks and benefits of GMOs. Many of them have established some regulatory policies, often with the help of experts from industrialized countries. In trying to enact and implement these policies, they have been caught in conflicting pressures by big trading partners (notably the EU and the USA).

2.   Explaining differences in regulatory policy

Popular views on why Europeans are more hostile to GMOs than North Americans center on arguments about general technophobia and nutritional habits (culinary culture). Such arguments are largely invalid. For example, survey results on public attitudes toward technology do not support the claim that Europeans are more technophobic (e.g. Bernauer, 2003). Moreover, while the obesity rate in the USA is much higher than in Europe, Europeans smoke more than US Americans (despite higher cigarette taxes in Europe) (Cutler and Glaeser, 2006).

Arguments that, on average, scientific risk assessment and cost–benefit analysis play a greater role in US policy-making are probably accurate. But this claim is too generic to help us to understand what we observe in the GMO area. Recent research has thus focused primarily on institutional structures, the mass media, consumer perceptions, and NGO and industry behavior to explain regulatory differences (e.g. Shaffer and Pollack, 2007; Falkner, 2006; Bauer and Gaskell, 2002; Russell and Vogler, 2002; Gaskell and Bauer, 2001; Paarlberg, 2001).

Bernauer (2003) explains transatlantic differences primarily in terms of differences in consumer perceptions, activity of non-governmental organizations (NGOs), interests and behavior of biotech firms, farmers, processors and retailers, and institutional characteristics of the political systems concerned. This explanation takes into account market processes as well as domestic and international political processes. The explanation combines two theoretical perspectives. The first views regulation as the result of a struggle for political and market influence among different interest groups within the EU and the USA; i.e. among input suppliers (agri-biotech firms), farmers, processors and retailers, and consumer and environmental groups. It illuminates why these groups have different preferences, and when and why particular interests prevail in the policy-making process. The second perspective looks at the effect of interactions among political sub-units (EU countries, US states) in federalist political systems (the EU, the USA). The first perspective focuses on societal influences operating from the individual or firm level upward (bottom up). The second centers on the effects of system-wide political structures and institutions (top-down perspective). In the EU, both processes have operated in ways that have driven GMO policy toward greater stringency. In the USA, they have operated in ways that have sustained GMO-friendly regulation. As to the first perspective, Bernauer's (2003) analysis shows that the collective action capacity of environmental and consumer interests has varied substantially between the EU and the USA. This variation can be traced back to differences in public perceptions of agricultural biotechnology, consumer trust in regulatory authorities, and institutional settings. Due to more negative consumer attitudes toward GMOs and lower public trust in regulatory agencies, the collective action capacity of GMO-adverse European environmental and consumer groups has been higher than the capacity of their US counterparts. Transatlantic differences in the extent and nature of NGOs' GMO campaigns reflect this variation in collective action capacity. GMO-adverse groups in Europe have thus been more successful in shaping markets for the technology than GMO-adverse groups in the USA. Negative public attitudes towards GMOs in combination with more institutional access due to more fragmented (multi-level) policy-making has also enabled GMO-adverse interests in Europe to exert more influence on policy-making. In the USA less negative public attitudes toward GMOs and a centralized regulatory system for GMOs have acted against GMO-adverse interests.

The collective action capacity of pro-GMO interests has also varied substantially between the EU and the USA. In Europe, negative public attitudes and NGO campaigns have driven a wedge between biotech firms on the one hand and food processors, retailers and farmers on the other. Thus they have reduced the collective action capacity of pro-GMO interests. The pro-GMO coalition in Europe has been crippled not by protectionist 'piggy-backing' by some producers (notably farmers) – a key claim in US attacks on the EU's GMO regulation. It has been weakened because those firms most vulnerable to market pressure spearheaded by NGOs, notably food processors and retailers, have been pushed toward support for stricter regulation. In contrast, in the USA a cohesive and well-organized pro-GMO producer coalition has prevailed due to more positive public attitudes and weaker campaigns by GMO-adverse NGOs. Differences in industrial structure (particularly higher concentration, in both economic and organizational terms, of the EU than the US retail sector) also play a role in explaining why the pro-GMO producer coalition has been much weaker in the EU than in the USA.

The interest group explanation does not account for differences in interests and policies of individual EU countries and US states, and their implications for variation of policies at the EU and US level. Hence the second perspective views EU and US GMO policies as outcomes of interactions between political sub-units (member states in the EU, states in the USA) within a larger (federal) political system where these sub-units can to varying degrees act autonomously. It concentrates on whether political sub-units within the larger political system can, by unilaterally installing stricter or laxer regulation of GMOs, push the stringency of system-wide regulations up or down. The analysis of GMO policy-making in the EU and the USA shows that in the EU we observe a substantial 'ratcheting-up' effect, whereas 'centralized laxity' has prevailed in the USA. EU countries are bound by supranational rules that guarantee the free flow of agricultural goods within the EU's internal market. But they maintain considerable national autonomy in closely related policy areas, such as environment, health and safety regulation. For example, in many areas they have safeguarded the right to establish regulation that is stricter than minimum standards set by the EU or that deviates from the principle of mutual recognition. These conditions apply to agri-biotechnology as well.

When the forces described and explained by the interest group perspective began to drive up the stringency of regulation in more GMO-adverse EU countries, the more GMO-friendly nations as well as the EU Commission faced a dilemma: how to satisfy demands, in some countries, for stricter GMO regulation and, at the same time, safeguard the EU's internal market for agricultural products. Variation across countries in approval and labeling standards for GM products threatened to disrupt agricultural trade in the EU. In view of strong public support for strict GMO regulation in around half of the EU's member countries, downward harmonization to levels acceptable to pro-GMO countries was impossible. Pro-GMO countries in the EU have thus regularly caved in to the demands of GMO-adverse countries. They have done so because, in their view, the costs of market disruptions are higher than the costs of restrictive GMO regulation. In this 'ratcheting-up' process GMO-adverse countries have, step by step, moved toward more stringent regulations and have dragged EU-wide regulations upward in this process.

GMO policy is more centralized in the USA than in the EU, in terms of both political levels and institutions involved. It is largely in the hands of two independent federal agencies and one federal ministry (FDA, EPA, USDA). What might appear like a paradox in the EU case – that fragmentation of decision-making authority produces upward harmonization and not simply paralysis – does not come into play in the USA to the extent that it does in the EU. Bottom-up pressure for stricter regulation has in some cases led to diverging policy preferences among US states. But due to institutional and legal constraints, US states' options for stricter unilateral regulation of GMOs are much more limited than the options of individual EU countries. Even if public pressure for stricter GMO regulation grew in some US states, and if these states imposed some restrictions that were upheld by the courts, a 'ratcheting-up' trend would emerge much more slowly in the USA than in the EU. In other words, relatively positive public attitudes toward GMOs and weak NGO campaigns are primarily responsible for lax GMO regulation in the USA; and federal processes in the USA constitute an additional barrier to stricter regulation should bottom-up pressure increase in future.

3.   The WTO dispute on GMOs

To put the GMO dispute in perspective: WTO trade disputes are extremely rare events. Only around 2 percent of all pairs of WTO member countries (country dyads per year) ever get involved in a WTO trade dispute (Sattler and Bernauer, 2007). Of the 300+ WTO trade disputes since 1995, less than 10 percent concern environment, health and safety issues (Bernauer and Sattler, 2006).

The principal reasons why the USA has opted for escalation in the transatlantic disagreement on GMO policy are primarily the following (Bernauer, 2003). First, economic losses due to the EU's GMO restrictions (estimated to be in the order of several hundred million US dollars p.a.) are relatively large and concentrated on politically influential economic actors in the USA (chiefly large, export-oriented farmers and the biotech industry). Also, the US government has worried that other countries that are important export destinations for US agricultural products will follow the EU policy model for GMOs. Second, non-coercive policy measures for solving the problem are difficult or impossible to implement. Mutual recognition is unacceptable to the EU and the USA because it would undermine the legitimacy of both sides' respective policy. Compensation would founder on political legitimacy and financial grounds. All international harmonization efforts are deadlocked for the same reasons that have led to regulatory polarization. The same holds true for unilateral regulatory adjustment in the USA, which has helped to mitigate trade tensions but cannot, by itself, solve the problem. Third, the USA assumed that it would win the case. It also anticipated that the EU would make concessions before a WTO verdict or after a 'guilty' verdict, and that other important export destinations for US agricultural goods would thus be deterred from enacting EU-style policies for GMOs.

As noted in the introduction, the US-led plaintiffs won the case. The *de facto* consequences of the verdict remain open. The EU had initiated reforms of its approval process even before the USA lauched the trade dispute. These reforms were completed in 2004 and were meant to end the informal moratorium on approvals of new GM crops (1998–2003). With reference to the EU Commission's position, the WTO verdict is largely running into an open door. The Commission is relatively biotech-friendly and has for the past several years tried to emphasize risk-assessment criteria over political considerations in the approval process, without much success. However, the main problem lies in implementing the EU's revised legislation under conditions of adverse public attitudes toward GMOs and strong resistance of several EU member countries to lifting their unilateral bans on GM crops (six countries at the time of the WTO verdict).

In late 2007 the EU Commission proposed that the unilateral bans must be lifted, but the Council of Ministers failed to support this proposal. Only Italy has lifted its ban. Whether the former or the latter body of the EU will prevail, or whether the issue will be taken to the European Court of Justice, remains open. It is also unclear whether new risk assessments undertaken by EU member states that have put in place unilateral bans would make those bans compatible with the SPS Agreement and resolve the WTO dispute. The principal charge in the WTO ruling was that those unilateral bans were not backed up by country-specific risk assessment, and were not supported by risk assessments carried out at the EU level (the EU has been in favor of approving the respective GM crops) (Arcuri, 2007; Poli, 2007).

In any event, the EU experiences great difficulties in implementing its own GMO regulations and, by implication, also the WTO verdict. The approval process is unlikely to gain the momentum requested by the plaintiffs in the WTO case. Moreover, if the unilateral bans could be supported by country-specific risk assessments, which would presumably make them compatible with the SPS Agreement, this would still not satisfy the plaintiffs. Finally, even if more GM crops were approved and cultivated in Europe they would be greeted by fierce NGO campaigns, less-than-enthusiastic consumers, and risk-averse retailers. And all this would happen in a setting where, according to the law, GM products have to bear a clearly visible label (EU labeling regulation was not challenged in the WTO case). Hence it appears very unlikely that the WTO verdict will mark the end of the transatlantic trade conflict over GMOs.

In more general terms, a reversal of the EU's GMO policy is unlikely because of low public acceptance of GM food, low trust in regulators, pressure by NGOs, significant opposition to GM crops among farmers, strong incentives of food processors and retailers to stay away or withdraw from the market for labeled GM foods, and institutional inertia in EU policy-making. The dominance of GMO-adverse interests in the EU is bolstered by the characteristics of regulatory federalism in the EU. Decision-making structures in the EU allow GMO-adverse minorities to block efforts to relax existing standards. In addition, a combination of multi-level decision-making, substantial regulatory autonomy of EU countries, and concerns about safeguarding the EU's internal market encourage a 'ratcheting-up' of GMO regulations rather than downward harmonization.

The USA, for its part, is unlikely to move toward the EU model of GMO policy any time soon. Potential conflicts between US farmers and biotech firms in view of precarious export opportunities for GM crops have been reduced through increased government subsidies for US farmers. In addition to low interest group ('bottom-up') pressure for stricter agri-biotech regulation, the characteristics of US regulatory federalism act against more restrictive GMO policies. In the unlikely event that consumer pressure for tighter rules grew, heavily constrained regulatory autonomy of US states in agri-biotech matters, combined with centralized decision-making at the federal level, would slow down any 'contagion' effect that might emanate from individual US states trying to impose more restrictive policies.

4.   Consequences for other countries

Whether regulatory polarization and transatlantic trade conflict over GMOs will continue and for how long depends not only on domestic processes in the EU and the USA. It also depends on developments at the global level. If most countries other than the USA and the EU moved toward the EU policy model for GMOs, this would create pressure for stricter regulation in the USA. Pressure for more liberal rules in the EU would grow if most other countries moved toward the US model. But for the time being the world's two largest economies are clearly the principal drivers of worldwide regulatory activity on GMOs. Their policy choices limit the options of other countries, particularly those that are economically dependent on the EU, the USA, or both. Switzerland, Norway, and Central and Eastern European countries have thus aligned with the EU, and Canada with the USA. Other countries, which are less dependent on EU or US markets, e.g. China, Brazil, India, Japan and Russia, have adopted regulations whose stringency lies somewhere in between the EU and the US model. GMO policy in these countries is very recent and very much in flux. Both the EU and the USA have been battling for influence on the regulatory policies of these countries.

In the overall picture, the welfare implications (at the national, not the individual, level) of restricting or promoting GM crops in rich, industrialized countries are quite limited. There is no compelling need to increase agricultural productivity and the nutritional value of food in rich countries. The most important benefits (offered only in minor ways by current-generation GM crops, but potentially by future GM varieties) may come from reduced fertilizer and pesticide, use and improved soil and water conservation. However, the biggest gains from GMOs in rich countries are likely to materialize in medical and industrial applications. The needs of many developing countries are very different. They are plagued by low agricultural productivity, rapid population growth, food insecurity, and (related) disastrous levels of soil degradation and deforestation. Appropriate GM crops could contribute to the mitigation of these problems (Brooks and Barfoot, 2006; Cohen and Paarlberg, 2004; Conway, 2005; Victor and Runge, 2002).

Unfortunately, the transatlantic GMO dispute has forced many developing countries to take sides and has crowded out systematic and pragmatic domestic debates in these countries about the types of biotech applications they may want and need. At the policy level, advocates of stricter GMO regulation appear to have been more successful in recent years in exporting their approach to developing countries (Cohen and Paarlberg, 2004). They have operated primarily in the framework or at least in the name of the Cartagena Protocol on Biosafety, which was adopted in 2000 and has been ratified by more than 140 countries – among them all EU member countries, but not the USA. The Protocol seeks to protect biodiversity from risks posed by GMOs. It establishes an advanced informed agreement procedure, embraces the precautionary principle (PP), sets up a biosafety clearing-house, and offers assistance to poor countries in implementing the Protocol (Falkner, 2000). Many GMO-adverse NGOs and some government agencies, primarily from Europe, have explicitly or implicitly used the Cartagena Protocol process to support GMO-adverse stakeholders in developing countries and establish regulatory policies subscribing to strict versions of the precautionary principle (Cohen and Paarlberg, 2004; Paarlberg, 2001).

It remains unclear whether the current dominance of GMO-adverse support for developing countries will lead the majority of poorer countries to follow the EU model. In fact, many developing countries have recently become more skeptical about whether GMO policies modeled after those of the EU are in their best interest (de Greef, 2004). Surveys carried out in developing countries (e.g. Aerni and Bernauer, 2006; Pew Initiative, 2006; see also Hoban, 2005) suggest that stakeholders in these countries hold rather pragmatic views, particularly with respect to indigenous biotech applications that would avoid economic dependence on industrialized countries and their biotech industry. Positive attitudes toward GMOs are most pronounced in developing countries that are at the forefront of GMO research, e.g. China, India and South Africa (e.g. Gupta and Chandak, 2005). GM-crop acreage in some developing countries is also on the rise (ISAAA, 2007). These trends in developing countries may in fact bring back some sanity into the political rhetoric of interest groups from rich countries about what developing countries want and need. They are likely to push GMO-hostile interest groups into revising their claims about catastrophic health and environmental risks that are out of tune with developing-country demands and also the vast majority of scientific risk assessments. They will also make it more difficult for GMO proponents to sustain claims that GM crops will allow poor countries to leapfrog in agricultural development and achieve the 'end of hunger' (see, e.g.

Conway, 2005; Kleckner, 2006). In other words, to the extent that the transatlantic dispute does not suppress bottom-up processes in developing countries, we are likely to see, within the next few years, more pragmatism and recognition that some agri-biotech applications may, under particular conditions, indeed offer benefits to farmers and consumers in developing countries.

5. Normative dilemma and potential solutions

The transatlantic GMO dispute is interesting also from another normative perspective. Normative, in this context, does not refer to debates on whether GMOs are ethical in whatever sense. It refers to the question of who should be entitled to decide on the approval of GMOs or particular biotech applications for research, commercial cultivation and marketing. In essence, such decisions can be taken by the market (i.e. by producers and consumers), voters and/or their representatives (policy-makers), scientists, or any combination of the three.

The US approach to GMO policy relies heavily on the first (market) and third (science) element, the EU approach largely on the second (political decision) and third (science). In the EU, the political has clearly trumped the scientific element. This is most apparent in those cases where proposals by the EU Commission to force countries with unilateral bans on EU-approved GM crops to lift these bans have been rejected by the Council of Ministers – the Council is composed of ministers from all EU member-country governments. The reasoning of the majority in those cases has been, very explicitly, that they do not wish to overrule countries whose population and government do not want to import, cultivate and/or consume GMOs. The WTO's SPS Agreement (and also US policy), in contrast, operates with scientific risk-assessment criteria, with some room for maneuver left by the precautionary principle. Supporters of the scientific approach claim that 'sound science' is the only effective and non-arbitrary barrier to trade-restricting environment, health and safety regulations that serve protectionist, rent-seeking purposes. Critics of this approach argue that science cannot, in the case of GMOs, offer conclusive evidence on risks and benefits, and that science-based decision-making is tantamount to 'technocracy' rather than democracy (see Jasanoff, 2005).

Switzerland is the most extreme example of the political approach. In its system of direct democracy, the government must call a public vote on initiatives that are signed by at least 100 000 voters. In November 2005, an initiative imposing a five-year moratorium on all commercial cultivation of GM crops was approved with a 56% majority. Surveys carried out thereafter have established that around 10–15% of No-voters meant to reject GMOs and thus voted the wrong way (the reverse error was much less important). Hence the *de facto* Yes-vote was in the order of 70% (Hirter and Linder, 2005). Whether the moratorium will be extended will become clear in late 2010. Given that the WTO panel in the EU–US dispute found the EU's *de facto* moratorium from 1998 to 2003 as well as the unilateral EU member state bans to be in violation of WTO rules, the Swiss moratorium may well violate the SPS Agreement also: it is based on a purely political decision, and not a scientific risk assessment (although risk assessments on GM crops in Switzerland have been carried out). However, most proponents of the 'sound science' approach would concede that the Swiss decision was as democratic as such a decision can possibly be.

There is no obvious solution to this dilemma that would satisfy both 'sound science' and democracy requirements. We can primarily highlight that the dilemma exists, and that the

WTO system of adjudication tends to perform better – in terms of real economic outcomes, rather than legal verdicts – when dealing with claims of 'conventional' protectionism (e.g. discriminatory tariffs, taxation or subsidies) than with claims concerning environment, health and safety regulation. The only other WTO dispute resembling the GMO conflict is the EU–US dispute over growth hormones in beef production (Caduff, 2005; Kelemen, 2001). In that case the WTO decided in 1998/9 that the EU was in violation of global trade law. But instead of changing its regulation on growth hormones, the EU chose to subject itself to punitive tariffs by the USA and Canada (since 1999) in the order of US$100 million p.a. It is very likely that the EU would behave similarly should the plaintiffs in the GMO case seek and obtain WTO approval for punitive measures. Even worse, the value (in monetary terms) of such measures is likely to be higher than in the beef hormones case (the costs imposed by the EU's GMO policies on foreign producers are higher) and may thus cause all sorts of nasty side-effects in EU–US trade relations.

As shown in this chapter, escalation of the GMO dispute in the WTO will not generate a solution that helps producers in plaintiff countries. 'Out-of-court' solutions may in fact be more useful in this and other, similar, cases. Such a solution in the GMO case will probably have to involve some sort of labeling of GM products (see Weirich, 2007). While solutions outside the WTO are obviously not ideal, they should be viewed in perspective. As noted above, only a tiny fraction of all country pairs (country dyads per year) ever get involved in a WTO dispute. And the large majority of the more than 300 disputes taken to the WTO since 1995 were resolved quite effectively. If cases such as the GMO conflict were dealt with outside the WTO, this would not call into question the very positive overall record of the WTO adjudication system. Rather, it would protect the WTO system from problems it cannot effectively solve.

References

Aerni, Philipp and Thomas Bernauer (2006), 'Stakeholder attitudes toward GMOs in the Philippines, Mexico and South Africa', *World Development*, **34**(3), 557–75.
Arcuri, Alessandra (2007), 'Compliance is a hard nut to crack in the biotech dispute', *BioRes*, **1**, 11–13.
Bauer, Martin W. and George Gaskell, (2002), *Biotechnology: The Making of a Global Controversy*, Cambridge: Cambridge University Press.
Bernauer, Thomas (2003), *Genes, Trade and Regulation: The Seeds of Conflict in Food Biotechnology*, Princeton, NJ: Princeton University Press.
Bernauer, Thomas and Thomas Sattler (2006), 'Sind WTO-Dispute im Umwelt- und Verbraucherschutzbereich eskalationsträchtiger?', *Zeitschrift für Internationale Beziehungen*, **13**(1), 5–38.
Brooks, Graham and Peter Barfoot (2006), 'Global impact of biotech crops: socio-economic and environmental effects in the first ten years of commercial use', *Agbioforum*, **9**(3), 139–151.
Caduff, Ladina (2005), 'Vorsorge oder Risiko? Umwelt- und verbraucherschutzpolitische Regulierung im europäisch–amerikanischen Vergleich: Eine politökonomische Analyse des Hormonstreits und der Elektronikschrott-Problematik', dissertation, ETH Zurich, Center for International and Comparative Studies.
Cohen, Joel I. and Roberg Paarlberg, (2004), 'Unlocking crop biotechnology in developing countries: a report from the field', *World Development*, **32**(9), 1563–77.
Conway, Gordon (2005), 'Agenda for a doubly green revolution', *Food Technology*, **53**(11), 146.
Cutler, David M. and Edward L. Glaeser (2006), 'Why do Europeans Smoke More than Americans?', NBER Working Paper No. 12124.
De Greef, Willy (2004), 'The Cartagena Protocol and the future of agbiotech,' *Nature Biotechnology*, **22**, 811–12.
Falkner, Robert (2000), 'Regulating biotech trade: the Cartagena Protocol on Biosafety', *International Affairs*, **76**(2), 299–314.
Falkner, Robert (2006), *The International Politics of Genetically Modified Food*, New York: Palgrave Macmillan.
Gaskell, George and Martin W. Bauer (2001), *Biotechnology 1996–2000: The Years of Controversy*, London: Science Museum Press.

Gupta, Anil K. and Vikas Chandak (2005), 'Agricultural biotechnology in India: ethics, business and politics', *International Journal of Biotechnology*, **7**(1–3), 212–27.

Hirter, Hans and Wolf Linder (2005), *Analyse der eidgenössischen Abstimmungen vom 27. November 2005*. University of Bern, Political Science Department.

Hoban. Thomas J. (2005), 'Public attitudes towards agricultural biotechnology', ESA Working Paper No. 04-09. Rome: Agricultural and Development Economics Division, FAO, www.croplifeasia.org/ref_library/biotechnology/public_att_biotech_hoban.pdf (visited in November 2007).

ISAAA (2007), 'Global biotech area surges past 100 million hectares', http://www.isaaa.org/.

Jasanoff, Sheila, (2005), *Designs of Nature: Science and Democracy in Europe and the United States*, Princeton, NJ: Princeton University Press.

Kelemen, R. Daniel, (2001), 'The limits of judicial power: trade–environmental disputes in the GATT/WTO and the EU', *Comparative Political Studies*, **34**(6), 622–50.

Kleckner, Dean (2006), 'A call to green revolution, *Agweb*, 10/2006, http://www.rockfound.org/about_us/news/2006/100806call_green.shtml.

Paarlberg, Robert (2001), *The Politics of Precaution: Genetically Modified Crops in Developing Countries*, Baltimore, MD: Johns Hopkins University Press.

Pew Initiative on Food and Biotechnology (2006), 'Survey: public sentiments about genetically modified food', Washington, DC, http://pewagbiotech.org/.

Poli, Sara (2007), 'The EC's implementation of the WTO ruling in the biotech dispute', *European Law Review*, **32**, 705–26.

Russell, Alan and John Vogler (eds) (2002), *The International Politics of Biotechnology: Investigating Global Futures*, Manchester: Manchester University Press.

Sattler, Thomas and Thomas Bernauer (2007), 'Dispute Inititiation in the World Trade Organization', Manuscript, ETH Zurich, Center for Comparative and International Studies.

Shaffer, Gregory C. and Mark A. Pollack (2007), *Regulating Risk in the Global Economy: The Law and Politics of Genetically Modified Foods*, Oxford: Oxford University Press.

Victor, David G. and C. Ford Runge (2002), 'Farming the genetic frontier', *Foreign Affairs*, **81**, 107–18.

Weirich, Paul (2007), *Labeling Genetically Modified Food: The Philosophical and Legal Debate*, New York: Oxford University Press.

15 The politics of trade and environment in the European Union

Henrik Selin and Stacy D. VanDeveer

Introduction

What is today the European Union (EU) began with the founding of the European Coal and Steel Community in 1952 (Richardson, 2006). The signing of the Treaties of Rome in 1957, entering into force in 1958, built on this effort and created the European Economic Community and the European Atomic Energy Community, respectively. Following a period of slower regional policy developments in the 1960s and 1970s, intensified European political and economic integration with the adoption of several treaties amending the Treaties of Rome started in the mid-1980s. The Single European Act – signed in 1986 and entering into force in 1987 – expanded the Community's legal competence on environmental issues and set the goal of creating a single internal market by removing remaining physical, fiscal and technical barriers to trade among member states.

The Treaty on European Union – often referred to as the Maastricht Treaty after the Dutch city where it was adopted – entered into force in 1993 and created the EU. The Maastricht Treaty developed the roles and legal competences of the main EU organizations, and expanded the process of European integration into new political issue areas. The Treaty of Amsterdam, which was signed in 1997 and entered into force in 1999, facilitated further membership enlargement and deepening integration, including on environmental policy issues. The Treaty of Nice was adopted in December 2000 and entered into force in 2003. This treaty paved the way for a series of organizational reforms to adapt the EU to a host of new member states in 2004 and 2007. The EU is still 'less' than a traditional nation-state, but it is also much 'more' than any other intergovernmental organization (Schmidt, 2004).

The expansion of free trade within the internal market has been a core objective of European integration efforts since the creation of the European Economic Community. Recent EU treaties also recognize the necessity of environmental protection measures. Environmental policy-making is important for many issues of deepening integration: many environmental issues are transboundary; environmental policy goals intersect with the functioning of the internal market through the harmonization of standards and regulations and the fulfillment of economic and social goals; and much environmental policy-making competence has been transferred from national governments to the EU level (Weale, 1996; Weale et al., 2003; Jordan and Liefferink, 2004). As such, there are many areas where trade and environment issues overlap as the EU seeks to move down a path of sustainable development (European Commission, 2002).

EU policy-making and implementation

As of 1 January 2007, the EU consists of 27 member countries (see Table 15.1). Three more countries (Croatia, the Republic of Macedonia and Turkey) are engaged in formal

Table 15.1   EU membership growth

1957	Belgium, France, Italy, Luxembourg, the Netherlands and West Germany
1973	Britain, Ireland and Denmark
1981	Greece
1986	Spain and Portugal
1995	Austria, Sweden and Finland
2004	Cyprus, Czech Republic, Estonia, Hungary, Latvia, Lithuania, Malta, Poland, Slovakia and Slovenia
2007	Bulgaria and Romania

membership negotiations, and several others have expressed a desire to join. At 27 members, the EU population is approximately 485 million, meaning that approximately one in 14 people in the world live in the EU. The size of the EU economy – roughly $11 trillion – is similar to that of the USA (population 300 million). In parallel with a sharp growth in membership, the EU's legal and political authority has been greatly expanded through the Single European Act and subsequent EU treaties. This expansion of policy-making competence covers trade and investment issues within the internal market as well as most environmental policy issues.

The Maastricht Treaty divided EU policy into three 'pillars'. The first pillar consists of all the policy areas of the 'old' European Community. Over time, these have been expanded from a focus on free trade issues to include social and environmental issues. For first-pillar issues, new policies are developed in collaboration between the European Commission (the administrative bureaucracy), the Council of Ministers (member-state government representatives) and the European Parliament (members elected by European citizens). In contrast, for policy areas falling under the other two pillars – the Common Foreign and Security Policy (second pillar) and Police and Judicial Cooperation in Criminal Matters (third pillar) – cooperation is still primarily intergovernmental in character, with member states retaining important veto rights. EU policy remains divided into these three areas, but that may be changed by future treaty developments.

The European Commission is the EU's executive body, located in Brussels (Nugent, 2000). It has four main roles in EU affairs: (1) it has exclusive power to propose new EU legislation to be considered by the Council of Ministers and the European Parliament; (2) it oversees the implementation of all EU policy and manages the EU budget; (3) it enforces EU law and can initiate legal action against member states that fail to comply in the European Court of Justice; and (4) it represents the EU internationally. The Commission is bureaucratically organized in Directorates-General (DGs) and Services, with separate DGs for, for example, the internal market and services, competition, enterprise and industry, and environment. As a result, many organizational parts of the Commission are involved in overseeing overlapping trade and environment issues.

The Council of Ministers consists of government representatives from each member state. The Council meets in different configurations: for example, the Environment Council addresses environment and human health issues and the Competitiveness Council deals with issues related to the internal market. On first-pillar issues, the Council uses qualified majority voting, where each member state has a set number of votes roughly proportional to population size. Member states are also responsible for the implementation of all EU law. The Council passes EU law on first-pillar issues together with the European Parliament under the co-decision procedure. Members of the Parliament are appointed through national direct elections. Parliamentary seats are distributed among member states approximately according to their population size.

The European Court of Justice is tasked to ensure uniform interpretation and application of EU treaties and all joint legislation. The Court interprets EU treaties and legislation. Decisions by the Court have greatly facilitated European integration (Vogel, 1995; Koppen, 1993). Since the 1970s the Court has fairly consistently supported the view that the Community should have a broad legal competence on environmental issues and raise environmental standards as a means to improve standards of living. The most frequent Court procedure on environmental issues is Commission-initiated infringement procedures against member states for failing to implement EU law. Member states are expected to abide by Court ruling and generally do so. Yet if a member state fails to comply, its punishment is mostly restricted to political embarrassment since the Court has limited enforcement powers. However, the Amsterdam Treaty introduced the possibility of fines for member states failing to implement Court decisions (Wurzel, 2004).

Legal issues of trade and environment
Many political and economic factors drive European integration. In the aftermath of World War II, German-Franco collaboration was institutionalized through the European Coal and Steel Community in an effort to secure peace in Europe through the expansion of economic and political interdependence. Economic integration and the expansion of regional trade through the European Economic Community's internal market were seen as a means to both promote peace and stimulate economic growth as war-torn European countries tried to rebuild their domestic economies. The Treaty of Rome, with its focus on security and economic issues, contained no direct mention of environmental issues, and it did not explicitly identify any environmental responsibility for the European Economic Community.

Early legal developments
The Paris Summit in October 1972 – four months after the United Nations Conference on the Human Environment was held in Stockholm – marked the beginning of a more active Community engagement on environmental issues spurred by growing public concern with air and water pollution and the accelerating use of hazardous chemicals (Hildebrand, 1993; Krämer, 2006). Community political leaders in 1973 adopted the First Environment Action Programme with the stated goal to 'improve the setting and quality of life, and the surroundings and living conditions of the Community population'. Since then, five more environmental action programs have been adopted, outlining basic policy objectives and principles that should guide EU environmental policy-making and identifying priority areas for action. The current Sixth Environment Action Programme covers the period 2002–12.

Early environmental policy decisions were based on provisions pertaining to the operation of the internal market rather than environmental protection (Articles 100 and 235 of the Treaty of Rome). As a result, much early Community environmental legislation, such as the first directive on hazardous chemicals from 1967, focused more on the harmonization of regulations and standards across member states for the purpose of facilitating the development of the internal market than on issues of raising environmental and human health protection standards (McCormick, 2001). Nevertheless, some environmental policy developments were initiated in the late 1960s and 1970s, and the Commission also became increasingly active in monitoring and enforcing implementation of environmental provisions (Jans and Vedder, 2008).

By the end of the 1970s, the Commission had initiated several infringement procedures against member states for their failure to implement environmental policy. Reviewing these cases, the Court confirmed the legal legitimacy of Community environmental policy and determined that environmental protection measures fell within the sphere of competence of the Community even if the environment was not mentioned in the Treaty of Rome. Specifically, the Court stated in an infringement case against Italy in 1980 that competition on the internal market might be 'appreciably distorted' if national environmental provisions were not harmonized. In 1982, the Court in an infringement case against Belgium further argued that environmental measures might be necessary to achieve the fundamental objectives of 'an accelerated raising of the standard of living' as listed in Article 2 of the original Treaty of Rome (Koppen, 1993; Jans and Vedder, 2008).

Trade and environment law after the Single European Act
The Single European Act established formal legal authority for Community environmental policy-making covering environmental issues under two sets of articles (Axelrod et al., 2005). Article 100a authorized the adoption of harmonization measures to expand the internal market. Articles 130r, 130s and 130t focused on the need for environmental protection. Whether an issue was decided under Article 100a or Articles 130r, 130s and 130t had initially important implications for decision-making in the Council; decisions under Articles 130r, 130s and 130t were taken unanimously whereas decisions under Article 100a required only a qualified majority. In subsequent treaty reforms qualified majority voting was expanded to almost all environmental issues with a few remaining exceptions: environmental measures with fiscal implications; energy supply issues; land use; town and country planning; and quantitative management of water resources.

As EU policy-making was greatly expanded beginning in the late 1980s, it became increasingly necessary for EU organizations and member states to strike a balance between the functioning of the internal market and the right of member states to adopt their own environmental standards. Many of these cases directly intersected with efforts to develop the internal market and reduce remaining barriers to trade. Under EU law, the room for introducing or maintaining strict national (environmental) legislation is limited by the effects of such measures on the functioning of the internal market. Member states may develop domestic environmental policy in areas where there is no common policy, but must be mindful of how it interacts with the internal market. If EU policy is in place, member states may apply stricter national provisions for environmental and human health protection in certain cases.

Court rulings have established two guiding principles for addressing trade and environment issues: domestic restrictions on environmental grounds may be justified as long as they are non-discriminatory and proportional (Koppen, 1993; Jans and Vedder, 2008). As such, a member state may in the absence of common EU marketing rules restrict the import and use of a particular product in order to meet domestic environmental standards as long as such restrictions apply equally to domestic and imported products. In other words, domestic producers cannot be favored over foreign producers. The national restriction must also be proportionate to the identified environmental policy goal and be the least trade-restrictive option for achieving that goal. In addition, the Court has recognized that the exact balance between environmental and market interests is case specific; each case needs to be assessed individually.

European politics of trade and environment

EU organizations play many critical roles. The Commission has been instrumental in strengthening EU legal and political authority as a result of its growing role in setting European political agendas, developing policy proposals and supervising national implementation (Selin, 2007). The expansion of qualified majority voting in the Council has resulted in accelerated EU policy-making on a host of environment and human health issues. EU environmental policy-making has also benefited from an expansion of the Parliament's powers. The Maastricht Treaty and the Amsterdam Treaty established the existing co-decision procedure with formal decision-making equality between the Council and the Parliament on most environmental issues. The Parliament's Environment Committee has been particularly active in strengthening EU's environmental standards (Burns, 2005).

The development of the free movement of people, goods, services and capital on the internal market is one of the core tasks of the Commission. Thus the Commission develops environmental policy proposals and monitors national implementation of EU environmental law, simultaneously protecting the internal market. If a member state wants to restrict the import and sale of a particular product on environmental and human-health-related grounds, it has to demonstrate that such action meets the Court's established criteria of non-discrimination and proportionality. Trade and environment relationships are complex, however. Sometimes member states restrict the movement of a product on environmental and human health grounds. Other times, member states use the dynamics of the internal market harmonization to strengthen EU environmental and public health standards.

The Court in several early cases elaborated on the principles of non-discrimination and proportionality, striking down specific domestic regulations. This included a high profile German effort to restrict the import of the French liqueur Cassis de Dijon because its alcohol content was not high enough to meet the German definition – and thereby requirement for import – of a 'liqueur.' The German government, justifying this restriction on public health grounds, argued that the health of German consumers was threatened because alcoholic beverages with low alcohol strength induced excessive consumption, creating an increased tolerance for alcohol. The Court in 1979 ruled that a fixed minimum alcohol content exclusively for liqueurs could not be justified on human health grounds, and that an import ban was disproportionate (Koppen, 1993; Vogel, 1995).

Similarly, in 1984 the Court ruled against a German law restricting the import of beer containing additives based on domestic *Reinheitsgebot* rules. The case was brought by a French brewer complaining to the Commission that Germany prohibited the import of his beer, which contained additives permitted in France. Germany maintained that the law was designed to protect public health, while the Commission and other member states believed that it was largely an effort to protect domestic producers from foreign competition. The Court argued that because there were no common Community standards on additives, member states had the right to determine which additives could be used.

However, the Court did not believe that Germany had produced evidence that the beer additives were harmful – in fact, some were permitted in other German beverages – and found the absolute prohibition disproportionate (Koppen, 1993; Vogel, 1995).

In contrast, in the mid-1980s the Court largely upheld a Danish restriction on the use of certain beverage containers. The law stated that beer and soft drinks had to be sold in reusable containers approved by national authorities to reduce energy use and waste. At the time, no metal containers had been approved. The Commission challenged the law on the grounds that it made it difficult to export beer and soft drinks to Denmark. The Court, however, found the law to be non-discriminatory between domestic and foreign producers, and largely proportionate in scale. The Court stated that environmental protection was a core Community objective, and supported the national deposit-and-return system. The Court also agreed with Danish authorities that the use of a limited number of approved containers was critical to ensure their reuse and to meet stated environmental policy goals (Koppen, 1993).

Food safety has become a major area of EU trade and environment/human health politics (Ansell and Vogel, 2006). The detection of bovine spongiform encephalopathy (BSE) in British cattle in 1986 resulted in a series of Community legislative moves in the late 1980s and 1990s banning all movement of British beef and beef products. This trade ban, however, did not stop the spread of BSE to other EU countries, and was eventually lifted. BSE acted as an important incentive for the creation of the European Food Safety Authority in 2002, which develops and communicates risk assessments on BSE and other food- and feed-related issues. The EU also operates a scheme for testing animals for BSE. In an effort to balance food safety and trade concerns, the EU has agreed that member states in which BSE is detected will be subject to immediate short-term trade bans followed by monitoring to help determine when trade restrictions can be removed.

The case of genetically modified (GM) crops also illustrates important trade and environment debates and policy issues. Early EU legislation was based on the principle of substantial equivalence: if a new GM food or food component was found to be substantially equivalent to an existing food or food component, it could be treated in the same way with respect to safety and regulation. This legislation, however, allowed member states to invoke safeguard measures for environmental and human health protection. In 1997, Austria became the first member state to take such action banning a maize variety approved for cultivation in the EU. Similar actions on particular GM crops were subsequently taken by Luxembourg, Greece, France, Germany and Italy (Lieberman and Gray, 2006; Skogstad, 2006). This resulted in a patchwork of trade restrictive policies across the internal market.

In 1998 the Commission asked the Council to repeal the first bans on GM crops by Austria and Luxembourg, but member states' votes were split. The Commission was also divided: while DG Environment tended to side with sceptical member states and green advocacy groups, DG Science, Research and Development, DG Industrial Affairs and DG Agriculture took a more pro-GM stand closer to the view of the biotechnology industry. The Commission – because of internal differences, divisions among member states and strong public support for a restrictive GM policy – refrained from initiating infringement procedures. Instead, the EU in 1998 imposed a *de facto* (but not *de jure*) moratorium on the approval of new GM crops for commercial cultivation (but licensed GM crops and foods remained on the market and new food products containing already approved GM crops were granted licenses) (Lieberman and Gray, 2006).

To overcome differences among member states distorting the internal market, the EU began developing new laws. The moratorium on new GM crops was lifted in 2004, in part due to pressure from the World Trade Organization (WTO) based on a legal challenge by the United States and other large producers of GM crops (Lieberman and Gray, 2008). Replacing earlier legislation, a revised system for approving GM crops on a case-by-case basis taking into account the precautionary principle was set up. The EU also established a scheme for tracing GM products 'from farm to fork'. With this new set of legislation, the Commission began pushing member states to remove domestic controls restricting trade. Nevertheless, there remain noticeable differences in opinion towards GM crops among EU organizations, member states and stakeholder groups, affecting the functioning of the internal market.

In many prominent human health and environment cases, the precautionary principle is at the center of EU debate and decision-making. The Treaty on European Union states that all EU environmental policy should be based on the precautionary principle. This view is strongly supported by EU organizations and influential member states seeking to use the precautionary principle as a guide on issues of decision-making under uncertainty (European Commission, 2000; Harremoes et al., 2002; Eckley and Selin, 2004). However, member states sometimes differ in their interpretation and application of the precautionary principle, as seen in cases of GM crops. There, member states have drawn different regulatory conclusions from the same set of scientific data influenced by national debates. This has direct implications for efforts to harmonize regulatory requirements and product standards across all member states.

Yet member states have also initiated many progressive environmental policy developments. In fact, much early EU environmental policy was championed by 'leader states' such as Denmark, Germany and the Netherlands, working to upload their higher domestic standards to the European level (Liefferink and Andersen, 1998; Jänicke, 2005). When Austria, Finland and Sweden joined the EU in 1995, the group of green member states grew. Coupled with the shift to qualified majority voting on most environmental issues, this increased opportunities for the passing of progressive environmental policy in the Council. The Commission's DG Environment also has a long tradition of working closely with environmental leader states. In addition, leader states frequently place experts in the Commission to work on prioritized policy issues aiding efforts to expand EU environmental policy and upload domestic standards (Börzel, 2002; Selin and VanDeveer, 2003).

Higher-regulation states have multiple reasons for seeking to upload their higher domestic standards (Börzel, 2002). First, many environmental problems are transboundary, and concerted efforts are needed to meet domestic policy goals. Second, uploading of domestic standards reduces competitive disadvantages for domestic industry by creating a level playing field with foreign competitors. Third, the more new EU policy resembles domestic standards and fits domestic modes of regulation, the less new costly domestic implementation action is required. Fourth, voters supportive of progressive environmental policy expect elected officials to pursue such policies both domestically and within the EU. Fifth, the expansion of domestic environmental standards to the European level may create new export opportunities for domestic producers of green technology.

To these ends, environmental leader states have used the need to harmonize regulations across the internal market as a powerful leverage for raising European environmental standards (Vogel, 1995, 2003; Selin and VanDeveer, 2006). In many such cases, national governments and domestic firms share an interest in exporting domestic regulations even if the same firms were against the domestic introduction of those regulations in the first place. For example, new Community requirements under the 1988 Large Combustion Plant Directive pioneered by Germany created an increased demand for abatement technologies that were largely produced by German firms (Börzel, 2002). More recently, German and other leader states, together with domestic industries, have used market harmonization rules to upload domestic recycling mandates for electronic waste (e-waste) into EU law (Selin and VanDeveer, 2006).

Concluding remarks

Over the past two decades the EU has greatly expanded its body of environment and human-health-related legislation while at the same time reducing barriers to trade on the internal market. However, sometimes domestic policy making clashes with efforts on regional harmonization. In addition, member states often struggle with transposing EU environmental law into domestic practice, or sometimes even elect to ignore EU policy for domestic political reasons. As such, EU organizations and member states will have to continue to find ways to balance trade and environment concerns as member-state environmental policy-making and implementation may significantly affect the free trade of products on the internal market.

EU efforts to continue to deepen regional political and economic integration, expand trade, raise standards for environment and human health protection, and promote sustainable development are guided by a series of strategies, action programs and policies. Yet these efforts are not necessarily compatible (Carmin and VanDeveer, 2005; Pesendorfer, 2006). For example, EU economic and trade policies typically promote continuing consumption while EU environmental policy supports waste minimization and recycling. In this respect, EU organizations and member states face the critical challenge of formulating and implementing a more coherent strategy for promoting socially and environmentally sustainable economic growth throughout the internal market.

Its growing membership, economic size and population have also increased the EU's international influence. With a relatively affluent population of nearly 500 million and an annual market of about $11 trillion, there are few large multinational companies that do not operate or sell their products in the EU. In this respect, regulatory standards set in Brussels can have significant implications for international production and trade. In fact, the EU is increasingly replacing the USA as the *de facto* setter of global product standards. New EU policies – and similar policies being enacted in response in other parts of the world – are also engendering responses in international markets (Selin and VanDeveer, 2006; Buck, 2007).

With the adoption of higher EU standards in a multitude of areas, EU organizations, public officials and firms share interests in exporting EU standards to other countries and in uploading such standards into international agreements (Vogel, 1995). EU efforts to shape international policy and standards have a long history. As early as in the first Environment Action Programme in 1973, European political leaders identified it as critical to be active in international forums to achieve goals that cannot be obtained solely at a regional level (Weale et al., 2003). The growing actions of the EU in global politics of trade and environment are seen in a host of cases, including GM crops, hazardous substances and e-waste (Ansell and Vogel, 2006; Selin and VanDeveer, 2006; Vogler and Bretherton, 2006).

As the EU has become increasingly active in international trade and environment politics it has supported the inclusion of trade-related measures in a host of environmental agreements on hazardous wastes, hazardous substances and biodiversity protection (Schreurs et al., 2009). Of course, it is also highly active in the WTO. The EU will continue to be a major actor in international politics of trade and the environment. Consistent with past actions, the EU can be expected to pursue the uploading of many of its developing environment policies and standards in a host of international forums. At the same time, the Commission and individual member states will have to ensure that their developing protection standards are fully compliant with WTO and other global regulations.

References

Ansell, Christopher and David Vogel (eds) (2006), *What's the Beef? The Contested Governance of European Food Safety*, Cambridge, MA: MIT Press.

Axelrod, Regina S., Norman J. Vig and Miranda S. Schreurs (2005), 'The European Union as an environmental governance system', in Regina S. Axelrod, David Leonard Downie and Norman J. Vig (eds), *The Global Environment: Institutions, Law, and Policy*, 2nd edn, Washington, DC: CQ Press, pp. 200–224.

Börzel, Tanja A. (2002), 'Pace-setting, foot-dragging and fence-sitting: member state responses to europeanization', *Journal of Common Market Studies*, **40**(2), 193–214.

Buck, Tobias (2007), 'Standard Bearer', *Financial Times*, 10 July.

Burns, Charlotte (2005), 'The European Parliament: the European Union's environmental champion?', in Andrew Jordan (ed.), *Environmental Policy in the European Union: Actors, Institutions and Processes*, 2nd edn, London: Earthscan, pp. 87–105.

Carmin, JoAnn and Stacy D. VanDeveer (eds) (2005), *EU Enlargement and the Environment: Institutional Change and Environmental Policy in Central and Eastern Europe*, New York: Routledge.

Eckley, Noelle and Henrik Selin (2004), 'All talk, little action: precaution and European chemicals regulation', *Journal of European Public Policy*, **11**(1), 78–105.

European Commission (2000), *Communication from the European Commission on the Precautionary Principle*, Brussels: European Commission.

European Commission (2002), *A European Union Strategy for Sustainable Development*, Brussels: European Commission.

Harremoes, Paul, David Gee, Malcolm MacGarvin, Andy Stirling, Jane Keys, Brian Wynne and Sofia Guedes Vaz (eds) (2002), *The Precautionary Principle in the 20th Century*, London: Earthscan.

Hildebrand, Philip M. (1993), 'The European Community's environmental policy, 1957 to 1992: from incidental measures to an international regime', *Environmental Politics*, **1**(4), 13–44.

Jänicke, Martin (2005), 'Trend-setters in environmental policy: the character and role of pioneer countries', *European Environment*, **15**(2), 129–42.

Jans, Jan H. and Hans H.B. Vedder (2008), *European Environmental Law*, 3rd edn, Groningen: Europa Law Publishing.

Jordan, Andrew and Duncan Liefferink (eds) (2004), *Environmental Policy in Europe: The Europeanization of National Environmental Policy*, New York: Routledge.

Koppen, Ida J. (1993), 'The roles of the European Court of Justice', in J.D. Liefferink, P.D. Lowe and A.P.J. Mol (eds), *European Integration and Environmental Policy*, New York: John Wiley & Sons, pp. 126–49.

Krämer, Ludwig (2006), *EC Environmental Law*, 6th edn, London: Sweet & Maxwell.

Lieberman, Sarah and Tim Gray (2006), 'The so-called "moratorium" on the licensing of new genetically modified (GM) products by the European Union 1998–2004: a study in ambiguity', *Environmental Politics*, **15**(4), 592–609.

Lieberman, Sarah and Tim Gray (2008), 'The World Trade Organization's report on the EU's moratorium on biotech products: the wisdom of the US challenge to the EU in the WTO', *Global Environmental Politics*, **8**(1), 33–52.

Liefferink, Duncan and Mikael Skou Andersen (1998), 'Strategies of the "Green" member states in EU environmental policy-making', *Journal of European Public Policy*, **5**(2), 254–70.

McCormick, John (2001), *Environmental Policy in the European Union*, New York: Palgrave.

Nugent, Neil (ed.) (2000), *At the Heart of the Union: Studies of the European Commission*, 2nd edn, Basingstoke: Palgrave Macmillan.

Pesendorfer, Dieter (2006), 'EU environmental policy under pressure: chemicals policy change between antagonistic goals?', *Environmental Politics*, **15**(1), 95–114.

Richardson, Jeremy (ed.) (2006), *European Union: Power and Policy-making*, 3rd edn, New York: Routledge.

Schmidt, Vivien A. (2004), 'The European Union: democratic legitimacy in a regional state?', *Journal of Common Market Studies*, **42**(5), 975–97.

Schreurs, Miranda, Henrik Selin and Stacy D. VanDeveer (eds) (2009), *Transatlantic Environment and Energy Politics: Comparative and International Perspectives*, Aldershot: Ashgate.

Selin, Henrik (2007), 'Coalition politics and chemicals management in a regulatory ambitious Europe', *Global Environmental Politics*, **7**(3), 63–93.

Selin, Henrik and Stacy D. VanDeveer (2003), 'Mapping institutional linkages in European air pollution politics', *Global Environmental Politics*, **3**(3), 14–46.

Selin, Henrik and Stacy D. VanDeveer (2006), 'Raising global standards: hazardous substances and e-waste management in the European Union', *Environment*, **48**(10), 6–18.

Skogstad, Grace (2006), 'Regulating food safety risks in the European Union: a comparative perspective', in Christopher Ansell and David Vogel (eds), *What's the Beef? The Contested Governance of European Food Safety*, Cambridge, MA: MIT Press, pp. 213–36.

Vogel, David (1995), *Trading Up: Consumer and Environmental Regulation in a Global Economy*, Cambridge, MA: Harvard University Press.

Vogel, David (2003), 'The hare and the tortoise revisited: the new politics of risk regulation in Europe', *British Journal of Political Science*, **33**(4), 557–80.

Vogler, John and Charlotte Bretherton (2006), *The European Union as a Global Actor*, New York: Routledge.

Weale, Albert (1996), 'Environmental rules and rule-making in the European Union', *Journal of European Public Policy*, **3**(4), 594–611.

Weale, Albert, Geoffrey Pridham, Michelle Cini, Dimitrios Konstadakopulos, Martin Porter and Brendan Flynn (2003), *Environmental Governance in Europe: An Ever Closer Ecological Union?*, 2nd edn, Oxford: Oxford University Press.

Wurzel, Rüdiger K.W. (2004), 'Germany: from environmental leadership to partial mismatch', in A. Jordan and D. Liefferink (eds), *Environmental Policy in Europe: The Europeanization of National Environmental Policy*, New York: Routledge, pp. 99–117.

16 Environmental politics and global shipping trade: club goods as a solution to common-pool resource problems
Elizabeth R. DeSombre

Most goods traded internationally – whether measured by value or by weight – are moved from one place to another on ships (Steinberg, 2001, p. 14). The environmental impacts of ships are therefore important to consider, as well as the political processes by which these impacts are influenced. These impacts have been dramatic, from major oil spills that wreaked havoc with coastlines and wildlife to invasive species transported in ballast water that have destroyed ocean ecosystems.

The international political economy of shipping underpins any effort to understand its environmental effects. Changes in technology and globalization made a dramatic increase in global shipping trade possible, and the international regulatory structure – most prominently the role of 'flag-of-convenience' ship registries within which global shipping now primarily operates – has influenced the level and type of regulation to which ships are held.

The issue structure of ocean environmental issues is central to understanding the environmental politics of global shipping: for the most part, environmental issues pertaining to the oceans have the characteristics of common-pool resources, since they are both rival and non-excludable. This issue structure, combined with an international regulatory system in which states choose which international rules to adopt and a ship registration system in which ship owners can choose which state in which to register their ships, makes protecting the ocean environment especially difficult.

The actual environmental politics of shipping is primarily coordinated through the International Maritime Organization (IMO), a UN-affiliated organization under whose auspices most of the international agreements to protect the ocean environment from shipping have been negotiated. Ultimately, where the rules the IMO oversees have been most successfully implemented in the context of globalization and flag-of-convenience ship registration has been through efforts to change the structure of the regulatory issue. Although the environmental issues remain common-pool resources, a regulatory process that excludes actors from benefits they seek if they do not participate in protecting the resource gives important incentives to ships to uphold international rules. The processes that have succeeded in restructuring the regulatory issue have often done so through direct or indirect impacts on trade. In an area as difficult to regulate as the open ocean, efforts to work within the political and physical constraints underlying environmental problems have made some progress in protecting the resource.

Technology, globalization and international ocean trade
Technological advances – improvements in both shipbuilding technology and the technology of handling goods to be shipped – have reduced shipping costs over the last

half-century and contributed to the increasing reliance on ships for international trade. Shipbuilding has gone through several revolutionary changes over the years. The most recent began in the early 1970s. That decade saw a dramatic change in the scale of international shipping. A revolution in technology made possible sizes of ships that had previously been unimaginable. The capacity of oil tankers increased more than tenfold, cargo ships increased by a factor of 20 in a two-decade period, and new container vessels were seven times larger than conventional break bulk liners (Couper, 1999).

Technologies also developed over the past four decades that have significantly reduced the cost of shipping many categories of goods. One is the automation of port facilities – heavy machinery now does much of the work that stevedores and dockworkers used to (Kahveci, 2000). Another is the development of containerization. This technology involves putting goods in standardized containers. The containers are loaded onto the decks of purpose-built ships, and can be transferred to trains or trucks without being unpacked. This makes it faster to load and unload ships, and easier to track goods in shipment and in port (Levinson, 2006; Cudahy, 2006). Finally, recent developments in information and communication technologies have made it cheaper and easier both to track goods in shipment and to organize the shipping industry on a global scale.

The globalization of production and decreasing barriers to trade have also made shipping finished goods or parts thereof easier from a political and economic standpoint. And decreasing shipping costs mean that it makes more sense than it previously did to produce halfway around the globe and take advantage of lower production costs rather than produce in the intended market to avoid transportation costs.

At the same time the profit margins for those running ships have become increasingly narrow. States subsidized their shipbuilding industries and global shipping capacity increased, and by the 1980s there was more shipping capacity available than demand for it (Broeze, 1998). Many individuals borrowing money to finance the building of newer and bigger ships defaulted on their loans, and when ships were repossessed the governments or banks that now owned them continued to operate them (usually through the creation of management companies) rather than scrap them, which continued the downward pressure on freight rates. In addition, industries – such as oil producers and steel corporations – that had previously run their own shipping lines bowed out, preferring instead to hire the services of ships owned by others. Independent ship owners competitively reduced their fees in order to compete for this shipping business (Couper, 1999, p. 11).

These factors have combined to make global shipping increasingly concerned about keeping costs low. The main ways to do so are to avoid high fees and taxes involved with ship registration, and to avoid the costly equipment, rules and labor protections imposed by international rules.

Flags of convenience and international environmental law

International law is made by states. They collectively negotiate international rules, and only those states that accept the rules (most commonly by ratifying treaties that have been negotiated) are bound by them. The standards to which a ship is held are determined by the state in which that ship is registered. Under international law all ships must have a nationality; the ship is then bound by all the domestic and international regulations adopted by that state. Until the mid-twentieth century ship owners primarily registered their ships in the states in which they were citizens; in most cases that was the only option available to them. But beginning with Panama in 1916, and followed, especially after World War II, by a number of others, some states allowed ship registration by non-nationals. The number of these open registries has grown dramatically since World War II, as has the number and tonnage of ships registered in them (DeSombre, 2006).

The term 'flag of convenience' (FOC) is derogatory and intended to refer to those states that offer ship registration to non-nationals, charge low taxes and fees, and do not hold ships to high environmental, safety and labor standards. Although there is no universal definition of which states fit the label, the International Transport Workers' Federation (ITF), a global labor union with an anti-FOC campaign, designates registries as 'flags of convenience'; it has so designated 29 registries (ITF, 2005, pp. 3–4), although new ones emerge annually.

Registry states gain economic benefits from ship registration fees and taxes, so developing states saw the advantages of gaining income from luring ship registrations. (In Panama, the largest open registry, 5 percent of the national budget comes from ship registry earnings – Morris, 1996, p. 15). In order to persuade ships to register there, they promise low costs, keeping registry fees and taxes relatively low and – most importantly – choosing not to adopt costly environmental, safety or labor standards for ships. Open registries in general adopt fewer international environmental, safety and labor standards than do traditional maritime states, and the newest open registry states, trying to lure ship registrations away from existing registries, have the lowest standards (DeSombre, 2006, pp. 41–5).

Although in other contexts the evidence for a regulatory race to the bottom is decidedly mixed, the potential for such a race – or at least for more limited 'pollution havens' in the shipping industry – is notable. Because of the ease of changing registry – ships need not travel to the registry state and can generally register by mail or online – shipping is an easier industry to 'move' to an area of low regulation than would be the case for more traditional manufacturing industries. From the perspective of the low-standard state itself, running an open registry is politically and environmentally more appealing than serving as some other form of pollution haven, in which the pollution from low environmental standards would be felt domestically. An open registry bears no more of the environmental impact of its low standards than does any other state; in fact, it may be remote enough (or in some recent cases, landlocked) that it does not suffer from the potential oil spills or other environmental problems caused by ships that operate outside the international regulatory system.

Ship owners, especially those engaged in international trade, have been willing to register in open registries. At least 64 percent of the world's merchant fleet tonnage is registered in FOC registries, including 68.7 percent of bulk carrier and 64.3 percent of container ship tonnage (Institute of Shipping Economics and Logistics, 2004, p. v). That ship owners choose to do so is not surprising: substandard shipping confers a competitive advantage. An OECD study concluded that ship owners that do not implement international safety and environmental standards benefit economically (OECD, 1996). Another OECD study determined that owners of substandard ships externalize the costs of these ships and are rarely economically harmed from problems that arise because their ships do not follow international standards (SSY Consultancy and Research Ltd, 2001). This regulatory context is central to understanding the environmental politics of shipping.

Common-pool resources and ocean environmental issues

Most environmental issues pertaining to the ocean are common-pool resource (CPR) problems. In game-theoretic terms, CPRs have two central characteristics. First, they are non-excludable, meaning that access to the resource in question is open to anyone. Second, they are rival (also called subtractable), which means that the use of a resource by one actor can diminish the availability or quality of that resource for other actors (Barkin and Shambaugh,1999). Take ocean pollution as an example. The ocean is non-excludable because it can be difficult, legally or practically, to prevent a given actor from polluting the oceans. And it is rival because each additional amount of pollution put into the oceans diminishes their use for others.

Common-pool resources are difficult to manage successfully because of their defining characteristics. Since the resource in question is rival, all actors that could impact the resource need to be involved in its management. Any actor that does not contribute to addressing the problem can actively prevent it from being successfully addressed: if most states prohibit their ships from dumping toxic waste at sea, the one or two that still allow it can cause sufficient damage to ocean ecosystems to overcome any benefit from the majority of states that refrained. But because the resource is non-excludable, these actors that are unwilling to cooperate envionmentally cannot be kept from access to the resource if they refuse to participate.

For this reason, common-pool resources, unlike more standard public goods, cannot be adequately protected or provided by a sub-group of committed actors who, for self-interested or altruistic reasons, want to undertake more than their share of the responsibility. In order to truly protect the oceans, methods must be found to ensure the participation of the vast majority of states, or the ships registered in them, in regulatory efforts. In the context of international agreements that must voluntarily be taken on by states, open registries that can gain ship registrations by not taking on those rules, and ship owners that benefit from keeping environmental standards low, environmental protection on the oceans can be especially hard to accomplish.

The International Maritime Organization and environmental regulation

Although there are a number of international regulations that address the ocean environment that are negotiated as stand-alone environmental agreements, the institution with primary responsibility for the intersection of shipping and environmental protection is the International Maritime Organization. The IMO was founded in 1948 by the major maritime states to coordinate international policy relating to issues of shipping. The organization is affiliated with, but operates independently of, the United Nations. It has a decision-making structure that includes an assembly and a council, along with a number of committees that focus on such issues as maritime safety, maritime environmental protection, and legal and technical questions. Through this decision-making process it issues recommendations as well as codes (or guidelines) to its members.

More important are the intergovernmental negotiations it coordinates to reach the major international agreements pertaining to maritime safety and environmental protection. The resulting agreements operate as any standard international agreement, binding only those states that ratify (and requiring a certain number of ratifications – and, slightly more innovatively – ratification by states accounting for a certain percentage of registered shipping). The IMO also then serves as the secretariat for these agreements.

Agreements negotiated in this manner address the major environmental issues pertaining to shipping. These include agreements to prevent tankers from discharging oil from ballast water into the ocean, those to prevent or reduce the severity of oil spills, address pollution from hazardous substances, and reduce the environmental harm from chemicals used on the outsides of ships. New efforts address the movement of species from one ecosystem to another in ballast water. Other major ocean pollution agreements, such as the Convention on the Prevention of Marine Pollution by Dumping of Wastes and Other Matter, were not negotiated by the IMO but have been brought under its auspices.

Apart from the environmental regulations it oversees, the IMO is the primary organization addressing the safety of ships, in ways that have direct or indirect implications for their environmental effects. IMO conventions address such issues as safety equipment and training standards, and the organization runs the regularly updated International Convention for the Safety of Life at Sea (SOLAS).

The IMO regulatory process faces several hurdles in effectively raising environmental standards on ships. The first is the international regulatory context, in which states do not have to join international agreements and flags of convenience may choose to lure ship registrations by keeping low the standards they require of ships. The second is that, even when ships and states are bound by international rules, enforcing these rules can be difficult. While enforcement is always a potential problem in international law, regulation of ocean ships poses increasing enforcement difficulties of two types.

The first is the number of actors regulated: a rule that applies to behavior on ships must be implemented by thousands of ships on hundreds of voyages each. The potential for non-compliance by some subset of regulated actors is much greater than with a rule implemented at state level. The more actors whose behavior has to change to implement a rule, the harder it is to ensure that they are all doing so. Ronald Mitchell's work on the International Convention for the Prevention of Pollution from Ships (MARPOL 73/78) and its precursor agreements demonstrate that discharge standards, in which individual ships on each voyage had to regulate how much oil they discharged into the water from their ballast tanks, were regularly breached. Later regulations that required segregated ballast tanks, so that ballast water is carried in a tank separate from that used to carry oil, have made an enormous difference in the extent of oil washed out from ballast water. This change came about not only because those who use segregated ballast tanks comply with the rules by default, but also because the point of regulation – ship builders – meant that a smaller number of actors had to change behavior for the regulation to succeed (Mitchell, 1994).

The second, related, issue is that these regulated ships are, for the most part, traversing a large, empty space that is outside international jurisdiction. If they are behaving in ways contrary to the rules they are subject to, this can be extremely difficult to detect. When an oil slick is detected in the water, indicating that a ship has broken the rule in question, it can be nearly impossible to trace that slick to a particular ship. The issue of fisheries provides numerous examples of individual ships breaking rules they are bound by and avoiding detection.

The IMO has thus created a context of global environmental standards for ships, but even for those that have agreed to adopt these rules it can be difficult to ascertain whether they are actually applying them. And even more problematic are those states or ships that refuse to adopt them in the first place.

Port state control and club goods

To the extent that the CPR structure is a major underlying cause of ocean environmental problems, it should be no surprise that one potential solution is to attempt a regulatory process that changes the structure of the issue by the creation of club goods. A club (or toll) good has the opposite structure of a CPR: it is both excludable and non-rival. Free trade agreements are the quintessential example of club goods: those states that join the agreements gain the advantages of free trade with others in the agreement (a good that is not diluted – and, in fact, can even be improved by increasing numbers of participants), and those that remain outside of the agreement do not gain those benefits. To the extent that a club can be created for a CPR issue, states will have an incentive to conform to environmental protection norms to gain access to the club.

The club that has had an impact on pollution standards (including oil pollution) observed by ships is the process of port state control (PSC). Port state control has come to be important in determining the standards ship owners uphold, particularly with respect to environmental and safety regulation. Detaining ships in port is the first line of defense against substandard ships; states use their sovereign authority over their territorial waters to prevent substandard ships from accessing the location to which they intend to transport goods.

States in regional groupings have created Memoranda of Understanding (MOUs) for the inspection of ships when they come into port. The primary locus of authority for the broad jurisdiction of PSC comes from the United Nations Convention on the Law of the Sea (UNCLOS) (1982). The UNCLOS provisions build on nascent (but not previously well-developed) aspects of international law that see ports as part of the sovereign territory of a state and thus an area to which states have the ability to restrict access. The MOUs generally make no new laws pertaining to ships; they refer to existing international agreements, most under the IMO, on labor, safety and environmental protection that ship owners must uphold.

States within each regional MOU agree to inspect a certain percentage of the ships that enter their ports, and share information with the other states in the agreement about their findings. If a ship owner is not following the most important international rules with respect to ship safety (regardless of what obligations its flag state requires), and especially if the ship is currently in bad condition, the ship can be detained until its condition has been improved such that it does not pose a threat to the ocean environment or to the safety of those who work on it (Özçcayir, 2001).

One of the most important aspects of PSC is that the inspectors explicitly discriminate in how they choose ships for inspection. Because they can only inspect a portion of the ships that arrive and would prefer to inspect those with the greatest likelihood of posing environmental problems, they choose to inspect ships that they expect are most likely to exhibit problems. They have therefore created formulas of characteristics of ships that are suspected of being especially risky, including the ship's previous inspection and detention record. Another important characteristic is the record of the ship's flag state.

In the case of flag states, ships registered in states that are not parties to the international agreements covered by the MOU are more likely to be targeted. This practice provides an ironic twist on the way international law generally operates: through this process ships flagged in states that have not adopted international standards can nevertheless be held to them in the inspection process, even though their flag states do not require that they adopt these standards. The other main impact of the state a ship is registered in is that average detention rates are kept for all ships and are aggregated by flag state. An overall average detention rate (a three-year rolling average) for all inspected ships is calculated, and flag states whose ships exceed the average during that period are then identified as those that should be more frequently inspected. The Paris and Tokyo MOUs also list states on black, grey and white lists to indicate the overall level of risk by ships that fly that state's flag. (The Paris MOU black list is further disaggregated into levels of risk.) Other PSC systems maintain lists of states that have a higher-than-average detention rate for the previous three years and thus receive additional attention (DeSombre, 2006).

No ship owners want their ships to be inspected – even if they pass, the additional time can cause costly delays in an industry that runs on tight margins, and the risk that something will be determined to be deficient is always present when an inspection happens. As Julio Sosa, the Panamanian Maritime Consul in Houston, put it, 'No one wants to be in a flag where the coast guard is going to be fingering you all the time' (Morris, 1996, p. 15). Ship owners, even if they prefer to keep the standards on their ships low, do not want to be singled out for inspection. Similarly, flag states recognize that gaining a poor inspection record can harm their ability to attract ship registrations.

The earliest success of the nascent system just as it was being created was seen in its effects on the potential for accidental oil pollution. The Liberian registry, at the time the largest of the open registries, had a very poor reputation for oil spills. Owners of Liberian-registered oil tankers did not want to be singled out for inspection under this new system, and so worked to increase the standards of the registry, both by persuading the Liberian state to adopt a number of international environmental agreements pertaining to ships, and by developing their own inspection system to ensure that Liberian-registered tankers would gain an excellent safety and environmental record (while retaining the cost advantages of low tax and registration fees and low labor standards). This effort paid off for many: those that could not meet the newly increased standards of the registry moved their ship registrations elsewhere, and the Liberian flag gained an excellent PSC rating (DeSombre, 2006).

A similar trajectory can be seen with the standards and records of ships flagged in other open registries. The standards undertaken by the Marshall Islands and Vanuatu improved dramatically when their ships began to be singled out for inspection. The registries created their own inspection processes, adopted new international standards, and their records improved. Belize followed a similar trajectory. Most recently both Malta and Cyprus increased their standards to overcome poor PSC records when faced with threats from the EU that their membership applications would not be approved unless the environmental records of their registries improved. Not all registry records have improved: in a system that singles out ships for inspections based on their relationship to the average ship's record, someone will always be below average. Some registries, such as Honduras, seem to focus on maintaining low standards, and others, such as Panama – currently the world's largest ship registry – try to stay as close to average as possible. But even these states pay attention to where the average is and would prefer, if possible, to beat it (DeSombre, 2006).

Even after pressure on major open registries through the PSC system to raise standards, ships flagged in open registries are more likely to fail inspection. The PSC records under the major inspection processes (the Paris and Tokyo MOUs and the US Coast Guard

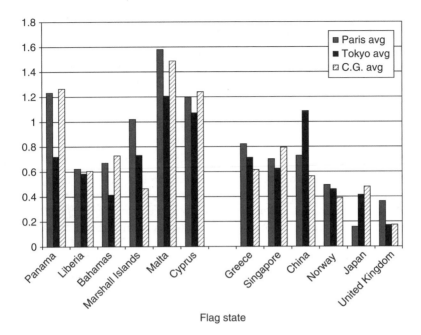

Flag state

Source: Calculated from: Paris MOU, 1986–2005; Tokyo MOU, 1995–2005; US Coast Guard, 1999–2005.

Figure 16.1 PSC records of detention ratios

inspection process – see Figure 16.1) indicates a worse record for open registries than traditional ones. The states shown on the left (Panama, Liberia, the Bahamas, the Marshall Islands, Malta and Cyprus) are the largest open registries; their PSC detention ratios are compared to the largest traditional registries on the right. A detention ratio above 1.0 indicates detentions above average for that PSC system.

The overall record is, nevertheless, impressive and improving. The PSC inspections systems have increased in stringency over time; the number of items for which they inspect has increased, as new treaty obligations have mandated new equipment, certificates and training, and the MOUs themselves have demanded higher standards.

In general the PSC process increases the incentive for flag states to raise their standards. It is true that as they do, new registries fill the low-standard void. One important pattern seen in the registries that have worked in recent years to raise their standards is that they have dropped ships from their rolls; in other instances ship owners whose ships could not meet the new higher standards have chosen to leave the registry. Owners of these low-quality ships, unfortunately, rarely leave the industry. Instead, they register in the newest and lowest-standard registries. But over time in these registries, at least those that choose to maintain open registries, they will be exposed to increased standards, and they will be detained and forced to fix their most egregious problems before they can sail. In this way, the standards of even the lowest-quality vessels are forced to inch upwards over time.

PSC was initiated by states concerned about the standards of ships that enter their ports, but they do so by creating a club good: access to (and ability to leave) ports. By selecting ships for inspection based in part on their registry state and their previous record, PSC creates a club of higher-standard registries that are less likely to be inspected and detained. It has provided an incentive for ship owners to register in states whose vessels are not singled out for increased scrutiny under the system. A number of flag states, in an effort to court ship registrations, have raised their standards, sometimes at the behest of ship owners. While the system does not prevent the existence of poor-quality ships, it does reduce the advantages to low-standard registries, and creates a mechanism to prevent some of the worst ships from sailing until they do not pose an immediate threat.

Conclusion

The environmental politics of the shipping industry are complicated by its increasing globalization and in particular the regulatory environment in which international shipping on the open ocean takes place. Since the ocean operates as a common-pool resource, a system in which most international trade is conducted on ships registered in flags of convenience creates serious problems for environmental protection of the ocean. Nevertheless, the system of international rules overseen by the IMO has been able to influence the standards on these ships, and thereby the overall environmental protection of the oceans, by creating an excludable good (unfettered access to major ports) that ship owners desire. That club good gives port states the ability to persuade registry states to take on, and individual ship owners to uphold, a set of environmental and safety standards that continue to rise. While this system does not prevent all environmental damage or ensure that all states and ships will adopt high standards, it has made a major difference in protecting the environment of the oceans from the damaging consequences of international shipping trade.

References

Barkin, J. Samuel and George E. Shambaugh (1999), *Anarchy and the Environment: The International Relations of Common Pool Resources*, Albany, NY: SUNY Press.
Broeze, Frank (1998), 'Containerization and the globalization of liner shipping', in D. Starkey and G. Harlaftis (eds), *The Internationalization of the Sea Transport Industries Since 1850*, St Johns, Nova Scotia: International Maritime History Association, pp. 867–76.
Couper, A.D. (1999), *Voyages of Abuse: Seafarers, Human Rights, and International Shipping*, London: Pluto Press.
Cudahy, Brian (2006), *Box Boats: How Container Ships Changed the World*, New York: Fordham University Press.
DeSombre, Elizabeth R. (2006), *Flagging Standards: Globalization and Environmental, Safety, and Labor Standards at Sea*, Cambridge, MA: MIT press.
Institute of Shipping Economics and Logistics (2004), *Shipping Statistics Yearbook 2003*, Bremen: ISL.
ITF (2005), *Campaign Against Flag of Convenience and Substandard Shipping, Annual Report 2004*, London: ITF.
Kahveci, Erol (2000), 'Fast turnaround ships: impact on seafarers' lives', *Seaways*, March, pp. 8–12.
Levinson, Marc (2006), *The Box: How the Shipping Container Made the World Smaller and the World Economy Bigger*, Princeton, NJ: Princeton University Press.
Mitchell, Ronald B. (1994), *Intentional Oil Pollution at Sea*, Cambridge, MA: MIT Press.
Morris, Jim (1996), 'Lost at sea: "flags of convenience" give owners a paper refuge', *Houston Chronicle*, **15**, 22 August.
OECD (1996), *Competitive Advantages Obtained by Some Shipowners as a Result of Non-Observance of Applicable International Rules and Standards*, OECD/GD(96)(4), Paris: OECD.
Özçayir, Z. Oya (2001), *Port State Control*, London: LLP.
Paris MOU, *Annual Report 1985–2004*, The Hague: Paris MOU.
SSY Consltancy and Research, Ltd (for the OECD) (2001), *The Cost to Users of Substandard Shipping*, Paris: OECD Directorate for Science, Technology, and Industry.
Tokyo MOU, *Annual Report on Port State Control in the Asia-Pacific Region 1994–2004*, Tokyo: Tokyo MOU.
US Coast Guard, 'Port State Control in the United States', *Annual Reports 1998–2004*, Washington, DC: US Coast Guard.

17 Fair trade, gender and the environment in Africa
Laura T. Raynolds and Jennifer A. Keahey

Introduction

Fair trade represents a promising approach to alleviating poverty and bolstering environmental sustainability in the global South through a strategy of 'trade not aid'. The fair trade model offers farmers and agricultural workers in the global South better prices, stable market links, and resources for social and environmental projects. In the global North, fair trade provides consumers with product options that uphold high social and environmental standards, and supports advocacy campaigns fostering responsible consumption practices. With its rising popularity, fair trade has come to represent an important counterpoint to the ecologically and socially destructive relations characteristic of the conventional global food system (Raynolds et al., 2007).

Fair trade joins a growing array of market-based initiatives that promote social and environmental concerns through the sale of alternative, often certified, commodities. In this sense fair trade is related to other environmental certifications found largely in food, forest and fiber products, and to other social certifications found largely in apparel, footwear and other manufactured items (Gereffi and Kaplinsky, 2001). Fair trade distinguishes itself from other efforts in its breadth in incorporating both environmental and social concerns, and in its depth in reshaping trade and production conditions (Raynolds, 2000; 2002). Although fair trade products continue to represent a minor share of the world market, certified sales are worth over US$1.4 billion and are growing rapidly (FLO-I, 2006a). Currently over 569 fair trade organizations across 54 countries in Latin America, Africa and Asia are registered, representing more than one million farmers and workers. There are over 18 fair trade certified products sold in 20 countries in Europe, North America and the Pacific (FLO-I, 2007a) and nascent markets are developing in middle-income countries in the global South, such as Mexico, Brazil and South Africa (Raynolds et al., 2007). The rapid expansion of fair trade certification into new commodities, regions and production relations brings with it substantial new opportunities but also new challenges.

This chapter analyzes the impacts of fair trade's efforts to narrow the global North–South divide, focusing particularly on the case of Africa. Africa is currently experiencing the largest growth in fair trade certified producer groups and products. Since Africa represents one of the most disadvantaged regions in the world, the need for fair trade to enhance environmental sustainability and social equality for farmers and agricultural workers is acute.[1] As we demonstrate, fair trade in Africa is closely linked to organic initiatives in seeking to halt environmental degradation in agro-export sectors. Fair trade's support for producer and organizational empowerment is linked explicitly to issues of gender equity, bolstering the initiative's social mandate. Although it is by no means a panacea, we conclude that fair trade provides an important avenue for addressing critical environmental and social problems in Africa today.

Fair trade principles and parameters

The fair trade movement has grown out of a set of North American and European initiatives seeking to transform North–South trade from a vehicle of exploitation to one of sustainable development (Renard, 2003). Operating initially in the handicraft sector, alternative trade organizations support disadvantaged producers by buying products at above-market prices and selling them directly to ethically aware consumers. In this way fair trade networks are designed to 'shorten the distance' between producers and consumers (Raynolds, 2002). Over the past 25 years, fair trade has expanded into major food commodities and fair trade certified foods are now sold in conventional retail venues (Raynolds and Long, 2007). Fair trade groups have aligned under the FINE umbrella,[2] forging a common definition of fair trade:

> Fair Trade is a trading partnership, based on dialogue, transparency and respect, that seeks greater equity in international trade. It contributes to sustainable development by offering better trading conditions to, and securing the rights of, marginalized producers and workers – especially in the South. Fair Trade organisations (backed by consumers) are engaged actively in supporting producers, awareness raising and in campaigning for changes in the rules and practice of conventional international trade. (FINE, 2003)

As this statement suggests, fair trade operates both 'in and against the market'. While it utilizes market channels to create new commodity networks for items produced under more favorable social and ecological conditions, fair trade operates against conventional market forces that create and uphold global inequalities (Raynolds, 2000; 2002).

Fairtrade Labeling Organizations International (FLO), the non-governmental organization that coordinates fair trade labeling, operates in 20 countries across Europe, North America and the Pacific. With earnings over US$1.4 billion per year, products certified under the FLO system comprise the lion's share of the fair trade market.[3] As noted in Table 17.1, the USA represents the largest and most rapidly growing market for certified fair trade products, with annual sales worth US$428 000 and a growth rate of 60 percent per year. The UK, Switzerland, France and Germany follow with the next-largest fair trade markets. Initially available only in small alternative shops, fair trade products are now sold by giant retailers and even by fast food chains (Raynolds et al., 2007). The rapid growth of fair trade sales has been fueled by increasing consumer concern over the environmental and social impacts surrounding global trade.

Table 17.1   Fair trade certified sales in major markets (US$1000)

	2005	% annual increase (2004–05)
USA	428 000	60
UK	345 000	35
Switzerland	178 000	5
France	136 000	57
Germany	88 000	23
Total	1421 000	37

Source: FLO-I (2006a).

Table 17.2   Growth of fair trade certified sales by commodity (metric tons)

	2003	2005	% growth rate, 2003–05
Coffee	19 293	33 992	76
Cocoa	2 698	5 657	110
Tea	1 522	2 614	72
Sugar	718	3 613	403
Honey	1 164	1 331	14
Bananas	51 151	103 877	103
Other fresh fruits	1 291	8 289	542
Fruit juice	2 193	4 856	121
Total*	80 632	168 476	109

Note: * Total includes other certified products measured in metric tons.

Sources: FLO-I (2005a; 2006a).

There are now 18 certified fair trade commodities, and additional items are being introduced each year. Coffee, fair trade's first certified product, remains the key commodity, generating roughly a quarter of all fair trade earnings (FLO-I, 2006a). As noted in Table 17.2, fair trade certification in cocoa and tea is also well established, with solid and expanding sales in these sectors. Bananas represent the second-most valuable fair trade labeled commodity and volumes are growing rapidly (Raynolds et al., 2007). Even more impressive is the sales growth in more recently introduced fair trade commodities such as processed fruits and juices, and fair trade fresh fruits, such as citrus, pineapples, mangoes, grapes and apples.

Fair trade certification standards establish norms of fairness and sustainability in production and trade relations.[4] Traditionally the domain of small farmers, fair trade has expanded to include hired labor enterprises. Small farmer standards require producers to organize into democratic cooperatives to facilitate collective development goals, while estate standards require workers to be represented by independent unions. In addition, estates must follow key International Labor Organization conventions, including freedom of association, freedom from discrimination, prohibitions on forced and child labor, and the maintenance of basic wage, occupational health and safety conditions (FLO-I, 2007b; 2007c). In the environmental realm, fair trade production standards establish basic criteria (including restrictions on agro-chemicals and land clearing, and the promotion of composting and other natural soil enhancement techniques) and seek to bolster further ecological improvements through the promotion of organic certification. Buyer standards uphold fairness and sustainability via the required payment of guaranteed minimum prices and social premiums and the provision of credit and long-term contracts (FLO-I, 2007b; 2007c). While fair trade's recent growth may extend producer benefits, the rapidity of this growth makes guaranteeing these benefit streams more challenging.

Fair trade production
Due to fair trade sales growth and the proliferation of certified commodities, fair trade is incorporating additional producer groups and regions. Between 1998 and 2004, the

Table 17.3   Fair trade certified production by region, 2004 (metric tons)

	Africa	Latin America	Asia
Coffee	4 386	24 932	764
Cocoa	2 073	1 889	0
Tea	1 620	0	766
Sugar	2 027	5 778	714
Honey	276	1 339	0
Bananas	1 317	64 670	0
Other fresh fruits	5 968	1 108	0
Fruit juice	8	2 943	11
Total	17 675	102 659	2 255

Source: FLO-I (2005b).

number of fair trade certified producer groups increased from 211 to 433, with producer countries expanding from 40 to 53 (Raynolds and Long, 2007). Latin America is the traditional hub of fair trade production, accounting for over 50 percent of all FLO certified groups and over 75 per cent of fair trade sales values and volumes. Table 17.3 highlights the importance of fair trade coffee in Latin America; the region also produces large amounts of bananas and cocoa. Asia, in contrast, is a relatively minor fair trade player, producing tea, coffee and sugar.

Africa is the second-most important production region for fair trade certified commodities, with exports valued at roughly US$24 million. This region is experiencing the most rapid expansion in fair trade production with the emergence of new certified commodities and producer groups. The number of FLO certified groups in Africa has risen dramatically, increasing from 78 to 171 between 2004 and 2006 (FLO-I, 2006b). Africa is the world's major supplier of fair trade certified tea and cocoa, and a secondary but critical supplier of certified coffee and bananas. As noted in Table 17.4, there are 33 producer groups involved in fair trade coffee production, 17 in tea and four in cocoa.

Africa has emerged as the major supplier of a number of new fair trade products, which have only become certified within the past five years. This region supplies the vast majority of newly certified fresh fruits (other than bananas), producing both tropical and temperate items. There are currently 40 groups growing these new fair trade fruits across seven African countries. South Africa is the regional and world leader, with 22 certified groups supplying fresh citrus, apples and grapes. This country is also a leading exporter of newly certified wine, which is now produced by 22 FLO registered enterprises. In addition, Africa is the world's largest producer of newly introduced fair trade cut flowers and ornamental plants,[5] with flowers grown largely in Kenya by 11 certified enterprises. What is striking about fair trade's growth in these new commodity areas in Africa is that almost all of this expansion is taking place in the large-estate sector. In South Africa, for example, only 7 percent of fair trade enterprises are within the smallholder sector (Kruger and du Toit, 2007). While this pattern of expansion threatens the traditional primacy of small-scale producers in fair trade, it may increase the standard of living for the large number of disadvantaged workers employed in African agro-export sectors and in some cases grant workers access to land or equity shares in estate enterprises (Tallontire et al., 2005;

Table 17.4 Certified fair trade producer organizations in Africa

	Coffee	Cocoa	Tea	Bananas	Other fresh fruits	Fruit juice	Flowers	Wine	Other*
Burkina Faso					2				2
Cameroon	2	1							1
Egypt					3				3
Ethiopia	3								
Ghana		1		1	8				
Ivory Coast	1	2							
Kenya			1				11		
Malawi									2
Mali					1				3
Mozambique					1				1
Rwanda	6								
Senegal					1				1
South Africa			5		22	2		22	1
Tanzania	7		6				2		
Uganda	12		4						1
Zambia	1								3
Total**	33	4	17	1	40	2	13	22	18

Notes:
* Includes honey, sugar, cotton, rice, herbs, vegetables and nuts.
** Includes countries not listed above.

Source: FLO-Cert (2005).

FLO-I, 2006a). In South Africa, for instance, fair trade estates must uphold national Black Economic Empowerment (BEE) policies, increasing black land ownership (Kruger and du Toit, 2007).

For small-scale producers in Africa, the most direct benefits from fair trade come from the higher guaranteed prices. The importance of these price guarantees is clearest in the case of coffee, where the FLO minimum price has far exceeded the world market price for most of the past 15 years (Raynolds et al., 2007; Tallontire, 2003). This price floor has meant the difference between survival and bankruptcy for many small-scale coffee growers. In addition to protecting producers from world price slumps, fair trade provides a social premium to be invested in community projects. The fair trade premium supports much-needed education, health, food self-sufficiency and farm improvement projects for small-scale producers. For large estates in Africa the FLO price floor provides economic stability, but it is the social premium that most benefits workers. This social premium funds the purchase of plantation ownership shares and supports educational, health, transportation and housing projects. For example, the Herkulu Tea Estate of Tanzania has utilized fair trade funds to repair workers' homes, improve school ventilation systems, build a medical dispensary and establish a fair trade shop so that workers may have access to essential food items at wholesale prices (Transfair USA, 2007a). Research suggests that both small farmers and estate laborers benefit most from fair trade's multifaceted informal and formal support for organizational capacity building (Raynolds et al., 2004).

Some question the benefits of fair trade in Africa, given the prevalence of national, regional and household food insecurity. Although the concern with local food production is well taken, it must be recognized that most African small-scale producers already produce market crops, often for export, and rely on their sale for household survival. This strategy of combining food and cash crop production is common particularly among small farmers. Fair trade standards require that producers be paid a better price for crops they already export and restrict the conversion of food croplands to export production or the clearing of new lands. As Barratt-Brown (2007) suggests, fair trade may foster food security in Africa directly through the investment of social premiums in environmental and household food production projects, and indirectly through the payment of higher prices for exports, freeing up resources for food crop production.

Although the potential environmental and social benefits of fair trade in Africa, as in other regions of the global South, are substantial, the increased geographic spread, product diversification and enterprise variation within certified networks makes realizing those benefits more difficult. The growth of certified fair trade production across Africa can bring substantial environmental benefits, particularly if this certification fosters organic production. This spread can simultaneously bring significant social improvements, especially as fair trade enters into commodity areas where women and other disadvantaged workers predominate, thus increasing their access to the flow of fair trade benefits.

Fair trade and the environment

Africa is a continent rich in biodiversity and natural resources. The livelihood of much of the African population depends on agriculture, yet increasing soil degradation, deforestation and desertification threaten current living standards and future production capacity (World Bank, 2001). According to the United Nations Environment Programme, regional poverty could be eliminated through more equitable and sustainable environmental resource management (UNEP, 2006). However, the expansion of the conventional global food system, foreign-agribusiness-dominated export sectors and disadvantageous trade policies are threatening the ecological resources upon which the poor depend (Gibbon and Ponte, 2005). The spread of chemical pollution, invasive species and genetically modified organisms (GMOs) further undermines agricultural sustainability, lending a contemporary twist to environmental degradation (UNEP, 2006; World Bank, 2001).

The growth of fair trade in Africa works to protect environmental resources in three key ways. First, fair trade certification standards require that producer groups uphold a set of general environmental criteria that address key ecological concerns in Africa.[6] Soil and water management standards prevent soil degradation and erosion, reducing the risk of desertification. Restrictions on wild species collection minimize natural resource depletion. Prohibitions against cutting virgin forests reduce deforestation, while buffer zone requirements serve to protect natural areas. In addition, fair trade encourages producer organizations to engage in environmental regeneration projects. Agrochemical restrictions and GMO prohibitions reduce the risk of chemical pollution and the entry of invasive GMO crops into local ecosystems (FLO-I, 2007b; 2007c; 2007d; World Bank, 2001). For instance, in the African cut-flower export sector – an industry renowned for its intensive agrochemical use and resulting detrimental impacts – the introduction of fair trade has restricted the use of hazardous agrochemicals, established buffer zone requirements and enhanced worker safety regulations (FLO-I, 2007e).[7]

The second way that fair trade is able to enhance environmental stewardship lies in its trade conditions. Fair trade goes beyond many other (often more rigorous) eco-certifications in ensuring that producers have the financial and organizational resources to uphold environmental standards (Raynolds et al., 2007a). While environmental standards may appear laudable on paper, if producers do not have the wherewithal to meet them, they are unlikely to have a significant impact on the ground. Poverty tends to exacerbate environmental degradation as people eke out a living in whatever way they can. By working to ensure that producers have a secure and livable income, fair trade reduces the need of impoverished households in Africa to overexploit natural resources. By promoting the organizational ability of producer groups, fair trade fosters collective capacity to address environmental problems (Raynolds, 2000). The fair trade social premium is often invested directly in environmental improvements. Indeed, in African cocoa and coffee sectors, fair trade premiums finance shade production systems and reforestation efforts, stemming erosion and providing critical wildlife habitat (FLO-I, 2007f; Transfair USA, 2007b; 2007c).

The third major way that fair trade works to protect environmental resources is by supporting the nascent rise of certified organic production in Africa. Although the global organic trade is booming, Africa currently trails other regions in supplying this dynamic market (Raynolds, 2004; Willer and Yussefi, 2006). In total, Africa has only one million acres of organic certified land. Twenty African countries export certified organic commodities and there is substantial opportunity for bolstering production given Africa's historical reliance on low-input farming practices and limited agrochemical use (Parrott et al., 2006).

Fair trade has proved critical in promoting certified organic production in Africa by providing the informational, organizational and financial resources necessary for producers to enter this demanding system. Although African producers may be farming in near-organic conditions, certification is a complex and costly process (Barrett et al., 2001). Fair trade networks help organizations bring their production practices into compliance with rigorous organic standards, typically funding required improvements in areas such as composting, terracing and buffer zone management.

Perhaps most importantly, fair trade capacity-building activities foster the administrative structures needed to create the internal monitoring systems required to verify compliance with organic certification standards. The fair trade social premium typically pays the substantial costs of internal and external organic monitoring (Raynolds, in press). As research in Africa suggests, without such external support few producers could afford organic certification (Parrott et al., 2006). Although certified organic products tend to garner a premium in world markets, these prices are not guaranteed and have fallen significantly over recent years due to increased global production (Raynolds, in press; Willer and Yussefi, 2006). In the face of eroding prices, fair trade's requirement that buyers pay a premium for organic certified commodities – above and beyond the FLO guaranteed price – has also proved critical.[8] In Ethiopia, for example, 11 Oromia coffee cooperatives have joined fair trade networks and invested their social premiums in acquiring organic certification, thereby gaining access to higher prices and fostering environmental sustainability in this ecologically fragile region (Fairtrade Foundation, 2007; FLO-I, 2007f).

Fair trade and gender inequality

A key facet of fair trade's social agenda focuses on promoting gender equity and bolstering the incomes of marginalized women workers and producers. Fair trade's gender sensitivity was established in the movement's inception in the predominantly female handicraft sector. As fair trade extended into agriculture, gender concerns were institutionalized into small-farmer and hired-labor standards. Given women's extensive engagement in African smallholder and estate farming sectors,[9] fair trade's growth in this region has opened up new possibilities for significantly improving the situation of women involved in agriculture.

Fair trade standards in the small-farm sector address gender concerns directly by requiring that certified producer organizations follow anti-discrimination policies and that programs related to recruitment, staffing and leadership work to improve the position of underrepresented groups, including women. In Africa, as elsewhere in the world, women have historically been excluded from important producer organizations and programs. This exclusion has meant that female farmers in Africa have significantly less access than their male counterparts to agricultural training, credit and other critical resources (FAO, 2005). By fostering non-discriminatory organizations and bolstering female organizational engagement, fair trade promotes women's independent access to key production inputs and to the equal rights and respect often denied them.

The Kuapa Kokoo Cocoa Cooperative in Ghana, for example, has addressed issues of gender equity on a number of fronts. Currently 30 percent of Kuapa Kokoo members are women and their representation continues to rise. Female cocoa producers in the region have gained recognition and respect as well as access to trade information and production credit. In fact women now serve in all cooperative leadership levels and are at least as likely as male members to represent Kuapa Kokoo in international forums (Tiffen et al., 2004). However, despite the increase of female membership within African fair trade cocoa cooperatives, the promotion of gender equity has been less successful within producer organizations operating in other export sectors such as coffee, where male dominance has been more firmly entrenched (Tallontire, 2000).

Even where African women are not members of small-farmer cooperatives, they may benefit from fair trade policies and programs. Fair trade's favorable price guarantees are intended to provide income security to entire families, while the fair trade social premium is designed to support a variety of social programs benefiting entire communities. Returning to the case of Kuapa Kokoo, we find that the fair trade premium has underwritten village water boreholes, corn mills, schools, meeting places and bridges (Transfair USA, 2007a). These efforts have eased female labor burdens in water collection, flour production and childcare across local communities.

Turning from the small farm to the estate sector in Africa, we find that fair trade addresses a set of critical gender issues in sectors where workforces are predominantly female. Women comprise the majority of workers in a number of African horticultural crops – such as fresh fruits and vegetables, cut flowers and wine (Barrientos et al., 2003; Dolan, 2005). Since these are some of the fastest-growing fair trade export areas, the labor standards required for participating enterprises may have significant positive gender impacts.

Fair trade's general estate standards build on key ILO conventions (FLO-I, 2007c). Gender equity is promoted first through non-discrimination and equal representation requirements as FLO requires estates to provide female workers with equal opportunities and access to fair trade benefits. Moving beyond an ILO labor protection strategy to a more empowerment-based strategy, fair trade standards require estates to develop capacity-training programs for women, sexual harassment policies, and to progress toward proportional gender representation in company leadership. The joint fair trade body is also required to be gender representative, ensuring that women's concerns are heard and women's organizational rights are advanced. The second key set of fair trade standards address gender concerns related to worker health and safety, and amplify ILO maternal health conventions. By fostering non-discriminatory practices, bolstering female engagement and requiring female leadership, these fair trade standards lay the basis for transforming the situation of historically disadvantaged female agricultural workers in Africa.

Finally, fair trade standards require enterprises to provide temporary workers with equivalent benefits and employment conditions. These regulations benefit large numbers of African women given their predominance in the temporary workforce in many export crops. Standards protecting temporary workers may be particularly important since non-permanent female workers are typically less aware of their rights, more vulnerable to discrimination and sexual harassment, and more likely to suffer from poor health and safety conditions (Barrientos et al., 2003; Dolan et al., 2003).

The cut-flower industry in Kenya provides a good illustration of fair trade's potential positive impacts on women workers. Conventional flower enterprises in Kenya are notorious for their poor employment conditions, health and safety standards, and treatment of female workers (Dolan, 2007). Partly in response to rising concerns over these conditions, fair trade has expanded rapidly in the cut-flower sector, with 13 certified African enterprises (see Table 17.4). Preliminary evidence suggests that fair trade engagement provides a number of benefits for large numbers of temporary and permanent female flower workers, and is fueling gender equity more broadly. In addition to more general employment gains, female workers in the fair trade flower sector benefit from important improvements in terms of maternal rights, safe housing and transportation services, and access to childcare (FLO-I, 2007e; Fairtrade Foundation, n.d.). Fair trade standards are likely to fuel positive impacts for women workers in other sectors of African large-scale agriculture as well. Yet despite these important gains, fair trade labor standards cannot be expected any time soon to erase deeply entrenched gender inequalities in Africa or elsewhere in the world.

Conclusions

This chapter outlines the contours of fair trade's recent rapid growth as it expands across Africa. While fair trade has historically grown on the basis of smallholder production of key tropical commodities, its current expansion, as we demonstrate, involves an array of new items produced predominantly by large hired-labor enterprises. Fair trade's expansion in Africa holds substantial promise given the region's historically severe trade disadvantage, ecological fragility and social development needs. As we demonstrate, fair trade enhances environmental sustainability in the region through the support for organic agriculture and standards that stem ecological degradation. What makes fair trade different from other ecological initiatives is that it provides communities with the financial security and resources necessary to engage in meaningful environmental stewardship. On the social front, we find that fair trade's support for producer and organizational empowerment incorporates key gender issues, enhancing the position of female producers and workers in Africa. What makes fair trade's efforts potentially more powerful than other labor standards efforts is the inclusion of temporary as well as permanent workers and the clear focus on women's empowerment and full representation. While by no means a panacea, fair trade provides an important avenue for addressing critical environmental and social problems in Africa today.

Notes

1. For an enlightening analysis of how trade relations fuel environmental and social problems in Africa, see Gibbon and Ponte (2005).
2. FINE is an acronym made up of the first letter of the name of its members: FLO, IFAT, NEWS! and EFTA.
3. Non-certified (largely handicraft) items account for an additional US$169 million in fair trade sales (Krier, 2005).
4. See Raynolds et al. (2007a) for a more detailed analysis of fair trade social and environmental standards in the coffee sector and comparisons with competing certifications.
5. For an insightful analysis of the growth of ethical certifications in the African flower industry, see Hughes (2001).
6. FLO environmental standards are specified by commodity but all follow these general guidelines; for crop specific rules, see FLO (2007g).
7. Despite the controversy surrounding industry practices, the African cut-flower and ornamental plant industry offers large-scale employment opportunities and is important for a number of national economies, including that of Kenya.
8. In coffee, for example, FLO standards stipulate that buyers pay a guaranteed minimum of US$1.21 per pound for conventional coffee, with certified organic coffee receiving an additional US$0.20 per pound (FLO-I, 2007a).
9. Women comprise 47 percent of the total agricultural labor force in Africa (FAO, 2005).

References

Barrett, H.R. et al. (2001), 'Smallholder farmers and organic certification: accessing the EU market from the developing world', *Biological Agriculture and Horticulture*, **19**, 183–99.
Barratt-Brown, Michael (2007), 'Fair trade with Africa', *Review of African Political Economy*, **112**, 267–77.
Barrientos, Stephanie et al. (2003), 'A gendered value chain approach to codes of conduct in African horticulture', *World Development*, **31**(9), 1511–26.
Dolan, Catherine S. (2005), 'Benevolent intent?: the development encounter in Kenya's horticulture industry', *Journal of Asian and African Studies*, **40**(6), 411–37.
Dolan, Catherine S. (2007), 'Market affectations: moral encounters with Kenyan fairtrade flowers', *Ethnos*, **72**(2), 239–61.
Dolan, Catherine S., Maggie Opondo and Sally Smith (2003), 'Gender, rights and participation in the Kenya cut-flower industry', NRI Report No. 2768, Chatham Maritime: Natural Resources Institute.
Fairtrade Foundation (n.d.), 'Fairtrade roses Q & A', available at http://www.fairtrade.org.uk/downloads/pdf/Fairtrade_roses_q_and_a.pdf.
Fairtrade Foundation (2007), 'Fairtrade Foundation producer profile: Oromia Coffee Farmers Cooperative Union Ltd (OCFCU), Ethiopa', available at http://www.fairtrade.org.uk/downloads/pdf/oromia_profile.pdf.
FAO (Food and Agriculture Organization of the United Nations) (2005), 'Impact of agricultural trade on gender equity and rural women's position in developing countries', available at http://www.fao.org/sd/dim_pe1/docs/pe1_051002d1_en.doc.
FINE (2003), 'What is FINE?', available at http://www.rafiusa.org/programs/Bangkok%20proceedings/12What%20is%20FINE.pdf.
FLO-I (Fairtrade Labelling Organizations International) (2005a), 'Annual report 2004/2005 – delivering opportunities', available at http://www.fairtrade.net/uploads/media/FLO_AR_2004_05.pdf.
FLO-I (2005b), 'Fair trade statistics', unpublished data, FLO.
FLO-I (2006a), 'Building trust: annual report 2005/2006', available at http://www.fairtrade.net/uploads/media/FLO_Annual_Report_01.pdf.
FLO-I (2006b), 'Number of fairtrade certified producer organizations by country', available at http://www.fairtrade.net/by_location.html.
FLO-I (2007a), 'Fairtrade Labelling Organizations International', available at http://www.fairtrade.net.

FLO-I (2007b), 'Generic fairtrade standards for small farmers' organizations', available at http://www.fairtrade.net/producer_standards.html.

FLO-I (2007c), 'Generic fairtrade standards for hired labor', available at http://www.fairtrade.net/producer_standards.html.

FLO-I (2007d), 'Trader standards', available at http://www.fairtrade.net/trade_standards.html.

FLO-I (2007e), 'Fairtrade standards for flowers and plants for hired labor', available at http://www.fairtrade.net/fileadmin/user_upload/content/Flowers_and_Plants_HL_March_2007_EN.pdf.

FLO-I (2007f), 'A success story: Oromia Coffee Farmers' Cooperative Union, Ethiopia', available at http://www.fairtrade.net/oromia_ethopia.html.

FLO-I (2007g), 'Product standards', available at http://www.fairtrade.net/product_standards.html.

FLO-I (2007h), 'Fairtrade standards for coffee for small farmers' organizations', available at http://www.fairtrade.net/fileadmin/user_upload/content/Coffee_SF_March_2007_EN_01.pdf.

FLO-Cert (2005), 'Fairtrade certification', PowerPoint Presentation, 29 November, prepared by Frank Brinkschneider.

Gereffi, Gary and Raphael Kaplinsky (eds) (2001), 'The value of value chains', *IDS Bulletin*, **32**(3), special issue.

Gibbon, Peter and Stefano Ponte (2005), *Trading Down: Africa, Value Chains, and the Global Economy*, Philadelphia, PA: Temple.

Hughes, Alex (2001), 'Global commodity networks, ethical trade and governmentality: organizing business responsibility in the Kenyan cut flower industry', *Transactions of the Institute of British Geographers*, **26**, 390–406.

Krier, J.M. (2005), *Fair Trade in Europe 2005: Facts and Figures on Fair Trade in 25 European Countries*, Brussels, Belgium: FINE.

Kruger, Sandra and Andries du Toit (2007), 'Reconstructing fairness: fair trade conventions and worker empowerment in South African horticulture', in Laura T. Raynolds, Douglas Murray and John Wilkinson (eds), *Fair Trade: The Challenges of Transforming Globalization*, New York: Routledge, pp. 200–219.

Parrott, Nicholas et al. (2006), 'Organic farming in Africa', in Helga Willer and Minou Yussefi (eds), *The World of Organic Agriculture: Statistics and Emerging Trends 2006*, Bonn, Germany: IFOAM, pp. 96–107.

Raynolds, Laura T. (2000), 'Re-embedding global agriculture: the international organic and fair trade movements', *Agriculture and Human Values*, **17**, 297–309.

Raynolds, Laura T. (2002), 'Consumer/producer links in fair trade coffee networks', *Sociologia Ruralis*, **42**(4), 404–24.

Raynolds, Laura T. (2004), 'The globalization of organic agro-food networks', *World Development*, **32**, 725–43.

Raynolds, Laura T. (in press), 'The organic agro-export boom in the Dominican Republic: maintaining tradition or fostering transformation?', *Latin American Research Review*.

Raynolds, Laura T. and Michael Long (2007), 'Fair/alternative trade: historical and empirical dimensions', in Laura T. Raynolds, Douglas Murray and John Wilkinson (eds), *Fair Trade: The Challenges of Transforming Globalization*, New York: Routledge, pp. 15–32.

Raynolds, Laura T., Douglas Murray and Peter Leigh Taylor (2004), 'Fair trade coffee: building producer capacity via global networks', *Journal of International Development*, **16**, 1109–21.

Raynolds, Laura T., Douglas Murray and Andrew Heller (2007a), 'Regulating sustainability in the coffee sector: a comparative analysis of third-party environmental and social certification initiatives', *Agriculture and Human Values*, **24**, 147–63.

Raynolds, Laura T., Doug Murray and John Wilkinson (2007b), *Fair Trade: The Challenges of Transforming Globalization*, New York: Routledge.

Renard, Marie-Christine (2003), 'Fair trade: quality, market and conventions', *Journal of Rural Studies*, **19**(1), 87–96.

Tallontire, Anne (2000), 'Partnerships in fair trade: reflections from a case study of Cafedirect', *Development in Practice*, **10**(2), 166–77.

Tallontire, Anne et al. (2005), 'Reaching the marginalised? Gender, value chains and ethical trade in African horticulture', *Development in Practice*, **15**(3–4), 559–71.

Tiffen, Pauline et al. (2004), 'From tree-minders to global players: cocoa farmers in Ghana', in Marilyn Carr (ed.), *Chains of Fortune: Linking Local Women Producers and Workers with Global Markets*, London: Commonwealth Secretariat, pp. 11–43.

Transfair USA (2007a), 'Producer profiles', available at http://www.transfairusa.org/content/certification/profiles.php.

Transfair USA (2007b), 'Environmental benefits: shade-grown', available at http://www.transfairusa.org/content/about/environmental.php.

Transfair USA (2007c), 'Kuapa Kokoo produces "Best of the best" cocoa and improves farmers' lives', available at http://www.transfairusa.org/content/email/ftbeat_may.htm#kuapa.

United Nations Environment Programme (UNEP) (2006), 'Africa environment outlook 2: our environment, our wealth', available at http://www.unep.org/DEWA/Africa/docs/en/AEO2_Our_Environ_Our_Wealth.pdf.

Willer, Helga and Minou Yussefi (2006), *The World of Organic Agriculture: Statistics and Emerging Trends 2006*, Bonn, Germany: IFOAM.

World Bank (2001), 'Sub-Saharan Africa regional environment strategy', available at http://iris 36.world-bank.org/domdoc/PRD/Other/PRDDContainer.nsf/All+Documents/85256D240074B56385256F490059BA BB/$File/AFREnvStrategy2001.pdf.\

18 The global waste trade and environmental justice struggles
David Naguib Pellow

The problem: electronic waste

For most people, the word 'pollution' conjures up images of smoke stacks, oil slicks in the Atlantic Ocean, or overflowing garbage dumps. Many US residents tend to go about their lives believing that environmental problems are 'out there' and disconnected from their daily routines. Unfortunately, the electronics that people use every hour of the day are also responsible for much of the world's pollution. The average US household owns 25 consumer electronics products, and since people typically replace these items in very short cycles, they create an enormous amount of electronic waste or e-waste.

E-waste is the most rapidly growing waste stream in the world, and experts project continued growth into the foreseeable future. European studies estimate that the volume of e-waste is increasing by three to five percent per year, which is almost three times faster than the municipal waste stream is growing generally.[1]

In the USA, 315 million computers became obsolete between 1997 and 2004 and about 100 000 every day since. The Environmental Protection Agency estimates that 130 million cell phones were discarded in 2005, resulting in 65 000 tons of e-waste. This creates a combined 300 000 tons of electronic junk annually. In all, an estimated 80% of our electronic waste ends up improperly disposed of in US landfills and incinerators, or recycled by prison labor under hazardous conditions (44 million pounds of electronic waste were recycled by prison labor in 2004), or shipped overseas, where some of the poorest and youngest citizens in places such as China, Nigeria and Pakistan might pick through our old printed circuit boards, printers, and other discards for a meager wage.

The USA remains the chief source of e-waste globally, since US consumers purchase more computers than the citizenry of any other nation. While the USA leads the world in consumption and disposal of these goods, the situation in Europe is not much better. For example, an estimated 1 million tons of electrical waste is produced in the UK each year and is increasing by 5 percent annually. Of this volume, 90 percent is thrown into landfills or incinerators.[2]

Environmental and public health risks

The electronics industry is the largest manufacturing sector globally, and, contrary to popular conceptions, it is generally not environmentally 'clean'. The IT sector creates large volumes of pollution and waste every year. And even when consumers try to do the right thing by recycling e-waste, the products are often shipped abroad for disassembly and then use in new manufacturing processes or are simply dumped.

E-waste is a problem not only of quantity but also one of toxic ingredients – such as the lead, beryllium, mercury, cadmium and brominated flame retardants – that pose major occupational and environmental health threats.[3] Computer or television displays (CRTs) contain an average of four to eight pounds of lead each. Monitor glass contains about 20 percent lead by weight. Cell phones also contain lead, as well as mercury, cadmium and other dangerous chemicals. When these components are illegally disposed of and crushed in landfills, the lead is released into the environment, posing a hazardous legacy for current and future generations. Consumer electronics already constitute 40 percent of lead found in landfills. About 70 percent of the heavy metals (including mercury and cadmium) found in landfills come from electronic equipment discards. These heavy metals and other hazardous substances found in electronics can contaminate groundwater and pose other environmental and public health risks. Lead can cause damage to the central and peripheral nervous systems, blood system and kidneys in humans. It accumulates in the environment, and has highly acute and chronic toxic effects on plants, animals and microorganisms. Children suffer developmental effects and loss of mental ability, even at low levels of exposure. Additionally, the mercury found in many electronics products often leaches when they are broken and dumped. The presence of halogenated hydrocarbons in computer plastics may result in the formation of dioxin if the plastic is burned. The presence of these chemicals also makes computer recycling particularly hazardous to workers and surrounding ecosystems.[4]

Worker safety and health concerns
The marketing of the electronics industry to cities and nations over the last three decades has relied on the claim that – by contrast to the old economic sectors of iron, steel and auto, for example – electronics production processes are clean and safe for ecosystems and workers. However, epidemiological studies conclude that electronics workers experience occupational illness three times the rate of workers in any other manufacturing sector and that employees face up to 1000 chemicals on any single workstation. Now that communities have become more aware of the toxicity of electronics, we see the most hazardous of operations reserved for immigrant workers in the USA and for communities and workers abroad.[5] Moreover, workers in e-waste recycling plants confront significant chemical hazards as well. One e-waste worker at a prison in Atwater, California, reported,

> Even when I wear the paper mask, I blow out black mucus from my nose everyday. The black particles in my nose and throat look as if I am a heavy smoker. Cuts and abrasions happen all the time. Of these the open wounds are exposed to the dirt and dust and many do not heal as quickly as normal wounds.[6]

Prison inmates reported that those who sought to improve conditions in the e-waste recycling facility faced discipline and the threat of job loss. Inmates worked for a rate of $0.20–1.26 per hour at the Atwater prison and were not allowed to unionize.[7] This is a clear issue of labor rights but extends into the realm of environmental justice since a disproportionate percentage of electronics workers are immigrants, women, people of color, and/or working class. The environmental justice implications of the e-waste crisis have strong spatial and geographic implications, as these discards are frequently shipped overseas to global South nations.

E-waste dumping: a global environmental injustice
The electronics industry is the largest manufacturing sector globally, and, as a chemical-intensive industry, creates inordinate volumes of pollution. What happens to the 300 000 tons of computers and other electronics goods we consume each year in the USA when

they are discarded? This electronic, or 'e-waste', is often shipped to urban areas and rural villages across Asia, Africa and Latin America for disassembly or dumping.

The practice of sending obsolete electronics abroad creates a massive transfer of hazardous waste products from rich nations to nations of the global South, and is responsible for impacting public health and the integrity of watersheds in countries such as Bangladesh, Brazil, India, the Philippines and Taiwan.

An estimated 80 percent of computer waste collected for recycling in the USA is exported to Asia, where it is generally dumped and recycled under very hazardous conditions.[8] Environmental activists have called this practice 'toxic colonialism' and a form of 'global environmental injustice'.[9] Jim Puckett directs the Seattle-based Basel Action Network (BAN) – an NGO – and argues that the global trade in e-waste is a problematic business that 'leaves the poorer peoples of the world with an untenable choice between poverty and poison'.[10]

E-waste in Asia: China and India

In 2002, the Basel Action Network (BAN), the Silicon Valley Toxics Coalition (another NGO) and several partners in Asia released a report and video that documented the growing international trade in toxic electronic waste from the USA to China, India, Pakistan and other Asian nations.[11] After months of strategizing with social advocacy groups to gain access to sensitive sites and interview workers in China, Pakistan and India, they completed and released the report, which sent shock waves through the electronics industry and was picked up by nearly every major media outlet in North America, Europe and Asia. The report and video centered on the way that computer monitors, circuit boards and other electronic equipment collected in the USA – sometimes under the guise of 'recycling' – are regularly sold for export to Asia, where the products are handled under hazardous conditions, creating tremendous environmental and human health risks. The report found that workers – including children – use their bare hands, hammers, propane torches and open acid baths to recover gold, copper, lead and other valuable materials. What is unused is dumped in waterways, fields and open trenches, or simply burned in the open air. *Exporting Harm* mainly focused on the situation in China, while acknowledging that the e-waste trade also heavily impacts many other parts of the world.

Like China, India has also embarked on a major modernization project. One of the primary paths to achieving this goal is through the embrace of information technology. But environmentalists and occupational health advocates are concerned that the Indian government's priority of increasing computer density among the population will ultimately contribute to the waste problem. As in the case of China's imports of e-waste from the USA, in India brutal global economics plays a major role. Recycling a computer in the USA costs about $20, but the same product can be sold in New Delhi for a mere $4.[12] E-waste recycling also creates dangerous working conditions for those involved in disassembling these goods. Ravi Agarwal, an activist with Toxics Link India, worries about the health impacts of exposure to plastics, for example:

> When you actually physically break them [computers] down, which involves burning, putting them in acid baths, these very low end, basic, labor intensive breaking practices, then people breaking them get high degrees of exposure, (that are) totally unacceptable in most parts of the world.[13]

Dr D.B. Boralkar, member-secretary of the Maharashtra Pollution Control Board, and an expert on e-waste in India, notes that the burning of materials to extract metals for recycling is a 'process [that] releases pollutants that cause diseases like silicosis, pulmonary edema, circulatory failure and suchlike'.[14] Ravi Agarwal argues that governments, industries and consumers in the global North and within India contribute to this kind of 'development', so it is a complex problem.

In a 2003 report by Toxics link India, it was revealed that the 'disposal and recycling of computer waste in the country has become a serious problem since the methods of disposal are very rudimentary and pose grave environmental and health hazards.[15] The import of hazardous waste into India is actually prohibited by a 1997 Indian Supreme Court directive, which reflects the Basel Ban on hazardous waste exports from OECD to non-OECD nations (see below). Northern nations, however, continue to export e-waste to southern nations such as India, rather than managing it themselves. So the trade in e-waste is camouflaged and is a thriving business in India, conducted under the pretext of obtaining 'reusable' equipment or 'donations' from northern nations.[16]

In 2004, the British Environment Agency (BEA) released a report indicting companies in the UK for sending tens of thousands of tons of e-waste illegally to India and other Asian nations. Kishore Wankhade of Toxics Link stated: 'The trade is absolutely illegal and against the spirit of the Basel Convention.'[17] His colleague, Ravi Agarwal, noted,

> We have been repeatedly stating for the past two years that tons of e-waste are landing in various Indian ports every year for recycling. In the absence of access to customs data, this could never be verified. The BEA report, however, squarely indicts developed countries like USA and UK.[18]

In 2004, K.S. Sudhakar, also of Toxics Link, found that a shipment of e-waste was mislabeled as 'metal scrap' when it arrived at the port in the city of Chennai, India. The mislabeling of toxics is one of the most common methods of getting such waste past the authorities and through loopholes in the Basel Convention, a UN-sponsored mechanism that prevents the export of hazardous chemicals from OECD to non-OECD nations. Toxics Link's research reveals that more than 70 percent of electronic waste collected in recycling facilities in Delhi was exported or dumped by northern nations such as the USA.[19]

This is high-tech environmental inequality, since the majority of these toxics flow from North to South, from wealthy to poorer communities. There are three primary reasons why e-waste is increasingly flooding southern nations:

1.   Labor costs are very low (in China e-waste workers earn only $1.50 per day)
2.   Environmental and occupational regulations are lax or not well enforced
3.   It is legal in the USA, despite international law to the contrary, to allow export of hazardous e-wastes with no controls whatsoever.[20]

The global movement for extended producer responsibility
A sophisticated transnational social movement effort has emerged to document these problems, and activists have had success in changing corporate environmental policies and passing local, national and international legislation to address the worst dimensions of the e-waste crisis. Many of the organizations mentioned above are taking the lead on these critical concerns.

The grassroots pressure that social movement networks exert on electronics firms comes not only from their own activist membership and staff, but also from the consumers of these technologies. Given that such a high percentage of citizens in the North are consumers of computer and electronic products, this provides a considerable pool of potential activists who might be mobilized to pressure or even boycott any number of companies.

The Basel Action Network (BAN), the Silicon Valley Toxics Coalition (SVTC) and other NGOs created the Computer TakeBack Campaign (CTBC), a national coalition to promote extended producer responsibility – the principle that manufacturers and brand owners must take responsibility for the life-cycle impacts of their products, including take-back and end-of-life management. The CTBC articulates an environmental injustice frame:[21]

> the recycling or direct dumping of the material results in a serious and immoral export of pollution to those countries [in the South]. Environmental protections in developing countries are usually poor, but regardless of the levels of protections, the export of pollution to countries due to their economic status is contrary to principles of environmental justice and moreover serves as a disincentive for manufacturers to prevent hazards and wastes upstream through product design. That is, rather than internalizing real environmental costs, manufacturers have been externalizing these costs to Asians and their environment.[22]

Activists from other NGOs who have worked on the e-waste problem concur. As a communiqué from the GrassRoots Recycling Network (GRRN) declared in response to the USEPA's decision to allow e-waste exports, 'Asian peoples are now asked to accept pollution that we have created simply because they are poorer.'[23] Responding to similar reports, Von Hernandez, a Philippines-based activist with Greenpeace and the International Campaign for Responsible Technology, stated, 'Asia is the dustbin of the world's hazardous waste.'[24]

BAN and SVTC have also contributed to successful efforts to pass such legislation in the European Union. They work closely on e-waste recycling campaigns with social movement organizations in many nations, including the Clean Production Network (Canada), Greenpeace International, Greenpeace China, Toxics Link India (India), Shristi (India), SCOPE (Pakistan), and the International Campaign for Responsible Technology.

A much broader umbrella network to which all these groups belong is the International Campaign for Responsible Technology (ICRT). To better coordinate transnational movement activities concerning the electronics industry, in 2002, 50 scholars and activists from around the world convened in San Jose, California to launch the group. They recognized that the development and sharing of information and critical knowledge across borders were key elements to ensuring a more just and sustainable high-technology industry. In addition to supporting advocacy campaigns and legal initiatives around electronics in the USA, Latin America, Asia, Africa and Europe, a central component of the ICRT's work involves documentation, research and publication. Toward that end, the network published *Challenging the Chip: Labor Rights and Environmental Justice in the Global Electronics Industry* – a book co-authored by more than 30 activists and scholars from a dozen nations in Asia, Europe, North America and Latin America.[25]

The ICRT is an international solidarity network that promotes corporate and government accountability in the global electronics industry. Ted Smith, one of the ICRT founders, explains how the network emerged from the Silicon Valley Toxics Coalition's work:

> It was late 1980s and early 1990s when we first got interested in the international angle of e-industry. At that time industry was moving out of Silicon Valley, particularly to the Southwest US, so we started working with SNEEJ (the Southwest Network for Environmental and Economic Justice) in particular and other groups in the US. But then it was pretty clear it was beyond that – internationally. We began to hear from people in other countries and we started to reach out to them in Europe and Asia. They started to deal with these aspects and we started making linkages and we started meeting at conferences. It was basically the same sets of issues – groundwater contamination and worker health, deregulation and corporate welfare – giving away of huge subsidies. In 1990 SVTC formed the Campaign for Responsible Technology, which later became the International CRT.'[26]

The transnational environmental justice networks that have evolved to track and combat the e-waste epidemic are clear in their framing of the problem as one rooted in inequalities by race, class and nation, and as perpetrated by both corporations and national governments. They articulate a challenge to global environmental racism and inequality in a political economy that benefits consumers, private industry and states in the North.

New directions in policy
The Basel Convention suffered from loopholes that allowed the shipment of hazardous wastes as long as they were officially for 'recycling'. In the 1990s, 77 non-OECD nations and China pushed heavily for a ban on the shipping of waste for recycling purposes. As a result, the Basel Ban was adopted, in order to end the export of hazardous waste from rich OECD nations to poor non-OECD nations, through 'sham recycling' operations. The USA has thus far refused to participate in the ban. In fact, the USA lobbied governments in Asia to establish bilateral trade agreements to continue dumping hazardous waste after the Basel Ban came into effect on 1 January 1998.[27] Hence it should be no surprise that the transnational export of e-waste remains a problem.

However, there is some cause for optimism. At the international level, the most progressive state action around e-waste yet is in the European Union. The EU passed two major policy initiatives, known as the Directive on Waste from Electrical and Electronic goods (WEEE) and the Restriction on Hazardous Substances (RoHS). These policies require electronics producers to take back products at the end of life and reduce the use of toxics in production. This should allow for products to be recycled and reused instead of being dumped into landfills or exported. Unfortunately, even with the WEEE legislation in place, if producers are not actually taking responsibility for recycling products domestically, many experts expect to see a continued rise in the export of hazardous e-waste to Africa, Pakistan, India and China and elsewhere in the global South. In 2003, record volumes of e-waste left the UK for such destinations – 23 000 tons of it. And government figures indicate that, more than ever, these materials are being shipped abroad. This is particularly acute since, in the UK, electronic goods are required to be recycled and barred from incinerators and landfills.[28]

Even the WEEE directive, while arguably the strongest such legislation anywhere, will not address the roots of the e-waste problem. Research by some environmental sociologists emphasizes the relationship between growth in markets and socio-environmental harm, and a critical examination of e-waste recycling might conclude that this practice will only enable that process.[29] Unless growth itself is challenged, the social and environmental ills activists bemoan will likely remain and worsen. For example, 'Given that the amount of WEEE [waste from electronics goods] is set to double by 2010, this means that the same amount now being disposed of to landfill and incineration may continue,' Gary Griffiths, environmental manager for RDC, a computer refurbisher in the UK, stated. 'We don't want any excuse for member states to be justified in increasing incinerator capacity, which is a long-term commitment and will divert funding from recycling,' Melissa Shinn of the European Environment Bureau noted.[30] Indeed, some have argued that the focus on recycling may be misguided because there is little sense in collecting volumes of recycled material unless there is a tax incentive or a legal obligation to use it. A perverse effect of the WEEE directive is that, as more material is collected for recycling, it may create a greater demand to export e-waste illegally to southern economies for dirty recycling. This is exactly what has happened with bans on e-waste in landfills – intended to encourage e-waste recycling – in the USA.

European nations have signed the Basel Ban on toxic waste exports – the USA. refuses to do so – but there are doubts as to whether it is being enforced. Since Europe agreed to stop exports, the BAN team has been back to China and reports that, while most e-waste comes from the USA, it is still 'flowing out of Europe'. BAN suspects that European waste more often ends up in India and Pakistan. 'So much harm has come under the green passport of recycling. Whenever someone says that word, it has the effect of making people swoon and think that everything is going to be lovely,' Jim Puckett stated.[31] Thus, as a result of the WEEE, 'ecological protection' in the global North may occur hand in hand with environmental injustice in the global South, as policies like this often shift hazards to poor nations.

Recently, environmental justice and labor rights activist networks such as the ICRT and CTBC (Computer TakeBack Campaign) have succeeded in pushing several states in the USA (Maine, Washington, California and Maryland), the EU, and companies such as Lenovo, Dell, H-P and Compaq, and even the entire University of California system to enact policies that: reduce toxic inputs in production processes; ensure a takeback of electronics at the end of life in order to recycle them; prohibit the use of prison labor for recycling; and prevent the export of these materials to other nations.

It might be said that electronics takeback systems constitute this social movement's success at institutionalizing a 'return to sender' policy among corporations and governments. While activists fighting other forms of transnational waste trading and dumping (e.g. municipal and agricultural wastes) have had to literally send the waste back to its nation of origin, it appears that e-waste activists have adopted another tactic: takeback systems that recycle products at the end of life.

But a state-by-state, company-by-company approach to environmental responsibility for our e-waste has created a patchwork of solutions that will soon become unwieldy and cumbersome for consumers, government and industry. These are positive signs, but alone they will never move us toward sustainability as a nation.

As local governments around the USA have seen this new waste-disposal problem emerging, they have begun to sound the alarm. Governments have taken on the burden until now, but states and municipalities are arguing that corporations should bear more of the costs. Michael Alexander, a senior research associate with the National Recycling Coalition of Alexandria, Virginia, points out, 'The question being raised everywhere is:

Should local government be saddled with this cost? And shouldn't manufacturers be involved? The question of manufacturer responsibility is now coming to the forefront.'[32]

In the 1970s and early 1980s, environmental organizations and farsighted elected officials in the USA led the way in developing state legislation that pushed companies to publicly report the extent of chemical substances they used or produced, so that nearby communities would be more aware of potential public health risks. The legislation was taken up by so many states that it became obvious that a national approach was the best way to go. This effort gave birth to the federal Emergency Planning and Community Right to Know Act of 1986, which led to significant improvements in safety across the nation.

Today, with rising volumes of e-waste and safety threats to public health and to the environment here and overseas, many activists and scholars believe it is time for a more sensible approach – a national policy on electronic waste. The US Congress could take a cue from the states and computer firms that have stepped up to the challenge and pass federal legislation. Like the EU, the USA could ensure that its electronics goods are safer for consumers and the workers who produce them, and that companies will take them back and recycle them responsibly (with non-incarcerated labor in the USA) when they are obsolete.

There are three policy initiatives that would likely improve the situation. First, the US Congress could finally ratify the Basel Convention and the Basel Ban on hazardous waste exports from OECD to non-OECD nations. The USA is the only OECD nation that has not yet ratified it among the 149 nations that have. Second, the US Congress could strengthen the federal Resource Conservation and Recovery Act (RCRA) – the main law that regulates hazardous waste in the USA. The problem is that RCRA currently exempts more and more hazardous wastes from export bans because if the waste managers declare that it is destined for recycling in another nation, it is considered non-hazardous. This happens with circuit boards and CRTs that would otherwise be declared hazardous. Thus RCRA – a domestic policy – contributes to global environmental inequality by allowing hazardous waste exports to less affluent nations. Third, and finally, the federal government might consider implementation of legislation similar to that which is in place in the EU, which facilitates the reduction of toxics in electronics goods and a national program for the takeback and recycling of electronics goods funded by industry. This would also go a long way toward addressing the USA's global impacts on environmental inequality.

Notes

1. Christopher Reuther (2002), 'Spheres of influence: who pays for e-junk?', *Environmental Health Perspectives*, **110**(4).
2. Andrew Osborn (2002), 'Britain accepts recycling deal', *The Guardian*, 12 October.
3. Basel Action Network & Silicon Valley Toxics Coalition (2002), *Exporting Harm: The High-Tech Trashing of Asia*, Seattle: BAN, p. 1.
4. Silicon Valley Toxics Coalition (2001), *Poison PCs and Toxic TVs: California's Biggest Environmental Crisis that You've Never Heard Of*, San Jose, CA: SVTC. p. 3.
5. David N. Pellow and Lisa Sun-Hee Park (2002), *The Silicon Valley of Dreams: Environmental Injustice, Immigrant Workers, and the High-Tech Global Economy*, New York: New York University Press. See also Ted Smith, David Sonnenfeld and David N. Pellow (eds) (2006), *Challenging the Chip: Labor Rights and Environmental Justice in the Global Electronics Industry*, Philadelphia, PA: Temple University Press.
6. Computer TakeBack Campaign (2003), 'The solutions: electronics recylers pledge of true stewardship', June. http://www.computertakeback.com/the_solutions/prison_sum.cfm.
7. Ibid.

8. GrassRoots Recycling Network (2003), 'EPA: keep toxic PC's out of Asia', 6 July, Madison, WI: GRRN.
9. Jim Puckett interview with the author, 5 March 2002. For an excellent analysis of the problem of global environmental inequality see Peter Newell (2005), 'Race, class, and the global politics of environmental inequality,' *Global Environmental Politics*, **5**(3), 70–94.
10. Neil Gough (2002), 'Garbage in, garbage out: castoffs from the computer age are a financial windfall for Chinese villagers. But at what cost?', *Time Asia*, 11 March.
11. BAN & SVTC, *Exporting Harm*.
12. *The Times of India Online* (2004), "NGO sounds e-waste alert," 16 March.
13. Quoted in 'India: Fears that IT hub Becoming Electronic Waste Dump', Asia Pacific, http://www.abc.net.au/ra/asiapac/programs/s 886414.htm, accessed on 29 July 2003.
14. Seema Kamdar (2004), 'E-waste gives citizens a big headache', *India Times News Network*, 19 July.
15. Toxics Link India (2003), *Scrapping the Hi-tech Myth: Computer Waste in India*, New Delhi, India, p. 5.
16. Ibid., p. 6.
17. Kishore Wankhade (2004), 'British Environment Agency report reveals 23,000 tons of e-waste being illegally exported to developing nations, including India', Toxics Link, New Delhi, 17 December, http://www.toxicslink.org/mediapr-view.php?pressrelnum=18. For the definitive text on the politics of the Basel Convention see Jennifer Clapp (2001), *Toxic Exports: The Transfer of Hazardous Wastes from Rich to Poor Countries*, Ithaca, NY: Cornell University Press.
18. Wankhade, 'British Environment Agency report'.
19. Ibid.
20. BAN & SVTC, *Exporting Harm*, p. 8.
21. Stella Capek (1993), 'The "environmental justice" frame: a conceptual discussion and an application', *Social Problems*, **40**, 5–24.
22. Computer TakeBack Campaign, 'The Solutions'.
23. GrassRoots Recycling Network, 'EPA: keep toxic PC's out of Asia'.
24. John Vidal (2004), 'They call this recycling, but it's really dumping by another name', *The Guardian*, 21 September.
25. Smith et al., *Challenging the Chip*.
26. Ted Smith, interview with the author, Spring 2002.
27. SVTC, *Poison PCs and Toxic TVs*, p. 18.
28. Vidal, 'They call this recycling'.
29. See Schnaiberg and Gould (2000), *Environment and Society: The Enduring Conflict*, West Caldwell, NJ: Blackburn Press.
30. *The Guardian* (2003), 'The e-waste land', 30 November.
31. Basel Action Network (2005), *The Digital Dump: Exporting Re-use and Abuse to Africa*, 24 October.
32. Reuther, 'Spheres of influence'.

PART III

TRADE AND ENVIRONMENTAL POLICY

19 An introduction to the trade and environment debate

*Steve Charnovitz**

Introduction

This chapter offers an introduction to the trade and environment debate. Readers of this *Handbook* will encounter many different approaches to these complex issues. What I seek to do here is to provide historical, political and legal context for analysts who try to understand and, ultimately, to solve trade and environment problems. Following this introduction, the chapter has two sections. The first puts the contemporary debate in historical context and explains how the trading system got to the point where it is today. The second section provides a legal guide to the provisions of World Trade Organization (WTO) agreements that relate directly to the environment.

History and context

International policies on trade and on environment have always intersected. The earliest multilateral environmental agreement (MEA), the Convention for the Protection of Birds Useful to Agriculture, signed in 1902, utilized an import ban as an environmental instrument.[1] The earliest multilateral trade agreement to pursue trade liberalization, the Convention for the Abolition of Import and Export Prohibitions and Restrictions, signed in 1927, contained an exception for trade restrictions imposed for the protection of public health and the protection of animals and plants against diseases and against 'extinction'.[2]

As environmental regimes evolved over the twentieth century, trade instruments continued to be used by governments seeking workable environmental protection. When the postwar multilateral trading system was designed in 1947–48, governments recognized the need for some policy space to accommodate the use of trade measures as instruments to safeguard the environment and health. The General Agreement on Tariffs and Trade (GATT) of 1947 contained provisions in Article XX (General Exceptions) to accommodate governmental measures necessary for the protection of life and health, and measures relating to the conservation of exhaustible natural resources. Although it never came into force, the Charter of the International Trade Organization provided an exception for measures taken 'in pursuance of any inter-governmental agreement which relates solely to the conservation of fisheries resources, migratory birds or wild animals . . .'.[3]

In these first-generation 'trade and environment' policies, the two regimes recognized some linkage to the other, but did not actively look for ways to enhance each other's goals. For example, the Convention on International Trade in Endangered Species of Wild Fauna and Flora (CITES), signed in 1973, uses trade bans as a central instrument for the management and enforcement of wildlife policies. For many years, however, CITES was not fully attentive to how controlled trade could enhance sustainable management. Similarly, the GATT system was often not attentive to how its normative activities to address non-tariff barriers were being perceived in the environmental community as a challenge to the legitimacy of environmental measures.

With few exceptions, until the early 1990s, there was very little communication between trade officials and environment officials operating at the international level and not much more at the national level. As a result, the trade effects of environmental laws and regulations were often not considered by the governments imposing them. Similarly, the environmental effects of trade and investment liberalization, and the impact of trade law disciplines were often not considered.

As a result of the new 'trade and environment' debate beginning in the early 1990s, there is now much greater understanding of these linkages. Trade officials at the WTO and in national capitals are much more aware of the linkages between trade and environment, and say that they are committed to avoiding conflicts. Similarly, there is greater recognition by environmental officials as to how trade restrictions can be overused or misused in the pursuit of environmental goals. Considerable credit should be given to many foundations, non-governmental organizations (NGOs), institutes and business groups that devoted attention to these issues from the early 1990s onward.

Of course, the fact that international policy on the 'trade and environment' is more coherent and constructive now than it was in the 1980s and 1990s does not mean that this level of progress is sufficient or that the underlying problems have been solved. Environmental problems will always be a challenge on a planet where governmental units do not exactly match ecosystems. Another way of saying this is that so long as the policies in one country can impose externalities on others, and so long as prices in the market are not fully reflective of environmental costs, there will be a need for international governance to manage the transborder conflicts that will inevitably ensue. In a recent speech, WTO Director-General Pascal Lamy explained that governance 'is a decision-making process that through consultation, dialogue, exchange and mutual respect, seeks to ensure coexistence and in some cases coherence between different and sometimes divergent points of view' (Lamy, 2006). That will be a key challenge for global governance in the twenty-first century.

Because all major ecological problems affect the world economy – for example, climate change, biodiversity, forestry, fisheries and pollution – linkages between the world trading system and environmental policies are inevitable. In Lamy's paradigm, there is a need for governance because individual governments acting alone will not, as a practical matter, adopt policies that are efficient on a global scale. Although individuals can act in a self-interested way in the market knowing that an invisible hand exists to help generate efficient outcomes, the same overall pro-efficiency dynamic does not automatically ensue in global politics if governments act only in a self-interested way toward other countries.

One of the contributions of environmentalist Konrad von Moltke, about 20 years ago, was the dictum that 'unmanaged environmental problems become trade problems'. There are two insights in this dictum. The first is that major environmental problems can never be definitively solved; new developments will always spawn new problems that require new solutions and better management. The second insight is that governments need to cooperate to solve environmental problems, and when such cooperation is not forthcoming, a government stymied in getting the cooperation it seeks may resort to a trade measure. This dynamic of environmental problems spilling out into the trading system can be seen in many of the major trade–environment conflicts to date.

Recently, this danger has become apparent in the proposals being made for a climate tax or tariff to be imposed on imports from countries that have not ratified the Kyoto Protocol to the UN Climate Change Convention or are not controlling their greenhouse gas emissions (Bennhold, 2007, p. 10). Because many governments are not cooperating on addressing greenhouse gas emissions and other energy conservation challenges, frustration is spilling out into the trade arena. In the case of climate change, trade measures are being suggested as a way either to level the playing field between countries with different levels of energy tax or to induce free-riding countries to cooperate gainfully.

Because the WTO is a functional international organization with a mandate for trade, WTO law does not generally address government policies beyond trade, but rather leaves those issues to environmental institutions. This approach has clear advantages and disadvantages. The advantage is that the WTO sticks to its technical competence and leaves environmental decisions to organizations with that technical competence. The disadvantage is that in trade and environment, the WTO looks only at one side of a problem. For example, in the *United States–Shrimp* case, the WTO considered the appropriateness of the US import ban directed at countries that the US government believed were not adequately protecting sea turtles. But the WTO did not consider whether the complaining governments were adequately protecting sea turtles. Because it is partial rather than holistic, WTO dispute settlement may not be able to achieve a satisfactory solution to complex disputes regarding the 'ecolonomy', that is, the overlay of the world ecology and economy.

This legal point has an analogue in the economic critiques of international trade law and WTO negotiations that point to the uncertainty as to whether trade liberalization will always benefit the participating countries. For example, the impact of services regulation on an economy will depend to some extent on whether the liberalizing government has an adequate regulatory regime in place. In other words, an adequate regulatory regime can be viewed as a precondition of fully benefiting from trade liberalization. The same point can be made regarding whether a government has in place an adequate legal system, adequate competition policy, adequate openness to investment, adequate adjustment assistance for workers and farmers, and adequate environmental controls. All of these policy preconditions have in common the fact that the WTO generally does not have rules assuring that non-trade policies are adequate for trade liberalization.

Beginning with Agenda 21 (1992), governments have affirmed that trade and environment policies should be 'mutually supportive in favour of sustainable development'.[4] This mantra is inscribed in the Doha Ministerial Declaration where the WTO members state: 'We are convinced that the aims of upholding and safeguarding an open and non-discriminatory multilateral trading system, and acting for the protection of the environment and the promotion of sustainable development can and must be mutually supportive.'[5] This phraseology has been adoptable because there is something in it for all sides of the debate. Those who view the trading system as already supportive of the environment can point to the way that trade can positively contribute to environmental goals. On the other hand, those who are skeptical of the benefits of trade for the environment see the mutual supportiveness as a commitment by the WTO to carry out the Doha agenda in a way that actually does deliver some environmental benefits. My guess is that if there is a Doha Round agreement, it will contain significant environmental language (Lamy, 2007).

Guide to WTO treaty provisions addressing the environment
This section examines the various provisions of WTO law that address the environment. The Marrakech Agreement Establishing the World Trade Organization (WTO Agreement) mentions the environment and sustainable development in its Preamble. The Appellate Body has stated that the WTO Preamble informs the interpretation of the WTO covered agreements, and the jurists used the language above in the *US–Shrimp* case to help interpret the WTO provisions at issue (Cameron and Campbell, 2002, p. 30).

The foundational WTO Agreement on trade in goods, the GATT, contains General Exceptions to all rules in that Agreement, including the disciplines governing import bans, domestic taxes and border tax adjustments. Although most environmental measures can be carried out without infringing WTO rules, a trade-related environmental measure (TREM) may come into conflict with trade rules.[6] With respect to the environment, Article XX (General Exceptions) states:

> Subject to the requirement that such measures are not applied in a manner which would constitute a means of arbitrary or unjustifiable discrimination between countries where the same conditions prevail, or a disguised restriction on international trade, nothing in this Agreement shall be construed to prevent the adoption or enforcement by any contracting party of measures:
> . . . (b) necessary to protect human, animal or plant life or health;
> . . . (g) relating to the conservation of exhaustible natural resources if such measures are made effective in conjunction with restrictions on domestic production or consumption. The introductory paragraph to Article XX, known as the 'chapeau' has been interpreted by the Appellate Body as a condition for the use of any of the Article XX exceptions. The chapeau is examined after a disputed measure is found to qualify provisionally under one of the specific exceptions. Both the (b) and (g) exceptions would be usable for an environmental measure. A panel adjudicating Article XX should first consider the threshold question to see if the governmental measure being litigated fits within the range of policies covered by the exception. If so, then the specific discipline in that exception would be examined. The Appellate Body has allocated the burden of proof to the defendant government for all steps of the Article XX analysis.
> For measures regarding human, animal, or plant life or health, the (b) exception requires that the measure be 'necessary', and that term has been applied strictly. In *EC–Asbestos*, the Appellate Body found that the XX(b) exception could justify the contested measure. According to the Appellate Body in that case, the term 'necessary' in Article XX(b) requires that there be no reasonably available and WTO-consistent alternative measure that the regulating government could reasonably be expected to employ to achieve its policy objectives. To determine whether a potential alternative is reasonably available, a panel will engage in a 'weighing and balancing process' that considers: (1) the extent to which the alternative measure 'contributes to the realization of the end pursued', (2) whether the alternative measure would achieve the same end, and (3) whether the alternative is less restrictive of trade.[7]

The Article XX(d) exception could also be relevant to environmental measures. That exception is for measures necessary to secure compliance with certain laws or regulations that are not GATT-inconsistent. In the *Mexico–Taxes on Soft Drinks* case, the Appellate Body held that this exception is designed only to secure compliance with a WTO member's own laws and regulations. This holding would seem to preclude the use of the XX(d) exception to justify laws, such as the US Lacey Act,[8] that prohibits importation of fish taken in violation of any foreign law.

For measures regarding the conservation of exhaustible natural resources, the (g) exception requires that the disputed measure be 'relating to' such conservation. In *US–Shrimp*, the Appellate Body ended the controversy as to whether 'exhaustible' natural resources were distinguishable from renewable resources (such as turtles) by holding that exhaustible natural resources includes both living and non-living resources. The issue of whether there is an implied jurisdictional limit to Article XX(g), that is, whether the natural resources being protected by the contested measure must be within the territory of the defendant country, remains unresolved. In the *US–Shrimp* case, the Appellate Body seemed to suggest that there had to be a 'sufficient nexus' to the defendant country.[9] The term 'relating to' has been interpreted by the Appellate Body to require an examination of whether the general structure and design of the measure is reasonably related to the ends sought and are not disproportionately wide in scope. In addition, the (g) exception further requires that a measure applying to imports be made effective in conjunction with restrictions on domestic production or consumption. In *US–Gasoline*, the Appellate Body held that this clause requires 'even-handedness' in the imposition of restrictions, in the name of conservation, upon the production or consumption of exhaustible natural resources.[10]

The applicability of GATT Article XX to process-related measures (PPMs) is controversial. In the *US–Shrimp* case, the Appellate Body ultimately ruled that a US import ban on shrimp from Malaysia was WTO-consistent even though it was linked to Malaysia's conservation practices.[11] On the other hand, the WTO Secretariat continues to declare that 'trade restrictions cannot be imposed on a product purely because of the way it has been produced'.[12] The issue of process-related taxes can also raise questions regarding the exceptions in Article XX as well as the underlying GATT rules on the imposition of taxes on imported products and border tax adjustments on imported or exported products. If taxes get used more widely as an instrument to address climate change and to promote the use of clean energy, some tax disputes may be brought to the WTO. The availability of Article XX to justify measures against so-called eco-dumping or against MEA violations has not been litigated.

As for all WTO rules, the WTO dispute settlement system prescribes trade sanctions as an instrument to induce compliance when trade rules are being violated. Ironically, the WTO is the only international organization (other than the UN Security Council) to use trade sanctions in that manner. The implementation system for MEAs relies more on the soft powers of persuasion and capacity-building. When MEAs use trade controls, the only trade blocked is the natural resource being regulated by the MEA.

Violations of GATT obligations were found in the *US–Gasoline* and *US–Shrimp* cases, and in both instances the US government corrected the violation without sacrificing its environmental policies. The experience in both cases demonstrates the focus of panels on the means used to achieve an environmental aim, not a second-guessing of the ends sought to be achieved. Of course, one should note that both of these cases involved an Appellate Body decision that reversed the lower-level panel on key points. The original panel decisions, if carried to their logical conclusion, had seemed to undermine the right of a government to carry out environmental regulation that affected trade.

The only pending environmental case is *Brazil–Measures Affecting Imports of Retreaded Tyres*. This is a complaint filed by the European Communities about Brazil's import ban on retreaded tires. In June 2007, the panel issued a report rejecting Brazil's invocation of the GATT Article XX(b) exception. As of this writing, that panel report has not been adopted.

Besides the GATT, several other WTO agreements supervising trade in goods also include provisions pertaining to the environment. For example, the Agreement on

Agriculture declared that fundamental reform is an ongoing process and committed parties to begin new negotiations in 2000. These negotiations are to take into account the so-called 'non-trade concerns, including food security and the need to protect the environment'.[13] The Agreement on Agriculture contains a so-called 'green box' list of subsidies that have an exemption from reduction commitments, so long as they have at most minimal trade-distorting effects or effects on production.[14] The WTO Secretariat has opined that this green box enables governments to 'capture positive environmental externalities'.[15] Yet I am unaware of any research on the true value for the environment of green box subsidies.

The Agreement on Technical Barriers to Trade (TBT) contains a complex set of rules regarding government and private regulatory systems. A central rule is that technical regulations not be more trade restrictive than necessary to fulfill a legitimate objective. The TBT Agreement includes, among an illustrative list of objectives, the 'protection of human health or safety, animal or plant life or health, or the environment'.[16] Furthermore, TBT requires governments to use international standards as 'a basis for' technical regulations except when such standards would be an ineffective or inappropriate means for the fulfillment of the legitimate objectives pursued.[17] The applicability of this requirement to international environmental standards has not been well defined or litigated.

Despite the mention of processes and production methods (PPMs), the extent to which these come within the scope of the TBT Agreement remains unclear. For example, would the sustainable fisheries label devised by the Marine Stewardship Council be a TBT measure? Another ambiguity in the TBT Agreement is whether the rules for conformity assessment by non-governmental bodies would apply to organizations such as the Forest Stewardship Council and Green Seal.

The Agreement on the Application of Sanitary and Phytosanitary (SPS) measures governs trade and domestic measures imposed to prevent risks to life or health from pests, diseases, additives, contaminants, toxins and disease-causing organisms. The governmental responses to epidemics, in so far as the ensuing policies involve trade in goods, are also governed by the SPS Agreement.[18] The SPS Agreement was written with a focus on food safety and veterinary concerns, and, at one time, trade law commentators thought that environmental regulations would be governed by the TBT Agreement rather than the SPS Agreement. Yet in 2006, the WTO panel in *EC–Approval and Marketing of Biotech Products* gave a broad interpretation to the scope of the SPS Agreement and emphasized that the Agreement could cover 'certain damage to the environment other than damage to the life or health or animals or plants'.[19] This precedent may mean that the disciplines of the SPS Agreement, which are among the strictest in the WTO, will collide more with TREMs in the future.

When a measure is covered by the SPS Agreement, it is subject to numerous rules. For example, SPS measures affecting trade have to be based on a risk assessment and cannot be maintained without sufficient scientific evidence.[20] SPS Article 3 directs governments to base their SPS measures on international standards, but allows governments to set a higher level of protection than exists in the international standard. The Appellate Body has taken note of 'the delicate and carefully negotiated balance in the SPS Agreement between the shared, but sometimes competing, interests of promoting international trade and of protecting the life and health of human beings'.[21] In that holding, the Appellate

Body seems to view the SPS Agreement as embodying a choice between trade and life/health. Another rule in the SPS Agreement is that regulatory measures (for example, a maximum residue limit on pesticides) not be more trade restrictive than required to meet the importing government's appropriate level of protection.

The Agreement on Subsidies and Countervailing Measures (SCM) supervises the use of domestic and export subsidies by governments, and the imposition of countervailing duties against subsidies. The SCM Agreement does not contain disciplines exclusively for environmental subsidies. Nor does it incorporate the polluter-pays principle. As negotiated in the Uruguay Round, the SCM Agreement contained an article (Article 8) making certain subsidies non-actionable. Listed among the non-actionable subsidies were financial contributions by governments for adapting existing facilities to new environmental requirement (subject to specified conditions). In so far as these subsidies are used to address market failure, the SCM Agreement manifested some sensitivity to the fact that some subsidies may be justifiable for economic reasons even if they distort trade. At the end of 1999, however, SCM Article 8 expired. With the expiration of this provision, an environmental subsidy can be 'actionable', which means that if a subsidy is 'specific' and causes 'adverse effects' to the interests of other WTO members, then that subsidy would violate the SCM Agreement.[22] The remedy for such a violation would be for the subsidizing government to withdraw the subsidy or remove the adverse effects.

The foundational agreement on trade in services, the General Agreement on Trade in Services (GATS), contains General Exceptions to all rules in the Agreement. The structure of the GATS General Exceptions, found in GATS Article XIV, is similar to the structure of GATT Article XX in having a chapeau like the one in Article XX and a list of specific exceptions. The GATS includes an exception for measures necessary for the protection of life and health, but does not include an exception regarding conservation or the environment. So far, this omission has not proved significant because no environment-related service measure has been challenged in WTO dispute settlement. The Preamble to the GATS recognizes 'the right of [WTO] members to regulate, and to introduce new regulations, on the supply of services within their territories . . .'[23] Nevertheless, that language did not impede the finding of a violation in the *US–Gambling* case, which involves a US ban on internet gambling without regard to whether the gambling services originate domestically or in other countries. In that dispute, the Appellate Body held that the challenged measure came within the scope of the GATS General Exception, but further held that the US measure did not qualify for an exception because the US government had not demonstrated that, with respect to horseracing, the regulations on remote gambling were not less favorable to foreign suppliers than to domestic suppliers.[24] If this decision means that government consistency is a precondition for a right to regulate, then that principle could work against the integrity of environmental regulations.

The foundational WTO agreement on intellectual property rights, the Agreement on Trade-Related Aspects of Intellectual Property Rights (TRIPS), does not contain an overall environmental exception. Article 8 of TRIPS states that WTO members 'may' adopt measures necessary to protect public health and nutrition, provided that such measures are consistent with TRIPS. Thus this provision is merely circular and lacks any content. The rules in TRIPS that would seem most likely to be in interface with environmental regulation are the requirements in Part II, Section 5 regarding the granting of patent rights to nationals of other WTO member countries. Section 5 provides that WTO members may exclude from patentability inventions if 'necessary' to 'protect human, animal or plant life or health or to avoid serious prejudice to the environment', and further provides that members may exclude from patentability plants and animals other than microorganisms provided that plant varieties receive protection either through a patent or an effective *sui generis* system.[25] The meaning of these optional exclusions from patentability has not yet been explicated in WTO dispute settlement.

Conclusion

So much for the legal details; I conclude this chapter with a thought for the future. What can environmental policy-makers learn from the trading system? For some, the answer is the importance of the principles of non-discrimination and free trade. In my view, that misses the point because the WTO rejects these principles as much as it embraces them.[26] The real lesson from the WTO is the success of an international regime that uses higher law to enable governments to enact and lock in optimal policy changes that would otherwise be hard to adopt because of vested interests. As Daniel Esty noted many years ago, importing that approach can be beneficial for environmental law (Esty, 1994, p. 230).

Notes

* Parts of this chapter draw from a study prepared for the World Bank Institute in 2007.
1. Convention for the Protection of Birds Useful to Agriculture, 19 March 1902, 102 BFSP 969, art. 2 (no longer in force).
2. Convention for the Abolition of Import and Export Prohibitions and Restrictions, 8 November 1927, 97 LNTS 391, art. 4, ad art. 4 (not in force).
3. Havana Charter for an International Trade Organization, 24 March 1948, art. 45.1(a)(x) (not in force), available at http://www.wto.org/english/docs_e/legal_e/prewto_legal_e.htm.
4. UN Conference on Environment and Development, Agenda 21, para. 2.21(b).
5. Doha Ministerial Declaration, WT/MIN(01)DEC/1, 14 November 2001, para. 6.
6. A TREMs is a measure in an environmental treaty, law or regulation that affects trade. Disputes about TREM can be lodged in the WTO. For example, the *EC–Asbestos* case involved a complaint by the Government of Canada about a French decree that banned the manufacture, sale, or importation of asbestos fibers and any product containing such fibers. The purpose of the decree was to prevent harm to human health. TREMs that inhibit trade are regularly used for environmental purposes. Of course, most measures that inhibit trade are trade measures, not environmental measures. For example, tariffs, quotas and countervailing duties are trade-related trade measures.
7. Appellate Body Report, *European Communities – Measures Affecting Asbestos and Asbestos-Containing Products*, WT/DS135/AB/R, adopted 5 April 2001, paras 162–72.
8. 16 USCS §3372(a)(2)(A).
9. Appellate Body Report, *United States–Import Prohibition of Certain Shrimp and Shrimp Products*, WT/DS58/AB/R, adopted 6 November 1998, para. 133.
10. Appellate Body Report, *United States–Standards for Reformulated and Conventional Gasoline*, WT/DS2/AB/R, adopted 20 May 1996, pp. 20–21.
11. Appellate Body Report, *United States–Import Prohibition of Certain Shrimp and Shrimp Products – Recourse to Article 21.5 of the DSU by Malaysia*, WT/DS58/AB/RW, adopted 21 November 2001.
12. WTO, 'The environment: a specific concern', available at http://www.wto.org/english/thewto_e/whatis_e/tif_e/bey2_e.htm. The Secretariat does not cite any legal authority for this assertion.
13. Agreement on Agriculture, Preamble recital 6, art. 20 (c); Doha Declaration, para. 13.
14. Ibid. Agreement on Agriculture, art. 6.1, Annex 2, paras 2(a), 12. Among the listed subsidies are infrastructure works associated with environmental programs and payments under environmental programs. Eligibility for such payments has to be determined as part of a clearly defined government environmental or conservation program and be dependent on the fulfillment of specific conditions. Moreover, the amount of payment has to be limited to the extra costs or loss of income involved in complying with the government program.
15. WTO, 'Relevant WTO provisions: descriptions', available at http://www.wto.org/english/tratop_e/envir_e/issu3_e.htm.
16. TBT, art. 2.2. See also ibid., art. 5.4. This requirement also applies to voluntary international standards.

17.   Ibid., para. 2.4.
18.   Measures to control cross-border travel of natural persons supplying or consuming services would be governed by the WTO Services Agreement. It is interesting to note that the World Bank counsels that trade and travel restrictions could be appropriate instruments to address an avian flu epidemic (World Bank, 2007, p. 146).
19.   Panel Report, *EC – Measures Affecting the Marketing and Approval of Biotech Products*, WT/DS291/R, para. 7.209, adopted 21 November 2006.
20.   SPS arts 2.2, 5.1. In instances where scientific evidence is insufficient, a government may provisionally impose SPS measures based on pertinent information. See SPS art. 5.7.
21.   Appellate Body Report, *EC–Asbestos*, ibid. para. 177.
22.   SCM Agreement, arts 1.2, 2, 5.
23.   GATS Preamble.
24.   Appellate Body Report, *United States – Measures Affecting the Cross-Border Supply of Gambling and Betting Services*, WT/DS286/AB/R, paras 371–2, adopted 20 April 2005.
25.   TRIPS arts 27.2, 27.2(b).
26.   For example, the WTO permits preferential trade agreements and antidumping duties against low-price imports.

References

Bennhold, Katrin (2007), 'France tells U.S. to sign climate pacts or face tax', *New York Times*, 1 February, p. 10.
Cameron, James and Karen Campbell (2002), 'A reluctant global policymaker', in Richard H. Steinberg (ed.), *The Greening of Trade Law*, Lanham, MD, and Oxford: Rowman & Littlefield Publishers, pp. 23–50.
Esty, Daniel C. (1994), *Greening the GATT*, Washington, DC: Institute for International Economics.
Lamy, Pascal (2006), 'The World Trade Organization: a laboratory for global governance', Malcolm Wiener Lecture, 1 November, available at: http://www.wto.org/english/news_e/sppl_e/sppl47_e.htm.
World Bank (2007), *Global Economic Prospects 2007: Managing the Next Wave of Globalization*, Washington, DC: World Bank.
WTO (2007), 'Lamy urges support for environmental chapter of the Doha Round', 5 February, available at: http://www.wto.org/english/news_e/sppl_e/sppl54_e.htm.

20 The WTO, services and the environment
Robert K. Stumberg

Global environmental services

The WTO's agreement on services – the General Agreement on Trade in Services (GATS) – sets rules for the most dynamic sector of every country's economy. But what exactly is the service economy?

Consider the energy sector. The demand for natural gas far exceeds the supply in North America. One solution to this shortage is to import liquefied natural gas (LNG) from other continents. The companies that manage global supply chains have evolved into networks of services – communications, financing, logistics, transport, transactions – that are powerful enough to compete on a global scale.

In the USA, five LNG ports are in place. Federal agencies have approved 23 new ports with 15 more pending (FERC, 2007). The ports dock tankers that carry LNG from Indonesia, Qatar, Algeria and Trinidad (EIA, 2007). The tankers are floating thermos bottles as long as three football fields; their LNG decompresses 600-fold into 5 billion cubic feet of natural gas (EIA, 2007). But this efficiency comes with risk.

The risk was apparent in 1944, when one of the first LNG plants leaked a cloud of gas that ignited and incinerated 131 people in Cleveland (Bureau of Mines, 1946). Since then, the industry has seen only eight marine leaks and a few onshore explosions (Foss, 2004). The most recent, an Algerian facility in 2004, killed 27 people over a square-mile area (Mobile Register, 2004). This was a rare accident, but it carries a post-9/11 message: LNG terminals are a target for terrorism. The film *Syriana* depicted this risk in a scene where jihadists steered their suicide boats into the hull of an LNG tanker.

Syriana was produced in California, which supplies only 15 percent of the natural gas it consumes. Governor Schwarzenegger and the state's energy regulators all agree that without new LNG ports, the economy will suffer and consumers will pay more (Feinstein, 2005). An Australian firm proposed building an LNG port, Cabrillo Port, not too far from Hollywood near Ventura. BHT Billiton designed the port to mitigate the security risk by locating it 14 miles offshore. However, that did not quell the public debate about how far evaporating gas could spread – one mile or 30 miles – before it ignites into a 'small nuclear explosion', to quote the Chairman of Lloyd's of London (Reynolds, 2004).

Starting in 2003, the regulatory process was complex. There was an environmental impact study and then an EPA finding in 2004 that Ventura County air pollution standards would apply. In 2005 that finding was reversed, and there was considerable public opposition on security grounds. Finally, in 2007, Governor Schwarzenegger exercised his authority (delegated to governors in the federal Deep Water Ports Act) to reject the port on grounds that it would harm California's air quality and marine life. The governor said he 'strongly oppose[d]' EPA's preliminary decision not to apply Ventura County air standards, which also apply to off-shore oil rigs (Schwarzenegger, 2007). BHT Billiton

Source: Photo courtesy of the Federal Energy Regulatory Commision (FERC)

Figure 20.1   LNG security near Boston

protested that the state and federal governments were working at cross-purposes (Wood, 2006). Yet as messy as it was, this regulatory process was legal and constitutional. BHT Billiton had no recourse in US courts.

Throughout 2006 and 2007, the Australian government was a leading advocate at the WTO for a set of trade rules, called 'disciplines on domestic regulation'. Article VI of GATS authorizes these negotiations (WTO–GATS, 1994). There may be no direct connection with Cabrillo Port. But if adopted, the disciplines would help companies such as BHT Billiton. Among other things, Australia proposed that licensing criteria must be based on objective criteria (e.g. not political pressure from public hearings), and licensing procedures must be as simple as possible (e.g. not a web of federal, state and local stages of review) (Australia et al., 2006).

In sum, the story of Cabrillo Port shows how:

- environmental goods such as LNG are delivered by global service industries;
- environmental services are highly regulated under laws that reflect a deliberate balance of power among local, state, federal governments;
- GATS covers governments at all levels and how they regulate, purchase, provide, or subsidize services;
- existing or proposed trade rules under GATS can conflict with traditional governing authority.

This chapter provides an overview of GATS as the legal framework for global trade in services and summarizes the debates over who should regulate the service economy. Then the focus shifts to how GATS could affect environmental policy. One section covers commitments in several environmental sectors, and another covers negotiations on new disciplines for domestic regulation.

GATS in a nutshell

WTO trade disputes
WTO agreements do not automatically nullify or pre-empt domestic laws. Rather, they are enforced through trade disputes between nation-states. The agreements obligate national governments to 'ensure' compliance by sub-national governments (GATS art. I(3)). A dispute panel hears and decides a case, and the losing country may seek review by the WTO's Appellate Body (WTO–DSU, 1994). The country that wins a WTO dispute may impose trade sanctions in order to prompt the losing country to repeal or amend the offending law. Sanctions include imposing punitive tariffs or ignoring patents or copyrights. Since trade sanctions are often applied to commerce outside of the sector in dispute, they work like a secondary economic boycott. When a WTO panel decides a trade dispute, it must answer three questions that reflect the structure of trade agreements, including GATS.

1.   Is the measure covered by a trade agreement?
2.   If covered, is the measure consistent with trade rules?
3.   If not consistent, is the conflict excused by a general exception?

Coverage
GATS covers measures that affect trade in services, except for services supplied under 'government authority'.[1] However, this carves out only some government services: those that are neither commercial (e.g. free) nor in competition with another supplier.

Some GATS rules cover measures in all sectors, and some apply only where a WTO member has agreed to 'commit' a particular service. Countries make commitments for particular sectors and 'modes' of supplying services, for example, establishing commercial presence of a subsidiary company.[2]

The USA has commitments in many sectors that manage or affect the environment, including pollution control, wastewater, solid waste, hazardous waste, construction, services incidental to mining and services incidental to energy distribution, to name a few. The USA has offered to make new commitments in sectors that would cover the infrastructure of LNG ports, including bulk storage of fuels and pipeline distribution of fuels (USA, 2005; USTR, 2007e)

Existing trade rules
The most significant GATS rules are:

●   *Most favored nation* – MFN prohibits discrimination for/against certain countries. It covers all sectors (art. II).[3]

- *National treatment* – NT prohibits discrimination against foreign suppliers, including laws that change conditions of competition, even if they do not formally discriminate. It covers committed sectors only (art. XVII).[4]
- *Market access* – MA prohibits various limits on service suppliers including quantitative limits (monopolies, quotas, excusive suppliers, economic needs tests, number of operations, volume of service, number of employees) and legal status of a supplier. It covers committed sectors only (art. XVI).[5]

Negotiations on expanded coverage and trade rules

When the Uruguay Round of trade negotiations ended in 1994, the most controversial GATS proposals were deferred for future negotiations. GATS includes a built-in agenda for negotiations on sector commitments (art. XIX), new trade rules on domestic regulation (art. VI), procurement (art. XIII), subsidies (Art. XV) and emergency safeguards (Art. X). The negotiator for the USA is the US Trade Representative (USTR), whose staff is part of the Executive Office of the President.

Exceptions

GATS Article XIV excuses conflict with a trade rule if a measure is:

- necessary to protect public morals;
- necessary to protect human or animal health;
- necessary to protect privacy or prevent fraud;
- necessary (in the view of each country) to safeguard essential security interests.

GATS debates

GATS regulates government 'measures' such as laws and agency regulations if they affect trade or investment. In most environmental sectors, government does not just regulate services; it also owns or regulates investments and their external impact. The GATS debate is about the power of government to pursue environmental objectives, to reverse a decision to privatize or deregulate, and to regulate at the subnational level.

Environmental objectives

The WTO's agreement on trade in goods (GATT, the General Agreement on Tariffs and Trade) has a general exception to preserve policy space to promote conservation of exhaustible natural resources. GATS does not have this general exception, and its critics warn that GATS could be used to challenge environmental measures that are beyond the reach of GATT (Waskow, 2003). GATS defenders assert that environmental measures are safeguarded by a footnote that excludes 'inputs' from an MA rule that prohibits limiting 'outputs' (e.g. limits on intake for water services) (GATS art. XVI(c)).

So will GATS trump a greener GATT? The test will come in a sector where GATS and GATT overlap. This is where an environmental good (e.g. LNG) is delivered in a sector where a country has a GATS commitment (e.g. bulk storage or distribution of fuels).

Privatization and deregulation

GATS critics warn that the agreement pushes privatization and promotes back-door deregulation (Sinclair, 2000; Sinclair and Greishaber-Otto, 2002). The WTO responds that countries are free to choose when to commit to trade rules, which sectors to cover, and what limits to set on those commitments.

GATS critics point out that countries can open up their markets without locking into GATS rules. They ask, what if privatizing water services results in higher rates and lower service, which happened in Atlanta? Or what if deregulating electricity results in higher rates but no increase in service capacity, which happened in California (Waskow, 2003; Menotti, 2006)? If market liberalization does not work, it might be prudent for government to reverse course and re-regulate or revert to public ownership. However, to reverse course could violate a GATS commitment and incur the risk of a trade dispute.

So why take on the added risk of trade conflict by making GATS commitments? The WTO asserts that locking in commitments to liberalize trade will produce a 'win–win–win' (hereafter, just 'win'). With environmental services, the first win is expanded trade in environmental technology at lower cost. The second is better environmental quality due to these goods and services. The third is help for developing countries to deal with environmental challenges of economic growth (WTO, 2007b).

In short, countries can use GATS to advertise their 'lock-in' in hopes of attracting foreign investment. The lock-in makes their long-term policy 'credible'. As the World Bank's analyst put it, 'the freedom to change one's mind can be a nuisance' (Mattoo, 2001). GATS may not force privatization or deregulation, but it does make it difficult to back out of a decision to privatize or deregulate, even if the results are bad.

Subnational authority
Which mayor would volunteer her harbor to be the site of an LNG port? Conversely, at the national level, which president would not like to see more LNG ports, to diversify energy sources? Different levels of government respond to different constituencies.

GATS supporters stress that the agreement allows countries to preserve state or local authority by avoiding sectors that are governed at the subnational level or by limiting commitments regarding subnational measures. GATS critics say that national trade negotiators rarely defer to subnational authorities. They also note that the GATS preamble imparts a federal bias as it recognizes the right to regulate for national, not subnational, objectives (Gould, 2002a; 2002b).

Negotiations on environmental sectors
GATS includes several built-in agendas for ongoing negotiations. The first is for rounds of 'progressive liberalization' to add new sector commitments. Current negotiations began in the year 2000 using a 'request–offer' process. Countries that want to export a service make a 'request', usually on behalf of a particular company. They are requesting another country to respond with an 'offer' to make a GATS commitment. The offer is notice that a country is willing to lock in 'commitments' at the end of negotiations. The commitment is an enforceable promise to follow GATS rules on market access (no quantitative limits) and National Treatment (no discrimination). Negotiations may take place between two countries ('bilateral') or a group of countries ('plurilateral'), but once they lock in, they make the same commitment to all WTO countries. Because of the MFN rule, every nation gets the 'most favorable' treatment (WTO–CTS, 2001).

The European Commission initiated its work on the GATS 2000 negotiations by stating: 'The GATS is not just something that exists between Governments. It is first and

Table 20.1   Environmental sectors

Sector in GATS Schedule	Status in GATS Negotiations			
	Provisional CPC	US Schedule	Commitments in 1995	Plurilateral Requests
Environmental services				
Wastewater management	9401	Commit	29	Environment
Solid/hazardous waste mgmt	9402, 9403	Commit	29	Environment
Ambient air and climate abatement	9404	Commit	27	Environment
Remediation of soil and water	9406	Commit	30	Environment
Noise and vibration abatement	9405	Commit	26	Environment
Biodiversity and landscape	9406	Commit	27	Environment
Other environmental services	9409	Commit	21	Environment
Environmental impact – selected sectors				
Bus servs – incidental to fishing	8820	Commit	33	
Bus servs – incidental to ag/forestry	8811, 8814	Commit	8	
Bus servs – incidental to mining	883, 5115	Commit	20	Energy
Bus servs – incidental to energy dist	na	Commit	8	Energy
Construction/related engineering	8672	Commit	14	
Distribution – agents/elec brokers	62113	*Offer*	21	Distribution
Distribution – retail	632	Commit	33	Distrb, Energy
Distribution – wholesale	622	Commit	34	Dlstrb, Energy
Tourism –guide services	7472	Commit	54	
Tourism – travel agency /tours	7471	Commit	89	
Transport – marine transport	721	No commit	39	Maritime
Transport – pipeline transport	7131	*Offer*	3	
Transport – bulk storage of fuels	7422	*Offer*	37	

foremost an instrument for the benefit of business' (EC, 2000a). Soon after came EC requests for countries to open their environmental markets to multinational corporations.

The WTO describes the response to such requests as 'disappointing'. Yet the service-exporting nations remain ambitious. They seek expanded commitments in as many as 20 environmental sectors. This chapter explores two kinds of sectors. The first is what the GATS classification calls 'Environmental Services', with subsectors that include pollution abatement, wastewater and solid waste. The second includes other sectors with an environmental impact such as energy distribution. Table 20.1 provides an overview of both sets and notes whether the USA has a commitment or a pending offer.[6]

Consider pipeline transport as an example. The subsector is Land Transport Services. By referring to section 7131 of the Commercial Product Classification (CPC), negotiators make clear that a commitment covers pipeline transportation of petroleum and natural gas. This US 'offer' is pending at a time when only three other countries have made commitments, and pipeline transport is not part of the plurilateral request on energy services. In other words, a US commitment would lock in or 'bind' current levels of regulation even though other countries are not reciprocating with commitments in this sector.

The following sections summarize the state of play in several sectors. We start with the WTO's environmental service category, followed by renewable energy as an example of other services that have an environmental impact.

Pollution abatement
The 'win' scenario for pollution and noise abatement predicts that expanded trade in services will support job creation in other sectors where the pollution is being abated. Pollution services mitigate the adverse impact of development. The market for pollution abatement is driven by government regulation (International Trade Commission, 2005a).

Pollution and noise abatement are non-traditional sectors in which private industries serve other private industries. Unlike public services, commitments in this subsector have not sparked a debate about privatization, job loss or higher rates. The US International Trade Commission reports few trade barriers to pollution control services in either developed or developing countries (International Trade Commission, 2005a). In such a new market, the purpose of GATS commitments is not to promote deregulation or privatization; it is to bind the existing level of regulation and constrain future regulation.

The USA is the leader in pollution control, followed by Europe and Japan. The largest export market is China, which already accounts for 15 percent of global demand (USITC, 2005). China limits its commitment on Market Access to allow for joint venture requirements (China, 2002).

In this and the other subsectors under Environmental Services, the USA stops short of a full commitment. The US schedule of commitments redefines each subsector with a narrower list of services where the USA has an export advantage:

> US commitments are limited to the following activities: implementation and installation of new or existing systems for environmental cleanup, remediation, prevention and monitoring; implementation of environmental quality control and pollution reduction services; maintenance and repair of environment-related systems and facilities not already covered by the US commitments on maintenance and repair of equipment; on-site environmental investigation, evaluation, monitoring; sample collection services; training on site or at the facility; consulting related to these areas.

The list avoids committing an entire subsector, which could imply a commitment to privatize public utilities. Privatization is what heated up the debate over traditional utility services, especially water and wastewater.

Water and wastewater
The world's largest private water companies are based in Europe: Suez and Veolia, both French, control two-thirds of global private operations (Thomas and Hall, 2006). In 1999, the European Commission (EC) proposed adding water as a subsector of GATS commitments under Environmental Services. Specifically, the EC proposed changing the original sector called 'Sewerage' to 'Water for human use and wastewater management' (EC, 1999; Joy and Hardstaff, 2003).

The EC, the OECD and the WTO promoted water services as a 'win' strategy. Water treatment is capital intensive. Countries that need water to develop do not have the capital, and Europe's global companies offer economies of scale in financing and technology. The win scenario is that these companies will invest in treatment plants, take a financing burden off of governments, transfer technology to communities, and then transfer ownership back to governments after they recoup their investment (OECD, 2000).

GATS critics seized the EC's water bid to headline a 'Stop GATS' campaign, predicting that privatized companies would cut costs by cutting jobs (Deckwirth, 2006). In developing countries, analysts warned that investors were seeking a legitimate risk premium through profits, but low-income consumers could not pay it. This would put pressure on governments to subsidize the poorest consumers, but they would not be able to do so after signing away their ability to tap the wealthiest consumers for a cross-subsidy (Kessler, 2004).

As the GATS debate was building, the toll of troubled projects to privatize water systems mounted, including Buenos Aires (a Veolia subsidiary), Manila and Atlanta (both Suez subsidiaries). These failures fueled the GATS critics and bore out their predictions (Food and Water Watch, 2003).

On the defensive, the WTO published *GATS Fact and Fiction*, which stated, 'The WTO is not after your water', and then explained that the way to avoid pressure to privatize is to avoid making a GATS commitment (WTO, 2007b). The GATS critics would probably accept that conclusion.

In 2003, US negotiators announced that they would not offer a commitment on drinking water, stating: 'GATS is not the appropriate vehicle for pursuing privatization of U.S. public services' (USTR, 2003).

By 2005, the European water companies were losing their zeal for owning foreign assets, preferring 'public private partnerships' with service contracts (Deckwirth, 2006). After Germany's electric power company RWE acquired ownership of water suppliers in 25 US states through its UK subsidiary, Thames, it sold Thames a few years later (Food and Water Watch, 2006).

The EC eventually tempered its market access request, seeking a full commitment only on services supplied by private industry to private industry. The EC explicitly deferred to any government's preference for providing 'exclusive' service through a contract or reverting to public provision after a contract expires. When governments do purchase services, the EC asked for national treatment (no discrimination) (EC, 2005).

The US offer on wastewater is not so explicit. To avoid the privatization debate, US negotiators covered a list of services that is less than the full bundle that public utilities provide. They also limited coverage to services 'contracted by private industry'. US negotiators said their intent was to liberalize the market for services that are purchased by industry while leaving the public sector free to choose its own path (USTR, 2003). However, the US schedule does not say, '*purchased* by industry', and the 'contracted by industry' language is ambiguous.

Black's *Law Dictionary* (2004) defines a 'contractor' as a supplier. So when government purchases a wastewater service from private industry, the service is arguably 'contracted by' private industry. The US list of services includes some that private industry supplies to public utilities, notably maintenance of facilities and onsite monitoring.

GATS Article XIII(a) states that market access commitments do not cover government purchasing so long as it is 'not with a view to use in the supply of services for commercial sale'. But that is what public utilities often do; they buy services from various contractors to supply the ultimate consumer for a user fee.

Negotiators from the USA, the EC and Australia have acknowledged that services 'contracted by' public utilities could well be covered by GATS. In a joint statement, they openly ask how a market access commitment would apply to the range of contracting formats (Australia et al., 2005). The formats include (1) concessions to operate a utility, (2) 'public–private partnerships' to operate certain facilities, and (3) contracts to support specific functions such as maintenance within a utility. In each of these formats, the private contractor is a single supplier.

The EC request resolved this conflict by explicitly not asking for market access commitments for government purchasing. The EC asked only for national treatment commitments. The US schedule retained a market access commitment based on an interpretation that services purchased by public utilities are not covered by GATS. If US negotiators were wrong and the EC was right, then a public–private contract that triggers coverage under the US commitment would violate market access rules. That is because it sets up a single service supplier. Perhaps the reason that US negotiators do not want to adopt the EC's clarification is that doing so would signal similar issues with parts of the US schedule outside of Environmental Services. Energy distribution and health facilities come to mind.

The GATS issues in wastewater also arise in solid and hazardous waste, but the environmental impact of GATS could be greater on solid waste.

Solid waste

Like the water industry, the waste industry is capital intensive and dominated by multinational firms (WTO, 1998). The 'win' scenario for solid waste promises greater access to the cleanest technology to burn, contain or recycle waste; reduced costs; and the ability to co-generate heat or power for industries and communities (OECD, 2000; International Trade Commission, 2004).

The controversy in this sector is about burning, as illustrated by the case of Ebara, a Japanese firm. Ebara promoted a state-of-the-art incinerator in Malaysia as environmentally friendly. But the environmental critique was stiff: opponents charged that the facility would destroy tropical rainforest, harm a water catchment area for two million people, and emit four persistent organic pollutants (POPs) that Japan has promised to eliminate under the Stockholm Convention on POPs (International POPs, 2005). Environmental advocates are critical of perverse incentives in this industry; massive investment in incinerators generates demand for waste to incinerate, and operators become less likely to pursue recycling or ways to avoid waste (Reichert, 2006).

The challenge of waste management is to get the optimal mix of technologies and conservation systems to meet unique local needs. A country might seek balance by licensing some incinerators while limiting their total number. But such a limit on the number of suppliers or operations would violate a country's commitment under GATS market access rules. Once the door is opened to private operators or contractors, then any attempt to limit the number of incinerators or operators could be challenged.

In the USA, there are approximately 140 commercially operated waste incinerators, 22 of which burn hazardous waste (EPA, 1996; 1999). The US commitment on solid waste covers the services 'contracted by private industry' within the list quoted above, for example, maintenance and monitoring.

Similar concerns have been raised in other sectors such as services incidental to mining, oil extraction, pipeline transportation or distribution of natural resources. GATS will permit limits on inputs (e.g. a volume of water or other resource being extracted), but not on the number of service suppliers or service operations (e.g. incinerators, wells or pipelines) (Waskow, 2003).

Hazardous waste

Hazardous waste management is covered by the same GATS subsector as solid waste, so the same issues arise with respect to coverage. Coverage of hazardous waste sets up a potential conflict with measures that implement the Basel Convention, an agreement that regulates international handling of hazardous waste, including a ban on transport to countries that are not party to the convention (Basel Convention, arts IV and XI).

The Basel Convention formally discriminates between nations based on their treaty status and their domestic regulations. Such least-favored treatment is not consistent with MFN under GATS, which is a general obligation that does not require a sector commitment in order to be effective. This kind of conflict between a WTO agreement and a multilateral environmental agreement (MEA) is the subject of negotiations in the WTO's Committee on Trade and Environment. The Basel conflict is on the agenda, but negotiations are still at an early stage (WTO–CTE, 2007).

One way to implement the Basel Convention is simply to ban all imports and exports of hazardous waste in order to avoid discriminatory effect. While that would avoid the MFN issue under GATS, a ban could be challenged as a 'zero quota', which arguably violates the US commitment on MA (WTO–*US – Gambling Services*, 2005; Pauwelyn, 2005). Countries could avoid this kind of treaty conflict by limiting their GATS commitments to not cover Basel measures.

GATS requires countries that want to limit or withdraw a commitment to compensate other countries by offering to commit additional sectors (GATS art. XXI).[7] Limiting is less expensive than withdrawing a commitment, but neither is likely. US negotiators value their GATS commitments as an 'offense' tool to press other countries for access to their service markets. In their view, introducing new defensive limits on commitments invites back-sliding by other countries.

That said, the recent internet gambling case presents one scenario in which the USA might limit a GATS commitment: if it loses a trade dispute. Losing a trade dispute creates an external threat of sanctions, and the WTO becomes the villain. Since most trade rules are inherently vague, US trade officials can criticize a WTO dispute they lose as flawed logic. A search of the USTR's website shows 317 documents that criticize an interpretation as 'deeply flawed' (USTR, 2007c).

Environmental impact – focus on electricity

Renewable energy offers a strong 'win' scenario. Expanded trade (transmission, distribution, incidental services) can connect consumers to renewable sources of electricity that are distant, sometimes across borders. By reducing dependence on coal, renewable energy can dramatically cut pollution, acid rain and greenhouse gas emissions. Now a small part of the energy economy (2 percent global share in 2002), renewables offer a way to avoid the environmental consequences of burning coal, and they create diversified jobs. Like pollution abatement, it is a market driven by government regulation and commitments under international environmental agreements (ITC, 2005b).

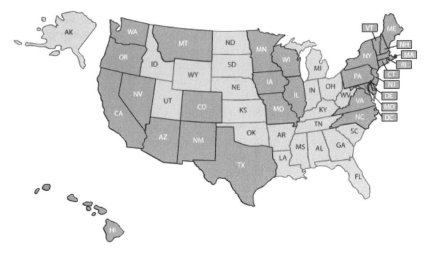

Source: DOE/EERE.

Figure 20.2   States with RPS (in dark grey), June 2007

'Renewable energy' is not a GATS sector, *per se*, and generation of electricity is not likely covered by GATS because it is seen as production of a good. However, the USA is fully committed under 'Services incidental to energy distribution' (USA, 2005, modes 1, 2, 3). In addition to local distribution of electricity, this commitment covers transmission in commercial markets (WTO, 2007a; USA, 2000).

Twenty-eight states (see Figure 20.2) have developed Renewable Portfolio Standards (RPS) as a way to stimulate development of renewable sources. RPS obligates distributors to purchase a minimum and growing percentage of their electricity from renewable sources, including wind, solar, geothermal, biomass and small-scale hydro (less than 30 MW) (DOE/EERE, 2007). RPS governs purchases by retail distributors (among others), so it is likely covered by the US commitment.

The US International Trade Commission reports few barriers to trade in renewable energy services, but the ITC did not study hydroelectric generation or transmission. Canada is eager to offer both: vast hydro capacity and a transmission grid that reaches the northern tier of US cities.

Ninety-six percent of Canada's electricity comes from large dams (greater than 30 MW), which RPS rejects as non-renewable. Large dams block salmon migration, cause sedimentation and concentrate toxins. However, Canadians think that the impact on Canadian rivers is their issue to manage. Canada's trade ministry argues that state RPS laws discriminate: they deny national treatment under NAFTA and GATT, which cover electricity as a good (DFAIT, 2007).

Several analysts reason that RPS does not flunk the national treatment test for two reasons. First, they argue that renewable electricity is not a 'like product' that can be compared to non-renewable electricity, but this interpretation has yet to be tested before the WTO. Second, under GATT, a violation of national treatment could be excused by GATT's general exception for resource conservation. The WTO's Appellate Body recognizes that protecting the atmosphere is a legitimate use of the GATT exception (Hempling and Rader, 2002).

GATS has no such general exception. Hence some analysts anticipate that claims that would fail under GATT might succeed under GATS (Waskow, 2003). That might explain the efforts of US market leaders, Enron and Halliburton, when GATS negotiations started in the year 2000. They organized a WTO Energy Services Coalition, and within a few months, US negotiators published a proposal for GATS commitments including wholesale energy trade, services incidental to transmission, and energy brokering.

The EC responded with a nearly identical proposal. The EC and US proposals on electricity alarmed state regulators. The proposals were similar to market integration policies that the Federal Energy Regulatory Commission (FERC) had advanced, which were policies that the states had successfully resisted. On this very point, a group of state officials met several times with US negotiators. They explained how commitments on wholesale trade and transmission services could shrink the policy space that Congress had preserved for states to adopt RPS policies and decide their own course on deregulation (State and Local Working Group, 2005).

In the midst of these negotiations, California's deregulation experiment failed, Enron collapsed, and energy traders were caught trying to manipulate supply and prices. Not surprisingly, only a handful of countries (besides the EU) showed interest in GATS energy commitments. As of May 2005, US negotiators refrained from commitments on wholesale trade and transmission services, limiting their offer to 'electricity brokering'.

To defenders of state initiatives such as RPS, moving from a broad GATS commitment on wholesale trade to a narrower one on brokering was progress. Yet the prospect of GATS coverage remains. One test is whether RPS affects 'brokering' (WTO–US – Gambling Services, 2005). This can be argued either way. The argument that GATS does not cover RPS is that RPS stimulates buyers and sellers, but brokering is neutral: it is merely a transactional service. The argument that GATS does cover RPS is that RPS creates the market for matching renewable buyers with renewable sources. How can RPS *not* affect brokering?

It can also be argued that electricity brokering is already covered by the US commitment on 'exchange agent' services. If so, the issue is whether the existing commitment should be limited. Either way, insertion of electricity brokering into the US schedule could preserve Enron's original proposal to cover electricity trading. This includes not only RPS, but a range of regulatory issues that 'brokering' could describe, including energy transactions, futures contracts and even the computerized trading systems that have replaced human brokers.

A commitment that covers future energy markets could apply to more than questions about market access (e.g. should monopolies be unbundled?) and National Treatment (e.g. should RPS include large-scale hydro?). A commitment could also trigger new disciplines on domestic regulation, which are part of the GATS built-in agenda.

Negotiations on domestic regulation

The built-in agenda for negotiating new rules under GATS has broad implications for environmental policy. On subsidies, new rules could help control unsustainable fishing, but they could also impede subsidies to build infrastructure for renewable fuels. On procurement, new rules could speed up or slow down markets for 'environmental goods'.

While important in the long run, the negotiations on subsidies and procurement are far from producing results. Meanwhile, a third forum has advanced through several drafts of a complete text of new GATS 'disciplines' on domestic regulation.

Article VI:4 of GATS authorizes the WTO's Council on Trade in Services to adopt disciplines that the WTO's staff describes as a yellow light for the right to regulate, specifically for regulations that are not discriminatory (WTO, 2006; Gould, 2008). Article VI implies that the disciplines could apply to government measures in all sectors. However, the Working Party on Domestic Regulation (WPDR) reached a consensus on applying any new disciplines only in sectors where countries have commitments under Market Access or National Treatment (WTO–WPDR, 2007).

After six years of plodding negotiations, the chairman of the WPDR pushed through several drafts in an effort to forge a consensus between two opposing camps. The demandeurs are led by big-island economies that are the most trade-dependent. Australia, Hong Kong, New Zealand and others want strong disciplines including 'necessity' tests. The Appellate Body has interpreted 'necessary' to mean that measures must be least trade-restrictive, or as applied to service suppliers, least burdensome (WTO–*US – Gambling Services*, 2005; WTO–*Korea – Various Measures on Beef*, 2000).

A necessity test would reverse the constitutional deference that US courts give to economic regulations. So long as they are not discriminatory, regulations in the USA need only be rational, almost the opposite of 'necessary' (Supreme Court, 1985). With encouragement from state and local governments, US negotiators have opposed necessity tests and held to the position that the only disciplines that are necessary at this time are those that promote transparency (USTR, 2007e).

At the outset, developing countries championed tough disciplines as a way to push back against developed countries. But within a few years, developing countries were redefining their self-interest to preserve policy space to regulate complex service industries (Tayob, 2006). This puts Brazil, the Philippines, the Africa Group, Venezuela and Cuba on roughly the same side of the argument with the USA, an awkward alliance for some (Kwa, 2006).

In early 2006, the WPDR chairman started presenting a series of draft disciplines that included necessity tests. US negotiators responded by restating their opposition to 'operational necessity tests'. As an alternative to 'ensuring that measures are necessary', US negotiators stated their willingness to support a more balanced purpose of recognizing the right to regulate so long as it is not used to avoid trade obligations (USTR, 2007d).[8]

In later drafts, the chairman dropped the necessity test. Yet what remains are more than 40 other disciplines that would cover laws that neither discriminate (covered by national treatment) nor set quantitative limits (covered by market access). Examples include disciplines (WTO–WPDR, 2008) that require regulations to be:

- pre-established (para. 11);
- relevant to the supply of services to which they apply (para. 11);
- based on objective criteria (para. 11); and
- as simple as possible (para. 18).

Pre-establishment test   In the USA, courts presume that legislation has a prospective effect. Yet environmental licenses do not grant rights to operate a service or use resources until a decision is final. It is constitutional to change licensing criteria up to the point that a license is granted (Woolhandler, 2006; Prebble et al., 2006). After a license is granted, domestic law permits government to change technical standards for ongoing operations. Under this discipline, applicants for a license could argue that licensing requirements are not pre-established:

- when regulators change requirements while a license is pending (before it is granted);
- when regulators impose conditions on a license at the end of the process; and
- when license requirements change before renewal of an existing license.

Relevance test   By linking relevance to services, this discipline could be interpreted to limit regulation based on environmental impacts that are external to the service. For example, states issue coastal development permits based on criteria including environmental protection, recreational access, historic values and scenic vistas – all of which are external to the development (e.g. a desalination facility, a utility plant or an LNG terminal). Arguably, scenic vistas are not relevant to the service of supplying natural gas.

Objectivity test   A likely definition of 'objective' is 'not subjective'. In the USA, legislatures delegate to public utility commissions broad plenary power to apply subjective standards such as serving the 'public interest' or achieving 'just and reasonable' rates. A working group of state and local officials explained that:

> On the surface, objectivity is a desirable goal. To raise objectivity to the level of an international obligation, however, undermines the ability of domestic regulators to deal with the inherent complexity of service industries. An international objectivity test moves in the direction of standardized and technocratic regulation and away from regulation in the public interest by legislatures and utility commissions that are accountable for balancing diverse public interests. (State and Local Working Group, 2006).

Balancing diverse public interests may well be the kind of subjective judgment that the WTO negotiators seek to prohibit.

Simplicity test   International suppliers other than BHT Billiton complain that the LNG regulatory process is complex and burdensome (Hanson, 2007). In addition, some states enable the public to vote on the desirability of a project that could affect safety, property values, or the environment (NARUC, 2005). In short, environmental regulations could flunk a test that regulations must be as simple as possible.

These proposals could be described as 'best practices' for government. But there is a reason that the US Congress has not imposed such disciplines on federal agencies or the states. Each proposed GATS discipline creates a spectrum of potential meanings – a degree of relevance, timeliness, objectivity or simplicity – that on one extreme would curtail the scope of government authority in ways that the Constitution does not. To illustrate, consider how a relevance test might apply to requirements for a coastal development permit for an LNG port.

On the left end (most relevant) of a relevance spectrum (see Figure 20.3) are license requirements that are intrinsic to the supply of a service (e.g. storage capacity). On the

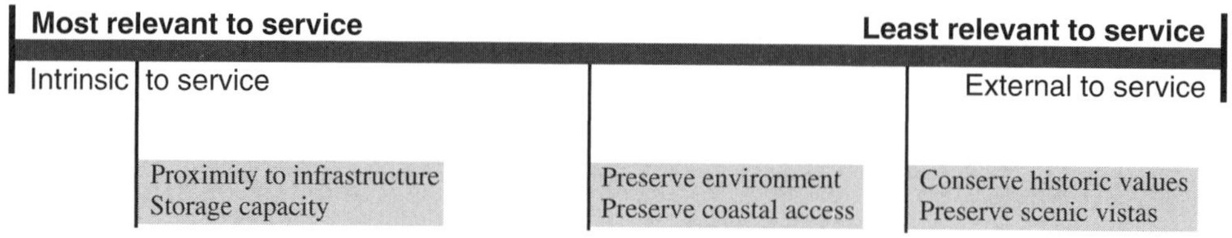

Most relevant to service		Least relevant to service
Intrinsic to service		External to service
Proximity to infrastructure Storage capacity	Preserve environment Preserve coastal access	Conserve historic values Preserve scenic vistas

Figure 20.3   *Relevance test applied to licensing requirements for coastal development of*
  LNG port

right end (least relevant) are requirements that relate to external impacts (e.g. preserving scenic vistas) and not the service, *per se*. If the purpose of this discipline is to 'ensure that . . . measures are necessary to ensure the quality of the service', which is permanent language in GATS Article VI:4, dispute panels could reject requirements that are not intrinsic to the service.

As with 'necessity', one end of the spectrum would require measures to be least burdensome, while the other end would tolerate measures that are more burdensome. Negotiators avoid resolving their differences on this spectrum by creating vagueness or ambiguity in the text, which kicks the real interpretation into the future, into the hands of WTO dispute panels. However, a discipline such as 'relevance' need not be so vague. Negotiators could define relevance to include external impacts as well as inherent quality of a service.

Conclusion

Since GATS became effective in 1995, its coverage has been interpreted by the WTO to overlap with GATT with respect to distribution of goods. Trade disputes that would fail due to GATT's exception for conservation of resources could be brought under GATS, which has a much more limited provision on environmental inputs.

GATS rules on market access have been interpreted by the WTO to prohibit not only limits on service suppliers, but also 'zero quotas' or bans. For example, GATS could prohibit limits on the number of incinerators or other service operations.

GATS negotiations on sectors have been controversial. After an international campaign to 'Stop GATS', the European Commission withdrew its proposal on water services. The EC still seeks commitments on infrastructure services that are purchased by public utilities from private industry, while the US position on public–private contracting is ambiguous. The USA is proposing energy commitments that would cover LNG facilities and electricity brokering. With one major exception, gambling, US negotiators have resisted proposals to limit such commitments so as to safeguard domestic regulation.

GATS negotiations on domestic regulation have received little public attention. But proposals being debated could constrain environmental regulation through relevance tests, objectivity tests, pre-establishment tests and simplicity tests. GATS is evolving to regulate the regulators of the service economy.

As its influence expands, GATS is attracting scrutiny from subnational officials, environmental advocates and developing nations. They all seek to balance the 'offense' trade agenda with a 'defense' governing agenda. In the words of the South Centre, 'Setting regulatory parameters based on foreign values or best practices ignores the unique historic, cultural, political and other important characteristics that shape the type of governance that is successful for a country' (South Centre, 2006).

The service economy is becoming a network of global companies. GATS is the framework for opening their markets, while constraining the authority of government to regulate, purchase, provide or subsidize services. Providing that framework for governance is also the function of national constitutions. They now have competition from GATS.

Notes

1. GATS Article I, Scope and Definition, states:

    1. This Agreement applies to measures by Members affecting trade in services.
    2. For the purposes of this Agreement, trade in services is defined as the supply of a service:

        (a) from the territory of one Member into the territory of any other Member;
        (b) in the territory of one Member to the service consumer of any other Member;
        (c) by a service supplier of one Member, through commercial presence in the territory of any other Member;
        (d) by a service supplier of one Member, through presence of natural persons of a Member in the territory of any other Member.

    3. For the purposes of this Agreement:

        (a) 'measures by Members' means measures taken by:

            (i) central, regional or local governments and authorities; and
            (ii) non-governmental bodies in the exercise of powers delegated by central, regional or local governments or authorities;
            In fulfilling its obligations and commitments under the Agreement, each Member shall take such reasonable measures as may be available to it to ensure their observance by regional and local governments and authorities and non-governmental bodies within its territory;

        (b) 'services' includes any service in any sector except services supplied in the exercise of governmental authority;
        (c) 'a service supplied in the exercise of governmental authority' means any service which is supplied neither on a commercial basis, nor in competition with one or more service suppliers.

2. Commitments are finely tuned, not just within subsectors, but with separate commitments to National Treatment and Market Access, which are made specifically for each of four modes of supplying a service (GATS art. I:2):

    ● Mode 1 is cross-border services.
    ● Mode 2 is tourism and other services supplied to consumers who cross the border.
    ● Mode 3 is commercial presence, including investment and subsidiary companies.
    ● Mode 4 is movement of natural persons who cross the border to deliver a service.

3. GATS Article II:1, MFN treatment, states:

    1. With respect to any measure covered by this Agreement, each Member shall accord immediately and unconditionally to services and service suppliers of any other Member treatment no less favourable than that it accords to like services and service suppliers of any other country.

    Article II allows countries to schedule exceptions to MFN treatment, but they must negotiate any new exceptions with other countries (GATS Art. II:2, Annex on Article II Exemptions).

4. GATS Article XVII, NT, states:

    1. In the sectors inscribed in its Schedule, and subject to any conditions and qualifications set out therein, each Member shall accord to services and service suppliers of any other Member, in respect of all

measures affecting the supply of services, treatment no less favourable than that it accords to its own like services and service suppliers.

2. A Member may meet the requirement of paragraph 1 by according to services and service suppliers of any other Member, either formally identical treatment or formally different treatment to that it accords to its own like services and service suppliers.

3. Formally identical or formally different treatment shall be considered to be less favourable if it modifies the conditions of competition in favour of services or service suppliers of the Member compared to like services or service suppliers of any other Member.

5. GATS Article XVI, MA, states:

1. With respect to market access through the modes of supply identified in Article I, each Member shall accord services and service suppliers of any other Member treatment no less favourable than that provided for under the terms, limitations and conditions agreed and specified in its Schedule. [Fn 8 omitted]

2. In sectors where market-access commitments are undertaken, the measures which a Member shall not maintain or adopt either on the basis of a regional subdivision or on the basis of its entire territory, unless otherwise specified in its Schedule, are defined as:

    (a) limitations on the number of service suppliers whether in the form of numerical quotas, monopolies, exclusive service suppliers or the requirements of an economic needs test;
    (b) limitations on the total value of service transactions or assets in the form of numerical quotas or the requirement of an economic needs test;
    (c) limitations on the total number of service operations or on the total quantity of service output expressed in terms of designated numerical units in the form of quotas or the requirement of an economic needs test; [Fn 9: Subparagraph 2(c) does not cover measures of a Member which limit inputs for the supply of services.]
    (d) limitations on the total number of natural persons that may be employed in a particular service sector or that a service supplier may employ and who are necessary for, and directly related to, the supply of a specific service in the form of numerical quotas or the requirement of an economic needs test;
    (e) measures which restrict or require specific types of legal entity or joint venture through which a service supplier may supply a service; and
    (f) limitations on the participation of foreign capital in terms of maximum percentage limit on foreign shareholding or the total value of individual or aggregate foreign investment.

6. This table is based on the following sources:

1. Provisional CPC sections are from the UN's Commercial Product Classification – Provisional, available at http://unstats.un.org/unsd/cr/registry/regcst.asp?Cl=9&Lg=1, viewed 18 September 2007.

2. US Schedule is from USA (2005). A user-friendly alternative to reading the US Schedule has been composed by Ellen Gould and Mary Battari; it is *Public Citizens' GATS Directory*, an automated directory of GATS sectors, commitments and links to UN classification codes. It is available at http://www.citizen.org/trade/forms/gats_search.cfm, viewed 18 September 2007.

3. Commitments in 1995 for Environmental Services: WTO Secretariat, Council for Trade in Services, Background Note, Environmental Services, World Trade Organization, Doc. No. S/C/W/46 (6 July, 1998), pp 26–7.

4. Commitments in 1995 for Environmental Impact: (a) Fishing is from Agritrade, Liberalization of 'Services Incidental to Fishing' could damage fishing communities, April 2007; (b) Forestry is from WTO, Predefined Report, Developed Countries, Services Incidental to Agriculture, Fishing or Forestry; (c) Mining is from US International Trade Commission, Oil and Gas Field Services: Impediments to Trade and Prospects for Liberalization, Investigation No. 332–444, USITC Publication 3582, March 2003, c. 5, p. 5; (d) Energy is from WTO Secretariat, Council for Trade in Services, Background Note, Energy Services, World Trade Organization, Doc. No. S/C/W/52 (9 September 1998), p. 28; (e) Construction is from WTO Secretariat, Council for Trade in Services, Background Note, Construction and Related Engineering Services, World Trade Organization, Doc. No. S/C/W/38 (8 June 1998), p. 10; (f) Distribution is from WTO Secretariat, Council for Trade in Services, Background Note, Distribution Services, World Trade Organization, Doc. No. S/C/W/37 (10 June 1998), p. 28; (g) Tourism is from Secretariat, Council for Trade in Services, Background Note, Tourism Services, World Trade Organization, Doc. No. S/C/W/51 (23 September 1998), pp. 23–4; (h) Maritime transport is from WTO Secretariat, Council for Trade in Services, Background Note, Maritime Transport Services, World Trade Organization, Doc. No. S/C/W/62 (16 November 1998), pp. 11–16; (i) Pipeline transport is from WTO

Secretariat, Council for Trade in Services, Background Note, Energy Services, World Trade Organization, Doc. No. S/C/W/52 (9 September 1998), p. 29; (j) Bulk storage is from WTO Secretariat, Council for Trade in Services, Background Note, Land Transport Services: Part I – Generalities and Road Transport, World Trade Organization, Doc. No. S/C/W/60 (28 October 1998), p. 23.

5. Plurilateral requests: (a) Environment is from EC, Plurilateral Request – Environmental Services (undated 2006); (b) Distribution is from EC, Collective Request on Distribution Services (undated 2006); (b) Energy is from EC, Collective Request in Energy Services (undated 2006); (d) Maritime is from Japan Ministry of of Land, Infrastructure and Transport, Collective request for Marine Transport Services (undated 2006).

7. The first use of this process to withdraw a commitment was when the EU accepted 13 new countries in 1995 and 2004, some of which did not want to conform their public services to the EU's GATS commitments (EC, 2007). The second was when the USA announced that it would withdraw its commitment that covers gambling services (USTR, 2007d).

8. The excerpt of the US statement on necessity tests and the purpose of disciplines is:

> The United States does not support any type of operational necessity test or standard in any new disciplines for domestic regulation. However, we share the concerns raised by many Members that the right to regulate should not be used in practice to avoid trade obligations. In that regard, we remain open to discussing non-operational language in the preamble, expressing that Members' objective in developing any new disciplines is to establish that principle. (USTR, 2007b)

References

Australia et al. (2005), 'Communication from Australia, the European Communities, Japan, New Zealand, the Separate Customs Territory of Taiwan, Penghu, Kinmen and Matsu and the United States', TN/S/W/28, 11 February.

Australia et al. (2006), 'Communication from Australia; Chile; Hong Kong, China; Korea; New Zealand and the Separate Customs Territory of Taiwan, Penghu, Kinmen and Matsu', *Article VI:4 Disciplines – Proposal for Draft Text*, JOB(06)/193, 19 June.

Basel Convention on the Control of Transboundary Movements of Hazardous Wastes and their Disposal, 22 March 1989.

Bureau of Mines (1946), *Report on the Investigation of the Fire at the Liquefication, Storage and Gasification Plant of the East Ohio Gas Company, Cleveland, Ohio, January 20, 1944* cited in Michelle Michot Foss (2004), 'Introduction to LNG', Center for Energy Economics, February, available at www.beg.utexas.edu/energyecon/lng/documents/CEE_INTRODUCTION_TO_LNG_FINAL.pdf, viewed 16 September 2007.

China, People's Republic (2002), Schedule of Specific Commitments, GATS/SC/135, 14 February 2002, available at http://www.wto.org/english/tratop_e/serv_e/serv_commitments_e.htm, viewed 18 September 2007.

California Coastal Commission (2005), *Seawater Desalination and the California Coastal Act*, March 2004, http://www.coastal.ca.gov/pubs.html, viewed 18 September 2007.

Deckwirth (2006), 'GATS and Water', Corporate Europe Observatory Briefing, 26 May, available at http://www.tradeobservatory.org/search.cfm, viewed 18 September 2007.

Department of Energy, Energy Efficiency and Renewable Energy, States with Renewable Portfolio Standards (June 2007), available at http://www.eere.energy.gov/states/maps/renewable_portfolio_states.cfm, viewed 18 September 2007.

Department of Foreign Affairs and International Trade (2007), 'Canada's International Market Access Report – Renewable Energy', 1 June available at http://w01.international.gc.ca/CIMAP/FicheDetail.aspx?Fiche_ID =1333, viewed 18 September, 2007.

Energy Information Agency (2007), 'LNG exporters', available at http://www.eia.doe.gov/oiaf/analysispaper/global/exporters.html, viewed 16 September 2007.

Environmental Protection Agency (1996), Technical Support Document for HWC MACT Standards, Volume I, Description of Source Categories, February, available at http://www.epa.gov/combustion/cmbust.htm, viewed 18 September 2007.

Environmental Protection Agency (1999), Fact Sheet, Proposed Rules for Commercial and Industrial Solid Waste Incineration Units, December, available at http://www.epa.gov/ttn/oarpg/t1/fact_sheets/propfact.pdf, viewed 18 September 2007.

European Commission (1999), Communication from the European Communities and their Member States – Classification Issues in the Environmental Sector, S/CSC/W/25, 28 September, available at http://docsonline.wto.org/gen_search.asp?searchmode=simple (search document symbol, viewed 18 September 2007).

European Commission (2000a), Opening World Markets for Services – Towards GATS 2000, European

Commission website (no longer loaded); quoted in Corporate Europe Observatory (2001), 'GATS: undermining public services worldwide', *CEO Observer*, Issue 9 (June 2001), available at http://www.corporateurope.org/observer 9/gats.html, viewed 18 September 2007.

European Commission (2005), Summary of the EC's Revised Requests to Third Countries in the Services Negotiations under the DDA, Brussels, 24 January, available at http://trade.ec.europa.eu/doclib/html/121197. htm, viewed 18 September 2007.

European Commission (2007), Bulletin EU 3–2007, Common commercial policy (2/5), World trade organization 1.29.2, available at http://europa.eu/bulletin/en/200703/p 129002.htm, viewed 18 September, 2007.

Federal Energy Regulatory Commission (2007), Existing and Proposed North American LNG Terminals, 6 August, available at http://www.ferc.gov/industries/lng.asp, viewed 18 September 2007.

Feinstein, Dianne (2005), Remarks on Senate Amendment 841, Energy Policy Act of 2005, 151 Cong. Rec. S6980-04, 22 June.

Food and Water Watch (2003), *Water Privatization Fiascos: Broken Promises and Social Turmoil*, available at http://www.foodandwaterwatch.org/water/pubs/reports/fiascoes, viewed 18 September 2007.

Food and Water Watch (2006), *The Future of American Water*, available at http://www.foodandwaterwatch.org/ water/pubs/reports/american-water, viewed 18 September 2007.

Foss, Michelle Michot (2004), 'Introduction to LNG', Center for Energy Economics, available at www.beg.utexas.edu/energyecon/lng/documents/CEE_INTRODUCTION_TO_LNG_FINAL.pdf, viewed 16 September 2007.

Gould, Ellen (2002a), 'The good and the bad news for local governments', 28 May, available at http://www.tradeobservatory.org/library.cfm?RefID=25526 , viewed 18 September 2007.

Gould, Ellen (2002b), 'TACD Background paper on Trade in Services', Transatlantic Consumer Dialogue (October), 1, available at http://www.tacd.org/cgi-bin/db.cgi?page=view&config=admin/docs.cfg&id=190, viewed 18 September 2007.

Gould, Ellen (2008), 'Developments in the GATS Domestic Regulation Negotiations', (Canadian Centre for Policy Alternatives, 14 February).

Hanson, Christopher (2007), 'Sound Energy Solutions decries decision to kill LNG report as bad precedent', Press-Telegram, 9 February.

Hempling, Scott and Nancy Rader (2002), Comments of the Union of Concerned Scientists to the Commission for Environmental Cooperation in response to its 'NAFTA Provisions and the Electricity Sector' Background Paper to its 22 October 2001, Working Paper entitled 'Environmental challenges and opportunities of the evolving North American electricity market', available at http://www.hemplinglaw.com/topics/ucs_nafta.pdf, viewed 18 September 2007.

International POPs Elimination Project (2005), Consumer Report on the Broga Incinerator Project – A Contribution to the Public Debate on the Use of Incineration for Managing Municipal Discards in Malaysia, available at http://www.ipen.org/ipepweb1/library/ipep_pdf_reports/2mal%20malaysia%20broga% 20incinerator%20project.pdf, viewed 18 September 2007.

International Trade Commission (2004), 'Solid and hazardous waste services: an examination of U.S. and foreign markets', Investigation No. 332–455, Publication 3679, April, available at http://hotdocs.usitc. gov/docs/pubs/332/PUB3679.pdf, viewed 18 September 2007.

International Trade Commission (2005a), 'Air and noise pollution abatement services: an examination of U.S. and foreign markets', Investigation No. 332–461, Publication 3761, April, available at http://www.usitc.gov/ publications/abstract_3761.htm, viewed 18 September, 2007.

International Trade Commission (2005b), 'Renewable energy services: an examination of U.S. and foreign markets', Investigation No. 332–462, Publication 3805, October, available at http://www.usitc.gov/publications/pub3805. pdf, viewed 18 September 2007.

Joy, Clare and Peter Hardstaff (2003), 'Whose development agenda? An analysis of the European Union's GATS requests of developing countries', April, available at http://www.wdm.org.uk/resources/reports/trade/index. htm, viewed 18 September 2007.

Kessler, Tim (2004), 'The pros and cons of private provision of water and electricity service: a handbook for evaluating rationales', Citizens' Network on Essential Services, January, available at http://www.servicesforall.org/html/Services/Privatization%20Issues%20Module1.pdf, viewed 18 September 2007.

Kwa, Aileen (2006), 'Analysis and update on the agriculture, NAMA and services negotiations', *Focus on the Global South*, 8 December.

Mattoo, Aaditya (2001), 'Shaping future GATS rules for trade in services', Policy Research Working Paper 2596; World Bank, Development Research Group; available at http://www-wds.worldbank.org/external/ default/WDSContentServer/WDSP/IB/2001/06/08/000094946_01052404350414/Rendered/PDF/multi0page. pdf, viewed 18 September 2007.

Menotti, Victor (2006), *The Other Oil War: Halliburton's Agenda at the WTO*, A policy brief on the energy services negotiations at the WTO, International Forum on Globalization, June, available at http://www. ifg.org/reports/WTO-energy-services.htm, viewed 18 September.

Mobile Register (2004), 'More bodies found at LNG blast scene', *Mobile Register*, 21 January, available at http://www.al.com/news/mobileregister/, viewed 18 September.

NARUC (2005), 'The need for effective and forthright communication planning for LNG facility siting: a checklist for state public utility commissions', 7, http://www.naruc.org/displaycommon.cfm?an=1&subarticlenbr=313, viewed 18 September 2007.

OECD (2000), Trade and Environment Directorates, Joint Working Party on Trade and Environment, *Environmental Services: The 'Win–Win' Role of Trade Liberalisation in Promoting Environmental Protection and Economic Development*, OECD Doc. COM/TD/ENV(99)93/FINAL(Sep. 2000).

Pauwelyn, Joost (2005), 'Rien ne va plus? Distinguishing domestic regulation from market access in GATT and GATS', Duke Law School Legal Studies Paper No. 85, *World Trade Review*, **4** (2), 131–70, available at http://ssrn.com/abstract=638303, viewed 18 September 2007.

Prebble, John, Rebecca Prebble and Catherine Vidler Smith (2006), 'Retrospective legislation: reliance, the public interest, principles of interpretation and the special case of anti-avoidance legislation, 22 *New Zealand Universities Law Review* 271.

Reichert, Tobias (2006), 'Turning pollution into money – environmental services and GATS', Institute for Agriculture and Trade Policy, 23 June, available at http://www.iatp.org/iatp/search.cfm, viewed 18 September 2007.

Reynolds, Mark (2004), 'Lloyd's executive likens LNG attack to nuclear explosion', *Providence Journal*, available at http://www.projo.com/massachusetts/content/projo_20040921_ma21lng.134600.html, viewed 18 September 2007.

Schwarzenegger, Arnold (2007), letter to Maritime Administrator, 18 May, available at http://epa.gov/region09/liq-natl-gas/index.html, viewed 18 September 2007.

Sinclair, Scott (2000), 'GATS: how the World Trade Organization's new 'services' negotiations threaten democracy', Ottawa: Canadian Centre for Policy Alternatives.

Sinclair, Scott and Jim Greishaber-Otto (2002), *Facing the Facts: A Guide to the Gats Debate*, Ottawa: Canadian Centre for Policy Alternatives.

South Centre (2006), *The Development Dimension of the GATS Domestic Regulation Negotiations*, Analytical Note, SC/AN/TDP/SV/11(August 2006), available at http://www.southcentre.org/publications/publist_issue_area_TradeInServices_index.htm, viewed 18 September 2007.

State and Local Working Group on Energy and Trade Policy (2005), *GATS & Electricity*, National Association of State Legislatures, 15 April.

Supreme Court of the United States (1985), *City of Cleburne v. Cleburne Living Center*, 473 U.S. 432, 440.

Tayob, Riaz (2006), 'Developing countries voice opposition to "necessity test" in GATS', Geneva, 21 November, in TWN Info Service on WTO and Trade Issues (3 December 2006), available via search at http://www.twn.org/, viewed 18 September 2007.

Thomas, Stephen and David Hall (2006), 'GATS and the electricity and water sectors', Public Services International Research Unit (PSIRU), March, available at http://www.pisru.org, viewed 18 September 2007.

United States (2000), *Classification of Energy Services*, 7, 18 May (S/C/W/27).

USA (2005), Revised Services Offer, TN/S/O/USA/Rev.1.

USTR (2003), *'Initial US services offer to the WTO: free trade in services'*, available at http://www.ustr.gov/Trade_Sectors/Services/2003_US_Services_Offer/Section_Index.html, viewed 18 September 2007.

USTR (2007a), 'Outline of the U.S. position on a draft consolidated text in the GATS Working Party on Domestic Regulation', undated (posted on 27 March 2007), available at http://www.ustr.gov/Trade_Sectors/Services/Section_Index.html, viewed 18 September 2007.

USTR (2007b), Statement of Deputy United States Trade Representative John K. Veroneau Regarding U.S. Actions under GATS Article XXI 5 May, available at http://www.ustr.gov/Document_Library/Press_Releases/2007/May/Statement_of_Deputy_United_States_Trade_Representative_John_K_Veroneau_Regarding_US_Actions_under_GATS_Article_XXI.html, viewed 18 September 2007.

USTR (2007c), Search using the term, 'deeply flawed', available at http://www.ustr.gov/, viewed 18 September 2007.

USTR (2007d), Statement on Internet gambling, 21 December, available at http://www.ustr.gov/Document_Library/Press_Releases/2007/December/Statement_on_Internet_Gambling.html, viewed 11 March 2008.

Waskow, David (2003), 'Environmental services liberalization: a win–win scenario or something else entirely?', *International Law*, **37**, 777.

Wood, Thomas, counsel to BHT Billiton (2006), Letter to EPA, 28 November.

Woolhandler, Ann (2006), 'Public rights, private rights and statutory retroactivity', *Georgetown Law Journal*, **94**, 1015, 1019–22.

WTO (1998), *Environmental Services*, Background Note by the Secretariat, S/C/W/46, 6 July, available at http://www.wto.org/documents, viewed 18 September 2007.

WTO (2007a), 'Eliminating trade barriers on environmental goods and services', available at http://www.wto.org/english/tratop_e/envir_e/envir_neg_serv_e.htm, viewed 18 September 2007.

WTO (2007b), *GATS Fact and Fiction* (undated but available since 2000), available at http://www.wto.org/english/tratop_e/serv_e/gats_factfiction_e.htm, viewed 18 September 2007.

WTO–Council for Trade in Services (2001), *Guidelines for the Scheduling of Specific Commitments under the General Agreement on Trade in Services (GATS)*, S/L/92 (28 March).

WTO–Council for Trade in Services (2005), 'Managing request-offer negotiations under the GATS: the Case of Environmental Services', in Special Session, Report of the Meeting Held on 27 and 30 June and 1 July 2005, Note by the Secretariat, TN/S/M/15, 15 September.

WTO–CTE (2007), Committee on Trade and Environment, Matrix on Trade Measures Pursuant to Selected Multilateral Environmental Agreements, Note by the Secretariat, Revision, WT/CTE/W/160/Rev.4, TN/TE/S/5/Rev.2, 14 March.

WTO–Division of Trade in Services (2006), Overview of GATS Disciplines & Negotiations on Domestic Regulation (slide presentation), available at http://www.tinyurl.com/3328zp, viewed 11 March 2008.

WTO–DSU (1994), *Dispute Settlement Understanding*, Understanding the Rules and Procedures Governing the Settlement of Disputes, Marrakesh Agreement Establishing the World Trade Organization, Annex 2, THE LEGAL TEXTS: THE RESULTS OF THE URUGUAY ROUND OF MULTILATERAL TRADE NEGOTIATIONS 354 (1999), 1869 U.N.T.S 401, 33 I.L.M 1226 (1994).

WTO–GATS (1994), *General Agreement on Trade in Services*, 15 April, Marrakesh Agreement Establishing the World Trade Organization, Annex 1B, THE LEGAL TEXTS: THE RESULTS OF THE URUGUAY ROUND OF MULTILATERAL TRADE NEGOTIATIONS 284 (1999), 1869 U.N.T.S. 183, 33 I.L.M 1167 (1994).

WTO–*Korea – Various Measures on Beef* (2000), Appellate Body Report, Korea – Measures Affecting Imports of Fresh, Chilled, and Frozen Beef, WT/DS161/AB/R (11 December).

WTO Secretariat (2000), *Energy Services: Background Note by the Secretariat*, 3, 9 September 1998 (S/C/W/52).

WTO–*US – Gambling Services* (2005), Appellate Body Report, United States – Measures Affecting the Cross-Border Supply of Gambling and Betting Services (WT/DS285/AB/R).

WTO–WPDR (2007), Working Party on Domestic Regulation, Draft Disciplines on Domestic Regulation Pursuant to GATS Article VI: 4, Informed Note by the Chairman, 18 April (Room Document), available at http://www.tradeobservaatory.org/library.cfm?refID=98264, viewed 18 September 2007.

WTO–WPDR (2008), Working Party on Domestic Regulation, Revised Draft, Disciplines on Domestic Regulation Pursuant to GATS Article VI:4, Informal Note by the Chairman, 23 January (Room Document), available at http://www.tradeobservatory.org/library.cfm?refID=101417, viewed 25 January 2008.

21 Biodiversity, intellectual property rights regime and indigenous knowledge system at the WTO: revisiting the unresolved issues

Sachin Chaturvedi

Introduction

In the last decade, interlinkages between the intellectual property rights (IPR) regime, biodiversity and the indigenous knowledge system (IKS) have emerged as one of the most contentious issues in the current round of World Trade Organization (WTO) negotiations. In fact the discontent among developing countries with the legacy of Uruguay Round in the realm of IPR has been so intense that debate on these interlinkages has overshadowed the Doha Round and has emerged as a major component of the negotiating agenda from the South, behind which all could rally.

The debate on these issues takes place at several multilateral fora, including at the World Intellectual Property Organization (WIPO), which established an Inter-governmental Committee (IGC) on Intellectual Property and Genetic Resources, Traditional Knowledge and Folklore,[1] apart from at the International Treaty on Plant Genetic Resources for Food and Agriculture (ITPGRFA), under the aegis of FAO which further encouraged protection and promotion of farmers' rights and indigenous knowledge system (IKS). Currently, this WIPO IGC is also discussing draft provisions for the enhanced protection of traditional knowledge and traditional cultural expressions against misappropriation and misuse.

However, it is at the Council for Trade-Related Aspects of Intellectual Property Rights (TRIPs) that the intensity of debate is very high. Since the Doha Ministerial, the deliberations on TRIPs have hovered around three major issues of concern to various members: the review of the provisions of Article 27.3 (b); the relationship between the TRIPs agreement and the Convention on Biological Diversity (CBD); and the protection of traditional knowledge and folklore. The recent Norwegian proposal[2] for amending the Agreement on TRIPs to make it mandatory for patent applicants to disclose any biological resources or associated traditional knowledge used in the inventions has given a new push to the demands from the developing countries for an equitable distribution of the gains appropriated through IKS and biodiversity.

With the advent of biotechnology, the economics related to biological resources and related IKS has triggered a major global debate on prior informed consent (PIC) and access and benefit sharing (ABS).[3] It is estimated that the global market for the pharmaceutical sector using genetic resources stands at US$300 billion per year.[4] The advances in biotechnology have facilitated faster identification of compounds as time taken for screening several plant samples for ranges of tests and their molecular characterization for further development of drugs has been curtailed to a great extent. In the context of WTO negotiations, access to biodiversity and sharing benefits derived from it is proposed to be addressed differently. Several countries have proposed a national access and benefit-sharing regime that may also require explicit statement on disclosure of origin,[5] while the USA and others have suggested exploring options within the existing IPR system, preferably through bilateral contracts between traditional knowledge holders and the companies or persons wishing to access and use that knowledge.[6] Some APEC members have also suggested relying on a market-oriented approach based on clear delineation of property rights to undertake bioprospecting in developing countries and developing a market whereby such rights can be freely traded.[7] As these issues are being debated at multilateral fora, another major concern emerging is the TRIPs Plus regime taking place through various FTAs led by the USA. This has posed a major challenge not only to the spirit and intention behind the Convention on Biological Diversity but has also gone far beyond the TRIPs agreement.

In this chapter we discuss some of these issues. The next section provides details of the various international treaties governing the IPR regime and access to genetic resources and IKS. A further section looks into the prevailing impasse at the WTO, followed by a case study of the Kani tribe that assesses the viability of ABS. The last section draws conclusions.

Framework of international treaties

The issues related to access to biodiversity and sharing of resultant benefits have been part of the debate on biodiversity resources and IPR protection since the early 1990s. At the Rio Summit, the issues related to the contribution of the indigenous community, particularly their knowledge, occupied the centre stage. The CBD reflected several elements of this debate, as did some other international treaties, such as ITPGRFA. However, at the same time the TRIPs appeared at the WTO, and later the Substantive Patent Law Treaty (SPLT) was proposed. The provisions of these agreements and treaties gave an impression that they were in conflict with the CBD. In this section, we look into some of these issues.

Convention on Biological Diversity
The CBD was adopted by more than 150 governments at the Rio Earth Summit in 1992. One of the three objectives of the CBD was to achieve equitable sharing of the benefits arising out of the utilization of genetic resources, for example by appropriate access and by appropriate transfer of relevant technologies. Article 15 of the Convention sets out a framework to achieve this objective. It recognizes the sovereign rights of respective countries over their natural resources and suggests that the national agencies/authority should set the conditions for determining access. There is a categorical recognition that access to genetic resources should be subject to PIC and that the national authorities should ensure that mechanisms are in place for sharing of benefits, in a fair and equitable way, arising from the commercial and other utilization of genetic resources. CBD Article 8(j) encourages national governments to develop such mechanisms in respect of the benefits arising from the utilization of knowledge, innovations and practices of indigenous and local communities embodying traditional lifestyles relevant for conservation and sustainable use of biological diversity.

The CBD, through its Conferences of Parties (CoP), has been discussing various issues related to ABS. Since the adoption of CBD eight such conferences have already been organized. At these meetings efforts have been made to assess user and provider experience in accessing the genetic resources and undertaking benefit-sharing so as to identify approaches for involvement of stakeholders. The major achievement of this consultation process is the adoption of the Bonn guidelines. At the last meeting, CoP-8, at Curitiba, Brazil, in 2006, it was further decided to establish a group of technical experts to explore and elaborate the possible options for developing an internationally recognized certificate of origin and analyse its practicality, feasibility, costs and benefits, with a view to achieving the objectives of Article 15 and 8(j) of the CBD. There is a Working Group on ABS already in place to develop indicators for assessment. This group held its fifth meeting in October 2007 for finalization of these indicators, and to look into issues related to certificate of origin and measures to support PIC requirements and material transfer agreement.

WIPO

The World Intellectual Property Organization (WIPO) has also been attempting to look into the ABS-related issues through the IGC since 2001. The final report of the group was expected by the end of 2007.[8] However, the IGC proceedings have not so far identified any point of convergence between the differing views of the members. The IGC objective was to forge a consensus on the issues related to the protection of traditional knowledge and evolving mechanisms for PIC and ABS. At the Curitiba meeting of the CBD, WIPO was invited to brief the meeting about the emerging views at IGC. This was one of the important initiatives to bridge the working of CBD and WIPO. WIPO has basically three treaties: the Patent Law Treaty (PLT); the Patent Cooperation Treaty (PCT); and a new one, which has been proposed as the Substantive Patent Law Treaty (SPLT). Apart from IGC, WIPO has also initiated discussion on ABS through fora such as PCT and SPLT.

FAO

The conclusion of the ITPGRFA under the aegis of the FAO further encouraged protection and promotion of farmers' rights and the indigenous knowledge system. This legally binding treaty covers all plant genetic resources relevant to food and agriculture. It is in harmony with the CBD. Its objectives are the conservation and sustainable use of plant genetic resources for food and agriculture and the fair and equitable sharing of benefits derived from their use, in harmony with the CBD, for sustainable agriculture and food security. In this way it further reinforces the dialogue at the CBD. The Treaty contains specific suggestions for ABS.[9] Article 17 suggests establishment of a global information system (GIS) for facilitating dissemination of information on plant genetic resources along with details on access to technology for improving them. There is also a provision for capacity-building for absorbing all the benefits from such a transfer of technology (art. 13.2c). Apart from this, Article 13.2d refers to sharing of monetary and other benefits out of the commercialization of plant genetic resources (PGR) and related knowledge.

CBD and IPR regime: current impasse at WTO

At the Doha Ministerial the developing countries joined the debate on IPR issues in a major way. In this debate, several developing countries contributed through their submissions on, for example, biodiversity and indigenous knowledge. The impetus for the inclusion of these additional issues also comes from the Doha Development Agenda

(DDA) (para. 19) where members agreed to exercise the relationship between the CBD and the production of traditional knowledge and folklore. The DDA asked specifically to look into the relationship between TRIPs agreement and the CBD. As discussed earlier, the debates at other fora had an impact, and additional issues related to IKS and ABS were also included in the TRIPs debate.

In relation to CBD and TRIPs, the views from members have been on different lines when it comes to assessing the relationship between them. The analysis from the WTO Secretariat (IP/C/W/368/Rev.1) has classified these views into four different groupings. Some of the countries that are not signatories, such as the USA, think that there is no conflict between TRIPs and CBD and, in fact, they are mutually supportive provided national measures are taken to implement their mandate.[10] On the contrary, some members suggest that there is an inherent conflict between the two, and that there is a need to review the TRIPs agreement so as to remove conflicting provisions.[11] These members demanded that the TRIPs agreement should be amended to reflect the spirit and commitments of the CBD. In order to achieve this, they recommended that disclosure of source and 'country of origin' of the biological resource or traditional knowledge used in an invention be made mandatory at the time of filing the patent. They also suggested obtaining PIC from a competent authority in the country of origin and entering into an equitable ABS. In addition some countries do not think that there is a conflict between TRIPs and the CBD but believe that there is a need to explore the possibility of international action. However, this group differs in terms of its prescription, as one sub-group suggests action in relation to the patent system while the other is not sure whether or not an amendment is needed to the TRIPs agreement for promoting the objectives of the CBD.[12]

Although it is widely acknowledged that Article 15 of the CBD recommends an ABS arrangement on mutually agreed terms, the spirit is not to confine this arrangement to the national level. It has international ramifications, particularly since, with the rapid economic liberalization and opening up of borders and removal of trade restrictions, the transboundary movements of genetic resources (GRs) and IKS usage may assume significant proportions. Many companies acquire GRs or IKS in one country and apply for a patent in another. This would become difficult to manage if only national instruments were used for governing contractual arrangements. Since provisions of the CBD do not bind all members of the WTO, there are no obligations under any international law to ensure commitment for ABS or PIC. Even if national contractual arrangements have international orientation, lack of a framework at the international level would adversely affect effective implementation of desired objectives of ABS and PIC.

Moving for bioeconomy

It is important to contextualize the emergence of the ABS instrument in light of the CBD-debate on protection of biological resources and the related IKS. Later in this section we look at the international arrangements that gave rise to ABS arrangements in an institutional framework. This was also the time when bioprospecting emerged as a major issue to articulate various efforts by the companies in the North to tap into southern biodiversity. Since, in the middle of 1990s, biotechnology also emerged as one of the key options for utilization of biodiversity, a view appeared that synergistic relationships should be targeted for larger global gains (see Table 21.1).

Table 21.1   Potential synergies between biotechnology development and value-added bioprospecting

Scientific and technical linkages	Common policy and programmatic issues	Reciprocal benefits
Biochemistry	Foreign investment policies	Creation of conservation incentives
Genetics	Technology licensing arrangements	Additional sources of funding and technical assistance
Cell and tissue culture	Intellectual property rights to isolated biochemicals	Broader allocation of policy and programme development costs
Fermentation techniques	Coordination of public–private R&D activities	Diversification of market opportunities
Recombinant production of natural products	Finance and business development for start-up enterprises	
Prospecting for genes conferring valuable agronomic traits or coding for valuable enzymes and other products	Access and benefit-sharing for use of wild biodiversity	

Source: Artuso (2002).

According to this view, technology from the North and bioresources from the South provide a perfect match for the development of new products. In Table 21.1 some of these cases are discussed in light of advancements in recombinant and fermentation technologies, including those in cell and tissue technology. This offered development of the bio-economy was seen as a 'win–win' for all the stakeholders. In the year 2000 USPTO granted 17 239 patents on 119 medicinal plants and the number rose to 20 835 in 2002 and to 23 956 in 2004–05.[13] According to a World Bank study, trade in medicinal plants would reach $5 trillion per year by 2050.[14] Indications are that plant-based chemicals will be the single important source for drug development.[15] According to the WHO, global sales of herbal remedies surpassed $21 billion in 2004.[16] There are also efforts to regulate the standards of herbal medicines. The WHO reports that, in 2003, 53 countries were regulating herbal medicines while 42 are in the process of developing such regulations.

In this context a large number of developing countries moved and supported a proposal for relevant changes in the TRIPs agreement so as to ensure norms for disclosure. There are three important constituents of this proposal, as follows:

1. The source and country of origin of the biological resource and of the traditional knowledge used in the invention.
2. Evidence of prior informed consent from the authorities under the relevant national regime.
3. Evidence of fair and equitable-benefit sharing under the relevant national regime.

In light of this proposal, the burden of proof has shifted on to the patent applicant, who may be intending to use biological resources and/or traditional knowledge. In its proposal (IP/C/M/47) Brazil has suggested that if there is no national regime to provide such permission, then consent from a competent national authority in that area should be procured. In this context, the legal effects of non-disclosure or inadequate or wrongful disclosure leading to revoking of patents, apart from the possibility of a judicial review, are some of the issues as yet unsettled.

Viability of ABS models

A framework for access to genetic resources and benefit-sharing from such access has been one of the most important achievements of the CBD. Article 8(j) makes states responsible to ensure that equitable sharing of benefits, arising from the utilization of knowledge, innovations and practices of indigenous and local communities embody traditional lifestyles relevant for conservation and sustainable use of biological diversity. The CoP-4 of the CBD, by their decision IV/8, decided to establish a panel of experts appointed by the member governments, composed of representatives from the private and public sectors, as well as representatives of indigenous and local communities. The panel, at its first meeting in 1999, reached broad conclusions on prior informed consent, mutually agreed terms, information needs and capacity-building.

However, until the CoP-8 at Curitiba, Brazil, in 2006, the Group could only agree on establishing a group of technical experts to develop internationally recognized certificate of origin/source/legal provenance and analyse its practicality, feasibility, costs and benefits, with a view to achieve the objectives of Article 15 and 8(j) of the CBD. At the same meeting it was also decided by the CoP that the Bonn Guidelines would be adopted for use while member governments develop and draft their legislative, administrative or policy measures on ABS.

In this context the Indian experience of sharing the benefits from a drug developed from the plant Arogyapacha, known to the Kani tribe in Southern India, has assumed major significance as a model for ABS.[17] The drug is 'Jeevani', and was developed by the Tropical Botanic Garden Research Institute (TBGRI). Jeevani is useful as an anti-stress and anti-fatigue agent. While the TBGRI was sharing the royalty with the tribal community, one company in the USA acquired the Jeevani trademark and started marketing it under its own banner. This adversely affected the earnings of the trust, established on the initiative of TBGRI for the welfare of the tribal community. This shows how important it is to have an international IPR regime that fully recognizes the IKS. The TBGRI model of ABS has otherwise worked well and has entered Phase II of its operations. Through the earnings of the trust, Kanis have acquired a small community centre, a school and a vehicle to take their forest produce to the nearby market.[18] In Phase II elaborate efforts were made to ensure fair and ethical implementation of the PIC regime in the contract through detailed participation of the tribal community.

Conclusion

The debate on incorporation of prior informed consent and ABS in the formal IPR instruments has expanded in the last few years. In light of ongoing resistance to the key demands of PIC and ABS, it is important to evolve a strategic response covering international mechanisms and national policy initiatives. As is clear, it is necessary to ensure incorporation of the CBD spirit in the upcoming IPR instruments both through the TRIPs and within the bilateral trade agreements. The FTAs among developing countries may produce elaborate statement of intentions supplemented by an action plan. This is being discussed at the CoPs. There is a need to bridge the knowledge gap between trade-negotiating documents and statements at CoP by developing countries, which can be achieved through advancing the interaction between trade and environment ministries and civil society actors across developing countries.

Some trends in biodiversity-related international patents have caused concern among developing countries, for instance the broad patents being granted in the USA and other developed countries, covering genetic material in their natural state, especially in the context of microorganisms and also in terms of blocking further research and application of the related knowledge which forms part of prior art. The granting of such erroneous patents on inventions is based directly or indirectly on genetic resources or traditional knowledge that does not qualify as being novel or inventive. These may foreclose R&D opportunities as patent rights over genetic resources may restrict research by third parties and may also deplete the indigenous community's benefit from their knowledge.

There is much to be done at the level of the developing countries as well; for instance the aggressive position of developing countries on issues related to the ABS, PIC and IKS needs to be adequately backed by necessary evidence. As discussed, initiatives have been launched to collect details on biopiracy etc. through digital library and other instruments. This process should be strengthened and consolidated further. Patent examiners worldwide could also use such databases of genetic resources and traditional knowledge when examining patent applications. Similarly, it is important that information on biodiversity and the indigenous knowledge system is put together and digitized as a source for consultation on prior art. This may help to ensure appropriate implementation of Article 8(j) of the CBD. In this regard, options suggested such as post-grant opposition, re-examination and revocation proceedings may not be very effective as the cost of monitoring may be extremely high for the developing countries. The Kani case has demonstrated that a mere national-level benefit-sharing arrangement would not be sufficient for deriving actual benefits. It would need to be supplemented by international arrangements (WTDR, 2007). The debate on the Kani experience assumes significance as the ABS has emerged as an important stumbling block at the TRIPs committee of WTO and also at WIPO. The fact that NutriScience could get a trademark in the USA and could market the drug at a price 11 times higher than what the Kani tribe was getting from the local pharmacy is itself suggestive of such a need. That the seventh CoP of the CBD in the decision VII/19 recommended an *ad hoc* open-ended working group for evolving such a mechanism is an important step (CBD, 2004). One of the strong recommendations of the CBD is to ensure technology transfer and capacity-building with the community facilitating access to genetic resources (WTO, 2000; 2005).

In the light of the wider debate on the access to technology for tracking down the usage of or applications of biotechnology to biodiversity or genetic resources, it may be worth exploring options for developing open sourcing mechanisms. This may help to ensure that common property is not about genome scientists or access to biotechnology in developing countries, but about finally prioritizing a common ownership that is specific to genetic resources. This may also attribute the ownership of genome research to communities, and explore commonality with the genomics networks to gain a more recognizable identity in regard to the current humanitarian views on bio-technology.[19]

Notes

1. This Committee began its work in 2001.
2. WT/GC/W/566.
3. ICTSD (2006); Dutfield (2006); Burrows (2005).
4. Ten and Laird (1999).
5. Sarnoff and Correa (2006).
6. US (2001; 2002; 2003).
7. Oxley and Bowen (2005).
8. WIPO (2006).
9. http://www.fao.org/AG/cgrfa/itpgr.htm.
10. US (2004). See also proposals in Australia (2001) and Japan (2000).
11. African Group (2003); Kenya (2005); Brazil (2004); India (2000).
12. Australia (2005); Canada (2005); New Zealand (2005); Andean Community (2002), para. 231; Brazil (2000); China (2005), para. 57.
13. Ghosh (2005).
14. Saha (2005).
15. Ibid.; *Economist* (2006).
16. Voigt (2006).
17. Chaturvedi (2007a).
18. Ibid.
19. Deibel (2006).

References

African Group (2003), *Taking Forward the Review of Article 27.3 (b) of the TRIPs Agreement*, Joint Communication from the African Group IP/C/W/404, 26 June, Geneva: WTO.

Andean Community (2002), *Minutes of the Meeting held in the Centre William Rappard on 17–19 September 2002, Addendum*, IP/C/M/37/Add.1, 8 November.

Artuso, Anthony (2002), 'Bioprospecting, benefit sharing, and biotechnological capacity building', *World Development*, **30**(8), 1355–68.

Australia (2001), *Communication from Australia*, IP/C/W/310, 2 October, Geneva: WTO.

Australia (2005), *Minutes of the Meeting held in the Centre William Rappard on 14–15 June 2005*, IP/C/M/48, 15 September.

Brazil (2000), *Review of Article 27.3(b)*, Communication from Brazil, IP/C/W/228, 24 November.

Brazil (2004), *Elements of the Obligation to Disclose the Source and Country of Origin of the Biological Resources and/or Traditional Knowledge use in an Invention*, IP/C/W/429/Rev.1, 27 September, Geneva: WTO.

Burrows, Beth (2005), 'Preface', in Beth Burrows (ed.), *The Catch; Perspectives in Benefit Sharing*, Washington, DC: The Edmonds Institute.

Canada (2005), *Minutes of the Meeting held in the Centre William Rappard on 8–9 and 31 March 2005*, IP/C/M/47, 3 June.

CBD (2004), *Analysis of Existing National, Regional and International Legal Instruments Relating to Access and Benefit-Sharing and Experience Gained in their Implementation, including Identification of Gaps: Note by the Executive Secretary*, Ad Hoc Open-Ended Working Group on Access and Benefit-Sharing, Third Meeting, Bangkok, 14–18 February 2005, UNEP/CBD/WG-ABS/3/2, 10 November.

Chaturvedi, Sachin (2007a), *Kani Case*, A Report for GenBenefit, available at www.uclan.ac.uk/genbenefit.

Chaturvedi, Sachin (2007b), 'TRIPS, indigenous knowledge and geographical indications', background paper for *World Trade and Development Report*, New Delhi: Oxford University Press, Research and Information System (RIS).

China (2005), *Minutes of Meeting held in the Centre William Rappard on 8–9 and 31 March 2005*, IP/C/M/47, 3 June.

Deibel, Eric (2006), 'Common genomes: open source in biotechnology and the return of common property', in Gudio Ruivenkamp and Joost Jongerden (eds), *Tailoring Biotechnologies*, **2**(2), Center for Tailormade Biotechnologies and Genomics.

Dutfield, Graham (2006), 'Protecting traditional knowledge: pathways to the future', *ICTSD Issue Paper No. 16*, ICTSD Programme on IPRs and Sustainable Development, June.

The Economist (2006), 'Psychedelic drugs: the God pill', *The Economist*, 15 July.

Ghosh, P. (2005), 'Traditional knowledge: a legal and market conundrum', *Financial Express*, 7 September.

ICTSD (2006), *Biodiversity and Trade Briefing Series*, COP-8 Briefings on Trade and Biodiversity, Geneva: ICTSD.

India (2000), *Protection of Biodiversity and Traditional Knowledge – The Indian Experience*, WT/CTE/W/156, IP/C/W/198, 14 July.

Japan (2000), *Review of the Provisions of Article 27.3(b) – Japan's View*, Communication from Japan, IP/C/W/236, 11 December, Geneva: WTO.

Kenya (2005), *Minutes of the Meeting held in the Centre William Rappard, 8–9 and 31 March 2005*, IP/C/M/47, 3 June, Geneva: WTO.

New Zealand (2005), *Minutes of the Meeting held in the Centre William Rappard on 8–9 and 31 March 2005*, IP/C/M/47, 3 June, Geneva: WTO.

Oxley, Alan and Bill Bowen (2005), *Developing an Effective International Regime for Access and Benefit Sharing for Genetic Resources: Using Market-based Instuments*, The Australian APEC Study Centre, Monash University.

Saha, R. (2005), 'A civilised solution still seems a far cry', *Financial Express*, 7 September.

Sarnoff, J.D. and C.M. Correa (2006), *Analysis of Options for Implementing Disclosure of Origin Requirements in Intellectual Property Applications*, Geneva and New York: United Nations.

Ten, K.K. and S. Laird (1999), *Commercial Use of Biodiversity*, London: Earthscan.

US (2001), *Communication from the United States*, IP/C/W/257, 13 June, Geneva: WTO.

US (2002), *Technology Transfer Practices of the US National Cancer Institute's Departmental Therapeutics Programme*, Communication from the United States, IP/C/W/341, 25 March, Geneva: WTO.

US (2003), *Access to Genetic Resources Regime of the United States National Parks*, IP/C/W/393, 28 January, Geneva: WTO.

US (2004), *Relationship between the TRIPs Agreement and the CBD, and the Protection of Traditional Knowledge and Folklore*, Article 27.3(b), IP/C/W/434, 26 November, Geneva: WTO.

Voigt, Kevin (2006), 'Cash crops: how traditional remedies are being turned into profit – part two of our look at Asia's burgeoning herbal industry', *Wall Street Journal*, 7–9 July.

WIPO (2006), 'IGC addresses core issues for the protection of traditional knowledge and traditional cultural expressions', Press Release 470, Geneva, 12 December.

WTO (2000), 'Protection of biodiversity and traditional knowledge – the Indian experience', Submission at WTO by India, WT/CTE/W/156, IP/C/W/198, 14 July.

WTDR (2007), *World Trade and Development Report*, New Delhi: Oxford University Press, Research and Information System (RIS).

WTO (2005), *Minutes of Meeting held in the Centre William Rappard, 8–9 and 31 March 2005*, Submission at WTO by Kenya. IP/C/M/47, 3 June, Geneva: WTO.

22 Investor rights and sustainable development
Chris Tollefson and W.A.W. Neilson

Introduction

Controversy surrounding the protection of investor rights through international investment agreements (IIAs) is longstanding. This has been particularly so in the context of the relationship between developed countries (DCs) and their less developed country (LDC) counterparts. From an LDC perspective, such protections have traditionally been seen as a substantial derogation from state sovereignty, fettering not only the ability of a host state to determine domestic policy priorities (most notably with respect to resource management and development) but also, more generally, its ability to regulate the activities of transnational corporate investors. The constraining impact of IIAs on domestic policy space has also been a thorny issue within the more developed economies. Here the overriding concern has been the impact of IIAs on the ability of governments to enact measures to protect the environment and public health. Given these various concerns, it is perhaps not surprising that, over the last 20 years, three successive initiatives to broker broad-based multilateral investment treaties (under the auspices of the United Nations, the OECD and most recently the WTO) have ended in failure.

Yet despite this pervasive skepticism about and resistance to IIAs, the last two decades have nonetheless seen a dramatic consolidation of investor rights in the realm of international law, accompanied by an unprecedented expansion in global foreign direct investment (FDI). During this period, both FDI flows and FDI stock have expanded over 15-fold (UNCTAD, 2006). In keeping with historical patterns, the predominant share (approximately 60%) of FDI has flowed from North to South (ibid.). This dramatic growth in FDI has been paralleled by the emergence of a highly complex and burgeoning international investment governance regime. This regime comprises a complex global network of well over 2500 IIAs, over 1500 of which have been concluded within the last 15 years. The vast majority of these IIAs are bilateral investment treaties (BITs) between DCs and LDCs, although there are also a handful of regional investment treaties, most notably those contained in the 1994 North American Free Trade Agreement (NAFTA). The volume and magnitude of investor claims being submitted to arbitration has also risen sharply. As of June 2006, the total number of known investment-related arbitrations was 248, two-thirds of which were filed after 2001 and most of these seeking damages in the tens or hundreds of million dollars (Newcombe, 2007).

This chapter considers the implications of this emerging IIA network for the ability (and indeed the appetite) of states to pursue domestic sustainable development policies. In framing our topic in this way, we have been mindful of the need to consider the relationship between IIAs and the capacity of governments to protect the environment and public health, and likewise the relationship between IIAs and resource management and development. As it has evolved in international law scholarship, the concept of sustainable development not only embraces these concerns but emerging public participation, good governance and human rights norms (French, 2005; Newcombe, 2007). In what follows we reflect on the nature and extent of the tension between domestic sustainable development policy in this broad sense and investor rights under the emerging IIA regime.

Although both the scholarly literature and the jurisprudence in this area remain in their infancy, some preliminary lessons can be drawn particularly from the experience under the NAFTA, where academics and tribunals have been grappling with the relationship between investor rights and sustainable development policies for well over a decade. We also propose to explore the emerging experience under the ever-expanding network of BITs, a context in which this issue is increasingly focusing global attention. In the next section, we provide an overview of the tension between investor rights and domestic sustainable development, and the competing values and interests underlying this tension. Then we describe the architecture and procedures of the IIA governance regime with a view to elucidating the claims of its critics and supporters. Finally, we reflect on the growing debate with respect to how the current IIA regime can be reformed to achieve a better balance between investor rights and sustainable development norms.

The tension between investor rights and sustainable development
In the years following the watershed 1999 protests at the WTO trade meetings in Seattle, few issues have stirred more controversy within the broader globalization debate than investor rights. During this period, investor rights and their implications for domestic sustainable development initiatives have become front-page news in jurisdictions around the world. Many of the most recent suits have targeted LDCs. Argentina has been particularly hard hit, facing close to about 30 such suits, many arising out of its financial restructuring of 2002 (Anderson and Grusky, 2007). Within the last two years alone, arbitral tribunals have ruled against it on four occasions. Other Latin American countries (including Ecuador, Bolivia, Peru and Mexico) have also faced or are facing investor suits, as are several former Soviet republics and African states (Anderson and Grusky, 2007; Newcombe, 2007).

Ongoing high-profile claims include a suit brought by UK-based water TNC Biwater, seeking damages from Tanzania for canceling a water and sewerage privatization deal; a suit by EU investors against South Africa seeking compensation for legislation aimed at bolstering black participation in the mining sector; a suit by the oil giant Occidental Petroleum against Ecuador in connection with the cancellation of oil leases due to allegations of environmental degradation and human rights abuses; and a suit by Texas farming interests claiming that Mexico has infringed their water rights. Frequently the damages sought, and in several recent cases awarded, have been in excess of $100 million (Newcombe, 2007).

Developed states have also been increasingly been forced to defend themselves from analogous investor claims. Canada and the USA have each been sued close to a dozen times under NAFTA's investor rights provisions (Chapter 11) for various government measures in the realms of environmental protection, public health and resource management. In two of these cases, Canada has ended up paying compensation (one an out-of-court settlement of a claim arising from a ban on the import of the fuel additive MMT (Methylcyclopentadienyl manganese tricarbonyl); a second involving an arbitral ruling that a federal ban on the export of PCB (polychlorinated biphenyl) waste violated NAFTA). To date, the USA has enjoyed more success, most notably in its successful defense of a claim arising from a fuel additive ban in the *Methanex* litigation. However, several environmental-protection-based claims are pending against both countries, including a suit against Canada for banning the pesticide Lindane, and another against the USA targeting environmental measures imposed by the state of California on an open-pit gold-mining operation licensed to a Canadian mining company (Newcombe, 2007).

Environmental and social justice NGOs and scholars critical of the emerging IIA regime have voiced a variety of concerns with respect both to the substantive rules embedded in the regime and the process by which these rules are enforced. They contend that the IIA regime represents a neoliberal-inspired Economic Bill of Rights for TNCs that undermines the sovereignty of host countries (often LDCs desperate to attract FDI) to determine and implement key environmental and sustainable development priorities. It is also contended that IIAs are asymmetrical: conferring rights but imposing no correlative responsibilities on investors. Moreover, critics claim that the legal uncertainty surrounding the scope and ambit of investor rights, combined with the economic risks and costs associated with defending potential claims, has a chilling effect on governments' willingness to regulate in the public interest. Finally, it is argued that the arbitral processes and fora currently in place to adjudicate these cases (ICSID – International Centre for Settlement of Investment Disputes; UNCITRAL – UN Commission on International Trade Law; and other bodies originally constituted to deal with private international commercial disputes) are ill suited to deal with what are fundamentally public policy matters (Van Harten, 2007).

Defenders of the current IIA regime typically reject the 'sovereignty critique' described above out of hand. While it is generally conceded that such agreements significantly strengthen the hand of TNCs when dealing with host states, most would strongly contend that entry into the regime is itself an exercise of sovereign will, reflecting a reasoned political judgment that the supposed costs of entry are outweighed by the benefits in terms of increased FDI. They also point out that accession into the IIA regime is not an all-or-nothing proposition since governments are allowed to reserve (exempt) from such agreements certain economic sectors or non-conforming measures. Further, although some regime defenders will concede that the IIA jurisprudence is inconsistent and unpredictable, and that many early investment treaties failed adequately to recognize the right of host states to regulate in the public interest, most strongly assert that it is premature to draw conclusions about what remains an embryonic regime (Newcombe, 2007). Indeed, it is claimed that tribunals 'get it right' most of the time, even in cases frequently cited by opponents as illustrations of where they have erred (Soloway, 2003). Likewise, arguments about 'regulatory chill' are characteristically dismissed as unproven and premature (Soloway, 2003; Franck, 2005). And while there is some acceptance in these quarters of the need for procedural reform, most argue that the necessary changes can be incrementally accommodated within existing arbitral institutions (Franck, 2005).

Investor protection architecture and procedures

IIA regime overview
Given the limitations of early treaties of 'Friendship, Commerce and Navigation' and the difficulties of securing multilateral investment treaty agreements (Franck, 2005, pp. 1525–7), countries in recent decades have turned to IIAs to promote and protect foreign direct investment. It is estimated that by 2006 over 2500 IIAs have been negotiated,

convincing evidence of their primacy as the principal public international law instruments governing foreign investment (Newcombe, 2007). IIAs impose binding obligations on partner states with respect to their treatment of foreign investment as a major beneficial force for economic development. Enforcement of these protection and facilitation standards occurs through direct investor-state arbitration. Successful claims result in an award of damages in favor of the investor that are largely immune from meaningful appeal or review (Tollefson, 2002b).

The great majority of IIAs follow a standard pattern in detailing the obligations of the host state's treatment of an investment. The investor rights provisions found in NAFTA's Chapter 11 are illustrative. Under NAFTA, these rights (also known as disciplines), which when breached entitle an investor to sue a host state for damages directly, include: the right to national treatment and most favoured nation treatment (art. 1102 and 1103); the right to international minimum standards of treatment (arts. 1105); the right to be free from certain performance requirements (art. 1106); and the right to be compensated for expropriation of their investment (arts. 1110).

Neither under the NAFTA nor in most other IIAs is the legal relationship between these private rights of action by aggrieved investors and the right of states to pursue sustainable development policies directly addressed (Tollefson, 2002a, p. 151). At the same time, such agreements typically provide a remarkably broad berth for investor rights. For example, under the NAFTA the range of governmental 'measures' that can trigger an investor claim includes 'any law, regulation, procedure, requirement or practice' emanating from any level of government (municipal, provincial or federal) or other arms of the state including the judiciary (Cosbey, 2005, p. 154). Indeed, there is no requirement that the complained-of 'measure' have legal force or effect. Likewise, 'investments' eligible for protection include not only direct investments but also debt security or loans to an enterprise or equity securities in an enterprise. A NAFTA tribunal has even held that a company's 'market share' is a protected 'investment' (ibid., p. 155).

Conferring upon investors a broad right to sue host states directly for damages in a legally binding, international adjudicative forum represents a seismic shift in international law. Before the emergence of IIAs, investors were forced to seek redress either by persuading their home state to champion their claim or to pursue litigation in the not always hospitable venue of the host state's domestic courts. Under provisions of modern-day BITs, investors are transformed into 'private attorney generals' (Franck, 2005, p. 1538) empowered to press their claims before arbitral tribunals organized under the auspices of a variety of fora including: ICSID (International Centre for the Settlement of Investment Disputes), the ICC (International Chamber of Commerce), the SCC (Stockholm Chamber of Commerce) and UNCITRAL (ibid., p. 1541).

Most IIAs set out a relatively standard set of procedures, including a notice of dispute to the host government, the selection of the particular tribunal, followed by the appointment of the panel of arbitrators and the conduct of the arguments by memorials, the exchange of evidence and the oral hearing itself in a non-public forum. Arbitrators tend to be trade law scholars, retired judges or members of the commercial arbitration bar. Each party to an arbitration proposes a list of acceptable arbitrators from which its counterpart must select. The two arbitrators selected in this fashion then confer with a view to selecting a Chair. Increasingly, critics have questioned whether this method of appointment adequately ensures arbitral independence (Franck, 2005).

(In)consistency between the IIA regime and sustainable development goals
As a result of tribunal rulings under NAFTA's Chapter 11 as well as the growing torrent of litigation under various BITs, the emerging IIA regime has increasingly been characterized by critics as a serious impediment to sustainable development. A frequent point of departure for this critique is the asymmetric nature of the obligations IIAs respectively impose on host states, home states and foreign investors. While such agreements invariably impose on host states a broad range of legal responsibilities to investors, typically they contain no correlative obligations on investors. Moreover, they are generally silent with respect to obligations of the investor's home jurisdiction 'to ensure its nationals comply with standards of conduct in their operations abroad' (Newcombe, 2007, p. 14).

It is also contended that the content and uncertainty surrounding the investor rights that IIAs enshrine is inconsistent with sustainable development norms. The controversy surrounding the content of these new rights is considered in more detail below. Regardless of the ostensible intent underlying these provisions, however, few would dispute that the ascendancy of the IIA regime has created considerable uncertainty with respect to the ability of host states to address serious health, consumer and environmental concerns without incurring liability to investors. This is underscored by the experience under NAFTA where tribunals have enunciated interpretations of its national treatment, international minimum standard of treatment, and expropriation provisions that are much broader (and hence more favorable to investors) than is generally accepted in international law (Soloway, 2003, p. 5). Whether and to what extent this uncertainty has created 'regulatory chill' – causing governments to resile from enacting measures aimed at promoting sustainable development – is a matter of considerable debate (Soloway, 2003; Tollefson, 2003).

This uncertainty is compounded by the failure of most IIAs to address or define how investor rights are to be balanced against sustainable development considerations. A recent analysis of over 71 BITs confirms that references to sustainable development principles are the exception rather than the rule, even in non-binding, preambular language (Newcombe, 2007, p. 65232). Moreover, most IIAs, including NAFTA's Chapter 11, are silent with respect to the 'traditionally accepted prerogative of governments to protect public health and the environment' (Tollefson, 2002a, p. 151), resulting in considerable controversy over how and whether competing private and public interests are to be balanced. This is in sharp contrast to the GATT, where Article XX explicitly provides a justificatory basis for measures of this kind. A related source of uncertainty is whether host governments can invoke the precautionary principle to uphold legal measures against investors which it claims to have taken to protect legitimate public interests in health, consumer safety or environmental protection (Newcombe, 2007, p. 32).

A third area of concern relates to the arbitral process itself. Here the critique is twofold: that the tribunals that have jurisdiction over such disputes are poorly equipped and ill disposed to address the complex 'public' nature of issues raised; and that the prevailing arbitral processes lack transparency and openness in terms of access to documents, hearings and public participation. While some steps have recently been taken to alleviate this perceived 'democratic deficit', particularly in the NAFTA context, the tribunal competence and public participation remain key issues for many critics of the emerging IIA regime (Franck, 2005; Soloway, 2003, p. 5).

Drawing on the NAFTA experience, we now propose to canvass in somewhat more detail sustainable development implications of specific elements of the IIA investor rights regime.

National treatment (NT) and most favoured nation (MFN)   NT, as elaborated in the NAFTA and most BITs, requires a host state to 'accord to investments of investors of another party treatment that is no less favourable than it accords, in like circumstances, to those of its own investors'. The devil is in the interpretation of 'like circumstances' due to the fact that most IIAs do not specify in what circumstances this right is engaged. Critics have worried that tribunals will import a narrow, trade-law-inspired approach to this question that would restrict the capacity of host governments to implement *bona fide* environmental regulatory decisions that affect foreign investments differently from their domestic counterparts (Tollefson, 2002a, p. 152). This concern has been reinforced by some early jurisprudence under the NAFTA (notably *S.D. Myers*). While more recent NAFTA cases (notably *Methanex*) have adopted a more regulator-friendly approach, the potential for investors to invoke NT to seek damages for enterprise-, site- or project-specific regulation remains.

The companion MFN obligation means that a foreign investor is entitled to the better of how the host government treats investors from any other country 'in like circumstances'. Identical issues of interpretation to the NT obligation arise here. Also, an MFN argument may be raised on the part of a foreign investor that they can claim the advantages of investor treatment accorded by the host state in any of its BITs signed with other investor countries, a prospect that underlines the 'need to carefully consider the relationship between different treaties when they are drafted' (Cosbey, 2005, p. 160).

International Minimum Standard (IMS) of Treatment   Virtually all IIAs augment the relativist protections of NT and MFN with an absolute obligation to treat investors in a manner consistent with international minimum standards (IMS). For example, in Article 1105, NAFTA directs that investors shall receive treatment 'in accordance with international law, including fair and equitable treatment'. Historically, IMS has been regarded as protecting against egregious state conduct that was in violation of international customary law. In several recent cases, however, investors have sought to expand this protection by claiming damages for alleged violations of non-customary forms of 'international law' including provisions of various WTO agreements and even non-Chapter 11 parts of NAFTA. An interpretative statement by the NAFTA Commission in 2001 narrowed that possibility by pointing out that the obligation of fair and equitable treatment was to be in accordance with customary international law standards of treatment (Tollefson, 2002a, pp. 155–6), a position now codified in the new US and Canadian model BITs (Newcombe, 2007, p. 70). Whether and to what extent IIA jurisprudence will adopt this more narrow approach remains to be seen (Cosbey, 2005, pp. 161–3).

Prohibition of performance requirements
As noted above, IIAs are often criticized for giving rights to foreign investors without imposing on them correlative responsibilities: for example, to advance various community development objectives of the host government in areas such as local job creation, environmental protection, technology transfer and sustainable development (Peterson,

2007, p. 142). Indeed, most IIAs prohibit host states from imposing such obligations (commonly termed 'performance requirements') subject to some exceptions prohibited under Article 1106 (Tollefson, 2002a, p. 156). While Article 1106 specifically exempts 'environmental measures' taken by host governments, arbitral case law under comparable GATT Article XX language confirms that the government bears the onus of establishing that it is impossible to achieve its environmental protection goal in a less investment-restrictive manner. Also, it remains uncertain '[w]hether sustainable resource management measures can be justified under this exception' (Tollefson, 2002a, p. 157).

Expropriation
A key feature of IIAs is a requirement on host states to compensate investors where a governmental measure has had the effect of expropriating their investment. Under customary international law, this obligation is known as the 'Hull standard', which imposes a duty on expropriating states to pay 'full, prompt and adequate compensation' (Van Harten, 2007, p. 91 fn 120). Under the Hull standard, an obligation to compensate is only triggered when an investor's property is physically confiscated or nationalized, or its value drastically diminished or eliminated by arbitrary state action (Tollefson, 2002a, p. 159). Relying on the broad protective language dealing with expropriation that is typically found in IIAs, investors have sought protection that far exceeds the ambit of the Hull standard. In this regard, it is contended that a right to compensation arises where government regulation, even if enacted for a legitimate public purpose, substantially interferes with an investor's property rights or has incidentally reduced the value of their investment (Van Harten, 2007, p. 91).

In this area, perhaps more than any other, the IIA jurisprudence to date has been characterized by inconsistency. Once again the NAFTA experience is instructive. Some rulings have been disquietingly expansive. Notable in this regard is the approach adopted in *Metalclad*, a decision which, on judicial review, was described by the court as 'extremely broad', necessitating compensation for, among other things, a 'legitimate rezoning of property by a municipality or other zoning authority' (Ruling of BC Supreme Court in *Metalclad*, 2001). In contrast, in *Methanex* the tribunal interpreted the protection in much narrower terms, aligning it closely with prevailing US 'takings' and 'police powers' jurisprudence. Consequently, there is considerable uncertainty as to how future tribunals will differentiate legitimate regulation from indirect expropriation both under the NAFTA and other IIAs, causing one commentator to observe that 'left to the process of investment treaty arbitration, we shall be unlikely to reach a stable definition of expropriation for decades to come, if ever' (Van Harten, 2007, p. 93).

In response to this uncertainty, both Canada and the USA have developed interpretive statements that are now routinely incorporated into all BITs to which they are a party. These interpretive statements direct tribunals to apply a test similar to that articulated in *Methanex* that considers not only the economic impact of the government measure but also the extent to which the measure interferes with distinct, reasonable investment-backed expectations and the character of the government. Canada's current model BIT also contains new language affirming that non-discriminatory measures that are adopted and applied in good faith and that are designed to protect legitimate public welfare objectives will only constitute indirect expropriation in 'rare circumstances' (Newcombe, 2007, p. 402).

Procedural issues

Much criticism has also been leveled at the procedures currently in place to arbitrate investor claims. These concerns include the restrictiveness of current rules with respect to public participation and access to claim documentation, as well as broader critiques aimed at the legitimacy and accountability of the arbitral process. In this context, the ensuing debate has pitted the prevailing norms of the international arbitral regime against an emerging public expectation 'that challenges to regulation by private parties will be adjudicated in a transparent, public and open forum' (Newcombe, 2007, p. 43).

Historically, international commercial arbitration was conducted in private under strict conditions of confidentiality as 'investment arbitration was considered to be a private commercial matter between two disputants' (Cosbey, 2005, p. 152). As critics point out, however, the implications of investor claims frequently transcend the interests of the immediate parties, raising complex issues of science and democratic values that commercial arbitral fora are ill equipped to adjudicate (Van Harten, 2007, pp. 150–51).

Securing even basic information about past or pending investor claims remains difficult. There is no general requirement, for instance, that arbitral documents or decisions be made available to the public. Thus, while ICSID lists pending arbitrations on its website, as yet UNCITRAL does not. And while NAFTA parties maintain a public register of notices of intent to arbitrate, this information is often incomplete (Cosbey, 2005, p. 153).

An important step to enhance both transparency and legitimacy was taken by the NAFTA trade ministers in 2003 in their release of suggested guidelines for considering petitions for *amicus curiae* status in hearings. Both the USA and Canada have also indicated their support for the principle of public hearings in all future Chapter 11 arbitrations (Mann, 2005, pp. 11–13). However, these initiatives are not legally binding and their implementation may well depend on the joint consent of the government involved and the private investor. In the same vein, the new US and Canadian model BITs now authorize tribunals to accept and consider submissions by non-disputing parties, and amendments in 2006 to the ICSID Rules expressly permit a tribunal to accept written submissions from such parties 'regarding a matter within the scope of the dispute' (Newcombe, 2007, p. 49).

Concerns have also been raised about the coherence of emerging IIA jurisprudence. In the NAFTA setting, for example, commentators have observed that 'a sense of consistency and permanence' has thus far been lacking (Soloway, 2003, p. 23). The lack of *stare decisis* or appropriate appellate oversight has undermined both the sense of accountability and predictability of the process and has led 'to jurisdiction shopping and a sense of uneven application of the rules among different parties to an arbitration' (ibid.).

In addition, serious questions have been raised about arbitral competence and the arbitral appointment process (Van Harten, 2007, p. 121). Critics contend that arbitrators, typically drawn from the ranks of the international trade law community, tend to be predisposed to apply private law rules or rights-based norms imported from private commercial arbitration law and sometimes to labor under misconceptions of human rights law to render judgments about what Van Harten argues are 'core matters of public law' (Van Harten, 2007, pp. 150–51). This perception of systemic bias in favor of investor rights is further fueled by concerns about the arbitral appointment process, which arguably lacks many of the neutrality safeguards normally associated with appointments made in the judicial realm (ibid., pp. 174–5).

The debate over reforming the IIA regime in light of sustainable development norms
Although still embryonic and inchoate in form, the emerging IIA regime is confronting growing pressures for reform from a variety of constituencies and quarters. Some LDCs are now calling for fundamental reforms to both the governing rules and procedures of the current regime, are examining their options to exit from current agreements, and, in the meantime, are actively resisting regime expansion. They are also demanding that future agreements restrict investor access to mandatory arbitral dispute resolution and incorporate new obligations on foreign investors to transfer technologies and employ local inputs and labour (Anderson and Grusky, 2007). Regime reform has also become a key issue for the international NGO community although, as yet, no consensus has emerged as to what these reforms should entail. Even stalwart supporters of the prevailing regime have expressed concerns about the inconsistency of emerging IIA jurisprudence and the need to retool the procedures by which cases are adjudicated and decisions reviewed (Franck, 2005).

Some commentators contend that the current IIA regime is already evolving in a direction that lends enhanced recognition to sustainable development norms and values (Newcombe, 2007). Evidence relied on in support of this thesis includes interpretive statements issued by the NAFTA parties on the meaning of 'international standards of treatment' (2001) and 'amici participation' (2003), as well as recent rule changes at ICSID (2006) aimed at facilitating *amici* participation and ongoing discussions on this topic at UNCITRAL. Jurisprudentially, recent decisions such as *Methanex* have been interpreted in a similar light (Mann, 2005). It is likewise claimed that analogous developments are under way at the domestic level. For example, both Canada and the USA have amended their model BIT agreements (used as templates for BITs that are currently being negotiated) to provide better legal recognition of the need for investor rights not to trump the right of governments to pursue legitimate sustainable development objectives (see below). Both countries have also, of late, adopted a much more civil-society-friendly approach to public access to IIA information and NGO participation in tribunal hearings. And Canada and several other DCs have recently implemented policies requiring proposed new BITs to undergo an environmental impact assessment before being signed.

Yet while most critics of the current IIA regime welcome these developments, incremental reforms of this kind are unlikely to diminish the growing pressure for more fundamental reform. An approach being promoted by some of the NGOs that intervened in the *Methanex* litigation seeks to impose on investors affirmative obligations to abide by various internationally recognized labor, environmental and human rights standards. Under their proposed model IIA, investors would also be required to undertake environmental and social impact assessments with respect to their investments (Mann et al., 2005). While the model does not eliminate the right of investors to pursue arbitration, they would first be required to exhaust domestic remedies. Moreover, investors found to have breached any of their affirmative obligations under such an agreement would forfeit their right to arbitrate. The proposed model also contains a 'general exception' provision, analogous yet considerably broader than Article XX of the GATT. It provides that host states have 'the right to pursue their own development objectives and priorities' and 'the right to take regulatory and other measures to ensure that development in their territory is consistent with the goals and principles of sustainable development' as long as they act in accordance with international law (Mann et al., 2005).

This proposed model IIA, which emerged from a consultative process spearheaded by the Canadian-based International Institute for Sustainable Development (IISD), is being studied by the OECD and has been favorably received by several LDCs that are currently in BITs negotiations. In other quarters, it has met with criticism. Predictably, business interests have responded critically to the suggestion that investors should be subjected to affirmative duties or that they should be obliged to resort to domestic courts (Anderson and Grusky, 2007). Moreover, some NGOs active around trade and investment issues have also criticized the model for preserving the right of investors ultimately to pursue claims directly against host states (ibid.).

Another variation on the 'exhaustion of remedies' approach embodied in IISD's model would be to require investors to apply to their home government for approval to proceed to arbitration. This approach has reportedly secured the support of several key Congressional leaders, including former presidential candidate John Kerry (Franck, 2005). An even more restrictive approach would be to require the investor to secure the advance approval of both its home and its host governments. For some reformers, however, the only acceptable model for future agreements is to abolish investor suits and return to the old mechanism under which investment disputes were brought on a state-to-state basis, as currently prevails in trade disputes. Supporters of this 'abolitionist' approach invoke the Australia–US Free Trade Agreement of 2004 (AUSTFA). Under AUSTFA, a state-to-state investment dispute resolution process was ultimately agreed to due to Australian concern to avoid replicating the 'experiences of Canada and United States under NAFTA Chapter 11' (Dodge, 2006, p. 2).

Considerable attention and debate have also focused on how to enhance the efficacy and predictability with which the prevailing IIA regime operates. Given the breadth and pervasiveness of this regime, the incremental benefit of reform proposals that focus exclusively on the nature of and rules governing future agreements will be necessarily limited. In recognition of this dilemma, some have called for reforms that would allow domestic courts to assume a much greater supervisory role over rulings arising under current IIAs by empowering them to review arbitral decisions for errors of law and jurisdiction. This approach, critics argue, represents a minimum that is required 'to ensure independence and accountability in the interpretation of public law and in the award of public funds to private businesses' (Van Harten, 2007). However, such an approach is likely to lead to consistent results both due to the necessity for coordinated action throughout IIA regime states, and the ingrained tendency of courts to defer to arbitral awards, particularly in the international setting. For these and other reasons, reformers increasingly favor a strategy that would see the establishment of an international court with comprehensive jurisdiction over the adjudication of investor claims (ibid.). This court would assume jurisdiction based on an opt-in model that would allow states to attorn to its jurisdiction 'when the time is right for each' (ibid.). Given the enduring controversy and uncertainty surrounding the current IIA regime, both capital-exporting and -importing states would appear to have strong incentives to become closely engaged in the negotiation and development of such a model.

References

Anderson, S. and S. Grusky (2007), *Challenging Corporate Investor Rule*, Food & Water Watch, Institute for Policy Studies, available at http://www.ips-dc.org/reports/070430-challengingcorporateinvestorrule.pdf.

British Columbia Supreme Court (2001), 'Decision of Tysoe J. in *Metalclad Corp v. United Mexican States*', 89 B.C.L.R. (3d) 359, 2001 BCSC 1529, 2001bcsc1529.htm.

Cosbey, A. (2005), 'The road to hell? Investor protections in NAFTA's Chapter 11', in L. Zarsky (ed.), *International Investment for Sustainable Development*, London: Earthscan, pp.150–71.

Dodge, W.S. (2006), 'Investor-state dispute settlement between developed countries: reflections on the Australia–United States Free Trade Agreement', *Vanderbilt Journal of Transnational Law*, **39**(1), 1–38.

Franck, S.D. (2005), 'The legitimacy crisis in investment treaty arbitration: privatizing public international law through inconsistent decisions', *Fordham Law Review*, **73**, 1521–1625.

French, D. (2005), *International Law and Policy of Sustainable Development*, Manchester: Juris.

ICSID (Additional Facility) (2000), 'Final Award in the matter of *Metaclad Corp. v. The United States of Mexico*', 30 August.

Mann, H. (2005), 'The final decision in *Methanex v. United States*: some new wine in some new bottles', IISD, available at http://www.iisd.org.

Mann, H. et al. (2005), *IISD Model International Agreement on Investment for Sustainable Development*, IISD, available at http://www.iisd.org.

Newcombe, A. (2007), 'Sustainable development and international treaty law', *Journal of World Investment and Trade*, **8**, 357–407.

Peterson, L.E. (2007), 'Investment', in A. Najam et al. (eds), *Trade and Environment: A Resource Book* , IISD, available at http://www.iisd.org/pdf/2007/trade_and_env.pdf.

Soloway, J. (2003), 'NAFTA's Chapter 11: investor protection, integration and the public interest', *Choices* (IRPP), **9**(2), 1–47.

Tollefson, C. (2002a), 'Games without frontiers: investor claims and citizen submissions under the NAFTA regime', *Yale Journal of International Law*, **27**, 141–191.

Tollefson, C. (2002b), '*Metalclad v. United Mexican States* revisited: judicial oversight of NAFTA's Chapter Eleven investor-state claim process', *Minnesota Journal of Global Trade*, **11**, 183–231.

Tollefson, C. (2003), 'NAFTA's Chapter 11: The Case for Reform', *Choices*, **9**, 48–58.

UNCITRAL (2000), 'Partial Award in the matter of *S.D. Myers v. the Government of Canada*', 13 November.

UNCITRAL (2005), 'Final award in the matter of *Methanex Corporation v. United States of America*', 3 August.

United Nations Conference on Trade and Development (2006), *World Investment Report 2006*, New York: UN.

Van Harten, G. (2007), *Investment Treaty Arbitration and Public Law*, Oxford: Oxford University Press.

23 Does environmental policy affect trade? The case of EU chemicals policy

Frank Ackerman

Introduction

Do the environmental policies of developed countries function as barriers to trade? This question has been extensively debated for years, often with a focus on developing-country exporters in agriculture or other low-technology industries. This chapter addresses the question from a different perspective, looking at the effects of one of the most ambitious European environmental initiatives of recent years: REACH, the new EU chemicals policy (the name is an acronym for Registration, Evaluation, and Authorization of Chemicals).

Based on a series of research studies on the economic impacts of REACH,[1] I conclude that:

1. The costs of REACH, although measured in billions of euros, are very small compared to the massive EU market for chemicals.
2. The effects of REACH on many developing countries are concentrated in mining, a sector dominated by multinational and other large corporations that can easily afford to comply with European regulations.
3. For US exporters, compliance with REACH will be entirely affordable, and will be essential to avoid repetition of the losses that have resulted from ignoring foreign standards in other cases.

As a number of researchers have noted, environmental standards set by Europe and other developed countries have the potential either to harm or to help developing countries (Nadvi, 2003). Rich-country standards can function as barriers to poor-country exports, thus impeding development (Copeland and Taylor, 2004). For example, food safety standards may turn out to play a protectionist role in practice (Henson and Loader, 2001). On the other hand, standards set in export markets may serve as a spur to social and environmental progress for developing-country exporters. European retailers have played a crucial role in transmitting information and incentives to their overseas suppliers, as shown in studies of the cut-flower industry (Hughes, 2000), fruit production in Brazil (van der Grijp et al., 2005), and the leather industry in India, Pakistan and elsewhere (Jenkins et al., 2002; Khan et al., 2002; Tewari and Pillari, 2005).

Most of the case studies in the literature are understandably focused on agricultural exporters, or on industries, such as leather, which process local agricultural products; such industries play a large part in the economies of developing countries. In these sectors, it is common to find small-scale producers with limited information about export markets and foreign standards, and limited resources for responding to a changing international context. Questions of asymmetric information become crucial for such producers; the need for technical, and perhaps financial, assistance is clear.

REACH raises a different set of questions, because it applies to industrial chemicals, metals and minerals. Small village enterprises do not produce ethylene or aluminum; exports subject to REACH come almost exclusively from large, capital-intensive industries. Chemicals remain a high-technology sector, concentrated in developed countries; more than half of all EU imports that are subject to REACH come from the USA, Switzerland, Russia, Norway and Japan (Ackerman et al., 2006). Mining, of course, is located wherever the relevant ores can be found; the same companies that operate mines in the USA and Australia are often involved in Chile and southern Africa as well.

If REACH affects trade, therefore, its primary effects will be felt by chemical industries in developed countries, and by mining companies operating around the world. And wherever the effects of REACH are felt, they must have some relationship to the costs of compliance with the new rules. Seen in the proper perspective, those compliance costs turn out to be remarkably small.

Costs of REACH: billions of euros small

After an intense five years of debate, from the initial proposal in 2001 to the final adoption in 2006, REACH went into effect in 2007. During the first 11 years of REACH, from 2007 through 2018, all the 30 000 or so chemicals that are sold in the EU in quantities above 1 tonne per year will have to be registered and tested. Those that are found to pose health or environmental hazards, presumably a small minority of the tested chemicals, will be subject to additional regulations.

As regulations go, this is a big one, affecting every aspect of an enormous industry. Complaints about the cost of regulation are commonplace, and commonly exaggerated (Ackerman, 2006) – but could REACH be the exception, the regulation that actually is expensive enough to interfere with economic prosperity? Such fears were amplified by two early studies of the costs of REACH, sponsored by German and French industry associations. (Perhaps living up to national stereotypes, the German study was a ponderous, methodical, 200-page report, while the French study was released only in the form of colorful PowerPoint slides presenting its conclusions.) In the opinion of these industry groups, the German and French economies would be devastated by the adoption of REACH.

Numerous other studies of the costs of REACH were conducted – and no one else found the costs to be large enough to cause noticeable damage to European economies. The European Commission estimated the costs at €2.3 billion; a study I directed, for the Nordic Council of Ministers, used different technical assumptions and came up with an estimate of €3.5 billion. Other estimates were in the same range, usually between €2 billion and €4 billion (Witmond et al., 2004). (Our study, Ackerman and Massey, 2004 includes a technical appendix detailing the numerous methodological errors of the German industry study, which account for its much higher result.)

How small are a few billion euros? Most people have no real understanding of quantities in the billions; such figures are so large that they have to be compared to something in order to be usefully comprehended. If the default standard of comparison is your own finances, or even a small business or non-profit organization, then a few billion euros looks enormous; if they were piled on a table, they would make a very big pile of money.

But the costs of REACH – the costs of registering and testing 30 000 chemicals – are not piled on a table anywhere; rather, they are spread across the breadth of the European chemicals market, over the first 11 years of the implementation of REACH. One appropriate standard of comparison in this case is the sales revenue of the European chemicals industry over an 11-year period. On this basis, a cost of a few billion euros is tiny, less than 0.1 percent, or one part per thousand, of industry sales revenues. Our study found a ratio of 0.06 percent, or one-sixteenth of 1 percent, but it is the order of magnitude, not the exact number, that matters. In industry, costs are constantly changing by much more than 0.1 percent; an industry unable to deal with changes of this magnitude would not survive in the marketplace. Even if, as the chemical industry sometimes suggested, most of the costs of REACH would be borne by one-third of the industry, the same general conclusion applies: that affected third of the industry would face costs of only a fraction of 1 percent of its sales.

The fact that the costs of REACH are so small, relative to the size of the affected industry, sets the stage for the analysis of impacts on trade. Since costs are small for European producers, and since REACH applies identical standards to European and foreign producers, the impact on Europe's trading partners is small as well.

REACH and developing countries

During the long debate leading up to the adoption of REACH, one of the last major objections raised was the potential impact on developing countries. In particular, will REACH harm the economies of the group of African, Caribbean and Pacific (ACP) countries that historically have been connected to Europe?[2] In 2005, the ACP Council of Ministers adopted a resolution supporting the general goals of REACH, but expressing 'deep concern' about the 'potential negative impact of REACH on exports, particularly in commodities such as minerals and metals, from ACP to the EU'. The Ministers stated that they were 'convinced that REACH will be expensive to implement', that REACH will have a negative effect on small, medium-sized and micro-enterprises, and that the costs imposed by REACH could 'lead to disinvestment from ACP States', potentially resulting in loss of employment for millions of people (ACP Council of Ministers, 2005).

Responding to these and other concerns, the European Parliament commissioned a study to assess the potential economic impacts of REACH on the ACP states. In that study, we analyzed the flows of ACP exports that would be subject to REACH, examining the commodities, countries and companies involved in those exports (Ackerman et al., 2006). At one extreme, local enterprises exporting a wide range of products in small volumes might face a heavy regulatory burden from REACH; at the other extreme, multinational companies exporting a small number of products in huge volumes might experience very little impact from regulations. We found many examples of multinationals and other large firms involved in ACP's exports subject to REACH, although we did also turn up one small example of local enterprises that might find REACH compliance to be difficult.

ACP includes many of the world's poorest countries, as well as South Africa and some smaller countries that are at a middle-income level by global standards. As of 2003, ACP's population of 743 million people represented 12 percent of the world population, while its total GDP of €434 billion was only 1.3 percent of world output. South Africa, by far the largest and most industrialized economy in ACP, accounts for about one-third of the group's total GDP, and two-thirds of the group's exports subject to REACH.

ACP countries are heavily dependent on trade, and have historically strong connections to Europe. Nonetheless, more than two-thirds of ACP exports go to non-European markets, such as North America and East Asia. Exports to all regions amount to one-third of ACP's GDP, while total exports to the EU are 10 percent, and exports to the EU subject to REACH are just 6.5 billion, or 1.4 percent of the group's GDP.[3]

Only 24 of the 79 ACP countries have any significant exports subject to REACH, by any one of three standards:

1. REACH exports[4] are at least 1 percent of GDP.
2. The annual value of all REACH exports is at least €10 million.
3. For at least one category of REACH exports, the annual volume of shipments exceeds 1000 tonnes.

Other ACP countries are agricultural exporters, service-based (often tourist-oriented) economies, or producers of fuels and other commodities that are exempt from REACH.

Of ACP's €6.5 billion of REACH exports, some €5.9 billion, more than 90 percent of the total, consists of mining products. Almost all of the mining consists of a few familiar materials: gold, iron and steel, aluminum, platinum, cobalt, copper, manganese and nickel together account for the overwhelming majority of REACH exports from ACP. There are no small-scale exporters of these products to Europe; in most cases, multinationals such as Anglo American (based in the UK), BHP Billiton (Australia), Alcan (Canada) and Alcoa (USA) are involved, either alone or with local partners. Particularly in South Africa, some large national firms are also involved in mining.

There is one important example of small enterprises in ACP mining. In several countries, small-scale or artisanal gold mining exists alongside major commercial mines. Large numbers of people are engaged in searching for gold with only rudimentary tools, under 'gold rush' conditions where most participants earn very little. This style of mining apparently does not occur on a large scale in South Africa (the source of almost 80% of ACP's gold exports to Europe), or in mining for anything other than gold.

Serious issues of poverty, economic development and environmental health are raised by artisanal gold mining. Yet the existence of these impoverished freelance miners does not imply that gold (or any other mineral) is exported to Europe by ACP micro-enterprises. Small-scale gold miners sell their gold either on the black market, or to national government agencies that export gold to Europe. In Tanzania, the country best known for artisanal gold mining, three-fourths of the nation's gold output comes from subsidiaries of Anglo American and other multinationals, and one-fourth from hundreds of thousands of artisanal miners. The national government is obligated to buy the gold produced by the small-scale miners, and is building a government-owned gold refinery to handle their output. Thus it is the government of Tanzania, not the individual miners, that exports the country's artisanal gold.

ACP exports to the EU of chemicals subject to REACH amount to just €0.6 billion a year, more than half of which comes from South Africa. On balance, South Africa is a net importer of chemicals from Europe, but its industry does export a wide range of products to the EU. Three companies dominate the South African chemical industry; one is a subsidiary of Dow Chemical, and the other two are national firms that are as large as many multinationals (one has annual sales of €9 billion and is listed on the New York Stock Exchange). Of the chemical exports from other ACP countries, the majority are oil industry byproducts from Trinidad and Tobago and from Equatorial Guinea, two oil-producing nations.

REACH compliance appears to be well within the abilities and financial resources of the large firms that account for almost all of ACP's relevant exports. Not only are the companies sufficiently large to understand and comply with European regulations; the affected products are, in large part, familiar ones whose properties are well known. No one expects that REACH will lead to a ban on aluminum, platinum, or copper imports, nor on well-known oil byproducts such as ethanol and methanol. Indeed, many of the test results required under REACH may already be available for some of ACP's leading products.

However, there is one small category of 'chemical' exports subject to REACH that fits the classic image of struggling local enterprises, namely the essential-oils industry. Essential oils are products of plants giving the odors and tastes characteristic of the particular plant, such as cinnamon and lavender. ACP as a whole exported €26 million of essential oils to EU, and six ACP countries averaged more than 50 tonnes of essential-oil exports to EU in 2002–04. We examined the industry in Madagascar and Comoros; in both cases, the sector appears to consist entirely of small to medium-sized farmers and manufacturers. Madagascar is ACP's largest essential-oils exporter after South Africa.

Essential oils of cloves and vanilla are among the country's most important exports; other essential oils produced in Madagascar include ylang ylang, palmarosa geranium, niaouli and helichryse. Madagascar has at least 20 small to medium-sized companies that produce essential oils or related substances. Comoros, sometimes called the Perfume Isles, exports 80 percent of the world's supply of ylang ylang essence, a main ingredient in many perfumes. The essential oils of vanilla and cloves are other important exports. Local distilleries use their own crops but also buy additional supplies from smaller farmers.

The European Federation of Essential Oils, which represents importers to the EU and producers in the EU, has emphasized that their 150 members are mainly small and medium-sized enterprises and would have difficulty complying with REACH. They advocated, unsuccessfully, for exempting essential oils from REACH. However, the overall costs of REACH compliance for the essential-oils industry will be low, since only a limited number of essential oils are exported from ACP to the EU in quantities affected by REACH. According to one estimate, 300 essential oils are sold in the EU, of which 170 are exempt from REACH because they are produced in amounts less than 1 tonne per year. Another 120 essential oils produce below 100 tonnes per year and face limited testing requirements. Only ten essential oils fall in the higher-volume range requiring more extensive testing. Safety and toxicity information is already available for many of the best-known products, reducing the burden of additional testing.

This example, it should be emphasized, is the exception, not the rule: essential oils comprise less than 0.5 percent of all ACP exports that are subject to REACH, a mere €26 million (not billion!) per year – and we did not discover any other sectors affected by REACH that are dominated by small ACP exporters and small EU importers. It might be reasonable to expect the EU to provide assistance in cases of burdensome impacts on small ACP exporters; the cost of such assistance would be quite limited because there are so few actual cases.

US exports: national pride or market access?

At the opposite end of the economic spectrum, REACH poses new, but manageable, challenges for US exporters as well. On balance, the EU has a trade surplus in chemicals with the USA (and with Japan; Europe is clearly the world leader in the chemicals industry). However, there are substantial flows of chemicals in both directions. In a recent study, we estimated that US chemicals exports to the EU that are subject to REACH amount to $14 billion per year, and are directly and indirectly responsible for 54 000 US jobs (Ackerman et al., 2007). There is no reason to expect that REACH compliance costs for US exporters will be any greater than for European producers. Applying the same 0.1 percent estimate for compliance costs, as discussed above, suggests that US exporters might face REACH compliance costs of $14 million per year, for 11 years, in order to maintain $14 billion of annual sales.

This should be, as the saying goes, a no-brainer: spend $1 a year for 11 years, or lose access to markets worth $1000 per year? No advanced quantitative skills are required to come up with the answer that looks best on the bottom line. In fact, spending $14 million a year to preserve 54 000 jobs compares favorably with many state job creation programs. Yet US industry and the Bush Administration have devoted considerable energy to arguing against REACH, continuing well past the point by which European industry had accepted the inevitability of some form of REACH.

In 2002, then-Secretary of State Colin Powell cabled US diplomatic posts with instructions to 'raise the EU chemicals policy with relevant government officials' and to object to REACH as 'costly, burdensome, and complex' (for documentation of this account, see Ackerman et al., 2007). The Assistant US Trade Representative for Europe and the Mediterranean invited American chemical companies to develop 'themes' for the US government to cite in its communications with EU officials regarding REACH. The Bush Administration filed formal comments with the European Commission criticizing many features of REACH, and circulated a chemical industry estimate of $8.8 billion in lost exports – an estimate based on the false assumption that all US computer sales to the EU would be cut off by REACH. As late as 2006, when the decision was all but final, the US Diplomatic Mission to the EU organized a joint statement of the Missions of Australia, Brazil, Chile, India, Israel, Japan, South Korea, Malaysia, Mexico, Singapore, South Africa and Thailand, asking the European Parliament to reconsider the implementation of REACH. The joint statement argued that REACH procedures are opaque, that REACH could disrupt international trade, and that it will harm developing countries in particular.

Following such persistent opposition, is there any risk that the USA might refuse to comply with REACH, now that it has been adopted? To do so would be foolish: like it or not, those are now the rules for selling chemicals in Europe. National pride is a poor substitute for access to export markets; past experience has shown that even the USA can quickly be shut out of established export markets by failing to comply with foreign standards.

One cautionary tale is provided by genetically modified corn. Bt corn, a variety of genetically modified corn developed in the 1980s, won its first regulatory approvals in 1992 and burst onto the market in the mid-1990s. From 1.4 percent of US planted area in 1996, Bt corn rose rapidly to 32 percent in 2004 (Ackerman et al., 2003; Nadal and Wise, 2004).[5] US growers, distributors and exporters are not able to reliably separate conventional from genetically modified corn; this meant that the whole US corn crop had to be treated as genetically modified. Since European consumers have rejected genetically modified food of any variety, this was a death blow to exports: US corn exports to the EU were above $100 million per year in the early 1990s but essentially vanished soon after the large-scale introduction of genetically modified corn, falling to $8 million or less per year from 1999 on (FAS, 2006).

A similar but larger loss occurred in meatpacking, when US producers failed to respond appropriately to foreign consumers' fears of bovine spongiform encephalopathy (BSE), or mad cow disease. US annual beef exports were around $3 billion worldwide from 2000 to 2003. Then the discovery of mad cow disease in the USA in late 2003 led to worldwide rejection of US beef. Exports dropped to $550 million in 2004 and remained below $1 billion in 2005 (FAS, 2006).

In most countries that have faced BSE problems, the response has involved a high level of testing for the disease to ensure that the food supply is safe. US regulators, however, have insisted on testing only a sample, in most years only a small fraction of 1 percent, of all slaughtered cattle. Following the detection of two North American BSE cases in 2003, the pace of testing was temporarily increased, reaching an all-time peak of just over 1 percent of all cattle slaughtered in the USA in 2005 and early 2006, before dropping back to a much lower level in late 2006. By way of comparison, BSE testing is done on 48 percent of cattle slaughtered in Europe, and 100 percent in Japan (USDA, 2005).

Additional testing, which could have reassured foreign markets, was rejected by the USA, even when private parties wanted to perform and pay for the tests. In 2004, Creekstone Farms, a Kansas beef producer, negotiated an agreement with the Japanese government to resume sales in Japan if Creekstone voluntarily adopted Japanese BSE testing standards. However, the Department of Agriculture invoked old food safety laws (written to prevent too little testing, a century earlier) to prohibit any American producer from exceeding US government BSE testing standards. Over $2 billion of annual exports were lost for at least two years, in order to maintain the principle that US industry does not need to meet other countries' safety standards.[6] While US beef exports have now edged back up, some export markets may have been permanently lost to other beef producing nations such as Australia.

A different outcome occurred in the wheat industry, one of the most export-dependent sectors of US agriculture. Roughly half of the US wheat crop is exported, with exports of wheat and wheat products to the EU-15 fluctuating around $200 million in recent years (FAS, 2006). Monsanto, a leading supplier of seeds and agricultural chemicals, applied for permission to grow genetically modified 'Roundup-Ready' wheat in the USA and Canada in 2002. Recognizing the threat to export markets, advocacy groups throughout wheat-growing areas organized an effective campaign against genetically modified wheat. The campaign quickly gained support from the Montana Legislature, the Canadian Wheat Board and other major organizations in the region. In 2004, Monsanto announced the withdrawal of its application to grow genetically modified wheat (OCA, 2006).

The high price of failing to meet other countries' health and safety regulations is painfully clear in the recent histories of the US corn and beef industries: genetically modified crops mean a loss of access to foreign markets, and the prohibition on internationally accepted levels of testing for mad cow disease crippled the beef export business, including meatpackers that wanted to meet those testing levels at their own expense.

Wheat growers, in contrast, understood the importance of foreign markets and rejected a dubious innovation that would have jeopardized their export sales. As the USA faces the dilemma of a huge and mounting trade deficit, the conclusion must be that the wheat growers got it right, making the choices that maintained market access, while the corn and beef industries (and the Department of Agriculture) got it wrong, stubbornly losing foreign buyers who wanted a product that can meet higher and different standards.

Conclusion

As the USA has unfortunately demonstrated, environmental standards do affect trade, at least when exporters ignore them. Even the world's leading economies can lose access to foreign markets, essentially overnight, by failing to respond to their customers' environmental preferences and regulations. On the other hand, for those who set out to comply with other countries' standards, the costs of a regulation as ambitious as REACH amount to only a trivial percentage of sales. The total cost of a few billion euros for REACH compliance, spread across one of the world's largest markets over a period of 11 years, turns out to be an insignificant cost burden. US exporters can easily afford their share of these costs, as the price of maintaining market access.

Perhaps more surprising is the near-absence of any burden on developing countries. There are almost no examples, in the trade flows affected by REACH, of struggling, small-scale developing country businesses, the emerging enterprises for which northern standards are a potential obstacle to trade. While that paradigm may be of importance in agriculture and other low-technology, less capital-intensive industries, it has little role in mining and chemicals. The one exception that falls within the scope of this analysis, the essential-oils industry, is so small that the EU can obviously afford any necessary technical and financial assistance to the producers.

Developing-country economies include small local enterprises, to be sure – but they also include subsidiaries of multinational corporations, which often account for large shares of the country's exports. Helping local enterprises to grow and prosper is a worthy goal, but should not spill over into special breaks for multinational mining companies when they mine the same commodities in Africa rather than Australia or North America. The producers of ACP's REACH exports can afford to comply with REACH, just as well as European companies; in a number of important cases, they *are* European companies.

Notes

1. The studies address: the costs of REACH, for the Nordic Council of Ministers (Ackerman and Massey, 2004); the effects of REACH on developing countries, for the European Parliament (Ackerman et al., 2006), also described in (Ackerman et al., 2008); and the effects of REACH on the US (Ackerman et al., 2007). My forthcoming book on the economics of toxic chemicals and precaution (Ackerman, 2008) includes chapters describing all three studies.
2. On Europe's longstanding economic and political relationship the ACP states see Robins (1998), Holland (2002) and Adelle et al. (2006).
3. This and many of our data are 2002–04 averages, and are documented in Ackerman et al. (2006).
4. This is a term we introduced; it is shorthand for 'exports to the EU that would be subject to REACH.'
5. All varieties of genetically modified corn together amounted to 45 percent of the US corn plantings in 2004 (Nadal and Wise, 2004).
6. See 'US won't let company test all its cattle for mad cow', *New York Times*, 10 April 2004.

References

Ackerman, Frank (2006), 'The unbearable lightness of regulatory costs', *Fordham Urban Law Journal*, **33**(4), 1071–96.

Ackerman, Frank (2008), *Poisoned for Pennies: The Economics of Risk, Toxics, and Precaution*, Washington, DC: Island Press.

Ackerman, Frank and Rachel Massey (2004), *The True Costs of REACH*, Copenhagen: Nordic Council of Ministers.

Ackerman, Frank, Timothy A. Wise, Kevin P. Gallagher, Luke Ney, and Regina Flores (2003), *Free Trade, Corn, and the Environment: Environmental Impacts of US–Mexico Corn Trade Under NAFTA*, Medford, MA: Tufts University, Global Development and Environment Institute.

Ackerman, Frank, Rachel Massey, Brian Roach, Elizabeth Stanton, Raya Widenoja, Julien Milanesi, William Parienté, Bernard Contamin, Patrick Bond, Euripides Euripidou, Anne-Sofie Andersson and Per Rosander (2006), 'Implications of REACH for the developing countries', *Policy Department External Policies*, Brussels: European Parliament Directorate-General for External Policies of the Union.

Ackerman, Frank, Elizabeth Stanton and Rachel Massey (2007), 'European chemical policy and the United States: the impacts of REACH', *Renewable Resources Journal*, **25**(1), 15–20.

Ackerman, Frank, Elizabeth Stanton, Brian Roach and Anne-Sofie Andersson (2008), 'Implications of REACH for Developing Countries', *European Environment*, **18**(1), January–February, 16–29.

ACP Council of Ministers (2005), *Resolutions and Declarations of the 81st Session of the ACP Council of Ministers*.

Adelle, Camilla, Julia Hertin and Andrew Jordan (2006), 'Sustainable development "Outside" the European Union: what role for impact assessment?', *European Environment*, **16**, 57–72.

Copeland, Brian R. and M. Scott Taylor (2004), 'Trade, growth, and the environment', *Journal of Economic Literature*, **42**(1), 7–71.

FAS (2006), *FASonline: US Trade Internet System*, Washington, DC: US Department of Agriculture, Foreign Agriculture Service.

Henson, S. and R. Loader (2001), 'Barriers to agricultural exports from developing countries: the role of sanitary and phytosanitary requirements', *World Development*, **29**(1), 85–102.

Holland, Martin (2002), *The European Union and the Third World*, New York: Palgrave.

Hughes, A. (2000), 'Retailers, knowledges and changing commodity networks: the case of the cut flower trade', *Geoforum*, **31**, 175–90.

Jenkins, Rhys, Jonathan Barton, Anthony Bartzokas, Jan Hesselberg and Hege Merete (2002), *Environmental Regulation in the New Global Economy: The Impact on Industry and Competitiveness*, Cheltenham, UK and Northampton, MA, USA: Edward Elgar.

Khan, S.R., M.A. Khwaja, A.M. Khan, H. Ghani and S. Kazmi (2002), 'Environmental impacts and mitigation costs: the case of Pakistan's cloth and leather exports', in S.R. Khan (ed.), *Trade and Environment: Difficult Policy Choices at the Interface*, London: Zed Books, pp. 84–123.

Nadal, Alejandro and Timothy Wise (2004), 'The environmental costs of agriculture trade liberalization: Mexico–U.S. maize trade under NAFTA', GDAE Working Group Discussion Paper, Medford, MA: Tufts University, Global Development and Environment Institute.

Nadvi, Khalid (2003), 'The cost of compliance: global standards for small-scale firms and workers', *IDS Policy Briefing*, May.

OCA (2006), *Campaign to stop GM wheat*, available at: http://www.organicconsumers.org/.

Robins, Nick (1998), 'Steering EU development co-operations towards sustainability: the case of the Lomé Convention', *European Environment*, **6**(1), 1–5.

Tewari, M. and P. Pillari (2005), 'Global standards and the dynamics of environmental compliance in India's leather industry', *Oxford Development Studies*, **33**(2), 245–67.

USDA (2005), *Statistical Highlights of US Agriculture 2004 & 2005*, available at: http://www.usda.gov/nass/pubs/stathigh/2005/2005Stat.PDF.

van der Grijp, N.M., T. Marsden, J. Salete and B. Cavalcanti (2005), 'European retailers as agents of change towards sustainability: the case of fruit production in Brazil', *Environmental Sciences*, **2**(4), 445–60.

Witmond, Bart, Sandra Groot, Wim Groen and Ewout Dönszelmann (2004), 'The impact of REACH: overview of 36 studies on the impact of the new EU chemicals policy (REACH) on society and business', Workshop REACH Impact Assessment, 25–27 October, Netherlands: The Hague.

24 Environmental regulation, globalization and innovation[1]
Nicholas A. Ashford

Introduction

This chapter explores the complex relationship between environmental regulation, innovation and sustainable development within the context of an increasingly globalizing economy. It will be argued that industrial policy, environmental policy and trade initiatives must be integrated, with a deliberate focus on stimulating technological innovation if trade and globalization are not to undercut progress in sustainable development.

Health, safety and environmental regulation – herein collectively referred to as 'environmental regulation' – addresses failures of the free market to internalize many of the social costs of an industrialized or industrializing economy by requiring the adoption of measures to protect the environment, workers, consumers and citizens. Regulation is criticized and resisted by many industrial firms,[2] who argue that such measures force sometimes unnecessary 'non-productive' investment that could be better directed to developing better goods and services and to expanding markets. Further, one of the complaints made by trading firms in industrialized nations is that such measures are not required in industrializing countries that enjoy the competitive advantage of free-riding on the environment and conditions of work.[3] A more modern view of the effects of regulation on the economy that results in competitive advantage resulting from regulation-induced innovation derives from the work of Michael Porter and Class van den Linde (1995a; 1995b), Martin Jaenicke and Klaus Jacob (2004), Jens Hemmelskamp et al. (2000), and Ashford (1979; 1985; 2000), among others, who argue that there are 'first-mover' advantages to firms that comply innovatively with regulation, become pioneers in lead markets, and displace suboptimal products, processes and firms.

Globalization has indeed changed the economic landscape. It connects the national economies in new ways and denationalizes access to information, technology, knowledge, markets and financial capital. It has also opened up two distinct pathways by which a national sector or economy can compete in international markets: (1) by producing more innovative and superior technology that may or may not be first deployed in niche markets (Kemp, 1994; 1997) and (2) by adopting cost-cutting measures that involve increased economies of scale, by shedding labor, and by ignoring health, safety and environmental hazards. While some have argued that globalization also increases the demand for more protective measures worldwide (Vogel, 1995; Bhagwati, 1997), others have cautioned about a 'race to the bottom' and an ever-increasing tendency to trade on environmental (and labor) externalities (Ekins et al., 1994).

Thus we see that there are not only two drivers of economic growth, technology and trade, but that trade itself can take two diametrically opposed directions, innovation-driven competition and traditional cost-cutting competition.

Health, safety and environmental regulation is the means by which industrial development is forced to become more sustainable, but the absence of strong international regulatory regimes changes the balance between industrialization and environment. This chapter argues that strong national regulation can spur technological, organizational, institutional and social innovation resulting in trade advantages that exceed shorter-term gains from cost-cutting and trade expansion that would otherwise weaken environmental protection, and it can result in better environmental quality than that kind of trade as well. However, more than the 'greening' of industry is needed. Creative destruction in the Schumpeterian sense is required (Schumpeter, 1939; 1962).

Innovation's key role in competitiveness and environment

Technological change is a general – and imprecise – term that encompasses invention, innovation, diffusion and technology transfer. Technological innovation is the first commercially successful application of a new technical idea. It should be distinguished from invention, which is the development of a new technical idea, and from diffusion, which is the subsequent widespread adoption of an innovation beyond those who developed it. [4]

As industrial societies mature, the nature and patterns of innovation change (Abernathy and Clark, 1985; Utterback, 1987). New technologies become old technologies. Many product lines (e.g. washing machines or lead batteries) become standardized or increasingly 'rigid', and innovation, if there is any, becomes more difficult and incremental rather than radical.

Using language that is familiar to traditional innovation scholars, an incremental innovation involves a step-by-step co-evolutionary process of change, whereas radical innovations are discontinuous and possibly involve the displacement of dominant firms and institutions, rather than evolutionary transformation (Moors, 2000; Luiten, 2001; Ashford et al; 2002; Partidario, 2003). Christensen (1997) distinguishes the former as sustaining innovation and the latter as disrupting innovation, rather than 'radical'. He argues that both sustaining and disrupting innovation can be incremental, moderate, or radical. Unfortunately, the term 'radical' in the literature is used in these two different ways and is a source of confusion.

However, another issue is in need of clarification: sustaining or disrupting of what? Christensen uses the term disrupting in the context of a customer base that values certain product attributes, and whose changing desires can change the markets for technological variants in products. The context in which we shall use the term pertains to the product – and also other technological or system changes – from a technological, as well as a customer-based desirability-of-attribute perspective. In this regard, our use of the term disrupting is more in line with Chris Freeman's (1982) use of the term 'radical' or Nelson and Winter's (1977) idea of shifting 'technological regimes' (see below). Since we take Christensen's point that the term 'radical' should be reserved to describe the rate of change rather its type, we shall generally avoid the term as a synonym for disrupting. But more is needed. From a technological perspective, disrupting innovations can be intrinsic or they can be architectural. The former is a dramatically different way of achieving functionality, such as the transistor replacing the vacuum tube; the latter may combine technological ideas in a new artifact, such as the hybrid electric-internal combustion engine. Christensen et al. (1998) stress the latter and focus on product technology. Utterback and Acee (2005, pp. 15–16) observe that '[i]nnovations that broaden the market create new room for firms to start' and '[t]he true importance of disruptive technology . . . is not that it may displace established products. Rather, it is a powerful means for enlarging and broadening markets and providing new functionality'. The problem with restricting one's analysis to the market determinants of technological change is that it neglects the fact that markets may not respond adequately to sustainability concerns. For example, consumers may well be concerned with product safety but are likely to be unconcerned by the safety of the manufacturing process affecting those who made the product. More is needed than matching the technological capacities of firms with current societal demands. Our inquiry will distinguish between sustaining innovation and disrupting innovation in a broader technological and societal context.

Product lines/sectors that are well developed, and that have become standardized, experience incremental innovation for the most part. Changes are focused on cost-reducing production methods – including increasing the scale of production, displacing labor with technology, and exercising more control over workers – rather than on significant changes in products. Gradually, process innovation also declines as manufacturing or production processes are standardized. A useful concept related to individual product lines is that of 'technological regimes', which are defined by certain boundaries for technological progress and by directions or trajectories in which progress is possible and worth doing (Nelson and Winter, 1977).

Sometimes, however, the dominant technologies (such as the vacuum tube and mechanical calculator) are challenged and rather abruptly displaced by significant disrupting innovations (such as the transistor and electronic calculator), but this is relatively rare, although very important (Kemp, 1994; Christensen, 1997). We shall argue that disrupting innovations may be what is needed to achieve sustainability. As industrial economies mature, innovation in many sectors may become more and more difficult and incremental, regulatory and governmental policies are increasingly influenced, if not captured, by the purveyors of the dominant technology (regime) which becomes more resistant to change. However, occasionally, traditional sectors can revitalize themselves, such as in the case of cotton textiles. [5]

Other sectors, notably those based on emerging technologies, may experience increased innovation. The overall economic health and employment potential of a nation as a whole is the sum of these diverging trends, and is increasingly dependent on international trade. Whether nations seek to increase revenues based on competition in technological performance or alternatively rely on cost-cutting strategies can have an enormous impact on both employment and the environment. As will be discussed below, health, safety and environmental regulation, structured appropriately, as well as new societal demands, can also stimulate significant technological changes that might not otherwise have occurred at the time (Ashford et al., 1985).

A technological innovation can be characterized by its motivating force, by its type, and by its nature. The motivating force behind technological change can be the result of an industry's main business activities or it can evolve from the industry's efforts to comply with or respond to health, safety, or environmental regulations and pressures (Ashford et al., 1979). Regulation, market signals and anticipated worker or consumer demand can affect any of the characteristics of innovation. There is ample evidence that the most significant driving force for technological change identified by business managers is environmental legislation and enforcement (Ashford and Hall, 2009).

Concerning the type of innovation, four different levels of technological change need to be considered: (1) product changes, (2) process changes, (3) shifts from products to product-services, and (4) more far-reaching system changes that not only include technological innovation, but also effects on employment, the organization of the firm, and societal demands. Innovation can be of a product-oriented type, meaning that it involves changes in the design of the final product or service. It can extend further to include shifts to product services, in which the firm envisions delivering a desired service or benefit to the customer in creative new ways, with a goal of minimizing resources, energy use and pollution. An example is selling copier services to customers – in which the copier company owns the machine and performs all maintenance and service on it while in use – instead of selling copy machines. This kind of change is described subsequently in more detail. Technological innovation can also be of a process-oriented type, meaning that it can occur as part of the production process of a product or the delivery of a service.

System changes are the deepest and broadest in scope. They extend outside the boundaries of the firm to include many actors, including suppliers, competitor and collaborator firms, government authorities and civil society. They involve the reconceptualization and reordering of entire production chains and stakeholder networks, for example, shifting from non-local industrial agriculture to locally grown organic food systems, or simultaneously altering production, employment, distribution and transportation regimes to move people and deliver goods more efficiently, with less energy use and pollution.

In the context of product change, the nature of a technological innovation can be evaluated according to whether it serves either to sustain or disrupt established product lines and value networks of customers with well-defined demands (Christensen, 1997). Christensen's concept of a 'value network' is 'the context within which a firm identifies and responds to customers' needs, solves problems, procures input, reacts to competitors, and strives for profit'. In Christensen's formulation, sustaining innovations occur when established firms push the envelope to continue to satisfy existing consumers with improved products within the prior but expanded technological trajectory. Disrupting innovations cater to different, perhaps not yet well-defined, customers with product attributes different from those in the established producer–consumer networks.[6] Alternatively, the distinction between sustaining and disrupting innovation might be focused on the technological nature of the change, a distinction that invites incentives focused not only on product changes (which may be the main driver in market-pull innovation), but also changes involving process changes, shifts to product services, and wider system changes. This is not to downplay the importance of consumer demand, but to put it in a proper context, since many desirable technological changes will need to come from more interventionist and regulatory approaches if sustainable development is to be achieved in a timely fashion. We explore these ideas further in the next section.

Another way of comparing sustaining and disrupting innovation is to depict three different pathways that innovation could take. In Figure 24.1, the various performance levels of an existing technology regime (for example, various internal combustion automobile engines with different fuel efficiencies) are shown as a function of cost. The most efficient existing engine is represented by point 'A' at cost C_1. New improvements (sustaining innovations) to internal combustion engines can be developed within the same technological regime in two different ways. First, improvements could be made, extending the capacity of existing technology, but at higher cost, as depicted by the dashed line. Second, a significant innovation could occur within the same technological regime, giving

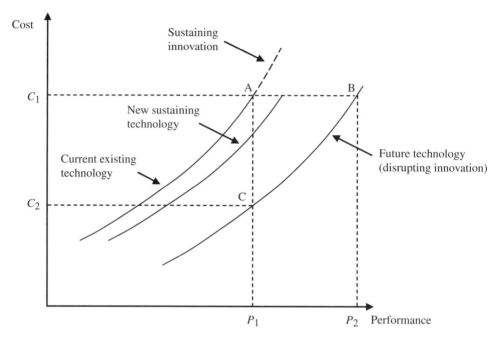

Figure 24.1   The efficient frontier for current and future technology contrasting sustaining and disrupting innovation

rise to new performance–cost relationships as depicted in the second curve, shifted to the right in Figure 24. 1. Third, a power system based on a different concept of innovation (a disrupting innovation) could be developed, represented by the 'future technology' curve, depicted by the right-most curve. At some point, fuel-efficient engines can be developed that provide the best old-engine efficiency, but at a lower cost C_2 represented by point 'C' – or better efficiency can be achieved at the same cost C_1, represented by point 'B'. Anywhere in between on the future technology curve represents a 'win–win' situation over the sustaining innovations on the dashed line.

Regulation's role in benefiting the economy and the environment

The ideology of *laissez-faire* suggests that government regulation is mostly unhelpful or inefficient, but there is increasingly persuasive evidence that regulation – properly designed – is not only necessary to achieve sustainable economies; it can actually stimulate innovation leading to improved competitiveness, employment and to an improved environment. Early MIT research stimulated more focused research into the effects of government regulation in the USA. It was found in a number of MIT studies beginning in 1979 that regulation could stimulate significant fundamental changes in product and process technology which benefited the industrial innovator, as well as improving health, safety and the environment, provided the regulations were stringent, focused and properly structured (Ashford, 1976; 2000; Ashford et al., 1985). This empirical work was conducted 15 years earlier than the emergence of the so-called Porter hypothesis, which argued that firms at the cutting edge of developing and implementing technology to reduce pollution would benefit economically by being first movers to comply with regulation (Porter, 1990; Porter and van den Linde, 1995a; 1995b).

The Porter hypothesis could be described as having both a weak and a strong form. Porter himself discusses only the weak form, essentially that regulation, properly designed, can cause the (regulated) firm to undertake innovations that not only reduce pollution – a hallmark of production inefficiency – but also save on materials, water and energy costs, conferring what Porter calls 'innovation offsets' to the innovating firm. This can occur because the firm, at any point in time, is sub-optimal. If the firm is the first to move by complying in an intelligent way, other firms will later have to rush to comply and do so in a less thoughtful and more expensive way. Thus there are 'learning curve' advantages to being first and early. Porter argues that in the international context, first-mover firms benefit by being subjected to a national regulatory system slightly ahead of that found in other countries. The strong form of the Porter hypothesis was not put forth by Porter at all. It (and the weak form as well) was first proposed by Ashford and his colleagues at MIT (Jaffe et al. 1995) after years of cross-country and US-based studies that showed that stringent regulation could cause dramatic changes in technology, often by new firms or entrants displacing the dominant technologies. The replacement of dominant technologies by new entrants, rather than incremental change by existing technology providers, has been the source of the most important radical innovations this century.

MIT research found paradoxically that the only government policy that affected innovation was health, safety and environmental regulation, not strategies devised by government as a part of its industrial policy. Moreover, the effects of regulation on innovation turned out to be positive, not negative as expected by the conventional wisdom at that time. Stringent regulation could stimulate entirely new products and processes into the market by new entrants with the displacement of dominant technologies rather than the transformation of technologies by existing firms. One of several vivid examples is the displacement of Monsanto's PCBs in transformers and capacitors by an entirely different dielectric fluid pioneered by Dow Silicone. Regulation can thus encourage disrupting innovations by giving more influence to new 'value networks' or 'customer bases' in which demands for improvements in both environmental quality and social cohesion are more sharply defined and articulated. Of course, industries that would fear disrupting new entrants would not be expected to welcome this regulation. This explains in part their resistance to regulation and their propensity to try to capture regulatory regimes, surreptitiously or through direct negotiation (Caldart and Ashford, 1999).

In principle, regulation can be an effective and proper instrument for government to guide the innovation process. Well designed, regulation that sets new rules changes the institutional framework of the market and can be an important element in creating favorable conditions for innovation. This enhances environmental sustainability and creates incentives for the development of powerful lead markets which pull innovation towards that sustainability. With regard to regulation, what seems to matter is not only the stringency, mode (specification versus performance), timing, uncertainty, focus (inputs versus product versus process) of the regulation, and the existence of complementary economic incentives, but also the inherent innovativeness (usually in new entrants) or lack of it (usually the regulated firms) (Ashford and Heaton, 1983; Ashford et al., 1985). The importance of new entrants is missing in the analysis offered by Porter.

In order for innovation to occur, the firm (or government itself) must have the willingness, opportunity/motivation, and capability or capacity to innovate (Ashford, 2000). These three factors affect each other, of course, but each is determined by more fundamental factors.

Willingness is determined by (1) attitudes towards changes in production in general, (2) an understanding of the problem, (3) knowledge of possible options and solutions, and (4) the ability to evaluate alternatives. Improving (3) involves aspects of capacity-building through the diffusion of information, through trade associations, government-sponsored education programs, inter-firm contacts and the like. Changing attitudes towards changes in production (1) often depends on attitudes of managers and on the larger culture and structure of the organization, which may either stifle or encourage innovation and risk-taking. Factors (2) and (4) depend on internal intellectual capacities. In the context of disrupting innovation by firms representing the dominant technology, willingness is also shaped by the (rare) commitment of management to nurture new approaches that are at odds with its traditional value network or customer base.

Opportunity and motivation involve both supply-side and demand-side factors. On the supply side, technological gaps can exist between the technology currently used in a particular firm and the already-available technology that could be adopted or adapted (known as diffusion or incremental innovation, respectively), or alternatively the technology that could be developed (i.e. significant sustaining or disrupting innovation). Consciousness of these gaps could prompt firms to change their technology, as could the opportunity for cost savings. Regulatory requirements could also define the changes that would be necessary to remain in the market. On the demand side, three factors could push firms towards technological change – whether diffusion, incremental innovation, or major innovation. These are (1) opportunities for cost savings or expansion of sales, (2) public demand for more environmentally sound, eco-efficient and safer industry, products and services, and (3) worker demands and pressures arising from industrial relations concerns. The first factor could result from changes in the customer value networks. All these factors, however, may stimulate change too late in the dominant technology firms, if new entrants have already seized the opportunity to engage in developing disrupting innovations.

Capability or capacity can be enhanced by (1) an understanding of the problem, (2) knowledge of possible options and solutions, (3) the ability to evaluate alternatives, (4) resident/available skills and capabilities to innovate, and (5) access to, and interaction with, outsiders. Knowledge enhancement/learning (2) could be facilitated through deliberate or serendipitous transfer of knowledge from suppliers, customers, trade associations, unions, workers and other firms, as well from the available literature. The skill base of the firm (4) could be enhanced through educating and training operators, workers and managers, on both a formal and informal basis, and by deliberate creation of networks and strategic alliances not necessarily confined to a geographical area, nation, or technological regime.

Interaction with outsiders (5) could stimulate more radical and disrupting changes. This last method of enhancing the capacity of firms to undertake technological change involves new 'outsider' firms and stakeholders with which the firm has not traditionally been involved. Capacity to change may also be influenced by the innovativeness (or lack thereof) of the firm as determined by the maturity and technological rigidity of particular product or production lines (Ashford, 2000; Ashford et al., 1985). Some firms find it easier to innovate than others. The heavy, basic industries, which are also sometimes the most polluting, unsafe and resource-intensive industries, change with great difficulty, especially when it comes to core processes. New industries, such as computer manufacturing, can also be polluting, unsafe (for workers), and resource and energy intensive, although conceivably they may find it easier to meet environmental demands.

The different dimensions or factors of willingness, opportunity and capability offer a variety of starting points for government policies for stimulating technological and organizational innovation. This represents an opportunity as well as a problem. The opportunity is that government does not depend on a few specific instruments, but may have command of a large variety of instruments. These include removing regulatory barriers to innovation, stimulating innovation by getting the prices for natural resources right, using government regulation to stimulate innovation, procurement and investment to develop new markets, advancing knowledge transfer from universities to small and medium enterprises, implementing proactive programs for the education and training of labor for a knowledge-based economy, and encouraging management and labor to bargain before technological changes are planned and implemented, and last but not least, cultural activities to enhance openness and willingness to engage in change (Ashford, 2000).

The problem is that these instruments must be integrated in a systematic approach or they will create various contradictory and conflicting effects – as is often the case with uncoordinated public policy. The coordination of a variety of policy instruments is often a complex task which exceeds governments' capacities. The real challenge, thus, is to find effective approaches and methods to coordinate a complex variety of instruments with complex impacts in a systematic way. We address this problem and its solution in the final section of this chapter.

Trade strategies, the environment and employment
Charles and Lehner (1998) argue that 'the type of innovation which is the key to new employment is one which develops markets in new directions and creates new markets and thus enhances a strong leading-edge economy'. One could make the same observation for the enhancement of the environment. As Schumpeter has pointed out, companies in the leading-edge economy can exploit a temporary monopoly resulting from their superior products and services (Schumpeter, 1939; 1962). Advanced-industry economies in their innovative sectors have already shifted in the last 10 to 15 years from technocentric to anthropocentric production systems – those that capitalize on human intelligence and are designed for continuous improvement and learning. Instead of a cost-driven strategy that calls for reduced labor costs, Charles and Lehner recommend that industrial economies aim for an innovation-driven strategy, which depends on a large number of human interfaces in the company that are likely to produce organizational learning, creativity, new ideas – and well-paying jobs. An innovation-driven strategy also affords an opportunity to modernize and improve products, processes and services.

Sustainable development should be seen as a broad concept, incorporating concerns for the economy, the environment and employment. All three are driven or affected by both technological innovation (Schumpeter, 1939; 1962) and globalized trade (Diwan and Walton, 1997; Ekins et al., 1994). They are also in a fragile balance, are interrelated, and need to be addressed together in a coherent and mutually reinforcing way. Technological innovation and trade drive national economies in different ways (Charles and Lehner, 1998). The former exploits a nation's innovative potential, the latter its excess production capacity. Innovation-based performance is enhanced by technological innovation and changing product markets, characterized by fluid, competitive production. Cost reduction strategies are enhanced by increased scales of production and/or automation, usually characterized by rigid, mature monopolistic production. Economies seeking to exploit new international markets may enjoy short-term benefits from revenues gained as a result of production using existing excess capacity, but they may ultimately find themselves behind the technological curve. Performance-driven markets may be slower to gain profits, but may outlast markets driven by cost reduction strategies. The consequences for the environment and for workers may differ as well.

Innovation-based performance competitiveness presents opportunities for environmental improvements and for skill enhancement and building optimal human–technology interfaces, while cost reduction strategies focus on lean production (with worker displacement and usually designed without health, safety, or environmental performance in mind), flexible labor markets, and knowledge increasingly embodied in hardware and software rather than in human capital. The consequences for the environment and for workers are different for these two strategies. The former strategy can lead to more environmentally sustainable technologies of production and also reward and encourage skill acquisition for many, with appropriate financial benefits for those workers. The latter may seek to minimize environmental improvement costs and create a division between workers, some of whom are necessarily upskilled and many whose job content is reduced. Different national strategies might be pursued, reflecting different domestic preferences and culture, but there are further implications, depending on the extent to which trade drives the economy.

The changing global economy presents challenges for all nations as concerns for the number of jobs, job security, wages, and occupational health and safety increase and compete for attention with environmental concerns. In the private sector, labor needs a role in choosing and implementing information-based technologies. In the public sector, there is a need for integrating industrial development and trade policies with those of employment, occupational health and safety, and the environment.

The need for integrating industrial, environmental and trade policies
Articulating policy approaches to sustainability requires more than an understanding of the challenges to sustainability posed by the international context. Integrated sustainability policies must utilize, alter or supplant existing policies (and the institutions that administer them) in the areas of economy, trade, environment and employment.

Recalling that a sustainable future requires technological, organizational, institutional and social changes, it is likely that an evolutionary pathway is insufficient for achieving factor ten or greater improvements in eco- and energy efficiency and reductions in the production and use of, and exposure to, toxic substances. Such improvements require more systemic, multidimensional and disruptive changes. We have already asserted that the capacity to change can be the limiting factor – often crucially missing in optimistic scenarios.

Successful management of disruptive product innovation requires initiatives and input from outsiders to produce the expansion of the design space that limits the dominant technology firms. Especially in sectors with an important public or collective involvement, such as transportation, construction and agriculture, this means that intelligent government policies are required to bring about necessary change.

Rigid industries whose processes have remained stagnant also face considerable difficulties in becoming significantly more sustainable. Shifts from products to 'product services' rely on changes in the use, location and ownership of products in which mature product manufacturers may participate, but this requires significant changes involving both managerial and social (customer) innovations. Changes in socio-technical 'systems', such as transportation or agriculture, are even more difficult. This suggests that the creative use of government intervention is a more promising strategic approach for achieving sustainable industrial transformations than the reliance of the more neoliberal policies on firms' shorter-term economic self-interest.

This is not to say that enhanced analytic and technical capabilities on the part of firms, cooperative efforts and improved communication with suppliers, customers, workers, other industries and environmental/consumer/community groups are not valuable adjuncts in the transformation process. But in most cases these means and strategies are unlikely to be sufficient by themselves for significant transformations, and they will not work without clear mandated targets to enhance the triple goals of competitiveness, environmental quality and enhancement of employment/labor concerns.

Government has a significant role to play, but the government cannot simply serve as a referee or arbiter of existing competing interests, because neither future generations nor future technologies are adequately represented by the existing stakeholders. Government should work with stakeholders to define far-future targets – but without allowing the agenda to be captured by the incumbents – and then use its position as trustee to represent the future generations and the future technologies to 'backcast' what specific policies are necessary to produce the required technical, organizational and social transformations. As mentioned earlier, this backcasting will have to be of a next-generation variety of backcasting. It has to go beyond its historical focus on coordinating public and private sector policies. It must be multidimensional and directly address the present fragmentation of governmental functions – not only at the national level, but also at the regional level in closely allied nations such as those in the EU, and at the international level through multilateral environmental and labor agreements and within revised trade regimes such as the WTO and NAFTA.

There is a great deal of serendipity and uncertainty in the industrial transformation process, and the long-term prospects may not be sufficiently definable to suggest obvious pathways or trajectories for the needed transformations. Thus it may be unreasonable to expect that government can play too definitive a 'futures-making' role. What follows from this is that rather than attempting tight management of the pathways for the transformations that are sustainable in the broad sense in which we define it in this chapter, the government role might be better conceived as one of 'enabling' or 'facilitating' change, while at the same time lending visionary leadership for co-optimizing competitiveness, environment and employment. This means that the various policies must be mutually reinforcing. This newly conceptualized leadership role, focused on 'opening up the problem space of the engineer/designer', is likely to require participation of more than one ministry and more than one division of the industrial firm, with the assistance of professionals trained in a more multidisciplinary way (see Ashford, 2004).

Notes

1. Copyright © 2007 Nicholas A. Ashford. This chapter draws heavily from a book in progress: Nicholas A. Ashford and Ralph P. Hall (2009), *Technology, Globalization and Sustainability*.
2. Here the term 'industrial firms' is broadly defined to include those engaged in the extraction of energy and material resources, manufacturing, transportation, agriculture and services.
3. I argue elsewhere that the three pillars of sustainable development include competitiveness, environment and employment, although this chapter is concerned primarily with environment, broadly construed. See Ashford (2000).
4. The distinction between innovation and diffusion is sometimes hard to draw, however, because innovations can rarely be adopted by new users without some modification. When modifications are extensive, i.e. when adoption requires significant adaptation, the result may be a new innovation.
5. Under the economic threat of more stringent worker protection standards for cotton dust exposure, the leading US textile firm decided to redesign and modernize its technology to reduce occupational exposure to both cotton dust and noise, and to improve production efficiency. It stands out as one of the rare instances where an industry reinvented and replaced itself.
6. The creation of new products in this case is not a wave built upon prior waves of technological advance, but rather occurs in an entirely new trajectory, often creating a new market.

References

Abernathy, W.J. and K.B. Clark (1985), 'Innovation: mapping the winds of creative destruction', *Research Policy*, **14**(1), 3–22.
Ashford, N.A. (ed.) (1976), *National Support for Science and Technology: An Examination of the Foreign Experience*, MIT Center for Policy Alternatives, CPA-75-12 (I & II), 15 May.
Ashford, N.A. (2000), 'An innovation-based strategy for a sustainable environment', in J. Hemmelskamp, K. Rennings, and F. Leone (eds), *Innovation-Oriented Environmental Regulation: Theoretical Approach and Empirical Analysis*, ZEW Economic Studies, Heidelberg, New York: Springer Verlag, pp. 67–107.
Ashford, N. A. (2004), 'Major challenges to engineering education for sustainable development: what has to change to make it creative, effective, and acceptable to the established disciplines', *International Journal of Sustainability in Higher Education*, **5**(3), 239–50.
Ashford, N.A. and R.P. Hall (2009), *Technology, Globalization and Sustainability*.
Ashford, N.A. and G.R. Heaton (1983), 'Regulation and technological innovation in the chemical industry', *Law and Contemporary Problems*, **46**(3), 109–57.
Ashford, N.A., G.R. Heaton et al. (1979), 'Environmental, health and safety regulations and technological innovation', in C.T. Hill and J.M. Utterback (eds), *Technological Innovation for a Dynamic Economy*, New York: Pergamon Press, pp. 161–221.
Ashford, N.A., C. Ayers et al. (1985), 'Using regulation to change the market for innovation', *Harvard Environmental Law Review*, **9**(2), 419–66.
Ashford, N.A., Wim Hafkamp, Frits Prakke and Philip Vergragt (2002), *Pathways to Sustainable Industrial Transformations: Optimizing Competitiveness Employment, and Environment*, Cambridge: Ashford Associates.
Bhagwati, J. (1997), 'The global age: from a skeptical South to a fearful north', *The World Economy*, **20**(3), 259–283.
Caldart, C.C. and N.A. Ashford (1999), 'Negotiation as a means of developing and implementing environmental and occupational health and safety policy', *Harvard Environmental Law Review*, **23**(1), 141–202.
Charles, T. and F. Lehner (1998), 'Competitiveness and employment: a strategic dilemma for economic policy', *Competition and Change*, **3** (1/2), 207–36.
Christensen, C.M. (1997), *The Innovator's Dilemma*, Cambridge, MA: Harvard Business School Press.
Christensen, C., J.M. Utterback and F.F. Suarez (1998), 'Strategies for survival in fast-changing industries', *Management Science*, **44**(12), S207–S220.
Diwan, I. and M. Walton (1997), 'How international exchange, technology and institutions affect workers: an introduction', *World Bank Economic Review*, **11**(1), 1–15.
Ekins, P., C. Folke and R. Costanza (1994), 'Trade, environment and development: the issues in perspective', *Ecological Economics*, **9**(1), 1–12.
Freeman, C. (1982), *The Economics of Industrial Innovation*, London: Frances Pinter.
Hemmelskamp, J., K. Rennings, and F. Leone (eds) (2000), *Innovation-Oriented Environmental Regulation: Theoretical Approach and Empirical Analysis*, ZEW Economic Studies, Heidelberg, New York: Springer Verlag.
Jaenicke, Martin and Klaus Jacob (2004), 'Lead markets for environmental innovations: a new role for the nation state', *Global Environmental Politics*, **4**(1), 29–46.
Jaffe, Adam B., Steven R. Peterson, Paul R. Portney and Robert N. Stavins (1995), 'Environmental regulation

and the competitiveness of U.S. manufacturing: what does the evidence tell us?' *Journal of Economic Literature*, **33**(1), 132–63.

Kemp, R. (1994), 'Technology and environmental sustainability: the problem of technological regime shift', *Futures*, **26**(10), 1023–46.

Kemp, R. (1997), *Environmental Policy and Technical Change: A Comparison of the Technological Impact of Policy Instruments*, Cheltenham, UK and Lyme, USA: Edward Elgar.

Luiten, E.E.M. (2001), *Beyond Energy Efficiency: Actors, Networks and Government Intervention in the Development of Industrial Process Technologies*, Utrecht: Utrecht University.

Moors, E.H.M. (2000), *Metal Making in Motion: Technology Choices for Sustainable Metals Production*, Delft: Delft University of Technology.

Nelson, R.R. and S.G. Winter (1977), 'In search of a useful theory of innovation', *Research Policy*, 6, 36–76.

Partidario, P.J. (2003), '*What-if*: *From Path Dependency to Path Creation in a Costings Chain: A Methodology for Strategies towards Sustainable Innovation*, Delft: Delft University of Technology.

Porter, Michael (1990), *The Competitive Advantage of Nations*, New York: Free Press.

Porter, Michael E. and Claas van den Linde (1995a), 'Green and competitive: ending the stalemate', *Harvard Business Review*, September/October, 120–34.

Porter, Michael E. and Claas van den Linde (1995b), 'Towards a new conceptualization of the environment–competitiveness relationship', *Journal of Economic Perspectives*, **9**(4), 97–118.

Schumpter, J.A. (1939), *Business Cycles: A Theoretical, Historical and Statistical Analysis of the Capitalist Process*, New York: McGraw-Hill.

Schumpeter, J.A. (1962), *Capitalism, Socialism and Democracy*, New York: Harper Torchbooks.

Utterback, J.M. (1987), 'Innovation and industrial evolution in manufacturing industries', in B. R.Guile and H. Brooks (eds), *Technology and Global Industry: Companies and Nations in the World Economy*, Washington, DC: National Academy Press, 16–48.

Utterback, J.M. and H.F. Acee (2005), 'Disruptive technologies: an expanded view', *International Journal of Innovation Management*, **9**(1), 1–17.

Vogel, David (1995), 'National regulation in the global economy', in *Trading Up: Consumer and Environmental Protection in a Global Economy*, Cambridge, MA: Harvard University Press, pp. 1–23.

25 Trade and environment policy-making in the Arab region

*Carol Chouchani Cherfane**

In November 2007, an expert meeting on trade and environment priorities facing the Arab region was convened in Cairo, Egypt under the auspices of the Kingdom of Saudi Arabia. The meeting involved delegates from ministries of environment, trade, industry and economy from nearly all Arab countries, as well as representatives from regional organizations, the private sector and civil society. The conference was organized by the League of Arab States (LAS), United Nations Economic and Social Commission for Western Asia (ESCWA) and the United Nations Environment Program Regional Office for West Asia (UNEP/ROWA). Discussions focused on key issues, including the liberalization of environmental goods and services; the impact of environmental requirements on market access and competitiveness; the effects of globalization and trade liberalization on the environment; trade and environment policy coordination; and climate change.

The meeting illustrates the wide range of topics that have now become mainstream trade and environment concerns in developing countries, as well as the number of different stakeholders involved in the process of trade and environment policy-making in the Arab region. While the event built upon of a series of meetings conducted on varied trade and environment topics over the course of several years, it is worth noting that this gathering concluded with a number of recommendations that were subsequently adopted by the Council of Arab Ministers Responsible for the Environment (CAMRE) in December 2007.[1] The Council also mandated that the recommendations be submitted to the Arab Summit for Development for consideration by the heads of state in 2008. Such an outcome would have been unimaginable in the region a decade earlier.

Regional background

The introduction of trade and environment issues on to the policy agenda is a relatively new phenomenon in the Arab region. The change in appreciation is due in large part to the growing recognition that trade and environmental issues should be addressed within an integrated policy framework that seeks to achieve sustainable development.

Before the 1990s, trade and environment issues were generally defined in terms of trade-related multilateral environmental agreements (MEAs) as government and civil society mostly thought about the topic in terms of managing natural resources and mitigating the negative effects of trade on the environment. Military conflicts in the developing world raised the profile of these interlinkages by exposing how a power vacuum can provide fertile ground for wayward traders seeking to dispose of hazardous materials in countries in crisis, such as in Lebanon during its long civil war. The threats associated with illicit trade in these substances led to the signing of the Basel Convention on the Control of Transboundary Movements of Hazardous Wastes and their Disposal in 1989, which most Arab countries have ratified. At the Arab regional level, the political aspects of these cross-border environmental concerns related to trade were addressed by CAMRE, which was established in 1987. However, economic decision-makers in the region paid little attention to these policy linkages during this period.

Preparations for the Rio Summit on Environment and Development (1992) raised awareness about the impacts of increased production and consumption patterns on sustainable development and the associated effects that increased trade flows would have on the environment. It also contributed to the establishment of the Joint Commission for Environment and Development in the Arab Region (JCEDAR) as a multi-stakeholder advisory committee to CAMRE. The inclusion of sustainable development as a key tenet of the World Trade Organization (WTO), as stated in its enabling charter signed in Marrakech, Morocco in 1995, and the subsequent activation of the WTO Committee on Trade and Environment (CTE) prompted economic policy-makers in the Arab region to take notice of trade and environment linkages. However, rather than viewing the issue from the perspective of trade impacts on environmental sustainability, they joined other developing regions who raised concern regarding the implications that non-tariff barriers (NTBs), including environmental, health and safety requirements, might have on restricting market access and reducing international competitiveness. Some oil-exporting Arab countries also signaled their concern that trade-distorting environmental measures, such as energy subsidies and taxation schemes, could be implemented in a discriminatory manner and harm the competitiveness of petroleum exports relative to other energy sources, including those that may present a greater environmental risk.[2]

These developments contributed to a chain of events that helped to institutionalize coordination and capacity-building mechanisms on trade and environment policy issues in the Arab region. Chief among them was the adoption of the Plan of Implementation of the World Summit for Sustainable Development (2002), which calls on countries to:

- enhance the delivery of coordinated, trade-related technical assistance and capacity-building programs, including those that promote market access opportunities (Section V.45(e));
- enhance the mutual supportiveness of trade, environment and development (Section IX.91);
- encourage efforts to promote cooperation on trade, environment and development, including the provision of technical assistance by international and regional organizations (Section IX.91(c));
- encourage relevant committees of the World Trade Organization (WTO) to debate the developmental and environmental aspects of negotiations (Section IX.91(a)); and
- promote mutual supportiveness between the multilateral trading system and multilateral environmental agreements (MEAs) (Section IX.92).[3]

This was complemented by the adoption of the Sustainable Development Initiative in the Arab Region (2002), which seeks to:

- call upon the international community to support the efforts of Arab countries to avoid the negative effects resulting from globalization on the economic, technical, environmental and social levels; and

● strengthen the competitiveness of Arab commodities and to endeavor to abolish all forms of subsidies, assistance and barriers imposed by the industrial countries to impede the access of Arab commodities in international markets.[4]

The initiative led CAMRE to request

> ESCWA and UNEP to coordinate and cooperate with the Technical Secretariat of CAMRE to develop a regional program for Arab capacity building on trade and environment issues, especially to address measures that hinder Arab export competitiveness in international markets and that relate to trade negotiations and adjusting to the rules and regulations of the World Trade Organization related to the environment.[5]

Based on consultations with Arab countries, the noted institutions subsequently drafted the Program for Trade and Environment Capacity Building in the Arab Region, which was adopted by JCEDAR and CAMRE in 2003.[6] The program focuses on assisting Arab states in three thematic areas, namely market access, international competitiveness and building capacity in dispute resolution, including mechanisms to ensure the mutual supportiveness of trade-related MEAs and the multilateral trading system.

The institutional context
Following the establishment of the WTO, a first generation of working groups on trade and environment issues emerged in the Arab region, namely in Egypt and Kuwait, who became members of the WTO upon its establishment or closely thereafter. These coordinating mechanisms were created within the framework of existing committees responsible for WTO issues and were thus led by ministries of trade. As such, the scope of their activities was mostly limited to topics included within the CTE work program. These committees have tended to be more focused on interministerial coordination, while the input of experts is also solicited on a needs basis.

As awareness about trade and environment linkages grew, environmental stakeholders sought to mainstream environmental issues into national development agendas. A new set of committees on trade and environment emerged, this time led by environmental agencies. Morocco, Saudi Arabia and Tunisia established national committees during this period to foster interministerial and public–private sector dialogue on trade and environment topics. These committees included relevant government ministries as well as representatives from private industry, chambers of commerce and nongovernmental organizations. CAMRE took note of these initiatives in 1999 and recommended that other Arab countries seek to establish national trade and environment committees.[7] Jordan and Syria have since sought to activate participatory trade and environment committees in their respective countries. Yemen established a National Committee on Environment and Trade in May 2006, which is supported by an Environment and Trade Unit based at the Environment Protection Authority that provides secretariat support to the committee. These committees have helped to foster formal and informal networks across ministerial lines and open channels of communication with the private sector and civil society. The committees have also provided a forum to raise awareness and enhance understanding about these issues in the region, often with support provided through the Program on Trade and Environment Capacity Building in the Arab Region.

Trade-related MEAs have also established consultative and coordinating mechanisms at the regional and global levels, with national focal points identified in environmental agencies. Until recently there was little appreciable interaction between trade-related policy advisors and MEA focal points, which echoed the situation in multilateral forums. However, networks fostered by national trade and environment committees and current negotiations before the WTO regarding the standing of trade-related MEA secretariats before the CTE have helped to increase the exchange of information and dissemination of views between these institutions. The 2007 CAMRE resolution reiterating support for national trade and environment committees in the Arab region specifically recommends that the national focal points of the trade-related MEAs serve as members of these national committees.[8]

Part of the difficulty of establishing institutional mechanisms for trade and environment decision-making stems from the fact that governments in the Arab region often change, as is the case in many developing countries with parliamentary systems. Changes at the ministerial level often result in associated shifts in responsibility for trade and environment files. This dynamic situation increases the time allocated to capacity-building and priority-setting among new counterparts, and reduces resources available for substantive policy analysis and formulation among senior staff.

Slow or ineffective institutional lines of communication also impede consultation with counterparts on trade and environment issues. The situation reduces the ability of negotiators to solicit policy positions and supporting technical input from relative stakeholders in a timely manner. For example, reports prepared by national missions to the WTO participating in CTE sessions in Geneva are usually submitted to the ministries of trade or foreign affairs in country capitals, which do not necessarily forward these documents to environmental agencies; outcomes from meetings of trade-related MEAs are also not necessarily shared with trade counterparts. While national committees on trade and environment are gradually helping to reduce these information transaction costs through more regular debriefing mechanisms and formal and informal networking arrangements, the strengthening of formal communication channels and consultative arrangements is necessary to facilitate greater policy coordination and policy coherence in the region.[9]

The policy-making process
Today most policy advisors in the Arab region understand that trade and environment policy linkages are part and parcel of the sustainable development policy framework and need to be addressed in an integrated manner in order to deal with new emerging issues presented by increased globalization and trade liberalization. However, the process of policy integration remains a challenge.

The policy-making process involves a variety of steps that begin well before a policy objective is identified. Indeed, when addressing a relatively new area of policy formulation, the first stage often involves raising awareness and increasing understanding about the policy context. In the case of trade and environment policy-making, this begins with garnering support for integrated sustainable development policy. While important advances have been made in encouraging integrated thinking about sustainable development topics in Arab countries through the development of national and regional strategies for sustainable development and associated action plans, the design, implementation and monitoring of policy instruments remains difficult. The process is also often subject to power politics between ministries with disparate financial and human resources, with environmental agencies most often representing the weaker institution.

As such the stages of the policy-making process comprise raising awareness; increasing understanding about basic principles governing international trade and multilateral environmental agreements; agreeing upon policy goals; identifying policy priorities; conducting policy analysis; assessing policy options through consultative arrangements; forging agreement on policy approaches through coordination and consensus-building; and adopting coherent policy positions. Trade and environment policy-making in the Arab region to date remains mostly concentrated in the initial stages of the policy process, with progress being made in the areas of policy identification, consultation and analysis of priority issues.

Regional priorities

Trade and environment priorities in the Arab region are generally associated with concerns regarding market access, competitiveness and the implementation of trade-related MEAs in a manner consistent with international trade rules. Two regional priorities identified by Arab countries are elaborated below to illustrate components of the policy development process in the region.[10] The first examines compliance with environmental, health and safety standards, while the second looks at the proposed liberalization of environmental goods and services.

Compliance with environmental, health and safety standards
The positions taken on trade and environment issues in Arab countries have often differed from the stance taken by countries in the North, which were the initial proponents of incorporating trade and environment concerns into multilateral agreements. This has been primarily due to differences in the development priorities between countries in the North and South, and the weight given to short-term socio-economic dimensions of achieving sustainable development. These differences in perspective are manifested in the increased commitment to consumer health and safety in the North, compared to growing concern regarding technical barriers to trade (TBT) and sanitary and phytosanitary (SPS) measures that are impeding market access of exports from the South. While an environment and trade issue, the challenge is also closely tied to sustainability priorities associated with income creation, employment generation and the competitiveness of small producers, which are also development priorities in the Arab region.

The globalization of the marketplace and international supply chains has changed the way that business is conducted. Key export sectors for the Arab region include agro-food products, fisheries, garments, electronics and chemicals. Compliance with mandatory standards associated with these sectors is required to access foreign markets. Such measures are allowable under the WTO provided that they are scientifically based and justified for the purpose of protecting the environment, human health and safety. The resulting requirements often influence the entire production line from raw materials to processing, packaging, labeling and disposal. For example, EU Directive 2002/95/EC restricts the use of certain hazardous substances in the production of electronic equipment, while Directive 2002/96/EC regulates the recycling of waste from electrical and electronic equipment. National producers as well as importers are subject to these environmental requirements; however, the cost of complying with these regulations is relatively higher for SMEs from outside the region than for producers based in Europe.

The financial and human resources needed to formulate technical regulations are also significant and often beyond the means of developing countries. While calls for harmonization with international standards are proposed as means to assist developing economies to overcome this challenge, the interim effect remains a loss of market share due to the inability to comply with measures that are beyond the technical, technological and financial capacity of SMEs in developing countries. Harmonization of standards also assumes that standards exist for products of strategic export interest to developing countries. This, however, is not necessarily the case for niche products and alternative crops that are not produced in most developed countries, such as exotic fruits and certain herbs. Standards to guarantee food safety do not also necessarily consider differences in diet and climate in different regions. For example, titanium dioxide in tahini is allowed in higher concentrations internationally than in Lebanon, where hummus and related food items are considered dietary staples. Standards related to the use of genetically modified organisms, reused water, and packaging also differ between Arab countries, and thus compliance with standards adopted in the North does not necessarily guarantee access to a neighboring country's market.

Additionally, an increasing array of voluntary standards has also emerged that influences the competitiveness and ability of small and medium-sized producers in developing countries to reach consumers in industrialized countries. Compliance with industry-based standards and consumer preferences is increasingly influencing the ability of exporters to enter international supply and distribution chains. While the opportunity to secure regular contracts with large retailers and multinational conglomerates encourages compliance with these more rigorous voluntary requirements, most manufacturers have not been able to take advantage of the opportunities presented by the global marketplace. For instance, while there has been an expansion of fresh and processed food exports from the Arab region in recent years, only six producers in the Arab region are certified under GlobalGap (formerly EuropGap), three in Egypt and three in Morocco, despite the fact that an increasing number of European supermarket chains impose EuropGap requirements as a precondition on their vendors. Rather than turning towards Europe, Arab exporters are instead looking to other retailers in other regions to market their goods. For instance, Arab exports to China have increased exponentially in recent years. As this may have implications for consumer protection in other parts of the world, greater assistance is needed to help producers comply with a necessary set of baseline standards to ensure food safety and environmental protection.

The solution, however, is not so easy. The cost of compliance with environmental requirements is further complicated when the cost of conformity assessment is incorporated into the equation. In this case it is not only compliance with an appointed set of standards that poses the difficulty, but also the cost and time associated with demonstrating compliance with these standards in the absence of adequate conformity assessment infrastructure. While the situation in the Arab region is improving, with new food-testing laboratories established in Egypt, Oman, the United Arab Emirates and Morocco, and Tunisia establishing laboratories for testing garments and fabrics, the demand for these services still outweighs supply. Additionally, many testing facilities are not accredited by international bodies, which allows potential importers to question the validity of their results.

The cost and time associated with securing the necessary certificates can thus be significant, particularly for manufacturing SMEs operating within modest margins. To provide a sense of scale, in Lebanon, the cost of tests needed to comply with food safety requirements in accordance with the Hazard Analysis and Critical Control Point System (HACCP) for olive oil is a minimum of US$705 per batch, while testing fresh orange juice can reach US$990 per batch.[11] An associated food safety lab can cost US$540 450 in terms of equipment and supplies in Lebanon,[12] while in Yemen the cost of establishing a fish quality assurance lab is estimated at US$246 961.[13] In Yemen, such an investment would need to be multiplied manifold in order to provide an adequate number of labs near ports along the country's lengthy coastline where the fisheries sector is a major source of income for local producers. Yemen is the third-largest producer and exporter of fish in the Arab region.[14]

Ensuring adequate access to information about mandatory and voluntary standards, enhancing the capacity of national standard-setting institutions, improving local infrastructure available for conformity assessment, as well as facilitating access to financial resource and technology transfer arrangements are ways to offset trade and environment challenges associated with compliance with technical regulations. Interestingly, policy initiatives to address these challenges are often formulated by ministries of industry, agriculture and economy responsible for SME development and called for by chambers of commerce or industrial syndicates. This illustrates the importance of insuring an inclusive approach to trade and environment policy-making in the region and the need for sound policy analysis, integration and consultation with relevant stakeholders.

Liberalization of environmental goods and services
The introduction of environmental goods and services onto the negotiating agenda of the Doha Development Round was advanced by industrialized countries that had correctly identified the market for environmental technologies as a burgeoning new industry capable of reaping significant trade dividends. Developing countries generally perceived the inclusion of this item for negotiation with skepticism, and mostly as a strategy devised for extracting additional concessions from developing countries on goods mostly produced by the North. There was also concern that industrialized countries were seeking to secure preferences for environmentally preferable products based on production and process methods (PPMs), which are measures opposed by most developing countries since they run counter to international trade principles associated with non-discrimination between like products and have the potential to create a new series of NTBs to restrict market access.

The difficulty of the negotiations stems from the lack of consensus regarding what constitutes an environmental good, since no definition or classification code for environmental goods exists with the Harmonized System (HS).[15] Generally speaking, two groups of products have emerged as likely targets. The first group comprises environmental technologies and related inputs that support the provision of environmental services, which consist of a varied group of products proposed by the Organisation for Economic Co-operation and Development (OECD) and the Asia-Pacific Economic Cooperation (APEC). The second group includes environmentally preferable products (EPPs) based on their final characteristics and use so as not to run counter to non-discrimination principles, as formulated by the United Nations Conference on Trade and Development (UNCTAD). Qatar was among the first developing countries to recognize a strategic opportunity presented by liberalizing trade in this second group of products and proposed natural gas as an environmental good based on its environmentally preferably use as an alternative to more carbon-intensive energy sources, such as petroleum and coal.[16] A similar logic is applied by Brazil when proposing biofuels as an environmentally preferable energy source. While the proposed liberalization of energy commodities has not been well received by industrialized countries, the Qatari proposal exposes a proactive policy position taken by an Arab country on a trade and environment topic based on strategic interests.

Following this lead, the CAMRE Technical Secretariat undertook a similar proactive effort to formulate guidelines for assisting Arab states to identify environmental products that could be proposed for liberalization. The resulting Arab Reference List on Environmental Goods offers a set of criteria for differentiating environment goods into five groups. The list includes products in the two groups of environmental goods discussed above, as well as many others.[17] Interestingly, the guidelines propose positive and negative criteria for justifying whether liberalization of a certain product should be pursued. For instance, the guidelines suggest that products banned under trade-related MEAs should never be considered for liberalization, which is the first time that negative criteria have been incorporated into guidelines to support policy-making on the liberalization of environmental goods.[18] While many of the items proposed for liberalization include minerals and chemical compounds (which WTO member states have now generally agreed to exclude from the negotiations), the list represents an important contribution to trade and environment policy discussions in the region.

Upon finalization of the list, trade analysis of these different proposed groupings of environmental goods was conducted by ESCWA at the request of Arab countries to further inform the negotiations and policy-making process. The analysis reveals the expected finding that while Arab imports of environmental goods under most definitions have been increasing, the largest share of these imports is sourced from industrialized countries. However, while the Arab region represents the smallest market for environmental goods, there has been a surprisingly sharp increase in the import of environmental goods in recent years, with figures doubling and even tripling based on classifications proposed by the Arab Reference List. The analysis finds, interestingly, that Arab exports of environmental goods have also been growing, albeit not as sharply as imports. Growth in exports has been mostly directed towards developing regions, with ESCWA member countries exporting to Asia or within the region. This demonstrates that despite common perceptions to the contrary, some degree of complementarity exists between environmental goods produced by developing countries. This presents an opening for enhancing South–South trade through the liberalization of certain environment goods, which supports regional policy goals for increasing interregional trade and exports.[19]

Emerging issues

The trade and environment policy-making process in the region has thus been concentrated on enhancing understanding of the major issues and increasing knowledge and analysis about priority concerns. These priorities have been focused on improving market access, enhancing competitiveness and ensuring the mutual supportiveness of trade-related MEA and the multilateral trading system. Emerging issues of concern to Arab countries also include trade in hazardous, harmful and illicit goods that can adversely affect the environment and human health. This challenge was initially raised within the context of increasing production and consumption patterns, and managing associated waste streams. However, developing countries, including those in the Arab region, still do not have the legal framework, regulatory enforcement mechanisms or appropriate technologies to dispose of these hazardous materials. The problem is being multiplied by the import of poor-quality goods, short-lived electronic items and second-hand goods that are no longer accepted by northern markets. Increasing investment in environmental services will thus be needed to mitigate this solid waste problem, as well as manage chemical and industrial waste generated from new industries.

Climate change is also an important challenge facing Arab policy-makers, given the region's vulnerability to climate change impacts generated by unsustainable production and consumption patterns. Apart from the evident impacts on freshwater quantity and quality, disease vectors moving northward from Sub-Saharan Africa due to temperature increase are already threatening some of the region's least developed countries. Land degradation is also being exacerbated, which is fueling rural to urban migration, unemployment, threats to food security and the loss of biodiversity. Warmer climates in Europe also impact growth in the Arab tourism and real-estate sector, with some countries noting concern that Europeans may start staying home rather than enjoying the sunny landscapes of the Southern Mediterranean and the Gulf. Climate change can thus have important implications for trade and investment in goods and services, as well as for the region's sustainable development.

Arab countries thus need to identify their strategic interests, assess their vulnerabilities, strengthen institutions and forge coalitions at the national, regional and international levels on shared policy goals in order to strengthen their position and secure benefits from integrated trade and environment policy-making.

Notes

*   The views expressed in this chapter are those of the author and do not necessarily reflect the views of the United Nations.
1.   19th Regular Session of CAMRE, 6 December 2007, Resolution 273, Article 4.6.1.
2.   See WTO, 'Energy taxation, subsidies and incentives in OECD countries and their economic and trade implications on developing countries, in particular developing oil producing and exporting countries – Submission by Saudi Arabia to the Committee on Trade and Environment and the Committee on Trade and Environment Special Session', WT/CTE/W/215; TN/TE/W/9, 23 September 2002.
3.   United Nations (2002), *Report of the World Summit on Sustainable Development*. Johannesburg, South Africa, 26 August – 4 September 2002, New York, A/CONF.199.20.
4.   League of Arab States (2002), 'The Sustainable Development Initiative in the Arab Region', p. 4.
5.   14th Regular Session of CAMRE, 24 October 2002, Article 2.2.
6.   15th Regular Session of CAMRE, adopted 9 December 2003, Resolution 190Q, Article 3.
7.   13th Regular Session of CAMRE, adopted 18 October 1999, Resolution 125Q. The recommendation was reiterated in subsequent CAMRE resolutions, including the 18th Regular Session of CAMRE (Algiers, 20 December 2006, Resolution 252, Article 2.2) and the 19th Regular Session of CAMRE (Cairo, 6 December 2007, Resolution 273, Article 4.5.2).
8.   19th Regular Session of CAMRE, 6 December 2007, Resolution 273, Article 4.5.2.
9.   It is interesting to note that the Ministry of Foreign Affairs plays the leading convening role in national trade and environment committees in Finland, Canada and other developed countries established to coordinate national policy positions prior to participation in international forums. This is not the case, however,

10. These priorities were identified during the 'Regional Workshop on Trade and Environment Capacity Building', organized by ESCWA, UNEP/ROWA, the CAMRE Technical Secretariat, the Ministry of Regional Municipalities, Environment and Water Resources of Oman and Sultan Qaboos University, 25–27 March 2006 in Muscat, Oman.

in the Arab region, where these committees are generally convened by ministries responsible for environment and/or trade.

11. See ESCWA, 'Background paper on financial implications of food quality control and suggested arrangements for setting up an analytical laboratory', presented to the Regional Seminar on Sustainable Development and Competitiveness in the Agro-Food Sector, convened by ESCWA in Beirut, Lebanon, 1–2 December 2005, pp. 16 and 18.

12. Ibid., p. 27.

13. ESCWA, *Trade and Environment Dimensions of the Fisheries Sector in the Arab Countries: The case of Yemen and Oman*, United Nations: New York, E/ESCWA/SDPD/2007/W.2, 30 October 2007, p. 24.

14. Ibid., pp. 4–5, compiled from FAO, Fisheries and Aquaculture Department, 'Total production 1950–2005 dataset', extracted from FishStat Plus in 2007.

15. The other important area preventing progress entails overcoming implementation constraints associated with managing trade in certain 'environmental goods,' such as the inclusion of products that require specificity beyond the six-digit HS level to allow for differentiation between products, and related concern regarding the multiple use of certain environment goods for non-environmental purposes after they have been imported under a preferential tariff scheme.

16. See WTO, 'Environmental goods – Submission by the State of Qatar on Paragraph 31 (iii)' to the WTO Committee on Trade and Environment Special Session, TN/TE/W/14, 9 October 2002; and WTO, 'Harmonized System (HS) classification codes of gas-related goods – Submission by the State of Qatar on Paragraph 31 (iii)' to the WTO Committee on Trade and Environment Special Session and Negotiating Group on Market Access, TN/TE/W/27 and TN/MA/W/33, 25 April 2003.

17. LAS, CAMRE Technical Secretariat, 'Arab Reference List on Environmental Goods', Final Report (available in Arabic), March 2007.

18. Note that the LAS does not have standing before the WTO, although the LAS serves as secretariat of the Greater Arab Free Trade Area (GAFTA) and its request for observer status in September 2000 was supported by Arab countries (see WTO, CTE, 'Request for observer status by the League of Arab States', WT/CT/COM/5). As such, these guidelines were not formulated with the intention to prepare a submission for Arab countries to the CTE, but rather to inform the policy-making process at the regional level so as to assist Arab countries to establish their respective negotiation positions.

19. For further elaboration, see ESCWA, *The Liberalization of Trade in Environmental Goods and Services in the ESCWA and Arab Regions*, United Nations: New York, E/ESCWA/SDPD/2007/WP.1, 22 October 2007 (available in Arabic and English).

26 Trade and environment institutions
J. Samuel Barkin

Introduction

This chapter looks at those multilateral institutions that oversee international rules regulating the relationship between trade and environmental issues. Some of these organizations, particularly the World Trade Organization (WTO), have already been discussed elsewhere in this volume. The purpose of this chapter is not to review these discussions, or to look in detail at the workings of any particular institution. Rather it is to provide a typology of institutional approaches to mediating the relationship between international trade and the environment. The term 'multilateral institution' here refers to those institutions (referred to in this chapter as international organizations, or IOs) that are created by states, and the primary membership of which is states. They are multilateral if they are broad-based (as opposed to bilateral, if they have only two members). The classic example of a multilateral institution is the United Nations (UN), and most of the IOs discussed in this chapter are part of the UN system, broadly defined.

The institutions discussed in this chapter are those that mediate in some way between international trade rules and rules governing the management of the natural environment, whether these latter rules are international or domestic. These rules come into conflict when trade rules interfere with the ability of states to manage the environment as they see fit, whether individually or collectively, or when environmental rules discriminate against the trade of particular countries. Different IOs deal with this interference and discrimination differently. There are four general categories of IOs that deal with trade and environment issues. The first of these is trade institutions, the primary function of which is to oversee international trade rules, and which deal with environmental issues only in so far as they interact with trade rules. The second category is environmental institutions, the primary function of which is to create international rules for environmental management, and use trade as a mechanism to enable or enforce those rules. The third is regional integration institutions, which are not designed primarily as either trade or environment IOs, but that regulate both none the less. The fourth category is IOs that help states (particularly developing states) to navigate the relationship between international trade and environmental management, but are not regulatory institutions. The key members of this category are development organizations.

Trade institutions

'Trade institutions' refers here to those IOs whose primary function is to create rules governing international trade that are binding on member states. From the perspective of environmental management, there are two potential problems with these sorts of rules. The first is that they limit states' ability to create domestic environmental rules: to the extent that these rules have the effect either of discriminating against imports generally, or of affecting different member countries differently, they may run afoul of trade rules. The second problem is that multilateral trade rules may give incentives to states to generate comparative advantage by undermining their own environmental rules, thereby making production cheaper. If other countries cannot discriminate against them for doing so, then this sort of environmental 'race to the bottom' can give a country a comparative advantage in international trade over countries with stronger environmental protections. It should be noted that these two problems are in a way the opposite of each other. The first problem is that states may not have enough flexibility to create their own environmental regulations, while the second is that they may have too much.

There are two general models through which trade institutions have dealt with these problems. The first model deals with the environment as an exception to the rules, whereas the second creates explicit rules delimiting members' freedom of action in changing their environmental rules. The classic example of the first model is the WTO, while the classic example of the second model is the North American Free Trade Area (NAFTA). These two models are not mutually exclusive – the WTO is discussing the creation of more explicit environmental rules, and NAFTA does allow for environmental exceptions. But it remains the case that the two models represent clearly different approaches to dealing with environmental issues in trade institutions.

In the exceptions model, exemplified by the WTO, states are allowed to create barriers to trade when these are necessary for the purposes of environmental management, as long as they do not interfere with trade more than necessary to achieve the environmental goal (GATT, 1986, Article XX; Barkin, 2005). Disagreements among member states as to whether a particular national environmental regulation is unnecessarily trade-distorting are resolved through arbitration, and if this does not succeed, through a trade court (in the case of the WTO, the Dispute Settlement Mechanism, or DSM). Because the WTO rules do not specify in any detail what constitutes legitimate grounds for environmental exceptions, the details have tended to develop judicially, through DSM findings. In practice, the DSM has generally accepted any stated need for environmental management as legitimate, but has forcefully supported the requirement that the rules created to meet the need not be unnecessarily trade-distorting (DeSombre and Barkin, 2002).

The WTO does deal with the relationship between trade and the environment politically, as well as judicially. It has a Committee on Trade and the Environment (CTE), which is charged with examining the relationship, and with recommending appropriate changes in trade rules to deal with the need for environmental stewardship. The CTE is a political body, in that it is made up of representatives of member states acting as voices for their states, rather than for the CTE or WTO as institutions. Because the CTE, like the WTO, works on a consensus basis, the CTE is rarely able to generate any specific recommendations that can be acted upon. A good example of this deadlock is the relationship between the WTO and multilateral environmental agreements (MEAs), the institutions discussed in the next section of this chapter. Developed countries generally prefer a rule that explicitly states that trade-distorting MEA rules constitute exceptions to WTO rules (see WTO, 2004 for an overview both of the CTE and of the WTO/MEA relationship). Developing countries generally prefer that this not be a rule. Since consensus is unlikely, the interpretation of the status of MEAs in WTO rules is likely to be made by the judicial mechanism, the DSM, rather than the political mechanism, the CTE.

The second model for dealing with environmental issues in trade institutions, exemplified by NAFTA, is by creating explicit rules. NAFTA in fact incorporates the environmental exceptions of the WTO (NAFTA, 1993, Article 2101), although it also includes requirements that governments compensate companies hurt by changes in environmental rules that may mean that the exceptions are in practice less environment-friendly than they are in the WTO context (NAFTA, 1993, Chapter 11). But the environmental innovation in NAFTA is a side-agreement, called the North American Agreement on Environmental Cooperation (NAAEC), that addresses environmental regulation explicitly (CEC, 1993).

The NAAEC has two key components. The first is a requirement that members of NAFTA effectively enforce their own environmental laws. The Agreement does not specify what those laws should be. It notes that 'each Party shall ensure that its laws and regulations provide for high levels of environmental protection' (CEC, 1993, Article 3).The Agreement does not define what it means by high levels, but it does require that individuals and corporations hurt by poor enforcement of environmental rules have legal recourse. The second key component of the NAAEC is the creation of a new institution, the Commission for Environmental Cooperation (CEC) to oversee the trade and environment aspects of NAFTA, and to help with the coordination and enforcement of environmental law within the NAFTA area. The CEC differs from the CTE in that the former has an executive rather than a legislative function. It is staffed with people who answer to it, rather than to member governments, and its job is to implement policy rather than create it. There are differences of opinion about how effective the CEC has been since its creation a decade and a half ago (Kirton, 2002), but few would disagree that it represents an approach to dealing with trade and environment issues that is distinct from the WTO exceptions model.

Of the two potential problems noted at the beginning of this section, the exceptions model of dealing with the effects of trade rules on environmental management is on the whole more effective at protecting the ability of states to define their own level of appropriate environmental management. Meanwhile, the environmental rules model is more effective at preventing states from defining their level downwards to create comparative advantage. The exceptions model evolved in the context of a broadly multilateral agreement, in which developed countries were the key players. The environmental rules model was developed in the context of a more limited trilateral negotiation, in which a powerful developed country (the USA) was concerned about the lowering of levels of environmental regulation as a tool for creating comparative advantage by a developing country (Mexico). In other words, in the first case the more powerful developed countries were more concerned about maintaining their own freedom to regulate, and in the latter case the key developed country was more concerned about limiting the freedom of the relevant developing country to negotiate. We can therefore expect a tendency towards the exceptions model in more multilateral trade institutions, where the more developed countries involved are more concerned about each other than about the less developed countries. Meanwhile, we can expect the environmental rules model when there are fewer countries involved, and when the richer ones are more concerned with the poorer ones than with each other.

The pattern of existing organizations seems to bear out these expectations. Following NAFTA, the USA has engaged in a series of bilateral and small-group trade negotiations with developing countries. These agreements tend strongly to include explicit environmental side-agreements modeled on the NAAEC, although without the creation of a new bureaucracy modeled on the CEC (e.g. USTR, 2006, ch. 18). The developing countries in question tend not to prefer such side-agreements, but the USA tends to present them with a take-it-or-leave-it template. Other regional trade agreements, such as the free trade area negotiated under the auspices of the Association of Southeast Asian Nations (ASEAN) tend to follow the WTO exceptions model (ASEAN, 1992, Article 9). The agreement between the USA, five Central American countries, and the Dominican Republic (DR-CAFTA) takes a middle route, borrowing language about races to the bottom in environmental regulation and the need to enforce environmental law from NAFTA, but failing to create institutional mechanisms for enforcing these environmental exhortations (USTR, 2004, ch. 17).

Environmental institutions

There are hundreds of environmental IOs, institutions designed to generate international cooperation in dealing with particular environmental challenges, or in some cases designed to promote environmental cooperation more broadly. These are the MEAs referred to in the previous section. Many of these IOs have no real impact on international trade. But some of them have rules that explicitly call for interference in international trade in ways that contradict the WTO's basic rule of non-discrimination. They do this either to prevent trade in particular goods altogether, to use trade discrimination as an inducement to countries to join the institution, or to use trade discrimination as an enforcement mechanism.

An example of the first of these three reasons for interfering in international trade can be found with the Convention on International Trade in Endangered Species of Wild Fauna and Flora (CITES). This agreement is an example of an MEA that interferes with trade in particular species of wildlife for the direct purpose of preventing trade in those species. It prohibits member countries from engaging in international trade in species that are deemed to be threatened with extinction. The prohibition is on any international trade in the species, whether live specimens or processed parts (there are milder restrictions on trade in species that are deemed endangered but not immediately threatened with extinction) (CITES, 1979). CITES does not mandate domestic conservation measures for the relevant species. The choice of which species count as threatened with extinction is made within the institution, and individual countries are able to get exceptions for particular species (ibid., Article XV). There is no enforcement mechanism *per se* for countries that fail to live up to their obligations under CITES. But some countries, particularly the USA, have used various forms of pressure to convince non-complying countries to improve their enforcement (DeSombre, 2000, pp. 173–9).

An example of the second of the three reasons for interfering in international trade, to use trade discrimination as an inducement to join an environmental IO, can be found with the Montreal Protocol on Substances that Deplete the Ozone Layer. This agreement regulates the production of a variety of substances, such as chlorofluorocarbons (CFCs) and halons, that deplete the stratospheric ozone layer. It prohibits trade in any of these substances between member countries and non-members. It also allows significant time lags, of a decade or more, between the requirements to reduce production of the relevant chemicals in developed countries and the requirements for developing countries (Benedick, 1991). The combination of these two elements, the prohibition on trade with non-members and the time lag, was designed to provide an incentive for developing countries to join the agreement. The logic was that if developing countries were allowed to produce and trade in these chemicals from within the institution, even if only for a limited time, they were less likely to stay out of the institution and lose their ability to trade in chemicals with members. While it is impossible to know how key a role this particular incentive played in bringing developing countries into the Montreal Protocol, it may well have played a significant role (DeSombre and Kauffman, 1996).

The third of the reasons for interfering with international trade in the context of an MEA is as an enforcement mechanism. An example of this use in action can be found in the Catch Documentation Scheme, a mechanism developed by the Convention for the Conservation of Antarctic Marine Living Resources (CCAMLR) to help enforce its quotas on catches of Patagonian toothfish (also known as Chilean seabass). This agreement calls on member states to import only those fish that are certified as caught within the quotas agreed to within CCAMLR (CCAMLR, 2006). Non-certified fish, even though they are otherwise identical, are thereby refused legal entry into most of the world's biggest fish markets. As a result, the price of certified fish is far higher than the price of non-certified fish, punishing fishers for fishing outside of quota and giving them an incentive to fish within (DeSombre, 2005). This mechanism overlaps with the second reason, in that it provides an incentive for non-member states to join, thereby giving their fishers access to a broader range of markets. But it affects the incentives of individual fishers as well as those of states, and thus acts as enforcement mechanism as well as an inducement.

These are only three examples of some 20 MEAs that have trade-affecting provisions (WTO, 2007). All of these provisions exist for one, or a combination, of these three reasons. The relationship between the provisions and international trade rules, particularly the rules of the WTO, is unclear. To this point, no complaint about trade restrictions undertaken because of MEA commitments has been brought to the WTO (WTO, 2007). On the one hand, this suggests that countries adversely affected by such restrictions are not confident that they could win such a case in trade court. On the other hand, it means that there is no explicit precedent that MEA trade restrictions are compatible with international trade rules. As noted above, this issue is under negotiation at the WTO, but there is at this point no indication that a consensus among members can be reached. As such, it may well be the case that the relationship between trade-affecting MEAs and international trade rules remains unclear for the foreseeable future. At the same time, though, DSM jurisprudence seems to suggest a strong bias toward deference to multilateral environmental cooperation (DeSombre and Barkin, 2002).

Most environmental IOs, like the three examples discussed here, are designed to deal with specific issues. But there are some that are designed to oversee international environmental cooperation more broadly. One of these, the CEC, has already been discussed, having been created in the context of the NAFTA environmental side-agreement. The biggest of these general-purpose environmental institutions, with the broadest remit, is the United Nations Environment Programme (UNEP). Unlike the MEAs discussed above, UNEP tends not to regulate state behavior directly. It generally oversees the creation of new special-purpose MEAs to deal with specific issues (and often acts as secretariat for these MEAs), rather than regulating in its own right (on UNEP and its relationship with MEAs, see DeSombre, 2006). As such, it does not affect international trade rules directly. But some scholars of international environmental politics argue that it should be expanded to include (or replaced by an institution that includes) a direct trade-affecting role. This expanded or new institution is often referred to as a World Environmental Organization (WEO) or Global Environmental Organization (GEO) (Biermann and Bauer, 2005).

A key argument in favor of a WEO is that it would provide an institutional counterweight to the WTO. Some scholars of international environmental politics see an imbalance between the WTO, a fully fledged organization in the UN's terminology that oversees trade rules broadly and that creates binding rules, and UNEP, a mere programme, that has neither the powers nor the resources of the WTO. A WEO, on this view, would be better able to create and support regulations that contradict international trade rules than the current plethora of single-purpose MEAs (Biermann and Bauer, 2005). A key counter-argument is that creating an overarching WEO modeled on the WTO risks creating in the field of international environmental management the sort of deadlock currently found at the WTO, which has been trying since 1999 to update international trade rules, with little success. Precisely because a proliferation of issue-specific MEAs lacks the comprehensiveness or the political heft of a WTO, they allow for progress that might otherwise not be possible in regulating particular environmental issues (Barkin, 2005). A WEO would help to clarify the status of trade-affecting multilateral environmental rules, but such clarification does not require the creation of a major new IO. In any case, a WEO is unlikely to be created in the near future, making the debate about it academic.

Regional integration organizations

The practice at most IOs, including all those discussed above, is for member countries to create a common set of rules that they are all then bound by, administered with some assistance from the IO. In these institutions states remain the primary players. Regional integration organizations are institutions that create regulations that member countries are bound by, meaning that the members may end up having to enforce regulations that they did not explicitly agree to. Because of this feature, regional integration organizations are sometimes referred to as sovereignty-pooling institutions (e.g. Koenig-Archibugi, 2004). To the extent that such institutions have the authority to regulate in issues of international trade and the environment, they create a different dynamic in the relationship between the two issue areas than that found in the relationship between traditional trade agreements and MEAs.

At this point there is only one regional integration organization that has meaningful powers to regulate both international trade and environmental management: the European Union (EU). Several other institutions officially aspire to regional integration characteristics, including ASEAN, the African Union (AU), and the Southern Common Market (Mercosur), an agreement among six South American countries. While these three organizations have achieved different levels of success in managing international trade among their members, as well as cooperating on other political and security goals, none has yet made meaningful steps towards a pooling of sovereignty that would allow real regulation at the regional level. Furthermore, at present the AU and ASEAN seem to be making little if any tangible progress towards regional integration, and Mercosur if anything seems to be losing ground.

The EU, with 27 European countries as members, has gone quite far toward regional integration and pooled sovereignty in both international trade and environmental regulation. In both issue areas basic decisions are made at the EU level (this involves a complicated decision-making process involving both national governments and authoritative EU-level institutions such as the European Commission and the European Parliament. For an overview, see Dinan, 2005). In international trade, sovereignty has been pooled to the extent that it is the EU, rather than its member countries, that negotiates international trade agreements. The situation with MEAs is more complicated, with the EU representing member countries at some environmental IOs, and the member countries representing themselves in others.

Internally, the EU is officially a single economic area. This means that there are in effect no international trade rules governing goods and services exported from one country to another within the Union. Economically (in principle, at least) there are no borders to cross. Since a good made in one EU country can enter and be sold in other EU countries without having to pass through an economic border, there is no real way for environmental rules to discriminate between domestically produced goods and those produced elsewhere in the EU. This makes any rules governing the relationship between trade within the EU and environmental regulation moot. The EU is also in many ways a single environmental area (e.g. Andonova, 2003; Carmin and VanDeveer, 2005; Oberthür and Gehring, 2006). Key decisions about the overall direction of environmental policy, as well as many detailed regulations, are promulgated at the Union level. This level of government also controls many resources that are controlled by countries elsewhere, such as fishery resources in the Union's Exclusive Economic Zone (EEZ). Thus when one studies the relationship between trade and the environment, the EU looks much more like a federal country such as the USA or Canada, where different levels of government have authority over different aspects of environmental policy, than like traditional international trade and environment IOs.

Because of their pooled-sovereignty aspect, successful regional integration organizations allow for much stronger levels of environmental protection than are feasible with traditional MEAs, and to a large extent obviate the trade and environment tension in the way that this tension is discussed in the context of traditional IOs. From outside the integration organizations, they look more like countries than IOs with respect to trade and environment issues. But referring to 'organizations' in the plural may be misleading – it may well be the case that the EU is an anomaly. In any case, none of the other IOs that claim to be heading towards regional integration are likely to get there in any meaningful sense in the foreseeable future.

Non-regulatory organizations
The final category of IO relevant to the nexus between international trade and environmental management is institutions that provide countries with technical and financial advice and assistance in dealing with this nexus. This category includes both IOs focused primarily on trade issues, and those that focus primarily on environmental issues. It should be noted that many of the institutions discussed above also provide advice and assistance to smaller and poorer countries that would otherwise have trouble meeting their commitments under international agreements. For example, the WTO provides technical assistance by providing training in international trade law and policy for officials from member countries (e.g. WTO, 2006). The Montreal Protocol includes a Multilateral Fund that provides financial assistance to countries to transition to non-ozone-depleting chemicals (DeSombre and Kaufmann, 1996). As such, the line between the first two

categories, above, and this one is not always clear. But beyond the advice and assistance provided by institutions that also generate rules, there are IOs for which advice and assistance is the primary role.

An example of such an organization is the UNCTAD. This institution plays no regulatory function. It was created originally to provide a political voice to the trade concerns of developing countries. As that political bloc has fragmented, UNCTAD has gradually found a new role in training officials from poorer countries in how best to interact with the international trading system, and in setting up the bureaucracies necessary to allow these countries to master the regulatory framework of international trade and thereby participate fully in it (Barkin, 2006,pp. 109–10). Development organizations, such as the United Nations Development Programme (UNDP), provide both technical and financial support for economic development, which affects both the trade patterns and environmental management in recipient countries. The UNDP, which, along with the rest of the UN system, has explicitly accepted the principle of sustainable development (e.g. UNDP, 2006), is increasingly cognizant of the need to minimize the environmental impact of development. This is true throughout the multilateral development community, both of IOs like the UNDP that give grant aid, and development banks such as the World Bank that primarily lend money.

Being non-regulatory, these institutions are not directly implicated in the relationship between international trade rules and environmental management in the way that the trade and environmental institutions discussed above are. But they are important none the less for the relationship between trade and environment, for two reasons. The first is that they assist countries that could otherwise not do so effectively to fulfill their international obligations, both in terms of trade regulation and in terms of environmental management. The second is that they have the potential to create a more sustainable path to development, one that may well in the long term increase the proportion of countries committed to international trade rules that allow for effective environmental stewardship. As such, ensuring that these institutions maintain and, it is hoped, increase their commitment to the environment can help to defuse the tension between trade and the environment in the long term.

Conclusion

The array of IOs to be found at the nexus of international trade and environment issues is complex and bewildering. In part, this is because the issues themselves are complex and multifaceted. IOs tend to proliferate on an issue-by-issue basis (Shanks et al., 1996), and groups of like-minded countries are free to start new institutions when the existing ones fail to fulfill a particular purpose. It is easy to portray the relationship between international trade and environmental management as a zero-sum game. But the array of international institutions involved in the nexus between the two issues suggests that this need not be the case: there is a variety of ways in which the two issues can interrelate, and the future direction of this relationship, mediated through IOs, is not at this time entirely clear.

References

Andonova, Liliana (2003), *Transnational Politics of the Environment: The European Union and Environmental Policy in Central and Eastern Europe*, Cambridge, MA: MIT Press.

ASEAN (1992), *Agreement on the Common Effective Preferential Tariff Scheme for the ASEAN Free Trade Area*, Jakarta: The Association of South-East Asian Nations Secretariat.

Barkin, J. Samuel (2005), 'The environment, trade, and international organizations', in Peter Dauvergne (ed.), *International Handbook of Environmental Politics*, Cheltenham, UK and Northampton, MA, USA: Edward Elgar, pp. 197–210.

Barkin, J. Samuel (2006), *International Organization: Theories and Institutions*, New York: Palgrave.

Benedick, Richard (1991), *Ozone Diplomacy: New Directions in Safeguarding the Planet*, Cambridge, MA: Harvard University Press.

Biermann, Frank, and Steffan Bauer (eds) (2005), *A World Environmental Organization: Solution or Threat for Effective International Environmental Governance?*, Aldershot: Ashgate.

Carmin, JoAnn and Stacy VanDeveer (eds) (2005), *EU Enlargement and the Environment: Institutional Change and Environmental Policy in Central and Eastern Europe*, Oxford: Routledge.

CCAMLR (2006), *Conservation Measure 10-05: Catch Documentation Scheme for Dissostichus ssp*, North Hobart, Tasmania: CCAMLR.

CEC (1993), *North American Agreement on Environmental Cooperation Between the Government of Canada, The Government of the United Mexican States and the Government of the United States of America*, Montreal: Commission for Environmental Cooperation.

CITES (1979), *Convention on International Trade in Endangered Species of Wild Fauna and Flora*, Geneva: CITES.

DeSombre, Elizabeth (2000), *Domestic Sources of International Environmental Policy: Industry, Environmentalists, and U.S. Power*, Cambridge, MA: MIT Press.

DeSombre, Elizabeth (2005), 'Fishing under flags of convenience: using market power to increase participation in international regulation', *Global Environmental Politics*, **5**, 73–94.

DeSombre, Elizabeth (2006), *Global Environmental Institutions*, Oxford: Routledge.

DeSombre, Elizabeth and Samuel Barkin (2002), 'Turtles and trade: the WTO's acceptance of environmental trade restrictions', *Global Environmental Politics*, **2**, 12–18.

DeSombre, Elizabeth and Joanne Kauffman (1996), 'The Montreal Protocol Multilateral Fund: partial success story', in Robert Keohane and Marc Levy (eds), *Institutions for Environmental Aid: Pitfalls and Promise*, Cambridge, MA: MIT Press pp. 89–126.

Dinan, Desmond (2005), *Ever Closer Union: An Introduction to European Integration*, 3rd edn, Boulder, CO: Lynne Rienner.

GATT (1986), *General Agreement on Tariffs and Trade: Text of the General Agreement*, Geneva: WTO.

Kirton, John (2002), 'NAFTA's trade–environment regime and its Commission for Environmental Cooperation: contributions and challenges ten years on', *Canadian Journal of Regional Science*, **25**, 135–63.

Koenig-Archibugi, Mathias (2004), 'Explaining government preferences for institutional change in EU foreign and security policy', *International Organization*, **58**, 137–74.

NAFTA (1993), *North American Free Trade Agreement*, Ottawa: NAFTA Secretariat.

Oberthür, Sebastian and Thomas Gehring (eds) (2006), *Institutional Interaction in Global Environmental Governance: Synergy and Conflict Among International and EU Policies*, Cambridge, MA: MIT Press.

Shanks, Cheryl, Harold Jacobson and Jeffrey Kaplan (1996), 'Inertia and change in the constellation of international governmental organizations, 1981–1992', *International Organization*, **50**, 593–628.

UNDP Environment and Energy Group (2006), *Making Progress on Environmental Sustainability: Lessons and Recommendations from a Review of over 150 MDG Country Reports*, New York: UNDP.

USTR (2004), *The Dominican Republic – Central America – United States Free Trade Agreement*, Washington, DC: Office of the United States Trade Representative.

USTR (2006), *Final Text of the United States – Peru Trade Promotion Agreement*, Washington, DC: Office of the United States Trade Representative.

WTO (2004), *Trade and Environment at the WTO*, Geneva: World Trade Organization.

WTO (2007), *The Doha Mandate on Multilateral Environmental Agreements*, available at http://www.wto.org/english/tratop_e/envir_e/envir_neg_mea_e.htm.

WTO Committee on Trade and Development (2006), *Technical Assistance and Training Plan 2007*, WT/COMTD/W/151, Geneva: WTO.

27 Redesigning the world's trading system for environmentally sustainable development

Alejandro Nadal[1]

Introduction

In a relatively short period of time, human activity has brought the world to the brink of a major ecological disaster. One manifestation of this is a massive biotic crisis (Eldredge, 1998; Myers and Knoll, 2001; Wilson, 1993). The other is the anthropogenic impact on global average temperatures, with effects on rising oceans, disruption of rainfall patterns, and extreme climate variability (Houghton et al., 2001; McCarthy et al., 2001).

At the same time, social disparities and inequality mark the world's social and economic landscape, at both the national and international levels (UNFPA, 2002; GPM, 2004). Economic performance in the past 30 years was marked by slower growth rates for higher- and middle-income countries, and modest growth rates for lower-income economies. Also, the ecological footprint of the richest countries is still unduly heavy. Although greenhouse gas emissions rates have been going down, absolute levels of emissions continue to increase. The absolute volume of natural resources used by developed countries continues to increase and material flows' analyses reveal the presence of environmental cost-shifting.[2]

The structure of world trade provides a sobering backdrop for the assessment of WTO performance. Although developing countries' exports have increased, world trade remains heavily lopsided. Average trade deficits for all developing countries during the 1990s were higher than those in the 1970s by three percentage points of GDP while growth rates were lower by two percentage points (UNCTAD, 2003). This has serious negative implications for developing countries' current accounts and indebtedness, consolidating the trend towards greater disparities between rich and poor countries.

Before the world embarks on a new round of multilateral trade negotiations, existing trade agreements should be carefully evaluated. Developing countries should carry out their own assessment with the support of the international community. The central message is that WTO should be subordinated to the overarching objectives of sustainable development.

This chapter concentrates on reforms needed in the world's trading system in order to enhance its contribution to sustainable development. The first section presents five themes that need to be re-examined when assessing the world's trading system. The second section discusses the relation between macroeconomic and trade policies. The third section focuses on the regulatory regime for agricultural trade, while the fourth section looks at international commodity agreements, intellectual property and investment rights.

Perspectives for reform

The myth of the market
Any reflection on how economic, social and environmental affairs have been managed in the past 20 years cannot fail to observe that this period is dominated by the consolidation of the myth of the market as a device for efficient resource allocation. The evidence to back this up is lacking.

A casual observer might think that economic history confirms the idea that free markets bring economic prosperity. However, economic history shows that it is impossible to discern where the market stops and where state intervention begins. Subsidies of all types, protectionism and strict regulations on capital and labor mobility are inseparable from the operation of market forces over the past 200 years (Habbakuk, 1962; Landes, 1969; David, 1975). This does not mean that markets and prices are unimportant, but markets are not alone in explaining prosperity in Europe or the USA.

On the other hand, economic theory shows that efficiency (in the form of Pareto optimality) is a feature of equilibrium positions only. Unfortunately, there is no satisfactory theory explaining just how general equilibrium prices are attained.[3] Thus there is no rational foundation for the belief that the market is the best system for the allocation of resources.

Trade theory is not a scientific truth that comes out in favor of free trade; it is marked by the flaws of general equilibrium theory. And the simplicity of international trade models is misleading. Proofs of the basic theorems depend critically on initial assumptions, and when these are relaxed, conclusions are quite different (Ackerman, 2004).

Perhaps the most important lacuna of all WTO agreements is lack of reference to market concentration, oligopolies and anti-trust enforcement measures. Where collusion, unfair business practices and market concentration have real impacts on international market prices, WTO has really nothing to offer. In fact, its promotion of trade liberalization in the context of imperfect competition often leads to further concentration and intensified oligopolic structures.

Macroeconomic policy and trade
The last three decades have witnessed the separation of financial flows from international trade: short-term transactions in the world's currency markets are 50 times greater than trade flows. Any assessment of the performance of the world's trading system and its relation to social and environmental sustainability needs to take into account growth of international monetary and financial relations.

In general, however, trade policy analysts have been focusing too narrowly on their subject, without giving adequate consideration to the fact that trade liberalization is part of a bigger macroeconomic policy package. Thus they may have inadvertently left out of their analysis the critical relationship between trade and monetary and fiscal policies. The relation goes beyond the simple references to exchange rate over- or undervaluation, and involves the wider issues surrounding finance, capital flows and the policy space in the context of capital account deregulation.

The false dichotomy between monetary aggregates and real sector variables needs to be abandoned. A new type of economic analysis, integrating both dimensions, will be more policy-relevant. This implies redefining the contents of macroeconomic policy for developing countries, in both its monetary and fiscal components. Without this, there will be few benefits accruing to developing countries from reforms in the trading system.

Special and differential treatment
Special and differential treatment (S&DT) is based on the idea that fairness should be an important guiding principle in international economic relations. It is also linked to the recognition of existing international asymmetries between rich and poor nations. In the context of WTO it is linked to the idea that developing countries should not reciprocate in trade concessions because they need more time to adjust to the economic forces unleashed by trade liberalization.

S&DT is recognized by the original GATT in several of its articles, and these principles were picked up in various rounds of multilateral negotiations and in several WTO agreements. In practice, however, S&DT has really not provided the conditions needed by developing countries to adjust. A few extra years in certain transition periods, or a few tariff points below developed countries' concessions, have not been able to redress existing asymmetries. In addition, the scope of available economic policy instruments has shrunk as a result of structural adjustment policies, WTO and several regional agreements. It would seem that developed countries have kicked the ladder that enabled them to climb to higher living standards.

A new S&DT framework should recognize that developing countries need more room for policy-making. In particular, the world's trading system must allow developing countries to access the industrial policy instruments developed countries used in the past. These are especially important to attain dynamic competitive advantages which are skill and technology based. Without this, developing countries run the risk of remaining in the low-productivity trap of natural resource exporters and vulnerable to the long-term trend of declining prices for primary products (Ocampo and Parra, 2003).

The second component of S&DT is that financial assistance is essential to get to the level playing field. Foreign direct investment (FDI) flows cannot replace financial assistance. FDI is heavily concentrated in a few developing countries and up to 30 percent of total FDI is made up of mergers and acquisitions (M&A) of already existing companies. Financial assistance is a different instrument with a rationale of its own, oriented towards long-term investments under preferential conditions and should be part and parcel of trade agreements.

Process and production methods (PPMs)
Most developing-country governments are hostile to the notion of using environment-related PPMs within the WTO system. They argue that this leads to eco-protectionism, not to adequate environmental defense. But the problem is not with PPMs but with unilateral imposition of regulations and standards (Nadal, 1994).

WTO members should start a program of consultations with organizations such as UNEP in order to determine if and how PPM-based trade restrictions can be used, and under what types of circumstances they can be invoked. Defining criteria and accompanying disciplines should be the outcome of multilateral negotiations and not unilateral imposition. This is the only manner in which PPMs can be incorporated into the trade and environment agenda without fears that it will lead to unjustified neo-protectionism.

Production processes that are liable to have global or transboundary effects, for example, could be separated from those with purely domestic effects. The first could be candidates for trade regulations and even restrictions under certain circumstances and disciplines. But the most important point here is that all parties should engage in a process of multilateral negotiations that would tackle three important issues: sectors and products, disciplines and financial mechanisms to assist developing countries.

Precautionary principle (PP)
The precautionary principle is defined in the Rio Declaration as follows: 'Where there are threats of serious or irreversible damage, lack of full scientific certainty shall not be used as a reason for postponing cost-effective measures to prevent environmental degradation.' The PP recognizes the existence of critical ecological thresholds and seeks to prevent breaching those thresholds. The application of the PP requires weighing the risks of inaction with the costs of preventive actions. It is an important and necessary guiding principle in the relations between economic affairs and the environment, but it has generated a major controversy due to fears that it might serve neo-protectionism or that it can stifle technological innovations that could be good for the environment.

Part of the problem arises from the ambiguities that surround the implementation of the principle. Difficulties in determining where uncertainty and risks begin and where reasonable doubt stops make the PP an awkward tool. If improperly managed, it could lead to arbitrary and abusive decisions. For example, there are no easy answers to the question of how to deal with 'exaggerated claims of hazard'. And although 'science by consensus' does not necessarily lead to the best policy advice, it seems that dialogue and ventilation of differing viewpoints is unavoidable in the presence of disputes.

The precautionary principle does not hold a monopoly over vagueness. But vagueness and uncertainty is precisely what it is designed to deal with. And in order to use this principle adequately, without transforming it into an instrument of discrimination, it must be accompanied by legitimacy. This is only brought into the system through intensive and protracted multilateral *bona fide* negotiations. If we look at examples where the precautionary principle has been successfully used, this is the salient feature.

Macroeconomics and trade
Globalization and the expansion of trade go hand in hand with financial deregulation. Capital flows underpin the expansion of trade and trade liberalization relies heavily on deregulating the capital account. This was supposed to bring about better resource allocation and lower cost of capital. Savings from developed countries would flow to developing countries, spurring growth and productivity. Deregulation in financial and banking systems would also allow for greater investment rates and better services through greater competition and lower interest rates.[4]

But treating money and financial instruments as products that can be exchanged in a marketplace just like any other commodity is a fallacy. As Keynes pointed out, money and financial instruments lack intrinsic value; they are extremely sensitive to swings in confidence as to the future evolution of their value. Thus financial liberalization increased market volatility, opened new avenues for speculative investments and led to lower investment rates. The result was slower growth and rising unemployment rates in most countries.

In interdependent financial markets, capital flows are conditioned by domestic, as well as external, factors. Domestic factors include the real interest rate and expectations about the future evolution of macroeconomic aggregates and the performance of the current account. External factors include the international rate of interest, the state of other markets, and changes in the regulatory framework in other economies. Recognizing this single fact is of utmost importance for its theoretical and policy implications.

The International Monetary Fund (IMF) should allow countries to discourage excessive short-term capital inflows. This can be done through capital controls that can smooth cycles in the capital account and reduce overall economic vulnerability. Capital controls allow policy-makers to regain some autonomy for a countercyclical monetary policy.

The experience of the past 20 years demonstrates that premature and abrupt liberalization of the capital account is inappropriate for developing countries. Even when strong regulatory regimes continued to exist, most developing countries have found it difficult to adapt to the volatile environment of international capital flows. A flexible approach in this domain can play a key role in bringing about stability with adequate foreign investment levels.

The role of capital controls is to smooth the cycles of the capital account, enhance stability and allow for greater independence of monetary policy. This objective can also be attained with the use of balance of payments provisions within the WTO framework. Although these measures were reaffirmed in Marrakech, they have been left in the backwaters of policy-making thanks to opposition from dogmatic quarters in the WTO, the IMF and the US Treasury. These provisions can provide a constructive response to external accounts' crises (Nadal, 1996) and should be reconsidered as an important tool in the intersection between trade and financial flows.

Fiscal policy needs to go beyond the shortsighted objectives of providing primary surpluses that serve only to transfer resources from the real sectors of the economy to the sphere of financial services. This is the typical IMF recommendation and is normally achieved not by increasing fiscal revenues, but by cutting expenditures. Thus, precisely when adjustment to trade liberalization enters its critical stages, a restrictive posture in the realm of fiscal policy will have negative effects on producers. Trade and fiscal policy need to be reconciled and an approach linking public expenditures to the objectives of attaining dynamic competitive advantages should be one of the highest priorities.

Agriculture
The urgent task of reforming the world's agricultural system lies at the crossroads of trade, social responsibility and the environment. What we do today to the agricultural system of the world will determine the history of our future as a species. Yet the world has been unable to reconcile adequate food production and distribution systems, improving living standards and environmental sustainability of the agricultural system.

The strategic objectives of the Uruguay Round's Agreement on Agriculture (URAA) were to open up the markets of several highly populated countries to exports from the USA and Europe, and to maintain a façade of discipline in the relations between these two giant agricultural producers. It envisaged the reduction of subsidies, but allowed payments that are decoupled from production. It preserved the capacity of developed countries to maintain highly deleterious export subsidies close to US$ 300 billion per year (Stern, 2002). The URAA failed to open market access for developing countries' products, leaving unsolved the complex questions of food rights, economic development, social responsibility and environmental stewardship.

All of this ignored the fact that the 'invisible hand' metaphor does not work in agriculture. Income elasticity for food doesn't allow for expansion of demand as prices drop. On the supply side, aggregate crop output changes little with price because farmers use all their productive capacity all of the time and cannot influence prices. Summarizing, the current policy based on the false premise that we need to let markets operate freely is unsustainable and should be replaced by adequate supply management policies (Ray 2004; Ray et al., 2003).

Since 1996, world prices for America's chief farm exports have plunged more than 40 percent, but US crop exports did not increase (Ray, 2004). This led to dramatic losses in farm income and increases in government payments to farmers. This spelled trouble for small producers in developing countries as dumping practices destroyed markets, impoverished rural communities throughout the world and benefited vertically integrated agribusinesses. This is why the difference between consumer prices and the price that producers receive is out of any reasonable proportion.

The system that the URAA helped enshrine must be drastically redesigned. In the first place, developing countries must have the right to use quantitative restrictions (QRs) as a protection from dumping practices and to de-link their key strategic sectors from the paradigm of the URAA. These QRs are compatible with WTO and are recognized by Article XVIII of the original GATT. Safeguards should also be made available for developing countries.

Because global agricultural trade is in disarray, a radically new approach is required. We must replace the old system based on the URAA's naïve illusion concerning free markets with a sound institutional and legal framework that blends sound supply management policy measures with adequate support mechanisms in developing (and developed) countries. The world needs adequate crop prices that contribute to a healthy and vigorous worldwide agricultural sector (Ray et al., 2003).

A new institutional arrangement, perhaps a new framework convention, needs to tackle the issues of sustainable agriculture, biodiversity, food security and access to genetic resources, not on a piecemeal basis, but in one single undertaking in order to reconcile the objectives of food security and responsible environmental stewardship. The new convention should restate the fundamental right of nations to defend themselves from dumping practices and from the market distortions brought about by the concentration of corporate power. Countries would be allowed to determine the level of support to their domestic producers and be subjected to trade-distorting disciplines explicitly defined in this agreement. Support systems should not be considered as *a priori* market-distorting.

Commodity agreements, intellectual property and investment

Over the past century, real prices of primary products experienced a significant declining trend (Ocampo and Parra, 2003). The vulnerability of many countries relying on a few basic products for exports puts undue pressure on people and the environment. International commodity agreements (ICAs) can help reverse this trend and increase market transparency in agricultural trade. In the past, UNCTAD's mandate was to use ICAs to arrest the deterioration of terms of trade and to stabilize markets whenever there were large fluctuations. Several agreements were set up but this role was destroyed in the 1980s in the aftermath of the debt crisis and was never restored.

ICAs can reduce market distortions through the supervision of operations where giant corporations control more than 20 percent of the market. They can stabilize prices at levels that are fair for consumers and producers and dovetail certification and other resource management schemes with commercial trends. Producers that receive a fairer deal through ICAs can be more easily persuaded to improve quality and adopt cleaner process and production methods without exacerbating tensions between trade partners. ICAs can also blend trade concerns with technical and financial assistance that improve standards while restoring the notion of special and differential treatment. New multilateral agreements should combine sustainable management of resources and the recognition of the legitimate rights of indigenous peoples and other local communities. A new generation of international commodity agreements could explore ways and means to increase value-added of raw commodities, providing developing countries assistance to take advantage of new economic opportunities, from processing to packaging. Adding value to these commodities will create forward and backward industrial linkages that generate employment opportunities and have healthy multiplier effects in commodity production chains.

Intellectual property rights and trade
Contrary to the views of trade policy analysts, the objectives of 'free trade' clash violently with those of 'intellectual property rights'. The first require competition to attain efficient allocations of resources. The second create monopoly rights that may entail loss of welfare. Original patent protection treaties required members only to set up a patent system. Those legal instruments accepted restrictions in areas such as public health and the environment. There was no uniform standard regarding patent life. This changed during the Uruguay Round. The Agreement on Trade-related Aspects of Intellectual Property (TRIPs) imposed on WTO member countries the obligation to grant patents for a wide variety of items, a 20-year life term for patents and almost eliminated compulsory licensing. For countries investing very little in R&D, as most developing countries, TRIPs spelled bad news.

Economists have embraced the idea that patents are incentives for inventive activity. This is inaccurate. Intercapitalist competition is the main engine for innovations (Baumol, 2002) and patents serve primarily as instruments in corporate strategies, rewarding rent-seeking behavior and raising entry barriers for potential competitors. Thus, patents serve primarily the purpose of segmenting markets in order to extend monopoly rents.

Strengthening IPRs in developing countries will not necessarily increase R&D investment (Kumar, 1996). In addition, industrial policy instruments that could be used to enhance assimilation of technological capabilities have been curtailed by the WTO system. This makes technological development very difficult and a strong patent system will not modify this. Restoring elements of rationality in the international patent system should be accompanied by restoring the capacity of developing countries to design and implement industrial policies.

Returning to a more rational IPR system requires de-linking intellectual property rights from trade agreements. This is needed in order to redefine a global patent system that is less market-distorting and protects inventors' rights. It should not impose wide patentability and long duration for patents, and it should abolish patents on life forms, a major element distorting the patent system that has negative effects on human health and access to genetic resources.

Investment and trade (TRIMs)

Through the agreement on Trade-related Aspects of Investment Measures (TRIMs), developing countries are forced to forego the use of important industrial policy instruments. Policies aimed at increasing local content in value-added, or limiting imports to a certain proportion of exports, are not allowed under the current version of TRIMs.

Thus, instead of protecting developing countries against the effects of market concentration, TRIMs shield powerful multinational corporations against public policies in host countries. Some of the policy instruments eliminated by TRIMs are critical in order to obtain technological capabilities and go into higher value-added exports. They are essential to building forward and backward inter-industry linkages, and those linkages are the carriers of economy-wide multiplier effects (see UNCTAD, 2003b).

Chapter 11 of the North American Free Trade Agreement (NAFTA) is an example of unprecedented rights bestowed on private firms against government decisions perceived as detrimental to investors' rights. Firms can start a binding dispute resolution process in special arbitration courts that can lead to compensations paid with taxpayers' money. Panels do not offer the standard transparency guarantees of standard national courts. In a twist of priorities, special and differential treatment is accorded to private multinational firms to the detriment of public interest in host countries. This needs to be reformed, allowing developing countries more policy space. Also, a revision of the TRIMs is required to incorporate the need for greater market transparency through the monitoring of operations of multinational corporations.

Final comments

The international trading system is not leading to greater prosperity and economic justice. Empirical evidence shows that rapid trade liberalization coexists with slower GDP growth rates and a very large number of poor people across the world. It also coexists with rapid and severe environmental degradation. Evidently, something is not working as standard economic models of free trade predict (lower prices and greater welfare). The trading system has concentrated on the elimination of barriers to trade and has ignored the task of building up development capabilities of poor countries. In addition, trade agreements are not focused on building a regime for stable prices and fair terms for trade.

Free trade *per se* should not be the top priority of the world's trading system. It is just a tool to further integrate the world's economy into a single entity. But in this process, it is urgent to recognize social and environmental responsibility as the central priorities of the international agenda. Profit-making should stop being the leitmotif around which the world's trading system revolves. If the world's most powerful countries do not shift the balance towards sustainability, the negative consequences of today's irresponsibility will return to haunt us. The question of survival of our species is involved here.

Notes

1. I wish to acknowledge support from the John D. and Catherine T. MacArthur Foundation for my research on alternative development strategies.

2. Muradian et al. (2001); Muradian and Martinez-Alier (2001).
3. The best references are Fisher (1983), Sonnenschein (1973), Debreu (1974) and Mantel (1973).
4. Financial liberalization was forced upon the world's economy in order to hedge against the risk of fluctuating exchange rates after 1973. It was also driven by the symptoms of a global recession at the end of the 1970s and a fall in productivity and profit rates in most developed countries.

References

Ackerman (2004), 'An offer you can't refuse. Free trade, globalization and the search for alternatives', in F. Ackerman and A. Nadal (eds),*The Flawed Foundations of General Equilibrium. Critical Essays on Economic Theory*, London and New York: Routledge, pp. 149–67.
Baumol, William J. (2002), *The Free-Market Innovation Machine: Analyzing the Growth Miracle of Capitalism*, Princeton, NJ: Princeton University Press.
David, Paul (1975), *Technical Choice, Innovation and Economic Growth*, Cambridge, UK: Cambridge University Press.
Debreu, G. (1974) 'Exess demand functions', *Journal of Mathematic Economics*, **1**, 15–21.
Eldredge, N. (1998), *Life in the Balance: Humanity and the Biodiversity Crisis*, Princeton, NJ: Princeton University Press.
Fisher, Franklin (1983), *Disequilibrium Foundations of Equilibrium Economics*, Cambridge, UK: Cambridge University Press.
Global Poverty Monitoring (2004), available at:www.worldbank.org/research/povmonitor/.
Habbakuk, H.J. (1962), *American and British Technology in the 19th Century*, Cambridge, UK: Cambridge University Press.
Houghton, J.T., Y. Ding, D.J. Griggs, M. Noguer, P.J. van der Linden, X. Dai, K. Maskell and C.A. Johnson (2001), *Climate Change 2001: The Scientific Basis*, Intergovernmental Panel on Climate Change, Cambridge, UK: Cambridge University Press.
Kumar, Nagesh (1996), 'Intellectual property protection, market orientation and location of overseas R&D activities by multinational enterprises', *World Development*, **24**(4), 673–88.
Landes, D.S. (1969), *The Unbound Prometheus. Technological Change and Industrial Development in Western Europe from 1750 to the Present*, Cambridge, UK: Cambridge University Press.
Mantel, R. (1974), 'On the characterization of aggregate exess demand', *Journal of Economic Theory*, **7**, 348–53
McCarthy, J.J., O.F. Canziani, N.A. Leary, D.J. Dokken and K.S. White (2001), *Climate Change 2001: Impacts, Adaptation, and Vulnerability*, Intergovernmental Panel on Climate Change, Cambridge, UK: Cambridge University Press.
Muradian, Roldan and Joan Martinez-Alier, (2001), 'Trade and the environment: From a 'southern' perspective', *Ecological Economics*, **36**, 281–97.
Muradian, R., Martin O'Connor, and J. Martinez-Alier (2001), *Embodied Pollution in Trade: Estimating the 'Environmental Load Displacement' of Industrialised Countries*, Milan: Fondazione Eni Enrico Mattei, Available at: http://www.feem.it/web/activ/_activ.html.
Myers, Norman and Andrew H. Knoll (2001), 'The biotic crisis and the future of evolution', *Proceedings of the National Academy of Sciences*, **98**(10), 5389–92, 8 May.
Nadal, Alejandro (1994), 'The tuna–dolphin association in the Eastern Pacific Ocean tuna fishery: international trade and resource management issues', in E. Mann Borghese, N. Ginsburg and J.R. Morgan (eds), *Ocean Yearbook 11*, Chicago: University of Chicago Press, pp. 120–43.
Nadal, Alejandro (1996), 'Balance-of-payments provisions in the GATT and NAFTA', *Journal of World Trade*, **30**(4), 5–24.
Ocampo, José Antonio and María Ángela Parra (2003), 'Los términos de intercambio de los productos básicos en el siglo XX', *Revista de la CEPAL*, 79, 7–35.
Ray, Daryll E. (2004), *Agricultural Policy for the Twenty-First Century and the Legacy of the Wallaces*, John Pesek Colloquium on Sustainable Agriculture, 3 March, Ames, Iowa: Iowa State University, p. 45.
Ray, Daryll E., Daniel de la Torre Ugarte, and Kely J. Tiller (2003), *Rethinking U.S. Agricultural Policy: Changing Course to Secure Farmer Livelihoods Worldwide*, Agricultural Policy Analysis Center (APAC), The University of Tennessee, 68, also available at: www.agpolicy.org.
Sonnenschein, H. (1973), 'Do Walras' identity and continuity characterize the class of community exess demand function?', *Journal of Economic Theory*, **6**, 345–54.
Stern, Nicholas (2002), *Dynamic Development: Innovation and Inclusion*, Munich Lectures in Economics, Munich, Germany: Ludwig Maximilian University, available at http://econ.worldbank.org/files/22048_CES_Munich_Lecture_Nov_19.pdf.
UNCTAD (2003a), *Trade and Development Report 2003*, United Nations Conference on Trade and Development, New York and Geneva: United Nations, available at www.unctad.org.

UNCTAD (2003b), *Foreign Direct Investment and Performance Requirements: New Evidence from Selected Countries*, United Nations Conference on Trade and Development, New York and Geneva: United Nations, available at www.unctad.org.

UNFPA (2002), *State of the World Population 2002: People, Poverty and Possibilities*, New York: United Nations Population Fund, available at www.unfepa.org/swp/2002swpmain_spa.htm.

Wilson, E.O. (1993), *The Diversity of Life*, Cambridge, MA: Harvard University Press.

Index

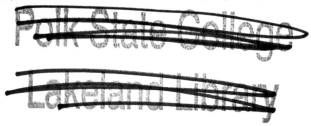